A *Quiet* Revolution

The First Palestinian Intifada
and Nonviolent Resistance

by Mary Elizabeth King

Introduction by President Jimmy Carter

Nation Books
New York
www.nationbooks.org

A QUIET REVOLUTION:
The First Palestinian Intifada and Nonviolent Resistance

Copyright © 2007 Mary Elizabeth King

Published by
Nation Books
An imprint of Avalon Publishing Group, Inc.
245 West 17th Street, 11th Floor
New York, NY 10011

AVALON
publishing group incorporated

Photograph information:

1. Feisel Husseini (waving): Credit: Hashomer Hatzair Archive,
Givat Haviva, Rachamim Israeli, al-Hamishmar Collection.
2. Ghassan Khatib: Credit: Hashomer Hatzair Archive,
Givat Haviva, Isaac Harari, al-Hamishmar Collection.
3. Hanna Siniora: Credit: Hashomer Hatzair Archive,
Givat Haviva, Rachamim Israeli, al-Hamishmar Collection.
4. Human chain (holding hands): Credit: Hashomer Hatzair Archive,
Givat Haviva, Rachamim Israeli, al-Hamishmar Collection.
5. Gene Sharp: Credit: The Albert Einstein Institution.
All other photographs courtesy of the author.

Nation Books is a copublishing venture of the Nation Institute and Avalon Publishing
Group, Incorporated.

Library of Congress Cataloging-in-Publication Data is available.

ISBN-10: 1-56025-802-0
ISBN-13: 978-1-56025-802-5

9 8 7 6 5 4 3 2 1

Interior design by *Ivelisse Robles Marrero*

Printed in the United States of America
Distributed by Publishers Group West

Dedicated to my husband
of thirty-three years,
Peter Geoffrey Howard Bourne,
whose interest and fascination with my work
has continually sustained and encouraged me.

About the Author

Mary Elizabeth King is professor of peace and conflict studies at the UN-affiliated University for Peace, and distinguished scholar with the American University's Center for Global Peace, in Washington, DC. She is visiting research fellow at Oxford University's Rothermere American Institute, in Britain.

In 1988, she won a Robert F. Kennedy Memorial Book Award for *Freedom Song*. In 2002, New Delhi's Indian Council for Cultural Relations released the second edition of *Mahatma Gandhi and Martin Luther King, Jr*, which chronicles nine contemporary nonviolent struggles, originally published by UNESCO in 1999. Her work has taken her to more than 120 developing countries.

As a presidential appointee in the Carter administration, King had worldwide oversight for the Peace Corps and other U.S. volunteer service corps programs. In the U.S. civil rights movement, Mary King worked alongside the Reverend Dr. Martin Luther King, Jr. (no relation) in the student wing of the movement, an experience which defined her life. She co-authored "Sex and Caste" with Casey Hayden, a 1966 article now viewed by historians as tinder for the second wave of feminism. King's doctorate in international politics is from the University of Wales at Aberystwyth. In 1989, her alma mater Ohio Wesleyan University honored her with its highest award, and in 2003 she received the Jamnalal Bajaj International Prize for the promotion of Gandhian values.

Contents

Preface

ALL OVER THE WORLD, groups struggle in civilian movements that have at their core the refusal to obey and cooperate with unjust authority. They are a formidable force for justice and human rights. Nonviolent movements have for millennia altered the course of history—from protests against the Roman caesars, to home rule in India, to the U.S. civil rights movement, to this century's popular dissent for free and fair elections in Serbia and Ukraine, and nonviolent resistance in Belarus, France, Iran, Lebanon, and Zimbabwe. Adapting an alternative to passivity and violence with vigils, boycotts, demonstrations, and strikes against authoritarian bureaucracies and despotic regimes, ordinary persons have changed their societies through organized dissent relying on action methods deliberately chosen because they do not utilize guns or military weaponry.

Civil disobedience—a form of power with ancient roots—was during the nineteenth century viewed as a way of remaining personally true to one's beliefs; the individuals or groups who used it had little intention of producing broad political transformations. During the twentieth century, peoples seized upon this ability to exert themselves in collective action aimed specifically at political change. Direct action disheartened British colonialism in India, broke the bars of racial discrimination in the United States, and helped to bring down the Berlin Wall.

On virtually every continent, nonviolent movements for social and political change are attempting to forge peaceful transitions to democracy, guarantee human rights, secure justice, bring down repressive dictatorships, and end military occupations. They are not always successful. Outside the framework of liberal democracies, independent citizen-based action may be cruelly crushed. In Burma in 1988 and into the 1990s, and in China in viii • A *Quiet* Revolution

1989, such movements were brutally quelled, with no perceptible modifications of the respective regimes in response to the people's grievances.

The behavior of participants defines nonviolent action, not their convictions or adherence to a creed. Nonviolent action does not entail or condone violence against persons or the threat of physical assault. Rather, it implies an active response in which the taking of action is not violent. Conventional warfare, armed struggle, and guerrilla warfare seek to achieve their goals through producing fear or capitulation, as injury to life and limb demoralize their opponent, or with expressly violent subjugation. In contrast, nonviolent struggle employs strategies for applying sanctions to bring about results; it does not seek to accomplish its goals through physical harm, injury, killing, or bloodshed.

• • • •

Nothing in my personal background predisposes me to favor either the Arabs or Israelis in the Eastern Mediterranean, and I can identify with the suffering and grief of both peoples. I am also deeply concerned about the tragedies endemic in this part of the world and elsewhere, when parties to conflicts in effect make pacts and agree to a policy of violence. My family background does not incline me to prejudice on either side. Yet it disposes me to political defiance and resistance against unjust authority. I am a direct descendant of an officer with Nathaniel Bacon in the failed rebellion of 1676 against Governor Alexander Spotswood, the British representative in colonial Virginia, which served as dress rehearsal for the successful American Revolution a century later. A number of officers ended up at the gallows, although I don't know if my ancestor was one of them. When Spotswood returned to Britain for an audience with King Charles II, according to our family oral history, the monarch told him, "Governor, you have hanged more men in Virginia than I killed to avenge my father's death," referring to the execution of Charles I. I am also a collateral descendant of Henry Clay, the twice-unsuccessful Whig candidate for president in 1832 and 1844, who famously said, "I would rather be right than president," and freed his slaves in his will.

After being graduated from Ohio Wesleyan University in 1962, where I had organized a student committee to support the sit-ins against racial segregation then roiling the South, I worked alongside the Reverend Dr. Martin Luther King, Jr. (no relation) in the student wing of the U.S. civil rights movement, for the Student Nonviolent Coordinating Committee. My job, working with Julian Bond, was communications—getting out the news about deaths and atrocities of African Americans that editors preferred to suppress. The *New York Times* later called me part of "a tiny handful" of white, female, "heroic, unsung organizers of the Southern civil rights movement."[1]

The four years that I spent at the vortex of the civil rights movement mark the start of lifelong awareness and study of nonviolent resistance. I was educated in how to fight for civil and political rights without violence from the same individuals who taught Martin Luther King, Jr. Indeed, everyone in this midcentury mass mobilization had to become competent in the nonviolent theories and practices that are inextricably linked, because nonviolent struggle must be learned—it is neither instinctual nor intuitive. Since 1975, as my professional work has taken me to more than 120 developing countries, I have become increasingly conscious of the applicability of nonviolent collective action under varying circumstances, not solely in liberal democracies. My belief that this method of fighting for social justice holds portentous potential was later at the core of my doctoral studies, as I became a political scientist of international politics and academician of peace and conflict studies.

In 1988, as the Palestinian intifada stirred, I visited Israel/Palestine with a Washington, D.C., private philanthropic foundation. Meeting with a broad spectrum of Israelis, we held discussions with reservists and conscripts who opposed the military occupation of lands set aside for the Palestinians by the United Nations and refused to serve there, military generals who feared that the occupation endangered Israel's security, members of the Knesset of all stripes, leaders of a host of Israeli peace groups, social scientists, authors, journalists, and government officials. In Arab East Jerusalem, although we did not fully recognize that we were meeting with leaders of the uprising, we had discussions with key individuals who were then influential in shaping the Palestinian intifada. In one gathering in particular in the elegant American Colony Hotel, a former Turkish pasha's residence, many of the persons you will meet in this book were present for the discussion. In 1989, the foundation returned again, having supported several of the U.S. solidarity groups of the Israeli peace camp. The precise spark for this book was tindered by these direct personal explorations with the Palestinians, and their Israeli counterparts, who comprised what I shall call an epistemic community—a group that shares knowledge in common. As I listened intently, I discerned similarities to the very concerns that had perplexed us deep within the internal controversies of the U.S. civil rights movement almost a quarter of a century earlier. Just as the canvas of an oil painting can sometimes reveal the *pentamenti* (traces of previous sketches or strokes) left by the artist beneath the contours of the final work, I could see in the arguments and deliberations of the Palestinians who were trying to create a path away from armed struggle to down-to-earth strategies of nonviolent action the agonies of our own debates and quandaries. Intrigued, I recognized vexing questions about the connection between the ends and means, hearing again the precisely pinpointed self-questioning of the validity of an action and whether it held potential for persuading the target group to bring about alterations. As we visitors were made privy to discussions on weighing the cost of reprisals against the benefits of an action, my memory ricocheted. The debates where ideas met action among the Israeli peace groups and with the Palestinian activists (and sometimes between them) on goals and purposes, reminded me of Atlanta in the 1960s. A distinctive sense of imminence, foreordination, and predestination comes from wrestling with action that carries great personal risk, because of the knowledge that violence may be used against you, despite your own prohibition against hurting the life or limb of the adversary.

Despite closely following reports of foreign correspondents in the Washington, New York, and London newspapers, it took dozens of meetings for me fully to grasp that a mass nonviolent movement was underway in the Palestinian uprising, one with trenchant parallels to comparable mobilizations in other times and places. I determined to embark on the research necessary to examine the linkages disclosed in the encounters of the two trips. This book is the result, in gestation since 1988.

Nonviolent struggle operates in the extralegal or extraparliamentary realm, often when institutionalized political channels such as government, justice systems, courts, and legislatures have failed or no longer function. Such power, implemented through popular participation, is frequently misunderstood or missed altogether. Since deeds and actions of the protagonists, rather than a moral code or creed, determine whether a struggle is nonviolent, this has made it difficult if not impossible for many spectators to look upon the first Palestinian intifada and see it for what it was: a remarkably coherent nonviolent mobilization to end a military occupation.

Misperceptions were common even among Palestinians. Some Palestinians living abroad viewed the uprising as merely an artful device. Not understanding what had changed since their families left British Mandate

Palestine in 1947 or 1948, or in 1967, they saw it as the last resort of a broken people. Others, enthralled by the secret Palestinian armed bands that took up bloody revolt after 1929, admiringly portrayed the first intifada as a violent rebellion and as originating from the Palestine Liberation Organization (PLO) in Tunis.

The first phase of what can be called the modern Palestinian national movement began in the years immediately prior to World War I, specifically 1916, following a series of bewildering, conflicting pledges and ambiguous obligations by Britain, France, and Russia, as they agreed on the dismemberment of the Ottoman Empire. In the mid-1930s, faith in some quarters was placed in Arab states to stanch the losses of Palestinian Arab land to Zionist colonies, a belief supplanted in the 1940s by hope that Arab League intervention might help.[2] When Arab unity produced few fruits, Palestinians stressed self-reliance and armed struggle as basic principles.[3]

What may be seen as a second stage of Palestinian nationalism began in approximately 1957 with the establishment of political and armed resistance movements, such as Fateh, culminating in the formation of the PLO in 1964. By July 1968, the Palestinians had adopted armed struggle as the *only* means of liberating Palestine, and codified it in the Palestinian National Covenant, or Charter, a revision by the fourth Palestine National Council (PNC). This meant that the register of Palestinian resistance to Zionism was framed within the concept of "armed popular revolution."[4] Guerrilla warfare evolved as the principal means of executing this policy, an approach that remained substantially unrevised until the first intifada.

Why, then, has the intifada not been universally comprehended as standing in stark contrast to the policy enunciated in the 1968 charter? The question is salient, because as Anders Boserup and Andrew Mack note, "one reason why nonviolence 'works' is precisely that the action is less violent than the opponent would have expected."[5] Study of the calculations, planning, and thinking that underlie nonviolent struggle has nowhere enjoyed the high estate of military strategy. History is often the narrative of wars, and military historians enjoy esteem and prestige, whereas the chronicling of how societies have achieved major accomplishments through nonviolent resistance is scant by comparison.

The belief of Fateh, the dominant faction within the PLO, in the necessity of armed struggle to stimulate political struggle and its ideological insistence on the use of "all available means" to advance its fight had the effect of limiting, rather than enhancing, effectiveness.[6] Its idea that tactics could be "mixed," with armed and nonviolent approaches intermittently alternated or combined, only impeded the prospects for what might be accomplished through disciplined, coherent nonviolent resistance. Many in Fateh viewed the use of militant nonviolence during the 1987 uprising with suspicion, because of an erroneous presumption that nonviolent direct action is a creed, or faith, something based on Love, a matter of spirituality, or a system of morality. It *can* be an article of faith, and is often preferred for its ethical attributes in forging social change without shedding blood, but not necessarily. Others thought nonviolent struggle was pacifism. Neither idealism nor pacifism is a prerequisite for effective nonviolent strategic action.

Palestinians in the occupied territories resisted the introduction of weapons because of fears that guns would negatively alter the "wide participatory nature of the *intifada*," Palestinian journalist Daoud Kuttab states.[7] His observation reveals an important and intrinsic democratic property of nonviolent struggle: although coercion may sometimes have been improperly used to dragoon persons into supporting boycotts or strikes, in theory no one person can make the decision for someone else to incur the risks in what Walter Lippman called the "political equivalent of war."[8] Clearly the intifada was "extremely militant,"[9] but more to the point, so was its use of revolutionary nonviolence.

Struggle within a Struggle

Nonviolent movements tend to be unilaterally devised, and it is not uncommon for the target group to respond violently to them. Such is the case of the Palestinian uprising, although observers generally overlooked its preponderant nonviolent resistance and failed to peer below the surface at the important organizational and intellectual changes that allowed nonviolent strategies to emerge in competition with military prototypes. In this process, a nonmilitary technique of striving for political rights trumped the old and established the framework for more than the first two years of the intifada.

The decision and process of struggling nonviolently resulted from a battle waged by a small group of Palestinians inside the territories militarily occupied by Israel since 1967. They changed the discourse surrounding the "liberation of Palestine," believing that the time had come to stop talking about *liberating* the Palestinian areas and to adopt nonbelligerent and solely political methods of asserting Palestinian rights; and they worked during the late 1970s and throughout the decade of the 1980s to do so. This is not to say that by the start of the intifada they had constructed a flawlessly nonviolent movement. Perfection is unlikely in any human social mobilization. Yet, in the pre-uprising skirmishes and contacts of a group small in size yet big in ideas, lies a more accurate understanding of the intifada than those generally offered.

What distinguishes the 1987 uprising is the extent to which a small cohort was able to hold a mass movement to a nonviolent template of struggle, despite countermeasures and reprisals. In looking at this "struggle within a struggle," the careful observer can discern a pivotal moment in contemporary world history, when a conflict long defined by violence created from within itself an upheaval of popular dissent based on the avoidance of violence, with significant changes in mind-sets that could eventually lead to diminishing a proclivity to choose violent conflict as the way to fight for one's cause.

Introduction
by President Jimmy Carter

THE UNITED STATES HAS changed so much since the 1960s civil rights movement that it is difficult now to realize how much hatred and visceral prejudice abounded in the South of my childhood. I am not speaking of my family, but as I approached adulthood I remember hearing slurs and epithets of hate and loathing towards African Americans. When the civil rights movement came to southwest Georgia, with its voter registrations, marches, boycotts, and organization of small institutions, many white people felt threatened. They feared change and losses to their way of life. Some dismissed the nonviolent discipline of the movement as "riots" and "violence," since the federal courts and Congress still espoused "separate but equal" as the law of the land.

Yet it was the movement's reliance on nonviolent resistance that was able to put the black community on equal footing with the powerful establishment that was committed to segregation. Fighting with nonviolent methods was also practical—black people were greatly outnumbered in the population as a whole, and were without a presence on juries or in police and security forces. It also was common sense to seek a way of struggle that would not make things worse, as violence tends to worsen an already bad situation. The movement's results were far greater than breaking the color bar. The laws denied basic human rights to black persons and *had* to be changed, yet in addition to rectifying legalized wrongs from the past, the gains from nonviolent action spilled over from the black community to encompass all people. White citizens could now hold their heads high because southerners could feel proud that their region had resolved a predicament of centuries with relatively little bloodshed. The stigma against the South began to dissipate, as the civil rights movement changed the equation of American life. The southern states prospered. The long journey for civil rights became a national struggle for rights and reform instead of a regional upheaval, and made it possible for me as a white southerner to be elected as the thirty-ninth president of the United States.

Similar injustices and hurts afflict people on both sides in the Israeli-Palestinian conflict. For thirty years, I have committed myself to bringing about peace with justice, including obtaining historic security for Israel. In March 1977, I called for the Palestinians to have their own homeland. In many trips to the area, I have spent hours in conversation with Israelis and Palestinians, including in the territories militarily occupied since 1967. In considering the Middle East, I am not making a simplistic equivalence between harms and grievances in two different settings half a world apart, but rather suggest that nonviolent struggle involves thinking and more complex solutions than violence, and that among its outgrowths can be social and political change that benefits all parties to a conflict. Nonviolent action, if sometimes contentious and defiant, favors outcomes of reconciliation and democracy, things that military approaches and guerrilla warfare cannot claim. While military actions and armed struggle stimulate a thirst for vengeance, revenge, and retribution, the use of concerted nonviolent action offers a basis for transformation of conflict to peace building.

The Palestinians' nonviolent resistance in the first intifada, documented here, contested military occupation from a store of classic methods used on every continent in today's world, as people fight for human rights and justice with concern for the connection between the ends and means. The joint grassroots Israeli-Palestinian committees were imagining a future that can yet be created. As Palestinian local leaders rebutted the empty premises of violent ideologies, strong efforts should have been made by the international community to fortify their resolve, which could have weakened the extremism that brought violence. How little encouragement was offered to those who were working for abandonment of the mythologies of violence! The intifada produced remarkable opportunities for resolution of the Israeli-Palestinian conflict, but these were wastefully squandered on all sides, including the United States.

Nonetheless, we can discern from these pages that it is not too late to strengthen the nonviolent peacemakers who are working to find solutions for all contenders, without the burdens of bankrupt violence

Jimmy Carter

Chapter 1

The First Intifada: A Variety of Perspectives

THE DEATHS OF FOUR Palestinians at an Israeli checkpoint on December 9, 1987, in Gaza touched off a landslide of primarily nonviolent Palestinian resistance that had been in the making for generations. Prior to the intifada, Palestinian efforts to achieve recognition of their civil and political rights and lift the military occupation had always failed to coalesce into a sustainable mass mobilization. The intifada constituted for the Palestinians a major shift in organization, thinking, leadership, and purpose. The Palestinians determined in essence to discard a tradition of armed struggle—which included some of the twentieth century's most notorious attacks on civilian and military targets—in favor of civilian, nonmilitary measures of struggle last tried in the 1920s and 1930s. These changes also explain how, for more than two years, Israeli actions and reprisals failed to alter the fundamental refusal of the Palestinians to use weaponry against the Israeli soldiers in their midst.

How could observers not have realized that the first intifada differed significantly from all the other Israeli-Palestinian "incidents" that had come before it? The decades of Palestinian hijackings and armed struggle broadcast around the world through mass media made it predictable that conventional wisdom would hold the uprising to be a violent rebellion against the state of Israel. Yet, to the contrary, nonviolent strategies of opposition to military occupation characterized the intifada for more than two years.

Civil Society, Innovative Symbols, and Ideas from beyond the Middle East

Three major developments laid the groundwork for the Palestinians' adoption of nonviolent struggle in the late 1980s: (1) a strengthening of civil society prepared the way for popular involvement; (2) a group of intellectual activists introduced innovative symbols through joint Israeli-Palestinian committees, ideas of coexistence, and a view that both Israelis and Palestinians have rights over the land they contest; (3) and external influences led to a reexamining of the reasoning and methods for challenging military occupation.

Organizational changes affecting Palestinian civil society began to take place after the 1967 Israeli military occupation of East Jerusalem, the West Bank, and the Gaza Strip—the remaining lands allocated for the Palestinians in 1947 by the United Nations. Political organizing took root in 1969, when the Palestine Communist Party violated Israeli prohibitions on such activities and set out to build small nonmilitary institutions based on the conviction that local governance and the organizing of civilian community entities were necessary preparations for independence. The formation of thousands of committees and groups into networks of popular mobilization—a direct result of the conditions of occupation—had the effect of creating a civil society. Innumerable voluntary associations—professional associations, student and faculty unions, and women's committees—evolved to fill voids created by military occupation, as well as to oppose it.

Authority fragmented during the 1970s, as a handful of movements composed of youths, university students and faculties, women from diverse social classes, and prisoners in Israeli jails assumed responsibility for opposing the military occupation themselves, rather than waiting for intervention by Palestinian exiles or Arab states as had previous generations. These movements were deliberately and markedly nonviolent. Palestinians who called for armed rebellion through military cadres sponsored by the PLO came to comprise but one cluster among the dispersing centers of power. Grassroots leaders shaped within these civilian movements expressed novel ideas about pressing for civil and political rights. They challenged monopolies of power and truth based on armed struggle, viewing nonviolent sanctions as a more realistic alternative.

Popular participation in nonmilitary clubs, professional societies, and civilian movements introduced and familiarized groups of Palestinians with parliamentary procedures, balloting in elections, group decision making, and the basics of nonviolent struggle. Large networks of committees prepared themselves to carry on, if their elected leaders were arrested. The activity of such committees was essential to the construction of the capacity for widespread confrontation with the Israeli military occupation. Without it, the sustenance of a popular uprising on the scale of the first intifada, with its breadth of popular participation, would have been impossible.

In transforming Palestinian political goals, some two dozen activists and intellectuals in Arab East Jerusalem effected the means of achieving them. Many of these Palestinians were writers and advocates who had risen to leadership positions in university student and faculty movements in the 1970s. Their forming of Israeli-Palestinian committees, begun in 1981, represented the first visible indication of the approaching intifada, as the activist intellectuals broke with tradition and pressed for direct negotiations with the Israelis. In reevaluating the use of armed resistance, their analysis concentrated on what the Palestinians might accomplish politically, including the idea that the employment of nonviolent strategies might improve the chance of statehood arising from a negotiated settlement. Publishing formally and speaking publicly in Arabic, English, and Hebrew forums and outlets, their advocacy of nonviolent tools, self-reliance, and insistence on direct talks held the potential to elicit sympathetic responses from Israelis.

Imagined solidarity between Israelis and Palestinians—in which what is forgotten is as important as what is remembered—and a conception of the military occupation as mutually humiliating to Israelis and Palestinians were two of the alternative ideas and symbols the activist intellectuals introduced to Palestinian society. Over a period of years, they also proposed that they, the Palestinians, would need to share the land, given the implausibility and impracticality of expelling the Israelis from it. Pointing to investment in political goals, they suggested that the South African experience, with its acceptance of rights for all South Africans of whatever race to participate in the country's economies and institutions, had more to offer the Palestinians than did the model of the Algerian war, in which the indigenous population expelled the French colonists. Allying themselves with Israeli sympathizers, the activist intellectuals situated Palestinian civil and political rights within the arena of widening international norms of human rights.

By advocating a negotiated two-state solution, these intellectuals recast statehood as a matter of citizenship. They envisioned it as a cognitive entitlement, rather than the literal return to their grandparents' lost citrus groves. They sought to redefine the dogma of the guerrilla cadres and to transform ideologies and recruitment mythologies of armed struggle by the few into forms of struggle that relied on the many. They believed that the political fate of the Palestinians resided with themselves, and that through their own exertions they could create the compromises necessary for living side by side with Israel.

External inspiration influenced the mix of ideas and methods being debated. The turn to political, rather than military, means represented by the intifada rested primarily on withdrawal of Palestinian obedience to the Israeli military occupation. Beginning in 1983, awareness that occupations are sustained by the people's submission began to spread into West Bank villages and refugee camps. Palestinians began to distribute among themselves literature on the theories and methods of resistance from successful nonviolent movements elsewhere in the world. Workshops, lectures, translated materials, and experimental applications of nonviolent direct action led growing numbers of Palestinians to recognize that they could withdraw their cooperation from the web of contacts through which the government of Israel administered the occupation. The realization dawned among the Palestinians that their compliance with the occupation upheld it, and conversely, that they possessed the power to refuse to submit to it.

The transmission of ideas occurred much as did the circulation of similar concepts prior to the "Velvet Revolution" of the Czechs and Slovaks against communist rule during roughly the same period, when fliers disseminated through kiosks would appear surreptitiously overnight. Among the Palestinians, an informal exchange of booklets, pamphlets, and translations of documents took place seemingly mysteriously as well. In contrast to a separate flow of exquisitely argued and published opinions of the Palestinian activist intellectuals, these street handouts were never destined for publication. Communicating how other peoples had empowered themselves and fought oppression without arms, they shared information on nonviolent movements throughout the twentieth century, translated into Arabic and summarized for rapid, pell-mell popular consumption.

Unlike the activist intellectuals, a group in the Palestinian Center for the Study of Nonviolence stood apart from the factions that had been established from the late 1950s onward. They passed insights from other movements into villages and refugee camps through mimeographed pamphlets, lectures, workshops open to anyone (Palestinian or Israeli), and handouts and translated materials. Pilot marches, parades, and demonstrations put words into action. For four years prior to the intifada, a handful of catalytic agents argued that the Palestinians should stop using violence in their efforts to fight the occupation, because it confronted a belligerent presence where the Palestinians were at their weakest. Tendering no political blueprints, they maintained that taking action was better than inaction, that nonviolent resistance was less costly than armed struggle and fit the limited abilities of the disarmed Palestinians, and most important, that such civil resistance would be more successful in redressing fundamental injustices and could more readily lead to a lasting solution.

This growing civil society, introduction of innovative symbols and ideas, and influences from beyond the Middle East made possible an opposition to the Israeli military occupation that would prove to be more effective than any claim to national rights that the Palestinians had made since Lord Balfour signed his letter to Lord Rothschild in 1917 promising a "national home" for world Jewry in Palestine. The unarmed uprising that broke out in 1987 emerged from this confluence of circumstances, which had reshaped Palestinian logic.

Initial Reaction to the First Intifada

Two schools of thought evolved to explain the Palestinian intifada: sudden unrest, or instigation by the PLO in Tunis.[1] Neither is correct. Those who saw the uprising as mayhem hoped for its early collapse, whereas those who thought it was externally controlled argued that coercive measures could end it.[2] Israeli officials did not differentiate between the turn to nonviolent struggle represented by the intifada and the operations of the military cadres that had been carrying out cross-border sorties since 1965. For four years, the Israeli government acted as if the uprising were violent rioting that had to be suppressed ruthlessly by military action, rather than a political struggle against which militarized retaliation would not work.

What became the intifada was the Palestinian response to the December 9, 1987, deaths of four laborers from the Gaza Strip who were crushed when an Israeli truck collided with their two vehicles as they waited to pass through an army roadblock after a day's work in Israel. The funeral for three of those killed drew four thousand mourners and protesters. Although Israeli officials called the crash an accident, rumors spread among the Palestinians that the deaths were in retaliation for the murder of an Israeli in the center of Gaza City the preceding day.

By December 10, smoke from barricades of burning tires covered much of Gaza. Demonstrations materialized in the Jabaliya refugee camp, and when Israel Defense Forces (IDF) troops arrived on the scene, young Palestinians pelted them with stones. Some soldiers blindfolded and tied two teenaged boys to the hoods of military jeeps, and Israeli television broadcast footage of a man in civilian clothes—later identified as a member of the Israeli internal security service, Shin Bet—firing his Uzi into a group of stone-throwing Palestinians.[3] On December 11, soldiers in the Old City of Nablus killed two Palestinian youths. In the Balata refugee camp, near Nablus, harassment of worshippers leaving Friday prayers ended with soldiers killing a woman, a teenaged girl, and a preteen boy.[4] So began the intifada and, with it, a debate on the "children of stones."[5]

In the next few weeks, seemingly unorganized protests by Palestinians erupted across the occupied territories, blocking roads and impeding Israeli army movements. Despite the tear gas and rubber-coated bullets used against them, demonstrators remained in the line of fire, throwing stones and advancing toward the soldiers. In Gaza, some thirty-five thousand Palestinians attended a funeral in Khan Yunis.[6] Israeli censors seemed to think that they could control media coverage of the intifada by restricting access to the Palestinians or expelling foreign news correspondents who disobeyed their ground rules.[7] The U.S. news media, in particular, accepted explanations from the Israeli government that defined the intifada as violent rioting.[8] After several years, the Israeli government came to recognize the intifada as a political phenomenon and move toward negotiations, but by that time a perception of the 1987 uprising as violent rebellion had become entrenched. The opening sentence of a study by Eytan Gilboa, an Israeli professor, on U.S. public opinion, reads for example, "One of the main goals of the Palestinian uprising . . . was to alter U.S. policy through a political communication process based on violence." It describes the uprising as "mass violent demonstrations and riots."[9] For years, in Israel and the United States, commentators routinely characterized the intifada using violent terminology. The Palestinians offered little clarity on the matter, in part because the illegality of resistance activities could lead to the arrest of legitimate spokespersons, but also because of divisiveness and fragmentation among Palestinian factions, which did not speak with one voice. Some factions wanted to abandon or refused to adopt the nonviolent strategy. PLO chairman Yasir Arafat increased the confusion by invoking the vocabulary of armed military ranks by referring to the youth of the intifada as "generals."

Israel never used tanks to suppress the first intifada, as had for example China—in ending the pro-democracy hunger strikes, sit-ins, boycotts, and demonstrations in Tiananmen Square—and other governments facing nonviolent action.[10] Instead, the state issued a swift and arbitrary order on January 3,

1988, to deport nine Palestinians said to have been involved in street disorders.[11] Israeli prime minister Yitzhak Shamir of Likud (Unity; an Israeli political bloc that came into being in 1973) ordered unprecedented displays of a "heavy hand" by the IDF to contain the rebellion.[12] Although Shamir did not coin the term "iron fist," he often associated himself with it. David Ben-Gurion, Israel's first prime minister (and simultaneously defense minister) had used the expressions *yad hazaqah* (strong hand), and *barzel Yisrael* (iron of Israel), and Israeli officials frequently voiced them during the uprising.[13] Yitzhak Rabin, Labor Party leader and the coalition government's defense minister, acted in what an Israeli journalisat called a "policy of naked terrorisation of the Palestinian population."[14] In the occupied territories, as many as five helicopters hovered over a given area at a time; snipers shot demonstrators in the legs. An unusual directive to Israeli soldiers to shoot at lower limbs appeared merciful, but it also presented the temptation to use excessive force, because IDF policy permitted shooting in non-life-threatening circumstances. Human Rights Watch declared it was "impossible to prevent this from becoming a shoot-to-kill policy," which "led to a large number of unjustifiable killings with only rare adverse consequences for the soldiers."[15]

After two thousand arrests, an Israeli defense reporter noted, "either new 'troublemakers' were blossoming as fast as the old ones were being plucked off the streets, or the wrong people were being detained."[16] Some IDF soldiers recognized that they faced "the enemy within—a difficult transition for a fighting force equipped, trained and psychologically honed to defend Israel from external threat."[17] Binyamin Ben-Eliezer, a retired brigadier general and a former battalion commander under General Ariel Sharon when the IDF had used force to quell turbulence in Gazan refugee camps in 1971, warned that Israel faced a popular uprising and that suppression would not work against "a generation without hope, a society that feels it has nothing to lose."[18] Nonetheless, on January 19, Defense Minister Rabin espoused what became the government's formal policy for responding to the intifada: "The first priority is to prevent violent demonstrations with force, power, and blows."[19]

A week after Rabin's statement of policy, Prime Minister Shamir told the right-wing Herut Party that the task before him required that he reinstill the fear of death among Palestinians. Having been criticized for shooting demonstrators, the army distributed wooden and metal clubs to soldiers, in addition to Galil assault rifles,[20] and authorized the breaking of limbs.[21]

Armed with wooden truncheons, Israeli soldiers "methodically" beat Palestinians, some "pounding their prisoners into unconsciousness."[22] News accounts described Israeli soldiers as "cruel, brutal and ruthless, simply breaking the hands, arms and legs of suspected ringleaders of the riots."[23] By January 23, a check of hospitals and clinic records by the Israeli newspaper *Haaretz* revealed that 197 Palestinians had been treated for fractured limbs within three days of Rabin's "break their bones" mandate.[24]

Near Nablus, in the village of Salim, on February 2, Israeli soldiers and settlers broke up a procession after prayers at a mosque, beating and trampling four youths before a master sergeant ordered a military bulldozer (used for sealing the village's gateway) to bury the youths alive. The driver, who had refused an order to run them over, instead agreed to cover them with a meter of dirt. Villagers were able to dig them out after they lost consciousness and before they suffocated, but could not take them to the hospital until the following day because of a blockade and curfew.[25] On February 8, Khader Tarazi, a nineteen-year-old from a prominent Roman Catholic family in Gaza, ducked into a house to wait out a demonstration. Israeli soldiers followed him, beat him with gun butts, and when he tried to flee, four or five soldiers put him on the hood of their military vehicle and beat him still more. Neighbors told the family that the soldiers then tossed his lifeless body into the vehicle and drove off.[26] At his funeral the next day, Israeli soldiers teargassed six hundred mourners.[27] By that time, two months after the start of the intifada, 51 Palestinians were reported to have been killed; as of April 30, the number had risen to 179.[28] In early 1989, reports cited plastic bullets in the deaths of 47 Palestinians and the wounding of 1,500 in the previous six months. Israeli pediatrician Ruchama Marton accused the Israeli government of impeding medical services as a form of collective punishment, as reports confirmed rubber-coated bullets to be lethal at close range.[29]

The prevailing, official Israeli view held that the intifada was a "war" that must be won. So said Justice Minister Dan Meridor in justifying Israel's use of collective punishment as deterrence.[30] A U.S. Department of State report on human rights lent credence to this view: "The Israeli government has regarded the uprising as a new phase of the 40-year war against Israel and as a threat to the security of the state."[31] According to Reuven Gal, an Israeli former chief psychologist of the IDF, the Israeli officials considered the intifada a military action: "the best proof is in the fact that Israel never handled the intifada by police forces or semi-military forces, but handled the intifada by brigades and divisions of the army—mobilizing full brigades, full divisions. . . . Not police, not riot control."[32]

On February 8, 1988, at the village of Jamain, near Tulkarem, Israeli troops pushed three young men, bound and tied, out of helicopters from a height of three or four meters.[33] Jamain villagers responded by staging a three-day sit-down and hunger strike.[34] Even before this event, a few Israeli journalists discerned a departure from the past:

> They have learned the power of the international media, the intricacies of Israel's internal divisions and the nature of Pan-Arab politics. They are graduates of high schools, teacher-training colleges, and universities their parents could not attend. . . . Today's "enemy" has used no weapon more sophisticated than a Molotov cocktail. Their fury has not been directed against Israeli civilian populations. They have taken no orders from the PLO. It has taken the defense establishment weeks to recognize the changes. The army has been slow in adapting to new realities.[35]

A feature of the intifada, making it an historical and political phenomenon worth examining, rather than single event or aberration, is the small number of Israeli soldiers killed in numerous daily encounters with the Palestinian populace.[36] One year into the uprising saw seventy thousand Israeli soldiers deployed in the occupied territories.[37] Daoud Kuttab, asked by London-based international news syndicates to cover the uprising, reported that the Palestinians had executed a predominantly nonviolent strategy "almost perfectly" in the first year. Israeli data support his conclusion that the number of incidents involving lethal weapons in Palestinian hands was "very small."[38] As the days of uprising turned into months, and the months became years, restraint persisted. Two years into the intifada, an Israeli journalist wrote, "[P]ractically no weapons have been used against the occupation army. No one doubts that secret arsenals of guns exist in the occupied territories—they are, in fact, used to execute informers—yet the decision not to use them against the occupation soldiers has been generally obeyed. This is all the more remarkable, and perhaps even unique, if one considers that thousands of close relatives of people killed, maimed and imprisoned are seething with rage."[39]

A Palestinian human-rights monitoring group concluded "not a single Israeli soldier . . . [was] killed in the first year of the uprising. . . ."[40] IDF sources officially reported the following: Four Israeli soldiers killed in the West Bank and none in Gaza in 1988; two soldiers killed in the West Bank and two in Gaza in 1989; two soldiers killed in the West Bank and one in Gaza in 1990; and one soldier killed in the West Bank and none in Gaza in 1991. Against the twelve Israeli soldiers killed during this four-year period, the IDF spokesperson said, Israelis killed 706 Palestinian civilians.[41]

Although the IDF reported the killing of nine Israeli civilians in the West Bank during 1988-89, the data suggest a deviation from the long-standing pattern of refusal by the PLO to distinguish between civilians and military forces. Most of the PLO's armed resistance historically had been against civilians.[42] From 1967 to 1970, Palestinian operations resulted in 115 Israeli civilians being killed and 687 wounded.[43] Between 1969 and 1985, the various PLO factions took responsibility for more than 8,000 attacks.[44] They mounted 435 of these overseas, killing 650 Israelis, some three-fourths of them civilians.[45]

These civilian targets form an important backdrop for the tale to be told. The emergence of a nonviolent mass movement against military occupation by Palestinians in 1987 occurred in the wake of decades of a Palestinian policy of armed struggle, much of it specifically aimed against civilians. The Israeli reaction must in part be seen in this light. Moreover, the conflict to many Israelis was not and is not solely between themselves and Palestinians, but between themselves and the entire Arab world. Their overreactions, existential fear, and counter-brutality—particularly among an older generation of leaders—and notwithstanding intermittent appropriate responses, flowed from a perception of Israel as a fragile state and fear of its possible destruction. Until the balance of power shifted in 1967, this was an unwavering concern and cannot be detached from their reactions to Palestinian mobilization. This perception comprised a major share of the strategic dilemma for the Palestinians.

This book is not about the statistics of death tolls, human-rights breaches, or violations of international treaties. Rather, to borrow a phrase attributed to the writer Hunter S. Thompson, it concerns the "Geneva Conventions of the mind." An entire society living under military occupation unified itself with remarkable coherence based on changes in popular thinking about how to transform their predicament, the very nature of which was extralegal and on which international conventions had had little or no effect. In the words of one reporter, the uprising was "waged more with radio broadcasts, clandestine printing presses and local underground committees than with stones."[46]

Chapter 2

The Significance of Nonviolent Struggle: Strategies and Potential

REVOLUTIONARY VIOLENCE WAS ONCE considered the only way for oppressed peoples to change draconian circumstances, because fighting for principle assuaged feelings of impotence. Bloodshed often seemed warranted, especially when justified by the widely held judgment that what was taken by violence can only be retrieved by violence. It has become clear in recent decades, however, that armed insurrection is not the only route available for aggrieved groups and societies.

Nonviolent movements across the world today have produced successes against heavily armed military regimes and seemingly invincible internal security machinery. They have brought down communism, oligarchies, and totalitarianism. The rising effectiveness of nonviolent mobilizations may paradoxically be shown by increasingly ruthless and sophisticated official repression against such movements in parts of the world at present. Yet lack of understanding of nonviolent resistance as a category of struggle, or defense, is widespread. This gap in knowledge not only led to misconceptions about the first Palestinian intifada, creating missteps in policy responses, but it also hampered the fullest possible implementation of nonviolent struggle by the Palestinians after the mass movement took hold in 1987 in the Israeli-occupied territories.

Not All Conflicts Can Be "Solved"

When disputing parties possess severely asymmetrical power, the smaller, weaker side may find it difficult to obtain a hearing apart from staging a nonviolent struggle, which has the potential to bring parity to the unbalanced relationship. Peace will remain out of the question in some conflicts until the depths of humiliation and pain are addressed to the satisfaction of the aggrieved, which may be one or both or several parties. Without such an undertaking, negotiations may eventuate, but would be ineffective on their own. Or, nonviolent resistance may be the only way to reach negotiations. This insight evolved as commonplace wisdom during the 1960s U.S. civil rights movement. In even the most remote hamlets, sharecroppers understood that nonviolent struggle might be the only way to effect negotiations. The Reverend Dr. Martin Luther King, Jr., articulated this realization in 1963:

> "Why direct action? Why sit-ins, marches, etc.? Isn't negotiation a better path?" You are exactly right in your call for negotiation. Indeed, this is the purpose of direct action. Nonviolent direct action seeks to create such a crisis and establish such creative tension that a community that has constantly refused to negotiate is forced to confront the issue. It seeks so to dramatize the issue that it can no longer be ignored.[1]

The technique of nonviolent action carries within it the potential for benefiting both parties to a conflict, because it does not seek to accomplish its goals by wounding or harming the adversary except politically. By the 1970s, Boston scholar Gene Sharp had demonstrated that a move away from pugilistic methods to nonviolent struggle improves the odds of reaching negotiations and can lay the groundwork for reconciliation.[2]

Professional negotiators often require bargaining skills and ambiguity in expressing ultimate goals, they test the waters on what might be capitulated, probe to find possible concessions, and exaggerate claims that can later be reduced in order to reach a compromise. In contrast, nonviolent struggle in the twentieth century has tended to rely strategically on clearly enunciating ultimate goals. This approach flows from a basic insight that one cannot expect the antagonists to see the dispute from the point of view of the nonviolent protagonists and to change behavior or alter policies and practices without full light being cast upon the underlying grievance. In nonviolent conflict, it is preferable that the adversary change from within—having become persuaded of the validity of the dissenters' perspective or the cost of inaction—and accept or come to terms with the nonviolent challengers' view. If such an alteration exists as a possibility, clear communication contributes to a preservation of the energy, psychological strength, and forbearance of the nonviolent participants—conservation of which represents a significant part of the planning for nonviolent struggle. Since nonviolent challengers operate without artillery, their arsenal of weapons consists of human beings—a resource that cannot be squandered in jockeying.

Long History of Nonviolent Struggle

Nonviolent resistance predates the time of Christ.[3] In 411 B.C.E. in an Athens depleted by the long and costly Peloponnesian War, Athenians paused for a theatrical festival. The sensation of the fête was *Lysistrata,* a mirthful and topical farce in which the comic genius Aristophanes devises a sex strike by the war-weary women of Athens to end hostilities. In the Roman Empire, Jews and Christians disobeyed the orders of the Caesar and his army, never acknowledging "civil disobedience." Peasants have long used "go-slows," underreported harvests, rumors and communications in covert language, evasion of taxes, and work stoppages to raise wages and improve working conditions. They carried out these actions despite their illiteracy and isolation. Peoples of the Caribbean continue to use the "road block," a nonviolent action from the days of slavery in which obstacles were placed in roadways, a way of exerting power and slowing deliveries. In 1880 in County Mayo, Ireland, Captain Charles Cunningham Boycott, a legally appointed land agent for an English lord, had eleven tenants evicted from the baron's land, and as a result, the Irish peasants and merchants shunned and socially ostracized him. The blacksmiths refused to shoe Boycott's horses, local laundresses would not wash his laundry, shopkeepers declined to serve him, and his servants quit. Yet long before the word *boycott* came into use, consumers had at times stopped buying from unfair merchants.[4]

Entitlements now considered to be universal human rights had first to be fought for through nonviolent struggle, for example, freedom from slavery and enfranchisement for the vote. Nineteenth-century movements on both sides of the Atlantic fought to abolish the slave trade with nonviolent action methods. Historian Carleton Mabee believes the first support for sit-ins and protest rides in the United States may have been in 1838, when the Antislavery Convention of American Women adopted such a policy for their work on abolition of slavery.[5] By 1893, New Zealand had become the first self-governing country to grant all adult women the right to vote, and as the twentieth century began women's rights movements gained strength and fought for women's suffrage with nonviolent action—utilizing petition drives, demonstrations, marches, and sit-ins—around the world. Women's rights movements gained strength in China, Iran, Japan, Korea, the Philippines,

Russia, Sri Lanka (then Ceylon), Turkey, and Vietnam. Women's nonviolent activism during the first two decades of the twentieth century led Fred Halliday, an expert on international relations, to describe the struggle for women's suffrage as one of the most remarkable transnational movements of the modern age.[6] Another twenty years, and women were enfranchised from Uruguay to Austria, the Netherlands to Turkey, and Germany to Ceylon. The practice of nonviolent action developed during the twentieth century into a means of projecting immense and effective political power.

Although labor unions have used strikes throughout recorded history as nonviolent measures of economic noncooperation, countless indigenous struggles for justice with nonviolent means have gone unrecorded. Possibly because of deficiencies in comparative political analysis or linguistic barriers in understanding the history of ideas, extraordinary holes exist in the writing of history on nonviolent struggle despite innumerable and major accomplishments achieved using the technique. For example, no English-language book offers an anatomy of the Norwegian nonviolent struggle that won the Nordic nation its independence from Sweden in 1905.[7] The first extensive work on the various forms of nonviolent resistance against Hitler did not appear until 1985, when Jacques Semelin analyzed nonviolent resistance to the Nazis by teachers and church leaders in Norway, physicians in Holland, church leaders in Germany, academicians in Poland, Czech and Slovak students and professors, and strikes by industrial workers and miners in Belgium and France, during World War II.[8]

A preference for military chronicles has greatly overshadowed the national European nonviolent mobilizations in opposition to the Nazis that required widespread involvement of the citizenry. The way Danish society unified to save its Jewish citizenry from Nazi removal and death led social philosopher Hannah Arendt to observe, "One is tempted to recommend the story as required reading in political science for all students who wish to learn something about the enormous power potential inherent in nonviolent action and in resistance to an opponent possessing vastly superior means of violence."[9] Arendt says that of a total of 7,800 Jews in Denmark, only 477 were seized by the Nazis, as virtually the entire society joined together in sequestering Jews. "It is the only case we know of in which the Nazis met with *open* native resistance."[10]

The Boston Tea Party and resistance to the Stamp Act were only part of the political defiance of the British Crown by American colonists, but what happened in Boston harbor and the refusal to pay the importation stamps required by London are usually not explained to schoolchildren as nonviolent struggle—as civil disobedience or tax resistance. On December 16, 1773, colonists disguised as Mohawks boarded three British ships and destroyed their cargo of 342 tea chests, chopping them to pieces and dumping the tea in the harbor. They did so to express their opposition to the imposition of a tea tax by Parliament, in which the colonists had no representation.[11]

The Stamp Act of 1765 sought to raise revenues by taxing coffee, sugar, textiles, and wine, partly to service the debt from sustaining ten thousand British troops garrisoned in the United States. "Stamps"—individually embossed sheets of vellum or parchment upon which a stamp of a certain denomination was imprinted—were required for clearing papers for ships, licenses, and deeds, and were obtained from official distributors.[12] The press became the first major institution to refuse the use of stamps, a nonviolent act of noncooperation.[13]

In these and numerous other instances, the colonists employed nonviolent sanctions enforced by extralegal local committees. British and American scholars working with original documents in archives on both sides of the Atlantic have shown that in nine, or perhaps ten, of the thirteen original colonies, de facto independence had been won from Britain through nonviolent sanctions by 1775—a full year prior to the outbreak of the revolutionary war.[14]

Two centuries later, from the 1980s into the twenty-first century, the televised spectacle of dictatorships hemorrhaging fascinated onlookers. Peoples everywhere watched authoritarian regimes tumbling or the populace refusing to obey the tyrant: the Polish Solidarity union 1980-89, the Philippines democracy struggle in 1986, the "mothers of the disappeared" in Argentina, the fall of the Berlin Wall, and the struggles against political oppression in Serbia in 2000 and Ukraine in 2004. Nonviolent action continues to offer potential in closed systems with a post–cold war security apparatus, yet the significance of nonviolent struggle is often found in more ordinary stuff.

When constitutional measures fail, protection of representative democracy categorically demands a way of fighting without resort to violence. Laws written by democratically elected legislators may deny or infringe on basic human rights, particularly relating to minorities. Nonviolent action is fundamental to democracy, functioning in its absence, but also acting as a means of democratic empowerment.[15] Respect for guarantees of fundamental human rights may be more significant for democracy than is majority rule, Michael Randle insists: "To resist the encroachment of basic rights by a duly elected government is not to deny democracy but to uphold it."[16] When liberal democratic principles are threatened or grievances rub raw in representative systems, the people may turn to extraparliamentary nonviolent demonstrations, picketing, civil disobedience, strikes, and tax resistance. More than 3 million persons repeatedly marched in cities throughout France in April 2006 to protest a law that allowed the firing of workers aged twenty-six years or younger for any reason; under intense pressure, the government yielded.[17] In Thailand that same spring, the premier surrendered his post after two months of large demonstrations, including round-the-clock gatherings of 100,000 citizens protesting corruption.[18] In the United States, also in April, festive demonstrations in dozens of cities rallied millions in asking for fairness in immigration policy.[19] The rallies far surpassed in size anything seen during the civil rights movement of the 1960s. Such action techniques are not the possession of any ideology, nor are they the domain of the Left or the Right.

Little is known about what actually happens inside nonviolent social campaigns, in part because of the failure of universities, social scientists, news media, and policymakers to study them systematically and interrogate the power of nonviolent sanctions and the dynamics of organized efforts to employ them. Take for example the U.S. civil rights movement. This mass movement of hundreds of thousands of persons was in fact a movement of movements, as each county, city, or region of a state produced homegrown community mobilizations with local leaders and organizers. Yet fewer than a dozen credible firsthand accounts from within the upheaval have appeared. Most studies by historians emphasize the leadership of the Reverend Dr. Martin Luther King, Jr., an eminently worthy subject, but not illuminating on questions of why local leadership was exceptionally strong in some places; how decisions were made; why distinctive action methods were newly developed; the role of freedom songs unique to specific settings and varieties of symbols; the leadership of women; or how the movement's far-reaching nonviolent resistance has in the decades since affected virtually all dimensions of U.S. political life.

Over the past thirty years, a literature of social-mobilization theory has developed that helps to explain important frameworks and procedures of social movements. Yet even such pathfinding studies do not necessarily explain the workings of ordinary people using nonviolent direct action for highly instrumental political change, dynamics in the vortex of such movements, or how the thinking and action strategies within specific nonviolent struggles have reflected diverse pressures, strategies, and leadership issues. Despite deficits in documentation, it is now the case that concepts, knowledge, and skills related to nonviolent struggle are spreading more swiftly and widely than ever. Options for sharing documents and cinemaphotography have increased, as electronic technologies have opened the sluice gates of translation and circulation. As Ronald Bleiker writes, popular dissent is shaping aspects of global politics and has become a "transversal phenomenon," a political technique that transgresses national boundaries and questions the spatial logic of boundaries in international relations.[20]

Mohandas Karamchand Gandhi's conceptualization of nonviolent resistance was complex and intermingled with his faith, yet he never expected that a mass nationalist movement could be built on a credo of nonviolence. Drawing heavily from other historical examples of nonviolent struggle, Gandhi was a shrewd political operative, and saw nonviolent resistance as practical—the best way to reach popular national goals. He did not expect that all, or even most, individuals would be able to adhere to the intense commitments that he demanded for himself. Jawaharlal Nehru and members of the working committee of the Congress Party viewed nonviolent struggle not as a spiritual persuasion or ethical conviction, but as a pragmatic method for achieving the political goal of independence. Most of Gandhi's colleagues accepted nonviolent methods in opposition to foreign rule, and as late as 1928 Nehru considered the possibility that violent revolt might be necessary to free India of the British. Nehru never became a "Gandhian," historian Judith M. Brown notes. He did not accept creedal nonviolence as an absolute ideal; nor was he persuaded of the "absolute priority of nonviolence, or of its guaranteed efficacy in practical politics."[21] Gandhi—with few colleagues accepting his severe political, religious, and personal self-discipline—sought agreement on a *policy* of nonviolent action not as an ethic, but as a strategy. Historian Balram R. Nanda stresses no mass movement in India could have been conducted on the basis of nonviolence as a creed.[22] An expedient preference for nonviolent action as practical and more likely to accomplish the objectives was sufficient to Gandhi as a matter of policy.[23] The adoption of a policy of nonviolent action by those who did *not* share Gandhi's personal spiritual beliefs and regimen was paramount for the successes of the decades-long mobilization.

No mass movement can be structured on the basis of nonviolence as an article of faith. Nonviolent resistance was often viewed through the lens of pragmatism in the 1955-65 U.S. civil rights movement. After the 1955 Montgomery bus boycott began, the Fellowship of Reconciliation sent Bayard Rustin and Glenn E. Smiley, seasoned professional trainers in nonviolent resistance, to tutor Martin Luther King, Jr., and introduce him systematically to Gandhian theories and methods, with which he had little familiarity.[24] Two months into the boycott, Smiley reported King's bodyguards had "an arsenal."[25] Rustin observed a gun left lying on a parsonage chair.[26] Within six weeks, as a result of studying the readings, King had banned guns for himself, his security guards, and the nascent movement, given the contradiction of his leading a nonviolent movement while also authorizing the use of weapons to protect himself. The Southern Christian Leadership Conference (SCLC) and Congress of Racial Equality (CORE) were both founded on explicit Gandhian thought, but contemplation of whether nonviolent direct action was a creed or a matter of pragmatism was constantly debated in the more ingenious Student Nonviolent Coordinating Committee (SNCC). Within SNCC (pron. *snick*), one amorphous wing viewed nonviolent struggle expediently, while another that originated in Nashville embraced normative nonviolence as an all-encompassing way of life.

In the rural, agrarian Deep South, with its lingering frontier ethos, African-American communities were armed. Guns were readily available for killing hogs, to put a horse out of its misery, or to hunt game for food. When civil rights workers came around, residents emptied rifle racks in pickup trucks and put away any guns that were normally out in the open where they resided. Local black Mississippians explained that they were doing so "to please the freedom riders." Unbeknownst to civil rights workers, local black youths sometimes stood guard with guns, sleeping under porches or on rooftops with rifles. The best that could be hoped was that the local people would leave their guns at home. The principled and the practical could neither be isolated nor contained.

Defining Nonviolent Movements: Behavior, not Belief

Offering the choice of action rather than inaction, and nonviolent rather than violent means of contention, nonviolent struggle balances political responsibility and ethics with the ultimate in efficacy and pragmatism.

Sociologist Kurt Schock, in examining what he terms "unarmed insurrections in nondemocracies," has shown that nonviolent movements succeed by forcing their opponents to take action rather than persuasion based on moral grounds. It is not the viewpoint of the opposition or oppressor, or its readiness to employ repression that decides the outcome of struggles that rely on nonviolent action; assumptions that political contexts determine the outcomes of collective struggles are misleading.[27]

The supposition that nonviolent resistance only works against mild repression or with "gentlemanly" opponents, such as the British in India, holds no validity whatsoever. The British colonial authorities in Mandate Palestine made mass arrests and introduced the demolition of homes as punishment of suspected dissidents, practices that the Israelis now use. In some cases British troops fired at unarmed Palestinians. During roughly the same period in India, on April 13, 1919, soldiers under the orders of British Brigadier General Reginald E. Dyer fired on more than 20,000 unarmed Indian peasants celebrating a Hindu festival in a sequestered walled garden in Amritsar. They killed 379 people and wounded more than 1,000.[28] As a point of comparison, the Amritsar massacre resulted in more deaths and casualties than when, in 1960, South African troops under the apartheid regime opened fire on unarmed peaceful demonstrators, killing 72 (of whom 40 were women, and 8 children) and wounding 186.[29] The incident, known as the Sharpeville Massacre, led to militant uprisings across the country that in turn resulted in the government banning antiapartheid organizations. The ban marked the end of decades of disciplined nonviolent action against apartheid that began after 1912. The methods of the antiapartheid movement then became "mixed," with Umkhonto we Sizwe (Spear of the Nation, or MK), the armed wing of the African National Congress (ANC), attempting armed struggle.

The armed sabotage of electricity lines, railways, and telephone lines in South Africa served as "an expression of dramatic propaganda, rather than full guerrilla or people's warfare," Bill Sutherland and Matt Meyer state; armed actions were more symbolic than nonviolent actions.[30] Few analysts believe that the antiapartheid violent struggle had any effect, apart from shoring up morale; the military prowess of the government vastly exceeded the capacity of MK. Yet reverberations from Sharpeville and its aftermath led to South Africa's withdrawal from the British Commonwealth, severance of diplomatic ties with South Africa by European nations, Canada, and the

United States, and boycotts of South African products. According to theologian Walter Wink, who conducted extensive interviews in the antiapartheid movement in South Africa in 1986, the most surprising result was that "a great many of the people simply do not know how to name their actual experiences with nonviolence."[31] A typical response to an inquiry about the action methods employed was "we tried [nonviolent resistance] for fifty years and it didn't work. Sharpeville in 1960 proved to us that violence is the only way left."[32] As Wink continued examining the most effective approaches in challenging the apartheid government, he discovered that his respondents

> produced a remarkably long list of nonviolent actions: labor strikes, slowdowns, sit-downs, stoppages, and stay-aways; bus boycotts, consumer boycotts, and school boycotts; funeral demonstrations; noncooperation with government appointed functionaries; non-payment of rent; violation of government bans on peaceful meetings; defiance of segregation orders on beaches and restaurants, theaters, and hotels; and the shunning of black police and soldiers. This amounts to what is probably the largest grassroots eruption of diverse nonviolent strategies in a single struggle in human history! Yet these students, and many others we interviewed, both black and white, failed to identify these tactics as nonviolent and even bridled at the word.[33]

Armed might and nonviolent action are often presumed not only to be distinct from each other, but also to be opposites. The relationship between them, however, is sometimes complex.[34] This is not to advocate the "mixing" of strategies, a strategic liability of some Palestinian factions during the intifada. Violent struggle and nonviolent action work in different ways; the two are not supplementary or complementary and cannot be blended. The injection of violence into a struggle destroys the potential for involving an entire people in self-reliant civil resistance, and thus affects mobilization and recruitment. Their combination also defeats the strategic advantage of a disciplined nonviolent movement, whose restraint can stand in sharp contrast to violent reprisals from the target group, thereby creating a condition in which the opposition reveals its own brutality. Acts of violence by the protagonists provide a pretext for reprisals and can lead to categorization as a terrorist organization. A British theoretician of military strategy, Captain Sir Basil Liddell Hart, interrogated German military generals after World War II and found "violent forms of resistance had not been very effective and troublesome to them." Yet the generals found it difficult to cope with the effectiveness of nonviolent resistance as practiced in Denmark, the Netherlands, and Norway. "They were experts in violence, and had been trained to deal with opponents who used that method. But other forms of resistance baffled them—and all the more in proportion as the methods were subtle and concealed. It was a relief to them when resistance becomes violent, and when non-violent forms are mixed with guerrilla action, thus making it easier to combine drastic suppressive action against both at the same time."[35]

Gandhi advised a resort to violence rather than submission if an individual could not summon the courage to resist nonviolently. He considered cowardice worse than violence, because it altered nothing, and the status quo ante remained intact. He believed nonviolent struggle to be the expression of strength, and in 1920 explains in "The Doctrine of the Sword,"

> [W]here there is only a choice between cowardice and violence I would advise violence. . . . I would rather have India resort to arms in order to defend her honour than that she should in a cowardly manner become or remain a helpless witness to her own dishonour. But I believe that non-violence is infinitely superior to violence. . . . Strength does not come from physical capacity. It comes from an indomitable will.[36]

Even if nonviolent action is only employed unilaterally, the number of losses and casualties is likely to be far less than in armed struggle, guerrilla warfare, or militarily insurrectionary methods of resistance. Scholar Richard Gregg spent years in India explaining its nonviolent struggles for Western readers, and wrote in 1960,

> In the Indian struggle for independence, though I know of no accurate statistic, hundreds of thousands of Indians went to jail, probably no more than five hundred received permanent physical injuries, and probably not over eight thousand were killed immediately or died later from wounds. No British, I believe, were killed or wounded. Considering the importance and size of the conflict and the many years it lasted, these numbers are much smaller than they would have been if the Indians had used violence against the British.[37]

If nothing else, the target group of the nonviolent challengers in an acute conflict is more likely to concentrate its attention on their actual grievance when not under the threat of violent attack.

Transmission of Knowledge

Historian David Hardiman asks how to explain that on virtually every continent nonviolent movements for social and political change are at work pursuing social justice, establishing democracies, realigning bureaucracies, securing human rights, unseating dictators, and throwing off military occupations, all based at least in part on a body of knowledge consolidated in India during the first half of the twentieth century?

That body of knowledge was itself infused with methods from India's past. Gandhi borrowed traditional cultural and religious customs, knowing the echo and resonance that they would have for the population. He reached back in time for the raw material of forms of mass collective action from India's past in formulating his techniques of struggle, including a nineteenth-century indigo revolt, movements against landlords, and tax resistance campaigns—peasant rebellions that had won support from members of the elite.[38] Gandhi was also writing about struggles elsewhere, such as the Hungarian nationalist struggle against the Hapsburgs from 1849 to 1867, and the Russian Revolution of 1905. Gene Sharp asserts:

> the Indian campaigns in South Africa, and Gandhi's own conceptions of appropriate means of struggle, were inspired or influenced by other recent cases of nonviolent resistance and revolution, including events in China, Russia, India, and South Africa. . . . Three cases which attracted Gandhi's attention in South Africa during this period were the Chinese boycott of American goods against the United States anti-Chinese legislation, the Russian 1905 Revolution, and the boycott movement in Bengal against British partition of that Indian state.[39]

Historian Sudarshan Kapur shows a steady flow of African-American leaders traveled by steamer ship to India during the 1930s and 1940s to learn the theories and methods of the Indian independence movements.[40] Upon their return to the United States, they gave lectures, wrote articles, preached, and passed key documents from hand to hand, to be studied by other black leaders. Their path exemplifies how the spread of knowledge concerning nonviolent action is often person to person.

Krishnalal Shridharani's *War without Violence* is particularly significant among the books circulated by the African-American leaders.[41] Shridharani, a Brahmin associate of Gandhi's, was one of the original seventy-nine adherents who trained with him for the 1930 Salt March and walked with him the 241 miles from Ahmedabad to the seacoast at Dandi. Derived from Shridharani's doctoral dissertation at Columbia University and first published in 1939, *War without Violence* is a firsthand analysis of Gandhian theories and methods. During the 1940s, such notable U.S. black leaders as A. Philip Randolph of the Brotherhood of Sleeping Car Porters and James Farmer studied *War without Violence*. Indeed, Farmer founded the Congress of Racial Equality on transference of Gandhian principles and techniques during the 1940s, and employed the sit-ins and freedom rides that would again be used in the 1960s. Martin Luther King, Jr., studied Shridharani's book during the Montgomery bus boycott, making it probably the single most influential document in the diffusion of knowledge from India to the United States and thence to the entire globe.

Transmission of knowledge from India by American black leaders is straightforward and indisputable. After King's death, his own voluminous writings combined with Gandhi's then-ninety volumes of mostly newspaper articles comprised a large collection, portions of which quietly spread into Latin America and the Philippines in the 1970s and into Eastern Europe and elsewhere during the 1980s to be translated into dozens of languages and studied wherever persons and groups contemplated taking history into their own hands through nonviolent action. It is now obvious that nonviolent resistance is not a Hindu specialization or technique solely effective in a Christian ethos; it has been practiced in many parts of the globe by atheists and Muslims and peoples of many other faiths, or none at all.

As access to the Internet broadens, wisdom is more accurately and exponentially spreading on how to plan and strategize the use of nonviolent sanctions. Focus on communications is crucial *within* and *without* nonviolent campaigns for reasons of morale and because of the necessity to explain grievances clearly. One cannot expect the target group to change unless the desired alterations are stated unmistakably. International third parties depend upon communications for their solidarity, a factor increasingly significant in nonviolent struggles. Tertiary sanctions can reinforce the strategy of a movement while making regimes aware that repressive actions will be broadcast and publicized.

During the late 1990s in Eastern Europe, the Serbian people (especially students) employed in their struggle against the dictatorial Slobodan Miloševic the lessons learned and shared with them by the Czechs and Slovaks' in their 1980s "Velvet Revolution." Toward the end of the 1990s, the Serbian students had begun studying the academic writings of Gene Sharp in skills-training workshops led by Colonel Robert L. Helvey, a retired U.S. military officer.[42] During 2002–3, the Serbian activists passed their knowledge and skills on to those in the Republic of Georgia (formerly Soviet Union) preparing for what would become the "Rose Revolution." Azerbaijanis, Kazaks, Ukrainians, and Zimbabweans, among others, are scrutinizing what their Serbian and Georgian counterparts studied and learned.

In virtually every part of the globe, the period since the 1980s has seen major nonviolent struggles produce political results. Such held to be true in the Baltic states, what is now the Czech Republic, the former East Germany, and elsewhere in Eastern Europe, Latin America, the Philippines, Poland, the former Soviet Union, and South Africa. Struggles in recent years have also been efficacious, and without large numbers of fatalities.

Chapter 3
Historical Review: Early Use of Nonviolent Sanctions by Palestinians

THE DIASPORA OF THE Jews began with the Babylonian exile in 586 B.C.E. Propelled by economic, demographic, and political pressures, and lured by opportunities, Jews began emigrating from Palestine to various parts of the Mediterranean. They flourished in Alexandria, Egypt, where approximately one million of them lived in the first century B.C.E. Large Jewish populations were established in different areas of the Roman Empire, especially in Asia Minor, and diaspora Jews outnumbered the Jews in Palestine, as they sought prospects in climes other than the poor country of Palestine. Over the centuries, Jewish communities spread throughout much of the world.

In the modern era, Jewish colonization of Palestine began in the 1880s, as economic displacement and waves of pogroms drove millions of Eastern European Jews to leave the Pale of Settlement and find new homes in western Europe, the United States, and South America. A small minority looked to Palestine for their new home.[1] The Zionist movement first arose in Russia coterminously with the development of Marxism in the late nineteenth century. As a political philosophy, it resembled the nationalist movements of Europe after the French Revolution, the benefits of which often eluded Jews. The concept of a nation-state during an era of European colonialism seemed an appropriate response for the protection of Jews from the discrimination and persecution of anti-Semitism, the Zionists thought. They also saw it as an attempt to correct centuries of Western anti-Semitism, currents of which would ultimately culminate in the Holocaust.

In Palestine, the first dispute between Jewish settlers and Arab peasants occurred in 1886 over land in Petah Tiqvah (Gate of Hope), the earliest Jewish colony, founded in 1878 near Tel Aviv.[2] Some forty violent encounters between Zionist immigrants and Palestinian Arabs would take place during the next three decades.[3] Although the Zionist leadership recognized the numerical significance of the Arab population from 1908 on, only after World War I did average persons among European Jewry realize the ethical and practical complications of the Zionist dream: half a million Muslim and Christian Arabs already inhabited Palestine.[4]

The newly arriving immigrants did not seek to integrate into the economies or institutions of the existing population. Their vision of a Jewish homeland entailed the development of their own structures and economic ventures, generally without Arab employees or consumption of Arab-produced goods. Sociologist Gershon Shafir explains that Jewish colonization rested on two doctrines: Hebrew labor, or conquest of labor, aimed to replace Arab workers with Jewish workers at all levels, and Hebrew land, or conquest of land, meant that Arab land, once purchased by the land-purchasing and development arm of the World Zionism Organization, could not be resold to Arabs. Historian Benny Morris adds, "The Arabs sought instinctively to retain the Arab and Muslim character of the region and to maintain their position as its rightful inhabitants; the Zionists sought radically to change the status quo, buy as much land as possible, settle on it, and eventually turn an Arab-populated country into a Jewish homeland."[5] With the loss of land and jobs associated with Zionist settlement and enterprises, conflicting interpretations of national rights arose and would be magnified by the colonial presence of the British. During the 1920s and 1930s, the Palestinian Arabs primarily drew upon the repertoire of nonviolent resistance in protesting the changes taking place around them and in fighting for what they regarded as their country. The same methods would reappear during the first intifada.

Palestinian Opposition to the 1917 Balfour Declaration

The modern Palestinian national movement is generally considered to have begun with the 1916 Sykes-Picot Agreement that divided the Ottoman Empire into British and French spheres of influence (with the concurrence of Imperial Russia) and continued through Arthur James Balfour's 1917 letter supporting a Jewish national home in Palestine, General Edmund Allenby's military entry into Palestine on December 9, 1917, after the Turks had evacuated,[6] and the acceptance of the British Mandate for Palestine by the League of Nations in 1922.

On November 2, 1917, Lord Balfour, the British secretary of state for foreign affairs, issued his letter to Lord Lionel Walter Rothschild, London leader of the Rothschild banking family and of British Jewry, containing the following:

His Majesty's Government view with favour the establishment in Palestine of a national home for the Jewish people, and will use their best endeavours to facilitate the achievement of this object, it being clearly understood that nothing shall be done which may prejudice the civil and religious rights of the existing non-Jewish[7] communities in Palestine or the rights and political status enjoyed by Jews in any other country.[8]

The negotiations leading to the letter had taken three years and six drafts to reach the final text.[9] Balfour had first met Chaim Weizmann, the guiding force of Zionism, in 1906.[10] Weizmann had moved to Britain because of his belief that of all the great powers, Britain would be most likely to give strong support to Zionism. Balfour, already sympathetic to Zionism because of his Scottish rearing and study of the Old Testament under his mother, was moved by the vision of a Jewish national revival in the Holy Land. It was not, however, Weizmann's elegant diplomacy that shaped events to come so much as the tract *Der Judenstaat* (the Jewish State), by Theodor Herzl, a Viennese dramatist and correspondent of *Neue Freie Presse* in Paris, which articulated the concept of political Zionism. On August 29–31, 1897, Herzl had brought together 197 Jewish "delegates" of varied political persuasions and from different areas of the world at Basel, Switzerland, and founded what became the World Zionist Organization, of which Weizmann was president for most of the British Mandate period.[11] The original program of the Basel congress called for establishment of "a publicly and legally secured home in Palestine for the Jewish people," that is, a Jewish state.[12] The wording was softened by this and subsequent congresses so as not to stimulate opposition, including that of Jews who preferred to assimilate themselves. Everyone in the British government knew that statehood was the goal, according to historian Barbara Tuchman, at least as early as 1903—the year that the British government offered the Zionists the right to colonize in East Africa—but the Zionists would deny until 1937 that there was any intention to establish a Jewish state in Palestine.[13] Apparently ignoring the efforts by Arabs and other national groups under the Ottoman Empire that were questioning the Porte's suzerainty, Herzl approached Constantinople pledging to the sultan the advantages of Jewish immigration. Turned down by the Ottomans, in October 1902 Herzl sought help from the British in assisting Jewish settlement in Palestine.[14]

The Jews had become acculturated during centuries of living throughout the world, most particularly on the continent of Europe, and despite persecution, had made dramatic contributions to the culture and politics of many countries. Yet they continued to be regarded as foreigners.[15] Support for Jewish migration to the Holy Land was buttressed by concealed bigotry and a desire to get rid of local Jewish populations. The issue of "alien immigration" had been raised in Britain by the arrival of large numbers of Jews from the Continent, many of them fleeing pogroms in Russia. Restrictive legislation was proposed in 1904 and reintroduced in 1905, and Jewish refugees were about to be barred from further immigration.[16] A vision of a restored Israel, with exiled Israelites returning to the Promised Land held great appeal not only for Balfour, but also for David Lloyd George (prime minister 1916–22), other ministers of government, and much of Western Christendom.[17] Support for Zionism thus resulted from "strange combinations of romanticism and strategic reasoning, zealotry and altruism, pro-Jewish sympathy and professed anti-Semitism."[18] Knowledge of Palestine in the West was mainly confined to the Bible, and it was felt appropriate to atone for anti-Semitism by affirming migration to Palestine, considered to be uninhabited desert. Herbert Louis Samuel, who would five years later become the first high commissioner of Palestine, wrote in March 1915 to the British Cabinet that Zionism would save the Christian Holy Places from the "vulgarization" they were suffering and open the Holy Land to "Christian travellers."[19] American Jewry, both individuals and institutions, gave money to buy land and provided strong political promotion for Zionism. Europeans and Americans who might otherwise have considered scriptural claims an inappropriate basis for international law, because of their shared Judeo-Christian tradition and identification with biblical accounts, supported the creation of a national home for the Jews.

Nostalgia and economic reasoning blended with strategic considerations.[20] Excluding any other European power from becoming a threat to the security of the Suez Canal was thought essential by Britain.[21] Leonard Stein authoritatively argues that expediency was the underlying force at work in Balfour's belabored letter. He observes:

> The war years were not a time for sentimental gestures. The British Government's business was to win the War and to safeguard British interests in the post-war settlement. Fully realising that these must in the end be the decisive tests, Weizmann was never under the illusion that the Zionists

could rely on an appeal *ad misericordiam*. Zionist aspirations must be shown to accord with British strategic and political interests.[22]

The relationship was contractual in spirit. With the gains of the German submarine war of 1917, the government in London sought assistance from all quarters. The Zionists offered the help of the constituency they claimed, in return for a British declaration of public law supporting their territorial goal in Palestine. The Balfour Declaration was the "winning card" in a "sordid contest between the two sets of belligerents" in World War I, Arnold Toynbee said, believing that his government's use of the term "national home" had been "deliberately ambiguous."[23] Other factors included the extension of the Pax Britannica of the Indian Raj, the civilizing mission of European imperialism, and the absence of mechanisms for expressions of Arab views.[24] It was generally thought that economic advantages would accrue to the Arabs as a result of Jewish settlement, that Arab hostility would dissolve as these economic benefits grew, and that the Arabs would eventually reconcile themselves to the contents of Balfour's letter.

By the mid-1920s, a number of Jewish philosophers were at work on ideas of binationalism that linked Jewish destiny to that of the Arabs, but no comparable philosophies developed that synthesized Arab nationalism with Zionism.[25] By the mid-1930s, the British oversaw the Suez Canal, while also protecting and maintaining an oil pipeline from Iraq with a terminus at the Haifa port, an air base at Lydda, communications flow by land and air to India, and British protectorates and possessions in the Mediterranean region.[26]

Between 1914 and 1918, Britain made a succession of promises to the Arabs concerning independence, self-government, and the principle of the consent of the governed.[27] Yet in 1919, Lord Balfour conceded that his pledges to Lord Rothschild for a national home for the Jews were incompatible with the rights of the Arab inhabitants. Furthermore, he writes:

> For in Palestine we do not propose even to go through the form of consulting the wishes of the present inhabitants of the country. . . . Zionism, be it right or wrong, good or bad, is rooted in age-long traditions, in present needs, in future hopes, of far profounder import than the desires and prejudices of the 700,000 Arabs who now inhabit that ancient land. . . . Whatever deference should be paid to the views of those who live

there, the Powers in their selection of a mandatory do not propose, as I understand the matter, to consult them.[28]

British policy in Palestine was in part shaped by belief that the Arabs could not govern themselves.

The Palestinian Arab response to the British colonial presence was, at best, recalcitrant. Although some Palestinian Arabs had accepted the idea of a parliamentary entity in which Jews residing in Palestine prior to World War I would enjoy proportional representation, they did not want to grant legitimacy to Zionist settlements or institutions, which they believed would encroach on their national rights. The Zionist leaders regarded it as essential to forge international recognition of their right to relocate in Palestine, and Jewish immigrants there thought of themselves as "a beleaguered minority endowed with historic rights."[29] Britain's Foreign Office gave the Zionists the use of the diplomatic pouch.[30] By contrast, the families of the Arabs' traditional aristocratic leadership were unknown in international capital cities. They had never been organized locally on any basis comparable to that of the Jews, nor had they established "any equivalent" in institutions.[31] The creation of legal structures comparable to the growing Zionist entities might have represented their point of view; however, by establishing formal entities to represent themselves before the colonial authorities, they would have been recognizing the legitimacy of the Zionist settlements defended by the colonial powers. According to a study by Palestinian-American historian Rashid Khalidi of how the Arabic print media between 1908 and 1914 treated Zionism in twenty-two newspapers and periodicals in Palestine, Cairo, and Beirut: "In no article among the more than 650 examined for this analysis of the press and Zionism was there a call for armed resistance to the colonizers, although . . . in a few areas the peasants had already spontaneously engaged in such resistance."[32]

Six Palestine Arab congresses convened between 1919 and 1923 in opposition to the Balfour Declaration.[33] Even before the official disclosure of Balfour's letter to the residents of Palestine, a large peaceful demonstration of hundreds of Palestinian Arabs assembled in opposition to its rumored contents in Jerusalem on February 27, 1920, with the knowledge if not assent of the British colonial authorities.[34] On March 8, a second demonstration took place, this time with speeches of a "violently political character," and stones were thrown.[35]

Opponents of the reported letter again held a demonstration on March 11, despite the British having proscribed public protests under pressure from the Zionists.[36] The Palestinians' popular dissent began peaceably, with 1,500 demonstrators rallying in Jerusalem, 2,000 in Jaffa, and 250 in Haifa. Exhibiting coordinated, nationwide action, Palestinians also closed shops and submitted petitions to British authorities.[37] By the end of Easter Week 1920, however, such modest protests boiled over into a violent clash between Arabs and Jews in which nine persons were killed.[38] Following the seven days of the yearly al-Nabi Musa celebrations, processions of delegations from across Palestine proceeded south from Jerusalem toward Jericho, destined for the mosque considered by Muslims to stand above the grave of Moses. After feasting by the Dead Sea, they returned to Jerusalem for closing prayers. The speeches at the annual ceremony on April 12 were of a "flagrantly political character" and the presence of agents provocateurs considered "extremely probable," the British military's Palin Report noted on events of that day.[39] The gathering eventually turned into a demonstration against the Jews. Five of them were murdered and 216 injured, while 4 Arabs were killed by firearms and 21 wounded.[40] Protests erupted across Palestine against the ratification of the Balfour Declaration at San Remo on April 25, 1920[41] and in opposition to the separation of Palestine from what was then Greater Syria, an alliance thought by young militant Palestinians to be the best vehicle for independence (and one nullified by the creation of the French and British mandates in 1922).

Britain's Peel Commission, headed by Lord William Robert Wellesley Peel, later concluded about the April 1920 riots: ". . . the causes of the trouble had been (1) the Arabs' disappointment at the non-fulfilment of the promises of independence . . . (2) the Arabs' belief that the Balfour Declaration implied a denial of the right of self-determination, and their fear that the establishment of the National Home would mean a great increase of Jewish immigration and would lead to their economic and political subjection to the Jews. . . ."[42] The violence had the effect of accelerating strides toward Jewish self-defense. Chaim Weizmann, the guiding force of world Zionism, called the riots a pogrom and argued that greatly increased immigration represented the only antidote to their repetition.[43]

Haj Amin al-Husseini, who for three decades would be the main Palestinian figure in opposition to Zionist political goals, was present at the speeches on April 12.[44] On May 8, the British, following the Ottoman custom of choosing a mufti, a religious jurist who acts as the head of the Muslim establishment, advised Haj Amin that they would grant him the position.[45] The British high commissioner had established a committee of Muslim leaders who in 1921 recommended the formation of the Supreme Muslim Council, and Haj Amin became its first president that year, an exceptional position of leadership in the Muslim community that had not existed under Muslim rule.[46] At Haj Amin's request, the mandatory government also granted him the more exalted title of grand mufti, *al-mufti al-akbar,* apparently considering the office a modest price for ensuring stability, which would last for eight years.[47]

During most of the 1920s, the Palestinians, led by Haj Amin and others in the often-feuding elite Palestinian Arab leadership, directed their resistance toward London and its support for the Zionist movement. They used the simplest and most basic nonviolent action methods of protest and persuasion: formal statements, declarations, petitions, manifestos, assemblies, delegations, processions, marches, and motorcades.[48] Although some of Haj Amin's biographers conclude that he primarily favored violence in the Palestinian struggle,[49] for the better part of the 1920s he advocated and employed rudimentary nonviolent sanctions.

Britain's military regime ended on June 30, 1920, and was replaced by a civil administration under Herbert Louis Samuel, later a viscount, a liberal Jewish ally of the Zionists who assumed office as the first high commissioner of Palestine, convinced that the Arabs would ultimately reconcile themselves to the program of the Zionists.[50] A boycott protesting Samuel's appointment ended weakly.[51] Violent outbreaks erupted only intermittently. Political parties had not yet begun to organize. With the Third Palestine Arab Congress (known as the Haifa Congress), held on December 13, 1920, opposition to the Balfour Declaration resulted in a deluge of manifestos to the League of Nations contesting the validity of British policy. A number of Muslim-Christian Association branches sent representatives from across Palestine to the meeting. In Haifa, the number of Christians signing public statements opposing the Balfour Declaration and joining protest actions often exceeded the participation of Muslims, and included landowners and wealthy merchants.[52] The Haifa Congress elected Musa Kazim Pasha al-Husseini to head the Executive Committee, a.k.a. Arab Executive, composed primarily of notable families. The public unified around the Arab Executive based on the hope of nullifying the Balfour Declaration through political action, a prospect that did not seem unrealistic at the time.[53] The thirty-seven delegates passed resolutions rejecting a national home for the Jews based on the Balfour Declaration, declaring their non-acceptance of the principle of Jewish immigration, and calling for the establishment of a national representative government.[54] Their resolutions represent the three basic doctrines of the Arab national movement at that time.[55]

The first Arab street demonstration under the civil administration took place in Nablus soon after the Haifa Congress to protest the Balfour Declaration. In Haifa, demonstrators defied a prohibition to march. When the governor of Jaffa rejected a request to march, Muslim shops closed in protest on March 28, 1921. In Jerusalem on the same day, another large, peaceful demonstration occurred. During a visit to Palestine, Winston Churchill, then secretary of state for the colonies, met with a Palestinian delegation from the Executive Committee of the Haifa Congress. Musa Kazim al-Husseini presented Churchill with a long memorandum from the congress dissecting the Balfour Declaration and requesting the abolition of the principle of a Jewish national home, the creation of a national government, cessation of Jewish immigration until an Arab national government could be formed, and the return of Palestine to its status prior to the proposed British Mandate under which it was unified with neighboring Arab states.[56] Churchill replied, "[I]t is not in my power" to repudiate the Balfour Declaration or halt Jewish immigration, "nor, if it were in my power, would it be my wish" and cited the right to rule based on military conquest.[57] During Churchill's stay, Palestinians held demonstrations in Haifa and Beisan.[58]

Jaffa, the main port in Palestine, sat adjacent to the growing Jewish neighborhoods of Tel Aviv and Petah Tiqvah. On May 1, Jaffa Arabs rioted.[59] Disputes over authorized and unauthorized May Day parades by Jewish socialists and communists had touched off the clash. Arabs congregating at the Jaffa side of an open area between the port and Tel Aviv misinterpreted police shots fired into the air to disperse the Zionists, who were gathered on the Tel Aviv side. A mob moved through the town, smashing Jewish shops and attacking pedestrians.[60] Rumor-mongering led to Arab attacks on Zionist settlements along the coastal plain and, after six days, 47 Jews had been killed and 146 wounded, while 48 Arabs lay dead and 73 injured, mainly by other Arabs.[61] High Commissioner Samuel was the first British official to grasp the magnitude of the Jaffa riots, which were attributed to increasing Jewish immigration and the resulting unemployment of Palestinians.[62] At a court of inquiry after the Jaffa riots, a representative of the Zionist Organization substantiated the fears felt by Palestinians, despite British blandishments, when he insisted "there can be only one National Home in Palestine, and that is a Jewish one, and no equality in the partnership between Jews and Arabs, but a Jewish preponderance as soon as the numbers of the race are sufficiently increased."[63] Large numbers of newly arriving immigrants disembarking at Haifa had begun changing this once "small roadstead" into a crowded harbor city. The Haganah (Defense), the Jewish self-defense organization founded in 1920 and later a people's militia, funneled guns through Haifa. Some members of the Jewish labor movement, including the carpenters' union, smuggled arms to the communists. In 1924, Jewish firms in the city were reportedly running arms from Danzig to Palestine.[64]

In July 1921, the first delegation of Arab leaders to travel to London protested to the Colonial Office, demanding abrogation of Balfour's pledge, an end to Jewish immigration, and the establishment of representative government rather than a mandate.[65] In February 1922, another delegation reiterated this position to the Colonial Office.[66] Churchill subsequently issued the White Paper of June 1922, a "cunningly balanced document" substantially drafted by Samuel. Its basic principles would formally stand until 1939.[67] It sought to limit the significance of the Balfour Declaration by interpreting the policy as not having the intention of subordinating the Arab populace or culture, and spoke of government plans to assist in the gradual establishment of self-government. The Palestinians rejected it, because British policy remained nonetheless based on Balfour. Shortly thereafter, following approval by the United States, on July 24 the Council of the League of Nations confirmed the British Mandate, explicitly including the Balfour Declaration in its second paragraph.[68] Also in July, a Palestinian delegation arrived in Mecca to orchestrate for the first time specifically Muslim support for their position. Their visit reportedly resulted in peaceful demonstrations by Afghan, Indian, Iranian, Javanese, Kurdish, Sudanese, and Turkish pilgrims to Mecca and Jidda.[69] Within Palestine, as the mandate became a fait accompli, the tone of Palestinian opposition changed from contesting the Jewish national home and delineation of the mandate to rejection of the entire mandate and assertion of independence.

Palestinian Noncooperation in the 1920s

On October 23, 1922, the British conducted the first census designating the religious faith of Palestine's population. Of the 752,048 people counted,

589,177 were Muslim, 83,794 Jewish, 71,464 Christian, and 7,028 Druzes.[70] The shift of dominion to a government supporting Zionist goals, and the increasing number of Jewish immigrants, led to changes in Palestinian thinking. Their opposition turned to action methods of noncooperation, in which cooperation and assistance are suspended, including withdrawal from the social or political system, strikes, resignations from jobs, slowdowns, boycotts of elections, and civil disobedience. Village *mukhtars* (similar to mayors) began to refuse to cooperate with government commissioners. Palestinians protested land grants to Zionists in a variety of areas and held a general strike on July 13 and 14, 1922, closing shops across the country. Villagers were encouraged not to tithe to a non-Muslim government, and prayers about the danger facing Palestine were offered in mosques. Haj Amin issued a fatwa, a legal opinion of Islamic jurisprudence, forbidding the sale of land by Muslims to Zionists or their agents.[71] Those who sold land to Zionist brokers or middlemen risked the sanction of excommunication—losing access to Islamic sites. Foreshadowing the division of opinion in the leadership of the first intifada almost seven decades later, by the summer of 1922 district governors split between two schools of thought—one favoring nonviolent methods of noncooperation, and the other preferring direct obstruction, confrontations, and armed guerrilla warfare.[72]

Palestinian leaders first used the nonviolent subcategory of political noncooperation when they refused to participate in a variety of conciliatory constitutional arrangements proposed by High Commissioner Samuel.[73] In response to the May 1921 Jaffa riots, Samuel had issued a temporary halt of Jewish immigration and was also prompted to attempt to reconcile Britain's irreconcilable obligations in the Balfour Declaration. Toward that end, he persuaded Churchill that a legislative assembly could provide a forum for the representation of Palestinian views to advise the civil administration. Later, on August 22, 1922, in Nablus, the Fifth Palestine Arab Congress voted to boycott Samuel's new Palestine constitution and proposed elections for a Palestine legislative council. With the constitution and council predicated on the Balfour Declaration—guaranteeing that the assembly would have a majority of non-Arabs and few powers—the fundamental Palestinian dilemma remained: participation could be construed as acceptance of the British Mandate and thus the Jewish national home, yet rejection of such a step toward self-governance would deny the Palestinians the possibility of moderating Jewish colonization (which to their minds would please the

Zionists).[74] In public pronouncements, they pressured the British to agree to their three basic demands.

In assembly elections held February 20–28, 1923, only 126 of the 722 seats allocated to Muslim and Christian Arabs were filled.[75] Throughout the country, only 1,397 votes were cast—1,172 of them by Jews, representing a turnout 50 percent Jewish, 18 percent Muslim, and 5.5 percent Christian.[76] With the elections "an embarrassing fiasco,"[77] Samuel declared them null and void: "In two out of the four districts into which Palestine is divided, the Arab population abstained . . . from submitting nominations and in the other two districts there was a partial abstention. This was due partly to voluntary action and partly to exercise of strong pressure by the organization opposing the election. The consequence, . . . [is that] His Majesty's Government have decided to suspend, for the time being, such part of the proposed constitution as relates to the establishment of a Legislative Council."[78] On March 12, 1923, Palestinians announced a work stoppage and shop closures to occur on the fourteenth, to underscore their withholding participation in the legislative council elections. The Sixth Palestine Arab Congress, held in Jaffa from June 16 through 20, passed resolutions restating old demands. Delegates discussed political obstruction and tax resistance.[79]

From 1920 to 1924, the Palestinian Arabs took the position that no elements of their society could cooperate with the British so long as its policy remained based on the Balfour Declaration. A contemporary account of a British colonel notes "wonderful self-control and exemplary behaviour of the local [Palestinian] Christians and Arabs" in response to Lord Balfour's first and only trip to Palestine, in March and April 1925, to inaugurate Hebrew University on Mount Scopus in Jerusalem: "Beyond showing their feelings by passing the day in prayer, with closed houses and places of business shrouded in black, and shunning the precincts of the new University, the Mohammedans made no hostile demonstration of any kind; and a similar attitude was taken by the Christian population."[80] The Palestinians had thus begun to combine nonviolent methods from the simplest category of protest and persuasion, with noncooperation methods that suspend obedience, such as the "stay-at-home." Blanche Dugdale, Balfour's niece and biographer, confirmed the one-day strike, noting that all the Arab shops closed and that Jerusalem's Arab newspapers ran borders in mourning black.[81]

As successive British Conservative and Labour governments inherited and retained the policy based on the Balfour Declaration, internal schisms deepened among Palestinians, as many of them arrived at the conclusion that nonviolent sanctions and persuasive appeals would be to no avail.[82] By the time the Palestinians reconsidered their position on a legislative body in 1928, the Zionists had rejected the principle.

The adoption of Islamic emblems for opposition to the Balfour policy emerged at the end of the 1920s. For Jews, the Western (Wailing) Wall (Kotel Maaravi), on the lower part of the outer wall of Herod's temple, and the sacred Temple Mount, represented the "last relic of their ancient sanctuary and of their national glory."[83] On September 24, 1928, the Jewish Day of Atonement, Yom Kippur, Jewish worshippers set up a partition at the outer wall of the temple in Jerusalem, dividing it into sections for men and for women. This rekindled an old dispute as complex as it was bitter, setting off a spiraling of events known as the uprisings of 1929.[84] In Muslim lore, the wall stood as part of the stable for the Prophet's winged horse, Buraq, who, according to tradition, carried Muhammad as he ascended into the heavens, as well as the retaining wall of the Haram al-Sharif (August Sanctuary), where Muhammad's skyward journey is said to have begun.[85] It had long been considered *Maghrebi waqf*. Maghreb refers to North Africa above the Sahara Desert and west of the Nile, and the term *waqf* (Islamic trust) is impersonally owned land set aside for pious purposes, which could not be sold or transferred under Muslim religious law.[86] This specific *waqf* was allocated to provide homes for Moroccan pilgrims to Jerusalem in the fourteenth century.[87] Since medieval times, the Jews had possessed the right to pray along the narrow pavement below the wall, and they believed that they were entitled to bring a screen, chairs, and scrolls. Muslims feared such measures, however, as the first steps toward a Jewish takeover of the Haram al-Sharif. On November 1, 1928, in Jerusalem, Haj Amin convened a General Muslim Conference (a.k.a. Islamic Congress), with seven hundred participants from across Palestine who promptly sent formal statements of protest to the League of Nations. They also established the Society for the Protection of the Muslim Holy Places.[88] The Colonial Office issued a white paper that month upholding the Ottoman position granting Jews the right to pray at the Western Wall, though without chairs, screens, or benches, out of concern that permitting the items to remain in place might establish a precedent and arouse the Muslims.[89] When the Jews refused to comply with orders to remove the partitions and various other articles, fights broke out with British officers.

Across Palestine, rumors spread about a possible rebuilding of the great Jewish Temple on the site of the al-Aqsa mosque atop the Haram al-Sharif.

Haj Amin originally intended to find a political solution,[90] but the mufti's efforts soon turned to bloodshed. The mandatory government failed to respond with legal approval for Muslim claims to the Western Wall, and a series of disturbances and counterdisturbances erupted during the following year. Jews marched to the wall on August 14, 1929, on the fast of Tisha Bav, to commemorate the destruction of the Second Temple in 70 C.E., and Arab demonstrations of possibly two thousand persons followed at the site the next day and again on August 16 for Mawlad al-Nabi, the Prophet's birthday.[91] During the next few days, skirmishes resulted in the wounding of eleven Jews and fifteen Palestinians, and the death of one Jewish boy.[92] These events culminated in what the Palestinian Arabs called the Buraq Revolt, rioting that lasted in the Jerusalem area from August 23 to 29, 1929. On August 23, armed with sticks, knives, revolvers, clubs, and swords, fellahin (peasant laborers) arrived at al-Aqsa for prayers. Following speeches by Haj Amin and others, the crowd charged into the area of the Western Wall; the police opened fire.[93] Mobs directed the worst of the violence at ancient Jewish communities in Hebron and Safed.[94] In Hebron, rioters massacred sixty non-Zionist Jews and injured one hundred members of the Old Yishuv, the old orthodox settlements antedating Zionism, who, pious and pacifist, did not fight back. By August 30, when the violence had reached Safed in the north, twenty Jews had been murdered and a hundred houses robbed. Across the country, 133 Jews had been killed and more than 300 wounded.[95] The catalyst may have been anti-Jewish sentiment—"mob action" to frighten the Zionists—but, as British troops began firing at Palestinians, residents of Arab towns including Acre, Gaza, Jenin, Nablus, and Tulkarem began to exhibit an explicitly anti-British bias.[96] In addition, Palestinian Arabs' implicit acceptance of non-Zionist Jews and for Judaism as a faith was broken.[97]

The British Commission of Enquiry, headed by Sir Walter Shaw, traveled around Palestine between October and December 1929, and found that a "National Home for the Jews, in the sense in which it was widely understood, was inconsistent with the demands of the Arab nationalists while the claims of Arab nationalism, if admitted, would have rendered impossible the fulfillment of the pledge to the Jews."[98] By the end of the year, reciprocal boycotts of Jewish merchants and Arab businesses were in place. The assessment by Sir John Hope Simpson—a former civil administrator in India who by the end of the decade had written two of the earliest modern studies on refugees—on October 20 verified "serious and widespread" Arab unemployment, some resulting from eviction of the fellahin, and inadequate land for agricultural cultivation by Palestinians already farming the land.[99] The Shaw and Simpson reports raised the question of Britain's obligations to the Zionists when they conflicted with its obligations to the Arabs under the Covenant of the League of Nations. The white paper of that same date— issued by the secretary of state for the colonies, Lord Passfield, better known as Sidney Webb—urged self-government along lines similar to those of Churchill's 1922 memorandum and called for proportional representation of Arabs and Jews.[100] This temporary reversal of policy, which might have allowed for an independent Arab state, reflected Britain's desire to retain control of the larger Muslim Middle East. In London, a "storm of protest" erupted among Jews and Conservative opposition leaders. The Zionists attacked the Passfield proposal because it allocated their seats according to their "actual population," the British governor of Jerusalem noted; "yet, if ever a people seem to deserve at least the opportunity of official public utterance, it is the Arabs of Palestine."[101]

The subsequent nullification of the Passfield White Paper in a letter from Prime Minister Ramsay MacDonald to Chaim Weizmann published on February 14, 1931—dubbed the "Black Paper" by the Palestinians—was viewed by Palestinians as regression and repudiation of the Arab Executive's moderate policies.[102] This advocacy of a position followed by its withdrawal intensified the misgivings of both Palestinians and Jews regarding British policy. Zionist land purchases proceeded unabated through the Jewish National Fund, established in 1901, which held land acquisitions in trusteeship, excluding non-Jews from controlling that land.

Palestinian Resistance in the 1930s
The 1930s brought the intensification and broadening of Palestinian opposition, with more general strikes and closures and the development of an extensive committee apparatus for support. Political parties emerged. A preceding decade of mostly nonviolent resistance by the Palestinians, led by aristocratic families, would be supplanted by a period in which popular, rural violence at times verged on the anarchic. These years witnessed the growth of armed Arab resistance, as the organization of Jewish armed resistance also accelerated.[103] The flow of Jewish immigrants was not an abstraction to the Palestinians, "as they saw entire regions of the country changing face."[104]

There had been calls early on for Palestinians to employ the nonviolent method of resigning from jobs in the mandatory government. As suspicions grew, however, that the Balfour Declaration could not be nullified and the British would not be departing, an opposing current sought instead to place Palestinian Arabs into these positions. In this, Christians had the advantage of higher levels of education, attained at schools run by religious orders or missionaries that had been able to function during the Ottoman period and had protected the study of the Arabic language and literature. Large numbers of Christian Arabs went to work for the civil administration. This resulted in Muslim unease, which, along with the rise of the Supreme Muslim Council, encouraged the organization of religious groups that did not adhere to the traditional approach of Muslim-Christian unity and downplayed the idea of a secular national identity common to Muslims and Christians. Exclusively Islamic entities developed, such as the Young Men's Muslim Association and youth scouting. At the same time, word spread from Damascus and Baghdad about concepts of Arab unity and independence, rousing a young educated elite whose status derived from education rather than clan.[105]

In the summer of 1931, a Palestinian conference in Nablus demanded the establishment of a defense organization and the procurement of weapons in response to help being given by the British for Jewish defense. The young activists (and the general public) denounced the policies of the Arab Executive for having selected lobbying as the approach to the British rather than armed means. Calls rose for independence in the context of Arab unity and the boycotting of imports not made by Palestinian Arabs.[106] It is probable that this July meeting was the first time that armed struggle (*al-kifah al-musalah*) was publicly expounded as the only means for contesting the completion of the goals of the Zionist movement. One of the conference delegates from Hebron proposed the formation of armed bands to fight both the British and the Jews; a three-person committee was appointed to procure weapons.[107] The committee apparently took no further action, but Nablus became the center of anti-British and anti-Zionist agitation in the summer of 1931, when young radicals seized the initiative from a fractured Jerusalem leadership. As armed bands mobilized to fight the British and the Zionists, debate focused on the concept of armed struggle, and a secret network began to develop.[108] In August, British authorities suppressed an attempted strike in Nablus and broke a collective action by taxi drivers.[109]

As the Ottoman army had retreated from Palestine toward the end of World War I, it left stockpiles of abandoned or purloined weaponry that ended up in civilian hands. Banditry and the pillaging of Christian pilgrims had flourished for centuries in the Eastern Mediterranean, and such plundering, coupled with the decline of the Ottoman Empire and the inadequacy of the central government, had resulted in the formation of gangs that created their own power centers. In addition, somewhere between 8,000 and 10,000 Palestinians—5 percent of the male population between twenty-five and fifty years of age in the mid-1930s—had already received basic training as soldiers or police through conscription or enlistment in either the Turkish army, the Arab "revolt in the desert," service to the British Mandate, or in the Transjordan Frontier Force.[110] A convergence of forces was at work: armed gangs were assembling, men with basic military training were available, and, as Zvi Elpeleg states, "Disappointment with the attempt to influence the British by political means prepared the ground for the evolution of militant, non-establishment organizations which were to influence the course of future events."[111] The call for armed struggle came primarily from two camps: those advocating pan-Arabism and confrontational strategies, and Muslim religious authorities and youth, many of whom were inspired by the grand mufti.[112]

In the winter of 1932, the first National Congress of Youth met in Jaffa, adopted a pan-Arab program, voted to establish branches in villages and towns, and passed resolutions advocating the promotion of local industries and products—a positive "buy-Palestinian" sanction, the opposite of a boycott. The congress reflected the developing national awareness of youth and its emergence as a separate political force.[113] A generation of educated Palestinian nationalists rising in the cities disparaged the impotency of the elite Jerusalem leadership after 1929. (Most of these young activists came from the north and the Nablus area.)[114] The ineffectuality of the Arab Executive reached a new level; some of its own members sold land to Zionists.[115] The new nationalist forces jockeyed for position, partisan news media raised their voices, and radical ideas and militant strategies became issues for debate. Renewed declarations called for Palestinians not to serve in an office of the mandatory government or cooperate with the government.

Political Parties

In 1932, the Istiqlal (Independence) emerged as the first modern Palestinian political party to organize along ideological lines rather than clan interests.

Founded by lawyer Awni Abd al-Hadi and appealing to pan-Arab elements, it summoned younger nationalists through "uncompromising concentration on the demand for national freedom."[116] The Istiqlal tried to stand apart from the competition between the Husseini family and the more gradualist rival clan of Nashashibis, but after only two years succumbed to factional infighting between pro-Saudi and pro-Hashemite elements. Its educated youth veered from its remains toward Husseini's leadership.[117] Before its demise, the party gave birth to a form of anti-British activism based on the assumption that by ending the mandate, Zionism would be denied its protector. The short-lived Istiqlal platform called for independence in the context of Arab unity, abolition of the mandate and Balfour Declaration, and parliamentary governance for Palestine.[118] These demands, although rooted in the idea of Arab unity, reiterated petitions of the previous decade with subtle differences. They remained the Palestinian position until Palestine ceased to exist on world maps. The idea that Arab unity could give birth to independence would not be abandoned until the years just before the first intifada.

As Jewish immigration exponentially increased at the start of the 1930s, Arabs of the Istiqlal idiom of Muslim militancy—anti-British, pro-Arab unity, opposed to the mandate and Balfour, and proponents of parliamentary self-governance—deliberated more subversive techniques for fighting it and its British protectors. Although the grand mufti did not openly countenance defying the authority of the mandatory government, many of his close associates supported the aggressive groups, and his newspaper, *al-Jamia al-Arabiyya* (Arab Society), steadily inveighed against the British. The new approach to propaganda and generally anti-British tone of leading Palestinians were different from Haj Amin's traditional anti-Jewish stance and influenced emerging youth organizations. The strategies of nonviolent resistance included social and political noncooperation: suspension of social activities, withdrawal from institutions, breaking contact with British administrators, resignation from official jobs, and civil disobedience—methods to be reasserted fifty years later in the street handouts of first intifada. When the Arab Executive convened an assembly of Istiqlalists and a youth congress on February 24, 1933, they attacked "lethargic leaders," condemned as traitors the brokers and middlemen who sold land to Zionists, and exhorted civil disobedience and boycotts of British goods as the only steps that might produce a response to their grievances from the mandatory government.[119] A March 1933 manifesto from the Arab Executive urged Palestinians to "get ready for the serious acts which will be imposed" by an assembly planned for March 26.[120]

At the Grand National Meeting on that date, using "every legal means" to end British rule included support for the principle of noncooperation.[121] The conference of five to six hundred Palestinians, held in Jaffa, was called the Noncooperation Congress (Mutamar al-La-taawun). The body adopted the principle of noncooperation, but limited its applications to three forms: social boycotts of government receptions, political boycotts of government boards, and a consumers' boycott of British and Jewish products. Attendees discussed nonpayment of taxes, but rejected such measures because landowners held sway. Although the meeting, which attracted "all classes and parties," decided to reject the authority of the government, internal strife prevented its resolutions from being implemented.[122] Haj Amin presented his opposition to civil disobedience and resignation from jobs, and the participants' decisions were never implemented.[123]

In 1933—the year the National Socialists won 44 percent of the votes in the March 5 German elections—Jewish immigrants from Germany numbered approximately 1,000 a month. Among the 15,000 that had arrived during the preceding six months, thousands possessed no immigrant permits and had either come as tourists and remained or had crossed borders illegally.[124] By the end of March, Hitler had assumed full dictatorial powers. On September 13, 1933, as the flow of authorized and illegal newcomers increased substantially, the Arab Executive staged a one-day general strike (without a permit) in Jerusalem that included figures from all persuasions, in a temporary uniting of clans and factions. Other towns staged strikes that same day. Palestinians scheduled a rally in Jaffa for four weeks later. A group from Nablus wrote to the high commissioner on September 30 threatening the adoption of self-defense against the Jewish newcomers.[125] On October 13, in Jerusalem, several thousand Palestinians demonstrated in defiance of the commissioner's orders.

The number of authorized Jewish immigrants to Palestine in 1929 had been 5,249; four years later, in 1933, as the Nazis took control of Germany, 30,327 legal Jewish newcomers arrived, a sixfold increase; by 1935, the number of authorized immigrants entering Palestine had reached 61,854.[126] Extralegal immigration particularly distressed the Arabs, and the lack of precise figures led to exaggeration and rumors.[127] As the percentage of Jews in the population climbed from 17 percent at the end of 1931 to 31 percent by the spring of 1936, Arab tensions rose. These numbers could be judged small if examined against the restrictive immigration policies of various countries toward Jews fleeing Nazi malevolence and murder, but such figures were large and threatening to the resident population of Palestine, which in 1936 stood at 1,336,518.[128] In four years alone, between 1932 and 1936, the Jewish population virtually doubled. By one calculation, if maintained at only half the number of incomers arriving in 1935 (a Jewish immigration rate of 30,000 per year), by 1962 the number of Jews in Palestine would exceed the Arab population.[129] Philip Mattar concludes:

> It seemed to the Palestinians that if the Yishuv continued to grow, they would inevitably find themselves dominated in their own homeland. They did not focus on the reason for Jewish immigration in the early 1930s, namely Nazi persecution, but on its effect on Arab economic and political power in Palestine. The increase in Jewish immigration . . . highlighted the bankruptcy of such moderate methods as petitions, delegations, and demonstrations.[130]

In Jaffa on October 13, 1933, approximately seven thousand demonstrators armed with sticks filled the streets; "so excited and so dangerous was the temper of the Arab rioters that the police were forced to use their firearms before order could be restored."[131] They killed 12 demonstrators and wounded 78; among police, one was killed and 25 wounded. A countrywide general strike was announced in response to what Palestinians called the "Jaffa massacre."[132] Street demonstrations broke out, as Palestinians across the country filled thoroughfares. In Nablus, riots erupted, and buildings and police were stoned. In Haifa, streets were barricaded and the train station attacked, as scores of casualties were exacted by police fire, Palestinian historian Abdul Wahhab Kayyali notes; a curfew was imposed, and Haifa's harbor was closed for three days.[133] Police were stoned. On October 28 and 29 in Jerusalem, violence claimed the lives of one police officer and 26 others; 187 were injured.[134] British troops occupied Nazareth, Safed, and Tulkarem on October 28.[135] The general strike lasted until November 2, when it was lifted.

The incendiary actions of 1933 were of a limited nature. The British mandatory government bore the thrust of the actions. The March noncooperation platform, October demonstrations, and the new militancy were intended to force a cessation of contacts between moderate leaders and the

British, so that any gradualists would be driven closer to armed struggle in resisting further immigration.[136] "Moderate Arab leaders . . . were reluctantly compelled to stand in with extremists," noted the British governor.[137] Militant Muslim organizations describing their purpose as the defense of Islamic holy places and mobilization against Zionism gained in members and influence during this period, as a decline of leverage ensued in the traditional Muslim-Christian societies that had been important during the 1920s and guided by the notable families and merchants of the major cities.[138]

The Rise of Qassamite Armed Resistance

By 1919, the secret anti-Zionist commando group al-Fidaiyya (Self-Sacrifice), comprised of Arab police and gendarmerie, had emerged.[139] The militant and clandestine al-Kaff al-Aswad (Black Hand), first became active in Jaffa as early as 1919 and may have had a branch in Haifa in which both Muslims and Christians participated.[140] A Muslim Self-Sacrificing Society was reportedly operating in Haifa in 1922, its aim being to "kill Britishers and Christians who were pro-British."[141] Small armed bands formed in greater numbers in the late 1920s and early 1930s. Among the main groups was the Green Hand (al-Kaff al-Khadra), which had appeared as early as October 1929 and circulated in the mountains among Acre, Nazareth, and Safed, gathering stolen or smuggled arms.[142] Joined by Druzes who had fought the French, they termed themselves mujahideen (warriors of holy struggle), and their blending of religious and nationalist purposes became common in rebel bands of the 1930s.[143] Although the Green Hand survived for only four months, it was indicative of the insurrectionary groups that would come to dominate the Palestinian political landscape later in the 1930s.

After the uprisings of 1929, Sheikh Izz al-Din al-Qassam had begun organizing secret armed cells in the Haifa area. "Dignified, charismatic and morally motivated puritanical," Qassam had moved to Haifa in 1921 from Syria, where his participation in guerrilla warfare against the French led to his flight.[144] Born in Syria in 1871 or 1880, while studying at al-Azhar University in Cairo before fleeing Syria, he may have been strongly influenced by Rashid Rida (1865–1935).[145] Rida was a Muslim leader who, during one of the most fertile periods of Islamic reform, propounded the idea that Islam needed its own political system in order to address Western Christendom, including a revived caliphate, the politico-religious institutionalized succession to Muhammad in a temporal sense that evolved after the death of the

Prophet in 632 C.E. As early as 1902, Rida determined that Zionist ambitions were political and aimed at national sovereignty, rather than spiritual, and he urged "promptitude in organising means of defence . . . acts and deeds, not talk and words."[146]

From 1921 to 1925, most land purchases by Zionists had been from absentee Palestinian landlords. Increasing numbers of peasants, however, began to be displaced as expanding Jewish immigration put pressure on Zionist institutions to acquire more land and allowed landowners to sell property at inflated prices to Zionist organizations.[147] By 1931 an estimated twenty thousand peasant families had been bought out or evicted. Driven from their land, and precluded from working under restrictive Zionist labor legislation, their way of life destroyed, they drifted to Old Haifa, where many of them encountered Qassam.[148] His challenge to British authority found keen popular support in Haifa, where accumulating social, economic, and political grievances were radicalizing large segments of society calling for aggressive confrontation. Although the mandatory authorities tended to regard any belligerency as the work of "brigands and lawless peasants," all classes of the Palestinian populace in the port city had become alarmed, as Jewish immigration "squeezed, altered and slowly phased out" its Arab character.[149]

Qassam gathered around him loyalists who combined faith and nationalism.[150] He preached against alcohol, gambling, prostitution, imperialism, and submission to the Jews and British alike, both of whom he considered aliens and infidels.[151] He regarded the lawlessness and unregulated violence of the uprisings of 1929 self-defeating and believed that political impact would be achieved by preparing cadres to strike selected targets.[152] These would include moderate Arabs seeking an accord with the Jews, insufficiently nationalistic politicians, and those suspected of selling land to the Zionists.[153]

Qassam believed only the poor peasants and wage laborers of Palestine were capable of prevailing against the colonialism of the British and Zionism. He taught literacy classes at night, and as a *madhun* (Muslim marriage official) traveled to villages. Both functions gave him credibility and access as he discreetly took his message of reform for Islam and its protection through holy war (jihad). His conception of jihad called for the religious preservation of the homeland and the lifting of oppression from the populace; he thought the pious might be the country's salvation. As it became evident that the nonviolent methods of protest led by the notable Palestinian families had been ineffective against British policy and Zionist settlements, Qassam recruited from among the displaced fellahin.[154] Secret organizations of youth and boy scouts became involved in clandestine arms acquisitions and target practice.[155] Radical groups received support from key figures of the Istiqlal, and both armed and unarmed forms of resistance assumed places among the progeny of the defunct political entity, of which Qassam is reported to have been a member.[156]

Al-Kaff al-Aswad formed during this period and led by Qassam, and another organization, Al-Jihad al-Muqaddas (Sacred Struggle), would strongly influence subsequent Palestinian armed struggle. Their cohorts were central to the "great revolt" (*al-thawra al-kubra*) that would last from 1936 to 1939. The reverses embodied in the so-called Black Paper of February 1931 emboldened both groups, as appeals went out to form clandestine paramilitary training centers. Al-Jihad al-Muqaddas emerged first, led by Abd al-Qadir al-Husseini, a relative of the mufti and the father of Feisel Husseini, who would prove to be a highly significant and influential figure in the story of the first intifada. Abd al-Qadir's father, Musa Kazim al-Husseini, was Haj Amin's uncle and had been mayor of Jerusalem and head of the Arab Executive. Abd al-Qadir organized and trained seventeen secret cells of young villagers in central and southern Palestine and armed them with weapons that he managed to procure. Others from similarly affluent families in Haifa and Safed did the same in the north. By one account, in 1934 there existed 63 secret cells, 400 cohorts, and 7 hidden training centers.[157] While Haj Amin kept one foot in the camp of nonviolent resistance, maintaining that he did not want to break his ties with the authorities, he also approved of Abd al-Qadir's army and later covertly became its leader.[158]

Nels Johnson argues that Qassam's movement catalyzed a shift in struggle because the dilemmas faced by the rural Palestinian fellahin, combined with the inability to alleviate them, led to the standard conditions for the emergence of a redemptive movement. The internal logic of Qassam's idiom of Islam proved powerful: ransom, or redeem, the evicted, landless, poverty-stricken, and alienated fellahin into a different form of resistance. Notions of *national* interests or nationhood were unfamiliar to the peasantry; the name "Palestine" had barely replaced that of "Southern Syria." Absorbing successive losses caused by immigrants of one faith and the administrators of another—both seeking dominion over land considered by Muslims to be second in holiness only to Mecca and Medina—the Palestinian peasantry turned to Islam. In Johnson's analysis, the path to redemption and restoration lay in the concept of jihad, because protecting the faith was a matter of conscience. For dispossessed laborers, Islam, as interpreted by Qassam, became the source of the coming mass resistance, much of it violent.[159]

Spurning classic nonviolent sanctions in response to the 1929 unrest, Qassam organized a secret gang that first struck in April 1931 and killed three Jews. Ikhwan al-Qassam (the Brotherhood of Qassam) had perhaps 200 trained adherents, and maybe 1,000 in its overall cellular structure.[160] After two additional murders, Qassam went underground, reemerging in 1935. In the wake of the discovery in Jaffa harbor of an illicit shipment of arms and ammunition bound for a Jewish merchant on October 18, Qassam gathered some of his followers on November 12 and told them that the time had come to show themselves. Police, however, intercepted and brought down Qassam and his associates in Yaabid, near Jenin, before they had fulfilled their mission of inciting the fellahin to revolt. When called upon to surrender, Qassam is said to have encouraged his adherents to "die as martyrs."[161] Qassam's death while battling the police pinpoints a turn toward armed militancy, including among the peasantry, together with a pattern of directing dissatisfaction toward the traditional leadership, none of whom attended Qassam's funeral. The Ikhwan al-Qassam survived their leader's demise, and its perspective gained in devotees, as growing numbers of Palestinian Arabs came to view the British, like the Zionist settlers, as enemies of the faith.[162]

Musa Kazim al-Husseini had died the year before, in 1934, resulting in the dissolution of the Arab Executive, which he had held together by dint of his personal influence. By this time, half a dozen political parties had formed.[163] Five days after Qassam's death, the leading figures in the five main parties (excluding the Istiqlalists) went together and met with the high commissioner to discuss another proposal for a legislative body. They also presented the high commissioner with a memorandum requesting a halt to Jewish immigration, cessation of land sales to Jews, and self-governance for the Palestinian Arabs. That they conveyed the memorandum with a notice of intent to pursue their purposes by other means should a suitable reply not be received within the month illustrates the extent to which momentum had already begun shifting away from nonviolent political methods and toward armed insurgency.[164]

In December 1935, one month after Qassam's death and probably not coincidentally, the British high commissioner, General Sir Arthur Grenfell Wauchope, proposed a new constitution laying out his duties and powers as well as the composition and powers of a legislative entity in which Muslims would elect 8 members, Jews 3, and Christians 1, with Arabic, English, and Hebrew to be used in the council's debates.[165] Even after the House of Commons criticized such a legislative council, following Zionist opposition to it, the Arab party leaders still hoped that a future delegation to London could persuade the government to implement the proposal.[166]

Qassam's example of guerrilla warfare through secret societies became the example followed during the revolt of 1936–39 by Islamic revivalist factions and in the present era. This represents the first appearance of nationalism among the peasantry and working classes, the first clear evidence that nationalism had overcome barriers of class, and the first *organized* use of violence. Qassam canonized the basic principles of fighting the mandatory authorities through ideological and organizational armed national resistance. According to Palestinian political scientist Ziad Abu-Amr, Qassam is the main source of inspiration for the current Islamic Jihad organization and perceived as the "first leader of the Palestinian armed resistance in the history of modern Palestine and the true father of the armed Palestinian revolution."[167] He became the standard-bearer of armed insurgency.

The "Great Revolt"

The "great revolt" of the Palestinian Arabs began with a general strike called at a nationalist conference that began in Nablus on April 19, 1936. Four days earlier, on April 15, a Qassamite group held up a convoy of ten automobiles on the Nablus-Tulkarem road and robbed its passengers. They took three Jewish passengers to the rear of a truck and shot them; two of them died. The next night, intruders broke into the home of orange-grove workers in Petah Tiqvah and killed two Arabs at close range, apparently in retaliation. In Tel Aviv at the funeral for the first Jew to die, cries rose for a Jewish army to be raised. On April 19 in Jaffa, Arabs were denied permission to march in a counter-demonstration. A mob formed at the news of the rejection of a parade permit and moved toward Tel Aviv, killing 9 Jews and 2 Arabs, and wounding 40 Jews and 10 Arabs. The refusal of the authorities to grant the permit was for the Palestinians the final straw and the immediate stimulus for the general strike. Legitimate, peaceful protest and persuasion were no longer permissible methods for Palestinians expressing their opposition to those gathering on their land while asserting their intentions to take it over with the assistance of the British, who for the time controlled it.[168]

On the day after calls went out for the strike, April 20, an Arab National Committee formed and resolved that a general strike should be sustained until Palestinian demands had been met. Similar committees organized in towns and villages in what would be the last attempt to mobilize all Arab political tendencies into an interlocking program of noncooperation, now that protest activities had been forbidden. On April 21, the leaders of the five main Arab parties ratified the decision taken at Nablus and appealed for a general strike of "all Arabs engaged in labour, transport, and shopkeeping" to begin the following day.[169] In Gaza, several hundred veiled Muslim women paraded on April 25.[170] Also on April 25, the Arab Higher Committee (al-Lajna al-Arabiyya al-Ulya) formed, creating a "cosmetic unification" composed of ten members, including leaders from the five main political parties, the Arab Youth Congress, and Christian representatives, with Haj Amin as its elected president.[171] It demanded a halt to Jewish immigration, restrictions on land sales to Jews, and establishment of a national government accountable to a representative council—in essence, an independent Palestinian state.[172] The committee issued a manifesto bidding "patience, quietness and determination until further notice," while exempting bakeries, cafés, clinics, flour mills, pharmacies, and transportation from the strike.[173] Two days later, national committees organized to secure relief provisions for the poor, raise funds, provide legal services, and promote Arab products in helping to sustain the general strike.[174]

In short order, *local* committees of the national body were organized. Although each committee had its own demands, the varying stipulations largely pertained to limiting immigration, regulating land sales, and establishing self-government in Palestine. A group of twenty-five Bedouin leaders traveled from Beersheba to Jerusalem with a petition that included pardons for imprisoned demonstrators. A Motor Transport Strike Committee functioned as an adjunct to the "Arab Car-Owners' and Drivers' Committee," and by late April had issued a manifesto urging nonpayment of taxes until the authorities concurred in limiting immigration.[175] On May 7, a convention of the strike committees and various leaders convened in Jerusalem, where it resolved to continue the strike, strive for "no taxation without representation," and articulated the aim of the overall struggle as "complete Palestinian independence within the framework of Arab unity."[176] It cited a stoppage to Jewish immigration (although not necessarily permanent) as a precondition for ending the strike, after which negotiations could begin anew on other demands, principally the formation of a democratic national government.[177] Sentiment was expressed for civil disobedience: "The [Arab Higher] Committee intimated that, while they were not responsible for it, the agitation in favour of 'civil disobedience' must be regarded as a spontaneous expression of national feeling, and they added that they could not use their influence . . . to call off the strike unless Jewish immigration were suspended."[178]

On May 10, student committees met in Jaffa and, along with women's organizations, became particularly active in the coordination of demonstrations. Far from holding an auxiliary role, women's groups were in the vanguard in April and May 1936 in urging more militancy.[179] They called for a boycott of Zionist- and British-made products and withdrawal from the British Boy Scout movement. The high commissioner's dissenting private secretary Thomas Hodgkin records at the time, "Resistance to the Government is not confined to men: women and schoolboys and schoolgirls have initiated demonstrations and presented protests in many of the towns. Most of the boys and girls attending Government schools in the towns have gone on strike and the schools have been closed down."[180]

Rural committees convened in Nablus and advocated nonpayment of taxes and established local branches of national committees in all Palestinian villages.[181] Younger militants called for a more confrontational approach.[182] Group after group joined with the local committees—Bedouins, chambers of commerce, labor groups, Muslim and Christian sports clubs, Arab "national guard" units, and the Jaffa boatmen's association—all guiding aspects of the strike in loose coordination with the Arab Higher Committee.[183] The rural areas were soon as well mobilized as urban quarters.[184] "Those few Arabs who kept their shops open or otherwise abstained from striking were soon won over or intimidated by representatives of the national committees, which, staffed largely by younger Arabs, kept a highly efficient watch on the conduct of the strike."[185] By May 11, authorities had arrested some six hundred Palestinians. That same month, British reinforcements began arriving, and by midsummer troops equivalent to an infantry division were garrisoned in Palestine.[186] On the eighteenth, the British set the immigration quota for Jews at 4,500 for the following six months, leading to eruptions of violence.[187] Five days later, they locked up 61 strike organizers, and in Nablus police killed 4 Palestinians.[188]

The local committees were largely autonomous, which may explain the strike's durability. As officials jailed one local leader, another took charge.[189]

Mayors met in Ramallah on May 30, and those from Bethlehem, Jaffa, Jenin, Lydda, Nablus, Shefaamr, and Tulkarem voted to lead their citizens on strikes at the beginning of June. The mayors of ten larger cities voted to follow suit the following week if the authorities did not heed their requests.[190] Palestinian officials in the mandatory government tithed their income for a strike fund.[191] Such employees could have incapacitated the government by going on strike, but ambivalence on the part of the Arab Higher Committee about such a crippling measure prevented it. Nonetheless, by month's end, 137 senior Arab officials in the mandatory government submitted a memorandum urging the government to accede to Palestinian pleas; soon after, 1,200 middle-tier Arab civil servants presented a similar request.[192] By the end of June, nearly all Palestinian businesses and transportation across the country had ground to a halt. The British responded by issuing collective fines, conducting mass arrests, and demolishing homes.[193] On June 2, they declared the strike illegal and began forcibly opening businesses and detaining strikers. On the nineteenth, Colonial Secretary William George Arthur Ormsby-Gore announced the detention of 2,598 Palestinians.[194] The British imprisoned as many as 400 leaders of strike committees. Still, the strike persisted.[195]

Haj Amin—having positioned himself as the leader of the Arab nationalist movement by holding the office of grand mufti and the presidencies of the Arab Higher Committee and the Muslim Supreme Council—straddled groups that favored continuation of the strike and those who wanted to break it. While the British pressured him to communicate a moderate line, and the citrus growers and shopkeepers clamored for an end to the strike, the young militants wanted him to head an armed revolt. Haj Amin, according to Zvi Elpeleg, was interested in a violent struggle against the Jews, yet one under his control that would avoid clashes with British forces. In June 1936, his posture was that he opposed bloodshed "because violence will not bring any positive results, and because . . . the government is more powerful, and it will put us down because it has the power to do so."[196] By the end of the month, however, an evolution from strike to guerrilla revolt had become evident, with the underground Qassamite armed bands in the vanguard.[197] Railway lines were blasted, two trains derailed, a bridge blown up, roads obstructed, and telephone wires sliced.

The most onerous development in the eyes of the British was the presence of bands of armed Arabs hiding on hillsides.[198] On June 16, Royal Air

Force airplanes had flown over the Old City of Jaffa—which offered sanctuary to the rebels with its tangled alleys and labyrinthine arrangement of houses—dropping leaflets warning of a two-week operation to demolish housing and clear roads to eliminate sniper roosts. The demolition process would take two weeks but, when finished, Jaffa was under control of the army.[199] Also on that day, three thousand Jaffa Jews evacuated to Tel Aviv.[200] Nablus, having brazenly defied the mandate, also was reoccupied.[201] The strike resulted in the strengthening of Zionist policies of economic self-reliance and Hebrew labor, as Zionist leader David Ben-Gurion declared that jobs vacated by Palestinians were to be permanently filled by Jews; markets for gravel, fruits, and vegetables previously served by Arabs be made Jewish; and reliance on the Arab port of Jaffa eliminated and services sought elsewhere.[202]

Violence intensified during the summer in response to incarcerations, house-to-house searches by the British, and the destruction of sections of Palestinian villages. Fortified by word that Syrian nationalists seeking independence from the French had attained concessions after a fifty-day strike,[203] the Palestinians pursued theirs through the summer. The strike produced a "sense of pride and power in the Palestinian camp," Elpeleg reports; after one hundred days had passed, a Palestinian newspaper in Jaffa described it as "one of the wonders of the world."[204] The tactics chosen by the various parties to the strike and directed against the mandatory government were partly aimed at equivocating Palestinian leaders mired in the interlinked politics of clan, municipality, nationalism, and Islam. On August 30, the Arab Higher Committee announced that it would persevere in the strike. In early September in London, the Cabinet resolved to crush the resistance. By mid-month, British emergency forces in Palestine comprised twelve battalions, engineers, and a signal corps to prepare for imposing martial law.[205]

"[D]espite the success of the general strike in many parts of Palestine it was never total," Zachary Lockman judges, "and the nationalist movement's inability to make it so undermined its effectiveness."[206] On October 10, a day after the monarchs of Iraq, Saudi Arabia, and Transjordan issued a joint appeal, the Arab Higher Committee ended the strike that had almost paralyzed the country. Palestinian leaders of the strike had invited the Arab leaders into the local matter to provide a pretext for calling off the strike.[207] The public had tired of the arduous demands of the sustained action. The strongest impetus for ending the strike came from Palestinian citrus grove owners, and stevedores and owners of boats at the Jaffa port.[208] The action had lasted more than one hundred seventy days—nearly six months: "When it finally ended . . . there was a feeling of real victory, and the Arab press was full of praise."[209] The Peel Commission had been appointed in August, but, "compelled" to postpone for nearly three months their departure from London, when the commissioners arrived on November 11 with the mission of determining the underlying causes of the unrest, they immediately faced a boycott of the ceremonial opening session by the Arab Higher Committee.[210] The commission would stay through mid-January 1937.

Ignoring the advice of the military, High Commissioner Wauchope decided not to attempt to disarm the rebels.[211] A relative calm had spread after the strike ended and prevailed until a few weeks before the release of the commission's report in July 1937, when leaked portions revealed that Lord Peel intended to recommend the partition of Palestine. Renewed rebellion erupted.[212] The revolt entered a second stage in early summer, when Palestinians realized that the commission's recommendation for partition had been accepted in London.[213] The Arab leadership split, with the Husseinis and their allies adamantly opposed to partition and the Nashashibi family and others who had wearied of the revolt willing to make terms with it. Ragheb Nashashibi resigned from the Arab Higher Committee, thereby ending all pretence at unity among the urban elite.[214] The Arab Higher Committee was declared illegal after the assassination of Lewis Andrews, the acting district commissioner for Galilee, in Nazareth on September 26.[215] The British arrested and deported several of its members, declared the national committees illegal, and mounted efforts to detain the mufti.[216] Haj Amin's stature rose among his people as he took sanctuary in the inviolate Haram al-Sharif in Jerusalem's Old City while remaining in contact with rebel leaders. Dismissed as president of the Supreme Muslim Council and disguised as a Bedouin, he fled to Lebanon from Jaffa port on October 13, 1937.[217]

After the harvest in November of that year, the Ikhwan al-Qassam launched a campaign in which some of Qassam's original followers emerged as commanders of the revolt's armed bands.[218] They directed their actions more against Palestinian Arabs than at anyone else, including the liquidation of people considered to be moderates or traitors, many of them intellectuals or members of old aristocratic families. Although the British had attempted to weaken the second phase of the revolt through numerous means, including by posing as leaders of rebel bands, by the autumn of 1937 little effort was necessary, as creedal, kinship, and intraregional disputes, personal resentments, and criminal deviance resulted in major rifts among the rebels.[219] Regardless, the armed bands sabotaged transportation and communications by destroying rail tracks, and rebels and gangs with weaponry seized control of towns, collected taxes, and held court.[220] Although the bands, such as the Black Hand and al-Jihad al-Muqaddas, had launched their paramilitary operations with the original intent of opposing and confounding the British and Zionists, they now played leading roles in a civil war raging among the Palestinian Arabs.

Yet another policy paper, issued from London in January 1938, deferred action on the Peel Commission's recommendations.[221] By April, more than 1,000 belligerent acts during a six-month period had been recorded, including 55 political killings and 32 attempted assassinations.[222] By August, even more chaos had overtaken events, with organized intimidation on the increase, civilian institutions collapsing, and roads and public buildings vulnerable. Extortion, kidnapping, and assassination were not uncommon, along with the arbitrary murder of intellectuals and those suspected of accepting the partition of Palestine. Communist and labor union leaders, as well as Druze and Christian communities, became targets.[223] The Nashashibi family and its supporters suffered violence. With Palestinian moderates the main victims of new waves of violence, "The unity achieved in early 1936 collapsed because of British intransigence which encouraged extremism and violence on the one hand and weakened the case for moderation on the other."[224]

During the autumn of 1938, the mandatory government lost control of Beersheba, Bethlehem, and the Old City of Jerusalem to the extent that the British had to recapture the Old City and other areas once under their suzerainty. The British Foreign Office, never enamored of the idea of partition (particularly if implemented by force), had in March 1938 appointed a committee chaired by Sir John Woodhead.[225] After reconsidering the Peel recommendations, the Woodhead Commission proposed abandoning partition, as published in its White Paper of November 9, 1938. London had decided that some concessions would have to be made to Arab demands, resulting in a dual policy of "appeasement and suppression of violence."[226] By early 1939, military suppression and proposed changes in policy had brought the rebellion to a close, although only after 547 Jews and 494 Arabs had been killed over three years, many of the deaths occurring in the closing months of the revolt.[227] During the turbulence, the British army had called on the Haganah to provide volunteers to serve in Zionist field squads and "special night squads," trained and commanded by Captain Orde Wingate, to help put down the revolt.[228] Trained and armed members of the Haganah also defended Jewish settlements.[229] The number of Arab gangs fell in number, and the Qassamite and Husseini organizers were defeated, but pillagers continued to operate in remote hills.[230]

The white paper published in London on May 17, 1939, envisaged a Palestinian state within ten years and limits to Zionist land acquisition and immigration. It held that the framers of the mandate had not "intended that Palestine should be converted into a Jewish state against the will of the Arab population of the country." In it, Britain's preference was defined as a binational state with independent Arab and Jewish states within Palestine. Its antecedents may have been less Arab in contour than the Palestinian Arabs believed was their due, yet it stated that Jews would not comprise more than one-third of the population, and Jewish immigration would be limited to seventy-five thousand over five years, after which none could continue "unless the Arabs of Palestine are prepared to acquiesce in it."[231] British acceptance of the Palestinian plea for majoritarian independence in ten years, limits on Jewish immigration, and a ban on land sales to Jews came about ironically, as Israeli sociologist Baruch Kimmerling and American political scientist Joel S. Migdal note, "just as the British finished the [Palestinians] militarily and destroyed their national leadership."[232] Both sides opposed the 1939 white paper. Beset by Nazism in Europe, Jews unanimously condemned it for placing them in a minority status in a hostile Arab state. Haj Amin's rejection of it—because it denied the Palestinians immediate independence—accorded with the position of the rebel leaders and was decisively influential with large numbers of his countrymen and women.[233]

After the first phase of the "great revolt" of 1936-39, the British government had recognized the situation as unworkable and irredeemable, as the Palestinian Arabs had consistently contended.[234] Although the general strike had been well organized and nonviolent—its boycotts and noncooperation methods carefully implemented through local coordinating committees—its discipline and restraint ultimately collapsed. The second phase scuttled the proposal for partition. In the meantime, the Zionists remained opposed to any curtailment of immigration or abandonment of partition. The second stage of the revolt had made reconciliation with the Palestinian Arabs appear impossible. While the Palestinians were crushed militarily, the Zionist armed resistance grew stronger. What may be called the first stage of the modern Palestinian nationalist movement ended in 1947 with the partition of Palestine, followed by defeat of the Arabs in a conflict increasingly referenced by a simple chronological name: the war of 1948.[235] Subsequent to the establishment of the State of Israel, 700,000 Palestinian refugees—half the Palestinian population in 1948—fled their homes or property and suffered other losses.[236]

• • • •

It has been professed that for the duration of the Arab-Zionist conflict the Palestinian leadership has unfailingly taken the most extreme, violent stands, thwarting resolution. A review of events of the 1920s and 1930s does not substantiate such a conclusion. Between the promulgation of the Balfour Declaration as policy and the onrushing events of World War II, which made the mandate unsustainable, the Palestinians utilized predominantly nonviolent strategies to preserve their way of life, which resulted in little if any effect on British policy or Zionist goals. The divisions among the Palestinian elite, and the politics of their respective parties, erected obstacles to effective action, but the conventional explanation for the failures of the Palestinians overlooks other, instrumental issues. The specific instances in which Palestinians actually influenced British policy involved wild bloody riots and paramilitary operations. High Commissioner Samuel temporarily suspended Jewish immigration after the riots of May 1921. The Passfield white paper, which would have reversed Britain's policy on self-government for the Arabs, proceeded from the uprisings of 1929. Proposed changes vis-à-vis the May 1939 white paper followed the slaughters of 1936-39. Yet, even these nods to legitimate Arab claims proved to be tangential and fleeting.

What stands out as more indicative of a pattern is the Palestinians' persistence, over two decades, in the use of classic, nonviolent sanctions, despite their inconsequential results. When use of "every legal means" and the most elementary nonviolent methods of protest and persuasion failed to produce basic changes in British and Zionist policies, Palestinians replaced these action methods in the late 1930s with noncooperation measures. When these, too, proved ineffective, Qassamite armed guerrilla operations and mass popular insurgency supplanted them. Neither the British nor the Zionists responded to the expression of Palestinian grievances when they employed nonviolent methods, thus reinforcing the alternative. By the autumn of 1938, historian

J. C. Hurewitz observes, "these events [had] taught the lesson that the use of violence as a political weapon produced results which otherwise appeared unobtainable."[237]

The turmoil of the Palestinian Arabs in response to the decision of the United Nations on partition did not subside, and two techniques for struggling for the protection of Palestinian patrimony evolved—one nonviolent, the other violent. The eclipse of the nonviolent action predominantly in use during the 1920s and 1930s by subsequent decades of a policy of Qassamite armed resistance only makes more trenchant the question of how nonviolent sanctions came to be reasserted in the early stages of the first intifada, where the unity of the uprising and its rejection of the use of arms contrast starkly with the bloody second phase of the "great revolt," and the carmine second intifada of 2000.

Chapter 4

Historical Organizing and Leading Precedents

A Myth of Armed Struggle to Liberate Palestine

In the 1950s, Palestinian resistance movements arose in the refugee centers of the diaspora, taking up the call to armed struggle because of the perceived failure of Arab unity to "liberate" Palestine. More than a decade later, inside the territories captured by Israel in the June 1967 war, the Palestinians began to organize themselves. Among the various Palestinian groups, only the communists accepted the idea of the UN partition plan—which endorsed the separation of Palestine into two states, Jewish and Arab—and did not adhere to the need for "armed struggle" to liberate Palestine, a position widely perceived as consensus. By the early 1970s, the communist policy of pursuing political rather than military methods by building small local institutions had goaded the most powerful of the Palestinian armed factions, Fateh, to focus on the occupied territories and turn toward civilian nonmilitary forms of mobilization. At the same time, prominent Palestinians inside the territories—where armed struggle held little attraction—began venturing a more conciliatory view of Israel.

Palestinian Exiles Adopt a Policy of Armed Struggle

As Zionism early in the twentieth century developed into a sophisticated global political movement fortified by a Great Power, most of the Arabic-speaking world remained under the European colonialism that replaced Ottoman rule after World War I. Independence had been promised and promised again to the Arabs, yet the idea of independent statehood for the Palestinians had not been coherently discussed apart from a loose concept compatible with the Balfour Declaration and Britain's strategic interests. A revised version of the Peel Commission's report, released in July 1937, was approved on November 27, 1947, in UN General Assembly Resolution

181 and called for partition. Two days later, the UN Special Committee on Palestine (UNSCOP), in its majority report, advocated partitioning Palestine into two adjacent states, with an economic union. The Jewish state was to have most of the coastal areas, western Galilee, and the Negev. The remainder was to become the Palestinian state. (The minority report urged a unitary state in Palestine along democratic lines.) The Jews were prepared for statehood, but the Palestinian Arabs, most of whose leaders had departed from Palestine as soon as UNSCOP left, were in no position to administer themselves, and Palestinian structures were insufficient for providing for the needs of an autonomous community, to say nothing of independent statehood. The Arabs rejected the UN partition plan because it allocated 55 percent of the land in Palestine to the Jewish minority, approximately one-third of the population, despite UNSCOP's estimation that Arab-owned land comprised 85 percent of Palestine.[1] The Zionists accepted the plan. The UN design lacked enforcement powers and implementation machinery, and as the world body turned its attention elsewhere, it was left to the parties involved to implement the partition. The Jews continued to fight for the land, claiming that they were defending Resolution 181, protecting their half, and operating under a UN decision. Palestinian resentment of what had been viewed since 1917 as foreign and colonial intrusion now manifested itself in armed fighting against what had been sanctioned by the UN resolution, although the Palestinians had in general been significantly weakened after the great revolt.

On December 1, Haj Amin al-Husseini and the Arab Higher Committee called a three-day general strike. Sniper shootings and armed attacks occurred in various parts of Palestine, and thus the Palestinians would be written into history as starting the war.[2] Only a few hours intervened between the passage of the partition resolution and the start of Arab hostilities. Israeli "new historian" Benny Morris observes "it was unclear to most observers, Jewish, British and Arab, that the two peoples, indeed, were now embarked on a war; most thought they were witnessing a recurrence of fleeting 'disturbances' à la 1920, 1929, or 1936."[3] Notwithstanding the fighting and chaos, a number of Arab villages instituted "peace meetings" with nearby Jewish communities, created formal peace agreements with neighbors, put local cease-fires into place, and concluded nonbelligerency pacts.[4] Most Palestinians were disinclined to take up arms.[5] The local cease-fires and peace agreements broke down, however, as a policy of destroying

Arab villages was implemented by the Haganah, one result of which was massive, fearful Arab flight. "[S]ecuring the interior of the Jewish State and its borders in practice meant the depopulation and destruction of the villages that hosted the hostile militias and irregulars," according to Morris.[6] A chain of operations was aimed at militarily occupying areas beyond the proposed state and driving out the Palestinians. War raged between Jews and Palestinians in the spring of 1948, although the Palestinians were greatly outnumbered, even with volunteers from Arab states.[7]

By the mid-1940s, as the enormity and tragedy of the Holocaust, in which Jews numerically were the primary victims, was publicly revealed, sympathy surged worldwide for concessions to Zionist claims upon the land of Palestine. On May 14, 1948, the Zionists proclaimed the State of Israel. The following day, the mandate formally ended, and British forces withdrew.[8] The conflict between Palestinians and Jews over land and immigration was transformed into a war between Israel and the major Arab states of Egypt, Lebanon, Iraq, Syria, and Jordan, which invaded on May 15. The Arab forces outnumbered the Israelis, but were ill equipped, poorly led, and disunited. In December 1948, the UN General Assembly passed Resolution 194 recognizing the right of Palestinian refugees to return to their homes and "live at peace" with their neighbors. During the hostilities, approximately half the area designated by the UN for a Palestinian state was subdued by Israel. Between late 1947 and early 1949, some 700,000 Palestinians became refugees.[9] In the course of the war, four hundred Arab villages were depopulated.[10] After the UN Security Council called a truce to end the fighting, and the warring parties signed general armistice agreements on the island of Rhodes in the Aegean Sea in February 1949, 77.94 percent of the land was Israeli-occupied.[11] "As an overwhelmingly agricultural society, what that meant," historian Michael R. Fischbach described, "was that in leaving behind their homes and villages, essentially you had a peasant society uprooted into exile without the material capital to rebuild their lives. You can displace a rich person and they can gain access hopefully to their liquid assets, but in farming societies, to leave behind one's land is to deprive oneself of the very material capital needed to reconstitute oneself in a host society."[12] "These Palestinians left behind homes, farmland, businesses, bank accounts, houses of worship, cemeteries, and shrines, not to mention farm and business equipment and personal property," Fischbach explains; most were "small-scale farmers before 1948 and therefore were rendered not merely refugees but propertyless refugees who lacked the capital necessary to eke out new existences in exile. The scope and scale of these losses was economically catastrophic."[13]

Following the establishment of temporary frontiers, the strategy of the Arab states evolved into forming an alliance to undo the effects of the 1948 war. The Arab governments remained theoretically in a state of war with Israel, their objectives being the establishment of a Palestinian state in what had been Palestine under the British Mandate and elimination of the Jewish national presence and the State of Israel. In December 1948, a Palestinian congress attended by luminaries and mayors in Jericho approved the annexation of the West Bank of the River Jordan by what was then called Trans-Jordan. A process of "Jordanization" began that affected major portions of the population. In official papers, King Abdullah substituted the phrase "West Bank of the Hashemite Kingdom" for the term "Palestine."[14] For approximately the next twenty years, Palestinian political aspirations flowed through the Hashemite Kingdom, which, according to Baruch Kimmerling and Joel S. Migdal, employed "active suppression and repression to prevent any public voicing of a national Palestinian identity."[15] Meanwhile, the Egyptians moved to exploit Gaza for their own purposes. Egypt viewed the All-Palestine Government established by Haj Amin al-Husseini in Gaza in 1948[16] and the Palestinian fedayeen, literally "self-sacrificers," or guerrillas, of the mid-1950s as instruments of opposition to Israel.[17] The Arab states, in the throes of decolonization, tended to act as competitors more interested in their own self-aggrandizement than in reaching a just solution on Palestine. Beyond the Middle East in the 1950s, the assumption grew in the United States and to a lesser degree in Europe that "the Palestinians would literally be absorbed into the Arab states," a view that subsequently gave way to a picture of them as "stateless exiles."[18]

The structure of Palestinian society had been semifeudal, ruled by a crust of landowning men, but was "a true peasantry rooted to the soil," the Palin Report explained, and the people were poor, uneducated, and in debt.[19] Throwing a sop at the despair of the Palestinians, the first Arab summit, held in Cairo from January 13 to 15, 1964, encouraged the formation of a "Palestinian entity" to take the lead on liberating Palestine, though the primary purpose was to circumscribe the Palestinian struggle to preclude the possibility that the Palestinians might drag the Arab states into unwanted war with Israel. For this reason, Egyptian president Gamel Abd al-Nasser was a driving force behind setting up the Palestine Liberation Organization (PLO). A secondary purpose was to neutralize pressure on delivering "liberation." Palestinian fury over Arab impotence vis-à-vis Israel led to vesting of hopes in the leadership of Nasser based on the belief that he could unite the Arabs, rescue the Palestinians, and destroy Israel. Ahmad Shukairy, a Palestinian lawyer who had served as assistant secretary-general of the Arab League, was chosen to set up the PLO and establish an executive committee. The grand theory was that Arab unity could bring about the restitution of Palestine.

The first Palestine National Council (PNC) since 1948 was held in East Jerusalem under the auspices of Jordan's King Hussein in May 1964. The gathering selected Shukairy to chair the Executive Committee of the PLO. The Palestinian National Covenant, or Charter (al-Mithaq al-Watani al-Filistini) issued on May 28 and approved on June 2, resolved among its thirty-three articles the "immediate opening of camps for military training of all Palestinians, in order to prepare them for the liberation battle which they affirmed could be won only by force of arms."[20] Regardless, under direction from Nasser—who rigidly controlled the Palestinians in the abutting Gaza Strip to avoid Israeli reprisals—the PLO prohibited commando operations against Israel.[21] Indeed, the new organization secured the support of Arab governments precisely because it was not violent.[22] The PLO leadership knew that raids were not contemplated, yet their rhetorical stance was that armed struggle was finally getting under way. Eventually viewed as a "tool" of the Arab states, the PLO became known for restricting Palestinian guerrilla activities.[23]

The Israeli military occupation in June 1967 of the remaining lands set aside by the United Nations for the Palestinians brought about a temporary loosening of controls exerted by the Arab regimes on those Palestinians in the diaspora dependent on their sponsorship.[24] By the close of 1967, Shukairy, whose rant just before the war that the Arab armies would drive the Jews into the sea is still incendiary,[25] had been relieved of his position by younger militants. Fateh, founded in the late 1950s by Yasir Arafat, nom de guerre Abu Ammar, and Khalil al-Wazir, nom de guerre Abu Jihad, moved to seize the initiative.[26] In February 1969, Fateh took over the PLO, gaining control of the administrative structure, the Palestine Liberation Army (PLA), and the Popular Liberation Forces, the guerrilla units formed from the PLA.[27] Arafat became chairman of the organization, remaining so until his death in 2004. The PLO under Shukairy had represented social sectors and geographic regions. Under Fateh's control, it became an umbrella, or front, sheltering political factions, divisions, and splinter groups of different ideologies while allowing each to retain its own Arab sponsors.[28] Thus the PLO developed an exceedingly high tolerance for divisiveness and fragmentation, as the patronage of the Arab states promoted each regime's interests rather than that of the Palestinians.[29] In the absence of coercion, unity among the Palestinian factions was improbable.[30] In an example of cross purposes, Austria, Greece, and Italy had arranged with Fateh not to carry out guerrilla operations on their terrain, but other factions ignored these agreements, undermining Arafat's ability to speak for the whole.[31] The PLO became perceived as ponderous and unwieldy.

Liberating Palestine Takes Precedence over Arab Unity

Fateh had begun training military cadres in the late 1950s, when it was the sole organization advocating armed struggle as the only way of liberating Palestine and the Palestinians.[32] In 1958 in Beirut, the Palestinian writer Tawfiq al-Huri and Yasir Arafat launched the newspaper *Filistinuna—Nida al-Hayat* (*Our Palestine—The Call of Life*), which editorialized for five years prior to the formal 1964 adoption of armed struggle that the time for action was near (due to disenchantment with the Arab regimes).[33] The successful end of the Algerian war in 1962 fired the imaginations of some Palestinians into believing that they could do the same thing, in their eyes to boot out the colonists.[34] Fateh sent its first reconnaissance team into Israel in 1963 after establishing military training camps in Syria and Jordan in 1963.[35] The June 1964 edition of *Filistinuna* posed the issue of "sacred violence," the chimera popularized by the Martinique psychoanalyst Franz Fanon.[36] In the same year, the Palestinian wing of the Arab Nationalist Movement (ANM), founded in Beirut in 1950, also established a military group to launch reconnaissance missions inside Israel.[37] The ANM arrived at this decision at a September 1964 conference that concluded that armed struggle was the only way to liberate Palestine.[38] Although Fateh was small and limited in the damage it could inflict,[39] it launched the first guerrilla operation against Israel on January 1, 1965,[40] based on a strategy of persuading the Americans and Israelis of "no end to armed conflict and political instability" until territorial forfeiture and recognition of the PLO.[41]

Fateh took the position that the liberation of Palestine would produce Arab unity.[42] The PLO held to the premise that Arab unity would attain the liberation of Palestine, and secondarily concluded that armed force was necessary to reach this aim.[43] Fateh's idea of "revolution" (*thawra*), substituted mass engagement for passivity and ideological speeches, and refocused attention on the Palestinians as the core of the Arab-Israeli conflict.[44] The Palestinian National Charter, as revised by the fourth PNC, which met in Cairo, July 10–17, 1968, codifies armed struggle as the means of achieving a democratic polity in Palestine. The charter proclaims, "Armed struggle is the only way to liberate Palestine and is therefore a strategy and not tactics. The Palestinian Arab people affirms its absolute resolution and abiding determination to pursue the armed struggle and to march forward towards the armed popular revolution, to liberate its homeland and return to it . . . to exercise its right of self-determination in it and sovereignty over it."[45]

The PLO's adoption of the principle of armed struggle represented a conscious resurrection of the thinking of Sheikh Izz al-Din al-Qassam.[46] It also marked a rebellion against the Arab bureaucracies that had exploited the threat of Israel for their own purposes (and then cited Israel's superiority as justification for their failure to stand up to it).[47] The PLO's doctrine on armed struggle was thought to magnify the plight of the Palestinians, which in theory would mobilize the masses, thereby triggering full-scale warfare between Israel and the Arabs. These goals were, as political scientist William Quandt notes, "shot through with contradictions," and Fateh in particular relied on the "mystique produced by activism" to offset the pressures from various Arab regimes.[48] Because the fedayeen were doing something, as opposed to nothing, it made it difficult for the Arab governments to voice objection or deny support. With Palestinian refugee camps situated near the guarded border between Israel and the remainder of Palestine, the refugees could sometimes observe as Jewish immigrants, lately become citizens of the state of Israel, assumed ownership of their farmhouses, former land, and assets. With some approbation from the Egyptians and Jordanians, the Palestinian refugees began conducting armed raids on settlements near the Gaza Strip and West Bank, sometimes killing the new owners of their properties, but for the most part returning unrewarded to their camps.[49] In time, the incursions became more organized, and the fedayeen units were supervised by the Egyptians and Jordanians. Ultimately these units comprised the beginnings of armed resistance, carrying out cross-border raids from emplacements in Lebanon and Jordan, bombings, and shellings of Israeli settlements. Such operations created strains for the Israelis but had little impact on the situation.[50]

Inside the Occupied Territories

In 1967, Nasser's closing of the Gulf of Aqaba and the Straits of Tiran provided an opening for Israel to take the offensive, and active warfare resumed. Six days of fighting ended with the Arab states bitterly defeated by Israel, which captured not only the West Bank and Gaza Strip, but the Golan Heights of Syria and the Egyptian Sinai Peninsula as well. The Israeli government declared these areas "territories under custody," in which military rule would apply, described as an "anemic" way of saying that people living in the territories had lost basic human and civic rights.[51] On September 23, 1967, the Israeli government renamed the occupied West Bank with the biblical names Judea and Samaria.[52] After 1968, Israel classified Gaza, the Golan, Sinai, and West Bank as the "administered territories." Arab East Jerusalem also came under Israeli authority, and large portions were appropriated. The "occupied territories" evolved as the most common appellation.[53] These changes were not acknowledged under international law.

Inside the occupied territories, the hostilities of June 1967 provoked some Palestinians into thinking that if they were ever to regain any of their land, they must do it on their own and without arms, because reprisals would be immediate and harsh. Humiliated and traumatized under military occupation, "average persons realized that they were being lied to by the Arab leaders."[54] Once the Jordanian and Egyptian administrations ended in 1967, the fate of the occupied territories lay squarely in the hands of the inhabitants themselves.[55] The refugee camps and communities created in 1948 were engorged by a new wave of displaced persons. The abysmal Arab performance in the war rendered collective action against the military occupation unlikely.[56] In the occupied territories, Israel forbade avowedly political activities by Palestinian organizations.[57] Officials dismantled the guerrilla organizations and disarmed the populace.[58] Yasir Arafat crossed into the West Bank in mid-August 1967 with a team of thirty, to foment armed resistance and establish covert headquarters in Nablus.[59] By early 1968, the severity of Israeli measures and the general disinclination of the populace to become militarily involved had led Arafat to return to the East Bank of the River Jordan, the notion of igniting armed revolution in the territories no longer alluring.[60] The Palestinians in the Gaza Strip posed the only real threat to Israeli authority. Arms caches remained from the period of Egyptian rule, and by the close of 1970 the fedayeen controlled the refugee camps and, by night, the towns.[61] This situation persisted until General Ariel Sharon smashed the guerrilla strongholds in 1971. After the 1967 war, the Israelis thought, for a time, that the Palestinians had become inconsequential to the Middle East: "[T]he Palestinians did not exist in the political consciousness of most Israelis."[62]

Since the 1950s, according to Ilan Pappé, the Israeli army had been preparing plans for rapid occupation of the West Bank, which were swiftly implemented to achieve this goal in 1967. Motivated by regret that Israel had in 1948 lost a chance to create more readily defensible borders, a group of "veteran kibbutzniks who enjoyed almost mythical status, . . . romantic nationalists who regarded the West Bank as the heart of ancient Israel," saw Nasser's actions as offering a ripe, postponed opportunity to reclaim Judea and Samaria.[63] With their predicament worsened, the Palestinians launched an internal effort to politicize the struggle for independence on a civilian basis, engaging in numerous nonviolent direct actions. In August 1967, teachers' associations implemented strikes to contest Israeli-imposed curriculum changes, and teachers signed protest petitions when asked to provide written endorsement of Israeli textbook censorship: "to cooperate with the occupation authorities is to allow them to strike deeper roots in the soil of our beloved country, and it gives the occupying power a justification for continuing its occupation." Most schools reopened in November after the Israelis made some concessions, but episodic strikes continued throughout the year.[64] The passage of UN Security Council Resolution 242 in November underscored a growing realization that the occupation would likely be protracted. In spring 1968, Palestinians called strikes in Jenin, Jerusalem, Nablus, and Tulkarem. Public demonstrations protested the demolition of homes in Hebron and Nablus, and the intrusion by soldiers into girls' schools in Ramallah. Major unrest swept the territories in autumn 1968, as Israel closed schools, imposed curfews, and deported eight Nablus teachers.[65] A general strike on the second anniversary of the June war led to the deportation to Jordan of nine strike coordinators from Jerusalem, Nablus, Ramallah, and Tulkarem.[66] The mayor of Nablus declared that a strike was a "peaceful and legitimate action," and "the only way to express the people's dissatisfaction."[67]

In Palestinian refugee camps in neighboring Arab countries, emphasis remained on the recruitment of guerrilla cadres, but as *political* organizing surged inside the occupied territories, the institutions established made no pretense to military solutions to the Palestinians situation. Although some organizing of secret military cells persisted in the territories,[68] armed cells there declined in the 1970s. The military factions increasingly saw themselves replaced in the Palestinian political imagination by the activism of the politically oriented communists,[69] the group that first revived organized Palestinian political activity in 1969.[70]

Foundational Arguments for a Two-State Solution

A Communist Alternative to Armed Struggle

The evolution of a two-state solution has its origins earlier in the century. The idea of binationalism began circulating in the mid-1920s, although it was often expressed as "equal representation" and "parity."[71] Unfolding in Zionist circles—some Jews hoped to change the status quo ante in their own favor—it was often associated with "moral justice," although the exact meaning of the expression varied.[72] Small, marginal movements asserted that a Jewish state must reconcile itself with the existence of the Arabs living in Palestine. Within the broad spectrum of Zionist thought, philosophers such as Asher Ginsburg, pen name Ahad Haam (One of the People), and Aharon David Gordon argued that Zionism represented not merely the physical migration of Jews to Palestine, but a renewal of Judaism in which the treatment of the Arabs posed a principal test of whether Zionism could rise to its moral imperative and justify its existence. Assumption of the validity of a Jewish nation with a right to return to Palestine was connected to an obligation to demonstrate justice.[73] The philosopher-theologian Martin Buber and the American-born rabbi Judah Magnes argued eloquently during the 1920s for brotherhood in a binational state.[74] "There was from the beginning of the movement another Zionism, now almost forgotten . . . except by scholars," in I. F. Stone's words, "which was prepared, from the deepest ethical motives, to face up to the reality that Palestine was not an empty land but contained another and kindred people."[75]

Within Palestinian families, concepts of either a binational or two-state solution had been under discussion for decades.[76] "Even in the 1940s, 1950s, and 1960s . . . you had people saying, 'We cannot live on the assumption or dream that we're going to be able to defeat Israel; Israel is a fact of life, and we have to . . . realize our political aspirations alongside Israel.' . . . There's always been a school of thought that—not really liking the fact—nonetheless saw that it was necessary to . . . make the best of it."[77] Political parties such as the Palestine Communist Party (PCP) proposed a vision of a "binational" state and the sharing of power and land. Throughout the 1920s, the PCP was overwhelmingly Jewish; the first Palestinian Arabs did not join the PCP until between 1927 and 1929.[78] From then until 1943—when the PCP split into two wings over the fundamental incongruities of Arab nationalism and Zionism, becoming the Israeli Communist Party and the National Liberation League (NLL)—the party consisted of Arabs and Jews who despite some disagreements generally endorsed a binational state and coexistence.[79] The Hashomer Hatzair (Young Guards Workers' Party) proposed a program of cooperation called "communal federalism" and a binational constitutional system with advisory councils that it believed could reconcile the national aspirations of both peoples.[80] Marxism had proffered that national divisions would eventually disappear as socialism evolved. Opposed to armed struggle, Palestinian and Jewish communists worked together, particularly on labor questions, each considering the other to be part of the overall equation. Even during the late 1930s in reaction to the great revolt, the PCP maintained a unified position, and when leafleting called for actions to be directed against the Jews it proclaimed that the revolt was on behalf of Jews as well as Arabs. Prevention of further bloodshed, the communists believed, required a united front of Jews and Arabs.[81]

The British mandatory government and world Zionism both opposed the PCP for its views on a "binational" state and the sharing of power and land. After the PCP's split, the NLL operated under the presumption that the interests and rights of both peoples could be met through a democratic secular state in Palestine. With the passage of UN General Assembly Resolution 181, the 1947 partition plan, however, the NLL accepted implementation in theory of the partition plan and the establishment of two states. Although separated in 1948 from the Arab communists living in Israel, the league maintained itself until 1951 and continued to advocate the establishment of a separate Palestinian state according to the partition plan. After the 1948 war, three distinct Palestinian communist entities evolved: in Israel proper, part of the NLL merged with the Israeli Communist Party; after Jordan's annexation of the West Bank, in 1951 the remainder of the league formed the Jordanian Communist Party (JCP); and in Gaza, the Palestinian Communist Party of Gaza (PCPG) formed.[82]

The wing of the PCP that had first become the NLL and later the JCP was the only significant political group to oppose the annexation of the West

Bank to Jordan.[83] Opposition took the form of leafleting,[84] until the NLL organized a peaceful demonstration in Nablus on March 31, 1950, to protest parliamentary elections proposed by King Abdullah that would effectively legitimize the process of merging the East and West banks of the River Jordan.[85] The JCP became the most powerful party of the 1950s among Palestinians, although at its peak, in 1956-57, the party never had more than a thousand members.[86] With an "independent Arab state" no longer imminent, the party adjusted to reality.[87] The JCP's program called for a two-state solution—a Palestinian state alongside Israel, not in place of it—to be worked out through political struggle and negotiations.[88]

The communists played a leading part in both large peaceful demonstrations and riots in 1955 and 1956, the aftermath of a communist-led national front having been disbanded by the Jordanian government in 1954.[89] On April 25, 1957, King Hussein outlawed political parties, and in his public broadcast announcing the measure specifically singled out the JCP for maintaining ties to Israel and calling for peace with the Jewish state.[90] The JCP's demand for the establishment of the independent state to which the UN partition plan entitled the Palestinians eventually became muted, along with talk of pacific coexistence with Israel, although the party continued to assert the right of refugees to return to their homes. Driven underground, the JCP split into two political wings. By late 1967, one had come to favor peaceful settlement of the conflict under UN Security Council Resolution 242, which was approved on November 22 to address the consequences of the war of that year and would become an internationally accepted basis for ending the occupation. The resolution mandates Israeli withdrawal from the occupied territories and is chiefly premised on the "inadmissibility of the acquisition of territory by war."[91] The other wing of the JCP advocated armed struggle and formed its own military unit.[92] Jealous of maintaining independence and a perception of parity with the PLO, the communists emphasized the building of institutions. By delivering social services, they were afforded "legitimacy they lacked as non-believers in a traditional religious society."[93]

In the late 1960s, opposition to armed struggle by Palestinian communists had less to do with principle than with the reality of the Israeli reprisals attendant to the sorties and infiltration from guerrilla fighters outside the occupied territories.[94] Although the notion of armed struggle had become a symbol for Palestinian refugees in Jordan, Lebanon, and Syria, the Palestinian populace of the territories, particularly on the West Bank, knew that cross-border guerrilla raids meant that Israeli retaliatory detentions and collective punishments would be aimed against them.[95] The Palestinian fedayeen had all developed outside the occupied territories, where the depth of support for the guerrillas and recruits appeared to be almost unlimited.[96] The communists also based their rejection of armed struggle on hopes of attaining long-range political goals that could only be achieved through comparably long-term changes in the social structure.[97]

After the 1967 war, JCP members in the West Bank were physically severed from their counterparts on the East Bank of the River Jordan. The political posture of the communists in the West Bank after the 1967 war condemned the Israeli de facto annexation of East Jerusalem and called for restoration of Jordanian sovereignty, meaning that they now stood in opposition to a Palestinian state. According to Ghassan Khatib, years later a minister of the Palestinian Authority and a former member of the communist party, the communists were then the only organized political group that not only concentrated its work in the occupied territories, but focused on popularly based activities and "nonviolent approaches and methods of struggle within the different strata of the Palestinian people."[98] The party argued "mass, popular, nonviolent struggle was the most suitable in our case, and would help us to survive," a viewpoint that gained adherents in the West Bank under the leadership of Bashir al-Barghouti, a journalist in Ramallah who was head of the communist party and editor of *al-Fajr* (the Dawn), a pro-Fateh English-language weekly.[99] Where the West Bank communists had once jealously protected their links to their East Bank confederates, by 1973 because of changed circumstances—the military occupation forcing them to function separately from the Jordanian wing for more than five years—the West Bank communists wanted independence from the Jordanian branch. By 1973, the West Bank communists had begun calling for an independent Palestinian state in the West Bank and Gaza Strip, and throwing their weight behind recognition of the PLO as the representative of the Palestinians.[100] Embracing Palestinian nationalism, the political organizing of the communists became even more assertive than before.[101]

1974: A "National Authority," and Conceptualization of a State alongside Israel

The idea of two states rarely figured in the public statements of exiled Palestinian nationalists during the 1970s, despite the Palestinian communists' more or less consistent support for an autonomous state and articles about two states in Palestinian newspapers in the occupied territories. In 1970, Nayef Hawatmeh, leader of the Popular Democratic Front for the Liberation of Palestine (PDFLP), had publicly argued for "dialogue" between Palestinian and Israeli socialists.[102] Just before the October 1973 war, Hawatmeh, at the time the only Palestinian leader of an armed faction with connections to the Israeli left, put forth the concept of a state in the West Bank.[103] Hawatmeh had, in 1969, founded the PDFLP, which, in that year, split from the Popular Front for the Liberation of Palestine (PFLP), founded in 1967 by George Habash. The PDFLP placed more credence in political rather than guerrilla activity.[104] In June 1974, at the twelfth PNC meeting, in Cairo, the DFLP ("popular" had been dropped) advanced the notion of a Palestinian state alongside Israel that would occupy only a portion of Palestine. The DFLP's initiative was adopted by Fateh and Arafat, although the 1974 resolutions were obscurely worded—a "national authority" on "part of Palestinian land to be liberated."[105] Prior to this benchmark, the goal of a "secular democratic state" in all of Palestine, enunciated by Fateh in 1969, had predominated, with its implicit suggestion of the dismantling of Israel.[106]

Although using a formulation discernible only to the initiated, in the early 1970s the PLO had embarked on a route toward conceptualization of a state alongside Israel. "The right of Jews to remain in Palestine was gradually asserting itself in Palestinian political thought," states journalist Alain Gresh.[107] Palestinian philosopher Sari Nusseibeh commented on this crucial but circuitous change of 1974: "It was in the context of destroying Israel, but constituted a formal turning point. When the leadership marketed the 'national authority' theory, they did so in a package that looked from an American or Western point of view unacceptable, because the authority would be set up to 'destroy.' Yet, within the Palestinian context, the opposition knew exactly what it was about!"[108] A new trajectory established the idea of partitioning Palestine, although the term *partition* was not used and a program for a two-state solution lacked clarity.[109] The trend toward accepting the irreversibility of the Israeli state had, nonetheless, begun.[110]

Moscow was also moving toward endorsement of the formation of an independent Palestinian state in the West Bank and Gaza Strip, and recognizing the PLO as speaking for the Palestinian people.[111] In autumn 1975, the communists in the occupied territories agreed with the JCP to organize the Palestinian Communist Organization (PCO) in the West Bank. Israel's

own interests led the government to lend the appearance of subdued tolerance for the communists, because the party's ideology emphasized Israel's
right to exist within its pre-1967 borders, and it received support from Arab
as well as Israeli communists in Rakah (the Israeli Communist Party), who
were functioning within the Israeli political system.[112] The communists
hewed to a commitment to an independent Palestinian state and leaned
toward political organizing.[113] With the PLO and Fateh showing only nom-
inal interest in political organizations on the ground, the communists had
few serious competitors.[114]

In 1982, the PCO announced the founding of a new, freestanding, and
independent Palestine Communist Party (PCP).[115] In April 1987, the PCP
would formally became part of the PLO's Executive Committee, at the
eighteenth meeting of the PNC, in Cairo, although never having been part
of the consensus on the validity of armed struggle.[116] After the collapse of
the Soviet Union and the end of the cold war, the PCP would rename itself
the People's Party.

Communist Stimulation of Nonviolent Organizing

In July 1973, 107 well-known Palestinians signed an appeal to the secretary-
general of the United Nations, demanding an end to the occupation and
affirming their right to "self-determination."[117] In August 1973, the Palestinian National Front was created as a coalition of groups, including the PLO
and its constituent factions and politicians, to resist military occupation and
to press for self-determination and the return of the refugees to their
homes.[118] Territories wide and clandestine, the multiparty National Front
combined political activity with military-style operations.[119] Although Fateh
was the "dominant ruling party" in the PLO,[120] after the military occupation began it came to believe that it could not maintain that position by
merely remaining a covert military organization in the occupied territories.
Sari Nusseibeh described the process:

> Fateh had always been a military organization. The only people who were
> not military were the communists. Immediately after the 1967 war, the
> communists acted on the political front—in labor unions, grass-roots
> organizations, everywhere—and they were the driving force behind the
> formation of first the National Front and then the National Guidance
> Committee [later formed to oppose provisions of the Camp David

accords]. They were trying to create . . . a leadership here on the ground to represent the people. That always met with opposition from the PLO, because the PLO felt that the politicization of the movement—taking it inside, into the occupied territories—basically meant disempowering the PLO, which was outside and was a military organization.[121]

The October 1973 war, in which Egyptians and Syrians fought Israel, raised hopes in the occupied territories, even though the hostilities ended with Israeli forces astride the Suez Canal and in control of still more territory on the Golan Heights. After October, the National Front's politicians linked their call for recognition of the PLO with explicit demands for an independent state in the West Bank and Gaza.[122] "For the first time in the history of Palestine after 1948, there was a political unity between the Gaza Strip and the West Bank," Abd al-Jawad Saleh recalled.[123] Saleh was mayor of al-Bireh and had in 1972 led teachers and instructors at schools and colleges in the Ramallah and al-Bireh area to join together cooperatively in community work programs. The front staged several instances of civil disobedience in the territories, although the mixing of political noncooperation on the one hand with acts of sabotage on the other held little potential for eliciting a positive response from Israel.

The National Front reflected the PLO's increasing emphasis on the occupied territories. Rivalry between the communists and Fateh heightened with the PLO's newfound focus,[124] but it also created a basis for cooperation with West Bank communists (although the relationship did not remain amicable for long). Having been routed during the upheaval of near civil war in Jordan during Black September in 1970,[125] when King Hussein sought to disarm the PLO in refugee camps, the PLO had lost its ability to retain a military presence in the Arab state with the longest border with Israel.[126] After moving to the refugee camps of Beirut and south Lebanon, where the absence of a cohesive central government and the competition among confessional groups offered relative autonomy, the PLO decided to refocus its attention on the occupied territories. There, a battle ensued for control of the labor unions.

Trade unions had been the domain of the communists since the 1920s. A Palestine Arab Workers' Society had begun to operate in 1925, and throughout the 1940s the Arab Workers' Congress was the largest union of Palestinian laborers, perhaps numbering twenty thousand.[127] In 1972, at the tenth PNC meeting, in Cairo, attendees passed the first resolutions calling for the organizing of trade unions, as they wanted to create new and additional unions under their wing, along with the provisioning of resources and assistance to institutions and organizations in the occupied territories.[128] When the DFLP and the PFLP took on the challenge of drawing the labor unions away from the communists and into the column of the PLO, they derived benefits from their ties to the PCP and also gained advantage from the rivalry between the PCP and Fateh. Fateh moved huge cash reserves into the resulting altercation during the late 1970s and early 1980s during the so-called war of the institutions.[129] Although an August 1981 split resulted in two different General Federations of Trade Unions, Fateh ultimately won over the unions.[130]

The disputes between the PLO and the communists were numerous and bitter, in part because of assumptions by Fateh that the communists were more interested in international Marxism than in Palestinian nationalism. Not only were the goals of the communists at issue, but also were their means.[131] The PFLP, on the other hand, still holding to armed struggle with the goal of eliminating Israel, withdrew from the National Front as it began to support ideas of limited territorial compromise and international efforts to bring Arab and Israeli contestants to the peace table. The front, which fell apart, was the last multi-pronged effort in the occupied territories until early 1988, when a multiparty leadership would coalesce to guide the first intifada.

Camp David

On November 19, 1977, President Anwar al-Sadat of Egypt reversed Egyptian policy and flew to Israel for an official visit. In December, Israeli prime minister Menachem Begin proposed a plan for Palestinian "autonomy" that the Palestinians perceived from the start as "a scheme for continued occupation under a more permanent guise."[132] Autonomy applied not to the land but to the people living on it, Israeli new historian Avi Shlaim notes.[133] On September 17, 1978, Egypt, Israel, and the United States signed the Camp David accords. On March 26, 1979, Egypt and Israel would sign a formal peace treaty.

"To allay Israel's stated fears, the option of a Palestinian state was . . . explicitly precluded" from the Camp David accords, according to William Quandt, who participated in some of the meetings in the Catoctin Mountains as a member of the U.S. national security staff, during President Jimmy Carter's thirteen days of meetings with Begin and Sadat that produced the agreement.[134] Although the Palestinians in the occupied territories were the main subjects of the "framework" in the Camp David accords, no one had consulted them or asked their concurrence.[135] Secretary of State Henry Kissinger had in 1975 devised a ban on official U.S. contacts with the PLO, and successive administrations had elected to maintain it, arguing that the PLO did not represent the majority of Palestinians, was committed to terrorism, and sought the destruction of Israel. Washington elected to consider conversations with anyone from the PLO as the equivalent of negotiations with and recognition of the PLO.[136] The framework offered lip-service on self-rule, but did not recognize the Palestinians as a people with rights to self-determination, and the accords would have the effect of furthering Israel's control of the territories, while encouraging an "Israeli-American preference for resolving the Palestine question without the Palestinians, and largely at their expense."[137] The West Bank and Gaza are only the "rump" of Palestine, diplomat Anwar Nusseibeh told scholar Ann Mosely Lesch, yet "we are denied even that rump."[138]

Between October 1 and November 7, 1978, the Israeli authorities allowed four public meetings throughout the occupied territories at which Palestinians were able to voice their dismay at the provisions of the accords. Five thousand people attended the final assembly, on November 7 in Nablus, after which Israel reasserted a ban on political gatherings.[139] From that point on, political expression moved underground, although occasional nonviolent demonstrations took place.[140] The October 1 session had adopted a resolution calling for the creation of a national guidance committee to coordinate opposition to the "autonomy" provisions in the Camp David accords. Formed before the end of the year, it was comprised of nine of the mayors who had been democratically elected when in 1976 Israel had allowed municipal elections[141] and the creation of some women's and students' organizations. Israeli authorities, U.S. political scientist Don Peretz writes, viewed the committee as "an 'arm of the PLO,' responsible for 'subversive activity,' 'political and ideological violence,' and 'deterioration of the security situation.'"[142] The leftist sympathies of the committee perturbed moderates in the PLO, while the communists would have preferred a more militant stance against Israeli military authorities.[143]

The belief of the communists in popular governance and organizing of community-level institutions as the best means of preparing for independence dovetailed with the need to safeguard against Israeli military intrusion into political activities. Protecting the prerogative of nonpolitical gatherings, Palestinians organized local women's, sports, cultural, and youth clubs and professional federations under the rubric of social or cultural agencies and societies,[144] rather than as the covert cells of the politico-military Palestinian factions. By 1979, the Union of Palestinian Medical Relief Committees had begun delivering health services to refugee and village neighborhoods, with the additional requirement that local committees be organized to establish community priorities and support the clinics. With health professionals volunteering their time, "the effect was electric"; having started with 10 professionals, by 1988 700 clinicians served 50,000 patients.[145] Of these, 52 percent of the health union's members were women, as were 32 percent of its physicians. The union "neither applied to the [Israeli] authorities for permission to operate, nor was it willing to admit to the need for such authorization for action to begin."[146] Collateral efforts in trade union organizing simultaneously led to a revival of the labor movement.[147] The structure and capacity for "new patterns of struggle" had begun to crystallize.[148] Social scientists acknowledge that developments within Palestinian society during the ten-year period prior to December 1987 made the first intifada possible.[149] Further examination reveals a more accurate estimate closer to twenty years.

Fateh Broadens Its Political Program

Since the PLO's founding in 1964, the organization had placed only a limited emphasis on popular mass organizing. It established a program of regional offices across the Arab world for *al-tanzim al-shabi* (popular organizing), although Arab opposition to the program's democratic slant and the PLO policy of conducting a census of Palestinians living in the host Arab states caused the effort to fail.[150] Despite having doubts, by the mid-1970s the PLO had begun to focus on mass mobilization by establishing new entities and reinvigorating existing ones, in addition to maintaining its customary military cohorts. By the late 1970s, the cumulative effects of the National Front, the electoral campaigns of 1976, and the National Guidance Committee—although limited in thrust and never able to organize a coherent program based on objections to the Camp David accords[151]—had reinforced Fateh's perception that focusing solely on military activities could cause it to lose politically. Political organizations came to be viewed as the best offense for coping with challenges from the communists.[152] Factions politically to the left in the PLO—principally the DFLP and PFLP—joined the front ranks of those leading popular mobilization in the occupied territories.[153] Fateh followed, and eventually took the lead, even while ambivalent about mass organizing. As Palestinian social scientist Musa Budeiri put it, the DFLP and the PFLP "chased the communists and started aping them, then Fateh joined them." The communists used traditional methods of mass organizing of women, students, and trade unions. This was in order to "channel people's energies," Budeiri summarized, "and to build their own organization, because this was a way of winning members. In a sense, the communists had no choice about the way they moved. . . . The left-wing groups, like the Democratic Front and the Popular Front, started to copy them, because they weren't getting very far with armed struggle, and they realized that Israel also distinguished between two kinds of activities—they put people into jail for three life sentences for using an explosive. The realization was seeping in that the territories were an important arena."[154]

Fateh's vacillation over political mobilization and continuing preference for guerrilla tactics may have been partially geographic and partly related to class. The movement had scant support among the West Bank political elite, and although Fateh had a number of intellectuals at its helm, many of the party's founders came from modest backgrounds; some had been born in Gaza or western Palestine, generally poorer than the West Bank.[155] Fateh was more "proletarian" than the "radical" PFLP or DFLP.[156] As the main military corpus of the PLO,[157] and having antedated its formation, Fateh had become the PLO's principal party because of its nationalist approach and "acute disdain toward ideology."[158] The vague political content of Fateh's doctrines was not accidental. Its ideologists sought to bring together all revolutionary elements and discourage "Byzantine discussions" concerning the social infrastructure after "liberation."[159] It tried to appeal to the left and the right, domestically and internationally.[160] A former commando wrote, "It was a fighting organisation in a time when others only talked about the theories of war."[161]

To the extent that Fateh and the PLO in the diaspora had an architect for a policy of civilian nonmilitary mobilization, it was Abu Jihad (Khalil al-Wazir).[162] Second in command of the PLO with responsibility for the occupied territories, Abu Jihad played a catalytic role in supporting the surge of political organizing and served as the main link between the PLO and the local groups that would be involved in creating an organizational infrastructure for the intifada. As if personifying the duality of the larger Palestinian strategic debate, he led Fateh's military efforts inside the territories, while endorsing the concept of a political direction. When the June 1982 Israeli invasion of Lebanon and evacuation of the PLO leadership from Beirut and Tripoli in August (after ten weeks of fighting) made the military option even more remote, Abu Jihad embraced more fully the hypothesis of mass political organizing in the occupied territories.[163] Sari Nusseibeh recalled, "He helped, as much as possible, to make those grass-roots movements grow and didn't really care about how many, or where, or how efficient . . . he helped everybody who came to him with a proposal to set up anything. He used to pour money into it. He knew that most of the money would probably be squandered on the way, but he used to say that even if a trickle reached [the people], that would be a major achievement . . . he wanted people to set themselves up—unions, student groups, federations—on every level."[164]

Fateh's success became linked to its ability to rebase itself in the territories after the 1982 débâcle in Lebanon. Although among PLO factions Fateh was the latecomer to political organizing, once decided it led the initiative. Fateh cadres "tipped the balance and mobilized the majority of West Bank and Gaza communities into conscious participation in the nationalist political effort."[165] Scale was involved, according to Bassam Abu-Sharif, an advisor to Yasir Arafat who had participated in one of the earliest hijackings of an airplane as a member of the PFLP, later the victim of a letter bomb presumed to be of Israeli origin, and who would become an advocate within the PLO for the turn away from armed struggle: "The communists, from 1967, started it, but when Fateh and the PFLP adopted civilian mobilization in 1973, in one year they did much more than the communists had done because they were more able. I am not saying that the communists are not able. Where Abu Jihad would have a budget of 20 million dollars for the West Bank and Gaza, the communists wouldn't have 20 thousand dollars. . . . Abu Jihad managed to build a network of social organizations and civil work that the communists would never have been able to do—clinics in the camps, clubs, football teams."[166] Fateh "could not remain aloof of the natural tendency of local Palestinians living under prolonged occupation to establish institutions of their own in order . . . to ameliorate their conditions."[167]

Aziz Shehadeh: Declare a Palestinian State

After the 1948 war, an individual emerged who has had a lasting impact. Although Aziz Shehadeh was instrumental in the evolution of a nonbelligerent view toward sharing land with Israel, he is rarely mentioned in historical accounts.

A British-trained attorney who had practiced law since the 1930s, Shehadeh was not the only individual to raise the issue of a Palestinian state with an implied acceptance of Israel, but he may have been the first Palestinian to be quoted publicly in the news media advocating such an approach. Shehadeh had broached the idea of two states side by side as early as 1948, when "the prevailing view was one of pan-Arabism, instead of narrow Palestinian nationalism."[168] By 1970, journalist Muhammad Abu Shilbaya in addition to Sheikh Muhammad Ali al-Jabari, former mayor of Hebron, and Dr. Hamdi Taji al-Faruqi of Ramallah, two other prominent Palestinians, also proposed such a state.[169] Those who suggested such compromise risked denouncement and in the worst case put their lives at risk.[170]

According to Jonathan Kuttab, a Palestinian-American lawyer who completed his legal training in Shehadeh's Ramallah law offices, the Jordanians considered Shehadeh's idea dangerous and suppressed it: "The official objection was that insistence on a Palestinian state at that time would diminish . . . the importance of pan-Arabism and the need to liberate all of Palestine."[171] The Hashemite Kingdom unofficially opposed the idea because it undermined Jordan's annexation of the West Bank and efforts at "Jordanization" of the territory.[172] In September 1967, after Israel's military occupation had begun, Shehadeh raised the concept again, having concluded that an Arab military victory against Israel was not possible. He thought a group should approach Israel, declare a Palestinian state in the occupied territories of the Gaza Strip and West Bank (including Jerusalem), and conclude a peace agreement with Israel on the basis of an Israeli state and a Palestinian state existing side by side. His proposal included Palestinian self-government with provisions for limited independence and the establishment of a parliament and other institutions of government. Timing was of particular concern: Shehadeh thought that such an action, to be successful, must be taken before attitudes hardened. As recounted to Kuttab, Shehadeh had told the Israelis, including defense minister Moshe Dayan, "The Jordanians are out of the picture now—it's you and us. You'd better make peace. To have one and a half million Palestinians within your borders will be a tremendous threat to you. There is no way that four million Israelis can rule over two million Arabs. . . . Every street will be a danger to you. Why don't you make peace with us? . . . We will be your bridge to the Arab world."[173] According to Shehadeh's son

Raja, shortly after the capture of Ramallah in 1967, two Israelis—Dan Bawly, a retired chartered accountant, and David Kimche, at the time associated with the Israeli intelligence services and later the secretary-general of the Israeli Foreign Ministry—visited his father.[174] They reportedly passed along Shehadeh's proposals to the Israeli government, where differences of opinion prevented their acceptance. Bawly and Kimche are believed also to have attempted to win support for the concept of two states from subsequent Israeli governments.[175] High-level Israelis came to the Shehadeh home to discuss such ideas.

Nationalists on salaries from Jordan might boycott the Israelis, Kuttab observed, but Aziz's perspective was practical.[176] As an example,

> Israeli control of zoning orders created many difficulties, at a time when the town leaders would have nothing to do with the Israelis. . . . Yet, as one poignant example, the graveyard in Ramallah was full, and there was no room for more graves. People asked Aziz to talk to the Israelis about granting a zoning permit to allow establishment of a new graveyard at a new site. On a matter as serious as burial, you must deal with those who have authority, never mind if it is unpopular.
>
> When the lawyers were on strike in 1967,[177] Aziz was the first to break it. People were besieging him . . . [for help]. Other lawyers might be proud that they were boycotting the military courts, but Aziz's response was, "These people need representation. . . . If the bar association thinks this is treason, that is their problem. This old man wants me to defend his son."[178]

Shehadeh held to the idea that Truth is Truth, Kuttab recounted, and this allowed him to negotiate with Israelis.[179]

"Military Solutions Have Nothing to Offer the Palestinians"

In the early 1900s, the Shehadeh family, which had resided in Ramallah, moved to Jerusalem, but once embarked on his law career, Shehadeh moved to Jaffa. The family of his wife, Widad, also a Shehadeh, was also living in Jaffa. Upon marrying, they moved into a new house in the coastal city and asked that the owner make renovations for them. When war broke out in 1948, the family fled back to Ramallah, yet continued to pay their debt for work on the house in which they now could not live. Raja remembered his father as a "visionary, moralist, ethicist, and determined man," who knew that his idea for resolution of the Israeli-Palestinian conflict "went against the grain, at a time when there was immense hatred of Jews and Israelis" for the losses that had been sustained by the Palestinians. "He was himself a refugee and had lost his property. . . . He had suffered as much as anyone and had the same emotions as everyone else—the difference is that he . . . had the capacity to overcome his emotions and think clearly about what should be done."[180]

Shehadeh was elected as an officer of the General Refugee Congress at a March 17, 1949, Ramallah meeting attended by five hundred delegates. This "marked the attempt of the refugees to take charge of their own affairs," Avi Shlaim records.[181] Borrowing money to go to Lausanne that same year to meet with the UN Conciliation Commission for Palestine, Shehadeh and three other Palestinians sought compensation for the refugees. The commission did not, however, allow Shehadeh, congress president Nimer al-Hawari, Yahya Hamuda—another deputy, nor Nasib Boulos, a member of the executive committee, to testify, although as Shlaim observes, they had been authorized to negotiate on behalf of the Palestinian refugees on all matters pertaining to them.[182] The General Refugee Congress delegation was refused recognition because it did not represent a state.[183] This formulaic response, devoid of human sympathy or substance, only reinforced Shehadeh's determination, according to Raja.[184]

Aziz wrote articles and made himself available to Israeli and foreign journalists. Critics thought it perfidious to consider giving up 70 percent or more of Palestine, even if the Palestinians retained Jerusalem. Defenders asserted that Shehadeh was not a politician and did not court ideological purity: "He would not soften language to make it saleable. . . . He was honest to a fault and a deep patriot. He really cared about Palestine, but he had no time or patience for patriotic talk that was full of slogans. . . . He was realistic [and thought] to hold on to empty slogans was not helpful.[185] The PLO opposed the idea of establishing a government on less land than Palestinians had once possessed and viewed Shehadeh with suspicion. Detractors accused him of attempting "to take Palestinian destiny into his own hands rather than leave it to the PLO."[186] In the 1970s, the Fateh leadership threatened a military tribunal to bring to trial those calling for a Palestinian entity solely in the occupied territories.[187] Raja Shehadeh recalled,

> The PLO was struggling for survival and the assertion of itself as the sole
> legitimate representative of the Palestinian people. . . . Aziz was seen as

enemy number one because he was trying to make a deal with Israel, and was not for armed struggle. . . . The PLO radio broadcast . . . threats against him. I remember very clearly a quote from somebody in the PLO, possibly Arafat, saying "we will never accept this mini-state," using a diminutive form of state, *duwayla,* to make it derogatory, because at that time, they were for *all* of Palestine. . . . They were also extremely worried about somebody calling for local leadership—a voice from within calling for a solution which would have rendered irrelevant their activity. . . . He suffered from opprobrium, was called a traitor, lost his Jordanian passport, was *persona non grata* in Jordan, and ostracized in local society.[188]

From the beginning, Aziz recognized the need for compromise, Raja asserted:

The generation of people that were born or were in their formative years in 1948 had great depth of anger. . . . Armed struggle was a way to release the anger. . . . [and turn] your back on your family's defeatism. . . . My father was trying to . . . develop life here, . . . to establish a national university, to improve the legal system and municipality. In the late 1970s, the idea of developing life here was looked on with suspicion, because the exiled leadership could survive only by remaining *the* leadership, and any attempt to have alternative leadership here could imply the creation of an alternative.[189]

Between 1969 and 1972, more than one hundred articles, a number of them by Shehadeh, appeared in *al-Quds* (Jerusalem)—the only East Jerusalem newspaper in 1969—on the idea of a Palestinian entity. Shehadeh also wrote articles for *New Outlook,* and other periodicals. Israeli political scientist Hillel Frisch calls Shehadeh's series of articles in the *New Middle East* (1968-71) "the most comprehensive series of articles in the English language by advocates of the Palestinian entity idea."[190] One of them urges Israel and the Arab governments to accept Security Council Resolution 242 and counsels the Arabs to negotiate with Israel on this basis: "Some among us have taken the course of military struggle against Israel; others, perhaps the majority, still believe in a peaceful solution . . . [and] hope Israel will . . . search for an honourable solution within the framework of the United Nations resolutions. . . . We Palestinians of all creeds . . . have been the principal victims of the stumbling, tottering and faltering leadership of the Arab states. They accept the Resolution [242] . . . but they refuse to negotiate the terms of the peace."[191]

Kuttab recalled Aziz arguing the Palestinians were never serious about armed struggle: "Aziz said, 'I am not a pacifist. If the Palestinians had really gone underground . . . there might be a point to it. But they were never serious, . . . it was just slogans, bombastic rhetoric, and an odd skirmish here and there, but no systematic, organized armed struggle. So why fool themselves and the world, pretending they wanted to liberate Palestine? . . . They never had a plan to liberate Palestine with armed struggle. . . . Don't talk about it if you are not doing it. Let's instead negotiate. . . . Let's talk about what we can achieve.'"[192]

In Shehadeh's envisioned Palestinian state, Palestinians could assert their identity and seek protection, returning when they chose, ceasing to be refugees "wandering in the wide world without a destination and no protection." He cautions, "Military solutions have nothing to offer the Palestinians and the call for such solutions can only create complications that would ultimately lead to the loss of everything."[193] Yet, Kuttab recalled, Moshe Dayan and the other Israelis with whom Shehadeh had met "were genuinely scared": "They really thought, Aziz said, that the idea made sense, but that the security problem would be too much. Unfortunately, they did not follow through with it, and soon found out how easy it was to rule the territories, that we were not much of a threat, and that we were not really serious about armed struggle. So, he said, they decided they could have their cake and eat it—they could keep the territories, plant settlements, and didn't need to negotiate with us."[194]

When U.S. secretary of state Cyrus Vance visited Israel in 1977, a year before the signing of the Camp David accords, he met with a group of Palestinians. Shehadeh gave him a letter stating, "It is imperative that both Israel and the Arab states recognize the basic rights of the Palestinian Arabs to set up a state of their own. . . . Israel and the emerging Palestine State would . . . sign a non-aggression pact, providing that none of the parties would invite foreign armed forces on its territories or enter into a military pact with a third party, without mutual consent."[195]

Shehadeh wrote not for purposes of scholarship, but to advance an argument.[196] The Arab Studies Society, established in East Jerusalem by Feisel Husseini in 1980, undertook to prepare an index of Shehadeh's personal papers—since disappeared—and Husseini, a key actor in the incipient intifada despite being under house arrest in East Jerusalem between 1982 and 1987, met frequently with Shehadeh in Ramallah. Jonathan Kuttab also played a key role in the years prior to the 1987 uprising. Referring to Husseini and Kuttab, Raja commented, "Though younger, these intellectuals and activists were more careful and circumspect than was Aziz. They are willing to work for a Palestinian state in stages, slowly. They are more cautious and guarded than was my father. He saw the Israeli settlements being built on a large scale and believed time was running out. He said, 'If we wait any longer, it will be impossible to have a Palestinian state, because there will be no land for a state.'"[197]

In a time of widespread opprobrium in Palestinian circles against talking with the "Zionist entity," Aziz Shehadeh believed that one should communicate with the Israelis precisely because they were the enemy.

• • • •

On December 2, 1985, Shehadeh was stabbed to death at the entrance to his Ramallah home. The perpetrator was never caught. Confidants of the family say that the outcome of the investigation by Israel—which bore responsibility for criminal justice, police, and security matters—was never disclosed. They believe that Shehadeh was killed by a collaborator.[198]

Although it would take until November 1988—eleven months after the start of the intifada—for the PLO publicly to propose the concept of a Palestinian state side by side with Israel, Aziz Shehadeh was influential with those actively working to introduce realistic alternatives to armed struggle and who would shape the uprising. Not the least of Aziz's lasting legacies was his influence on his son Raja, who, having been called to the bar at Lincoln's Inn in London in 1976 as a barrister, has practiced law in the West Bank since 1977. In 1979, Raja and others, including Jonathan Kuttab, established the first Palestinian human rights organization, al-Haq (Law in the Service of Man). Al-Haq allowed the reprimands of the Palestinians to be carried into transnational circuits through the center's affiliation with the International Commission of Jurists in Geneva.[199] Raja's conviction that Palestinians should fight for their rights by using the principles of the rule of law, and Israeli standards and military orders, has shaped a methodology that challenges Israel's legal claims on its own terms. They monitor the contradictions in thousands of Israeli civil and military administrative codes that circumscribe often benign or meaningless activity. This approach represents one of the earliest and most significant endeavors by Palestinians to use the nonviolent methods of documentation and denunciation to reveal the concrete nature of Israeli occupation.[200]

Chapter 5
Women at the Forefront of Nonviolent Strategies

Women Organize

Organizations for and run by women had existed since the Ottoman period, as had limited schooling for girls.[1] The first women's organizations included societies associated with different churches, such as the Orthodox Ladies Society founded in 1910 in Jaffa.[2] In 1911, the Christian Public Charity Society for Ladies was established in Haifa, and by 1919, the Arab Ladies' Associated was formed in Jerusalem. While the majority of such organizations focused on charitable efforts, a growing number increasingly turned to the political goals connected to the Palestinian national cause.[3]

By the start of the 1920s, Palestinian women were obtaining experience through exclusively women-led nonsectarian organizations in the largest cities, such as Jerusalem and Haifa, but also in Nablus, Tulkarem, Jenin, Acre, Ramallah, Bethlehem, and smaller towns. Notable among them was the Palestinian Women's Union, which by 1921 had headquarters in Jerusalem and Haifa.[4] While women elsewhere in the Arab world were challenging forced marriage, virginity and honor codes, cloistering, polygamy, and summary divorce, Palestinian Arab women were asking that the promises of independence by the British colonial authorities be honored. Women's groups in Tunisia and Egypt were specifically fighting against polygamy and summary divorce, at the time when the program of the women's union focused on retraction of the Balfour Declaration, cessation of Jewish immigration, and improved treatment for Palestinian political prisoners.[5] As early as 1920, women began writing protests to the government. A letter from women in the northern part of Palestine was sent to the chief administrator of what was then the Occupied Enemy Territory Administration, concerning the establishment of Jewish settlements.[6]

Activism by Palestinian women took shape in response to the circumstances created by the British Mandate, the growth of exclusive Zionist enterprises, and the influx of Jewish immigrants into the country. They would have been involved in an auxiliary sense in the three major episodes of violence discussed earlier: the May 1921 Jaffa riots, the uprisings of 1929, and the second stage of the "great revolt" in 1937 and 1938. Yet it was true for women, as it was for men and the community as a whole, that their predominant mode of involvement in trying to preserve their way of life was nonviolent action, generally with careful employment of the elementary methods of protest and persuasion. The women often acted independently on behalf of the nationalist movement, especially by the mid-1920s when their organizations began to assume more public roles. Although women's groups tended to identify themselves as charitable in nature, at a time when a transnational movement of securing the vote for women was sweeping the globe, their purposes and interests were concentrated on protecting life as they knew it. Palestinian women were active during all phases of the tumultuous early efforts for abrogation of the Balfour Declaration, and concerns for their rights and entitlements as women took second place.[7]

While women's leadership primarily derived from among the urban elite, their respective organizations encouraged collective action in the smaller towns and in rural communities, where the majority actually resided. They promoted cooperation across religious, political, and familial affinities, which contributed until 1938 to an avoidance of dissension and factionalism that was beginning to be visible among some Palestinians. The record is clear: men largely supported their activities. When Julie M. Peteet interviewed Matiel E. T. Mogannam, a prominent woman activist of the time, Mogannam explained, "Men encouraged the women in their protests and charitable work but did not direct their actions. Moreover, the women were financially independent of the national movement, raising money through bazaars and festivals, and collecting donations from religious institutions to pay for their expenses."[8]

Responding to the bloodshed resulting from the Western Wall disturbances, on October 26, 1929, at the Jerusalem home of Tarab Abd al-Hadi, more than two hundred women from across the country gathered as delegates to the First Arab Women's Congress of Palestine.[9] In the words of one of the organizers of the session, "It was a bold step to take in view of the traditional restrictions which, until then, prevented the Arab woman in Palestine from taking part in any movement which might expose her to the public eye."[10] The women protested the eviction of the fellahin from farmland that had been purchased by Zionist colonies and enterprises, while also asking for abrogation of the Balfour Declaration, an end to the mandate, and complete independence.[11] The Congress announced the formation of a fourteen-member delegation, the Arab Women's Executive Committee (AWE), which in its makeup displayed the diversity of membership that the women's organizations of the time were seeking. Mogannam was elected general secretary of the executive committee, and the congress was formally registered at the district commissioner's office, in accordance with the Law of Societies.

During the Congress, the delegation was received by the British High Commissioner Sir John Chancellor and Lady Chancellor at Government House and delivered a summary of the resolutions passed by the congress and the proceedings of the meeting, for transmittal to London: "To protest against the Balfour Declaration, which has been the sole cause of all the troubles that took place in the country, and which may arise in future. We consider that this country will never enjoy peace and tranquility as long as this Declaration is in force." The resolutions also protested collective punishment, "maltreatment by the police of Arab prisoners," and the donation of £10,000 sterling to Jewish refugees without a comparable contribution to help the Palestinian Arab refugees.[12]

The emotional content and gravity of the meeting was expressed when the Palestinian women, once seated, "simultaneously threw back their veils." This breach of Muslim tradition was not lost on the high commissioner, who reworked the section in his letter recounting the lifting of the veils to the secretary of state for the colonies, Lord Passfield, while the rest of his report on the meeting remained almost unchanged. When Sir John and Lady Chancellor offered coffee following the meeting, two of the women delegates refused it, declaring that Arab custom allows one to partake of refreshments only in the homes of friends. (Several later sent handwritten letters of apology to the high commissioner for this act of shunning, with an explanation that the two women who had refused the drinks were suffering from stomachaches.) The symbolism of the women's protest did not go unnoticed by the high commissioner: in his letter about the meeting, Chancellor notes, "Such a breach with the Arab traditions of the courtesy due to a host in his own house is significant of the bitterness of the hostility now felt towards the Government in certain quarters."[13] The semiotic potency of the "unveiling" caused a stir in the Muslim Palestinian newspapers for weeks.

Prior to the convening of the congress, several attendees met to discuss the possibility of holding a public demonstration in front of Government House, while the delegation was meeting with Sir John Chancellor. He summarily rejected their request for such a demonstration. Mogannam, in her capacity as general secretary of the AWE, posed a similar request to the governor of Jerusalem, who initially refused. Eventually he conceded, allowing the demonstrators to ride in automobiles.[14] He based his refusal on an argument that street demonstrations might incite others, particularly men, to riot. While men in solidarity and sympathy often joined demonstrations led by women, there may have been a thread of truth in the British concerns. Nonetheless, it is evident that the British administrators were also using the Arab tradition of separating men and women to encourage fragmentation. In several cases, British officials intentionally targeted Arab male sympathizers in order to discourage women's activism. In a handwritten account of the meeting regarding the preceding requests, Chancellor notes that male Muslim leaders initially "declined to intervene; but when it was explained to them that the demonstration would be stopped by force if necessary, and that they would have only themselves to thank if their women came into collision with the police the arrangements were altered."[15]

When the delegation of fourteen rejoined the ongoing congress, the participants conducted a motor cavalcade of 120 cars, which drove through the cobbled streets of Jerusalem, horns hooting, and pausing at diplomatic consulates to allow the women to give each foreign consul a copy of the summary of proceedings.[16] They sent a petition by telegram to Queen Mary and the colonial secretary in London:

> Two hundred Palestine Arab Moslem and Christian women representatives met on twenty-sixth instant in Congress Jerusalem, unanimously decided demand and exert every effort to effect abolition Balfour Declaration and establish National democratic Government deriving power from Parliament representing all Palestinian communities in proportion to their numbers; we beseech assistance in our just demands.[17]

Numerous memoranda sent by the executive committee to the government on behalf of prisoners went unanswered during this period, including a June 14, 1930, telegram to the Archbishop of Canterbury in London, but, eventually, three prisoners under life sentences were pardoned.[18] In the early

1930s, the AWE also drafted memoranda to the Mandatory Government regarding the growing debts of fellahin, their need to sell their personal property and lands, and the rising levels of arms being smuggled to Jewish paramilitary forces in the area. Palestinian women often sent cables to Queen Mary. References to such cables appear in documents of private collections in Jerusalem and published historical accounts, however, the registrar of the Royal Archives at Windsor Castle finds no cables from Palestinian women between 1929 and 1936, as "virtually nothing has survived from [Queen Mary's] official correspondence, sadly."[19]

The AWE in particular relied heavily on written correspondence as a method of protest, and the executive committee sent hundreds of letters to the British government, newspapers and news media outlets, Arab leaders, and other women's organizations. On January 28, 1932, for example, the AWE submitted a sixteen-page petition to the Permanent Mandates Commission at the League of Nations, to be sent through the office of the high commissioner. The memorandum accuses British authorities of discrimination with regard to dismissals of civil service officers, lack of reduced expenditures for which Arabs bear the brunt, and the failure to address previous grievances. The Palestine government eventually forwarded the petition to the League of Nations, as requested, but it was accompanied by a six-page memorandum of its own that strongly argued against each of the points raised in the petition.[20]

On April 15, 1933, as a way of showing disapproval of the policies of the British Mandate, Palestinian organizations boycotted the visit of Lord Allenby and Lord Swinton, while leading women organized a "silent demonstration" in the Old City, which they considered "unique in the history of Palestine."[21] According to the firsthand account of Matiel E. T. Mogannam, the procession moved to the Mesjid (Mosque) of Umar, which stood with its high minaret before the Church of the Holy Sepulchre. There, undeterred by heavy rains and watchful police, the first Christian woman to speak, Mogannam, offered a speech from the pulpit of the mosque. "We see before us the shadow of our complete extermination as a nation," she said, as she asked the "imperialistic administration" to fulfill its "national pledges" to the Arabs: "For fifteen years we have made repeated appeals to the Mandatory Government for a change of its destructive policy." In Mogannam's book, the demonstrators proceeded silently to the Church of the Holy Sepulchre, where, for the first time, a Muslim woman, Ouni Abd al-Hadi, gave her remarks, denouncing "the calamities which have befallen the Arabs in this country and the sufferings which they underwent in consequence of the unjust British policy" and British "failure to keep their promises" to the Arabs for liberty and independence.[22] Soraya Antonius refers to these women as "the inspirers and progenitors of the women activists of today."[23]

The 1929 first Arab Women's Congress of Palestine had the effect of stimulating the formation of women's societies and unions in both small and large municipalities across Palestine, starting with Acre, Haifa, Jaffa, Nazareth, Ramallah, Safed, and Tulkarem. Furthermore, women began to participate in activities alongside men as well. Women comprised a sizable portion of the October 13, 1933, demonstration in Jerusalem called by the Arab Executive Committee. A group of women activists organized a procession later that month in Jaffa, where Mogannam gave a speech that "excited the crowd."[24] To protest the brutality of police during these events, women's organizations sent yet another delegation to meet with the high commissioner at the end of that month. In the latter half of the decade, the role of women continued to expand within the nationalist movement. They acted as strike enforcers, demonstrators, and logistical coordinators. According to Ellen Fleischmann, the British officials were alarmed over what they considered troubling behavior and the prominence of women at these demonstrations.[25]

By April 1936, when the general strike was called that would eventually uncoil into the great revolt, Abdul Wahhab Kayyali records that women and students were playing significant roles in "maintaining morale and providing personnel for the organisation of relief, demonstrations and medical aid," and women were in the foreground of urging the boycotting of the government and refraining from entering negotiations with it until Arab demands had been conceded.[26]

Studiously nonviolent initiatives of women continued to develop into the next two decades, with entities such as the Jaffa-based Zahr al-Uqhuwan (The Lilies) in 1936, and the Women's Solidarity Society, in 1942.[27] The Arab Palestinian Women's Union (al-Ittihad al-Nissai al-Arabi al-Filastini) of Jerusalem, had been established in 1921. Perhaps the most prominent of the nonsectarian Palestinian women's organizations that were forming to challenge mandatory rule, the Arab Women's Union helped orphaned children, ran literacy and sewing classes for women, and by the late 1930s was aiding the nationalist cause.[28] In 1937 and 1944, the union was involved in the First and Second Pan-Arab Conferences for Women, which took place in

Lebanon and Egypt respectively.[29] The Eastern Women's Conference to Defend Palestine was held in Cairo, from October 15 through 18, 1938, under the leadership of Huda Sharawi, with women attending from Egypt, Iran, Iraq, Lebanon, Syria and Palestine. Of the twelve women who offered speeches from throughout the Middle East, five were from Jerusalem.[30]

As a point of objective comparison, although Mohandas K. Gandhi was a captive of a deeply patriarchal worldview that persists even today in India, because of his experiments during twenty-one years working in South Africa, he came to see the central involvement of women in political action as a core concept. Having returned to India, by 1921, the year that Palestinian women formed the Arab Women's Union, he was calling for women to become involved in the nation's political deliberations, to have the vote, and to enjoy legal status equal to that of men. The hand-looming of homespun roused the involvement of women by the millions in the fight for India's independence and put the nationalist struggle ahead of the hearth. By the late 1920s, some Indian women were leading local struggles. Gandhi's initiatives incorporating the political work of women became so pervasive that by 1931 the Congress Party passed a resolution committing itself to the equal rights of women. As Gandhi interprets the power underlying nonviolent resistance, even a frail woman, as well as a child, can pit herself on equal terms against a giant armed with the most powerful weapons. In his three major movements (1920-22, 1930-34, 1942), large numbers of women in different parts of India participated.[31]

Thus it is possible comparatively to note that in some ways the Palestinian women in the 1920s were ahead of their counterparts in India, and animated by their own efforts without a particular champion. Unaware of the malignity of the Nazis to their fellow Semites, throughout the period prior to the 1948 war, Palestinian women would remain active, often showing the way for nationalist Palestinians who were trying to preserve their way of life without bloodshed. In earlier decades, later during the 1970s and 1980s, and again in the first intifada, women would leave the home "to enforce pricing, boycotts, and strikes; to organize demonstrations; smuggle supplies; confront soldiers."[32]

"A Movement of Committees"

Miriam Cooke's study of what she calls the War Story—the universal memorializing of the fighting contributions of men, while understating the roles of women—shows through its literary analysis of writings by Palestinian women authors that women had grasped earlier than did men the futility of armed struggle in the occupied territories for addressing their dilemma.[33] Women knew, Cooke argues, that a different way of fighting would be entailed for success, and this contributed to the growth of nonviolent strategies of resistance, including the need to "recognize and negotiate with the humanity of the enemy."[34] Sahar Khalifa's post-1967 novels show "the solutions are in the hands of women who have invented a new kind of fighting."[35]

After 1967, as Palestinians in the territories militarily occupied by Israel came to realize that the occupation would not soon be lifted, as initially thought, and "a new social infrastructure" was built through committees, they developed broad political bases for themselves.[36] At the forefront were the women's committees. Until 1978, women's organizations had fallen into roughly two categories: traditional charities that reached back to the Ottoman era, while still-functioning branches of the Arab Women's Union formed the other.[37] Between 1948 and 1967, nine new organizations dedicated to addressing Palestinian social needs were created, almost all of them by women; although the numbers participating were small, their influence was great.[38] Anthropologist Rosemary Sayigh counted thirty-two such women's associations that had developed before 1967. In spite of the conditions associated with occupation, by 1976 she tallied thirty-eight involved in relief, health, child care, orphanages, elderly care, and the generating of income.[39] Separate all-female social-welfare institutions such as Inash al-Usra (Sustenance of the Family), political institutions, and work committees are not unequal, Ghada Hashem Talhami asserts: they are superior to comparable groups led by men.[40]

In the women's movements of the late 1970s and 1980s, the main way of becoming involved in national politics was through local work committees. As grassroots organizations formed themselves into volunteer work committees in association with the Community Work Program of Bir Zeit University, tens of thousands would participate in the nonpartisan voluntary committees during the 1970s, the vast majority of them not members of PLO factions or parties. Men and women worked with each other in these consequential community efforts that regularly brought young men and women into public association together.[41] Teachers and instructors at schools and colleges in the Ramallah and al-Bireh area joined cooperatively in 1972 under the sponsorship of al-Bireh's mayor Abd al-Jawad Saleh, who was criticized for departing from tradition:

In one of the mosques, the movement was condemned because of this [gender mixing]. So I went to the sheikh and told him, "Why don't you protest against laborers [who are] going to work in Israel? . . . You never shouted against [laborers working in Israel] as you have shouted against people working for their own country." . . . The next Friday, he preached in favor of voluntary work. . . . But my own sister said, "Brother, it is a great shame that you are working with these girls— people will talk against you."[42]

This path represented a novel progression since "mixed," that is, male and female, activities had been noteworthy and unusual before the 1948 war. The Ba'ath Party, Arab Nationalist Movement, and Jordanian Communist Party found new adherents in women; in Israel, Rakah similarly stimulated such organizing efforts.[43] The PLO had supported the development of the General Union of Palestinian Women (GUPW) (al-Ittihad al-Amm lil-Mara al-Filistiniyya) in 1964, but as an official section of the PLO both the Israeli and Jordanian authorities banned it in 1967.[44] Open recruitment of women for the fedayeen did not begin until after 1968.[45] From 1967 onward, Rosemary Sayigh writes,

Israeli occupation was followed by a sharp rise in women's participation in all kinds of resistance, from demonstrations and sit-ins to sabotage. In Gaza, women participated in a continuous insurrection between 1968 and 1971. They were killed and imprisoned. Many who were imprisoned were also tortured . . . others were deported, including Issam Abd al-Hadi, chairwoman of the GUPW's Executive Committee. Their acts of resistance were carried out in small groups or individually, without strong mass participation except in Gaza. Temporarily crushed in the occupied territories, resistance group organizing, still in its infancy, moved to Jordan.[46]

The women's movement that remained in the occupied territories proceeded to put down deep roots and became central to the process of civilian mobilization described here. The various decentralized and autonomous women's committees were able to gain greater significance than their counterparts in the diaspora.[47] As the first women's work committee was organized in Ramallah in 1978, and various groupings under the umbrella of the Palestinian Union of Women's Work Committees spread to the villages, they encountered in the rural hamlets a state of affairs in which girls' education ended prematurely at an early age, female descendants were disinherited, high rates of female malnutrition and infant mortality prevailed, and strong pressures to increase the birth rates of the Palestinians were applied with the result that twelve children might be born in thirteen years of marriage.[48]

"By the mid-seventies it was becoming very clear that there was a large sector that was still unmobilized even at the political level, and actually it was the women who discovered this fact," Rita Giacaman says. "A women's movement emerged that was trying to go to the villages instead of expecting the villages to come to it."[49] Literacy classes, nursery schools and kindergartens,[50] day care, and sewing workshops run by women's committees in refugee camps and villages seemed innocuous, yet, while seeking to address gendered exclusions and inequities, they were also avenues through which their members learned the rudiments of democratic self-governance and became part of the process of building a robust civil society.[51] These women were spearheading the diffusion of pluralistic societal power that would later help in withstanding reprisals, while contributing to changes in power configurations to allow the nonviolent contours of the first intifada to form. From 1978 onward, after the first such women's committee formed in Ramallah, a generation of women arose who were "capable of full participation in political life."[52]

With the entire society reacting both viscerally and cognitively to military occupation, a separate track of women's organizing also developed that was affiliated with the various Palestinian political factions.[53] On March 8, 1978, a group of approximately twenty women established the Women's Work Committees (WWC), which enlisted younger, educated women who had a grasp of issues related to class and sexual discrimination. An outgrowth of both the ferment from the voluntary work committees and the faculty and student activities at Bir Zeit University, many of its founders drew inspiration from the DFLP, the most energetic of all the PLO factions in advocating the transfer of resources to the territories, even though the WWC sought to define itself as broadly nationalistic.[54] One of its original organizers, Siham Barghuti, stated that she did not want "*us* working for *them*":

> We felt there was a need for a more broad-based women's organization, with no age limit, one in which decisions were not formulated from the top down, but one which encouraged the participation of rural and refugee women in the decision-making process. . . . We needed to work on several

levels to help women fight triple oppression at home, in the workplace, and under occupation.[55]

The WWC was "the first women's organization that attempted *mass* recruitment of women," according to Zahira Kamal, and by 1989, it had five thousand members in its committees.[56]

> When we organize women, our main aim is to improve their lives by empowering them. We never establish a committee in any village unless the women of the village request it and are willing to run it. . . . We see our role as informing women of their rights, urging them to keep land in their own names, and supporting them to withstand family pressures once they decide to do so. . . . The women's movement is part of the national movement. . . . [P]ersonal and national liberation go hand in hand. When both sexes are deprived of their freedom and national dignity by the Israelis, it would be inappropriate for us to deal only with sexual inequalities. On the other hand, we will fail both women and our cause if we do not understand that liberating women from discrimination will better equip them for waging a successful national struggle.[57]

As factional competition heated up in the early 1980s, splits accompanied the fledgling women's movement. Procommunist women set up the Union of Palestinian Working Women's Committees on March 8, 1981.[58] These committees ran unionizing workshops that addressed the economic problems of Palestinian women whose only income was from what Israelis call "black work"—jobs inside Israel unwanted by Israelis—plus seasonal agricultural work, and other unskilled labor jobs.[59] Another group, the Palestinian Women's Committees, was formed in 1982 and allied with the PFLP; in 1983, the Social Action Committee was established.[60] The WWC meanwhile decided to change its name to Union of Women's Work Committees, and by 1989 had become the Federation of Palestinian Women's Action Committees.[61] The largest of the women's organizations, it was constructed of tiers of committees, branches, district committees, higher committees, secretariats, executive offices, and a general conference—a structure difficult to interrupt through the removal of key leaders or organizers.[62]

The village women's committees and others in the popular movements of the 1970s and 1980s perfected a recurring pattern of forming committees that could continue operating, even as successive layers of elected leaders were imprisoned. It continued in the first intifada. The approach is identical to that developed in India during the yearlong civil-disobedience movement of 1930-31, part of the political program of the Indian National Congress for independence. When Nehru was locked up on April 14, 1930, his father took his place in the leadership, and, as ranking leaders across the country were rounded up, surrogates replaced them. Among the Palestinians, despite divisiveness and ideological disputes, factionalism among the women's committees was more restrained than in the labor unions, and there was less Israeli repression of the women's associations, possibly because of what Joost Hiltermann terms "the occupying power's patronizing conception of women and their role in society."[63]

The "discovery of the villages," as Rita Giacaman puts it, nine months before the outbreak of the first intifada, "proved to be crucial in developing a new movement . . . a movement of committees. . . . What's distinctive about this movement, especially the women's committees, is their structure and . . . function":

> Women from the village set up the committee themselves; it could be five women, ten. . . . One of these women is elected to represent her region in the national setup, . . . a structure where you have . . . previously invisible rural and refugee camp women, . . . representation of the poor by the poor. . . . With the women's committees, when several centers were closed down, the work went unharmed because it's a popular grassroots organization, . . . this kind of movement doesn't depend structurally on the presence of one or two or even ten people. And you can't put sixty to seventy thousand peasant women in jail. . . . This new form came as a great success against the military. . . . While these women are imprisoned[64] for only doing literacy work and are put under town or house arrest, the difference is that the work is extremely effective despite all that.[65]

The scale of involvement by women led political scientist Ghada Talhami to suggest that a form of de facto Palestinian governance by women-run organizations was in place by 1990:

> Deprived of state-supported social services, and hindered by the social climate from entering male-dominated institutions, Palestinian women . . .

have demonstrated a remarkable facility for creating their own institutions without any outside help. . . . The Occupied Territories are run by a network of women's social welfare organizations that have utilized the energies of women who are generally older and socially well-connected. Given the total absence of government-run social welfare organizations since 1967, these institutions . . . function as the informal government.[66]

As broad civilian mobilization solidified for the Palestinians the capacity for mass resistance that would later be manifested by the first intifada, among the foremost to take responsibility were women and women's groups.

Chapter 6
Movements of Students, Prisoners, and Work Committees

As EARLY AS 1968, four years after the formal establishment of the PLO, Eqbal Ahmad, a Princeton-educated Pakistani political scientist, asserted "highly organized, militant, nonviolent struggle" by Palestinians should be the preferred alternative to armed struggle: "The roads should be clogged with people lying down, offices blocked with hunger strikers. . . . Large marches should be organized into the West Bank and Gaza. Return home. When old men or women die, they wish to be buried in their ancestral villages. Funeral processions should move across the frontiers into Israel. The symbols of exodus must be reversed. A liberation movement seeks to expose the basic contradictions of the adversarial society."[1]

Ahmad, who had taught at the Pakistan Military Academy, held conversations with individuals in the PLO during the 1970s. In 1974 in Beirut, he proposed to Arafat and the PLO a variation of Gandhi's 1930 Salt March.[2] The PLO rejected Ahmad's suggestion of processions of tens of thousands of Palestinian refugees walking from the refugee camps of Amman to the Allenby Bridge.[3] It is doubtful whether such a plan would have worked anyway, because the PLO's political strategy had long been jeopardized by its military strategy.

Eqbal Ahmad instead called for "outadministering" the opponents—the aim being to undermine the legitimacy of a target government and institute a rival regime through the creation of "parallel hierarchies," also known as "alternative institutions" in the repertoire of nonviolent struggle. "The major task of the movement is not to outfight but to outadminister the government."[4] Outadministering the adversary "is a political, not a military undertaking, and is the essence of revolutionary struggle."[5]

"Previews of the Intifada": New Networks and Nonviolent Mobilization

Within the occupied territories, alterations in popular thinking were volcani-
cally shifting. Although hard to trace, changing political thought sometimes
reveals itself through organizational changes. A combination of political
stimulation from the communists, a need for alternatives to armed struggle,
probes on the acceptability of two adjacent states, and the activation of
previously uninvolved sectors of the populace was bringing about major
organizational changes in the occupied territories. These, in turn, had an
effect on their participants, encouraging further political modifications.

Accompanied by a surge of enrollment in secondary and higher education in the years after 1967, Palestinians by the thousands became involved
in the broad, popular mobilization of small social movements. They stopped
waiting for the PLO to act, and took responsibility for opposing the Israeli
military occupation themselves. As the old elite atrophied and centers of
power diversified, a new local leadership developed, and committees learned
how to function even if their leaders were imprisoned. Networks "outadmin-
istered" the military occupation by providing services to address neglected
needs, as Eqbal Ahmad had suggested. As the Israeli Civil Administration
failed to provide basic services and infrastructure, it turned a blind eye
toward the villages and committees that were openly organizing themselves
to provide needed services. In other words, for twenty years, a large proportion of the Palestinian population was developing the capacity for nonmilitary civilian-based defense, a form of nonviolent resistance, and laying the
organizational groundwork for the intifada.

The mass organizations formed during the 1970s and 1980s often had
emblematic connections to the main political-military factions of the PLO,
whose heraldic identification in families and clans was indisputable. Fedayeen
units were limited, secret, and mostly involving young men in their prime,
whereas the most prominent features of these civilian organizations is that
they were nonviolent, distinctly nonmilitary in ethos, they involved large
numbers including women, and they functioned with comparative openness.
Although lacking normal channels of institutionalized or constitutional
action, these nonmilitary groups in an emergent Palestinian civil society
sought to alter their condition by building social-welfare institutions to
address material needs, preserving cultural traditions, raising political
consciousness, and developing free-standing and often highly representative

institutions. Some reached out for international solidarity and offered the perspective of the Palestinians under occupation when possible in global forums.

Civil Society

The writings of twentieth-century Italian Marxist Antonio Gramsci were widely read by Palestinian intellectuals during the 1980s. He sees civil society in opposition to the state and the basis for revolutionary challenge, and, eventually, elimination of the difference between civil society and state. Rather than representing universal concerns, to Gramsci the state stands for particular interests. It holds coercive powers of control, domination, or violence, whereas the direction of civil society occurs through nonviolent means, principally through organizations. Gramsci defines civil society as "the political and cultural hegemony which a social group exercises over the whole of society, as the ethical content of the State."[6] He uses the term *egemonia* (hegemony), interchangeably with *direzione* (direction, meaning leadership), to explain how basic premises are diffused throughout a society, determining what is considered to be right or wrong, true or false, moral or immoral. The realm in which ideas and propositions collide with each other, and out of which hegemony or consent arises, is civil society.

Interest in Gramsci was in part related to eleven years that he spent imprisoned by Mussolini's fascist regime, and his opposition to the Bolshevik seizure of power through violence. Viewing civil society as the consensus that reigns over political society, or force, he saw it as the site of democratic struggles. His major contribution of hegemony, although often misunderstood, pertains to the notion that a certain worldview leads a society, encompassing economics, politics, ethics, ideology, linguistics, and power.[7] Hegemony was a live system of meanings and values. A hegemonic class gains the consent of other social forces by creating and sustaining a system of alliances through political or ideological struggle.

Intriguing to the Palestinians, the realm of civil society encompasses nearly all nonviolent organizational interactions between the citizens and the state. It has a life of its own.[8] Toleration of varying points of view is paramount; yet equally important is the use of nonviolent methods for its interactions. In the Arab world, the political liberalization that might open space for civil society has usually been introduced from above, rather than through popular forces below, often merely to ameliorate economic crises or isolate a regime's opposition.[9] This was not the case in the intifada.

A new political space opened during the 1970s with emergence of new networks and nonviolent mobilization, which represented the makings of a Palestinian civil society under military occupation and would become the bedrock of the uprising. For more than two years during the coming intifada, the methods of civil society would be utilized, while the rights required to support such an emergent society had still to be sought through the same techniques.

Five Tributaries Lead to the First Intifada

Five separate tributaries—predecessor movements of the 1970s—led to the civilian mobilization in the occupied territories, which coursed during the 1980s to the intifada.

1. Voluntary Work Committees

Among the first civil society organizations to form under occupation after 1967 were volunteer work committees, allied with the Community Work Program of Bir Zeit University in Ramallah.[10] Although the initiative for creating the committees came from the PCP, they were not party organizations. They were nonpartisan institutions in which participants of any persuasion were welcome; "tens of thousands of people participated in the voluntary committees in the 1970s, the vast majority of them not party members," Ghassan Khatib clarified.[11] The program began in 1972, when, Palestinian political scientist Lisa Taraki explains, numerous leaders of the student, labor union, and women's movements began to be introduced into national politics through this local movement.[12] It started as teachers and professors at schools and colleges in the Ramallah and al-Bireh area joined that year under the sponsorship of Abd al-Jawad Saleh, then mayor of al-Bireh, for meetings in the public libraries of both towns. A participating mathematics teacher recalled, "The mayors of Ramallah and al-Bireh encouraged us to use the public libraries and facilities of their municipalities for our activities. . . . The whole country was suffering from neglect; volunteer work in refugee camps and villages would be appropriate."[13] Participants planned work programs and discussed the writings of Arab and international literary or political figures. By the end of 1973, committees had begun to form in Nablus, Hebron, and Jericho to plan projects of manual labor, including the building of roads, agricultural reclamation, and help for farmers during the harvest.

The effort gained momentum after the Israeli government allowed municipal elections in 1972 and 1976, enhanced by Israeli cancellation of a 1955 Jordanian regulation that had prohibited participation by women in elections. Palestinians under occupation had retained a formal right to vote and run in elections, an allowance with little meaning since it did not include the right to form independent political parties. After the 1976 elections in the West Bank, leaders invited the involvement of work camp participants in municipal upkeep. Some let the students in the voluntary program work alongside the regular public works staff in municipal projects. Volunteers were soon running literacy programs in refugee camps and villages.

"Not only the voluntary work movement, but other movements, mass organizations, were really the backbone of the intifada," Saleh recalled. "Without it, without its spirit, without its mobilization, it might have broken, but not with its intensity and continuity."[14] Emanations of the coming uprising were visible in two distinctive features of the voluntary work committees: gender intermingling as men and women worked together side by side, and validation of manual or agricultural work

Manual labor was encouraged to break the class and social barriers between physical toil and intellectual work, and to span the isolation of towns and rural areas. For example, volunteers from Ramallah and Bir Zeit held a two-week work camp in the Hebron area, which resulted in the secluded hamlet of Udaysa becoming connected by a feeder road to Hebron and the world beyond its village gates.[15] "We were aware that by doing physical labor we were making a statement that all work, including manual labor, is valuable," commented a participant who worked with her sister to repair the playground of al-Amaari refugee camp school run by the UN Relief and Works Agency for Palestine Refugees in the Near East (UNRWA). "We wielded shovels and shared the work equally [with the men], and, eventually, other women joined us."[16] On foot or on tractors, entire villages took part: "children, women, men, old people, traditional people, students, teachers . . . reclaiming the land."[17] Its nationalist intentions, Saleh said, were indisputable:

We started it as . . . a way to work back to the land, preserve our identity, and to be able to resist the occupation. That's why . . . it spread all over. . . . We also started a committee to rehabilitate the victims of war . . . and I was the first mayor to get permission . . . to have food, fruits, and sweets brought to the prisoners. The whole town was involved—Ramallah and al-Bireh—it was really fantastic. . . . A traditional mayor saw me working with the volunteers and told me, "You brought shame to us, working with these sick people." . . . It was revolutionary—not accepted by some personalities who looked at public office for status, not serving the people.[18]

Among the impediments faced was the apparent interest of Israeli officials in inhibiting such development of national consciousness. Mukhtars were turned against the program, military checkpoints were set up near worksites to deter volunteers or deny them access, and the fact of Palestinian mayors working with local women was sensationally advertised by Israeli authorities.[19] As the movement began to spread, Israeli officials deported Saleh on December 10, 1973. Representatives from Nablus called on him the morning of his expulsion, before he had been informed of the deportation proceedings, to ask how they could build a voluntary work movement there.[20] Exiled for ten years, he recalls, "We formulated . . . a new form of struggle: voluntary work and a movement of nonviolent struggle against military occupation. The Israelis considered this very dangerous."[21]

After the deportation of Saleh, the voluntary work committees lost their national orientation and became divided along party lines, such that Fateh had its own committees and the communists had theirs.[22] Increasing factionalism beset West Bank organizing, and political competition began to lessen cooperation while, at the same time, paradoxically increasing the numbers of local committees,[23] although on a decidedly less utopian basis. By 1980, a Higher Committee for Voluntary Work had been established to coordinate among the 37 local committees and their 1,200 members. By 1982, only two years later, 6,500 participants from 96 local voluntary committees had recovered 6,000 dunums (a dunum is one thousand square meters, roughly equivalent to one-fourth of an acre) of land, planted 34,000 fig and olive saplings, retrofitted innumerable water pipes and sewage lines, and fixed countless roads.[24] While literacy remained a focus, during the 1980s the committees also tried to bolster the quality of Palestinian land management and agriculture, rendering confiscation by Israel of supposedly neglected or untended land a more complicated matter.

2. University Student Movements of the Late 1970s

Student activism—one of the few forms of political engagement allowed by Israeli military authorities—increased as university students saw a way to assume a major role in West Bank politics. The trend coalesced during the first decade of occupation.[25] By the late 1970s, student political activity had become a proxy for the normal political impulses of a civil society.[26] Bir Zeit University, twelve miles north of Ramallah, described by *al-Ayyam* (the Days) as the "backbone and main foundation" of student activism, became a meeting place for proponents from every conceivable political tendency—its vox populi demonstrated beyond doubt when it was singled out as one of the first targets in a crackdown after the Camp David accords.[27] Bir Zeit graduated thousands of Palestinians who formed a generation of youthful popular leaders. At new West Bank universities in Bethlehem and al-Najah, and a college newly built in Hebron, student activism went hand in hand with the growth of academia, and was often accompanied by the punitive closure of such institutions by Israeli military authorities for weeks or months:

> The level of political consciousness among Palestinians living under Israeli occupation is unmatched in the Arab world. . . . They learn the names of PLO leaders before they have learned to read and . . . can tell you the difference between Zionism and Judaism. . . . Soldiers, batons, tear gas, rubber bullets, arrest, torture, curfews, closure of entrances, administrative detention, and town arrest are all part of the refugee camp's daily dictionary. . . . From early in life, young Palestinians learn the language of resistance.[28]

While symbolic identification with the PLO was strong, it was not by fiat. Usually it was learned at the hearth. By the mid-1970s, student political groups were being set up to represent the various factions within the PLO. These were increasingly put together openly, with an emphasis on networking among the factions that is remembered as surprisingly cooperative. Contests among the different political groups were visible in the universities by the late 1970s, with "elections among the various factions, clubs, or societies, with people presenting themselves as Fateh, Popular Front, Democratic Front, or whatever," Sari Nusseibeh recalled. This was "a major step from Fateh's point of view, because . . . in the occupied territories at least, Fateh looked upon itself as secret, clandestine, military . . . with a cellular military structure."[29]

Until the 1967 war, student politics had been "sporadic, event-oriented, and reactive only to major political developments."[30] Palestinian students were ideally suited for political mobilization. They had time on their hands and lacked sufficient maturity to translate their political energies into power centers that could challenge the diaspora leadership.[31] Yet significant, if small, movements comprised of students who represented perhaps half of the population of the West Bank and Gaza, were able to set up, in Nusseibeh's words, "a good network, a collectivity, and could wreak havoc throughout the West Bank and Gaza." They did so, particularly during the years 1980-82: "The primary actors were the student activists. . . . You brought things into existence . . . by organizing. If you wanted a town to go on strike, you went there, and asked the mayor . . . to be involved. I've done it myself, personally, from the north to the south, asking people to show solidarity with us."[32]

A gap between the expansion of educational opportunity and a lack of jobs underscored the political activism.[33] In proportionally huge numbers after 1967, Palestinians entered high schools and universities. West Bank secondary schools had 17,682 students in 1969; six years later, 33,487. In the Gaza Strip, the number of secondary school students rose from 11,252 to 17,252 in the same period.[34] When the Israelis militarily occupied the territories in 1967, no universities existed, only post-secondary colleges. From a few hundred students enrolled in teacher-training and vocational institutes in 1968, the numbers in small Palestinian colleges and, later, universities had, by 1983, risen to 16,997.[35] By the following year, seven accredited universities were awarding degrees, and an additional seven teachers' colleges were functioning. In Gaza, a branch of Cairo's al-Azhar University opened; later, the Islamic University was established there, plus a teachers' college. Yet the jobs available were mainly manual labor stints in Israeli construction, industry, or services.[36] A youthful population mixed with endemic underemployment, made more painful by increasing educational opportunity, combined to create conditions conducive to popular participation.

Demographic shifts during the first decade of the Israeli occupation had seen the population of the West Bank and Gaza Strip rise by nearly 19 percent and, during the next decade this figure increased by another 20 percent. The population of 586,000 in the West Bank rose to 696,000 by 1977, and to 836,000 by 1986; the population in Gaza grew from 381,000 to 451,000 by 1977, and to 545,000 in 1986. The figure of greatest relevance for understanding the upsurge of popular mobilization is that by the mid-1980s, fully one-half the Palestinian population in the West Bank and Gaza was fourteen years of age or younger, and an additional one-third was between fifteen and thirty-four years of age.[37] Thus, four-fifths of the population of the territories had some education and was of high youthful energy, while facing bleak futures. By 1986, an estimated 7,000 Palestinians with thirteen years or more of education were yearly searching for jobs. As many as 10,000 university graduates may have been unemployed in 1984, three years before the eruption of the first intifada.[38]

3. Struggles against Israeli Military Orders 854 and 947

The territories edged toward open revolt when Israeli Military Order 854 was promulgated on July 6, 1980. With this order, the Israeli authorities assumed broad powers to restrict academic freedom. Amending a 1964 Jordanian law on education and culture, Order 854 brought institutions of higher learning under the purview of the law, imposing upon them restrictions that were usually placed only on elementary and high schools. The order gave the military authorities complete control in the licensing of teachers and institutions, supervision of curricula and textbooks, and decisions over who could be admitted to university.[39] Already roiling against the occupation, the student movements intensified their fervor. Sari Nusseibeh, recently returned from education abroad, joined the cultural studies faculty at Bir Zeit, and taught a course in Islamic philosophy at the Hebrew University for one year. The next year, while still at Bir Zeit, he taught the history of philosophy at Hebrew University. To Nusseibeh,

> Military Order 854 . . . was in direct confrontation with us—straightforward infringement of academic freedom. One of the first conferences held [by the faculty at Bir Zeit] on this order was as a faculty union in 1980 or 1981. . . . [T]he faculty union I belonged to and the student movement combined was perhaps *the* power in the occupied territories—far more than anything later, even the organization of Fateh. I was a founding member of the Higher Committee of Fateh, but we (in the faculty union during 1981 and 1982) had far more power because of the student numbers.[40]

The emerging student leadership, bellwethers of the intifada, arose mainly because of a Palestinian university system that had not existed before 1972. Prior to this date, university education was available for elite landowning families that were able to send their children abroad. By the start of the uprising in 1987, almost 16,000 Palestinians would be enrolled in seven

Palestinian universities, 70 percent of whom came from refugee camps, hamlets, villages, and small towns—a major alteration in the educated sector of Palestinian society.[41] Universities (and Israeli prisons) were the place where this group developed politically and built networks that would enable them to broaden their leadership skills during the 1980s and play formative roles in the intifada. Universities were also crucial in the "strategy of building embryonic institutions of power in the occupied territories," Palestinian sociologist Salim Tamari explains, because they were viewed as "institutional components of future power, so that a Palestinian state . . . [would] not arrive in a vacuum" and would have its own political and civic institutions to sustain it.[42] Relations between the military authorities and the universities, in the words of Meron Benvenisti, Israeli scholar and administrator from 1967 to 1973 of Jerusalem's Old City, were tense:

> This stemmed from the [Israeli] military government view of the universities as hotbeds of subversion in academic guise. The universities . . . regard their purpose as the training of a cadre of leaders and intelligentsia for the Palestinian state of the future. The Israeli view of all . . . political expression [was] as subversive activity aimed at the destruction of Israel, and the Palestinian view of Israel as an occupying power and illegitimate ruler, made the clash inevitable.[43]

Stringent enforcement measures in response to what Israel considered acts of sedition only served to heighten frustration and resistance, according to Benvenisti, thus inviting, in turn, harsher reprisal.[44] Regardless, the Palestinian fight against Order 854 was "consciously conceived as a civilian struggle." It was a major episode in the process of building the capacity for the intifada, one in a series of "parabolic waves."[45] In this emerging civil society, while some Palestinians embarked on nonviolent action, others expressed their spirit in folklore, songs, and pamphleteering.

A year after the issuance of Order 854, a Likud initiative undertaken by prime minister Menachem Begin further intensified popular mobilization. In response to the proposals for "autonomy" of the West Bank and Gaza Strip associated with the Camp David accords, Israeli Military Order 947 in November 1981 established a "civilian administration" to address the "civilian affairs of the inhabitants."[46] Just as the British had done in 1920 when Herbert Samuel became high commissioner, the Israelis instituted a "civil administration" that gave its military government the ruse of a civilian facade.[47] In the eyes of Zeev Schiff, *Haaretz* military correspondent, and Ehud Yaari, it was "one of those subtle devices that has enabled Israel simultaneously to practice occupation and to deny it."[48] The military government delegated some of its powers to a system of "village leagues," established under the Likud leadership in 1981-82, and supplanting the village councils created by Jordan in 1954; of such councils, ninety-six had been operating on the eve of the 1967 war.[49] Regarding the village leagues, Raja Shehadeh observes,

> Israel was trying to save face by implementation of its version of the "autonomy" plan and needed the presence of a local group through which it could claim popular acquiescence. . . . Members of the leagues are armed with sub-machine guns provided by the Israeli army and are trained by the army in the use of these weapons . . . . [R]ecruited from the lowest rank of society and from amongst society's outcasts. . . . , the leagues were meant to be developed into an army militia which would support the central Israeli policy of encouraging the emigration of the Palestinians from the West Bank . . . by making life intolerable.[50]

Village *mukhtars* were advised by military authorities that requests to the Israeli government needed to be approved by the leagues, which also dispensed favors for those who opposed the PLO.[51] These associations were strengthened when General Ariel Sharon became Israeli defense minister and in 1981 sought to turn rural areas against the PLO-allied larger towns.[52] In the autumn of 1981, Ramallah mayor Karim Khalaf, an attorney in the West Bank judiciary before becoming politically active, declared a policy of non-recognition and noncooperation in regard to Order 947: "This is being done against our will, and we shall not bow to coercion. No one will answer the call to work for such an administration, because that would amount to recognition of the Israeli occupation."[53] As the order was implemented in November 1981, Don Peretz asserts, the residents of the occupied territories were near "full-scale insurrection."[54]

Rebellion broke out against the occupation during 1981 and 1982, with burning tires, throwing of stones, demonstrations, and casualties exacerbated by the provocation of Israeli soldiers posted throughout the refugee camps. "The line had been stretched so thin that something would break," Nusseibeh recalled—"previews of the intifada" were everywhere—and the term *intifada* was being used by Palestinians for approximately three years prior to the start of the December 1987 uprising.[55] An Israeli policy of purging the local Palestinian leadership of PLO supporters was evident as leaders were expelled, collective punishments were imposed on villages and refugee camps,[56] and Palestinian economic life was marginalized, further disenfranchising the population. All the while the society was being bureaucratically enmeshed with myriad and often conflicting military orders—1,250 then in force in the West Bank and another 900 in Gaza.[57] In March 1982, Palestinian casualties heightened, as Israeli chief of staff Raphael Eitan increased personal and collective punishments. At the same time, the authorities were offering Israeli settlers who were building settlements in the occupied territories more license.[58] Zeev Schiff describes a April 21 demonstration as without parallel: "The demonstrators are not afraid as they were in the past."[59]

On May 1, twenty-five Palestinian West Bank towns issued a statement that threatened to close down municipal services unless the Israeli administration was abolished and the deported mayors who had been elected in 1976 were allowed to return.[60] The Likud government of Israel interpreted the "mini-intifada" of 1981-82 as having been instigated and organized by the PLO, and this episode of what was actually popular civil resistance became a principal rationale for Israeli's 1982 invasion of Lebanon, the major purpose of which was to destroy the PLO.[61]

Meanwhile, in December 1981, Prime Minister Menachem Begin had annexed the Golan Heights, despite having two weeks earlier signed a memorandum of understanding with the United States on strategic cooperation, an action that violated the principles of international law, UN resolutions, and the Camp David accords. After Israel's annexation, the Druze on the Golan, who consider themselves Syrian, adopted nonviolent resistance when in that same month Israel required that they carry identity cards.[62] The sect has Islamic origins and lives as a separate Arab community in the mountainous villages of the Golan. Unlike Muslim and Christian Palestinians, the Druze are conscripted and serve in the Israeli army, where they have acquired a reputation for ferocity in carrying out their instructions against Palestinians. Druzes petitioned against accepting Israeli citizenship, and when that failed announced plans for noncooperation. Laborers refused to work, the elderly and young violated curfews to harvest crops, and children were arrested. One village on strike took advantage of being at home and adopted the "reverse strike," digging trenches and a pipeline for which they had been refused permission and funds for years by Israeli authorities.[63] The Druzes' rejection of the order to accept Israeli identity cards was significant, because lack of one made travel and cashing checks difficult, and precluded the registering of marriages and births; it also increased the likelihood of random arrest.

Following four months of prolonged negotiations, Israel indicated a suspension of the plan to force the Golani Druze to accept Israeli citizenship and instead implemented military pressure. During a siege of forty-three days, 14,000 Israeli soldiers or more occupied the area, during which time authorities attempted to force the Druze to comply.[64] Israeli officials sealed homes, and demolished several. Electricity and water was cut to four villages with a combined population of 13,000. The close-knit community remained determined, as Israeli troops went door to door, confiscating villagers' old identification papers, and instead leaving Israeli identification papers. The next morning, the main squares of the various villages were strewn with the Israeli identity cards. In one demonstration, nine persons were wounded.[65] Yet, in another instance, Israeli soldiers refused their orders to fire on villagers demonstrating.[66] When five Druze were arrested for lacking identity cards, the entire village appeared for the trial—not to protest, they told Israeli authorities, but to turn themselves in for the same crime. The campaign made an impact on the Israeli troops, as villagers defied curfews to put tea and biscuits on their doorsteps for the soldiers, and some Druze chatted in Hebrew with them. "The soldiers were affected by this reception, and morale and discipline broke down," according to Brad Bennett; "The Israeli division commander complained that the Golan campaign was 'ruining' some of his best soldiers."[67] The Israeli government ultimately yielded.

In Washington, the Ronald Reagan administration temporarily suspended the memorandum of understanding and $300 million in arms sales to Israel, while in Israel defense minister Ariel Sharon, named by Avi Shlaim the "real driving force behind Israel's invasion of Lebanon," moved into center stage, with aims that were ruthless and wide-ranging.[68] Assisted by chief of general staff Raphael Eitan, Sharon set out an aggressive policy for Israel in southern Lebanon. It would exacerbate the already strained relations between Syrian forces in the Bekaa Valley, PLO fighting units relocated from the Mediterranean coast, and the Israeli army to the south, assisted by its own right-wing Maronite Christian militia, the Phalange.[69] Sharon's aerial bombardment of Beirut began on June 4, 1982, and continued through the fifth. On the sixth, Israeli forces embarked on a major air, land, and sea invasion of Lebanon, resulting in the occupation of one-third of the country, with a siege in the western sector of the city that cut supplies of electricity, food, medicine, and water to the civilian population.[70]

President Reagan's aide and confidant Michael K. Deaver would later recall that he had been troubled as the National Security Council for weeks advised Reagan that Israel would succeed in its goals: "I wondered, could we continue to stand by, publicly denounce the Israeli incursion, and privately encourage them even as civilian casualties mounted?" Having decided to resign due to his discomfort with the carnage, Deaver conversed with Reagan over his decision, and told the president, "All you have to do is tell Begin you want it stopped." As Deaver recounted, Reagan telephoned Begin, telling him, "It has gone too far. You must stop it." Twenty minutes later Begin phoned back and said he had issued orders to Sharon. "The bombings had ceased," said Deaver. Reagan hung up, marveling, "I didn't know I had that kind of power."[71]

The campaign lasted sixty-six days, until after September 1, when the remaining PLO fighters ensnared in Beirut evacuated the coastal city. The indignation of Arab allies led the Reagan administration to send a force to supervise a partial Israeli withdrawal, as U.S. diplomats negotiated the terms between the Israelis and Palestinians for a safe exit of the PLO's forces. They moved to Tunis, where Arafat established his headquarters in distant North Africa, far from his would-be homeland. The invasion foreclosed once and for all any dream of "armed struggle" as the means to "liberation," although the delusion would die hard, and then not until the uprising of 1987.

George W. Ball, undersecretary of state during the Kennedy and Johnson administrations observed, "Since the Reagan Administration lacked any coherent Middle East policy of its own it supported, without critical sensitivity, the policies, decisions and actions of the Israeli government, apparently unaware that Israel's objectives in Lebanon diverged sharply from America's . . . . [and thus] encouraged Israel in an adventure that was ill-conceived and disastrous for both countries."[72] The lowest point was still to come.

In September 1982, Sharon allowed commanders from the Phalange into the refugee camps of West Beirut. Sharon may have warned the Phalangists against attacks on civilian noncombatants, but the Israeli army is now widely believed to have barricaded the camps of Sabra and Shatila and created a path of entry for the Phalangists. If the Israeli soldiers reported their concerns of a massacre, nothing was done in response. Zeev Schiff says he learned of the massacre while it was underway and rushed to inform Mordechai Zippori, then minister of communications in Menachem Begin's Cabinet. Zippori, in turn, told foreign minister Yitzhak Shamir, and criticizes Shamir for ignoring this information.[73] The Red Cross tallied 2,750 unarmed Palestinian refugees who were massacred in Lebanese refugee camps at Sabra and Shatila, at the hands of the Phalangists on September 16. The teeming camps were surrounded by armed Israeli soldiers, and the killings took two days to complete.[74]

The war, the massacre, and the PLO's removal from Lebanon came to be viewed as a "turning point, the watershed that led to the *intifada*."[75] The net effect was to broaden the ranks of Palestinians who became active. Offering a "new Palestinianism," the grassroots committees won increasing support from a broad cross section of the populace.[76] The perceived link between the IDF and the slaughter led more than 400,000 Israelis to gather in a celebrated demonstration in Tel Aviv initiated by the Israeli peace group Shalom Achshav (Peace Now).[77] Sharon was forced to resign. A government commission of inquiry dismissed several senior officers who had been involved and ruled that Sharon was unfit to serve in such an exalted position (he would become prime minister in 2001).

The historical process—with its traumas associated with the events of 1948, ongoing land expropriation, and the military occupation of 1967—was intensifying a collective sense of betrayal in the territories.[78] Priorities of the PLO were questioned, as residents of the territories contended that they, rather than the exiles in the diaspora, should have been given precedence by the PLO after the military cadres were routed from Beirut and Tripoli in 1982. The cumulative deterioration found its expression in intensified organizing of the civil society structures that would implement and sustain the intifada.

4. Youth Committees

Among the structural developments was the movement called al-Shabiba (The Young People).[79] Youth "committees for social work" were established in 1980 in the Anabta refugee camp, near Tulkarem, by Adnan Milhem, who led the student council at al-Najah University and had spent years in Israeli prisons.[80] "These committees did not come from nothing," Milhem writes; "They are rather a realization of a phenomenon that was always very well known in our villages and towns, namely mutual aid. On this foundation, the youth committees have built . . . a new meaning for social work. . . ."[81] Diffuse and nonhierarchical, the committees may have been spawned by Fateh's first concrete attempt at political mobilization in the territories.[82] The Shabiba movement reached other refugee camps in 1982.[83] Firsthand accounts suggest training within some clubs started with youth aged twelve years. Unlike much of the mobilization taking place, the Shabiba set up separate branches for young men and women. From this group would come a socially oriented, disciplined, and politicized corps of youths pledged to community service for the intifada. In April 1987, months before the outbreak of the uprising, the Shabiba movement was deemed illegal, despite its having campaigned openly in student elections and never defining itself as a clandestine organization, unlike the cellular guerrilla cadres.[84] The Shabiba committees became especially strong in the Balata refugee camp near Nablus (from Balata street demonstrations in the West Bank would flow in immediate response to the outpouring from camps in Gaza that would launch the intifada).[85] By March 1988, arrests associated with membership in the Shabiba movement began in earnest.[86]

Such organizations were gaining the "popular legitimacy a national movement so desperately needs."[87] Localized women's committees, councils, societies, youth clubs, labor unions, professional groups, charities, and federations not only reduced vulnerability to Israeli reprisal, but also decreased the control exercised by Israeli authorities.

5. The "Prisoners' Movement"

Operating without any apparent mechanism for coordination, Palestinian political detainees[88] in Israeli jails, from north to south, were successfully able to call for collective actions on a given day and time. The "prisoners' movement" of the 1980s worked through "prisoners' clubs." Its leadership was annually chosen through committees elected in each prison cell. One hundred jail cells comprised one section, which, in turn, elected a committee. Ten sections elected another committee, and so on, with a final committee representing each prison facility. Each final committee in the prison elected a leader for that installation. The leaders from all the prisons elected a top committee, which had a single spokesperson. The seniormost prison committee in each facility coordinated with those in other penal institutions, despite the fact that no communications were allowed. Hunger strikes and other action methods of nonviolent struggle were coordinated across the length and breadth of prisons in Israel by this movement.[89] Among the favored methods were the banging of bars to make nerve-racking noise when a prisoner was beaten, and the "cold shoulder" technique, *den Kolde Skulder* (*Den Skolden*), used by the Danish unarmed resistance against the Nazis, in which representatives of the target group are ignored, snubbed, or sometimes stared at.[90]

The first coordinated mass prison hunger strike of the contemporary period occurred in Ashkelon in 1970. For fifteen days, the prisoners drank water and consumed salt, but ate no food. One prisoner, Abd al-Qadir Abu al-Fahem, died as a result. The second coordinated hunger strike took place in 1976, and lasted for forty-five days.[91] The third occurred in the summer of 1980, for a duration of thirty-three days. Two prisoners died in that fast—Rasem Halawah and Ali al-Jaafari.[92] By the 1980s, released prisoners had established prisoners' clubs throughout the West Bank and Gaza, comprised of former detainees and inmates, and actions inside the prisons thus had support from peaceful demonstrators outside the prisons. A fourth hunger strike was coordinated across Israeli prisons in 1984, three years before the outbreak of the intifada.[93] A prisoner's mother joined the demonstrators that summer:

> [M]y son was moved to a new prison, Jnaid. The prisoners went on a hunger strike, protesting their living conditions. A lot of women went to demonstrate in support of them. . . . There were about a hundred and fifty altogether, and other women joined us during the day. We were Muslims, Christians, and Jews all together. . . . I went without food for twelve days.[94]

Another hunger strike took place in March and April 1987, about which states a veteran of twenty such fasts: "All the detainees, all the prisoners, used the hunger strike as a last resort when they reached a breaking point. Hunger strikes were to defend yourself, to defend your rights as a human being."[95] Hunger strikes required preparation.[96] One had to know

> the hows, the whats, even the alphabet of the hunger strike: what the person will feel when he begins, . . . the movement of the stomach, the smell of the mouth, the taste, how we must go to the bathroom, how we must take water, how we must take salt, . . . how to maintain the strike even if they were placed in isolation or transferred. . . . We said that even

if they were released they must continue the strike with their colleagues who were still imprisoned.[97]

The "prisoners' movement" has not been documented as such,[98] yet it is important in explaining how the capacity for sustained popular dissent was developed by the Palestinians. A brief chronicling of the involvement of Qaddourah Faris will be useful. Faris was elected yearly to the leadership of the prisoners' movement starting in 1985, and through its pyramidal apparatus was repeatedly chosen as spokesperson for the entire population of politically active Palestinians imprisoned in Israeli jails. Having begun his career in elective office, so to speak, two years before the eruption of the first intifada, Faris was one decade later elected to the Palestinian Legislative Council. In 1992, while incarcerated in the Jnaid prison camp near Nablus, he led 15,000 prisoners on a hunger strike that was invisibly coordinated across major Israeli prisons. It began on September 27:

> Our demands were that we be allowed to kiss our children (touch and hold our children when they visited), that we be allowed to learn [study] while in prison, that we have more time for family visits, better health care, better medicine, operations [surgery], and more time outside [in the open air] for sports, exercise, and to see the sun.[99]

In response, according to Faris, family visits were instead suspended by prison officials and no time was permitted out of doors. Twelve days later, he claimed, three of the prisoners' demands were accepted, amid threats from prison wardens that they would break up and transfer committee members to other prisons. The practice of shifting committee members from one institution to another had no impact, according to activist Mahmoud Jasser, because second, third, and fourth tiers of the leadership were ready to take their place.[100] By Faris's account, Israeli minister of police Moshe Shahal visited him in prison and asked him to end the hunger strike. Three days later, Faris requested that the guards connect him by telephone with the minister, and told him that the prisoners were supporting peace, wanted the peace process to succeed, desired no violence outside the walls, and that if Israel wished the peace process to succeed, it should accept their humane approach. Following a four-hour meeting with prison authorities, Faris felt obliged to confer with all the committees from the other prisons before the fasting action could be halted. On Tuesday, October 13, the entire committee structure having been consulted, and every demand having been met, according to Faris—the hunger strike ended.

As a result of the strike, an arrangement was set up whereby 150 of the 3,500 Palestinian political prisoners who remained in Israeli prisons by 1996 could enroll themselves in the Open University of Tel Aviv University, at a fee of 129,500 NIS (new Israeli shekels), then equivalent to $29,000, allowing them to earn six hours of academic credit through correspondence courses.[101] The prisoners also won the right to teach themselves Hebrew or English in classes led by prisoners who already spoke the languages.[102] Faris, released in 1994 and elected to the Fateh Supreme Committee after fourteen years of incarceration, during half of which he led the prisoners' movement, stipulates the prisoners' clubs had no relationship with the Palestinian Authority and maintains they took no money from it. He and Jasser, while allied with Fateh, maintained that all funds for the movement were raised from their six thousand members, that is, former prisoners, who each paid 10 NIS (US$2.25), in annual dues.[103]

By governing themselves through reticulated links of elected representatives and committees, invisibly coordinating nonviolent actions such as hunger strikes, and learning Hebrew, Palestinians imprisoned in great numbers during the 1980s gained experience dramatically different from that of the commando cadres in the diaspora. Israeli prisons became hatcheries for ideas.[104] Since the occupied territories had been "hermetically sealed," the prisons were the one place where Palestinians from "different geographical and political zones" met.[105] The success of Faris as a candidate for parliamentary elections in Ramallah in 1996 came as a surprise to him since he ran as an independent, rather than on Fateh's list, and spent little money on his campaign.[106] Prison—the essence of nondemocracy, a vacuum of rights, compounded by circumstances of military occupation—became a place where democratic proceedings, processes of debate, parliamentary procedures, aspects of institutionalized political action, and mechanisms of citizenship were learned. "There is no legitimacy without elections," Faris stated on behalf the prisoners' clubs, which, he said, helped him to develop different objectives from those that he had championed while leading a military cell in the early 1980s.[107]

Networks Disperse the Centers of Power
Social mobilization diversifies a society's centers of power, laying the basis for broad resistance and social movements. "Effective action requires *corporate*

resistance and defiance," Gene Sharp argues, because the structural condition of a society determines its capacity to limit the rulers. When power is diffused throughout varying institutions in a society, such bodies provide restraints.[108]

Prior to 1967, Meron Benvenisti had counted 89 Palestinian charitable organizations on the West Bank that were among the loci of power; by 1983, he had tallied 166. He also noted that Israeli policy sought "to reduce the establishment of new charities as much as possible, as some are viewed as *fronts for subversive activities.*"[109] Catholic Relief Services officials in East Jerusalem describe more than one thousand indigenous Palestinian private, voluntary, development agencies in existence by 1994.[110] The tabulation may have run much higher. The head of the Palestinian Academic Society for the Study of International Affairs (PASSIA) in East Jerusalem, Mahdi Abd al-Hadi, told the *New York Times* that 45,000 committees were in existence by 1987 and able to act as the organizational base for the intifada, including student groups and trade unions.[111] One among many that assumed bland names to evade military intrusion is the aforementioned Arab Studies Society, set up in 1980 by Feisel Husseini. Located in Orient House, a once grand Husseini family home in East Jerusalem, the society's original purpose was to translate into Arabic articles published about the Palestinians that appeared in Israeli Hebrew-language newspapers, because, as Husseini explained, such news accounts often disclosed Israeli plans concerning the Palestinians.[112] In the society, "representatives from various Palestinian associations, not political organizations, which are forbidden, but things like labor unions, teachers unions, physicians unions, universities, and so on, would meet to discuss and make decisions."[113] The society includes archives, a library, and documentation center.[114]

Islamist Blocs

Antedating the Israeli military occupation by almost twenty years and the first intifada by forty, Islamist associations have never stopped being a subject of controversy. It should not seem extraordinary that such a force would develop in the wake of political Zionism, itself a revolt against the traditional pacifist values of Judaism, or that such blocs would arise in the shadow of Israel's theocracy, in which certain functions of the nation-state may be determined by rabbinical authorities. Nor would it be amazing that the "almost completely disenfranchised" Palestinians would spawn religious movements, including some with radical solutions.[115]

A process of building Islamic institutions had been underway in Gaza (and the West Bank) for half a century. The earliest branch of the Muslim Brotherhood, originally established in Egypt in 1928 to oppose British occupation, was set up in Jerusalem on October 26, 1945, and by 1947 there were twenty-five branches in Palestine.[116] During the great revolt of 1936-39, the Egyptian brotherhood organized committees to raise funds, carried out propaganda activities, and a few volunteers took part in armed raids on Zionist colonies in Palestine.[117] By 1948, perhaps one million adherents in Egypt were members, although the number of combatants was small.[118]

In the mid-1950s, the Muslim Brotherhood in Gaza and the West Bank was the first to express disillusionment with the notion of Palestine being liberated through pan-Arab unity, instead recommending self-reliance and military action by Palestinians in the West Bank.[119] Under the Hashemite monarchy, the Muslim Brotherhood obtained legal recognition, functioned openly, and was favored by the authorities, who hoped it could counteract the appeal of other political parties that were forbidden by law.[120] The perceived closeness between the Muslim Brotherhood and an unpopular Jordanian regime caused it to lose ground in the eyes of the Palestinian populace, and the relationship between the brotherhood and the Hashemites was often marked by mutual suspicion.[121] Political violence that in Egypt had been associated with the Brotherhood's activities was missing under the Jordanians.[122]

Following an Egyptian ban on the Muslim Brotherhood in 1949, its Gaza branch reorganized itself into an educational and religious center called the Society of the Oneness of God (Jamiyyat al-Tawhid). Between 1952 and 1954, the Brotherhood became viewed as the "party of the government," because of its good relations with those who ended monarchical rule.[123] After an attempt on Nasser's life, the Brotherhood was forced to adopt secret activities, leading to a disintegration of what had been one of the largest organizations in Egypt. In the aftermath of an attempted coup d'état in 1965, thousands were arrested, including Sheikh Ahmad Yasin, a disabled schoolmaster who would become a symbolic leader.[124] The 1967 defeat was particularly nettlesome for Palestinian Muslims. The Israeli presence changed from a specified Jewish national home to claims of divine sanction for new conquests, with the Hebrew Scriptures as justification for appropriating land, and a policy of the Judaization of Jerusalem.[125] Despite its tough rhetoric, the Brotherhood was neither prepared nor willing to undertake organized military operations against the Israeli occupation.[126] By the late 1970s,

Islamic revivalist organizations had quickened their educational and political activities and were focusing not only on mosques and places of learning and promoting religious education for youth, but were also offering a political alternative for families that wanted a faith-based movement. The ideological or religious appeal of Islamic organizations may have been less important for the Palestinians than their ability to offer services and support for the local population.[127]

The Muslim Brotherhood successfully enlisted large numbers of students in "Islamic blocs" at educational institutions in the West Bank and Gaza. Coinciding with the awakening of nationalist student movements, the relationships between these student organizations and the Brotherhood were often antagonistic. A series of violent clashes occurred at Palestinian universities during the early 1980s, chiefly between Fateh and the Brotherhood.[128] Irritation derived mainly from the Islamic groups' increasing tolerance for violent methods, or armed struggle, and lack of clarity in their ideology, largely consisting of advocacy for an Islamic state.[129]

Al-Jihad al-Islami (Islamic Jihad), a wing of the Muslim Brotherhood, was founded in 1980. Inspired by Sheikh Izz al-Din al-Qassam's conjunction of jihad, the holy struggle for God, with jihad for the sake of country, Islamic Jihad explicitly links nationalism and religion, rejects contact with Israel and the United States, and sponsors suicide missions defined as a path to martyrdom. Its origin within Palestine, on which it focuses as the central issue rather than a transcendent Islam, has given it notoriety. It is characterized, according to Ziad Abu-Amr, by its organization, discipline, and secrecy, particularly with regard to its armed operations.

Hamas resulted from a decision by the Muslim Brotherhood to participate in the intifada.[130] *Hamas* is a non-Qur'anic word meaning "zeal," and an acronym for Harakat al-Muqawama al-Islamiyya (the Islamic Resistance Movement). Its founding is usually dated to August 1988, when it published its covenant (*mithaq*), differentiating itself from the leaflets that were guiding the intifada and which appealed for recognition from Israel while at the same time confronting the state. A more likely date of origin would be the end of 1987, just after the outbreak of the uprising, when, under the spiritual leadership of Sheikh Ahmad Yasin, the group's patronage of kindergartens, clinics, and youth centers emerged.[131] Hamas was, indicates Abu-Amr, the idea of Sheikh Yasin, who sought a special offshoot from the Muslim Brotherhood to take responsibility for participation in the uprising.[132]

Controversy will likely never cease over the willingness of the government of Israel to allow certain concessions to Hamas.[133] The Islamists were able to bring funds of Saudi, other Gulf Arab, and Iranian origin into the territories.[134] It is alleged that they were given access to caches of arms and munitions, and that their cross-border movements were expedited by Israeli authorities. Salim Tamari claims that the Israeli security establishment had collaborated with other Muslim organizations as early as the 1970s.[135] The Israeli brigadier general in charge of Gaza told David Shipler of the *New York Times* that he had funded Islamic factions to strengthen them against the PLO.[136] According to Susan Hattis Rolef, retired Brigadier General Binyamin Ben-Eliezer, coordinator of operations in the occupied territories from 1983 to 1984, implied in interviews that Israel had a policy of encouraging Muslim forces to weaken the PLO.[137] The Israeli Foreign Ministry admitted in an interview that the welfare programs of the Islamic groups were among the justifications for Israel's support of Hamas in its early days.[138]

"Outadministering" the Opposition

Whether Islamist, nationalist, or local and not affiliated with any other group, Palestinian groups were compensating for the lack of political institutions by offering services and opportunities not provided by military authorities. Some groups stood in tacit opposition to occupation, while others, in a different context, would be called self-help.

Although Fateh was by 1982 giving attention to mass mobilization, many of those running for office as "Fateh" in various unions and organizations were not Fateh in a cellular sense, that is, the individuals did not belong to cells, as Sari Nusseibeh explained: "They were *generally* Fateh."[139] Whole student movements developed that were loosely associated with Fateh, but had no connection with the PLO. At Bir Zeit College, the Fateh student movement developed "primarily by itself, independently; although there were students who were operatives in Fateh, on the whole, the student movement was not."[140] Hillel Frisch explains, "[N]one of these movements contained an overarching secretariat or central committee that was responsible for all the organs within the movements," possibly with the exception of the communists.[141] While the underground military branches were tied to one faction of the PLO or another, each member carrying out commanders' orders, the diverse nonmilitary popular groups run by women, students, prisoners, and youth were offering services otherwise unavailable. From the latter grouping came the infrastructure, leadership, and corporate capacity at the local level for the intifada.[142]

In Gaza, the young who sparked the uprising were not even allied with the factions of the PLO and had grown up under the Israeli policy of what Sara Roy calls the "de-development" of Gaza.[143] Frisch reports, "The Israeli authorities were surprised to find that most of those incarcerated in the first months of the *intifada* in Gaza had no prior arrest record and no organizational past."[144] A classified survey, carried out after Israelis arrested the initial demonstrators in the Gaza Strip, showed that the vast majority of Palestinian participants in the protests considered themselves to be devout Muslims, this was their first arrest, and their first physical contact with Israeli soldiers. Most of those sampled did not listen to PLO radio broadcasts, nor were they familiar with PLO political platforms or slogans.[145]

After 1967, the traditional local elite was "overcome by political torpor," as political scientist Emile Sahliyeh puts it.[146] As diverse clubs and agencies arose, the old oligarchies were pushed to the side. Alternative institutions rising in their stead opened avenues for a Palestinian leadership that was not groomed in how to cooperate with the Israeli military regime. With the increasing significance of nonmilitary political organizations operating without clandestinity and the democratization brought about by widened access to higher education, the influence of the *mukhtars* and their urban counterparts withered as the networks of civil society organizations expanded after 1967, and receded still further in 1981-82, with the student movements' rebellion against the euphemistically named Israeli civilian administration. Not only was the legitimacy of the occupation questioned, but also the "legitimacy of an established hierarchy based on lineage."[147] The potency of youth in a stratified society increased as authority fragmented, accelerating the ascendance of students, women, youth, and those who had been arrested during the 1970s, to be released five to seven years later.[148] Clearly the leadership was local and unleashed by the mobilization after 1967.[149] To become a "leader," one had to serve the community and not flaunt privilege. Standing derived from service, rather than from inherited status or the privilege of class or clan.

Better educated than their parents, born under military occupation and in increasing numbers, and knowing no other existence, the young derived tangible experience through the webs of committees in providing vital community services. They gained hands-on experience in infant nurseries, reforestation, harvesting, retrofitting home plumbing, teaching literacy, road renovation, fixing cemeteries, cleanup of refugee camps, and bringing isolated villages into the electricity grid of the East Jerusalem Electric Company, still the most sizeable Palestinian endeavor in the territories. Once the intifada erupted, the impact on leadership was evident. A Gazan leader of the uprising told a Tel Aviv reporter two weeks after its outbreak,

> Of the 650,000 inhabitants of Gaza, the occupation forces have, as of now, arrested 47,000. Every one of them is already a leader in the place where he lives. The arrest creates the leader. . . . No fool should think that outside forces are directing what is happening. People belong to all kinds of organizations, which are really the political parties of the state-in-the-making.[150]

Israeli authorities had been able to keep themselves apprised of political activity in the universities and could study the groups that they viewed as fronts for subversion through Palestinian informers in schools and universities.[151] Yet much of the activities of the emerging civil society after 1967—voluntary work committees, women's organizations, youth clubs, trade unions, cultural societies, and professional associations—remained uninterrupted and possibly undetected by the Israeli authorities.[152]

Bir Zeit University political scientist Ali Jarbawi believes that the unions, clubs, and committees after 1967 disqualify themselves from civil society, because of their frequent association with the political factions of the PLO.[153] Yet even if the civilian organizing was often factionalized—an undeniable feature of Palestinian life under occupation—membership was voluntary. Recruits were neither conscripted nor gang pressed, although social pressures toward conformance within extended families or clans were strong. As Nusseibeh observed, individuals were *generally* loyal to factions.

Girls, boys, men, women, university students, labor unionists, and prisoners were involved in collective action—a wedging open of nongovernmental political space and development of institutions not under official purview—which represented germination of an evolving Palestinian civil society. Armed revolution held little attraction for Palestinians under occupation, not so much because of moral revulsion against violence, but because they would suffer the retaliatory consequences of cross-border sorties by the fedayeen. The ganglia of nonmilitary committees and movements increased logarithmically, both despite, and because of military occupation. Previously inactive communities and sectors galvanized themselves; most would not under any circumstances have been candidates for military cadres. As authority fragmented, ten thousand unemployed university graduates being among those who were available to participate, large numbers assumed responsibility for opposing the military occupation. In the course of participating in scores of nonmilitary clubs, some since the age of twelve, members became familiar with chairing meetings, electing officers, setting priorities, making decisions as a group, and nonviolent methods of struggle. Democratic procedures were learned by thousands of Palestinians in Israeli prisons. Committees learned how to structure themselves so that they could continue functioning when elected leaders were arrested. "Outadministering" the occupation, whether surreptitiously or openly, the committees not only precluded some aspects of Israeli control, but networks questioned monopolistic assumptions of armed struggle. Knowledge and strategies of nonviolent action began to seep into the interstices of doubts about the practicality of armed struggle.

The term *civilian mobilization* encompasses popular, nonmilitary organizing in which the centers of power became dispersed, and emphasizes the rising use of strategies other than paramilitary strikes and emergence of a leadership whose symbols differed from those of armed struggle. Civilian organizing to deter foreign military invasion or occupation is also one of the applications of the field of nonviolent resistance. Palestinians were learning its basics within view of an omnipresent military force. For the better part of two decades, the capacity for a massive and deliberate confrontation with military occupation was under construction. Without this period of popular activation, the sustenance of a movement on the scale of the intifada would have been impossible. The simultaneity and girth of the uprising stunned the world, yet inside the occupied territories the only surprise was that such upheaval did not occur sooner.

Chapter 7
"We Chose to Accept Occupation"

BY THE EARLY 1980S, handouts were appearing mysteriously in the streets of East Jerusalem, the West Bank, and Gaza. Fliers and pamphlets described how peoples elsewhere had empowered themselves and fought oppression without arms. Translations of scholarly writing and materials circulated from other social movements. Outside influences were mixing with local ideas on challenging the military occupation in the occupied territories.

Although not secret, neither were these booklets meant for publication. They resembled Thomas Paine's *Common Sense* and *Rights of Man*—pamphlets of eighteenth-century colonial New England. Brochures left lying on seats of buses used by Palestinians were bundled, as if to signal the dispersal of them. Mimeographed summaries on cheap paper, they were intended for brisk, pell-mell popular consumption. They proposed a theory of power and described nonmilitary methods that could be used by any Palestinian in the occupied territories. The distributed materials gave examples from other geographic areas of how to escape from the implicit pact to use violence against violence. Without offering political solutions, these pamphlets suggested that action was better than inaction, nonviolent resistance was less self-destructive than armed struggle and within the limited capacity of the disarmed Palestinians, and fighting with political weapons could be more effective then violence in redressing fundamental injustices.

Who was distributing the fliers? Despite the persisting claim of the PLO in exile in Tunis that it was guiding all social and political change inside the occupied territories, Mubarak Awad and two individuals associated with his work—Jonathan Kuttab and Gene Sharp—were among the *accoucheurs* for the Palestinians' catalytic alterations in thinking on nonviolent struggle, starting in 1983 and persisting until the uprising began in 1987 and the years beyond. These individuals had nothing to do with the PLO and its various factions, yet merely disproving the PLO's avowed "authorship" of the intifada would shed little light on the human agency and transmission of ideas that helped to shape the first intifada.

"People Are People, and There Is No Reason to Fear Them"

Mubarak Awad and Jonathan Kuttab

Born to a Greek Orthodox Palestinian family in 1943, Mubarak Awad spent his first five years peacably in the once-grand Musrara neighborhood of Jerusalem. His life changed at the sound of a rifle crack in 1948, when his father was gunned down by sniper fire. The child, his mother, and his six siblings, the eldest of whom was ten years old, were forced from their home in what became "no-man's-land," during the period following the war of 1948 until 1967. Awad's mother, Huda Kuttab Awad, a nurse, unable both to work to support her children and care for them at home, was forced to place them in orphanages and foster homes. Although scattered under many roofs, she still guided the closely knit family. The children never found out whether their father had been shot by an Israeli or an Arab sniper; his bones remain to this day where he fell. Mubarak Awad's conviction that one must fight injustice without bloodshed probably originates with his mother, who taught her children that killing was wrong and what had happened to them should never be the cause of another's death: "She told us never to seek revenge, but to work so that other mothers don't suffer."[1]

He and his brother Bishara went to an orphanage in the Old City of Jerusalem founded by Katy Antonius, widow of the historian George Antonius, author of *The Arab Awakening*. Called Dar al-Awlad (House of Boys), the orphanage was part of a growing network of Palestinian social services meant to help children whose parents had been killed or uprooted in the 1948 war. As a young boy, Awad organized a food strike to secure the addition of eggs to the diet of the schoolboys. Katy Antonius would be a powerful influence in his life, instilling in him the idea that "people are people, and there is no reason to fear them or their rank." In adulthood, he recalled hearing the *doyenne* in her parlor curse Jordanian monarch King Hussein for his approach to the Palestinians. Hers was considered the "most popular salon in Arab Jerusalem" during the British Mandate period, and when the boys visited the Antonius home, she taught them Arab history and culture.[2] If they failed to participate in the colloquies taking place, often among distinguished guests,

Mrs. Antonius would upbraid them afterward, telling them that their opinion was as valid as that of the other visitors. She arranged for Mubarak and Bishara to attend elite St. George's preparatory school in East Jerusalem. She also persuaded a young nuclear scientist, George P. Sakalosky, from the United States, to pay the boys' tuition fees at the school for ten years, until they were graduated.[3] At St. George's, Mubarak Awad developed friendships with boys from Jerusalem's venerable aristocratic families, such as the Husseinis and Nusseibehs, forming bonds that help to account for the ease with which he would share ideas and actions with them two decades later. His first arrest came at the age of twelve, for protesting against Jordanian rule. He was jailed by the Jordanian authorities on another occasion merely for asking questions about the budget of the Greek Orthodox Church.[4] He refused to carry a gun during the school's military training and was ridiculed for his decision. His friendship with the Paris-based studio artist Kamal Boullata dates to his preteen period when, as classmates at St. George's, their conversations on how to struggle without violence began. Subsequently, in a Hashemite prison cell, by then in his teens, Awad began to study the nonviolent movements of other peoples.

In 1960, he moved to the United States, where two colleges accepted him as a student. Knowing nothing of either, he turned down Yale University and chose the one that offered room and board as well as tuition—Lee College, a small Christian institution in Tennessee. With the civil rights movement in full gear, he began reading the writings of Martin Luther King, Jr. He was shocked by the standards of the students at the Tennessee campus in two particular ways: he could not understand how people who considered themselves to be Christian could defend racial segregation, and he was confused by the relaxed American attitudes toward sex. He decided to return home after only two years. Back in East Jerusalem, he taught English, mathematics, and religion at a Mennonite orphanage school for boys in the village of Beit Jala, a few miles south of Jerusalem and adjacent to Bethlehem, until 1969, when he was arrested by Israeli authorities for preparing leaflets that proposed resisting the military occupation, then in place for two years. Jailed for two months in an Israeli prison where, according to Awad, he was beaten, he bargained his way out of a ten-year prison sentence by agreeing to leave the place of his birth—his first exile. He had become interested in the study of militant nonviolence and returned to the United States in 1970 for the bachelor's degree at Bluffton College, a Mennonite institution in Bluffton, Ohio.

Upon his return to the United States, he found the country divided over the war in Vietnam, and watched the growing student resistance campaigns to end military conscription. At Bluffton, he came under the influence of professor Elmer Neufeld, later the college's president. Neufeld challenged him with a strongly stated conviction that God exists in every human being, and therefore one does not have the right to kill the Divine in another person. Awad internalized this principle, and years later would echo the professor when he wrote pamphlets on nonviolent resistance. While in Ohio, Awad intently studied the writings of Mohandas K. Gandhi and Martin Luther King, Jr.; in particular he parsed King's 1963 letter from the Birmingham, Alabama, city jail. He also began working with juvenile delinquents in state facilities, viewing counseling as implementation of his growing body of beliefs. Awad was awarded the master's degree in social work from St. Francis University in Indiana, in 1977. A Ph.D. in clinical psychology followed, from the now defunct International Graduate School in St. Louis, Missouri.

In 1978, the newly trained psychologist and social worker established the Ohio Youth Advocate Program (YAP), a treatment program for children with severe behavioral problems. Soon after, Awad pursued U.S. citizenship so that he could obtain an American passport. Having been initially denied citizenship because of his refusal to pledge allegiance to the flag, he appealed to an Ohio court, outlining his need for citizenship. Without the formality of his reciting the oath, the judge granted citizenship to him in 1983, when he explained that his allegiance was to Palestine. That year, at the age of forty, Awad took a leave of absence from YAP, and in March returned to Jerusalem to train psychologists and social workers who were counseling Palestinians.

As a result of his success as a clinician with American youth who had histories of extreme violence and deviancy—among them killers and arsonists—Awad determined to apply his knowledge to the chronic provocations faced by Palestinian youth. If American children needed support and therapy, Palestinian youths needed it possibly more than anyone else. "Under occupation, there is so much frustration, so much anger, so much enmity, that the children don't know how to handle it," he contended; "when they try to do something about it, they are likely to handle it with violence."[5] His fundamental theory was that individuals have the power within themselves to alter their situation, yet they must have willpower, courage, and the willingness to sacrifice.[6] Awad was troubled by what he considered pathological Palestinian hatred "so deep that the Palestinians are not functioning normally" as individuals or in groups, and viewed outside circumstances (the PLO and the Arab world) as exacerbating this condition, while Israel proceeds to "take everything from us without any resistance."[7] "With preparation and a systematic approach, we could achieve more than has been achieved by violence," he told a journalist: "We have reached such a point of despair, feeling that our identity is going without admitting it to ourselves. That is the moment for a nonviolent struggle."[8]

"Get Your Rights without a Single Bullet": Workshops

In East Jerusalem in the spring of 1983, Mubarak Awad set up the Palestinian Counseling Center. Questionnaires filled out by participants in a school counseling workshop in May had showed that the respondents ranked political problems as the area in which they most needed help, followed by problems of anxiety, alcoholism, divorce, alterations in moral values and traditions, the mental state of released prisoners, and gambling.[9] Awad also conducted a series of workshops on counseling skills for professional educators at the Young Men's Christian Association (YMCA) in East Jerusalem, attended by perhaps fifty teachers and social workers. He began to write, and he and his cousin, Jonathan Kuttab, coauthored a series of papers arguing the necessity for nonviolent resistance by Palestinians. Contending that nonviolent direct action would be more compatible with actual Palestinian capacity than armed struggle, their circulars argued that simply by choosing *not* to use weapons, the humiliation of occupation could be lifted. "Slowly," Kuttab recalled, "we developed the idea that we must work on a systematic and a conscious application of a nonviolence strategy. I say systematic and conscious because we concluded that there was a very strong inclination toward nonviolent struggle—a strong practice and history of nonviolent struggle in Palestine—none of it conscious, none of it articulated, and certainly none of it systematic. To the contrary, side by side with the widespread practice of nonviolence was a rhetoric of violence."[10]

Jonathan Kuttab had received the bachelor of arts degree from Messiah College in Pennsylvania, been graduated from the University of Virginia School of Law, and then left a Wall Street firm to return to Jerusalem in the late 1970s. In Ramallah, he completed his legal training with the lawyer Aziz Shehadeh. One of the first West Bank Palestinian lawyers to learn Hebrew and pass the Israeli bar examination, Jonathan Kuttab also become a member of the Jordanian bar. In 1979, he had joined with Raja Shehadeh to found al-Haq as the first Palestinian human rights organization.

Awad and Kuttab responded positively when Palestinian educators asked for additional training workshops in the autumn of 1983. Awad held a second course and ran child-care training programs in Bethlehem, where he tried to persuade administrators of the need for more counseling services. He also undertook a series of three workshops in the Arab East Jerusalem area from October 13 through 15, 1983, which were designed to tackle directly the political problems identified by Palestinians in the spring counseling workshops. Open to anyone, the first took place at the Young Women's Christian Association (YWCA), preceded by public announcements of its topic: How to Get Your Rights without a Single Bullet.[11] The session was contentious, a newspaper reported: "Awad's ideas were repeatedly challenged from the floor. One typical response was 'violence begets violence and, from a Palestinian point of view, Zionism is violence.'" Others argued that, while his ideas were intriguing, Palestinians "could not afford different forms of struggle and still had to acknowledge the predominance of armed confrontation."[12]

Awad's goal was reported as being to bring about a movement of nonviolent resistance among Palestinians. One journalist noted that the "predominant examples that he and others cited of non-violent struggle were those of Mahatma Gandhi and Martin Luther King."[13] According to Israeli journalist David Richardson, Awad was abruptly rejected as "another one of those American Palestinians with their imported ideas" or as a "CIA or an Israeli agent."[14] Awad insisted on the need for openness and told Richardson, "No one, like the Israelis or the organization [the PLO], can tell me that my approach is not allowed."[15] Although the PLO had long called for a medley "all means of struggle," and its main party Fateh had often lumped guerrilla operations with political activities, such a jumble absolutely did not mean an open invitation to voluntary citizen action. From beginning to end, controversy was associated with Awad's endeavors, not only because of his ideas, but also because of his independence.

When participants arrived for the second session of the workshop on the following day, the director of the YWCA announced that the Israeli authorities had denied permission for the meeting to take place. Awad escorted those who had shown up into buses and taxis. They shortly arrived at the front gates of the Friends' Girls School in Ramallah, to the surprise of the headmistress, an American educator and Quaker named Nancy Nye. Perhaps thirty individuals survived the shift in venue for rousing debates. On the third day, fewer attended because rumors had spread of probable arrests and reprisals.[16]

Palestinian activists and intellectuals and a sprinkling of Israelis active in political circles had attended, among them a young Palestinian, Nafez Assaily, and a youthful Israeli, Amos Gvirtz. Despite intimidation and the attempts to derail the workshops, news accounts reported "several hundred"— "far more" than expected by Awad, had heard him explain the theories and practices of nonviolent resistance.[17] In his coverage of the workshops, Richardson termed Awad's plan "a schedule for civil disobedience" and singled out for mention the methods of noncooperation that would "aim at the morale, psychology and mentality of the oppressors."[18] The October 1983 sessions were the first chance for distribution of the materials Awad and Kuttab had been writing. They handed out a six-page workshop program, which defined problems facing Palestinians and laid out a series of techniques for solving them. Reading it, one is struck by its stance—"we can be free from the Israeli military," however, "we chose to accept *occupation*."[19] Conceding that nonviolent action might seem unfamiliar, even "vague and mysterious," the program regrets the lack of articles in Arabic on the subject. Its definition of the term *nonviolence* is "social change—a method for social liberation from the Israelis." The goal of nonviolent struggle is described as "social justice and self-determination."[20] "Anyone seeking justice through law and action who wants to liberate himself/herself from the Israeli military rule" is welcome to join this citizen action, the program states.[21] Four methods are listed for accomplishing these goals: openness, personal risk, truthfulness, and self-suffering.[22] The techniques mentioned include negotiation, direct action, agitation, consumer boycotts, picketing, strikes, sit-ins, noncooperation, nonpayment of taxes, civil disobedience, and development of a parallel government. The program notes the following points for discussion:

1. Nonviolent struggle is not a method for cowards.
2. It does not seek to defeat or humiliate the opponent.
3. Attack is directed against forms of evil, not the person who commits the evil.
4. Nonviolent resistance requires a willingness to accept suffering without striking back.

5. Nonviolent struggle avoids not only external physical violence, but also internal violence directed at the spirit.

6. Nonviolent resistance is based on the conviction that the universe is on the side of justice.[23]

Neither scholarly credit nor attribution is given, yet these six points are recognizable from the writings of Mohandas K. Gandhi and Martin Luther King, Jr., and often verbatim:

(Point 1) Gandhi: "Cowardice is worse than violence."[24] King: "This is *not* a method for cowards; it does resist."[25] "The first thing that can be said about this method is that it is not a method of submission or surrender. . . . [I]t is a method that is very active in seeking to change conditions."[26]

(Point 2) Gandhi: "The end of non-violent 'war' is always an agreement, never dictation, much less humiliation of the opponent."[27] King: "The nonviolent resister seeks to lift or rather to change the opponent, . . . not seek to defeat him or to humiliate him."[28]

(Point 3) Gandhi: "My enmity is not against them, it is against their [British] rule."[29] "Man and his deed are two distinct things."[30] King: "You work to defeat evil systems, but not the individuals who are caught up in [them]."[31]

(Point 4) Gandhi: "What then is the meaning of non-co-operation in terms of the Law of Suffering? We must voluntarily put up with the losses and inconveniences that arise from having to withdraw our support from a government that is ruling against our will. . . . We may make mistakes; there may be avoidable suffering. These things are preferable to national emasculation."[32] King: "There are some laws unjust and the only way to call this to the attention of the community is to break them and suffer the penalty."[33]

(Point 5) King on Gandhi: "[Gandhi] would resist evil as much as the man who uses violence, but he resists it without external violence or violence of the spirit."[34] King: "Nonviolent resistance . . . avoids not only external physical violence but also internal violence of spirit."[35]

(Point 6) King: "The method of nonviolence is based on the conviction that the universe is on the side of justice."[36] "The arc of a moral universe is long, but it bends toward justice."[37]

The program for the October 1983 workshops recommends that if well planned, and with large numbers, nonviolent struggle could be viable for the Palestinians. It acknowledges that nonviolent resistance can fail. It suggests a rotating system of leadership, so that any persons arrested are replaced, and it suggests that taking action will have its own rewards: "With nonviolent action, Palestinians and (not the politician) but *every* Palestinian can participate. . . . By doing this we can overcome the feeling of impotence."[38]

At these autumn workshops, Mubarak Awab and Jonathan Kuttab also distributed a booklet in Arabic about wielding power to accomplish political goals.[39] By mutual agreement, the cousins decided that Kuttab's name would not be listed as coauthor, to avoid compromising his ability to practice law before the Israeli bar.[40] A draft of the booklet was given to former president Jimmy Carter on September 7, 1983, at a New York meeting of Habitat for Humanity, a private U.S. voluntary housing agency.[41] Shortly thereafter, Awad went to Atlanta, Georgia, to meet with Carter and ask his advice. Carter marked up the text of the booklet, emphasizing the need for an exclusively nonviolent approach.[42] Awad was fearful that word of the meeting in Atlanta might reach East Jerusalem, where, if known, his ideas could be rendered foreign; he nonetheless took the criticism seriously and made revisions:[43]

> The enemy in this battle is very serious and ferocious. There is no assurance and we cannot expect that he will himself be nonviolent. On the contrary, there are great sacrifices that are expected in the nonviolent struggle. . . . Nonviolent struggle is a real war and is not an easy alternative. Nonviolent struggle is not a negative or passive method. It is an active affirmative operation, . . . a form of mobile warfare. . . . It requires special training and a high degree of organization and discipline.[44]

According to the booklet, the institutions of a society strengthen the capacity for resistance. Efforts must be directed toward civilian structures, which are central and whose control must remain in the hands of the people— or resistance may be more difficult. To maintain such institutions (not including those overseen by the occupying regime) may mean defying orders or operating underground committees. Most activities contemplated would be illegal under the occupation. The booklet warns, "To bravely . . . accept persecution for one's belief brings one very close to the power of nonviolence. It neutralizes the effectiveness of the instruments of repression. . . . The most powerful weapon in the hands of the authorities is fear. A Palestinian who can liberate himself from fear and who will boldly accept suffering and persecution without fear or bitterness or striking back has managed to achieve the greatest victory of all."[45] Pressure and suffering must be accepted voluntarily in defense of principle, instead of letting suffering be imposed involuntarily. The booklet calls for extensive planning for civilian defense and applying an understanding of the intricacies of power. It also reveals a search for methods that might resonate with the target group, Israelis, and potentially split their official positions. It contends that the Israeli government is sensitive to public opinion, both local and international, and "Israel does not possess the internal resources which will enable it to bear international isolation for a long time."[46]

The materials distributed by Awad for four years prior to the outbreak of the first intifada had grown out of years of study and discussions. Helping clinicians and counselors to enhance their skills made Awad realize that counseling alone could not be sufficient to address the problems facing Palestinians—the workshops persuaded him that social problems could not be addressed until larger political concerns had been confronted. As Nancy Nye recalled, psychology and political activism blended in Awad's thinking, and drew upon the teachings of psychotherapist Carl Rogers that the solutions to one's problems come from within; "so it was natural that he would also say that each individual should assume responsibility for trying to end the occupation." Carl Rogers's approach to management of conflict emphasizes allowing both positive and negative attitudes to be aired, with a focus on attitudes rather than the content of the issues. Again and again, Awad would say, "The occupation of one's nation does not mean that one's spirit is also occupied."[47]

Gene Sharp's Writings and a Pragmatic Stance

Appended to the Arabic translation of Awad and Kuttab's 1983 booklet was a list of 121 methods of nonviolent protest, reduced from the 198 methods examined in Gene Sharp's three-volume *The Politics of Nonviolent Action*.[48] At workshops and lectures, Awad also routinely passed out an Arabic translation of a work by Sharp, written with no particular conflict in mind.[49] In it, Sharp argues that accepted precepts of power and defense demand reconsideration and that old formulations about systems of allies and military defense are proving fallible, even disastrous. Methods of civilian defense should rely on self-reliance and preparedness, breaking with the outmoded belief that defense is synonymous with military strength. Rather, defense requires a redefinition of the concept of power. The central thesis in the theory of civilian defense is that an entity occupying through military force has no true power without the consent and obedience of those who are occupied (even if such cooperation is obtained by force, punishments, or threats). Civilian-based defense—part of the subject of nonviolent resistance—requires no ideological basis for success, Sharp argues; it requires a desire on the part of the occupied to defend their society and way of life in a manner that offers limited destruction and harm. The translated text maintains that defense based on planned nonviolent direct action and noncooperation by the citizenry—along with a social infrastructure—offers an effective alternative to military response against foreign invasion and internal confrontations. The objective is to create a society that is ungovernable for the oppressor or attacker, thereby deterring aggressive behavior. Such an undertaking requires a definitive plan, Sharp writes, including strict adherence to a set of priorities focusing on the ability of the people to continue living under their accepted precepts—instead of militarily oriented goals of land acquisition or the causing of injury or death to the occupier's army. Extensive training and planning is essential, and must be accompanied by de facto support by the people's representatives. It concludes by urging the need to weigh costs and benefits.

Awad's booklet and Sharp's translated work circulated widely and informally throughout the Palestinian areas in the early and mid-1980s. During 1983-84, between 4,000 and 7,000 copies of the Arabic translation of Sharp were distributed.[50] Palestinians in the territories recall furtively reading the two documents, which seemed to be everywhere on the West Bank, including on Israeli-owned buses. Dog-eared copies were passed from family to family. In contrast to a separate literature of Palestinian-authored essays and articles that were being published for a wider audience in Hebrew and English, or the clandestinely printed and circulated underground documents of the uprising that would later appear, Awad and Sharp's works were comparable to the manifestoes and charters of movements seeking relief from Soviet hegemony that appeared in Eastern Europe in the same period.

During the 1980s, in what would later be called the Czechs' and Slovaks' Velvet Revolution, citizens copied or memorized position papers and manifestoes that were plastered on walls, for transmission to other areas of the former Czechoslovakia.[51] Clandestine publishing houses and underground journals flourished. Such unofficial publications, known as *samizdat* (Russian for self-published) were the stock-in-trade of the Czechoslovakian resistance after the country fell under Soviet domination in 1948, and included letters, books, appeals, periodicals, journals, opinion essays, or summaries detailing government persecution.[52]

Awad and his colleagues disseminated their *samizdat* through whatever means possible. He did not care if he were harassed, arrested, or injured in the process, because he thought it would draw more attention to the ideas presented in the handouts. He spoke as a street organizer, Kuttab later described: "He could be very influential, very effective, and reach many, many people without making an impact on the official political scene—either among the Israelis or with the Palestinian intellectuals or political speakers. The issue for Awad was just to get the ideas circulating."[53]

He believed that mixing nonviolent resistance with occasional violence would contribute to further Palestinian defeat. He wanted to attract Palestinians away from armed struggle for practical reasons. He wasn't saying that violence was morally wrong, an Israeli journalist notes, but that it was "smarter to use other weapons."[54] He argued that pursuit of nonviolent struggle does not dictate the terms of political solutions, yet, as David Richardson reports, "his talk of different strategies and another political 'movement' . . . incurred the wrath of PLO supporters, particularly those on the radical left and the Moslem Brotherhood in the West Bank."[55]

Awad's political detachment pleased no one. As time passed, he was increasingly pressured by the Palestinians to declare a position and by the Israelis to explain why he did not repudiate cross-border sorties, guerrilla raids, and terror tactics. He refused to condemn armed struggle, because he did not want it interpreted as blanket condemnation of the PLO and did not wish to be perceived as its opponent.[56] Newspaper reports from 1983 to 1988 show him resisting any endorsement of particular political frameworks, but by 1986 the Israeli news media reported that Awad had endorsed the 1969 goal of a secular democratic state in all of Palestine.[57] Although this position represented Herculean compromise with the PLO's earlier stances, because of its acceptance of sharing land that the Palestinians had considered entirely theirs, it still could be interpreted as carrying an implicit suggestion that Israel would have to be dismantled, and thus could be viewed as extremist. Israeli journalist Edward Grossman writes that Awad was honest enough to admit that his immediate goal was to end the occupation of the West Bank, Gaza, and East Jerusalem, but his other "long-term thing" was to "crack the Zionist set-up" and have it replaced by one state for Jews and Arabs.[58] By 1987, news outlets reported Awad as favoring a "unified, secular" state in which "no Jew would have to leave," yet Palestinians would have passports: "Call it Israel-Palestine or Palestine-Israel, and slowly build it, whatever it is."[59]

Another thorny problem was that Awad's booklet and seminars allowed a return to guns if the nonviolent strategy failed, again out of an apparent desire not to renounce persons who were supporting violent struggle. Awad claims that he was attempting to be realistic, to show that he was not asking for a spiritual commitment, but was saying let us try something with the potential for making us strong, that will not weaken us or rebound in even harsher retaliation. In acknowledging the possibility of regression—even as his own confidence never dimmed that nonviolent struggle was the only feasible approach—he created a predicament for himself in Israeli eyes. For Palestinians living in the West Bank and Gaza, he wrote that the most effective way to fight is strategic nonviolence, but this does not "constitute a rejection of the concept of armed struggle," nor "negate the possibility that the struggle on the inside may turn into an armed struggle at a later stage.[60] Some Israelis interpreted this to mean that his advocacy of nonviolent struggle was merely a precursor to armed struggle, or even a ruse. Awad's wording was indeed ambiguous and not much different from Fateh's tincture of "all forms of struggle." Since he does not use the subjunctive mood in English, nor speak Hebrew, Israelis listening to him heard what one reporter called "hesitant English."[61] His point, according to U.S. columnist Nat Hentoff, was that "nonviolent struggle will, at this time, be a more effective strategy in dislodging the Israelis" from occupation.[62] Numerous accounts appearing in print from 1983 to 1988 encouraged the perception that Awad spoke in contradictory terms, an observation that dogged his efforts.[63]

Ideas from Other Movements

A Center Opens in East Jerusalem

On March 16 and 17, 1984, in Washington, D.C., a meeting was held to discuss the deteriorating situation of the Palestinians living under occupation.[64] It was convened by Palestinian-American historian Hisham B. Sharabi of Georgetown University.[65] In addition to Mubarak Awad, Jonathan Kuttab, and Kamal Boullata, also in attendance was Eqbal Ahmad, the Pakistani political scientist who had first broached the subject of nonviolent direct action with the PLO in Beirut in 1974; Jim Fine, an American Quaker and staff in Jerusalem for the American Friends Service Committee; Gene Sharp; Beth Heisey Kuttab, representing the United Methodist Women; and R. Scott Kennedy, head of the Santa Cruz Resource Center for Nonviolence, formerly mayor of Santa Cruz, California.[66]

At the end of the session, Sharabi declared that someone must proceed to the occupied territories to open a center on nonviolent action.[67] Jonathan Kuttab was concerned that such a center be established cautiously, with the purpose of study rather than of stimulating direct action, a discomfort shared by Sharabi.[68] The professor privately raised $30,000 through the Jerusalem Fund, a tax-exempt nonprofit charity in Washington, D.C., and by autumn delivered a check to Awad to set up the center.[69]

Mubarak Awad married Nancy Nye in St. George's Cathedral in East Jerusalem, on April 29, 1984.[70] In March of the following year, he and Nancy went to India for a study tour of six weeks, traveling to Ahmedabad, Mumbai (Bombay), and Vellore. They met with Indians who had participated in the Indian independence struggles and asked their help in applying lessons from their movements to the Palestinians' losses. Muslims who had worked with Gandhi told them "nonviolence started with Islam," and said that they believed that what Gandhi was doing was Islamic.[71] Intrigued by nonviolence as a value in Islam and unconcerned about whether his Christian background might hinder him, Awad's contact with Muslim participants in the Indian independence movements only strengthened his resolve, and the couple returned from India by ship at the port of Haifa in April 1985. His clinical, religious, and political background had predisposed him to accept the challenge of the Washington group to establish a program in the occupied territories. The three-room Palestinian Center for the Study of Nonviolence (PCSN) officially opened its doors later in the month in a seedy walk-up called the Nuzha Building on Abu Obedieh Street in Arab East Jerusalem.

The first year of the center's modest existence was spent writing and publishing; holding discussions in villages and refugee camps; translating Gandhi, King, and Gene Sharp; and distributing information to an often skeptical audience. An early translation into Arabic was a biography of Khan Abdul Ghaffar Khan (1890-1988), *A Man to Match His Mountains.*[72] Ghaffar Khan had led the Pashtuns—Pashto-speaking Muslim people in areas bound by the Hindu Kush mountains of what are now Afghanistan and Pakistan—in nonviolent struggle against the British between 1930 and 1947. Despite their reputation as fearless warriors and sharpshooters, the Pashtuns did not use rifles and guerrilla warfare in opposition to the British, but instead fought a disciplined nonviolent struggle. Although Ghaffar Khan had formulated his conceptions of nonviolent action independently from Gandhi,[73] by the late 1930s he would become part of Gandhi's inner circle of advisors. Also known as Badshah Khan, the "Frontier Gandhi," he came from a family of landowners near Peshawar. In 1929, Khan formed the Khudai Khidmatgars (Servants of God), the "Red Shirt" movement of what was then the Northwest Frontier Province of India, a nonviolent nationalist force to fight for the independence of India from the British, awaken the political consciousness of the Pashtuns and establish an independent state for them, all the while opposing the partition of India. By 1938, the Red Shirt movement numbered more than 100,000 mountaineers famed for their militarism, who, according to a contemporary account, "threw away their arms" to join the movement.[74] In one of the most remarkable nonviolent struggles of the twentieth century, the Red Shirts shut down Peshawar for four days in 1930 in opposition to colonial rule, yet their seventeen-year story is not taught in Pakistani schools, nor does it appear in history textbooks in post-partition Pakistan.[75] Khan's chronicle allowed the center to introduce to the Palestinians an account of an Islamic people considered by the British to be notoriously violent, "hard men, who bore arms almost from the moment their mothers first set them on the earth."[76] The center's materials extolled the way they unified themselves in nonviolent struggle.[77]

Despite the suspicions and cynicism of many Palestinians, social ostracism, and allegations that Awad was a CIA agent, one year after the center opened eleven volunteers comprised the staff.[78] Nafez Assaily, having attended the 1983 workshops, became the center's initial volunteer staff member. Biweekly seminars were held around a circular table in the center's library, which was stocked with hundreds of books on and by Gandhi, Ghaffar Khan, Martin Luther King, Jr., Jawaharlal Nehru, Rabindranath Tagore, and others.[79] Although Awad was troubled by how little Palestinians actually knew about nonviolent resistance and the scarcity of literature in Arabic about its history, he did not try to Islamize it or use gimmicks to sell it to Muslims. Nothing sensationalizing Islam appears in any records about Awad's activities, although material alludes to the compatibility of Islam with nonviolent struggle, and Nafez Assaily cites Khan as a "perfect example of how a devout Moslem found his religion to be a source of nonviolent philosophy."[80]

The three-room office may have been physically small, yet there was nothing diminutive about the scale and audacity of ideas emanating from it. In early 1985, a leaflet was aimed primarily at Palestinians who lived inside the "Green Line." This is the boundary between Israel and the West Bank of the Jordan River—the 1948 border of Israel as agreed to in the 1949 armistice—named for its green color on official maps, as it was less conclusive than final borders marked on UN maps in black or occasionally purple.[81] The flier proposed "apology visits" by Palestinians to their ancestral homes.[82] Entitled "For Every Palestinian Who Lives in the Center of Palestine, for Those Who Have Lost a House or Field in Which Strangers Live Today," it said "let's talk in nostalgic terms about the appropriated houses of our parents." The leaflet called for Palestinians to make an "apology visit to the houses which still mourn their owners." It suggested setting aside one day annually for visiting their familial abodes. Awad told the Israeli newspaper *Hadashot* that the purpose of the appeal was to contradict the absolute Israeli claims that were derived from an exclusive Jewish past: "We have a much nearer past which continues to live in our hearts forever."[83] Palestinian children were counseled to knock on the doors of their ancestors' homes, potted rosebushes in arms, and politely explain to the current Israeli inhabitants that their grandparents, or great-grandparents, had built the house and they would like to plant a rosebush in the garden in their memory. Awad warned that the visits should not "cause hatred to those who are living in our houses, but sorrow for the lost humanity. We don't want them to be our enemies. We want to explain to them that these are our houses."[84]

In the autumn of 1985, a full two years before the eruption of the first intifada, the center distributed 1,500 leaflets in the West Bank and Gaza, calling for a campaign of economic independence, the centerpiece of which was the purchasing of "local" as opposed to Israeli goods. Leaflets and posters appearing in November called for the first Monday of each month to be Local Products Day, with coordinated action to begin on December 2, 1985.[85] The buy-Palestinian tactic had negligible impact on Israeli sales. Its purpose was to promote self-reliance and show families that they did not have to comply with the occupation.[86]

Among the major obstacles Awad encountered was a perception among Palestinians that nonviolent sanctions imply passivity or weakness. Some misconstrued his strategies as a call for submission, or appeasement. Reports said he was having trouble showing that nonviolent struggle is not for the weak—effective though it may be for those who lack conventional power.[87] Gandhi's theories had similarly been disputed by the Muslim community in India, where some interpreted them as cowardice or unmanliness.[88] Emphasizing the fact that spirituality is not necessary for nonviolent resistance, Awad repeatedly had to clarify that nonviolent action methods do not require religious beliefs. The simple desire to protect one's life and society is enough, he explained. The conservatism of rural Palestinian farmers inhibited their absorption of anything that seemed different, or radical, and some had forgotten the 174-day general strike of 1936, effaced as it was by the rebel violence and anarchy of the second phase of the great revolt. Villagers would say to the center's staff, "nonviolence is all right, but we need action."[89] Awad also encountered an aversion to ideas associated in the public mind with Gandhi, and some Palestinians thought Gandhi was opposed to the political aspirations of the Muslims in the subcontinent, because he had not readily accepted the British proposals of partition of India into Muslim and Hindu states. Mention of the U.S. civil rights tumult had its drawbacks, too. Palestinians who were knowledgeable about the writings of Martin Luther King, Jr., were dismayed by his silence on the rights and security of Palestinians, despite his frequent expressions of concern for Israeli rights.[90]

Among Awad's problems was the search for an Arabic term for nonviolent action that did not denote subservience or acquiescence. His Arabic-language skills had been diluted by years of living in the United States, and his English was not smooth. He tried using *sabr,* the name of the prickly pear that yields delicious fruit despite arid conditions, because of its implied reward—the fruits of patience as taught by the desert. This did not work. A Jew born in Israel is known as a *sabra* in colloquial Hebrew, with the same derivation. In Islamic texts, *sabr* has multiple shades of meaning, including postponement until one can strike again. The only term that stuck was *la-unf,* meaning "no violence."

His readiness to rely on the news media—often crucial to nonviolent mobilizations in building internal morale or arousing international sympathies—also caused problems and incurred criticism, especially from those who did not view communications as a tool of their struggle and criticized him as self-serving and hogging the media. He believed it crucial to avoid stealth. Intrinsic to nonviolent action is a strategic assessment that secrecy is counterproductive, whereas repetition and clarity of communication about the grievance or injustice is essential to conveying that a situation is intolerable and achievement of one's goals. "Publicity is important for me," Awad told a reporter; "we can influence Jews here who have been in much worse places than us. Not 'look what you are doing to us,' but 'look what you are doing to yourselves.'"[91] The center's occasional eight-page newsletter carried articles on leading Israelis who advocated coexistence, such as peace advocate Joseph Abileah and moral philosopher Yeshayahu Leibowitz.[92] An Israeli peace activist and advocate for nonviolent resistance, Amos Gvirtz, wrote several position papers for the center's use.

Coming from a family that believed that in remaining independent one could work with everyone, Awad never joined a Palestinian faction. According to his account, he was summoned to Cairo for two separate appointments with the PLO's second in command Khalil al-Wazir (Abu Jihad), in 1985. The meetings never took place, however; when he went to the designated place at the specified hour, no one was there, and he refused to wait. After agreeing to a third request, he was met at the plane in Cairo by Abu Jihad, who told him, "I believe in what you are doing." As Awad recalled, he countered by asking why, in that case, persons had been sent to vandalize the office. When Abu Jihad asked if they could work together, Awad responded that this would not be feasible, because Abu Jihad believed in guns.[93]

Although handicapped by organizational estrangement within the established Palestinian structures and nakedly lacking the sponsorship of the PLO, one significant asset Awad possessed was the protection extended to him by Feisel Husseini, scion of a patrician East Jerusalem family, and relative of Haj Amin al-Husseini, as noted in Chapter 3.[94] Husseini and his associates, such as the Palestinian newspaper editor Hanna Siniora, and others who sent representatives, attended Awad's East Jerusalem workshops. In order for his ideas to hold fast, Awad needed resonance within Fateh and other factions.

Unless key figures appreciated his concepts and encouraged others to listen—and defended him in Tunis against PLO attacks—his impact would be marginalized.[95] A symbiotic relationship developed: Awad generated plans and projects, while Husseini grafted them onto his own personal advocacy of nonviolent struggle, broadcast them through the Arab Studies Society he had founded, and generally sought to help Awad and neutralize any opposition from within PLO circles. Later Husseini would say that what he admired most was the range of Awad's ideas.[96] Most of the volunteers at the center were simultaneously working with Husseini, and relationships with Husseini were always excellent, according to Awad.[97]

Recovering Land through Nonviolent Direct Action

By 1985 Awad had begun a program of village outreach along the lines of Gandhi's "constructive program." Social and political problems of a protracted nature require a long-term response, thus the question for Gandhi was how to accomplish major institutional changes in the existing societal order without relying on the usual nostrums of seclusion, charity, generosity of others, or individual good works—none of which could affect national needs. Entitlements and actions would be distrusted, if proposed by an unjust state apparatus, and thus would not produce lasting institutional change. Nor did Gandhi want to emphasize strategies that had the effect of centralizing power, because his ideal was direct democracy, which he believed had its best guarantor in decentralization. His alternative involved creating a set of decentralized institutions to serve as the infrastructure of a preferred society, to supplant the old. New, entirely self-controlled institutions were to be constructed "brick by brick by corporate self-effort."[98] Gandhi's constructive program involved seventeen components, including hand-spun cloth of village production, cottage industries, adult education; advancement of women; and the development of labor unions committed to nonviolent action.[99] Were such a program accepted by a whole nation, Gandhi believed, it could lead to *poorna swaraj* (complete independence).[100] Formation of such "alternative institutions," or "parallel institutions," is an advanced method of nonviolent intervention.[101] Most significant for Awad, Gandhi's village-based work program was a concrete way to proceed toward a new social order in the midst of the old, meaning that even while the Palestinians were still living under a belligerent occupation, they could create self-reliance through the establishment of institutions that were beyond Israeli control. The alternative institutions would rival previous entities and ulti-mately replace them, and the Palestinians would take charge through nonco-operation and by creating new structures. The popular committees that would sustain the first intifada were alternative institutions. In Eqbal Ahmad's words, revolutionary movements

> must demonstrate, in practice, that there are alternative structures and arrangements which approximate the popular yearning for a just, com-munal, and participatory system. . . . [The] central objective is not simply to achieve the moral isolation of the enemy but also to confirm, perpetuate, and institutionalize it by providing an alternative to the discredited regime through the creation of "parallel hierarchies." The major task of the move-ment is not to outfight but to outadminister the government. The main target in this bid is the village.[102]

Awad's adaptation of Gandhi's constructive program included a library on wheels (a bookmobile is still operating on the West Bank and run by Assaily) and cleanup campaigns. Awad gathered about him several dozen volunteers who assisted in organizing visits to forty or fifty villages.[103] Some 60 percent of Palestinians were then living in villages on the West Bank, 30 percent in towns or cities, and the remaining 10 percent in refugee camps. Awad visited village after village, traveling by motorbike, spreading his ideas. Said Hafid Barghouti, "Mubarak was interested in working with the villagers to defend the land that the Israelis were going to confiscate, and helping villages to make work committees in their villages—to help the vil-lagers to have water."[104]

Early 1986 saw the start of a new direction for the center's work. An eld-erly man from the al-Asakreh tribe, in the hamlet of Tqu (Tekoa) near Beit Sahour and not far from Bethlehem, came asking for *la-unf* and demanding to see the technique that Awad had been describing in his rounds of the vil-lages. Rejecting pamphlets, books, and reprints, he said that he did not want to read or hear a lecture; he wanted to see nonviolence in action. Despite Awad's initial reservations about leading demonstrations—as advised by Hisham Sharabi and Jonathan Kuttab—he thought it prudent to prove the validity of the theories he had been advocating. The Tqu villager's request was for Awad and the center to help his family and fifteen thousand residents of his town take back several dunums of land seized by Israeli settlers. On January 10,

Israeli settlers from a settlement near Tqu had expanded their holdings by appropriating ten dunums of his family's land. Moving the settlement's iron gate, they had placed it in the center of the road that connected the village of Tqu with the nearby municipalities of Beit Sahour and Bethlehem, and had posted a sign on the gate indicating "use of road forbidden except for security vehicles." Bulldozers plowed through ten dunums (one and a quarter acres) outside the settlement fence, and the area was enclosed with wire.[105] The villager said that his sons wanted to kill a settler to avenge the land expropriation. He, however, did not want to kill anyone; he simply wanted his land back. Awad stipulated that nonviolent direct action meant sacrifices, no running away, and no guns. When the villager expressed readiness, Awad instructed the man to return to his village and gather between one hundred and three hundred individuals who would be willing to abide by the three guidelines. Three days later, the village leader brought news that he had amassed the willing villagers. Journalists were invited to watch.[106]

According to eyewitness accounts, the center's staff and Jonathan Kuttab, its lawyer, arrived on January 14 in Tqu, along with Israeli sympathizers and foreign guests. More than three hundred persons were waiting to take part in *la-unf*. Walking, Awad silently led the group toward the border fence and started to take it down. Israeli settlers began shooting into the air around the group, apparently to scare them. The villagers responded, "Go ahead! It will only show the world that you are killers!"[107] According to Haj Abd Abu-Diab, among the first volunteers to become involved in the center in 1985 and manager of the East Jerusalem Electric Company—the largest economic enterprise in the West Bank until the establishment of the Palestinian Authority—the Israeli settlers fired into the crowd, wounding seven youths.[108] None of the villagers fled; they kept working on the fence. Before long, settlers, border patrols, and the military governor arrived.[109] The governor suggested that the Palestinians take the case to court; the Tqu villagers said that the Israeli settlers should be the ones taken to court. Finally, the military governor agreed to the removal of the stakes and set a meeting in two days' time, to which the settlers could bring their maps and claims of a confiscation order dating to 1980. Two days later, the disputed metal gate was removed by the settlers, rendering the meeting with the military governor unnecessary. The villagers responded by planting olive tree seedlings and asked Kuttab to sue the settlers for the losses to their grain crop and damage to the land.[110]

Tangible results had accrued. In the public record, this was the first time that any West Bank village had recovered land that had been appropriated.[111] According to journalist Daoud Kuttab, brother of Jonathan, Israeli army officials looked into the land dispute and subsequently accepted the contention of the Palestinians.[112] Those Palestinians who participated in the action claimed that they had gained a sense that their own actions could produce results, even if the larger problem remained unresolved.[113] The Tqu episode changed the center's emphasis, and it began receiving requests from other villages asking how to fight nonviolently.[114]

Olive Trees at Qatanna

In 1986, the cautionary advice of Sharabi and Jonathan Kuttab to make analysis the priority of the center, rather than deeds, was abandoned. Awad soon was enmeshed in direct action that took the center into the land question at the heart of the Palestinian-Israeli struggle. On January 7 farmers from Qatanna, about nine miles northwest of Jerusalem near the Green Line, had visited the center. They claimed that in the preceding week laborers from the Green Patrol—the Nature Preservation Authority of the Israeli Ministry of Agriculture—had uprooted thousands of olive and almond trees on land that was owned and worked by eight families in Qatanna. Staff and volunteers from the center went to the village to photograph and document the uprootings. A team of reporters from *al-Fajr* newspaper, edited by Hanna Siniora, also visited the site on January 7, and found an Israeli crew of two bulldozers and six workers leveling a hillside and scooping up trees, in the process damaging topsoil and terraces. Two patrol cars of Israeli border police were pushing away angry villagers shouting, "This is our land. You can't destroy it like that."[115] An ITV filmmaker captured a wizened villager explaining that the robbed trees each yielded eight gallons of olive oil per year, perhaps two hundred dollars income per tree per annum.[116] Amina Mustafa, a sixty-year-old village woman, told a reporter that the trees dated to the Ottoman Empire. She described how, when the Israeli tractor came, she threw herself in front of it, a large dog was set upon her, and she was dragged away. "They took part of our land four years ago to make a road," she claimed; "now they've taken the rest . . . next time they will throw us from the house."[117]

An Israeli newspaper confirmed that the Nature Preservation Authority had uprooted the trees, but also cited Uri Baidats, director of Israel's Lands Administration, as saying that the trees had been planted there recently, illegally, and because the land belonged to the authority, he had asked for their removal.[118] Israeli officials asserted that the trees were inside the Green Line in what had become "no man's land" during the period of 1948-67, now claimed as "state land." The farmers produced tax records documenting their ownership of the property, which, the eight families told journalists, they had worked for as long as anyone could remember. The documents included a 1956 mortgage for olive-tree planting from the Jordanian government, verifying that the trees were between fifty and sixty years old. Kuttab checked the 1949 Armistice maps and found the property to be on the West Bank, rather than in "no-man's-land." He noted that the Israelis had classified the land under the jurisdiction of the Custodian of Absentee Property, meaning that Palestinians living meters from their own property were considered "absentees."[119]

The center's staff consulted the Israeli chapter of the International Fellowship of Reconciliation (IFOR), a pacifist organization formed in Britain at the time of World War I, whose branches now are a worldwide source of training for nonviolent resistance. IFOR agreed to contact its members. Coordinated by the center, on January 25—Tu Beshvat (the Jewish holiday of planting trees)—more than 150 Palestinians, Israelis, and foreign observers carrying borrowed hoes joined the villagers to replace the olive trees with five hundred seedlings. Volunteers distributed instructions banning the throwing of stones or any violence, no matter the provocation from soldiers.[120] While the Israelis and Palestinians worked—watched by armed Israeli settlers and military personnel—the settlers, who included U.S. citizens, pulled out the saplings as soon as they were planted and tossed them into the underbrush. A reporter noted that when the Palestinians and Israelis started planting the uprooted trees, the settlers began to break the saplings, until finally, "root balls smashed, leaving roots naked, leaves mixing with dirt," the planters sat around the saplings, protecting them with their bodies.[121] When a Major Amr arrived from the office of the Israeli military governor in Ramallah, it was mutually agreed that all parties would leave the area until a court of law resolved the matter. Major Amr guaranteed that not one tree would be touched, according to a news account. Following speeches, the villagers brought out fruit, bread, and olives; "Kuttab and Awad gave the soldiers fruit—embarrassed, they ate it."[122] According to Amos Gvirtz, no one was arrested.[123] There was no violence.

The next day, January 26, thirty of the original group returned to water the trees and found them gone, reported by villagers to have been pulled up one hour after the planters left the day before. The story aired on Israeli television, with Awad's commentary, "We lost those seedlings, but our action and the military response publicized what was happening all the time to the Palestinians—their land was being confiscated, their lives destroyed. So the villagers had proved that, in a nonviolent way, they could confront the authorities and their guns."[124]

The center discovered that some of the uprooted trees from Qatanna had been sold without benefit to the villagers, to municipal authorities and were planted in an Israeli memorial in West Jerusalem dedicated to the memory of Martin Luther King, Jr.[125] Rafi Davara, spokesperson for the Jerusalem municipality, confirmed that uprooted trees had been planted near the West Jerusalem memorial to the slain U.S. civil rights leader: "We needed some trees and when we called the Keren Kayemet, the Jewish National Fund, they asked us to send two trucks," claiming that the land belonged to the Israel Land Authority.[126] On March 3 a demonstration was held at the King memorial in West Jerusalem. As excerpts from King were read aloud, along with texts from the Qur'an and the Bible, seventy-five Palestinians, Israelis, and foreign visitors participated, among them Qatanna villagers. Holding hands, they sang "We Shall Overcome" in Hebrew, Arabic, and English, with one police officer joining in the refrain.[127]

In that spring of 1986, carefully planned noncooperation measures were laid out by the center, including refusal of Palestinian laborers to work in Israeli settlements, refusal to fill in governmental forms if required to be in Hebrew, refusal to comply with Israeli taxes, and plans for civil disobedience, such as forming human chains to block roads or lying prostrate in front of bulldozers at public works projects administered by the Israeli government. Such methods had a better chance of working than the military option, Awad maintained: "Palestinians here are so tired of having nothing to do for achieving their freedom. They don't want to throw bombs, but they want to do something. I am trying to offer them a revolution by nonviolence."[128]

Also in 1986, with the start of the first intifada still more than a year away, Awad brought the villagers of Yatta to plant trees on disputed land near the Israeli settlement of Sussia.[129] Another protest took place at the village of Bidya, north of Ramallah, after it lost more than one thousand olive trees.[130] On narrow technical grounds, it could be argued that these incidents made no impact on the overall situation, and that the center's tree-planting demonstrations had no effect on the larger conflict. In fact, it could be claimed that the four million olive trees planted by Palestinians on the West Bank during a ten-year period—a mid-1970s program for the mass distribution of olive and fruit-tree seedlings assisted by U.S. private charitable agencies—made no impression.[131] To be sure, these demonstrably nonviolent actions failed to stop what Ibrahim Matar calls the Israeli "outright seizure of private property."[132] Yet, episodes such as those at Qatanna, Sussia, and Bidya provide evidence that rural Palestinian folk living in the agricultural subsistence economies of isolated West Bank villages were being introduced to methods of standing up for their land that relied not at all on violence, and in which no violent imagery or retaliatory symbols were invoked. Such encounters exhibit a stream of activities flowing toward the first intifada, where nonviolent methods would predominate for nearly three years. In reconstructing what had occurred from published Israeli, Palestinian, and international news accounts, it is possible to discern the six principles cited at the 1983 workshops, including the rejection of anything that might humiliate the opponent and the directing of action against the "evil" rather than the persons involved.

Shopping in Hebron and the Committee on Family Reunification

On January 28, 1986, four Hebron shopkeepers approached the center and claimed that their businesses were being hurt because Israeli soldiers were searching and questioning anyone who wanted to enter their stores. Israeli settlers had established an enclave in the business district of Hebron, so the downtown Palestinian commercial areas had been cordoned off with barbed wire and patrolled by Israeli soldiers.[133] Soldiers at either end guarded a high-wire fence in front of a row of Palestinian shops. Shoppers were reluctant to pass through the secluded passage. Hebron's mayor, Mustafa Natsheh, agreed to join Awad and staff from the center in visiting shops behind the fence, as a symbolic action.[134] The episode occurred in front of British television cameras and international reporters, one of whom reported that access to three shops near the center of town "coveted" by the Israeli authorities had been made extremely difficult by the erection of a barbed wire fence, leaving a narrow passage a few feet wide, rimmed by boulders painted "blood red" stacked on tin drums alongside the fence.[135] Film showing body searches and Awad being forced to take off his shoes aired in British cinemas and on ITV.[136]

Shortly thereafter, the center developed plans for coordinated groups to go shopping at Hebron's Beit Hadassah and Daboiah Buildings.[137] The

Israeli branch of IFOR agreed to join, and its news release speaks of the shared risk to Palestinians and Israelis from the settlers—an effort to imagine a sense of community and a creative forgetting of the past. "The Israeli army considers these shops a security risk to the [Israeli] settlers above them," the Israeli cosponsor's news release notes; yet, "our group of Palestinians, Israelis, Jews, and foreigners considers the illegal settlers and the policy to protect them to be the real security risk."[138] In May, thirty volunteers from IFOR and the center went shopping at the stores, arriving in Arab taxis that proceeded through Israeli roadblocks without incident.[139] A leaflet urged "solidarity with those who are surrounded by wire fences and the guns of soldiers," and organized visits by Israelis, Palestinians, and expatriates were scheduled.[140] The joint PCSN and IFOR activities continued for several months.

In addition to piloting direct action campaigns, the center organized a Committee on Family Reunification to publicize the difficulties faced by tens of thousands of Palestinians who were prohibited from living with their families, because they lacked the identity cards issued by Israel in September 1967, shortly after the territories were militarily occupied. One member of the group, married to a Palestinian woman caught outside the occupied territories the previous June and therefore unable to return, recalled how the committee made contacts with Israeli members of the Knesset, to present the case of divided Palestinian families.[141] The committee organized events, such as a picnic and a march, six months before the start of the first intifada.[142] Speakers alluded to a parallel between Soviet Jewish and Palestinian families, because families in both settings were split by the refusal of powerful states to allow movement by populations under their control.[143]

On June 14, 1987, carrying placards in Arabic, Hebrew, and English, demonstrators presented U.S. consular officials with a letter to President Ronald Reagan, asking for humanitarian assistance for divided families, since husbands, wives, and children who were refugees in Arab countries could not join them due to Israeli policies. A permit for the protest was secured from Israeli police.[144] Petitioning of the authorities by the Committee on Family Reunification was aimed at Israeli sensibilities. Wrote Daoud Kuttab, "For the first time Palestinians demonstrated—legally—in front of the Israeli Prime Minister's office," and Awad penned letters to international leaders, including heads of state in Europe, North America, and the Soviet Union. He met personally with then–U.S. vice president George H. W. Bush to plead the case of broken Palestinian families, and visited the Knesset to speak to parliamentarians about family reunification cases.[145] Correspondence with the U.S. State Department publicized the predicament of divided Palestinian families.[146] The public record discloses these and other nonviolent actions and appeals of protest and persuasion were undertaken with a view to summoning sympathetic responses from Israelis. No threat was implied.

Gene Sharp and a Theory of Power

In November 1986, Gene Sharp traveled to Israel and the West Bank for the first time, where he spoke with Israeli strategic studies specialists in Tel Aviv and visited the Knesset. He met with Labor Knesset member Ephraim Sneh, a physician and former general who would later become minister of health, and who was at the time head of the Israeli Civil Administration in the West Bank, in hopes that he might try to influence Israeli policy "in case there was a major shift to nonviolent struggle by the Palestinians." Sharp expressed the view that it was in the interest of both Palestinians and Israelis for the Palestinians to adopt nonviolent struggle, which "would give greater power to the Palestinians in pursuing independence but would also relieve the Israelis of the problem of terrorism"; "hence, it would be in Israel's interest *not* to impose such severe repression as to drive the Palestinians back into violence."[147] Sneh recalled meeting with Sharp in his military office: "I was quite skeptical and didn't think the Palestinians would buy his offer. I remember a very strong argument, but felt it was not applicable to Palestinian reality."[148]

Having been present at the 1984 Washington meeting that resulted in the opening of the Palestinian Center for the Study of Nonviolence, Sharp now led several workshops for Palestinians and held meetings with the growing circle of activists who were becoming involved in the center's activities. He spoke widely and offered lectures, among them one at the Truman Institute at Hebrew University, attended by sixty persons.[149] He also met with youth in Qalandia refugee camp, which houses families that fled Israel in 1948 and is not far from the boundary that cuts off the occupied West Bank from Jerusalem.[150] Awad and Sharp joined a group who were building a new youth center. Qalandia youths no longer young would years later recall hammering nails, while talking with Sharp about the type of power that each person possesses.[151] The initial leaflet of the intifada would appear in Qalandia fourteen months later.

Sharp's lectures and discussions with Palestinians, Israelis, and mixed groups offered historical analyses of nonviolent struggle. He provided examples of how nonviolent resistance can split the ranks of the target group so that eventually some soldiers and police may be swayed by the underlying grievances; in contrast, violent struggle has the effect of uniting the target group against the challengers. He spoke of how a regime's repression against a nonviolent movement can paradoxically strengthen the nonviolent resisters. When speaking with Palestinian audiences, he focused on military occupation as rooted in and dependent upon obedience from civilians. Underlying his arguments, and on which partially rests his three-volume cross-cultural analysis of 1973, *The Politics of Nonviolent Action*—by then circulating for more than a year in the occupied territories and Israel in Arabic and Hebrew—are insights from the 1577 essay by Étienne de la Boétie, *Discours de la Servitude Volontaire*.[152] As a student at the university in Orléans, de la Boétie hypothesized that any form of government, no matter how despotic, relied on consent from the populace, and since cooperation with a bureaucracy is voluntary, it could be withdrawn. In his lectures and workshops, Sharp noted how acts of terrorism lead to international isolation, while nonviolent struggle engenders sympathy and support. He questioned the "blind faith" in violence held by some Palestinians, despite decades of disastrous results, and said that Jews throughout the world, and Israelis in particular, had adopted irrationally negative attitudes about the Palestinians because they feared violence, when they might have become allies in the quest of the Palestinians for a homeland. Unquestioning confidence in violence prevents the consideration of alternatives and criticism of failure, Sharp observed; besides, vastly fewer Palestinians could participate in violent struggle than in nonviolent struggle. Faith in violence thus threatened the future of the Palestinians.[153]

To Jonathan Kuttab, the most significant of Awad's contributions to the coming uprising was his interpretation and popularization of Sharp's theories.[154] Haj Abd Abu-Diab surmised, "Of all the things introduced by Awad, the most important was the idea of noncooperation."[155] This concept—termed in English "disengagement" during the intifada—took firm hold early in the uprising and became one of its central platforms.[156]

Self-Reliance

Awad's 1983 booklet considered any hope of salvation coming from the Palestinians outside the occupied territories implausible: "The military branches of the PLO are presently incapable of liberating the occupied territories by force and the Arab governments appear presently unable or uninterested in entering into a broad military confrontation with Israel aimed at liberating the military areas by force."[157] In Awad's view, "To tell me the only way to resolve this conflict is armed struggle is a bunch of baloney. If you don't have arms, don't say we are waiting for others to come liberate us. If you want to be violent, be violent. But don't play the game that 'we believe in armed struggle and are waiting for someone to come do it for us.'"[158] Compared to the asceticism, restraint, austerity, and self-discipline of nonviolent struggle, violence has hedonistic expressive appeal, stated Jonathan Kuttab. The Arabic language might be verbally aggressive, with the poetry and semantics of violence, yet the reality of Arab culture is not violent:

> We are not militaristic—even Saladin was a Kurd. The Arab civilization . . .
> never pioneered a single weapon, tactic, or campaign. Our battles were
> usually one-day assaults and skirmishes. The Prophet had an Ethiopian
> convert, who taught him how to build moats and trenches. Trenches! We
> have always compensated by militant rhetoric. In early Islam, there were not
> even regular armies.[159]

Although Awad personally believed in principled, ethical nonviolence, the public record shows that he did not argue on moral grounds, but presented nonviolent resistance as a practical and empowering technique that does not depend on interventions from others. It appears to have been of no consequence to him whether his ideas were accepted as a calculated concession, or matter of principle, so long as individuals adhered to the operational principles. He realized that some who joined him were making a tactical decision: "If we gave them tanks, they'd use tanks."[160] His clinical training led him to believe that changing behavior could have its own rewards: "Whenever the Palestinians start violence, we start losing," he said.[161]

As the notion of "liberation" by outside forces faded among the Palestinians, the idea of independence as something that could result from the exertions by those under occupation grew. The center encouraged a muscular activism to replace the perseverance of *samud*. Haj Abd Abu-Diab: "In 1985, Mubarak came to me with thirty Palestinian flags. He wanted to organize a flag-waving demonstration from a mosque in the Old City. I took the flags, layered them around my waist, and carried my coat in front of me. We went to the mosque together, handed out the flags, and a demonstration emerged."[162] Haj Abd recalled how Awad had showed the Palestinians that holding a quartered onion in front of one's nose was an antidote against tear-gas and how to organize "traffic stoppages":

> When the police told people to remove the Palestinian flags, they sat down. Once more than five hundred people sat down at the Damascus Gate to the Old City and the cars couldn't move for more than thirty minutes; meanwhile, we were issuing statements to the press. Mubarak showed how those in front should clench their hands together and wrap them with rubber bands, so that when the police moved one of us, ten persons had to be moved together.
>
> When the Israelis closed the boundaries into Jerusalem, Muslims were not allowed to go to the mosques to pray, and Christians were not allowed to go to the churches. We organized it so that the people would pray at the boundaries, in front of the soldiers and police. . . . We often timed it so that the Muslims were praying and the church bells were ringing at the same time. On other occasions, when the police came for the young people who were involved, instead we sent old women in their place.[163]

According to Awad, mutual fear was driving each side to want to destroy the other. Palestinians' fears were based on concern for survival as a people and worry that their national destiny was dependent on outside help, while Israeli mistrust derived from survival anxiety following upon the Holocaust.[164] Awad believed that nonviolent struggle could work to eliminate the causes of fear in Israel that were employed to justify militarization of the West Bank.

Awad's True Offense

Observers and activists alike impugned Awad's integrity, in one case referring to him as a "self-styled pacifist. . . . The latest in a parade of Palestinian phonies."[165] Yet pacifism played no role in the ferment underway. Its doctrine of resisting all wars held little relevance in the occupied territories, and neither he nor anyone else at the center advocated that the Palestinians remain defenseless. Awad told a reporter that although he, personally, was a pacifist in principle, his "campaign to sell nonviolence to his fellow Palestinians stresses practical self-interest, not religion or principle."[166]

While Awad's return to Jerusalem was viewed as "a new form of political sophistication" by those who believed he was striving to move the confrontation with the Jewish state onto "moral terrain,"[167] he was not moralistic enough for others, with his talk of self-interest and what will work. Don Peretz in his account of the first intifada deserves credit for noticing that there was a new discourse developing in the territories and for quoting sections from Awad's 1983 booklet, although he ignores the profound pragmatism and strategic intelligence that underscores the writings of Gandhi and King, when he says "though supposedly influenced by Gandhi and Martin Luther King, Awad's approach . . . was based more on practical than on moral considerations."[168]

In early summer 1986, Awad traveled to Plains, Georgia, to meet again with former president Jimmy Carter.[169] The discussion turned to the necessity to exclude all violence from any protests against the occupation, whatever the provocation. As a result of Carter's admonishment, Awad began openly to condemn the PLO whenever the front accepted responsibility for violence.[170] "I am completely against violence from the PLO and from the Israelis," he told three hundred religious Jews at the Beit Elisheva meeting hall in Jerusalem, just before the start of the first intifada.[171] Although acknowledged as "one of the few Palestinian leaders who openly condemns violence, and the only one who actively promotes and teaches nonviolent theories of resistance," Awad had initially confused Israeli observers by withholding complete repudiation of the use of violence.[172] Reluctance to condemn violence made it easy for an advisor to the Knesset's Tehiya faction to assert Awad viewed himself as the "complemental factor to terror."[173]

Other Israelis considered Awad "the first Palestinian to have publicly renounced violence against Jews," noting that he had never recommended entering a Jewish settlement on the West Bank to sever their electrical power wires.[174] Jonathan Kuttab believes that historical circumstances made it difficult for Awad to disavow armed struggle and retain legitimacy with Palestinians.[175] Lost in the reverberating claims and counterclaims[176] is the fact that the presence of violence or violent elements does not imply coordinated efforts between the protagonists of nonviolent sanctions and the perpetrators of violence. No linkage can be assumed.

Awad's Deportation Fuels Debate

When Awad returned from the United States to Jerusalem in 1983, he brought with him his old East Jerusalem identity card and, on May 15, 1987, sent it to the Interior Ministry for replacement. A letter of August 4 informed him that he had lost his Jerusalem residency.[177]

The Knesset's 1967 unilateral extension of Israeli jurisdiction over the entire area of mandatory Palestine, and annexation of East Jerusalem, had brought Arab East Jerusalem under Israeli civil law rather than military order. To get rid of Awad, the government could not rely on the emergency regulations that dated to the British Mandate, such as were being used to deport residents from the territories, because the Knesset had decided in 1979 that these regulations did not pertain in Israel, now interpreted to include annexed East Jerusalem.[178] The Interior Ministry maintained that, in Awad's case, Israel's Law of Entry pertained, in which a resident who remains abroad for more than seven years or takes citizenship elsewhere can lose his or her Israeli residency. A petition filed by Awad's lawyers, Avraham Gal and Jonathan Kuttab, and assisted by Hebrew University law professor David Kretzmer, argued that Awad's absence from 1969 to 1983 for academic study and his acceptance of U.S. citizenship did not alter the fact of his East Jerusalem residency. They maintained that he had not entered the country in 1967 but was already there, and that he was enrolled in the population registry and had been provided with an identity card.[179] After his three-month tourist visa expired in the autumn of 1987 and Israel refused to renew it—one of sequential visas he had used, each valid for three months—the question of deportation loomed. Without a residency permit and holding only an expired tourist visa, the issue became one of whether the High Court would judge the Interior Ministry to have exceeded its authority.

Awad was arrested by eighteen police officers who arrived at his home on May 5, 1988, six months after the uprising had started. On May 6, Prime Minister Yitzak Shamir ordered him deported. Shamir, who had defended terrorism for Jewish purposes, before the establishment of Israel,[180] released to the news media letters he had written about Awad in response to correspondence from U.S. senator Claiborne Pell and Coretta Scott King pleading Awad's right to remain in Israel.[181] Awad was "not a man of peace," Shamir claimed, and "his description of himself as a disciple of Mahatma Gandhi and Martin Luther King is not only an Orwellian inversion of language but a gross insult to the memories of those great leaders."[182]

Piracy of Awad's writings by Palestinians probably abetted his deportation. The media advisor to the prime minister, Avi Pazner, called him "the main brains of the intifada," alleging that he was one of the authors of the leaflets that served as "instruction sheets" for the Palestinian uprising, and that he supported the PLO's armed struggle.[183] Internal Israeli security documents declared that the purportedly moderate image projected by Awad was a cover that was incompatible with his real purposes. A court document sworn by a Shin Bet agent using the pseudonym Yossi, who was assigned to follow Awad, describes what he saw as the Palestinian's true designs:

a) Political objectives—the liberation of the Territories from Israeli rule and the subsequent establishment of bi-national Palestinian-Israeli state that would be Palestinian in nature.

b) Activity that constitutes civil disobedience—he expressed his ideas on this subject even before December, 1987, and most of his ideas have been incorporated in the leaflets that have been published by all of the forces behind the uprising. . . .

From the outset of the uprising in the Territories in December, 1987, his ideas began to find actual expression in the leaflets that were issued by the command of the uprising, resulting in actions taken by the inhabitants of the Territories.[184]

On May 24, Awad issued a statement through Jonathan Kuttab denying that he had authored the fifteenth leaflet of the intifada, as charged, and repudiating the allegation that the center received money from the PLO: "They say that I advocate violence. I do not. They say that I am working to get all of Palestine. . . . I favor a two-state solution. One state for the Palestinians and one for Israel."[185] Placed in solitary confinement for forty days while appealing to Israel's High Court, Awad's first week of incarceration was spent in Muscobiyya prison, also known as the Old Russian Compound, in West Jerusalem. He went on a hunger strike and stopped drinking water, as dozens of Palestinians and Israelis marched in protest outside.[186] In response, reported his wife Nancy Nye, the authorities removed the mattress from his jail cell.[187] Kuttab implored him to stop fasting. As Awad's attorney and the only person allowed to see him, Kuttab protested to Awad that he was "fat enough" to survive, but "there are supporters outside who are skinny, like Edy Kaufman, who could die because of their sympathy fast."[188]

As protesters swirled outside, under a mulberry tree in the parking lot of the compound, Edward Kaufman "set a precedent, as a Jew, by joining an imprisoned Arab friend in a hunger strike," to protest Awad's jailing.[189] Then at the Harry S. Truman Institute for the Advancement of Peace at

The Hebrew University of Jerusalem and professor of political science, Kaufman had earlier in the spring invited Awad to address his course on human rights. As Awad stepped on the stage, Israeli authorities arrested him.[190]

Secretary of State George P. Shultz wrote a personal appeal to Shamir, asking him to revoke the deportation.[191] On June 5, the High Court issued a sixteen-page decision that Prime Minister Shamir, as acting interior minister, could deport Awad, because East Jerusalem residents had the option of becoming Israeli citizens.[192] The following night, twenty members of the peace group called Israelis by Choice set fire to a copy of Israel's declaration of independence, saying that it had lost its meaning.[193] Thomas Pickering, U.S. ambassador to Israel, told Shamir that it was "incomprehensible" that Israel should deport an advocate of Palestinian nonviolent action; "you need more Awads . . . not fewer."[194] *Newsweek* magazine interpreted official U.S. concern as arising from the knowledge that between 2,000 and 3,000 Palestinians in the occupied territories held U.S. citizenship, casting light on the "statelessness" of the Palestinians: "Like thousands of other Palestinians, Awad chose to apply for and accept US citizenship in lieu of remaining 'stateless.'"[195] Awad's case reminded observers that more than 300,000 Palestinians who had resided in the West Bank or Gaza were exiled in the months following the June 1967 war, and a sizeable number of those who had been temporarily abroad had not been allowed to return—possibly a violation of the 1949 Fourth Geneva Convention.[196]

From solitary confinement, Awad wrote a statement for his wife to read publicly, were he deported before its release: "During the past years I have succeeded as a Palestinian from Jerusalem in encouraging Palestinians and Israelis to walk together even if they don't accept each other's opinions. Most of the activities of the Palestinian Center for the Study of Nonviolence involved Israelis, other Jews, and Palestinians. Through their assistance and mutual cooperation many relationships developed. Is this the real reason for my deportation?"[197] At a news conference at the National Palace Hotel in East Jerusalem on May 8, 1988, Nye read the statement: "The seeds of nonviolence have already spread, and we see them in the daily activities of the *intifada* as it moves towards a full campaign of civil disobedience."[198]

Before Israel's High Court, Awad declared that he accepted the legitimacy of the Israeli state and judiciary because peaceful means were the only way to achieve peace. Justice Aharon Barak's judgment went against him, but even so acknowledged Awad's urging of "reconciliation, including negotiations with the refugees for paying them compensation for their property, and the opening of a new chapter in the relations between the Jewish and the Palestinian peoples."[199] To the court, Awad said, "there can be no losers." Israelis and Palestinians must both be the winners; "If the uprising will not open your eyes and soul to tell you we need freedom I don't know what will. . . . As a Palestinian I never hated you. I don't hate you now. And I will never hate you.[200]

Israeli Reactions Spread Awad's Ideas

On June 13, 1988, Awad was expelled from Israel, yet not without a fight over whether the news media could record his departure. Mounting the steps to a waiting commercial aircraft, his fingers flashed a Churchillian "V" to the Israelis and Palestinians who had come to protest his deportation.[201] The "V for victory" sign, adopted by children in the intifada and a "password" required of adults, was but one of more than a hundred nonviolent action methods introduced by Awad in the 1980s. "Israel probably made a mistake by moving against Awad, a largely unknown Palestinian whose international stature was elevated by the deportation," an unnamed official conceded; "We probably shot ourselves in the foot."[202] The *Jerusalem Post* suggested if Awad had become a national hero to the Palestinians, it was Shamir who had thrust the crown on his head.[203]

The Israeli decision to expel Awad enhanced his credibility among the Palestinians, and his notoriety sped communication of his ideas to groups he might otherwise have been unable to reach. The Israeli public learned in its own news media about a Palestinian debate to which only its avant-garde intelligentsia and political left had been privy. Thus five years after initial distribution of the 1983 booklet, the excerpts quoted in the news awakened the Israeli public to his concepts, even if passages were distorted and interviews with Awad created even more upheaval. Quotations attributed to him were "violently torn out of context" and distributed by the prime minister's office, according to one newspaper.[204] An out-of-context statement by Awad was apparently taken from a document originating from Israeli lawyer Elyakim Haetzni, who also represented Israeli settlers in the settlement of Kiryat Arba, near Hebron. According to journalist Joel Greenberg, Haetzni was not only the source of such invalid quotations, but was also the lawyer who filed the legal petition to start Awad's deportation.[205] As disputes raged in Israeli newspapers about the validity of the Haetzni text, the *Jerusalem*

Post published a full transcript of the tape recording from which the incorrect extracts had been taken.[206] Haetzni evidently considered Awad's materials to be "incitement" and "sedition"; what especially angered him was the 1985 buy-Palestinian campaign, in which he alleged Awad had mimicked the Nazis by saying, "Don't buy from the Jews."[207] Haetzni was joined in the legal effort at expulsion by "right-wing activist" Shlomo Baum, who charged that Awad was one of the chief organizers and ideologues of the uprising. Haetzni filed legal complaints with Israel's attorney general, yet no action was apparently taken until 1987, when Awad was refused his new Jerusalem residence permit.

Awad's situation graphically raised the issue of a right of return for Palestinians. His case drew attention to the fact that Palestinians born in the West Bank and Jerusalem were treated like foreigners in the land of their birth, and were subject to stricter residency requirements than Jews who had never become citizens in Israel, yet came and went at will under the Israeli law of return.[208] What Awad did *not* represent may have been his true offense in Israeli eyes: "He does not represent an attitude of adjustment and submission. . . . Successive governments have sought a political myth—a representative local Palestinian leadership ready to capitulate."[209]

Amos Gvirtz believes Awad's deportation helped the legitimacy of nonviolent struggle among Palestinians.[210] One Palestinian youth, who at the age of twelve met Awad in 1986, recalled,

> No one accepted his ideas of nonviolence. The Israeli settlers were confiscating our land, and Mubarak said we should sit on the land and plant trees. I tried hard to understand what this meant. Originally I agreed with the villagers that we should fight with weapons, but I stayed in touch with the Center for the Study of Nonviolence. They encouraged me to be involved (I was already active with the Shabiba youth organization and Fateh). I organized demonstrations, youth groups, and nonviolent activities against the soldiers and settlers, and spent two years on Israeli wanted lists, much of it in hiding. I learned some techniques of action from the Shabiba and Fateh, but my principles and ideas came from the nonviolence center.[211]

Hanna Siniora who, from his post at *al-Fajr*, assured that the center's activities were reported, said, "Before the intifada, people would say Mubarak Awad was an Israeli agent or a CIA agent, but the intifada brought the awareness that nonviolent resistance is more important than military confrontation. . . . Mubarak brought a new trend, but the intifada itself expressed that at the beginning without the help of Mubarak Awad. He became a victim of the intifada, because he was targeted by the Israelis for preaching nonviolence, and this targeting by the Israelis brought his ways to the attention of the people."[212]

Israel's targeting intensified Awad's impact. No longer a nonconformist, his calamity was now the same as that of other Palestinians. He reached the Israeli public, and increased international awareness of the Palestinian dilemma. Sidra DeKoven Ezrahi, professor of Jewish literature at Hebrew University, who stood on the tarmac as Awad boarded the airplane, lamented: "a sense of human dignity . . . is being trampled underfoot by our stampeding tribesmen . . . lost in the xenophobic claims of collective destiny and chosenness.[213] Perhaps for the first time, U.S. officialdom publicly defended a Palestinian Arab.

Was Awad's contribution merely interesting, rather than important? Riad al-Malki, spokesperson for the Popular Front for the Liberation of Palestine (PFLP), a faction that sponsored some of the earliest Palestinian acts of terrorism, asserted that no one single person was behind the uprising.[214] This statement would apply to all mass movements. Such upheavals defy simplistic explanations of origin, yet human agency is important in nonviolent movements, and the outcome is not known in advance. Some official Israeli and Palestinian figures dismiss Awad, yet the evidence suggests that his role was catalytic. "His ideas, thoughts, and conceptions worked because he was able to convince key people—it was not intrinsic," Daoud Kuttab stated; "he has not received proper credit. It's no accident that the Israelis picked Mubarak to deport."[215]

Awad's refusal to repudiate Palestinians who were committed to military tactics left ambiguity in his statements, confusing Israelis who misinterpreted his refusal to condemn. He did not advocate the superiority of nonviolent strategies as if a contestant in a tussle of principles and ethics—although personally persuaded of the moral attributes of fighting with nonviolent resistance—but as a practical method for securing halts to Palestinian losses. Realizing that standard bearers for armed struggle also have convictions and moral codes, he intentionally restrained from ethical condemnations of armed insurrection, asserting instead the belief that nonviolent action has a better chance in the contemporary era. Awad's timing was astute, Jonathan Kuttab said:

He did not attack the politicos, he totally ignored them and went straight to the masses. . . . His ideas hit fertile ground. . . . The Palestinians lacked an articulation and a connection with a conscious, consistent strategy of nonviolence. There was nothing new about hunger strikes, commercial strikes, boycotting, self-reliance. The seeds have always been in the Palestinian community, . . . but were never . . . claimed as a strategy until Mubarak.[216]

To a community befallen by loss, ineptitude, and oppression, the idea of intentionally being willing to accept the penalties of arrest, injury, or death without retaliation—a core requirement for noncooperation—could not have been easy to explain. Yet not only did Awad take a stand against the presumed effectiveness of violence as a manifestation of power, he undermined its logic and that of the basic bargain to employ violence that has often characterized both sides in the conflict.

While the three-room Palestinian Center for the Study of Nonviolence spilled ideas, its propositions spread—chiefly its adaptation of Sharp's insight that a people's submission to a military occupation is required for its sustenance. External influences were thus affecting the mix of ideas and methods for resisting occupation, activating villages, and leading toward a conscious conclusion to reject the use of weaponry while strongly rising up against the occupation. The center's printed materials and experimental exercises showed Palestinians how to depend on themselves and use simple techniques of nonviolent direct action within their capacity. Awad's interpretations of Sharp's emphasis on self-reliance sped the diminution of expectations of outside help from the Arab world, a notion that would disappear in the first intifada.

Chapter 8

East Jerusalem Activist Intellectuals: New Ideas
Prepare the Way

Imagining Futures: The Committee Confronting the Iron Fist

Feisel Husseini

To the extent that the Palestinians living under military occupation after the 1967 war and subsequently had a "national" leader, it would be forty-two-year-old Feisel Abd al-Qadir Husseini. At the start of the 1980s, Husseini sought out Israeli political journalist Gideon Spiro. A former paratrooper who was decorated for his participation in the 1956 Suez war, Spiro had emigrated with his family from Berlin to British-controlled Palestine in 1939, and was among the Israeli soldiers who took military control for Israel over Arab East Jerusalem in 1967.[1] Later he became a founding member of Yesh Gvul (There Is a Limit), a movement of Israeli reserve soldiers who in 1982 refused to serve in the war in Lebanon and questioned that war's legality.[2] The two men, Palestinian and Israeli, began to work together through the Committee Confronting the Iron Fist (Lajnat Muwajahat al-Qabda al-Hadidiyya). The term "iron fist" was used by defense minister Yitzhak Rabin in reference to Israeli policies and had been employed for decades, including by Israel's first prime minister David Ben-Gurion and later by Yitzhak Shamir when he became prime minister. Husseini became the leader of the committee.[3]

The small group formed by Israelis and Palestinians is significant, because it marks a formal beginning to organized contemporary nonviolent action against the Israeli military occupation. The Committee Confronting the Iron Fist consolidated preexisting groups that had grown out of an Israeli peace group called the Committee of Solidarity with Bir Zeit University (CSBZ), initially formed by Israelis who opposed the involuntary closing of the Palestinian university by Israeli authorities in student unrest in late 1981.[4] Spiro had become the spokesperson for CSBZ. By 1980, a joint endeavor had become visible when a number of Palestinians around Husseini joined with Israeli activists enlisted by Spiro to protest the arrest of Abu Anish, a staff-person in the Arab Studies Society founded by Husseini.[5] Several successive committees followed, each named for a person whose impending deportation was being protested or for whom a defense was being arranged. Instead of retaliatory action, or speaking of retribution, the goal of the committees was to quicken Israeli sentiments and publicly raise awareness about individual cases of imprisonment or deportation of Palestinians. In 1985, the sundry committees merged and became the Committee Confronting the Iron Fist. Husseini explained,

> The Committee Defending the Rights of Abu Anish . . . was the first direct action—that is, announcing a committee which had inside it Palestinians and Israelis. Before that, we had committees created by Israelis . . . [or] a music committee,[6] but this was the first time that we had something polit-ical mixed together with Israelis and Palestinians. After that, we created the Committee Defending the Rights of Jabril Rajoub. Then eventually we decided why should we change names all the time? So we went on with our work, but we called it the Committee Confronting the Iron Fist.[7]

Rudimentary tools were used by the committees, each employing iden-tical methods of persuasion and protest, the simplest category of nonviolent action, including banners, documentation, demonstrations, group lobbying, letters of opposition, marches, news media releases, picketing, public speeches, signed public statements, and vigils.[8] Their methods were nearly identical to those being used in Eastern Europe's nonviolent movements against Soviet supremacy during the same period of the 1980s.[9] Documen-tation and denunciation were also the main methods utilized by the Mothers of the Plaza de Mayo in Argentina who, between 1976 and 1983, had organ-ized in opposition to the military generals' so-called dirty war, in which tens of thousands of students and opponents of the regime "disappeared."[10]

With the various committees consolidated into one overarching entity, Husseini and Spiro were chosen to act as spokespersons. Spiro recalled, "I started to think of ways to create real cooperation since we, as Israelis, have to pay the price for our occupation of another nation."[11] Among its pur-poses, the Committee Confronting the Iron Fist sought to persuade Israelis that there was a valid Palestinian perspective on rights and entitlements that they need not fear. The message was conveyed in a number of ways, including the fact that the committee operated in the open, without secrecy. The statements of the two spokespersons emphasized the idea of mutuality between occupier and occupied; in other words, military occupation causes harm to both the occupying forces and the occupied populace. Among the papers and minutes in the files of the committee, no hint of retaliation is expressed, no allusion made to military prowess, no coercive language employed, and no language of revolution can be found. In 1987, the group was described as

> Composed of Arabs, Israelis, Armenians, a sprinkling of Jewish and Arab-Americans and anyone else who cares to join, this organization of "peaceniks" engages in consciousness-raising politics. Its tactics embrace protest tunes, poetry, scathing speeches and hand-scrawled posters. Its members embrace vast enthusiasm and much idealism.[12]

The committee's protests were meant "to call Israeli and world attention to . . . intolerable conditions" of forced deportation, "prolonged holding of prisoners without charges," and "brutality during interrogation."[13] It declared itself as committed to ending administrative detention, cessation of torture, and the elimination of collective punishments, such as demolitions of homes. The group's members protested prison conditions, condemned house demolitions, and denounced the closure of schools, unions, newspapers, and other institutions by military officers. They hosted seminars, leafleted, held news conferences, picketed, staged demonstrations, and organized vigils. They issued fact sheets and news releases concerning deportations and administrative detentions. Their internal writings suggest that they were trying to save the lives of political prisoners who were believed to be maltreated or tortured, and attempting to lessen harassment of the families of the imprisoned by disclosing the reprisals that they faced.

Minutes from the steering committee for the Committee Confronting the Iron Fist in 1986 note that the case of Jabril Rajoub was discussed.[14] The committee considered plans for a demonstration to be held at the Israeli military command headquarters in the village of Beit Hanina thirteen days later, at which placards would carry the names of deportees and detainees in three languages: Arabic, English, and Hebrew. The group deliberated a "Day of Fast, Study, and Solidarity" with Palestinian Prisoners for April 17.

In Beit Hanina on February 1, 1986, 150 Israelis and Palestinians turned out for the demonstration at the central regional headquarters of the Israeli authorities to protest the expulsion of three Palestinians from the West Bank. Israeli members of the committee could obtain police permits for demonstrations, even though more than 100 Palestinians showed up as opposed to a few dozen Israelis. A newspaper called the protest "well organized," and reported that each demonstrator was carrying a placard with the name of an individual being held in administrative detention, written in Arabic, English, and Hebrew. Speeches criticized Israel's "iron fist" policy, the expulsion of 29 Palestinians, and imprisonment of more than 120 others under administrative detention. "The names of all detainees and deportees were chanted by the demonstration organizers," as the crowd answered "*samud,*" (meaning to remain steadfast), if the person was under administrative detention, and "*aid*" (returning), if expelled.[15] *Samud* had been a main political stance of Palestinians in the territories since the mid-1970s. It denoted *survival* as a form of resistance.

On March 21, 1986, the Committee Confronting the Iron Fist organized a demonstration at the Damascus Gate of Jerusalem's Old City.[16] Statements were read aloud in the three languages, concerning "intolerable conditions" in which Palestinians were being held at Israeli prisons, which were said to "lack sanitary conditions, lack healthy food and drinkable water, and lack fresh air." A member of the committee told hundreds of spectators that the protest sought in part to reassure political prisoners that they were not forgotten. A boldly lettered placard read, "Down with the iron fist, down with occupation."[17] On June 5, 1986, a demonstration by the committee protested the nineteenth year of occupation, with one hundred Palestinians, Jews, and international guests picketing for one hour outside the Damascus Gate leading into the walled Old City, as picketers carried posters in Arabic, English, and Hebrew protesting the Israeli military occupation.[18]

Gideon Spiro advised "Gandhi-style" resistance and suggested that a human wall of 200,000 Palestinians encircle Kiryat Arba—an Israeli settlement near Hebron. He hoped that the committee could dramatize the idea of coexistence, defined by him as the Palestinians being granted either independence or equal rights. He urged that curfews be greeted by an outpouring of Palestinians into the streets, rather than acquiescence to Israeli orders by staying at home.[19]

The basic platform of Husseini and Spiro's original committees reflected important alterations in thinking. One of the most significant conceptual adjustments was an acknowledgement of Israel's permanence. "On the basis of our belief that occupation is an enemy to both occupied and occupier, we address our call to the democratic and progressive forces in Israel to stand in solidarity with Palestinians in the struggle to end the occupation and to bring about a just peace in the region."[20] Despite the illegality of the committees under the political bans of occupation, the group recognized both the State of Israel and the humanity of Israeli citizens. Years later former chief psychologist of the IDF Reuven Gal would observe, however, that apart from the small number of Israelis who were directly involved, "very little of this came across into the Israeli awareness."[21] Equally, the Palestinians' increasing acceptance of a smaller Palestinian state than envisioned in the 1947 UN partition plan appears to have been missed, denied, or ignored in Israel.

Another significant conceptual development involved acts of imagination. The committees existed in actuality, yet the ideas that they manifested had to be imagined. According to anthropologist Benedict Anderson, nation-states are also imagined political communities. The citizens of the smallest nation will never know each other, yet the "image of their communion" exists in the mind of each.[22] Such imagining involves memory, yet it also requires forgetfulness. The committees had created an imagined political community in which what was forgotten was as important as what was remembered. Husseini and the group of Israelis and Palestinians who were involved with him were setting aside the mentality of "us vs. them," and were instead creating an outlook of a shared experience in which military occupation was harmful to both peoples, who, they argued, must share the land. They said both sides had an interest in dislodging something mutually hurtful. Rather than remembering the animosities that fuel quests for vengeance, they tried to forget them. Each side existed in the mind of the other in their shared futures. The "other" was part of a still larger kinship summoned by an act of imagination, in which both communities were aggrieved by the violence of military occupation:

> We decided that the main enemy is the occupation . . . the main enemy for the two communities—for the Palestinian community and for the Israeli community. . . . [T]he occupation can hurt the morale of the people who are controlling the occupation, no less than the people who are under it—maybe more. We reached an agreement that we must, as Palestinians and Israelis working together, end this occupation . . . [and] that it was in the interest of the Israelis to end this occupation as well as the Palestinians.[23]

Despite the significant departure that such visualization and imagina-tion represented from the culture of covert guerrilla cadres, the adoption of forthright, public, non-clandestine and nonviolent forms of struggle was considered by the Israeli government to jeopardize the public order and threaten the security of the state. Instead of seizing on the openings created by Husseini and the others, Israeli authorities imprisoned him for 15 out of 21 months between April 1987 and January 1989, under administrative arrest—the provisions for detention renewable for six-month periods without charge or trial, as provided by the Defense (Emergency) Regula-tions introduced by the British in 1945.[24] Israeli authorities often preferred administrative detention rather than criminal charges because they did not need to reveal intelligence sources in court.[25] When Husseini was impris-oned in the summer of 1988, hundreds of Israeli peace groups condemned his arrest. Members of the Israeli association Peace Now held a vigil against the government's action and sent protest telegrams to Yitzhak Rabin, despite the group's customary avoidance of confrontation with the IDF or security services. The mass membership organization also conducted a demonstration at Rabin's home in Tel Aviv, at which it was pointed out that Husseini had been speaking out for a two-state solution, meaning a recog-nition of the Israeli and Palestinian states alongside each other, and speakers declared that the government should be meeting with Husseini instead of locking him up.[26]

In his cell, Husseini's faultlessly polite behavior toward his prison guards showed indebtedness to a Gandhian principle in which acceptance of punishment offers an opportunity to influence the adversary. In prison, he reversed the "cold shoulder" technique used by the Danes in their resistance to the Nazi occupation, and would smile every time a guard passed. Upon release, Husseini explained how he told the guard, "I am in a cell whose walls don't smile, the ground is cold and frowning, your guards don't smile and even the sun you allow doesn't smile. I can't force any of them to smile, but I have full ability to keep my own smile."[27] In 1987, as the twenty-year anniversary of the occupation approached, reminding the residents of the West Bank and Gaza Strip of the futility of their situation, at a time when official PLO utterances were pompous and inflammatory, Husseini reached across constituencies and developed a reputation for tactful, plainspoken truthfulness.

Israeli Court's Refusal to Differentiate Terrorism
from Nonviolent Action

Husseini's heritage gave him legitimacy and strengthened his ability to assert nonviolent struggle as the best way for Palestinians to fight for their rights. His stature came from a number of sources, including an autonomy that had been enjoyed by Jerusalem's aristocratic families since the nineteenth century. Of special resonance was the fact that his father Abd al-Qadir al-Husseini had in the 1930s led al-Jihad al-Muqaddas (the Holy War). Husseini's father was also regarded as a legendary Arab hero of the 1948 Arab-Israeli war and was killed in action at al-Qastel on April 8, 1948.[28] Newspaper editor Hanna Siniora later mused, "Feisel has a special place as the son of one of the leaders of the 1948 war, a military leader who died in battle. People always remember that he comes from a family that fought for the country, and that his father paid with his life to defend the country. He had a good heritage and the sympathy of the public."[29] Husseini was also related to the controversial grand mufti of Jerusalem, Haj Amin al-Husseini.[30] His lineage included two former mayors of Jerusalem and a seventeenth-century mufti of Jerusalem, and he claimed descendancy from the Prophet. As Palestinian scholar Mahdi Abd al-Hadi put it, he possessed all the imperatives of leadership: wealth, credibility, Muslim credentials, "clean hands," and connections.[31] When Husseini argued that there was a better, nonmilitary technique to struggling for political rights, rather than armed struggle, his words had peculiar credibility. As early as 1968, he had started making public statements to the effect that peace could be achieved only through nonviolent approaches.[32] His authority exemplified a Palestinian moral order, allowing him to influence the society's production of symbols.[33] This "quiet, honest, ascetic man has none of the zeal of the extremist," reporter Sarah Helm notes:

> Not a charismatic leader, his solid somewhat dour countenance is that of a determined pragmatist. . . . In the 1960s Mr. Husseini took up the PLO banner, training in military camps in Syria. When he returned to live in Jerusalem after the 1967 Arab-Israeli war his first arrest was for storing weapons for the PLO. By the mid 1970s, however, Faisal Husseini was developing his own ideas about the way forward for the Palestinians, talking about non-violence and passive resistance and compromise, accepting a two-state solution early on.[34]

Yet in the same way that the British had failed to respond to the eighteen years of largely nonviolent Palestinian Arab protest and persuasion that followed the Balfour Declaration, reacting only to three major episodes of violence, Israeli officials in the 1980s offered no recognition that nonviolent methods were coming into use by influential Palestinians. Their actions belied a view of nonviolent action as undifferentiated from the violent resistance that the government was fighting through military measures.[35] "To Israelis it really doesn't make any difference if the *intifada* is violent or nonviolent," Israeli journalist Daniel Rubinstein later observed; "the problem is the goal of the Palestinians and not the means."[36] U.S. journalist Barton Gellman would later point out that Israeli commentators tended to brand as "terrorists" all of the 120,000 Palestinians out of the population of 2 million estimated by the Israeli government to have been incarcerated during the uprising from 1987 to 1993, even though only a few hundred were ever implicated in serious violence.[37] An official Israeli refusal to discern between the advent of nonviolent struggle and the PLO's guerrilla strategies can be seen in a decision of Israel's High Court of Justice upholding one of Husseini's administrative detentions:

> There is no actual physical violence in the activities of the appellant. He is not the one who places explosives, nor the one who sends those who place them, but . . . his coordinative activities between the organizations are highly important for the organization[al] structure which leads to the execution of the terrorist actions of the various organizations. . . . The counter-war of Israel must, therefore, focus on each unit of this wide range and hurt or weaken it.[38]

Feisel Husseini was perhaps a target for other reasons. He was the first Palestinian, or among the first, to speak and give lectures to Israeli audiences in Hebrew, having learned the language during a year spent in Dahnoun jail in Haifa, from November 1967 to October 1968.[39] Immediately after his release in the second year of military occupation, Husseini began having conversations with Israeli political parties on the left and offering interviews in Hebrew to the Israeli news media.[40] In the words of Israeli journalist Yizhar Beer, "The English and Hebrew in which he addresses Israeli and foreign audiences is not particularly good. But even with his limited vocabulary, Husseini comes across with intellectual clarity, strength, and precision. . . . Other

West Bank leaders acted in a factional manner, whereas Husseini stood out as a national personality.[41]

Husseini is often described in print as a Fateh representative, rather than a pivotal agent of broader social change.[42] This may be because Israeli policies were designed to prevent contact with anyone even remotely associated with the PLO. As Reuven Gal said, throughout the 1980s and even during the early years of the intifada,

> We didn't hear any of these names: Sari Nusseibeh, Feisel Husseini, Hanan Ashrawi, and others. The Israeli leadership, especially the leadership of the Mossad or the security services (who were activated by the Israeli political leaders) considered those leaders behind the scenes as the troublemakers who create rock throwings and cocktail bombs. They didn't consider them as partners for negotiation. . . . I see a lot of responsibility on the Israeli side for not being sensitive enough or insightful enough to see that, but I also put a lot of responsibility on the Palestinian side . . . for not being able to put across that this was a political struggle—that they were not trying to go back to Jaffa, or Haifa, or so on, but to sit down at the negotiation table and negotiate a future for the Palestinian people.[43]

Analysts of the Israeli peace constituencies writing subsequently have placed more importance than was previously accorded on Husseini's role, support for Israeli-Palestinian dialogue, and repudiation of violence. David Hall-Cathala, Reuven Kaminer, and Colin Shindler give him more credence than do most North American or European commentators.[44] Yet none of these accounts recognizes Husseini's role in initiating major realignments within his own camp. His committees represented the first consistent expression of coherent adoption of nonviolent action after the 1967 occupation and are one of the earliest harbingers of the political evolution underway in the territories that would result in the 1987 uprising.

Husseini's positions went against the stock revolutionary ideologies of the armed factions. Suspending his awareness of the indignities imposed by the occupied, virtually all of his peace-building activities were illegal under occupation. He spoke in the tongue of the adversary, and used neither linguistic tricks nor bombast. With his relative immunity from the conformity expected by the PLO, Husseini asked that the Israelis imagine themselves in a shared predicament. By the early 1980s, Feisel Husseini was opening room for compromise and creating symbols in which both Israelis and Palestinians have rights over the contested land, speaking of shared solidarity, and refusing to cast blame.

Ideas in Action: The First Authorized March

Palestinian intellectuals and activists in the occupied territories had learned the lessons of oral histories and knew that noncooperation methods without a political program would come to naught. At the same time, a view of action as the substantiation of ideas was developing among them. In other words, if one proposed a sovereign independent state, one had to act in such a way as to demonstrate that statehood was viable. The notion that ideas and action required integrated strategies was evolving at approximately the same time that the term *intifada* was coming into use during the student struggles of the 1980s, with its connotation of shaking off occupation, instead of the combative terminology of the 1950s and 1960s, which implied demolishing, destroying, or defeating. The word *intifada* implies motion and change, according to literature professor Hanan Mikhail Ashrawi, later elected to the Palestinian Legislative Council and minister of the Palestinian Authority.[45] Thus, among the influential adjustments by Husseini and his associates were changes in wording. Conjuring the building of a nation-state came to mean the development of institutions and freedoms, instead of *thawra* (revolution), which had been the dominant political rubric from the pan-Arab era. Gone, too, would be emotive and grandiose phraseology, noms de guerres, and Marxist slogans. Husseini's committees operated openly. Nonviolent mobilization in general tends to be porous, and for good reason. It is not possible to activate entire populations, or large sectors, and use secrecy. This factor alone was a revolutionary departure leading to the intifada.

In June 1987, the Committee Confronting the Iron Fist organized a march to protest the occupation and call for an independent Palestinian state with Jerusalem as its capital, implying that Jerusalem could serve as the capital of two adjacent states. This was the first political procession in Arab East Jerusalem to express opposition to Israeli policies for which the Israeli authorities granted permission.[46] Proceeding peacefully past the U.S. consulate on June 14, carrying sixty-seven black flags, representing the first year of the military occupation of 1967, some five hundred Palestinians and Israelis carried placards from a joint Israeli-Palestinian exhibit entitled Down with Occupation. Speeches called for the right of Palestinians to an independent state and proclaimed the PLO their representative, an assertion related to the bans against contact with the organization. Gideon Spiro told reporters that the march's significance came from Jews and Arabs joining together in opposition to the occupation.

This first authorized march is revealing, coming as it did six months in advance of the 1987 uprising. Sari Nusseibeh, a member of the committee, was criticized for obtaining the permit to march, because it admitted the authority of Israeli officials.[47] He replied,

> There is no difference in kind between obtaining a building permit and a march permit if both permits aim at helping the continued existence of Palestinians on their soil. . . . We will not physically push out the military authorities through a demonstration or a march, what we gain through these activities is to publicize our opposition to occupation.[48]

Nusseibeh declared his hope that the march "would be the first of many acts of passive resistance by Palestinians against 20 years of Israeli occupation." In using the phrase *passive resistance,* he invoked a quaint term that even Gandhi had rejected because of its incorrect implications of passivity, yet it probably reflected a judgment that the term would be understood as a call to nonviolent action.[49] His comments predict an intifada.

Although the June march was aimed against the occupation, its larger purpose was to prepare the way for a Palestinian state, something for which the organizers assumed there was no logical prospect through armed struggle. Since the activities of the Committee Confronting the Iron Fist were not covert and the public's participation was always invited, an underlying presumption reveals itself: the populace in the territories could through their own words and deeds influence a political outcome. Nusseibeh later described the transition: "[P]eople have come to realise that ideas and aspirations must be embodied in manifest acts if reality is to be changed."[50]

Husseini, Nusseibeh, and others were also urging the broad PLO apparatus based in Tunis to adopt a more utilitarian and consensual view of struggle. By the end of 1985, Husseini was in discussion with Khalil al-Wazir (Abu Jihad), "Our first talk was about *passive resistance,* but we didn't like the name [which connoted passivity], so we started talking about another [term] and we reached *aggressive nonviolence*."[51]

The PLO supported civilian organizing in the territories, but, importantly, as an accessory to military cells. In 1978 the PLO and Jordan had established the Palestinian-Jordanian Joint Committee, with representatives from the PLO, primarily from Fateh and Jordan, to distribute money from the Arab states. Although unable to collect 60 percent of what had been pledged, it nonetheless provided the West Bank and Gaza with 138 million Jordanian dinars in the seven years of its operation, 1979-85.[52] Abu Jihad sat on the committee, and, in addition to directing the military cadres, encouraged the diversification of civilian networks and committees. Yet the PLO remained locked in the contradictions of insisting on "all available means" of struggle.[53] By encouraging the use of nonviolent strategies only sporadically, and maintaining the mythology of violence, the PLO failed to recognize that strategic nonviolent action must exclude violent operations, and it left its basic doctrine on armed struggle intact.[54] Arafat appeared at the UN General Assembly in 1974, embodying such a tangled approach, when he said that he came "bearing an olive branch and a freedom fighter's gun" and declared political struggle to be an adjunct to armed struggle.[55] A farrago of "mixed strategies" held little possibility of persuasively affecting the power configurations in Israel, or influencing the international community.

Viewing nonviolent resistance as an adjunct or precursor to armed struggle misses one of the most potent properties of nonviolent struggle: the potential for exploiting disparities between the unarmed and the militarily dominant. Asymmetry between the Palestinians and Israel was deeply entrenched in the historical circumstances, yet the Palestinian failure to exploit fully the incommensurate relationship between Israeli military pre-eminence and their own lack thereof would make the road to political gains ultimately achieved by the first intifada more difficult and circuitous.

Shifting toward Negotiations

Husseini and Nusseibeh began to press for direct contacts with Israel in the early 1980s. Negotiations, of course, implied the recognition of Israel, a position officially still regarded as treachery by many Palestinians. Nusseibeh found it difficult even to broach the subject: "Those arguing in favour of recognising Israel (real peace) in exchange for the establishment of a Palestinian state were treading on such virginal political ground that, in order to maintain their credibility in their own constituency, they often resorted to what was necessarily a language that didn't make much of an impression on

Israel or on the world community."[56] The Israeli military general Yehoshafat Harkabi had in 1968 perceived in the writings of Fateh adherents living abroad a "lack of serious consideration of the relationship between the objective and the means to attain it." In the absence of a bridge between the aims and the actions, "violence becomes a goal for its own sake—violence for the purpose of satisfying psychological motivation and the urge for vengeance."[57] Inside the occupied territories, conversely, the activist intellectuals were by the late 1960s arguing a connection between the ends and means. This does not mean that they were free to engage in public debate on the matter. Deliberation on the means and ends is a customary and predictable element of preparation for nonviolent resistance. It echoed among Palestinians in the occupied territories, as ideas on direct negotiations with the Israelis—apart from their intrinsic value—began to affect the reevaluation of the validity of violent struggle. To speak of negotiations meant focusing on what might be achieved through talks and, so, the benefits of nonviolent struggle stood out.[58]

The gulf between the East Jerusalemites and the armed factions was great. Although a trend to accepting the irreversibility of the State of Israel had been underway since 1974, the continuation of Palestinian violent guerrilla behavior, with its indiscriminate effects and harm of civilians, caused Israeli retaliation to be brought down on the residents of the occupied territories, resulting in ambivalence and distrust—no basis for a popular movement. Nor would it reassure the Israeli public. According to Palestinian political scientist Yezid Sayigh, "[T]he form and logic of Palestinian military action in the 1974-82 period simply did not relate to the active political aims that the PLO strove to achieve, such as gaining American political recognition and bringing international pressure to bear on Israel to withdraw from the territories. The nature of Palestinian action (especially terrorism) tended to undermine, rather than reinforce, the PLO's political and moral message to Israel and the West."[59] Nusseibeh explained the disjuncture: "Palestinians essentially believe that any bargaining with Israel over Palestinian territory is like bargaining over stolen property with the very thief who stole it by force."[60] An earlier generation of Palestinians in exile believed "the road to Tel Aviv lies through Amman and Beirut"—that is, by vanquishing Israel through Palestinian military operations from camps based in Jordan and Lebanon.[61] In contrast, as Nusseibeh later phrased it, "Our own road to statehood is through Israel, through Israeli public opinion. . . . It is still our responsibility as Palestinians to emphasize to the Israelis that it is peace that we seek and coexistence, not the destruction of Israel. . . . Not for Israel's sake but for our sake."[62] Husseini's words were comparable: "We struggle for the liberation of our people, not to dominate any other people; we struggle in order to establish our own state, not to destroy any other state; we struggle in order to guarantee and secure a safe future for our coming generations and not to threaten the coming generations of any other people in the area."[63] He would maintain that reassurance was needed for the Israelis, rather than mixing messages: "We must convince Israelis that we are not going to destroy them or throw them in the sea, that they can live with the Arab world. . . . The only solution is to go on making it clear to the Israelis that the intifada is not using weapons. We have the means, but we are not using it, because we don't want to kill."[64]

As the Palestinians inside the territories increasingly adopted pragmatic political conceptions, they changed phraseology. Language reveals complex modifications in behavior, and foremost in the altered terminology was the adoption of *independence* instead of the old stipulation *liberation*. "Independence" meant self-governing and free, unlimited in potential, with unhindered horizons, and statehood, whereas "liberation" was insurrectionary, suggesting overthrow, and armed revolt. By the time of the intifada, the broad concept of independence would replace the idea of liberation along with its narrow objectives. Indeed, the word *liberation* would all but disappear during the uprising, releasing for a time the Palestinians in the territories from the albatross of armed struggle which had left them "struggling in diplomatic councils while being judged in the courts of terrorism."[65]

"Pens, Pictures, Images, and Dreams"

In the two decades following the 1948 war, those who subscribed to the use of terrorism viewed it as a weapon of political propaganda to "gain publicity for the movement and prevent it slipping into oblivion," while external world opinion was considered insignificant because "liberation" could, according to the ideologists, be won through their own masses.[66] The activist intellectuals around East Jerusalem instead saw international opinion as their ally, and by the mid-1980s a premium began to be placed on Palestinians who could express themselves not only to their fellow Palestinians but to Israelis and the international community as well. Palestinians began to publish in Hebrew or English, in hopes of reaching the global community.

Others who might normally have written for international periodicals turned to the local Arabic outlets, in hopes that their writing would be picked up by organs in Cairo, Amman, and Kuwait. Hanna Siniora later reviewed these developments:

> We in the local media did our best to carry the sentiments, the aspirations of our people to the international community, and that's why we published in English. . . . I encouraged my journalists and editors to become closely tied with the international press that was based in Jerusalem; many of my colleagues today work with Reuters, Agence France-Presse, AP, UPI, the BBC and other outlets.[67]

The Palestinians active in this dissemination of writings thought of themselves as instrumental and able to influence the course of events. Throughout the early and mid-1980s, their published pieces in Arabic, English, and Hebrew argued the necessity for compromise and direct negotiations between Israelis and Palestinians.[68] Moreover, by habitually understating estimates of numbers or projections of persons who participated in rallies, rather than embellishing them, they differentiated themselves from the wild exaggeration so characteristic of the armed factions from the late 1950s onward. Openly appealing to the occupier, essay after essay offers a rational discourse upon which negotiations might be built. At the same time, they were seeking to transform Palestinian rejectionist ideologies and pose alternative strategies for pursuit of their rights and entitlements among those who read the Arabic dailies and weeklies. One of the earliest to start advancing such ideas in this way was Ziad Abu Zayyad.

Ziad Abu Zayyad

A lawyer in East Jerusalem, Ziad Abu Zayyad was among the first Palestinians to speak to Israeli audiences in Hebrew, along with Feisel Husseini. After being graduated from Damascus University in 1965, Abu Zayyad discovered that he had the ability—talent, some would call it—to think and talk like an Israeli. He had taken an intensive Hebrew-language class created for recent Jewish immigrants, and then put his newly learned Hebrew to use as a translator for the Arabic newspaper *al-Quds*. By 1977, he was editing a Hebrew edition of *al-Fajr*, and in 1986 he started publishing a journal in Hebrew, *Gesher* (Bridge).[69] He favored coexistence based on mutual recognition and respect, believing that militarized force could not solve the problem.[70] As a result of Abu Zayyad's efforts, Palestinian and Israeli journalists made their first contacts, and the relationships that they formed endure to this day.[71] A member of the editorial board of *New Outlook,* a journal of the Jewish peace movement, he is also an editor of the *Palestine-Israel Journal of Politics, Economics and Culture,* a quarterly for both local and international audiences as a joint Israeli and Palestinian endeavor. Four times arrested and imprisoned, Abu Zayyad was detained by Israel in 1990 for involvement in the leadership of the intifada. He, Radwan Abu Ayyash, Sari Nusseibeh, and others would be imprisoned later that year based on an allegation that they were acting as spies for Iraq and passing information on missile sites to Baghdad.[72] A storm of international indignation resulted.[73] More than one Israeli would charge that the "real reason" was to discredit such newly emerging leaders in the eyes of international opinion.[74]

Radwan Abu Ayyash

To Radwan Abu Ayyash, the predicament of the Palestinians was partially of their own making. Born in a tent in the Askar refugee camp near Nablus sometime after 1950, to Palestinian parents from the village of Jamasin in what is today Tel Aviv, Abu Ayyash underwent a "psychological shift" following the 1967 Israeli occupation and concluded, "All that I had learned seemed to me to be lies, and not true."[75] Considering that a cycle of mutual elimination of Palestinians by Israelis, or Israelis by Palestinians, was "not a humane solution," he became a political columnist in 1975 for the daily *al-Shab.*[76] In 1979, he joined Raymonda Tawil in her local news agency, the Palestine Press Service (PPS), where he became editor in chief. Exposed to cooperation with the foreign news media—Agence France-Presse, the BBC, ITV, and U.S. television networks—he learned to deal professionally with Israeli journalists in the exchange of news.

While still at PPS, Abu Ayyash helped to found the Palestinian Journalists' Association and was responsible for running its public relations department for five years. In 1982, he had begun working for a weekly political magazine, *al-Awda* (The Return), until it was shut down by Israel in 1984.[77] In 1987, he created a local news agency, the Arab Media Center, and began to work on the creation of the Palestinian Broadcasting Corporation. Abu Ayyash was imprisoned for "precautionary" reasons on December 8, 1987, the eve of the intifada, for six months, in his third or fourth incarceration. Having grown up under occupation and knowing no other life, and although from a refugee background, he was now working to change Palestinian nationalist thought. Abu Ayyash perceived a situation in which

> We were slaves of our own slogans, that we had ourselves created. . . . We, the Palestinians, were not using the language of the world; it was a totally different language that we had created for ourselves, as if we had closed the door and were singing inside a closed room with no audience, no one hearing you, and you think that you are the best singer on earth. . . .[78]

He and others who were writing during the 1980s were speaking to a worldview that Ziad Abu Zayyad explained thus: "Palestinians have been living with the dream of turning the clock back to the pre-1948 situation, in other words, returning to the land and homes which were taken from them during the 1948 war and from which they were uprooted and driven away. They were not ready to accept the new reality. . . . For them, Israel as a state did not exist, and Palestinian literature from 1948 onward referred to it as the 'Zionist enemy,' or the 'invading enemy,' and Palestine was the 'robbed' or 'raped' homeland."[79] For Abu Ayyash, however, armed struggle held no attraction and the choice was clear:

> [T]he best way would be to find reconciliation. . . . I began to work on this concept. Many Palestinians said, "How come you believe in coexistence between Israelis and Palestinians? They are not going to be faithful." I said, "Yes, enemies can be friends. They need time." . . . I began to take the Israeli journalists, my colleagues, into the Palestinian refugee camps . . . in the late 1970s and early 1980s.[80]

In 1990, Abu Ayyash states, he went alone to West Jerusalem to meet secretly with Labor leader Shimon Peres, then out of power, at the behest of Peres, although he first informed Arafat. By his account, Abu Ayyash told Peres,

> We are soldiers for our people—but not by weapons. We are soldiers of pens, pictures, images, and dreams. . . . Before you built something called Israel, you were the Palmach, Irgun Zvai Leumi, and the Stern Gang—you were all terrorist organizations. If you are defining the word *terrorist*, you

will not reach any solution. Enemies can make peace; friends don't need to make peace because they are friends. Only enemies can make it.[81]

He, like Abu Zayyad, would again be arrested for involvement in the uprising in November 1990.[82] Abu Ayyash would later find himself at the helm of Palestinian television broadcasting, in Ramallah.

The 1987 uprising would bring "new questions, new ideas, new cadres . . . new forms of struggle. . . . a new ethos . . . a new language."[83] The language of the intifada would reshape the discourses of the Palestine-Israel conflict.

The Right of Return: Undergirding a Palestinian State

Sari Nusseibeh: Possibilities and Actuality

Sari Nusseibeh studied at St. George's preparatory school in East Jerusalem, and in Britain when his father, Anwar, was ambassador from the Hashemite Kingdom of Jordan to the Court of St. James.[84] His mother, Nuzha, was from Ramleh, in the central plains of what is now the heartland of Israel, where her father's property was confiscated by the British, against whom he was resisting. In the centuries since Saladin's recapture of Jerusalem on October 1, 1187, and its return to Muslim control, members of the extended Nusseibeh clan—among Jerusalem's oldest—have been the traditional custodians of the keys to the Church of the Holy Sepulchre.[85] This arrangement, whereby a Muslim family opens the massive doors to the church the night before Easter, sidestepped the problem of feuding between the Christian orders over which of them should take precedence in opening the locks.

Nusseibeh studied politics, philosophy, and economics at Christ Church, University of Oxford, from 1968 until he received his undergraduate degree in 1971. During his last year at Oxford, he began studying with A. I. Sabra, then of the Warburg Institute at the University of London. The Mutazilite school of theology fascinated him, with its preoccupations with rationalism, human responsibility, and freedom. "God being just, God also treats human beings with justice, which leads to the adoption of a theory of human responsibility. . . a rationalist theory. Dominant and popular to begin with, this school of theology was eventually cast out from Islamic society and was marginalized as mainstream theological schools came to replace them."[86]

Sabra, a student of the philosopher of natural and social science Karl Popper, was concerned with perception and theories of light, issues straddling physics and philosophy. Having moved to Harvard's history of science department, Sabra invited Nusseibeh to Harvard, an invitation joined in by Muhsin Mahdi of the Center for Middle East Studies, a student of political philosophy under Leo Strauss at the University of Chicago.

Nusseibeh's doctoral dissertation examined the philosophical system of the Islamic scholar Avicenna (Ibn Sina), and his reconciliation of possibility and actuality. Attracted by Avicenna, he studied his works on physics, logic, and language: "I tried to unravel his system, in which he attempted to reconcile on the one hand the universe of possibilities and, on the other hand, the actuality."[87]

In 1978, Nusseibeh received a doctorate in philosophy from Harvard University. Upon returning to Jerusalem and reluctantly reinvolving himself in political activism, he pondered why things were the way they were when the possibilities were unlimited. He probed the balancing of what is with what might be. By the early 1980s, he was centrally involved in the student and faculty movements in resisting Military Orders 854 and 947. He recalled steep incongruities:

> As the head of the faculty, I needed to approve political statements. I would look at the drafted statements and towards the end I would see a slogan. . . I would ask the person who had brought the draft to me, "What do you mean by this word *unconditionally?*" They would tell me, "*Unconditionally* means that we don't negotiate on this point." I would say that you cannot expect things to come up just by blowing a pipe. That was when I started to really look at our political positions and wonder whether they were properly constituted.[88]

The rising influence of academically-based individuals in the widening debate in East Jerusalem was linked to the standing of the faculty and student unions, which had become centers of power in the occupied territories after the Lebanon war in 1982, and throughout the student struggles of the 1980s. Israel's 1982 suppression of publicly pro-PLO Palestinian leadership had also resulted in a political void, which had the effect of enhancing the youth and student groups into becoming the dominant political force in the territories.[89] Nusseibeh recollected:

> Faculty unions were dependent on the system of the university. . .
> Al-Najah University had put together the employees and the faculty into

one organization and called it the Union of the Faculty and Employees. . . .
[I]nstrumental in doing that at al-Najah was the mathematician Adnan
Idris. I was at Bir Zeit and, through my connections with him, . . . we dismantled [our own associations], liberated them from their dependence on
the administration of the university, created a union—now a chapter of a
faculty and staff union throughout Palestinian universities. . . . Very quickly
we had a major organization throughout the higher-learning institutes, but
we didn't stop at that. We created a coordinating committee with the
teacher associations in the various schools in the West Bank and Gaza. . . .
[All] schools were linked to a coordinating committee of the faculty and
staff of the universities. The heart of political activity for the majority of the
active Palestinian political population was [now] in the student system,
the school system, and the university system.[90]

Such was the potency of these movements that in 1985, Nusseibeh had
the effrontery to write that the PLO should exist for the people and "not for
itself," and insist that it was "far worthier to risk the PLO for the chance of
a just political settlement than to risk the chance of a just political settlement
for the PLO."[91]

The Israeli public was first exposed to Nusseibeh's propositions when
he was thirty-six years of age and interviewed for the first time for an Israeli
periodical. On November 13, 1985, in *Koteret Rashit,* the Israeli inter-
viewer Michal Sela asked what the Palestinians would do if they did not get
a state. Nusseibeh's response was that Israel should annex the Palestinians
and give them rights, which would mean their obtaining between twelve
and sixteen seats in the Knesset. If they were not a majority at that time,
he claimed, within ten years the Palestinians would have a demographic
plurality. Asked whether he would prefer being an Israeli or a Palestinian in
a democratic state, Nusseibeh answered, "the ideal for me would be a state
which is Palestinian, democratic, and secular." The interview closed with
the declaration, "If you ask me unequivocally to choose between autonomy
and annexation, I say annex,"[92] rejecting the limbo of "autonomy." In the
interview, Nusseibeh repeated points already argued under his own byline
on October 19, 1985, in the East Jerusalem daily *al-Mawqif* (The
Opinion), of which he had been editor, working with Hanna Siniora, Ziad
Abu Zayyad, and Hebron mayor Mustafa Natsheh.[93] Despite the redun-
dancy of his remarks, the interview created an uproar, so much so that a

newspaper with a Jordanian slant, *al-Nahar* (The Day), claimed "Sari Nus-seibeh wants to become an Israeli soldier!"[94]

In Nusseibeh's writings, literal claims to land or homes granted titles under Ottoman rule, British Mandate, or Jordanian laws were modified from justiciable claims into metaphorical entitlements. Instead of arguing the right of individuals to return to their familial place of abode, he sought an histor-ical option that did not imply doing to the Israelis what had been done to the Palestinians.[95] He advocated a "return" that was neither destructive nor triumphalist. Writing in numerous local Arabic newspapers during the mid-1980s, Nusseibeh capsized conventional wisdom: "Arab strategy since 1948 has been based on the concept of 'regaining' or 'recapturing' land. This has been especially true since 1967. . . . What if Arab strategy were to be reversed? Instead of *returning* land as a tactical aim, what if Arab strategy were to be based on the concept of *returning* to the land?"[96]

Nusseibeh was not denying the need for negotiating the refugee problem that went back to 1947, nor was he overlooking the provisions of UN Gen-eral Assembly Resolution 194, or UN General Assembly Resolution 3236, passed in 1974 and affirming the "inalienable right" of the Palestinians to return to their homes and property. Much as the State of Israel was built on a doctrinal pillar of the right of return for Jews from anywhere in the world, Nusseibeh took a vision of Palestinians returning to mandatory Palestine and reconceptualized it in light of hundreds of villages that no longer existed and the new realities resulting from decades of displacement.[97] To Nusseibeh, "The idea of return should be in our minds—not return to the past . . . to the pre-1948 olive groves—but that *we,* the Palestinians, should return."[98]

Revised views on the right of return were a signpost on the road to the intifada. In thinking about their right to return, he said it was important that Palestinians distinguish between the past and the future: "If they, as a whole people, could not return, the individual could."[99] Still, the implication of persons returning, but not necessarily to their grandparents' house, repre-sented acceptance that the "liberation" of all of Palestine was impossible. The significance of such a position would be grasped by any schoolchild—it meant dropping the claim to the 77 or 78 percent of the land that had been historic Palestine prior to 1948.[100] Nusseibeh espoused no literal counter-part to the Israeli-claimed "right of return," but asked symbolic redress for the Palestinians' alienation from their land.[101] He wrote of the Palestinians as aborigines.[102] He envisioned a three-part system of rights in the "struggle for achieving Palestinian national aspirations," which he defined as existence or survival, repatriation or return, and equality (meaning Palestinian political rights identical to those of their Israeli counterparts). He surmised that obtaining these three categories of entitlements would require three stages of transition over an extended period of time. At the first plateau, human and political rights would be denied; at the second stage, a binational Israeli state would grant some rights; and, in the third, a democratic and secular state could be achieved, as Arabs became a numerical majority. Such a strategy could evolve naturally because of the population trend.[103] If it were not possible to have a contiguous Palestinian state, a strategy for a democratic binational state should be developed. On the basis of the right to exist, right to return, and right to be equal within such a binational state, Palestinians could call for alterations of the Israeli electoral system.[104]

Revising the Right of Return: Citizenship in a Palestinian State Could Substitute for Lost Land

In 1986, Sari Nusseibeh wrote that the Palestinian dilemma was reminiscent of South Africa, with two groups, "one a master group, and another a servant group, entwined together in one political system, which is effectively under the total control of the master group." The demographic threat of the Palestinians to Israel would be a "deterrent to continued occupation" only if combined with the threat of an antiapartheid strategy.[105] Success would come when the Palestinians in the territories decided to challenge the Israeli system in a more powerful way, by basing their national struggle on the South African example as opposed to the Algerian ideal.[106] The Algerian prototype referred to 1962, when Charles de Gaulle conceded independence to the Algerian armed rebels and abandoned France's 130-year old colony. "The Algerian model is one of colonialists: you go against them and get rid of them . . . 'kick the Israelis out.' . . . It's a pre-1948 mentality. . . . The other model is the South Africa model: do not shake off [the Israeli] people, but be yourself, integrate into the system."[107] To Nusseibeh, in the South African example, the indigenous peoples, having lost their ancestral lands to European colonists and become scattered, fight not to return to their original homes and habitats, but to assert their rights within the established institutions and economies of the country. He called for awareness that the Palestinians were living under an apartheid system, and, importantly, it was a configuration that could be changed:

To declare this to be a state of apartheid, and to address the Israeli political structure and the Palestinian problem as such is, in effect, to recast the
continuing reality of the integrative process into a winning strategy for the
Palestinians, a strategy which replaces the existing transitional two-states
program with a transitional program of one binational state on the way to
democratic secularism.[108]

Were it not possible to have the right of return, Nusseibeh suggested
that the Palestinians could demand their rights within Israeli polity—which
would eventually have to conform to them, because they would outnumber
the Israelis.

Nusseibeh warned a few months before the eruption of the intifada that a
disconnection had developed between the psychological and nationalist consciousness of the Palestinians and their economic integration into the Israeli
system, because their incorporation was happening without their being granted
accompanying rights. Either Palestinian behavior should conform to a nationalist strategy, or the nationalist strategy should coincide with reality, he contended. If Palestinian nationalism were expressed in behavior, "What we should
be finding is a reality of civil disobedience, of burnt ID cards, of abstention
from the payment of taxes."[109] Nusseibeh had first heard of the concept of
noncooperation while at Oxford. Later, when studying at Harvard, he visited
Walden Pond, the Massachusetts site of Henry David Thoreau's two-year
return to nature that embodied his withdrawal of support from the U.S. government for its acquiescence on slavery. Nusseibeh's first serious contemplation
on civil disobedience, however, was prompted by mathematics professor Adnan
Idris. In 1979, while teaching at al-Najah University, Idris wrote and circulated
a paper about the applicability of civil disobedience for the Palestinians living
under military occupation.[110] Four years later, in 1983, Bir Zeit professor
Musa Budeiri invited Mubarak Awad to speak to the cultural-studies faculty at
the university concerning nonviolent sanctions, and Nusseibeh attended.[111]

Key Palestinian thinkers around East Jerusalem were thus pressing for
political and economic involvement within the structures of the occupying
state, along with employment of nonviolent struggle, as the most effective ways
to obtain basic rights. Nusseibeh's arguments were addressed to all strata of the
society: you return yourself, participate politically in fighting for equal rights,
and reveal to the outside world a system in which people of Arab descent are
denied rights, despite their economic attractiveness in the Israeli system.[112]

Such thinking was manifested in June 1987, prior to the start of the intifada, when Hanna Siniora proposed to head a Palestinian list in the November municipal elections in Jerusalem—an idea attributed to Nusseibeh—stating: "This does not mean we relinquish sovereignty over East Jerusalem. I believe Jerusalem should be an undivided city with dual sovereignty, the capital of both a Palestinian state and of Israel."[113] In Israel, Siniora's statement was received as "revolutionary."[114] Yehuda Litani wrote in the *Jerusalem Post* that Siniora's step had showed the willingness in East Jerusalem "to give up the armed struggle," but was also a warning that since Israel had annexed East Jerusalem, Palestinians could start using electoral powers against annexation.[115] Litani observed:

> For the past 20 years Palestinians in the territories and East Jerusalem have called for either an armed struggle against Israel or a peace process involving the superpowers, the Arab states and the PLO. For the first time since June 1967 a resident of East Jerusalem, a Palestinian leader belonging to the PLO, is calling on his people to participate in the political process within the Israeli establishment.[116]

The prospect of seeking rights within the institutionalized political context of the Israeli system eventually proved too great a leap, however, and Siniora withdrew because of local Palestinian opposition to his bid. He later reflected on his original purpose,

> I tried, as a nonviolent approach, to have a say-so in the affairs of Jerusalem and called for participation in the municipal elections. I told the Palestinian public that local elections were different from national elections and, by taking action on the local level, we could prevent the expansion of Israeli settlements in the heart of Jerusalem. The perception—I believe it is a wrong perception—was that participation in local elections would mean endangering our political rights in East Jerusalem. . . . Some still believe that participation in local elections will weaken our position and claim over Jerusalem.[117]

In Helena Cobban's view, receptivity for application of the broad principles of human rights—including the freedom to develop and take charge of nongovernmental and human rights organizations—was probably more advanced by the mid-1980s among Palestinians than had been the case a decade earlier during the mid-1970s in the Soviet-bloc countries of Eastern Europe.[118] Nusseibeh's writings indicate such a hunt for a realistic system of thought for fulfilling Palestinian aspirations for human rights.

Accompanying the ferment in political thought in East Jerusalem was an upsurge of international Palestinian debate, as academicians such as Ibrahim Abu-Lughod, Rashid Khalidi, Walid Khalidi, Fouad Moughrabi, and Edward W. Said added their collateral thinking from the diaspora. A revolution in communications technologies was also underway, as television and global newspaper reports lessened the invisibility of the Palestinian problem. Telexes, and later fax machines, sped the flow of information.[119]

Willingness to compromise on the legal configurations for Jerusalem also suggested the new thinking in the city's eastern, Arab section. Looking forward one year into the intifada, this would become evident when Feisel Husseini would be released from prison on January 29, 1989. Once home, he reported to callers that while imprisoned he had conversations with Shmuel Goren, Israeli coordinator for the territories, in which he had discussed the Palestinians' right of return and the protection of Jerusalem as the capital of a future Palestinian state. The issue of the status of the city of Jerusalem could be solved by "either the return or arbitration," Husseini said, referring to a right of return, so long as it remained "one city and the capital of both countries." Some losses are so painful, he evidently told Goren, such as the April 1948 Israeli massacre at Deir Yassin, that the "hurt can only be healed if it is rebuilt and its people allowed to live there."[120]

The right of return and a two-state solution, in which Israel would be accepted, were linked. "The very idea behind creating the state is the establishment of a homeland where the Palestinian people can feel secure," Husseini said; "any Palestinian who lives in exile who wants to come to the Palestinian state . . . must be able to do so."[121] Husseini later addressed Jewish sympathizers of the Israeli peace camp in the United States:

> We are a people without a land, a people without a state. Any status which resolves only the problems of the inhabitants of the occupied territories is not a solution of the Palestinian issue; the Palestinians abroad would remain refugees, whatever their social or financial status. . . . The importance of the Palestinian state is that it would be clear that each and every Palestinian has the right to return to live in that state and to fulfill his

national aspirations within that state. Any other situation will engender more wars.[122]

By revising the right of return, citizenship in a Palestinian state could substitute for lost land.

Thought into Action

In 1977, only three years before Feisel Husseini and Gideon Spiro launched their first joint committee, the PLO's Dr. Isam Sartawi, a heart surgeon educated in the United States who had advocated recognition of Israel and had contacts with Israeli peace groups, was assassinated in Lisbon by a gunman sent by the notorious terrorist Abu Nidal, who was not associated with the PLO. Sartawi had suggested to Austrian chancellor Bruno Kreisky that the return of the West Bank and Gaza could translate into a state of nonbelligerency between a future Palestinian state and Israel so long as settlement could be reached on the "right of Palestinian refugees to return to their original homes, if they wished to do so, or to be compensated if they freely elected not to return."[123] Less than a year later, in London on January 4, 1978, Said Hamammi, Fateh member and PLO representative in London, another pioneer of dialogue with Israel, was also assassinated by Palestinians. He had suggested in *The Times* of London in 1973 that Palestinian Arabs believed in a binational state in which they could live together with Israeli Jews, called for mutual recognition between the two parties, and sought a peace conference.[124] In 1976, MK (member of the Knesset) Uri Avnery, editor of *Haolam Hazeh* (This World), helped found the Israeli Council for Israeli-Palestinian Peace and began efforts at dialogue with PLO figures, a stance that he has consistently maintained ever since.[125]

Dialogues between Arabs and Israelis under third-party academic or remote neutral auspices began to make their mark. Having remained involved with the faculty union and student movement until 1982 or 1983, Nusseibeh was invited to such a conference at Harvard University by professor Herbert Kellman. Soon after, he attended a meeting in Jerusalem, organized by representatives from the Israeli party Meretz.

> I made a decision that if I wanted to go on with politics, then the student movement, Bir Zeit, and the small uprisings against the occupation . . . were not enough, and I had to start being engaged in dialogue. . . . My

constituency was dead set against talking with Zionists, and I couldn't do it as the head of a union. So I severed my relationship with my constituency and union, and started on a long journey of open dialogue with the Israelis—whether in Israel or abroad. . . . I had become convinced that, on the one hand, we were powerful as a people, but, on the other hand, we needed to find out what the other side was prepared to give us. Negotiations were, therefore, necessary.[126]

By the early 1980s, Husseini and Nusseibeh were having periodic discussions with Israeli intellectuals and some government officials,[127] but these did not surface publicly until 1987. In April of that year, Nusseibeh was physically attacked by Bir Zeit students, following the revelation of his contacts with Moshe Amirav, a member of the Likud central committee:

The people who were involved in the beating were all actually Fateh people. Most of them afterwards came and apologized to me. . . . In the pro-Fateh group, there were internal schisms between . . . the Gaza and West Bank groups, and within the West Bank, there were different schisms. A lot of them were brought up to believe in the ideology of armed struggle in Fateh, so they were not happy about people like me talking about reconciliation, dialogue, and negotiations in the name of Fateh, . . . just as a lot of people weren't happy with Arafat when he spoke like this. Some said, "they didn't really beat Sari up, they beat Arafat up"—a radical message to Arafat that he shouldn't go too far. . . . Within the organization you work on instructions. These guys got an instruction.[128]

After the attack, the Bir Zeit University employees' union asked that Nusseibeh be dismissed from his academic post because he had also met with Israeli prime minister Shimon Peres.[129]

By July 1987, "back channel" talks began between Moshe Amirav and Nusseibeh, Feisel Husseini, and Salah Zuhaika, an editor of *al-Shab,* to discuss interim arrangements for broad self-rule for the Palestinians.[130] They were preparing the groundwork for discussions between prime minister Yitzhak Shamir, then heading a National Unity government, and chairman Arafat.[131] According to Nusseibeh, Shamir probably surmised that the Palestinians would reject talks, but Amirav took the position that negotiations were not possible without the PLO. The first of more than a dozen meetings that summer between Amirav, a seasoned member of Likud's Herut wing, and Husseini and Nusseibeh, took place at Nusseibeh's home.[132] Amirav also persuaded Knesset members Dan Meridor and Ehud Olmert, who would become future ministers in a Shamir government (Olmert would become prime minister nearly two decades later), to join some sessions.[133] On August 26, 1987, a memorandum was drafted, but not signed, in which Likud agreed to recognize the PLO and negotiate the establishment of a "Palestinian entity" whose "administrative" capital would be in Arab East Jerusalem. A planned meeting in Geneva between Amirav and Arafat, however, never occurred.

Everything fell apart as Husseini was once again arrested, and Amirav was expelled from the Likud party in 1988 by Shamir for his reformist views.[134] Zeev Schiff and Ehud Yaari call the episode a failure, a "naive effort" to bridge the gap between Likud and the PLO, and contend that Husseini and Nusseibeh learned that they were better off making unilateral moves.[135] To the contrary, the lasting significance of the aborted effort for Husseini and Nusseibeh was a deepened conviction about the necessity for direct negotiations. As Husseini put it, "It was as if these people were hearing our positions for the first time; they were surprised at what we said, which was the opposite of what they had been told by their leaders."[136]

The genesis for these particular Israeli contacts resulted from relationships established by Husseini, while in prison, with leftist political parties such as Ratz and Mapam. Through them, he had learned that Israeli politicians wanted to meet with him, including Amirav.[137] Nusseibeh and Husseini worked together closely, with concurrence from the PLO in Tunis. Nusseibeh recalled,

> I wanted to make sure that not only Abu Jihad was in favor, or Abu Ammar [Yasir Arafat] wanted it, but that people here [in the territories] were on my side. In the years before, I had learned the terrain quite well. I knew exactly where everybody was and how everything had to happen. So I made sure that I did not do anything with Amirav without coordination at every level.[138]

The elaborate synchronization and numerous sessions that occurred were not the result of personal interest, Husseini said, but "a Palestinian decision to explain our political positions to all Israeli political elements."[139]

Contact with Israelis—from the Ratz and Mapam parties on the left to Shinui on the right—affected the Palestinian activist intellectuals' thinking, if only to give them a sense of what might be accomplished through a negotiated settlement. The outlook of Palestinians inside the occupied territories was changing, affected by factors such as increased access to education, the study of Hebrew, and contacts with a more democratic and assertive society. Jordanian rule, for example, became unthinkable.[140] The changes occurring among the Palestinians were more profound than those in the Israeli community, Abu Ayyash mused.[141]

The "Fourteen Points

The cumulative effect of the new political thinking is corroborated by a document released at a press conference in East Jerusalem on January 14, 1988, almost five weeks after the initial outpouring of the first intifada. A list of demands was released, grouped into fourteen clauses, and presented by Palestinians from the West Bank and Gaza. The document has come to be known as the "Fourteen Points by Palestinian Personalities."[142] Among those stepping forward to issue it were Hanna Siniora, Hebron mayor Mustafa Natsheh, acting president of Bir Zeit University Gabi Baramki, Mubarak Awad, Jonathan Kuttab, and Sari Nusseibeh, who drafted this and other key documents.[143]

The Fourteen Points call for the convening of an international peace conference with the PLO acting as the sole legitimate representative of the Palestinian people at the convocation. The document lists fourteen demands for Israeli compliance prior to the commencement of the conference, in order to create an atmosphere of equality and also implying recognition of the national rights of the Palestinian people, including self-determination and the "establishment of an independent Palestinian state on Palestinian national soil."[144] Mentioning a renewed spirit, the document concludes that the occupation under which Palestinians lived is unnatural and would come to an end. No allusion was intended to U.S. president Woodrow Wilson's January 8, 1918 "Fourteen Points."[145] The fourteen demands speak to issues of military occupation, such as the need to abide by world conventions on human rights, including those concerning deportations, prisoners, imprisonment, actions by Israeli settlers and soldiers, and rights of political freedom; lift the "siege" of the refugee camps; cessation of settlement activity and confiscation of Palestinian land; the necessity to allow free movement of products from the occupied territories; and removing restrictions on political contacts between inhabitants in the territories and the PLO, to allow participation in the Palestine National Council and direct input into the making of decisions by the PLO.[146]

In Washington on January 27, 1988, Hanna Siniora and Gaza lawyer Fayez Abu Rahme delivered the Fourteen Points to Secretary of State George P. Shultz.[147] The Palestinians who signed the Fourteen Points were a few months later denounced as not speaking for constituencies, not representing the broad Palestinian spectrum, for supporting Fateh to the exclusion of other factions, and for being available to meet with anyone. Specifically singled out for castigation were Nusseibeh, Siniora, Abu Rahme,[148] and Natsheh as self-appointed, opportunistic, pro-PLO and pro-Jordanian mouthpieces, who raised the "art of political accommodation to new heights" and whose "contacts with parties perceived as enemies actually undercut any popular nationalist support they might nurture."[149] Doubtless, far more criticism was voiced than published.

The "Husseini Document"

The Israeli Knesset on June 27, 1967, had unilaterally extended "Israeli law, jurisdiction, and public administration over the entire area of the Land of Israel" creating a pretext for any subsequent Israeli determinations in the eastern portions of Jerusalem. Israeli civil law, rather than military order, was applied to the 70-square-kilometer (roughly 200-square-mile) area east of the 1948 armistice line,[150] so Palestinians resident in East Jerusalem were technically not under military occupation. This form of de facto annexation has still not been recognized by any of the world's sovereign states, all of which view this section of East Jerusalem as under occupation[151]—part of the West Bank—and insist that Israel must abide by international law governing occupying powers.[152] The legal status of Palestinians living under annexation in East Jerusalem and its environs mimicked that of Israeli Palestinians in Israel proper, who possessed more freedoms than those under military occupation or annexation, except that their citizenship and passports remained Jordanian. Consequently emergency laws were instituted to deny Palestinians freedom of the press, and onerous Israeli censorship, administrative detention, the closing of newspapers, and deportation of Palestinian journalists accompanied annexation.[153]

Palestinian reporters in East Jerusalem had initially thought they would be able to operate with freedoms unknown in the rest of the Arab world.

Some Israeli laws did bring benefits to journalists and publishers in Arab East Jerusalem which, while not exaggerating their scope, were both timely and helpful for those redefining what it meant to be a Palestinian. A few initially desired a Jerusalem identity card, because they thought East Jerusalemites would gain special treatment in any subsequent peace treaty under UN supervision, as envisioned in the 1947 partition plan. They came to view annexation as a liability, however, when emergency measures such as six-month administrative detentions supplanted the original forty-eight-hour administrative detentions. Even their Israeli number plates on their automobiles became a problem for them when traveling in the West Bank and Gaza.[154]

Feisel Husseini made a self-deprecating claim that his status as a Palestinian living in East Jerusalem meant that he had less to fear from being politically outspoken: "I carry a Jerusalem identity card, they can't deport me, which has enabled me to speak out more forcefully and to work more actively in the field than others; the price of my positions cannot be more than administrative detention or prison."[155] Orders for Husseini's house arrest by day and town arrest by night stood without change for five years, until the Israelis began to imprison him under administrative detention procedures.[156] Beginning in 1982, when the predecessors to the Committee Confronting the Iron Fist came into view, Husseini was often held under Israeli emergency provisions that allow detention without charges or trial proceedings. When he was arrested in April 1987, nine months prior to the outbreak of the intifada, numerous documents were confiscated from his office and lodgings at Orient House, home to the Arab Studies Society. On August 31, 1987, Husseini was arrested again. More papers were taken. One year later, eight months into the first intifada, at two A.M. on July 31, 1988—the same day that King Hussein announced the severing of ties between Jordan and the West Bank, and the demise of the so-called Jordanian option—Husseini was rearrested.[157] Among the documents confiscated this time from Orient House was one referred to as the "Husseini Document."

The Husseini Document is an outline providing for the declaration of independence of a Palestinian state that takes for granted that the state of Palestine has already been formed through the momentum of the popular uprising of the intifada. At its core is the stated objective of moving the conflict from one of throwing stones to one of diplomatic negotiations held on an equal footing with the Israelis. Leadership and administrative bodies are addressed along with steps to be taken toward each. Basic to the declaration is an understanding that it is creating "a Palestinian state in the homeland," not a government in exile. An essential precept is that the Palestinian people would create this state rather than waiting for outside assistance: "our people . . . hold the reins of the initiative"; neither Israel, the Arab nations, nor the world community would have a "way out of dealing with this reality created by the uprising." Basic points include guidelines for geographic boundaries; executives of state, legislative, and administrative bodies; and negotiations on such issues as water, Israeli settlements, and the right of return for refugees.[158]

On August 6, 1988, Israeli authorities leaked to the news media what they said appeared to be a secret draft declaration of Palestinian independence.[159] Nusseibeh was quoted the following day:

> The Palestinians should now use the King's [Hussein] speech to push one step further. The PLO can turn its offices around the world into embassies, and we can turn the underground committees here into ministries for health, education and municipal services. Having declared a state in the West Bank, we should then offer to negotiate with our neighbors—Israel and Jordan—the exact nature of relations.[160]

An Israeli journalist pointed out that what Nusseibeh had said was "strikingly similar" to the draft declaration, and that the ideas in the seized working paper had been circulating in Palestinian circles there for some time:

> The idea of declaring an independent state is part of a broader effort by Palestinian nationalist intellectuals to give new meaning to the uprising in the territories, to translate it into a political language which will win both international gains and sympathy in Israel. The idea is to confound Israel diplomatically, divide its public opinion. . . . The declaration, like the uprising, is a creation of the Palestinians in the territories.[161]

The document that had been appropriated from Husseini's house was indeed the first draft of a declaration of Palestinian independence, written not by Husseini but by Nusseibeh.[162] "Sari came to my house and gave it to me to review, but before I could read it or respond, the Israelis arrested me and seized it. I did not learn what was in it until I was in jail, and was surprised to hear about a paper named after me while watching television."[163] Why did the Israeli authorities name the confiscated document after him? Husseini's supposition: "Many Israelis had started viewing me as a moderate. The authorities knew that *Israelis* would start to demonstrate against my arrest. So they were trying to pull the rug out from under Israeli activists by reading the document on TV and calling it the Husseini Document."[164]

The ideas put forward by these intellectuals and activists included the expectation of popular mass participation in determining the political direction of the Palestinian people and the notion that through their own actions they could create a necessary compromise with Israel. As they redefined the meaning of the Palestinian "nation," they were also building the postulate that the Palestinian people living in the fraction of what remained of historic Palestine would be the ones to bring about change, rather than those leading from the diaspora. This was "part and parcel of the intifada strategy."[165]

The "Jerusalem Paper"

Once the intifada began, a document circulated that helps to explain how the Palestinian challenge to military occupation was diverted for more than two years from its inveterate rubric of armed struggle to nonmilitary civilian strategies. Any account of the transition represented by the first intifada should reference the "Jerusalem Paper," also called the "Jerusalem Document," or "al-Quds Paper." Its working draft is dated February 8, 1988, two months after the uprising broke.[166] The preamble declares,

> It is necessary to move the state of the intifada from the stage of strikes, demonstrations, and confrontations with the occupation authority to a new phase of quasi-separation from the system of occupation, in preparation for the proclamation of independence of the Palestinian people living on Palestinian lands in the West Bank and Gaza Strip. . . . The phase we have in mind is the one which the masses of the occupied land had created with their own will: the appropriate objective background for the proclamation of independence and the building of the state.[167]

The document represents shared viewpoints across a spectrum of Palestinian political parties and factions—with reservations from some tendencies.[168] Produced as a working paper from discussions within Fateh in East Jerusalem and the territories, consultations then took place with the other factions.[169] Once agreement was secured, particularly from the communist party and the Democratic Front for the Liberation of Palestine (DFLP), Sari Nusseibeh faxed[170] the document to Abu Jihad in Tunis, via the East Jerusalemites' pre-arranged intermediary in Paris, Muhammad Rabaia, nom de guerre Abu Tariq.[171] Having first circulated among formal Fateh circles in Ramallah and East Jerusalem, Abu Jihad "fine-tuned" it and subsequently promulgated it as a Fateh directive.[172] Concerning what he considers two major "landmarks" of the intifada—the Jerusalem Paper and the Husseini Document—Nusseibeh describes this paper as "the backbone of the strategy of the *intifada*."[173] Regarding the connections between the three documents, he recalled:

> The Fourteen Points were an outward manifestation of what was being dis-cussed and formed internally and would come out as the Jerusalem Paper, both drafted by the same person—me. They were not so much my writing as an articulation of what was going on. The Husseini Document was at the end of the same process as the Fourteen Points and the Jerusalem Paper. . . . My contribution was the articulation of what was going on inside [Fateh].[174]

The key idea the document expresses is that the population of the occu-pied territories could disengage itself from the occupying authorities through a number of steps preparatory to declaring independence. In ascending order, linked to the seriousness of the penalties to be expected in return, the document calls for a progression of nonviolent action steps moving from methods of protest or persuasion, such as conferences, marches, sit-ins, and demonstrations, to more severely punishable methods of noncooperation, such as strikes and boycotts, and finally proceeding to nonviolent interventions, such as refusal to submit to Israeli bureaucracy—in the form of disobeying orders, resigning from jobs, withholding taxes and payments for water and electricity—establishing underground printing presses, and most serious, burning the identity cards that were obligatory to pass through Israeli checkpoints. The document states an intention to strip the Israeli occupation of its "benevolent" face and arouse the inter-national community to "carry out its responsibilities in compelling Israel to recognize the rights of Palestinians to live in freedom in their own inde-pendent state."

Calling for the intifada, at the time two months old, to move to a new stage of civilian resistance, the paper suggests that the uprising must focus on a political process with stipulated targets. It argues that the mass movement cannot remain effective if it stays within the realm of strikes and demonstrations. At the same time, the people of the occupied territories would not gain anything by terminating the uprising, therefore, escalation offers the most promising path for independence. The document highlights responsibilities the Palestinians should be ready to assume in order to proclaim themselves an independent state. In its most significant passage, it contends that the military occupation functions with the implied consent of the Palestinians. Through refusal to cooperate, Palestinians in the occupied territories could withdraw their concurrence from the occupation, and once disengaged, the "only relationships left are those based on Israeli coercion, subjugation, and force." The document says that Palestinians should be prepared for hardships arising from such a severing of relations with the military authorities. Citizens could lose jobs, have their electricity cut off, or experience shortages of goods. Those living in the territories would need to understand and prepare for tribulations, and once such a path was embarked upon, there would be no turning back—because the situation would forever be altered.

The text specifies that there must be a balance between protesting occupation and harming the Palestinian community; therefore provision should be made for the people of the West Bank and Gaza Strip to support themselves and provide for their families. Acts of civil disobedience should be planned and coordinated by a committee of leaders to monitor the effects of the struggle on the community, and it would be vital for popular committees to be organized to inform the community about civil disobedience as well as to help in the creation and functioning of a Palestinian state. Most important for the intifada and the stepped-up phase advocated by the document would be the Palestinians themselves, as it would be only through their determination and fortitude that the uprising could continue until independence:

> The Jerusalem Paper is a program—a civil-disobedience program. If you read it today, it is elliptical, cryptic, but it has in it the seeds of both a beginning and an end—the initiation of a civil disobedience program leading eventually to a declaration of independence and, thereafter, negotiations with Israel. It was an attempt to politicize a mass movement.[175]

"Much of the strategy of the intifada leadership, the gradual step-by-step evolution, was actually an implementation, or partial implementation, of that paper," Nusseibeh recalled. "From the point of view of Fateh, we have clear evidence that there was a coherent, purposeful, holistic strategy, reaching out to the day of independence."[176]

Thus, in one of the seminal documents of the intifada, the term *armed struggle* does not appear.[177] Each action method is historically recognizable from a world body of nonviolent strategic action that might have been used in almost any country or any century. The paper shows a grasp of the properties of nonviolent resistance and its powers when applied to change the behavior and outlook of the target group. Inherent was the idea that military occupation was a web of contact points between occupier and occupied, the great majority of which were sustained by the implied submission of the occupied, and only a small proportion of which were based on force. To end the occupation, one had to change the state of submission, largely by cutting off the points of exchange maintained by the occupied, thereby revealing to the international community in clear form the force used by the occupier. This had been the strategy used against Military Order 854.

Evolutions in Thinking inside the Palestinian Territories

The twenty-year process of civilian mobilization after 1967 built the capacity for a mass movement, but the political contours of the coming intifada were shaped by the ferment of ideas and action from Arab East Jerusalem. With ideas cross-fertilized by education abroad, increasing awareness of other popular struggles, contact with Israeli sympathizers, and the stimulus from scholarship on nonviolent struggle, human agency was instrumental in preparing the groundwork through development of a new orientation on the assertion of Palestinian rights. Publishing in Hebrew and English was for purposes of reaching Israelis and the international community with news on the new conceptualizations. These included the imagining of Israeli-Palestinian solidarity in which what was forgotten was as important as what was remembered, and the occupation was recognized as degrading Israelis as well as Palestinians. The reimagining of a coexisting Palestine was later expressed by Nusseibeh: "The Palestinians and Israelis, living side by side as equals, not as occupier and occupied, each in their own state, can contribute far more to themselves and to the world at large than either of them can ever do as long as the sense of injustice prevails."[178]

The conceptual alterations represented by the Fourteen Points, the declaration of independence articulated in the Husseini Document, and the program outlined in the Jerusalem Paper signaled a turning away from the guerrilla strategies that had produced so little and undermined the political and moral need to resolve the Palestinian issue. Striding away from short-term tactical thinking, the East Jerusalem activist intellectuals sought to transform ideologies and recruitment mythologies of armed struggle by the few into forms of struggle relying on invigoration of the many. The willingness of this epistemic community to invest in elusively political goals, pragmatic advocacy of nonviolent tools, reliance on one's own exertions, and insistence on direct talks also held potential for a sympathetic response within Israel, while at the same time their longer-term strategies of building a state were being crystallized by the ongoing formation of civil society committees. The advocacy by the activist intellectuals of direct negotiations with the Israelis strategically affected the choice of nonviolent means of struggle. The growth of ideas on legitimizing rights and throwing off occupation—by bringing Palestinian grievances face to face with widening international norms on human rights—was accompanied by a doctrine of popular participation, manifesting a belief that the political fate of the Palestinians rested with themselves, and that they could, through their own exertions, create the compromises required to live side by side with Israel.

Chapter 9

The Intifada, or "Shaking Off"

"No Voice Rises above the Voice of the Uprising"

In spring 1987, the Israeli military detained scores of Palestinians without charge, closed universities, increased deportations, and shot unarmed students (one fatally), making that year one of the harshest in the two decades of occupation.[1] At Bir Zeit University in April, Israeli soldiers shot and killed a business student and wounded others when they came to the aid of two soldiers who had been cornered by protesters throwing rocks.[2] The incidents followed the death of Ofra Moses, a pregnant Jewish woman whose car had been firebombed at an Israeli settlement near Kfar Sava.[3] Friends and neighbors of the Moses family, plus other settlers, rampaged, destroying cars and damaging homes in Qalqiliya, a nearby West Bank Palestinian town. By summer, Palestinian prisoners held in Israeli jails had begun a three-week hunger strike to demand improved jail conditions. The strikers were among 4,000 Palestinians seeking recognition as political prisoners rather than as criminals.[4] Their protest triggered demonstrations among the 800,000 Palestinians under Israeli military rule on the West Bank and the 500,000 in the Gaza Strip.

The territories-wide intifada was sparked by the aforementioned December 9, 1987, collision of an Israeli truck with two vehicles carrying four Gazan laborers, who were waiting to pass through an army roadblock after a day's work in Israel. Four were killed and seven others injured. Four thousand mourners turned out for the funeral for three of those killed. Israeli claims that the crash was an accident were disregarded, as rumors swelled among the Palestinians that the deaths were in reprisal for the murder the preceding day of an Israeli in Gaza City. By the following day, barricades of burning tires spewed smoke over much of Gaza. Demonstrations poured from the Jabaliya refugee camp, where young Palestinians pelted with stones the IDF troops that arrived on the scene.

As apparently spontaneous protests by Palestinians broke out across the occupied territories, in Gaza, 35,000 Palestinians turned out for a funeral in Khan Yunis. Human walls of thousands obstructed roads, hindering Israeli army movements. Shoulder to shoulder in the line of fire, they advanced toward the soldiers while throwing stones, despite the tear gas, arms, and rubber-coated bullets used against them. By the first of January, 1988, the IDF had more troops in the territories than it took to capture them in 1967.[5] Weeks later, young unarmed Palestinians announced that they had "liberated" some areas and had taken control.[6]

Harmonization could soon be discerned, when action methods appeared in simultaneous use across the geographically separated West Bank and Gaza Strip that Palestinians could traverse only by crossing Israeli land, with no safe or simple passage. Syncopated events were occurring in dispersed communities.

The four deaths represented the low point in a series of occurrences that had added to a growing sense of calamity and gall in the Israeli-occupied territories. Evidence of disdain for the Palestinians as a people emanated from the east and the west. An Arab summit held in Amman in November 1987 had sidestepped the Palestinian predicament, while news media reported that U.S. and Soviet presidents Ronald Reagan and Mikhail Gorbachev had failed even to discuss the Israeli-Palestinian conflict during a summit in Washington.[7]

On November 25, shortly before the deaths at the Gaza checkpoint, a guerrilla from Ahmad Jabril's Popular Front for the Liberation of Palestine–General Command (PFLP–GC) had crossed from Lebanon into Israel by motorized hang glider. Landing at an Israeli military post, he killed six soldiers and wounded seven others before being shot dead. During the fourteen months prior to the start of the uprising, the radical revivalist Islamic Jihad organization had similarly carried out a series of ostentatious strikes in Jerusalem and Gaza, including one in which commandos wounded seventy Israeli soldiers. Such acts stirred the Palestinian populace, and their psychological impact was to suggest that the Israelis were not invincible.[8]

"People exploded," said Radwan Abu Ayyash, since by 1987 Likud policies under Prime Minister Yitzhak Shamir had driven Palestinians into despair, turmoil, and anger: "They had to challenge everything—no food, no work, no freedom of thinking, of talking, of moving, nothing—so they said, 'What the hell are we doing? Are we going to die slowly?' . . . The young people were full of despair: no tennis shoes, no playgrounds, no gardens, no books, only roadblocks, check-posts, prisons, torture."[9] Once the intifada erupted, the activist intellectuals and leaders in Palestinian factions began organizing to focus the energies of the populace and put to use the knowledge of non-violent struggle that had been spreading in the territories for years.[10]

The Unified National Leadership Command of the Uprising

Within the first two months of the uprising, Gabi Sheffer, a political scientist at Hebrew University, suggested that the Palestinians had learned a number of lessons from the mistakes of the 1936-39 great revolt. Unlike the earlier turmoil, he notes, the Palestinians proscribed firearms, and civil disobedience paid handsome dividends. They identified long-term goals, avoided violent internal quarrels, and the secret leadership of the uprising shunned the incompetence of a "roof organization" like the Arab Higher Committee of the 1930s with its figureheads.[11]

Local committees took the lead in guiding the uprising.[12] It is safe to say that all had been part of the grassroots mobilization of the 1970s. The success of these small bodies, initially called "support committees" and organized to respond to curfews, Daoud Kuttab writes, "triggered the establishment of a national Command that could continue to supervise donations and distributions," not only to formulate strategy, but to manage the situation so that no outside force could take control.[13] The leaders of innumerable such village support committees have never identified themselves, were not jailed, and may never be known.[14] A month of undirected disturbances passed before the coalescence of the Unified National Leadership Command of the Uprising (al-Qiyada al-Wataniyya al-Muwahhada lil-Intifada), in which representatives designated by Fateh, the Popular Front for the Liberation of Palestine (PFLP), the Democratic Front for the Liberation of Palestine (DFLP), and the Palestinian Communist Party (PCP)—the four main secular-nationalist factions in the occupied territories—began coordinating actions.[15] According to Fateh representative Hatem Abd al-Qader Eid, "All the time, we were four, but if we had something dangerous, and they wanted to be involved, then we would invite one member of Hamas. . . . But Hamas were not normally members of the command."[16] The inclusion of the PCP on a basis equal to that of Fateh testifies to the influence of the numerically small party from 1969 onward, as it led the way in organizing small self-sufficient institutions.

Multiple chronicles explain the origins of the Command. The DFLP regards itself as the prime mover not only in the organization of the intifada, but also in pioneering the formalization of the Command and the programming of the uprising.[17] Some contend that Samir Shehadeh, professor of Arabic literature at Bir Zeit, introduced the idea of a unified leadership group during a chance meeting in Amman with the PLO's Abu Jihad of Fateh, in his role as PLO liaison with the occupied territories.[18] Whenever a major issue had been pending, a meeting would be called of representatives from the four main factions. Informal coordination among the factions antedated the uprising, and after it began, Ghassan Khatib recalled, "coordination became regular and started to be called the unified leadership command of the intifada," such that the leaflets of the uprising bore this name *before* consultations as a formal "command" had actually begun.[19] Fateh was the first to issue leaflets in the West Bank under the name "Unified Leadership Command," but the PCP initially adopted the name in Gaza, with the DFLP later following suit, Khatib said. This convergence gave rise to "unified leaflets," as the notion of a unified leadership became settled.[20]

To the Palestinians, the name "Command" stood for coordination among the factions rather than a chain of command, in contrast to the military cadres' top-down hierarchical structures. Khatib clarified:

> It was not a leadership of persons, but of organizations. . . . Although the highest source of decision making was in the West Bank, there were joint meetings of the Command, many of which took place in Gaza, at the initiative of Dr. Haidar Abd al-Shafi, and in many cases in his house.[21] Representatives came with ideas from their groups, exchanged ideas, agreed on something, and went back to their groups, which started to work accordingly. . . .
>
> Individuals on the Command were not on a high level in their organizations, not even on the second level, but probably on the third level, because they were not meant to be a leadership. The leadership was in the factions and was not involved in the coordination on the Command directly as persons. The other reason for low-level persons was a security reason—it was known that they would be arrested, so instead of destroying the organizations, they "sacrificed" persons whose arrest would not be harmful.[22]

The strengths and the weaknesses of the Command were one and the same. Its multipronged and coalitional nature gave it resiliency, and it was egalitarian in allocating the key factions equal weight. This structure allowed it to survive imprisonments, because as the Israelis detained individual members, the factions appointed other representatives to it. This also made it vulnerable to disputes, mirroring the discordant operating styles that had characterized the Palestinian response to the 1948 war and events of the three decades that followed. Moreover, its egalitarian and representative nature meant that it could not adopt the style of a central, coherent executive body to make decisions on behalf of all factions.[23]

The Command survived at least four waves of arrests by Israel, yet the moment would come when only one of the original members of the Command remained, all others having been incarcerated.[24] Sari Nusseibeh maintained that the Israelis always left one representative from the preceding group as "a hook," therefore having at least one person whose activities they could watch who had straddled the previous and the current Command.[25] The ceaseless interruption of arrests helps explain the wide variations in the experiences and perspectives of those who served on the Command. For example, Fateh representative Abd al-Fatth Hamayl could not recollect a single face-to-face session of all four representatives. Instead, during his tenure, it "met" every two days without actually sitting, and its members sometimes did not know each other. "It was like a circle," said Hamayl, describing an arrangement in which the four representatives consulted two-by-two sequentially.[26] Other representatives, however, remember meeting continuously. Eid insisted, "We met weekly. . . . We met all the time. . . . If security was not good, the Command did not actually meet; but we were able to meet many times."[27] As the DFLP's Muhammad Jadallah described the process, "You planned something and then met with one of the factions, and then you moved to the second, and so on. In the first few days especially, it was not easy to have joint meetings—it was by lateral contacts."[28]

Following procedures similar to those of the communist cells of the 1950s, the representatives on the Command usually communicated through couriers who went back and forth between the first and second representatives, the second and third representatives, the third and fourth, and back around from the fourth to the first again, relaying the thinking of the others, passing along argumentation until a modicum of agreement had been reached. Debates within the Command thus took place between "faceless interlocutors across the factional fence," as Nusseibeh puts it.[29]

Few Palestinians have ever learned the names of all the persons appointed to the Command of the intifada. Among others, the representatives included former prisoners—who subsequently became students, teachers, or labor organizers—some of whom had associated themselves upon release with the pro-Fateh Shabiba movement.[30]

The activist intellectuals advised the consultations unofficially, without actually serving on the Command. They had revived the word *intifada* deliberately, as a linguistically nonviolent construction because it carries no implication of violence, from its earlier use in the student struggles of the 1980s, where it had begun to replace the confrontational vocabulary of the 1950s and 1960s, which implied ruin, damage, or downfall. *Nafada,* the Arabic verb from which *intifada* derives, expresses recovery or recuperation. The choice of this particular word goes beyond *samud* (steadfastness), the term previously used by Palestinians for the act of resisting by holding fast. *Intifada* is a more active term, one that implies the literal shaking-off of Israeli occupation, like "shaking off dirt from one's sandals."[31] Palestinian scholar Shukri Abed stresses the internal meaning of the word to Palestinians, signifying to tremble, shudder, or jump to one's feet.[32] To Palestinian cultural anthropologist Ali Hussein Qleibo, the term "connotes the removal of unnecessary elements; shaking off preexisting weaknesses, . . . updating and revitalizing the system."[33] The English word *uprising*—the most common translation of *intifada* and the word chosen by English-speaking Palestinians—fails to convey the sense of sloughing off passivity or of newly mobilizing elements in society's leaping to their feet to stand up for themselves. The recent catch-phrase *take back,* as in "take back America" (to work to restore, not destroy) is close to the spirit of *intifada.*[34] *Intifada* is one of the few Arabic words to enter the vocabulary of international politics.[35]

"An entire conceptual revolution was taking place," Nusseibeh wrote at the time, "as committed thinkers, intellectuals and activists sought a way of harnessing the *intifada* to maximize its effects."[36] He later surmised, "The intifada leadership was able to do two things: to translate what was going on into tangible demands, that is, 'we're not going on strike to regain Haifa and Jaffa' (although in the first two weeks anybody would have said that it was to regain Haifa and Jaffa). And two weeks into the intifada, the leadership was able to formulate a coherent political message and to give it the vehicle of civil disobedience, or what I would call the implementation of the 'Jerusalem Paper.' This was an impressive achievement, and it went on for a couple of years."[37]

The Command functioned through an ebb and flow of ideas and tactics. It was, Daoud Kuttab said, "a crucible for the population's ideas rather than a leadership trying to impose its own predetermined ones."[38] This stance reflected the influence of the communists, whose membership ranks swelled once the uprising began. Recognized as a mainline faction in the PLO after the eighteenth PNC in 1987, the communists were influential in their philosophical commitment to a strong role for the decentralized local committees.[39] Especially in the first two years, the Command shared power and direction with the popular committees.[40] It also retained a strong preference for representation that had been directly associated with the civilian mobilization. Such civilian leaders transferred political initiative from the traditional leadership to members of the poorer social strata, who had felt the effects of the occupation, and were now made representatives on the Command and leaders in the popular committees.[41] Its coordination exhibited more democracy than is acknowledged by the PLO, because it was the only way to adjudicate differences between the factions and achieve unity. The Command's most important functions were to move the center of action from one location to another, and to distribute pressure and prevent fatigue by devising different methods for popular dissent.[42]

The Leaflets: A "White Revolution"

The Command carried out its tasks of dispersing activities and innovating action methods through a flow of dated and numbered leaflets. On January 4, 1988, the first leaflet appeared in the Qalandia refugee camp in the West Bank and a few other locations.[43] Qalandia is where Mubarak Awad and Gene Sharp had two years earlier hammered nails into a new youth center while talking with young camp dwellers about the power at the command of ordinary individuals to fight tyranny and defend their way of life.

Although there is some dispute over the numbering, the first leaflet, printed at a shop in Issawiya, near Qalandia, represented the byproduct of an ad hoc agreement between "official" and "unofficial" tendencies in Fateh.[44] Persons in Fateh, in consultation with Sari Nusseibeh, wrote the leaflet without coordinating with the other factions.[45] The next leaflet maintained continuity with the first one, but was written by only one of the two signatories to the first, as the nationalist groups tried to keep pace with the initially impromptu surge of actions in Gaza and offer direction for the popular outpouring that was as massive as it was unfathomable.[46] Local Fateh member Samir Shehadeh, officially involved on behalf of his faction, drafted the third leaflet in consultation with Nusseibeh (speaking unofficially for

Fateh) and the DFLP.[47] As Nusseibeh explained: "The first two leaflets were created in total chaos with no clear policy, strategy, or coordination. . . . Everybody knew there was nobody in control. . . . The Israeli reprisal was so sudden, so intensive, and so quick, that from a security point of view, it was impossible to set up anything of lasting coordinating value to begin with. . . . With the third leaflet, you suddenly have organization. You can tell, because if you look at the first two leaflets, there was no format. Suddenly, with the third leaflet, you begin to have a format, and the format continues throughout two years of uprising."[48] With the third leaflet, the Command started draping the masthead with the proclamation "No Voice Rises above the Voice of the Uprising," and with the mantle of the PLO, at the initiative of the DFLP, according to Muhammad Jadallah, who recalled it as the most important leaflet. More than 100,000 copies were distributed in barely two or three hours in the West Bank and Gaza.[49] IDF forces would three months later close down twenty-one printing plants in Gaza alone in their search for the local printers of the leaflets.[50]

Fateh, the DFLP, and the PFLP—militant factions with origins in ideologies of armed struggle—viewed the leaflets, *nidaat* (appeals), as less directive in tone than *bayan* (manifestos or declarations) that they had traditionally issued to their cadres.[51] The PCP, however, regarded the leaflets as excessively directive in intonation, and as a result, formally withheld its endorsement of the first six enumerated leaflets. Adnan Dagher, a PCP representative, was asked by his party supervisor, Taysir Aruri, a professor at Bir Zeit University, to avoid language that militaristically gave orders.[52] Each faction took responsibility for the distribution of the leaflets to its constituency.[53]

Often contradicting previous statements and sometimes internally illogical, the leaflets, released approximately every two weeks, reveal conflicts between the various leaflet writers. Disagreements about strategies and methods are frequent.[54] Not only do the leaflets' calls appear in various permutations—apart from Israeli counterfeits[55] or competing Hamas leaflets—but paragraphs coexist in the same leaflet calling for knives or Molotov cocktails alongside others calling explicitly for nonviolent means.[56] Such combinations reflect a compromise between those on the Command who wanted a reversion to violence and those who wanted adherence to nonviolent strategies. The combining of military and nonviolent methods of struggle, the theory advocated by Palestinian theorists as "all means of struggle," was the main area of conflict within the Command and the issue that eventually became the most conspicuous disagreement between Palestinians in the territories and the PLO in Tunis.[57]

To sustain resistance, representatives on the Command valued feedback concerning the leaflets' appeals. Before the drafting of a leaflet, the representatives heeded voices in the street, shops, and markets as people went about their daily rounds.[58] Leaflets sometimes appeared in two or three editions, as word filtered back that an appeal might be too onerous to pursue.[59] Once the senior local leaders of the factions reached agreement on the general outlines of a direction, their representatives on the Command wrote a draft leaflet. The DFLP representative might write the first draft one month, the PFLP representative the next, followed by Fateh's representative, with the PCP designate taking the initiative in turn, moving in rotation. Next, the leaflet would be circulated for proofreading, to verify that factional viewpoints were accurately reflected.[60] The Marxist jargon from third world armed insurrections that had been slowly disappearing from the Palestinian discourse in the occupied territories throughout the 1980s is not to be found in the leaflets. Instead, they reflect an ongoing strategic debate, infused with a nod to Islam, as each begins, "In the name of Allah, the beneficent, the merciful."[61]

Nusseibeh credits the actual drafting to Izzat Ghazzawi and a group in Ramallah that included Samir Shehadeh and Samir Sbeihat, a former head of the Bir Zeit student council.[62] Nusseibeh would then fax the proposed leaflet from an East Jerusalem office that had belonged to his late father to Muhammad Rabaia (Abu Tariq) in Paris. He would, in turn, send it to Tunis.[63] Changes made in Tunis were minimal, Nusseibeh said, especially in the beginning, when they "dared" not make many suggestions.[64] By this he meant that the political center of gravity for the Palestinians had shifted from Tunis to those inside the territories so extensively that the exiles would not consider overruling the residents of the territories. Still, disagreements with the PLO in Tunis were common.[65] Hatem Abd al-Qader Eid remembered one dispute in particular, in which, after the end of the war between Iraq and Iran on August 8, 1988, members of the Command in the territories were glad to see hostilities cease and sent a fax to Tunis expressing this view: "Abu Ammar [Yasir Arafat] sent his answer: say that Iraq was victorious over Iran, and that we Palestinians were happy that Iraq was the victor. . . . I called a meeting of all of the parties in the Command, told them about the fax, and that Abu Ammar wanted a change. All four parties refused. They said that they were not against Iraq and not against Iran, but were simply happy that the war had ended. . . . I faxed Abu Ammar that I would not change it. . . . This happened many times."[66]

Substantial portions of the leaflets are immediately recognizable from Mubarak Awad's 1983 booklet *Nonviolence in the Occupied Territories,* if one lays out the first eighteen month's leaflets alongside it, with its appended translation of 121 of Gene Sharp's list of methods.[67] Joel Greenberg noticed that language in the leaflets was strikingly similar to Awad's previous urgings of sit-down strikes and home production of food in camps and villages: "His ideas seem suddenly relevant, and the uprising strategists seem to be picking up his themes, formulating them in almost identical language."[68] Awad said he did not have a hand in preparing the leaflets, but added, "If they use my writing, I'm proud of it."[69]

Conflicts sometimes occurred over leaflets even after agreed-upon versions had been released. Nusseibeh recounted a revealing incident over one leaflet's referring to a "white revolution."[70] This was the term used by Palestinian activist intellectuals inside the territories to propound their pursuit of bloodless systemic change. "I was surprised that the term 'white revolution' got through Tunis [was not contested]. Later, I discovered that in republishing this leaflet—in one or two of the magazines published outside by the PLO—one of the changes they introduced in re-editing was to delete this phrase—a kind of interference. . . . I remember thinking at the time that this [action was] influencing the spirit, because the use of 'white revolution' was very conscious in trying to convey to the people . . . that the intifada was an unarmed revolt. It was a conscious use of that term. And the elimination of it was also a conscious elimination of it, [meant] to show that unarmed revolution is just a phase in this process."[71]

The PLO's misguided preconception of nonviolent struggle as something merely to be tried for a while as a prelude to armed struggle had never been sufficiently analyzed within the ranks and rejected as strategically impossible. Divisions of opinion on this question would persist for the duration of the uprising. Eid explained,

> Fateh wanted to keep the political door open, but others wanted to shut the door and said we needed violence. . . . I sometimes refused to sign the *bayan,* not only about throwing stones, but about throwing Molotov cocktails, or opening fire on the Israelis. Bombs and any military activity, I refused, and Fateh refused. Part of the Command wanted to make the

intifada military. I thought to myself, this is not good for us—the intifada must be popular, civilian, not war, some stones, maybe a demonstration, but not opening fire, not throwing bombs. . . . This was our policy in the Command. Without me, they could not put it in the leaflet. Fateh was bigger, and without Fateh, those wanting armed struggle could not do anything.[72]

Displaying independence, those affiliated with the PLO in the territories expressed views of their own. Power had shifted to the territories, Daoud Kuttab wrote, with the Command having "discretion to decide how best to move things locally," while it was "willing and happy for the PLO to reap the political gains."[73] Kuttab told a foreign correspondent that the PLO "leave it up to their local people to decide whether the people are up to it or not. . . . It doesn't take long for people working in these situations to be mobilized without somebody pushing a button in Tunis."[74] Although the leaflets contained specific bids to different constituencies, such as shopkeepers, and calls for days of solidarity, or proposals for confrontation with the IDF, their appeals were broad, rather than fixed orders, so local organizers had leeway. A reporter wrote of this dynamic with the youths in Palestinian refugee camps: "The *shebab* [youth] are widely assumed to be linked to the PLO. But they appear to operate with relative autonomy."[75] The uprising would end the "waiting for instructions from outside," Salim Tamari argues, and "the Palestinian people were able to assume the reins of the decision making from inside."[76]

The Think Tank

Nonviolent resistance had fared poorly in the rocky terrain of the Israeli-Palestinian conflict, Reuven Kaminer states, because "there was no important, organized group which adopted these concepts as the starting point for their political program or strategy."[77] Although Kaminer apparently overlooked the communists, elements of truth remain to his historical observation. Even so, the evolution of an alternative school of thought on securing Palestinian rights and ending military occupation—led by East Jerusalem and Ramallah activist intellectuals—discloses a slowly developing critical mass of persuasion on nonviolent approaches. Behind the Command stood perhaps twenty Palestinian activist intellectuals, who, acting as a political think tank, recalled Muhammad Jadallah, had been grooming themselves in nonmilitary struggle and guided the uprising.[78] They comprised the core of a larger group of up to a hundred local individuals who were in a diffuse sense "running" the intifada, numbering twenty or so from each of the four main factions generally, in addition to independent individuals.[79]

Sources ranging from PLO officials close to Yasir Arafat to Israeli and other scholars have asserted that leaders in the territories did not make strategic decisions about the intifada, but only executed decrees originating elsewhere.[80] Although the premises of military-style organization and factional loyalty comprise part of this saga, adhering to this interpretation misses more significant developments. The two greatest deficits of such construal are the failure to fathom the nature of the interplay between the Command and the local popular committees and to understand that most of the decisions into the third year of the intifada emanated from the community of East Jerusalem activist intellectuals and their concentric circles around the Command.[81] In addition, they overlook the way in which, during the uprising, the Palestinians came to realize the link between ideas and the actions manifesting those ideas.[82]

Meetings of the so-called think tank took place in different locations, including, for example, at the Ramallah home of Hanan Mikhail Ashrawi, a political independent and then dean of the faculty of arts at Bir Zeit.[83] Along with representatives from the main factions, nonpartisan academicians and professionals also attended. The core group included surgeon Mamdouh Aker;[84] Muhammad Jadallah; Zahira Kamal, head of the Federation of Women's Action Committees;[85] Ghassan Khatib; educator Khalil Mahshi; Riad al-Malki; and Sari Nusseibeh.[86] Jadallah recollected, "There might be twelve or thirteen: six or seven people, sometimes nine, who were fixed, and four were coming and going. . . . There were two from the Democratic Front, one from the People's Party [communists], and one from the Popular Front. Of the independents, there were four or five. The Fateh people sometimes came in three or four, . . . [because] they had to show that they were the majority and had the right to be represented by more than one. Secondly, they had to satisfy many people within Fateh."[87]

In addition to molding the political presentation of the uprising, formulating ideas, and funneling concepts and options to the Command, the think tank also ran an informal speakers bureau. It arranged for speakers on the intifada to be impaneled at international seminars and conferences, meet with diplomatic envoys, spoke on the record to the media, maintained dialogue with Israeli peace organizations, and shaped an information campaign, including overtures to Israeli public opinion.[88] A similar but smaller group, affiliated with Bir Zeit, developed political approaches that Fateh might pursue. It included author Izzat Ghazzawi,[89] Samir Shehadeh, and Samir Sbeihat.[90] Nusseibeh, also involved with this group, claimed that one reason such a forceful coterie could develop within Fateh to call the shots for the intifada was the dearth of "infrastructure" in the occupied territories.[91] This situation led to the development of what came to be known as "unofficial Fateh." Hanna Siniora, another participant, explained: "Sari was never official Fateh. I was never official Fateh. We were Fateh-leaning. Official Fateh was underground; we were above ground. We tended to talk to the general public and not solely to partisans, because we felt that we had to talk to all the people, not just the party people, including Israelis. We encouraged dialogue and talking with everyone. . . . We became known as 'local' Fateh because we were working with the Fateh leadership outside."[92] Neither Nusseibeh nor Siniora had risen through military cadres. They declared themselves independent, stood on their own stature, and spoke from their individual credibility. They were not "party men."[93]

An "official" Fateh leadership existed in every city or town. In East Jerusalem it included Feisel Husseini and Radwan Abu Ayyash.[94] A comparable "official" group resided in Ramallah.[95] Such a division was probably a deliberate attempt to check power by curtailing the influence one individual might wield, Nusseibeh suspected; "maybe it wasn't conceived of to be like this, but eventually this is how it ended up, with the head separated from the body [for Fateh]. . . . The 'head' was the people in the forefront. . . . Other people were in the grass roots, building organizations. Sometimes you had people crossing, coming in and going out, but, basically, the division was there. And, in general, just at the outbreak of the intifada, there were a lot of people who were not happy in Fateh, not happy with how the organization was run."[96]

Although Nusseibeh was not part of official Fateh, he was sufficiently closely connected to the organization that he became entrusted with funds and could communicate with the diasporan leadership on the local organization's behalf.[97] He granted that, in the "channel of Fateh," he was "if not in control, at least in charge or in the know-how of everything."[98] Nusseibeh "supervised" the intifada, in Siniora's phrase: "Sari Nusseibeh for a certain period actually managed to have the leadership of the underground in the palm of his hand, and he guided the intifada for the first two years."[99]

Among Nusseibeh's roles was that of oversight for the leaflets, which came out of the "body," although the "head" guided them.[100] "I wasn't actually writing something myself in the leaflets," he said. "They often showed them to me and I would react, and would give final approval. I am not sure actually at what point this began . . . maybe by the eighth, ninth, or tenth leaflet."[101] In sum, says Nusseibeh of his part in the intifada,

> I tried, basically, to make use of the volcanic eruption . . . to give it a form that was presentable and understandable. Secondly, to make sure that this was the thing that would in fact lead eventually to a settlement with Israel, not to just have an intifada for its own sake—a heroic event in the life of Palestinian history—not another sacrifice. It had to lead somewhere. . . . The only real change, if you like, was among the elite, in Fateh, in the leadership of the intifada, who decided and got convinced of the value of using the unarmed tactics, specifically because such tactics seemed to be better to get to specific targets and specific solutions. They were in a position actually to show this through the program that they instilled into the leaflets and the direction of the intifada, right through the second year.[102]

By May 1989, Nusseibeh was reported to be a "paymaster" of the uprising, so named by an IDF prosecutor, and to have authored intifada leaflets. Court documents from Shin Bet "unmasked" Nusseibeh and Abu Ayyash as running the uprising.[103]

Mahdi Abd al-Hadi explained, "Feisel [Husseini] was the face of the intifada; Sari was the brains of the intifada."[104] Social movements—even if forced by circumstances to be clandestine—help to create their own leadership figures. "The whole Fateh organization rallied around Feisel and in a way made Feisel the important leader that he became," Hanna Siniora explained.[105] Haj Abd Abu-Diab recalled, "Feisel Husseini was in every single demonstration, in the lead. He was in every strike when he was out of jail, and in every hunger strike when he was in jail."[106] Husseini had spent six months at the start of the uprising incarcerated in a cell with Hatem Abd al-Qader Eid at al-Fara, a prison originally built as a British army camp near Tulkarem. Despite Husseini's jailing at this crucial stage in the uprising, the Command always had contact with him, Eid asserted, and Husseini never relaxed his obstinacy on the importance of negotiations.[107] Eid said, "I was in a small cell without anybody else except Feisel Husseini. I was not allowed to see any other prisoners. . . . Feisel told me that the intifada was very important to continue, because we needed a political solution. The intifada was not enough on its own. We needed the intifada to pressure the Israelis; but without additional political action, the intifada could not do anything. The intifada was . . . to open the political door and to make contact with Israel."[108] Husseini adamantly insisted that the intifada should be nonviolent so that it would lead to negotiations, and that it was not a military operation, but a movement to change consciousness."[109]

"We Don't Want Bodies": Disagreeing with the PLO

Mubarak Awad had predicted that if sufficiently large numbers of persons engaged in nonviolent struggle, the PLO would not be able to remain aloof.[110] Indeed, the PLO did become involved, but lacking the knowledge and skills in strategic thinking necessary for nonviolent resistance, its involvement might well compromise the effectiveness of the uprising. The PLO's ambiguity on the continuation of commando actions hung in the background as an ominous limit to the strength and forcefulness of the uprising. Although events in the occupied territories were altering some aspects of the PLO's thinking, the front did not share the perspective in the territories on the need to undermine the political rationales in Israel for extremist policies that played on fear.

So disturbed about differences in viewpoint between the residents of the territories (the insiders) and those exiled elsewhere (the outsiders) was Hafid Barghouti, editor of the Ramallah newspaper *al-Hayat al-Jadida* (New Day), that he traveled outside the territories in spring 1988 specifically to register with Abu Jihad the perturbation of Palestinians in the occupied territories about possible resumption of cross-border raids. "We don't want bodies," Barghouti emphatically told the PLO's second in command, fingers jabbing the air.[111]

The relationship between the Command inside the territories and the PLO in Tunis was fraught with disagreement, ironically restrained by the determination of the Palestinians inside the occupied territories to build up the stature of the PLO. Members of the think tank, and "official Fateh" and "unofficial Fateh," wanted reciprocity with the PLO. Difficulties in achieving such parity were compounded by a rift that developed between the "official Fateh" organization and the "unofficial Fateh" group, Nusseibeh recollected: "The people who were in charge of the official Fateh organization were not involved in the direction of the intifada, as was the *unofficial*

Fateh organization. . . . There was constant division."[112] Yet they all agreed on a strategy of empowering the PLO, to help it attain negotiations with the Israelis, based on the conviction that diplomacy represented the only way to produce lasting change for the Palestinians. A pincer movement developed based on the local leaders' expectations of the role to be played by the exiles in Tunis.[113] In their view, the PLO had "a supportive role," Daoud Kuttab explains, but would at the same time "collect the political fruits of the uprising."[114] As envisioned, the intifada would improve the PLO's stature, and consequently, its position in negotiations for a political settlement.[115] They also hoped that the cumulative effect of the uprising would be such that any political concessions the PLO might have to make would not undermine the gains made on the ground. Mamdouh Aker and Mubarak Awad counted themselves among those who believed that the uprising would succeed only if it remained utterly independent from the PLO inside the territories.[116] The PCP often protested the need to seek the PLO's approval. The local leadership omitted support from the Arab world from their calculus.[117]

The PLO used the intifada, and the uprising capitalized on the PLO in a relationship based on a division of labor that became increasingly complex as time passed, in part because the PLO feared that the independence and self-reliance of those involved in the uprising and the world attention focused on the rebellion could be turned against it.[118] Decades of Israeli efforts to fragment Palestinian leadership and avoid talking with the PLO, beginning with the creation of the Village Leagues in 1981-82, served to exacerbate this fear. Despite the legitimacy given to the PLO by the uprising, in Tunis anxieties lingered that the intifada might give birth to a leadership not beholden to it. Raja Shehadeh says the PLO's objective of winning recognition for the organization overrode all other considerations, in part because it felt vulnerable to the Palestinians in the territories striking a deal with Israel that would render them redundant.[119]

Meanwhile, the Command concentrated on sustaining the uprising. In leaflet after leaflet, it presented the Palestinian strategy as one aimed at peace, negotiations at an international conference, and creation of an independent state alongside Israel. "The overall political ideology of the Command could not have been more moderate or pragmatic," Nusseibeh subsequently wrote from prison, calling as it did for a two-state solution through "entirely civilian struggle."[120] Not one leaflet bade the destruction of Israel or death to the Jewish people. The Command never condoned in a leaflet the killing of the one Israeli soldier who lost his life in the initial year of the intifada (in Bethlehem and reportedly by another soldier).[121] When someone tossed a bomb on the outskirts of Jericho, setting fire to a Jerusalem-bound bus and killing an Israeli rabbi's daughter, Rachel Weiss, and her three sons, the local popular committee of the intifada issued a special leaflet lamenting the renegade action.[122] Villagers would disarm Israeli soldiers, strip them, and then return their clothes and guns to Israeli military authorities.[123] The uprising centered on the military occupation and denial of Palestinian rights: "Our uprising is not aimed at the destruction of Israel. It is aimed at establishing freedom for ourselves in our own state."[124] The "outside" PLO leadership was not needed for this, Nusseibeh insisted: "It was necessary [for them] to say clearly to Israel, 'This is what we want,' but it wasn't necessary for them to direct us. . . . There was enough going on here to create its own momentum, and an interplay between the various circles of power here—intellectual circles and organizational circles."[125]

Faxes sent by Nusseibeh to Tunis via Paris went to Abu Jihad, who then presented the issue to Arafat.[126] In the occupied territories, many, although not all, regarded Abu Jihad as a "corrupt-free and humble leader despite the large sums of money that he was personally responsible to dispense."[127] The key Fateh figure behind the Shabiba movement (declared illegal by the Israelis in 1987), Abu Jihad's position as chief on the Palestinian side of the Joint PLO-Jordanian Committee in Amman and responsibility for handling funds had cast him as a pivotal figure in academic, journalistic, municipal, professional, and trade union circles in the occupied territories. In Daoud Kuttab's judgment, those in Fateh seeking to shift their struggle to wholly nonviolent means saw him as a warrior who had accepted the need for compromise with Israel and could persuade the military cadres of that perspective.[128] So he remained until his assassination on April 16, 1988, in Tunis, by an Israeli commando squad.[129]

Local Fateh people trying to promote clear, open communication of information on political grievances and their proposed solutions viewed the killing of Abu Jihad as causing the loss of one of the very few in the diaspora who comprehended their nonviolent strategies.[130] "Abu Jihad may have been the only 'outside' leader who had studied the situation in the territories," according to a peer of the activist intellectuals, Marwan Barghouti, who was expelled by Israel to Jordan during the intifada, "He didn't just issue directives. . . . He listened to us. . . . When the Israelis killed him, they also killed a concept, a strategy, if you like, that held the two wings [military and political] together."[131] Leaflet no. 14, dated April 20, 1988, the first after Abu Jihad's death, called for a return to "all acts of struggle, using all potentials and means," declaring "the day will come when the Kalashnikov [a Soviet-designed assault rifle] rings out . . . its bullets."[132] Israeli officials knew, in the words of Yossi Melman and Dan Raviv, that "Abu Jihad was a great conciliator," who "helped hold the organization together, because both Arafat and his violent rivals would listen to him."[133] Little has surfaced in the intervening years to suggest that Israeli officials had calculated the effect of Abu Jihad's death on those who were trying to guide Palestinian resistance away from armed struggle and toward nonviolent strategies to reach a compromise with Israel. It is doubtful that they weighed such a factor at all.[134]

Before Abu Jihad's assassination, the seeds scattered by the intifada had taken root. Almost two months after his death, a storm erupted over the circulation of a position paper by Bassam Abu-Sharif, an advisor to Arafat, at an Arab summit held in Algiers, June 7-9, 1988. It talked about Israelis and Palestinians living side by side and called for a two-state solution through bilateral negotiations and a UN-sponsored international conference. Five factions denounced Abu-Sharif from exile as a "traitor."[135] Palestinians inside the territories, however, saw his affirmation positively and as firm evidence that the uprising had increased the political weight of the West Bankers and Gazans among the diasporan PLO.[136] Feisel Husseini and Radwan Abu Ayyash applauded Abu-Sharif's effort (for which Husseini landed in jail).[137] An ideologue behind early militant Palestinian campaigns of bombs and hijackings, Abu-Sharif had emerged to reconfigure the positions within the PLO, advocating what Aziz Shehadeh had been reviled for proposing twenty years earlier. According to one report, Arafat himself distributed his paper at the summit, suggesting readiness for direct negotiations.[138] The diaspora leadership was obligated to come forward, Nusseibeh insisted: "We couldn't do it all ourselves. The PLO had to come out with very clear calls for recognition, reconciliation, willingness to negotiate. . . . A lot of us made statements in public, calling on them to come forward." [139]

Six months after Abu-Sharif's paper, Hani al-Hassan, another Arafat advisor, spoke in London on December 11, 1989, to the Royal Commonwealth Society at the invitation of the Radical Society. There he mournfully admitted that since 1967 the Palestinians had realized that they would have to yield to Israel on land, but were abashed by the scale of the compromise required: "For us Palestinians the brutal, heartbreaking truth is that if we want peace and an absolute minimum of justice, we have to pay for it with three-quarters of our homeland."[140]

Inadvertent Results: "A True Example of a People's Revolution"

Within the first month of the uprising, Israel placed 200,000 Palestinians under curfew throughout the West Bank and Gaza; by December 1989, the second anniversary of its start, one million of them were confined to their homes or locations.[141] The curfews, "Israel's main weapon," political scientist F. Robert Hunter says, were applied on an unprecedented scale in an attempt to contain the uprising.[142] Yet in retrospect the curfews inadvertently boosted local organizing efforts and provided the kindling for rapid establishment of local support committees. In the words of MKs Yossi Sarid and Dedi Zucker of the Citizens Rights (Ratz) faction of Meretz, "A continuous curfew, and the hardships it creates, has had one effect . . . the degree of solidarity among the residents is immeasurably greater today than it was on the eve of the curfew."[143]

Committees outside curfewed areas collected food donations, while those inside restricted areas took responsibility for distribution. Health teams based their treatment on the assumption that residents must be prepared to withstand the situation for a long period of time.[144] In early morning, groups of women sneaked out of blockaded refugee camps and hid in nearby villages. During the day, they purchased scarce meats and vegetables and at night would slip back into the camps to feed their families. Elsewhere, butchers and grocers sold provisions from their homes.[145] Farmers' crops rotted, because their cultivators could not plow or tend them.[146] A strategy of self-reliance led Palestinians to rely on small home gardens, rabbit hutches, chicken cooperatives, bread baking, and beekeeping, described in Muhammad Muslih's study of civil society.[147] The baking of bread acquired novel status; wealthy matrons kneaded dough, to take part in the action.[148]

As an exercise of will, the leadership of the uprising had initially called for school attendance until noon only. In response, on February 3, 1988, Israeli military authorities closed 900 schools by military fiat, to prevent their being used to foment upheaval, affecting 300,000 students.[149] The closure of six major universities in the territories at the start of the uprising sent 14,500 students home, along with faculties.[150] All sixteen community colleges were issued closure orders in January 1988 (and only allowed to reopen on a gradual basis in March 1990). A military order that April broadened the Israeli decree to cover all educational institutions, including governmental, private, and UNRWA schools, for an indefinite period. For 17 out of the 28 months preceding June 1990, all 1,174 schools in the West Bank (excluding East Jerusalem) were forbidden to operate. This meant that 303,000 students, or approximately 35 percent of the Palestinian population, were denied access to formal education.[151] The closure of Bir Zeit University, the institution's seventeenth under occupation, would send 3,500 students home and last four and a half years.[152]

The IDF termed the school closings and curfews "environmental punishments" meant to quash the uprising through collective punishment of entire communities.[153] Although Palestinian educators decried the halt to education and the Command condemned the closings in Leaflet no. 9, the closures' unforeseen effects in retrospect help explain why a movement benefiting from the insights of sophisticated academicians and activist intellectuals so effectively was able to animate rural dwellers, including refugee camp residents in Gaza.[154] When students and faculty went home to their families, they reintegrated into village life, a strong causative factor in the breadth and depth of the uprising.[155] Virtually every account of the intifada has overlooked the crucial element of students and teachers' being at home. The imponderable effect of Israel's policy created an environment in which the mobilization could swell across social class divisions. With pupils and pedagogues at home, informed activists were dispersed throughout the villages, towns, hamlets, and refugee camps of the West Bank and Gaza.[156] Once there, they marshaled their families and friends. The happenstance of Israeli curfews and closures hastened the spread of ideas about Palestinian nonviolent resistance and contributed to an historic instance of intellectuals, academicians, and elite activists being joined with savvy young street organizers in common cause. The connection between the intellectuals and rural villagers was explicit, precisely as Antonio Gramsci, whose writings from prison were being savored throughout the territories among educated sectors, had advocated as the ideal for successful resistance.[157]

Palestinians communicated across generations and neighborhoods, as all strata of their society unified.[158] The presence of university instructors at home prevented disjuncture between the "thinkers" and the proverbial masses; as the doors of the universities shut, theoreticians joined with the families, popular committees, youths and children of the uprising. The physics professor worked with the baker to plan food distribution.

Students resisting Military Order 854 of 1980 (chapter 6) had used Israel's closing of universities for maximum effect, retooling an otherwise burdensome collective punishment to their advantage by taking the opportunity to rouse whole communities to involvement.[159] "In the early 1980s, we used to work consciously to get Israel to close us down so that we could go back home, which would make the students intermingle. This time, when things broke out, they broke out truly as a whole population. . . . Nobody asked anybody anything."[160] Nusseibeh recalled, "The students were not on campus—one of the reasons why the intifada happened—the students were already in the towns. . . . Everyone will tell you that we'd been preparing in a strategic sense, . . . yet the proof of what I'm saying is that even the local leadership (the local national leadership) took some time to see . . . It took time for the PLO to seize on what was happening . . . but the local leadership also was caught by surprise. . . . Everything was happening by itself. It was just as it should be . . . a true example of a people's revolution. It was everyone, not just student activists, but the carpenter . . . all were leaders. No one was waiting to be told what to do."[161]

On May 5, 1988, Israel announced its decision to extend school closings for another month, a measure that inadvertently modified the Palestinian educational system. Alternative popular education (*al-talim al-shabi*), taught by volunteers, began to take shape in neighborhood experiments run by local committees. This unorthodox tack was coeducational, with boys and girls attending class together in homes, mosques, churches, clubhouses, and gardens.[162] A Palestinian educational publication notes "community-based education presented a grave threat to the Israeli authorities since they were no longer in control of the process and contents of Palestinian education."[163] As October 1988 approached and the schools remained closed, the Command established an education committee to invigorate plans for alternative education. Leaflet no. 24 bids "all teachers, high school pupils and students, and especially elementary school pupils, to mobilize for the success of the popular education operation . . . in order to foil the authorities' policy of closing the schools and inculcating ignorance in our children. Popular education is a national responsibility."[164]

Not only did the Israelis oppose the reopening of regular schools, fearing that students would demonstrate, but defense minister Yitzhak Rabin also outlawed alternative popular education, establishing ten-year jail terms and fines equivalent to $5,000 for any teacher involved in it.[165] "If you are a teacher and you teach your neighbor's children," an UNRWA educator told a reporter, "they will treat [you] as terrorists."[166] UNRWA and private schools organized "teaching-at-a-distance" in October 1988, with study packets for home use. This, too, the Israelis deemed illegal.[167] Pressure within Israel from dismayed Israeli citizens and international condemnation resulted in Israeli officials reopening schools in July 1989, with the belated realization that shutting them would only serve to encourage the alternative education (and interpretation of history) that they had forbidden.[168]

Shuttered universities managed some stipends for the improvising professors, despite the absence of the tuition normally paid by students, and apart from grants and subsidies from abroad. For want of laboratories, science professors suffered most. The political content of alternative courses fortified the uprising, and underground education at the university level deepened the immersion of elites. Students lacking a few credits were graduated inconspicuously, without ceremony. Underground leaflets avoided announcing academic events for fear that Israeli soldiers would intrude; information spread by word of mouth.[169] Homebound scholars and intellectuals spoke directly to international media from their kitchen tables, despite Israeli prohibitions, and to the mass uprising as well. While academicians and writers helped the intifada to proceed, the uprising was also modifying their outlooks, as they brought their writings into step with the popular movement.[170]

With everyone at home, the efforts of women were vital and noticed, in an atmosphere of respect for leadership based on action and service regardless of social status. Rather than crediting the engagement of women as deriving from the larger Palestinian national quest, women as individuals and women's groups lent "infrastructure, experience and leadership to help the national movement."[171] As noted in chapter 5, Palestinian women's organizing antedated Palestinian nationalist mobilization, and, despite the constraints of a deeply patriarchal culture, women were at the forefront as a national movement developed in the 1920s and 1930s, not dependent on it. After the 1967 occupation, a coherent women's movement became organized, composed of committees. In the words of one scholar, "The uprising has been possible because of women's political agenda."[172]

In addition to playing a critical formative role in organizing committees in villages, refugee camps, and towns, the women's movement also took on responsibilities for helping carry out appeals from the Command.[173] Not only were women the backbone of the organizing of the popular committees, but between December 1987 and March 1988 they held more than one hundred demonstrations, such as one in Ramallah on March 8, 1988, in which five hundred women, ranging from teenagers to grandmothers, marched in silence.[174] Although women were indispensable to the popular committees, it is also true that meetings often took place in mosques or coffee shops where women did not go.[175] Role changes were nonetheless reported, such as women participating in political discussions with outsiders.[176] Women "confronted Israeli (male) troops; they shared in decision-making; they . . . did what the men did, without fear or complexes. Perhaps it would be still more accurate to say that because of the intifada, the role of men was altered."[177]

Knowledge and Techniques of Nonviolent Resistance

Nontraditional Transmission: Graffiti, Games, Poetry, and Sparklers
In the eastern part of the Mediterranean three main lines of faith meet, and an equal number of holy days are observed each week. The Muslims revere Friday, the Jews hold Saturday sacred, and the Christians keep Sunday. On Fridays, as worshippers prostrated themselves to prayer mats in mosques, hands reached into pockets to pull out bunches of underground leaflets and pass them to the next supplicant. Marches often began at a mosque after Friday prayers or after church on Sunday with the perusal of the latest leaflet. The fliers frequently made reference to mosques and churches and designated Sundays and Fridays as demonstration days.[178] Appeals to Christians, Jews, and Muslims were common. The multifaith perspective of the intifada—a form of political inclusivity, rather than interfaith activity—was shown by frequent references to the three great revealed religions in the leaflets. Following prolix opening rhetorical flourishes, Leaflet no. 21 states:

> Our people are invited to escalate and amplify the uprising, thus bringing us closer to total civil disobedience. The [Command] salutes those Jewish progressives, democratic, and peace forces which support our national cause, and calls upon them to intensify their activities. . . . We call upon the Organization of Islamic States, the Vatican, the United Nations and all friendly forces to stop the desecration of our Islamic and Christian holy places.[179]

Following turgid exhortations, the leaflets gave concise lists of action steps. More poetry than program, "you could see people skipping the verbiage and going straight to the end of the leaflet to read the instructions."[180] Couriers went from village to village carrying the leaflets, often in school bags or back-packs.[181] The rote learning to which the Palestinians had been exposed under Jordanian or Egyptian education systems became in the uprising an asset in transmission. Long passages were committed to memory and dictated to other youths, because, if intercepted by Israeli soldiers, it was beneficial not to have leaflets in one's possession. One of the Shabiba recalled, "I memorized the leaflets in order to be able to take them from one village to another without paper, although sometimes I would take the leaflets from village to village in my school bag. In the villages, I would get the young people out at nighttime to discuss them. At night, we had more freedom."[182]

The leaflets took on totemic proportions. They now comprise folklore of their own about the intifada. Parents and teachers found themselves helpless to ask children to go against the leaflets.[183] Said one father, the leaflets are the "only authority" to which the children respond.[184] Aired from southern Syria over the al-Quds radio station and from Baghdad on the Voice of the PLO,[185] with the passage of time radio replaced printed leaflets, because broadcasts could reach tiny hamlets unimpeded, a trend encouraged by counterfeit versions of leaflets disseminated by Israel.[186]

Graffiti reinforced the directives in the leaflets.[187] Writing on walls announced strike days and the rudiments from leaflets, and various political tendencies prescribed their political positions there.[188] "Any car that leaves for work [in Israel] tomorrow will be burned," read a dire warning on a wall.[189] The graffiti were similar to the manifestos and *samizdat* plastered on the walls and kiosks of Prague during the Velvet Revolution, to be copied or memorized for nighttime transmission to provincial Czech and Slovak towns.[190] Emblazoning graffiti was dangerous. An activist was killed by Israeli soldiers when the youth was scribbling graffiti on a Nablus wall.[191] Leaflet no. 20 of June 22, 1988, "stresses the need to ignore the [Israeli] authorities' instructions to remove national slogans from walls."[192] The significance of graffiti was also shown by an incident in the Qalandia camp after Abu Jihad's death, when the camp was placed under curfew, as a consequence of large numbers of Palestinians having demonstrated. Israeli soldiers angered by the graffiti there painted over it, replacing it with a Star of David. In short order, a Palestinian flag was daubed in its place, even though soldiers had purportedly been stationed at the site around the clock.[193]

Women sometimes raised their voices to confuse Israeli soldiers, or blew whistles. Much as in the prodemocracy struggle in Chile of the same period, they would sometimes bang on pots and pans to create a din.[194] Children's games were part of the broadcast process, including one called "Golani and the Intifada," in which children between six and ten years of age divided into two groups, with one playing the Golani Unit of the Israeli army, said by a leaflet to be the first to implement defense minister Yitzhak Rabin's break-their-bones directive, and the other playing Palestinians.[195] The Golani group carried sticks as guns and wore aluminum saucepans to mimic helmets, while the Palestinian group carried slingshots and wore kaffiyehs, the Arab checkered headdress.[196] The rules called for the second group always to win, while the children sang a song.

Music and poetry were often employed, such as a song by Ibn al-Jabal called "O Negev," composed in Ansar 3,[197] a detention center in the Negev desert referred to by Israelis as "Tsemach detention camp" after its commander. Although innumerable poems were penned, one is recalled as encompassing the meaning of the uprising. "Draw a mustache for Antar" was addressed to the children of the intifada by a Palestinian living in Australia. It says that they were the ones who put a mustache on Antar—the legendary Arab hero, a black slave who personified courage, bravery, and chivalry. "What the poem meant was that all these Arab leaders talk like Antar, but it took children to bring about manliness [the mustache]; it spoke to the contrast between the Arab regimes and the Palestinian children."[198] Meanwhile, an "artistic intifada" took root in East Jerusalem. Artists in theater, dance, and puppetry were able to work with comparative immunity and less fear of army raids and military censorship, as concerts and exhibits of art were held.

Cleverness and inventiveness in responding to the actions of the target group is a feature of nonviolent struggle. An example of minute, simple, and witty action was the setting of Palestinian watches to a different time zone from the state of Israel's—a symbolic step introduced by Mubarak Awad. In April 1989, daylight savings time was adopted by Palestinians two weeks in advance of Israel's customary turning forward of the clocks (although Palestinians who tried this silent protest got their wrists broken and timepieces smashed by Israeli soldiers).[199]

Leaflet no. 28 of October 30, 1988, announces a general strike on the seventy-first anniversary of the Balfour Declaration, and asks that at four o'clock on Palestinian Independence Day, November 15, 1988, everyone will "sing *Biladi, Biladi*—my homeland," and take part in scout parades, parties, dancing in the streets, and fireworks. On that day, darkness fell early, the electric current having been cut by Israeli authorities. Refugee camp dwellers made their own light shows. Steel wool for scrubbing saucepans substituted for fireworks. When the pads of steel wool were ignited, twirled, and thrown in the air, they sparkled.[200]

An Infrastructure Grows: Popular Committees and Self-Rule

The popular committees were comparable to the constructive program developed by Gandhi, a process of incorporating the entire population of India in its independence struggles. Mubarak Awad's 1983 booklet, *Nonviolence in the Occupied Territories,* had reinterpreted and popularized Gandhi's concept, with its notion of building a new society while still living under the old order. To this end, Palestinians needed to establish alternative, or parallel, institutions to replace the regime of the occupation. Awad stresses, "All attempts must be made to utilize existing loopholes and legal opportunities in creating new institutions . . . such as *ad hoc* popular committees which meet to coordinate, but then proceed to act separately without a recognized legal structure."[201] Five years later, the Jerusalem Paper stated, "The success of the disobedience plan requires . . . the formation of popular committees in various areas and neighborhoods."[202]

The roots of the popular committees date to 1936.[203] Local strike committees of the Arab National Committee sprang into being in April of that year to run the general strike that lasted for 174 days. These committees, like those of the intifada, possessed independence and individuality within the broader context of nationalist appeals for limiting immigration and establishing self-government in Palestine.[204] Decades later, the communists' persistence in working through small, localized institutions—initially advocated in 1969—had resulted in almost twenty years of collective experience in such organizing. DFLP organizing efforts antedated the intifada by a decade, Muhammad Jadallah emphasized: "The DFLP's women's committees and health committees founded in the late 1970s were really in the forefront of what later became the popular committees. We started, as the Democratic Front, the formation with others of the popular committees."[205] The civilian movements and nonmilitary mobilizations of the 1970s and 1980s broadened the number of Palestinians who came of age through the organizing of committees. Daoud Kuttab wrote in 1988, "Without having to go back to a central power or authority, local popular committees are deciding and acting on initiatives that are special to their communities. While these initiatives don't contradict the general guidelines of the Unified Leadership of the Uprising, they do reflect the strength and independence of the committees."[206] Demonstrations drew attention and international media coverage, but the more significant developments were to be found in the activities of the committees.

The committees were pivotal, Nusseibeh stated, in allowing the Palestinians to "disengage from the Israeli system, economically and administratively, and to effect a simultaneous takeover of the control of our daily activities."[207] They are described by Salim Tamari as "crucial transformations of consciousness," particularly so during the first year of the uprising, when a "new spirit" emerged as neighborhoods shared the weight of the occupation through the "creation of organizations, groups, patterns, and economic strategies of sustaining the people."[208] Muhammad Muslih credits the intifada with establishing "cooperative action as a recognizable feature of associational life" and notes its political pluralism.[209] Jonathan Kuttab explained, "The intifada introduced the attitude that everything is 'tryable.' When the Israelis once stopped petrol supplies to Jericho, I filled my car with petrol and drove to Jericho to share it with whoever needed it. A baker hung a sign, 'If you know anyone without food, take as much bread as you need.' No one was paying him to do this, and there was no accounting. In the refugee camps under siege, youths would throw stones as a diversion so that food trucks could come in the rear entrances to the camps. Nothing else in the Arab world compares with the intifada. We were all unified. The absence of hierarchism was different from Arab culture, and its spontaneity was different from Arab culture."[210]

The Husseini Document had called for the popular committees to "gain official status as branches of the new state, helping to continue the growth and development of the state apparatus."[211] Less than a year after the eruption of the uprising in December 1987, an alternative society had developed, the governance of which was Palestinian.[212] By March 1988, the committees had begun to function like local government.[213] Leaflet no. 18 of May 28, 1988, describes the intifada as "building the apparatus of the people's self-government through the popular committees with their various tasks."[214]

Awad's 1983 booklet had projected the "building of an entire infrastructure independently of Israel (universities, factories, institutions, libraries, hospitals, schools)" as the "nucleus for the coming Palestinian state."[215]

The committees operated through elected leadership that favored a democratic approach to decision making.[216] The popular committees ran themselves, with those in rural communities, where the clan structure was strongest, functioning best.[217] Efforts at regional coordination among committees proved to be unsuccessful because of variations in levels of commitment, yet as such consultations failed, the local organizations grew stronger.[218] The magnitude of Palestinian organization is indicated by the scale of Israeli authorities' disruption of thirty-seven committees in Gaza alone in August 1988.[219] The village of Beit Sahour (pop. 12,000) organized itself into thirty-six committees.[220]

Rita Giacaman viewed the popular committees as being overtly political, and others have recorded her concern that the committees became "bogged down" in factional disputes.[221] The popular committees, as opposed to innumerable smaller neighborhood committees, were clandestine and often heavily composed of activists from the various PLO factions, yet according to the network of committees called the FACTS Information Committee, these structures were not explicitly political.[222] Riad al-Malki of the PFLP agreed, and said the popular committees served no ideological purpose. They were consequential because they sustained communities through the ardors of resistance.[223] As the main instrument for organization in the intifada, popular committees continued the trend toward civil society begun after 1967.

The most important groupings among the committees concerned themselves with agriculture.[224] When night fell, fences moved on Palestinian land. An unenunciated Israeli policy of uprooting olive trees and burning crops became evident within the first six months of the uprising. Leaflet no. 21 reported the Israeli destruction of 3,690 olive trees in eighteen villages, fruit and nut trees, and wheat fields.[225] Agricultural responses to the intrusions of military occupation are in and of themselves nonviolent means of contention—they are clever, nonadversarial, and entail nonretaliatory thinking. Ingenuity manifested itself in the pursuit of self-sufficiency.[226]

In Beit Sahour, Jad Ishaq, a biologist at Bethlehem University, created an agricultural cooperative called the Shed, which sold seeds, tools, and insecticide at cost to plant "victory gardens."[227] Ishaq considered agricultural endeavors a strategy for survival.[228] "It was an act of economic defiance that echoed the non-violent strategy of Mahatma Gandhi."[229] Palestinians planted an estimated 500,000 fruit trees in the West Bank and Gaza during the first two years of the uprising as part of a strategy linked to "national feeling" and self-reliance.[230] Urban dwellers, the elite, and professionals learned how to farm in vacant lots, on roofs, in window-box gardens, and in backyards. Often neophyte in execution and lacking prerequisite technical and marketing skills, the process of developing home gardens helped to politicize the population, Azmy Bishara told Daoud Kuttab.[231]

In addition to growing vegetables and fruits privately, Palestinians practiced small-scale animal husbandry to raise lambs, goats, cows, and chickens. A farmers' cooperative in Beit Sahour bought twenty milking cows from an Israeli kibbutz in preparation for making the village self-sufficient, and hid the creatures to evade confiscation by Israeli soldiers. Moments of hilarity injected themselves, as the fugitive cows became the "local heroes of the *intifada*."[232] In 1988, Palestinian journalist Muhammad Zahaike accompanied Bob Simon of CBS News and Mubarak Awad to the Bedouin village of Kissan, near Bethlehem. While viewing animal barns and feeding bins demolished by Israeli soldiers, someone suggested organizing a demonstration of the now homeless sheep, goats, donkeys, and chickens. Jonathan Kuttab and Awad telephoned the Israeli police for permits for a march to start at the Friday market in Jerusalem, where cattle were weekly bought and sold. To be a "peaceful animal march," the beasts would wear signs on their backs in Arabic, English, and Hebrew asking authorities to stop demolishing their homes and allow their barns to be rebuilt. After several conversations, an Israeli officer granted permission, pending confirmation. When the official asked who would clean up after the animals, Awad said volunteers from the Palestinian Center for the Study of Nonviolence would do any needed mopping or scrubbing. Zahaike records, "He rang back to ask: 'What if the animals become violent, especially the donkeys, and they attack the security forces, who would then be responsible?' They answered that the protest was peaceful, nonviolent, and violence was guaranteed not to happen. . . . The officer phoned a third time and stated in a forceful manner that it was forbidden to have the animals demonstrate. As soon as he hung up, we exploded in laughter."[233]

On July 1, 1988, on Israeli television, General Amram Mitzna, the senior Israeli military commander, declared the popular committees to be illegal and asserted that the civil administration "is the only authority" in the occupied territories.[234] Israel made membership in the popular committees punishable by up to ten years in prison. After outlawing the committees, the Israeli army crushed them in Gaza, jailing their members,[235] and arresting another two hundred Palestinians in the West Bank for membership in the "organizational backbone of the uprising."[236] Deportation orders against twenty-five heads of popular committees made it "hard to miss the paradox of Israel's quickness to deport anyone who showed signs of genuine leadership while complaining [that] there were no Palestinians of stature with whom to negotiate."[237] As hundreds of popular committee members landed in prison, their prestige and importance within the community rose, and fresh participants replaced them. These prisoners became symbols of Israel's inability to crush the intifada. Not only did such reprisals not quell the uprising, they intensified the spirit of resistance.[238]

The Siege of Beit Sahour

Although as early as 1923 Palestinians had discussed withholding taxes to protest Britain's support for Zionism, it was not until the intifada that they successfully implemented such a measure. The tax resistance carried out by the village of Beit Sahour involved the implementation of a highly coordinated strategy. Anthropologist Scott Atran explains its emblematic value: "Because most taxes collected in the West Bank and Gaza go to paying the costs of occupation with little reinvested in social services to the Occupied Territories, Palestinians began refusing to pay the costs of their own repression. The hallowed principle of 'no taxation without representation' would carry a special appeal."[239]

For twenty-two years, some of Beit Sahour's citizens had refused to pay taxes to Israel.[240] The determination of the entire village of Beit Sahour collectively to engage in economic noncooperation with the Israeli tax collection system began in mid-1988 and was in full swing by the summer of 1989. This ancient nonviolent action method produced a public relations fiasco when Israel moved to suppress it harshly and resulted in "an existential crisis of sorts in a nation [Israel] more comfortable responding to acts of violence than to peaceful acts of civil disobedience."[241] Israeli authorities cracked down hard on what Hanna Siniora termed the "almost perfect" nonviolent campaign by a "valiant village."[242]

What has been called the "siege" of Beit Sahour lasted from September 22 to October 31, 1989.[243] Adjacent to Bethlehem on the West Bank, the village was placed under 24-hour curfews during the first five days and was considered a closed Israeli military zone, leaving residents to survive solely on their own resources; they could not leave, and no one could enter. Subsequent curfews lasted from five o'clock in the afternoon to five o'clock in the morning. Israeli soldiers conducted surveillance from rooftops. Authorities severed telephone lines, rounded up scores of residents, ransacked homes and stores, and barred the news media, along with the consuls general of Belgium, France, Greece, Italy, Spain, Sweden, and the United Kingdom.[244] Tax authorities seized furniture and furnishings as well as Jad Ishaq, one of the key organizers, imprisoning him in Ansar 3 for six months, uncharged, for organizing the Shed.[245] Atran writes troops "seized and proceeded to auction off personal goods worth many times the value of the taxes ostensibly owed."[246] Feisel Husseini told reporters the village had "raised the flag of nonviolence," while the Israeli administration attempted to force it to "abandon this flag." More than NIS 1 million in confiscated goods were put to auction, as tax raids followed "a civil disobedience campaign that has been uniquely successful," according to Joel Greenberg. Not one of the merchants in the village capitulated to the paying of taxes.[247] After Israel lifted the siege, Palestinians held an ecumenical service at the Beit Sahour Roman Catholic Church in the mostly Christian village and invited Israeli peace proponents who had ventured to the village to join them in comaraderie. On November 12, 1989, a truckload of trees and saplings arrived from Israeli sympathizers.[248]

In the words of Scott Atran, "So fearful was the Israeli administration of the economic and symbolic value of nonpayment of taxes that it went to extraordinary measures to crush the 'tax rebellion.'"[249] Under international condemnation, the Israeli government changed tactics, thereafter conducting tax raids as discrete lightning strikes against individual villages, which thereby did not have time to organize synchronized strategies for self-sufficiency.[250]

Noncooperation and Civil Disobedience

Total civil disobedience—a course urged by Mubarak Awad and advocated in the Jerusalem Paper—was propounded early in the intifada. The degree of adherence by East Jerusalem businesses to calls for strikes showed how deeply the concept of noncooperation was being absorbed and the influence of the Command. During the initial three months of the intifada, the Palestinians generated momentum by holding demonstrations almost daily.[251] Stores closed as planned. The Israeli army responded by "breaking open shops and forcing the owners to stand inside," a measure that failed to prevent strikes, as the soldiers "could not compel customers to buy from the shops."[252] As a struggle ensued to force businesses to remain open, the army began breaking into shops and leaving them open. Jonathan Kuttab recalled this also had no impact: "There was no looting after the Israeli soldiers broke locks, so strong was the solidarity. The Israelis thought there would be riots and looting if they broke the locks on shops that had voluntarily closed in accord with the call of the intifada. Instead, volunteer welders fixed the broken locks, and youths carried the new keys to the homes of the shopkeepers."[253]

Eventually the shopkeepers did not bother to lock their shops at all, and street committees kept watch over them.[254] Israeli officials then ordered the opposite of whatever appeals the Command issued.[255] In May 1988, the Israelis demanded that shops close for three days; in an excess of zeal, merchants instead closed for more than twenty-four consecutive days and more than fifty days intermittently.[256] As the shop closures progressed, the Command, in its fifth communiqué, asked store owners to open for two or three hours a day, usually in the morning, except in times of a complete strike. The request arose because Palestinians would, otherwise, be forced to purchase goods from Israeli shops in West Jerusalem. "Everyone wanted to participate, and there was no question of going against it," Lucy Nusseibeh recollected; "any shop that stayed open, if shop closings were called, was boycotted."[257]

Seven brothers in the Balata refugee camp, near Nablus, came up with the idea of alternating the hours of strikes, to defy the Israeli-ordered hours: "The change from total strikes to intermittent strikes first occurred in Balata. . . . You had to have *some* time in which people worked. . . . This camp was the source of many acts of innovation and organization, which, in the early days, caught on simply by virtue of the fact that they made sense. People in Balata would do it, and soon it would become widespread. . . . There was a group of very enlightened and strategic-thinking people there."[258] The shop closings were "about demonstrating who is in charge"—defiance of Israeli orders, which were aimed at breaking compliance with strikes and challenges called for by the Palestinian leadership.[259] Joel Greenberg saw them as an effort to "sever contact" between the Palestinian populace and the Israeli authorities.[260]

The participation of merchants was intrinsic to the nonviolent strategy.[261] For example, early in the uprising, on February 2, 1988, shopkeepers from

Ramallah and al-Bireh called a news conference to announce six demands, including an international conference with PLO participation, an end to deportations, the freeing of Palestinians arrested in the uprising, and abolishment of the taxes that the Israeli government had sought since their enterprises had been closed. They stated, "You can't tax someone if he's not selling anything."[262] An unusual unanimity prevailed, with little expectation of outside help.

The clandestine leadership sought to spread the uprising's activities to as many locales as possible to appear ubiquitous, harmonizing actions to disperse the Israeli response and arranging for the uprising to show itself in many forms. Leaflets urged the writing of poetry, songs, and slogans and taking part in information campaigns.[263] Nullifying earlier norms of authority, they stressed "democratic emergent leadership from the people."[264] Prison became a rite of initiation, so much so that if one had not been imprisoned, his or her loyalty might be questioned, and prison records earned by the young replaced the stature once enjoyed by the elders. A leadership tested by survival under occupation and service to the community replaced the patronage system of the village patriarchs. A new status system meted out prestige based on action. The parents of activists were often chosen to lead the committees entrusted with donations, Salim Tamari observes, because of the sensitivity of handling money, and they would be entrusted with fair distribution of food and donations.[265] No division existed between rural farmers or refugee camp dwellers and the elite of East Jerusalem, retailers, and business owners, whose counterparts during the great revolt of 1936-39 had become its victims. Geographic and cultural differences were forgotten between "cool" East Jerusalem—the "brains" of the uprising—and a "hot" city like Nablus, the "heart" of the intifada, which had in 1931 been the center for student militancy.[266] Yehoshua Porath observed to Benny Morris that political unity was a defining feature.[267] Competing nationalist movements and parties shared a commonality of interest and worked together. Such unification was essential to separating the Palestinians from Israel, Tamari continued: "New sectors of society, until that time largely marginal, participated in the political struggle. . . . These strikes were voluntary and brought to the fore the idea of the impossibility of controlling the West Bank and Gaza Strip through military force. . . . The call to boycott Israeli products was also successful, . . . despite the Israeli military strength against it."[268] Differences between the nationalists and the Islamic revivalist movements were suspended. No one was allowed to claim credit for the intifada or to publish their own leaflets.[269]

On May 12, 1988, the Command noted success in forgoing Israeli products, quitting jobs in the civil administration, curtailing consumer spending, implementing community teaching, and creating committees on health, education, agriculture, food supplies, and information. Leaflet no. 16 states the popular committees are "making the day of full civil disobedience much nearer."[270] Eleven days later, a statement on civil disobedience similarly described the uprising as "proceeding on its steps toward full civil disobedience in all the occupied territories," depicted as the most effective way to weaken the occupation and speed establishment of a right of return, self-determination, and establishment of an independent state.[271] The Command called for suspension of all dealings with occupation authorities and the replacement of its services by those who possessed "popular authority," boycotts of Israeli products, abstention from paying taxes, and the burning of Israeli identity cards at a later stage. Apart from declining to call for withholding payment of electric and water bills, the appeal followed the program laid out by the Jerusalem Paper. The Command did not call for nonpayment on water and electricity accounts, noting that such delinquency would be the most difficult aspect of civil disobedience, because it would result in the termination of services. The May 23 statement reiterates the chance of worse retaliation from Israeli officials, while warning "civil disobedience is not a magic wand."[272]

Breaches inside the Command concerning political noncooperation disclosed themselves with the appearance of two versions of Leaflet no. 17 in late May. The first advocated a one-day strike in memory of Abu Jihad; the second materialized two days later and called for an eight-day strike and preparations for the civil disobedience campaign. According to Ian Black, Fateh's representative on the Command initially argued for a strike long in duration, but representatives of the DFLP and PCP opposed such a measure on the ground that the bulk of the Palestinians would be unable to sever all connections to the occupying authorities. Fateh capitulated, so the first leaflet went out calling for limited action. Appearance of the second edition suggests that other Fateh activists had wanted full civil disobedience but lacked the final say. A separate PFLP version of the latter, however, called for opening operational fronts for armed struggle and rejection of UN Resolutions 242 and 338.[273]

The resignation of twenty-two Palestinian officials from their jobs in the traffic and motor vehicles department in Ramallah on May 31, 1988, was extolled as the first piece of the civil disobedience program. The rapid response of department heads and employees to calls in the leaflets may have been related to increasing Israeli harassment through the rejection of licenses and registrations. The partial strikes that had characterized the initial stages of the uprising, with merchants opening shops for only a few hours a day, were reaching their limits in the battle over who would be heeded—the intifada Command or Israeli military authorities. Hardships began to affect families trying to acquire necessities under conditions of curfew and limited shopping hours. The resignation of six hundred police officers from their jobs represented the "pinnacle" of this phase.[274] In addition, some 120,000 Palestinian laborers refused to cross the Green Line for daily subsistence work.[275]

The wording of Leaflet no. 20, called the "Jerusalem Leaflet" of June 22, 1988, indicates progress had resumed toward the civil disobedience program, recognizing the merchants' withholding of taxes: "Despite the tax raids being carried out by the Israelis . . . we affirm the essentiality of not paying taxes, and . . . ask our merchants to organize sit-ins." It bade assigning Palestinian names to replace those on schools and buildings, and additional resignations as a step toward the comprehensive boycotting of Israeli institutions.[276] The Israeli reaction to such timeless noncooperation methods was as intense as it was broad, ranging from nighttime tax raids, special levies on cars and olive presses, the linkage of permits (such as drivers licenses and birth certificates) to the payment of taxes, the cutting of telephone links,[277] curbs on internal and foreign travel, closure of wholesale markets, a partial ban on exports to Jordan and Israel, a two-week ban on fuel oil and gasoline to Palestinian distributors—all designed to make civil disobedience impossible.[278] Leaflet no. 21 of July 6, 1988 reiterated the goal of *total* civil disobedience and lauded the hunger strikes and noncooperation being used by five hundred prisoners in the Dhahiriyeh detention center near Hebron. It affirmed boycotts, the withholding of fines and bail, withdrawal of funds from Israeli banks, increased output from local Palestinian industries, and labor unions' contracting with local enterprises; warned against collaborators; and urged that popular committees (instead of Israeli authorities) be contacted in emergencies.[279]

The leaflets—rather than being seen as edicts from a subordinated middle command or dicta issuing orders—should be recognized as revelations from an underground literature of an ongoing strategic debate in a covert movement in which virtually all dimensions of protest activity are illegal. In this light, it is significant that civil disobedience was debated for the entire first year of the uprising and well into its second. In Daoud Kuttab's view, Palestinian organizers had two options at the beginning of the uprising's second year: escalate nonviolent struggle to total civil disobedience, or turn to armed struggle, neither of which he viewed as practicable: "The Palestinian community which would have had to bear the brunt of a campaign of civil disobedience was not willing to go along with it, especially as the people saw that little progress had been made after the first year of the uprising. At the same time it was almost unanimously agreed that armed action was simply not feasible. There are few weapons, almost no opportunity to train and . . . armed action would be crushed very quickly and brutally."[280]

Leaflet no. 32, appearing in early 1989, urged Palestinians to stock up on food and necessities in the event of long sieges or strikes. Employment of a full spectrum of noncooperation methods would require substantial preparation, training, depth in popular support, and readiness by the Palestinians to cut ties entirely with Israeli authorities.[281] Lively disputations followed on whether the declaration of independence in the Husseini Document should follow or complement the civil disobedience program.[282] Preparation of the populace had been discussed, as leaflet after leaflet broached the suffering that civil disobedience would exact, including the need to forgo automobiles. Supporters of civil disobedience expected their fellow Palestinians to use animals for travel and were unconcerned about factories closing, because they believed this would prompt the establishment of small family-owned businesses that would be almost impossible to crush.[283]

Yet, ultimately, the population remained wary of full-scale civil disobedience. Haj Abd Abu-Diab concluded it could never be implemented, because of lack of understanding or agreement to it, the enormity of the burden it would impose, and the likelihood of reprisals more severe than those already experienced.[284] Extensive civil disobedience would also require far-reaching infrastructure. The role of the PLO in Tunis was perhaps the paramount reason for the failure to implement total civil disobedience. In a refrain voiced by a numerous local leaders of the intifada, Muhammad Jadallah explained, "1988 and 1989 were two pure years organized by local leadership, but when the interference of the [PLO] leadership started taking place, things started to suffer. . . . [Prior to 1990] the interrelations among the [factions] were great, with high responsibility, good cooperation, coordination, and there was space and place for everyone to operate separately. There was room for joint work, and there was room for individual work, so everybody was involved. This was the case until the [PLO] leadership took over. . . . By [March] 1990, it was their intifada. This is when the uprising was aborted. The intifada was strangulated by Palestinians, before it was strangulated by the Israelis."[285]

Until March 1990, the leaflets, with their deliberations on civil disobedience, were written in East Jerusalem—if polished via fax to Tunis—but after March, when the Israelis arrested members of the last autonomous Command, operatives in Tunis unfamiliar with nonviolent struggle composed them.[286] Calls for preparations for civil disobedience disappeared.[287] For approaching three years, the Palestinian activist intellectuals had succeeded in overcoming the nearly insuperable problem of factional disunity, while moving toward a "white revolution," teaching their compatriots to press for entitlements through nonviolent struggle. Their pursuit was not the *thawra* (armed revolution) of the post-1948 period, but the end of armed struggle and negotiations with Israel.

Aziz Shehadeh, attorney in Ramallah, West Bank, proposed the idea of two states side by side as early as 1948, with implied acceptance of Israel.

(Below) Raja Shehadeh, who in 1979 established the first Palestinian human rights organization, al-Haq (Law in the Service of Man), affiliated with the International Commission of Jurists in Geneva.

Feisel Husseini established the Arab Studies Society in East Jerusalem in 1980, one of thousands of civil society organizations that would make the intifada possible seven years later.

Gideon Spiro (left), Israeli former conscript paratrooper, who in 1980 cofounded with Feisel Husseini (right) the Committee Confronting the Iron Fist.

Palestinian-American clinical psychologist Mubarak Awad (right) and Gideon Spiro (left) shared a core insight into the power of refusal to cooperate. Awad's 1983 booklet *Nonviolence in the Occupied Territories* was influential.

Jonathan Kuttab, Palestinian-American lawyer who coauthored a series of papers in the early 1980s arguing the necessity for nonviolent resistance by Palestinians.

Amos Gvirtz, one of the Israeli volunteers of the Palestinian Center for the Study of Nonviolence, attended Mubarak Awad and Jonathan Kuttab's 1983 workshops on nonviolent struggle.

Daoud Kuttab, key Palestinian reporter, whose reportage was critical in explaining the first intifada.

Philosopher Sari Nusseibeh's writings throughout the 1980s led to a guiding role in the intifada.

Lucy Austin Nusseibeh worked then and now for a "white revolution," meaning pursuit of political goals without bloodshed.

Ghassan Khatib was among the communists who argued that the best way to fight military occupation was through small, localized non-military institutions—initially advocated in 1969.

Hanna Siniora, Palestinian newspaper editor, who encouraged his reporters to cover the manifestations of new Palestinian political thinking.

Scholar Gene Sharp, who traveled in 1986 and 1989 to meet with Israelis and Palestinians, and whose writings were distributed by the thousands in the West Bank and Gaza during the 1980s.

Hanan Mikhail Ashrawi hosted some meetings of the "think tank" at her home.

In late 1989, a human chain was organized by Peace Now, Israeli women's organizations, some members of the Knesset, Feisel Husseini, and other Palestinians. It encircled the Old City of Jerusalem.

Mary Elizabeth King (author) receiving the 2003 Jamnalal Bajaj International Award for promotion of Gandhian values, Mumbai, India.

Chapter 10
The Israelis

A NUMBER OF ISRAELIS had embarked on their own protestations of military occupation, and others proved receptive, as Palestinian activist intellectuals reached out to them. As some walked together in combined demonstrations, others held joint press conferences, and a few Israelis participated in hunger strikes. The bonds reinforced the concept of Israelis and Palestinians living and working side by side, lending validation to the two-state solution proffered by the East Jerusalem activists. Eventually, an intifada of scholars would occur, as Israeli and Palestinian academicians began meeting together for the first time to compare notes. Despite the mutual risks, both Israeli and Palestinian activist intellectuals insisted on working with their counterparts. Such cooperation and cohabitation had occurred historically, even at the height of conflict, but its narrative was often lost to sight. In November 1931, for example, Palestinian and Jewish truck drivers went on strike together against the steep taxes that had been imposed on motorists, especially truck drivers, to compensate for the loss of business from the railway system as buses and motor vehicles became preferred. Having paralyzed much of the country for eight days, the government reduced the taxes.[1]

A Seminar on Mount Carmel
Two months after the outbreak of the intifada, on February 9, 1988, Gene Sharp traveled again to Israel and the occupied territories. It had been two years since his last visit there. At the behest of Eugene Weiner, a sociologist at Haifa University, he spoke at the Israeli Institute of Military Affairs (IIMA), at Zichron Yaakov on Mount Carmel, to a seminar organized by Reuven Gal, the institute's head. Weiner, a founding director of the institute, had met Sharp at the home of psychoanalyst Robert K. Lifton, in Wellfleet, Massachusetts, where Sharp had described his research.[2]

The purpose of the session on Mount Carmel, on nonviolent resistance, was to introduce Sharp to key Israeli strategists and analysts: "There was something they had not yet grasped [about the intifada], and Gene might help them understand it from other precedents in the world, such as Burma, India, South Africa."[3] Retired general Aharon Yariv, formerly head of military intelligence and later a government minister for prime minister Golda Meir, attended, along with Israeli luminaries from the social sciences and military studies.[4] Sharp argued that limited options were available to Israel: (1) heightening repression; (2) tightening administrative controls; (3) maintaining repression at current levels; or (4) "Israel might openly, or while claiming it was not doing so, increasingly recognize elements of Palestinian independence and progressively reduce Israeli repression in extent and type."[5] A fifth option was the purview of the Palestinians: the pursuit of an intensifying but strictly nonviolent intifada. Detailing how the first three alternatives would be "disastrous for everyone concerned," Sharp explained that the fourth and fifth options offered hope for both peoples, particularly if facilitated by Israeli reparations for lost Palestinian land, which would cost far less than decades of continuing military build-ups.[6] As Gal pointed out, Sharp's projections stemmed not from specific immersion in the intifada, but from analyses of prototypical nonviolent struggles, which had led Sharp to conclude that the fourth option was the most likely to occur:

> Gene foresaw the end result, . . . in much the same way that it is inevitable that there will be a Palestinian state. Many Israelis still do not think it is possible. For many, it is still a nightmare to think of such a possibility, but anybody who has their mind in the right place can see it happening, . . . as Gene Sharp said in his fourth corollary or option. Gene had a big advantage [with his] cases to show that it was almost an inevitable process. Most of us Israelis . . . did not recognize the power of nonviolent struggle. . . . When you deal with nonviolent strugglers, one of their powers is that they gain sympathy. They certainly gain sympathy from third parties, but they may also gain sympathy from their opponent.[7]

Sharp asserted that the Palestinians' grasp of nonviolent resistance was thin and lacked depth, and the government of Israel thus had to be cautious and careful about the way it reacted. If reprisals against the uprising were harsh, he said, it could affect the ability of Israelis to bring an end to terrorism.[8]

Yet neither Weiner nor Gal would subsequently recollect the meeting as being particularly persuasive or productive. Regarding Sharp's presentation, Weiner said: "They thought that the Arabs couldn't develop such techniques. They thought that the Arabs were so inherently violent that they would never be able to adopt such strategies. They basically rejected the scenario expressed by Gene. They regarded his research as interesting, but not in line with the cultures of the Middle East."[9] Sharp's analyses were, in sum, rejected by the Israeli cognoscenti.

General Matan Vilnai was responsible for the Gaza Strip as the chief commander of what the Israelis called the Southern Command. Gal considered Vilnai powerful, influential at high levels in Israeli military circles, and a personal friend. Surmising that Vilnai might be interested in the substance of the February seminar, he contacted him. In March or April 1988, Gal met General Vilnai at the Eretz entrance to Gaza, in early morning, and joined him for a half day of rounds and meetings with troops and commanders. During the hours together, he tried to transmit Sharp's conceptualization of nonviolent struggle. He shared with the general Sharp's rendition of its principles and properties, "most importantly, the incapability of military forces to put it down," how it can make the nonviolent protagonist stronger than the target group, and how "when you have struggle like this, there is no way that the military can put it down, because it is not a military issue."[10] Gal recalled,

That afternoon, Vilnai gathered all of his chief commanders—thirty or forty of them—high rank, brigadiers, all the senior ranks that were dealing with the intifada. He gave me the floor, . . . "Tell them what you told me." I spoke for a long time. They were very attentive. I think it was the first time that any serious [group in] the military was . . . learning [of] nonviolent struggle as a . . . socio-political phenomenon. This should be granted to Gene Sharp. This is his contribution, even though not directly.[11]

Even this indirect exposure to Sharp's analysis eventually resulted in minimization of Israel's military engagement with the Palestinians, as, by 1991, in Gal's view,

[Israeli] instructions had moved 180 degrees to become, "Try to minimize contact with the Arabs. If they set fires in tires, let them do that. If they throw rocks or stones, move back. Try to avoid physical contact." . . . The

military started to understand that the uprising was not a military affair—
where the one who has the most offensive, is the one who wins—but,
really, the other way around. . . . But as I say, it took the Israelis three or
four years to digest this, . . . until 1991.[12]

The following year, in July, Weiner persuaded Gal to invite Sharp back
as guest speaker for a seminar on the impact of the intifada.[13] The IIMA had
been renamed the Carmel Institute for Social Sciences: "You may call this
one of the outcomes of the intifada," Gal mused; "We felt uncomfortable
being identified as an institute for military studies."[14] Weiner recalled that he
was eager for the second discussion in 1989, because, he believed,

> Gene's predictions had been close enough to the truth for it to have been
> an impressive analysis. . . . Despite the rejection of Gene's concepts [in
> 1988], his comments had been borne out. He had claimed that the Arabs
> had become more sophisticated and more capable. The response from my
> fellow Israelis was that the intifada was violent, that it was anything but
> nonviolent struggle, and that the Arabs were using whatever weapons were
> available. Much of the discussion the second time was over whether the
> intifada was violent insurrection or civil disobedience.[15]

Meanwhile, some army commanders started to admit to reporters that
quashing the uprising in the West Bank and Gaza Strip was a "hopeless task,"
no matter what tactics they tried, and a few military leaders, including
defense minister Yitzhak Rabin, granted that the uprising would end only
through a political solution.[16] On July 10, 1989, in the seminar, noting that
Israeli control measures had failed to end the intifada, Sharp called attention
to statements by Israeli military commanders conceding that no military
response could suppress the uprising. He called for reconsideration of reality
by both sides, and noted that the Israelis would not be packing their bags.
He told of learning in a Palestinian refugee camp that the young had been
and were willing to live peacefully in an independent Palestine alongside
Israel, long before it would become PLO policy. He said that the Palestinians
were not going away either, but would continue to struggle until they won
the independence and respect that Israel had gained. He made an observation that some Israeli policies he had witnessed had hurt the long-term goal
of a free Israel and discussed options.[17] Although among the Israelis neither

Weiner nor Gal remember their colleagues as having been fully persuaded, Sharp's analysis found more attentive listening than in the first seminar. "There was an aura," Weiner said. "Sharp had been vindicated, because the sympathies of the world [judged] the intifada less violent than were the Israelis; therefore, the uprising was, comparatively speaking, nonviolent."[18]

Official Israeli Countermeasures in Response to the First Intifada

Kimmerling and Migdal assert the "bloodthirsty stereotype" resulting from the PLO's "emphasis on terror" had over the years exacted a high cost in the loss of "Israelis who might have sought accommodation." Moreover, Israeli leaders could point to the terrorism as evidence that the Palestinian Covenant involved not solely the elimination of Israel, but of Jews generally, and "the world's revulsion enabled these leaders to delegitimize Palestinian national claims."[19] The government of Israel officially regarded the intifada as another phase of protracted Arab hostilities against Israel, although, as Efraim Inbar points out, Yitzhak Rabin never toyed with the purely military solution advocated by Israel's right wing.[20] Tanks and troops were never deployed in the 1987 uprising as China had responded to the student nonviolent pro-democracy movement in Tiananmen Square in Beijing, concurrently in 1989. Rather, military operations by Israel against the "motley outbreaks of civic Palestinian resistance"—Inbar and coauthor Stuart A. Cohen's description of the uprising—fell into a category designated in 1896 by the British military analyst C. E. Callwell as "small war." Used to pursue extensive goals, including political aims, Callwell's small war was for purposes of subjugating the enemy rather than annihilation. In this scenario, small units of force would be employed to bring about attrition.[21] Initially attempting to use force in an "annihilatory mode" through beatings, Israeli policy makers eventually adopted an "attritional approach," combining "limited force" with a lower profile in the territories.[22] Israel's political goals were twofold: to prevent its having to withdraw from the occupied territories and establishment of an independent Palestinian state.[23] Israeli military historian Meir Pail confirms this view, noting that the response of the Israeli leadership was to try to wear the Palestinians down and paralyze the intifada, without formulating political moves toward Palestinian self-determination.[24] Israel avoided reprisals that might have cost thousands of lives, yet preclusion of mass killings may have arisen more out of concern over creating polarization among its citizens and Jewish communities around the world than was already evident.[25] Had the endurance of the Palestinians been correctly assessed by the Israeli authorities, who from the start believed the uprising to be a brief "passing phase," more repressive measures might have been used.[26]

Meron Benvenisti, former deputy mayor of Jerusalem, contended that although the "impressive manifestation of communal power" of the uprising was "not directed at the destruction of Israel," but at assertion by the Palestinians, Israel still defined it as "a problem of law and order."[27] As Reuven Gal observed, it took years for the Israelis to recognize that the uprising had political rather than military goals. The extreme ten-year penalties against membership in the Palestinian popular committees resulted from the perception that "for the Israelis, especially in the beginning of the intifada, the first two or three years, this was seen as a military uprising, a violent uprising. So even though the committees talked about distributing food, the Israelis took them to be distributing propaganda and fuelling violence. For the Israelis, the humanistic aspects—distributing foodstuffs and so on—were considered only a cover story for the real aims of propaganda."[28] Discerning "no distinctions between mainstream, dissident, or renegade PLO factions," Israeli politicians alleged that the "terrorist" aims of the PLO had not changed.[29] This insistence led innumerable Israelis to see the uprising as a tactical effort masking more sinister plans.[30] Palestinian pleas for peace were read as treachery by many Israelis. Successive prime ministers had defined the Israeli response as brutal and unforgiving. The first official U.S. criticism of Israel did not appear until February 7, 1989, in the U.S. Department of State Country Reports on Human Rights.[31]

"My government makes a great effort to show that the intifada is violent," stated Daniel Rubinstein, correspondent with *Davar* (Word).[32] Jerusalem city manager Aharon Sarig expressed a widespread outlook that the uprising was led by "children who are controlled by terror organizations."[33] Israeli claims that Palestinian parents had forced their offspring into confrontations with Israeli soldiers were said to have absolved the IDF of responsibility for high casualty rates among the young. Israel was determined not to accept any Palestinian opposition, be it violent or nonviolent, according to Daoud Kuttab.[34]

The policy of beatings had reached "monstrous dimensions," noted Citizens' Rights Movement MKs Yossi Sarid and Dedi Zucker, who toured Gaza on January 21, 1988, and compiled a report. They were referring to Yitzhak Rabin's exhortation to use "might, force and beatings," in what Avi

Shlaim calls the "kind of arrogant and aggressive attitude that had provoked the uprising in the first place."[35] Sarid and Zucker state, "The results of the defense minister's policy can be seen on the hands, backs, and heads of hundreds of youths and old people in the Gaza Strip."[36] The heart of the problem, expressed an ABC News correspondent, "is the greed, the extremism, the opportunism that have . . . driven Israeli policy in the occupied territories and the weakness of more moderate leaders to stand up to these forces of darkness or even to recognize them for what they are."[37] Likud's defense minister Moshe Arens in 1989 replaced his predecessor Yitzhak Rabin's policy with instructions to the security forces to keep a low profile of restraint, avoid unnecessary provocations and confrontations, and minimize armed force.[38]

Israeli elections in the autumn of 1988 polarized the society, and the balloting came to represent a referendum on Palestinian self-determination.[39] By the beginning of the third year of the intifada, after 750 Palestinians had been killed (along with 42 Israelis during the same period), a Palestinian activist in Nablus told a reporter that several hundred more would have to die before Israel would come to the negotiating table.[40]

The First Intifada and Mechanisms of Change in Israel

The intifada occurred in specific response to the military occupation imposed after the June war of 1967, yet the exact nature of the uprising has been difficult to discern, partly because of emotionally charged historical complications, starting with what Scott Atran calls the "surrogate colonization" of Palestine.[41] Scriptural text had been used as the basis of international law.[42] The stark and unbearable consequences from the mid-twentieth century genocidal Holocaust unavoidably obscured perceptions of the intifada.

Israeli responses to the first Palestinian uprising can be clarified by explaining four mechanisms, or processes, defined over the years to differentiate the effects of nonviolent struggle generally.[43] They explain what can be aimed for in nonviolent struggle, and how results can be realized.

In conversion, the first mechanism, the target group reacts to nonviolent direct action by accepting a new point of view and adopts the goals of the nonviolent protagonists. The opponents' emotions and belief systems are, hence, "converted." This mechanism is exceedingly rare. Israelis in small numbers and constituencies came to see themselves as occupiers and acknowledged the Palestinians as human beings who merit sympathy and respect. Astute and perceptive Israeli observers contend that some deep-seated changes in perception occurred.[44] (Concurrently, Feisel Husseini believed that through the intifada Palestinians moved toward acceptance of Israelis as persons.[45] Some Palestinians recognized that they in the occupied territories could not seek a solution that would displace 3.5 million Jews.[46])

With accommodation—the most customary mechanism of change and occurring most frequently historically—the target group in a nonviolent struggle chooses to yield on demands and adjust to the new circumstances produced by the nonviolent challengers, yet without necessarily changing their positions on the underlying issues. This second mechanism, accommodation, most accurately describes the Israeli response, in which some Palestinian demands might be granted without any apparent alteration in Israeli mind-sets.[47] Such a response can quiet internal dissension, preserve decorum, avert a worse predicament, limit damage, or cut losses—an acknowledgement that outright refusal to accede to the demands of the nonviolent movement would be too taxing and not worth the cost politically. Rather than transforming the thinking or the convictions of the target group, it results in an alteration of the situation. Numerous Israelis, rather than changing their belief systems or intentions, saw the issue merely as one necessitating different techniques for containing the Palestinian problem.[48] Accommodation is typical of trade union strike settlements, heavily influenced by the extent of power that each side can wield.

The third mechanism, nonviolent coercion, occurs when the members of the target group remain in place with their policies unchanged, yet they are no longer able to manage the system without the cooperation of the nonviolent protagonists. Internal divisions erupt. Repression is ineffective, because of massive noncooperation by the populace, or because the police and security apparatus in the camp of the opponent will no longer dependably carry out orders. This can happen without the will or consent of the target group, which may retain control of the structures of power and the capability to use them, even as its capacity for containing the nonviolent resisters may wane or be circumscribed, because of defiance by the citizenry. The nonviolent protagonists may achieve their objectives against the will of the adversary yet fall short of dismantling the system of the target group. If soldiers and police mutiny, bureaucracies refuse to function, or the populace withdraws authority and support, the ability of the target group to apply repression can be thwarted or even eliminated.[49]

The fourth mechanism, disintegration—the collapse of the opponent's power system—did not occur.[50] The Israeli army did not refuse to obey en masse.

A process known as *political jujitsu* is rare, but linked to the mechanisms. With careful strategic planning, a nonviolent movement can decide to aim for a particular mechanism, and then chart a progression of action methods to try to achieve it. Harder to establish as an objective, political jujitsu cannot be sought simplistically. By deliberately refusing to meet violence with more of the same, and by sustaining nonviolent behavior despite repression, the nonviolent protagonists can throw the target group off balance by causing its repressive measures to be seen in harsh light. As cruelties increase, the opponent's regime comes to appear more despicable. Its ranks can split. The conflict can shift, becoming, instead, an internal dispute over the infliction of violence on unarmed peaceful protesters. The target group becomes unsure of how to respond to the deliberate refusal of the nonviolent actors to reciprocate with violence. Sympathies of the police or troops may begin to flow toward the nonviolent actors. Meanwhile, if the nonviolent proponents maintain discipline, they may gain self-assurance. They cannot use violence or they will fuel their opponent's determination, furnish pretexts for harsher crackdowns, while weakening themselves. Even if brutal repression results, the nonviolent challengers may still move toward a solution. Disagreement by the populace and with the atrocious measures witnessed can turn on itself, resulting in a withdrawal of support from the adversary and backing for the nonviolent resisters. Third parties—whose espousal and economic assistance the opponent regards as important—may turn away or lose commitment. In exceptional cases, the opponent's own security or police forces may come to oppose the reprisals being unleashed against the nonviolent challengers and disobey orders. *Political jujitsu* thus describes a phenomenon in which the use of brutality against a nonviolent group, rather than breaking its determination, can instead rupture the base of the opponent. The changes induced through jujitsu do not operate in isolation, and are complementary to other political, social, economic, and psychological alterations. If the defiance and solidarity are sufficiently broad, it can be impossible to crush the nonviolent movement.[51]

Israeli soldiers never felt compelled to mutiny, switch allegiance, or go over to the Palestinian side in political jujitsu. Although some segments of Israeli society experienced sympathy for the unarmed Palestinians who were being disproportionately killed by armed soldiers, no mass movement or upheaval of Israelis developed against military service in the occupied territories.

The Israeli Left Stirs

Israeli peace groups reactivated or were formed anew in response to the intifada. High school students who refused to perform military service in the occupied territories had organized themselves in 1978 under the name of the Group of 27.[52] The 1982 war in Lebanon had elicited the first refusal of members of the Israeli military to serve in the armed forces.[53] Colonel Eli Geva, for example, asked to be relieved of his command of a tank brigade.[54] A professional soldier, he was the highest-ranking officer who decided to leave Lebanon, on grounds that what he had been ordered to do was militarily unacceptable. He was not the only one who said that the ten-week siege and Battle of Beirut was a mistake that had led the soldiers into catastrophe.

Yesh Gvul, an organization of Israelis in the armed forces who selectively refuse military service, started with a 1982 petition signed by 2,500 reservists, who asked not to be assigned to military service in Lebanon. Its first activity was a letter signed by 86 reservists to Begin and Sharon, declaring their refusal to serve there. Of the reservists who had petitioned, 150 were court-martialed and sent to prison. "Some were court-martialed again and again," Gideon Spiro, one of the founders that year of Yesh Gvul, and who with Feisel Husseini had led the Committee Confronting the Iron Fist in the early 1980s, notes: "They would serve thirty days in prison, be called again to duty, and then be court-martialed and locked up again, sometimes several times, just to harass them."[55] Established in 1982 to protest the war in Lebanon, Spiro recalls:

> What was unique about Yesh Gvul is that *refusal* had been unknown in Israel until that time. The army was sacrosanct, a sacred cow. Refusal had never even been debated in Israel. No right to conscientious objection is recognized by law for men. What was most difficult for Israelis to accept is that we were advocating *selective* refusal. We were saying was that we understand the need for defense, and we have taken oaths to defend the country, but we do not want to be part of aggression. This was very difficult for Israelis to accept.[56]

Later, Yesh Gvul took issue with the military occupation of lands reserved by the Unted Nations for the Palestinians: "We were ready to defend our country," Spiro said, "but not ready to carry out abuses of human rights. It was not our duty to oppress the Palestinians or defend the settlements, which are defined as war crimes in international law. We said that we will not defend an apartheid regime."[57]

The Israeli intelligentsia became active, as "writers and artists, psychologists and mental health professionals, social workers, doctors, journalists and . . . joint Israeli-Palestinian committees" protested the occupation.[58] MK and sociologist Naomi Chazan estimated that eighty-six new Israeli peace groups came into being as a result of the intifada. A projected 40 percent of all Israeli protest activity after the start of the 1987 uprising came from newly formed groups.[59] Existing and moribund protest movements were emboldened. A cacophony of organizations pleaded for revised government policies.

Some groups were outrightly condemnatory of Israel's position, such as Dai L'Kibbush (Down with the Occupation). Within two months of the start of the uprising, 160 Israeli army reservists signed a declaration refusing to "take part in suppressing the uprising in the occupied territories"; among their ranks were three majors and five captains.[60] By June 1988, according to Mordechai Bar-on, twenty members of the Israeli armed services were in jail for refusing to serve in the occupied territories.[61] Peretz Kidron believes refusals by Israeli soldiers to serve in the occupied territories due to their government's response to the uprising probably eventually ran into four figures.[62]

A number of soldiers eventually adopted civil disobedience as a necessary step for opposing the occupation.[63] Eight months into the first intifada, defense minister Rabin confirmed that 120 army reservists and 5 army regulars had refused to serve in the territories. The government of Israel imprisoned 29 of them, including 3 officers. It would eventually release as many as 100 soldiers for refusing to serve.[64]

In the beginning, Yesh Gvul would not accept committed pacifists as members. In its posture, what Reuven Kaminer terms "patriotic anti-militarism," it wanted to emphasize the readiness of its members to accept military service, while making clear their disagreement with the post-1967 military occupation.[65] Yet as time went on, it broadened its membership to admit pacifists.[66] By January 1, 1988, shortly after the intifada started, Yesh Gvul published the names of the reservists who had put their appelations on a declaration of intent "to refuse to take part in suppressing the uprising and insurrection in the Occupied Territories."[67] Among the signatories were three majors, five captains, one medical officer, and a Jerusalem municipality councilor; a number were veterans of combat units, and there were a "large number" of junior and noncommissioned officers.[68] By early summer 1988, the number of potential "refuseniks" stood at six hundred. One of the leaders of Yesh Gvul, Adi Ophir, a lecturer at Tel Aviv University, called attention in a letter to defense minister Rabin to the difference between the defense of Israel and the "continuing enslavement of another nation."[69]

Gideon Spiro described the mission of Yesh Gvul as follows:

> Israelis were and are the victims of blind obedience, and we in Yesh Gvul made it our mission to break such blind obedience. Nobody in Israel (from any political angle) would question that *refusal* in Nazi Germany was justified. We asked the question: do we have to wait until we have reached the stage of Germany under Nazism to start to refuse, or do we have to begin much earlier before we have reached the stage of such dictatorship? There are war crimes which are not equivalent to those of Nazi Germany, and still it is justified to refuse to participate in them. For example, against the apartheid regime of South Africa, the U.S. war in Vietnam, the U.S. invasion in the war against Iraq, the 1982 Israeli war in Lebanon, or in the occupation of the Palestinians starting in 1967, refusal is justified.
>
> Between 1933 and 1939 [even before the "Final Solution"], Nazi Germany was a brutal, racist regime. I think that large numbers of Israeli society, and Israeli ruling circles, sometimes resemble those of Nazi Germany in the 1930s, especially in their adoption of racist principles.
>
> I am a survivor of *crystalnacht,* the night of shattered glass, when Germans in 1938 rampaged Jewish shops and synagogues. When I see Israeli soldiers and Jewish settlers in the occupied territories, they are very often acting more brutally that what was happening when I was a small child during that period [1933-39] in Nazi Germany. Israel is the classic example of a beaten child, who became a beating parent. Jewish racism and Jewish war crimes are not less ugly because they are Jewish.[70]

Shalom Achshav (Peace Now) grew exponentially during the intifada. It had initially been formed in July 1978, tracing its existence to a letter written to then prime minister Menachem Begin and signed by 348 army reserve officers and combat veterans, some of whom had been decorated in three wars.[71] They never sent the missive, which asked the premier not to place maintenance of the occupied territories above the pursuit of peace, but it appeared instead in *Haaretz*—"the better to make its point."[72]

Several dozen distinguished retired senior Israeli military officers formed the Council for Peace and Security in March 1988, and urged an end to the occupation by pressing the idea that Israelis must compromise to gain real security.[73] Their reasoning was different from that of Yesh Gvul and the Israeli peace movements, as Gideon Spiro notes: "The first consideration of Yesh Gvul and the peace groups was the 'crime of military occupation,' but the generals were concerned about Israeli security. They presented a view that occupation was an endangerment to the Jewish state, because, if busy as an occupying power, the army would deteriorate, jeopardizing the Jewish state."[74] Arguing publicly that the territories were no longer worth holding, the generals said the Gaza Strip alone was requiring more troops to be deployed than were needed to occupy all of the territories in 1967.[75] In January 1989, by which time 350 Palestinians and 15 Israelis had been killed, the generals spoke openly of the psychological damage being caused to those in military service by being forced to fill the role of riot police, rather than soldier. An elite paratrooper unit assigned to Nablus angrily confronted Prime Minister Shamir in the same month, complaining that during the intifada they had been forced to brutalize Palestinians.[76]

When General Amram Mitzna led a discussion of the Kibbutz Artzi movement, a coalition of eighty-six kibbutzim, reserve officer Eli Ben-Gal protested, "The Palestinians are making us kill them, and faced with this the Jewish people have become morally paralyzed. We won't last. We won't be able to. They are destroying us by making us the guilty ones."[77] The uprising "broke the I.D.F.," an Israeli military historian told a reporter.[78] Israeli military and civilian psychologists and psychiatrists notified the country's leadership that conscripts were suffering psychological stress as a result of a self-perception that they were part of an occupying force, not soldiers defending Israeli security.[79] Israeli scholar Yeshayahu Leibowitz would later remark that at last there was recognition in Israel that the "status of violent domination over another people cannot endure."[80]

While some activists arranged street demonstrations, others protested symbolically, undertook documentation of abuses, or made secret contacts with the PLO. On December 30, 1989, a human chain encircled the Old City of Jerusalem, a demonstration involving Peace Now, Israeli women's organizations, Ratz MKs, and Feisel Husseini and other Palestinians.[81] The distance around the Old City is 4,010 meters (just under two and a half miles). Peace Now estimated that at least 25,000 persons walked together, of whom two-thirds were Israeli.[82] Organizers said they were demonstrating in favor of a Palestinian state and a Jewish state side by side.[83] Although no one threw stones, Israeli police used rubber bullets, tear gas, water cannons, and truncheons to break up the crowds.[84] Horses trampled women, and protesters were targeted with gunfire, water cannon, and tear gas.[85]

One group has since become an international movement. Women in Black started in Jerusalem in January 1988, a month after the start of the intifada, when a small group of women began carrying out a simple act of denunciation. Condemning the military occupation, and opposing the use of excessive force by Israeli troops against the young Palestinians who protest it, each week, every Friday afternoon, they hold a small vigil in Paris Square, a hundred yards from the prime minister's residence, at a busy five-way intersection near downtown West Jerusalem. Evoking images of widowhood, and wearing black to signify mourning and loss of morality and reason, they raise black signs in the shape of a hand saying "Dai L'Kibbush," or Down with the Occupation! The wearing of black also blends perceptions of who is an Arab and who is Israeli. The idea spread rapidly and spontaneously to other parts of the world. At least twenty-four spinoffs in Europe, North America, and South America now similarly hold vigils in solidarity or in denunciation of other issues of discrimination, racism, or sexism.

Leaders of Israeli peace organizations claimed that their nation's moral standing and the tenets of Judaism were compromised by the government's harsh treatment of the Palestinians. "The fiber of our country is threatened by denying the Palestinians' rights—it's morally wrong, politically wrong—and destructive for us and for them," stressed Galia Golan, who in 1988 chaired Peace Now; "we both have claims to this land; we both have rights to this land."[86] Israel had professed a posture of ethics involving a central concept of justice that had historically been associated with Judaism—in the words of historian and theologian Gerardus van der Leeuw, "the religion of Will and Obedience."[87] Some Israelis were perturbed by the moral issues arising from militarily fighting a civilian uprising.[88] Israelis also paid a price, as sources of alternative information about changes in Palestinian political thinking were closed down by Israeli officials. The Israeli Alternative Information Center and the Palestine Press Service were among nearly a dozen outlets shut by

Israeli authorities during the uprising.[89] Moreover, Israeli civil liberties were sacrificed, as when Israeli songs protesting the occupation were banned.[90]

By 1990, the Israeli rubber bullets used against the intifada had killed an estimated 125 Palestinians, according to Michael Posner of the Lawyers Committee for Human Rights, and Kenneth Roth of Human Rights Watch.[91] It became harder to assert that Israel presided over a benign occupation or espoused democratic values. As Gideon Spiro put it, "The Palestinian uprising dealt the final blow to Israelis who believed in an 'enlightened' occupation."[92] A residual sense of tragic victimhood left by the Holocaust had been replaced in the international worldview by a perception of the Palestinians as the victims. It had become clear that even when the penalties were extreme, Palestinians in the territories would not remain quiescent, and Israel could not suppress the seething in the camps, villages, and cities. In addition to the damaged morale in the military, the army was in conflict with Israel's civilian leaders, who insisted that the army develop a military solution for a problem whose "roots and essence are political," according to Dan Shomron, IDF chief of staff. He told a Knesset committee, "There is no such thing as eradicating the uprising because in its essence it expresses the struggle of nationalism."[93]

Chapter 11
The End of the First Intifada

Unintended Consequences, Uncertainties, and Collapse

The choice of a nonviolent strategy had unpredicted results for all parties. Among the Palestinians, disagreement raged on what constituted a nonviolent approach. Was the throwing of stones included, or not? Representatives on the Command vacillated. The Islamist blocs, while disagreeing on the overall plan, used some of its tactics. Israeli officials refused to differentiate anything new in the nonviolent action methods. The PLO was quick to seize the benefits of the positive international response to the display of nonviolent sanctions inside the territories, while simultaneously contradicting its own declared support. Hamas enjoyed Israeli support, yet the champions of nonviolent struggle met ambivalence, and worse.

Mixing Violent with Nonviolent Strategies

A two-part analysis of the first thirty-nine leaflets of the Command shows that more than 90 percent of the appeals in the initial eighteen months of the intifada called for classic nonviolent methods, such as strikes, demonstrations, marches, the withholding of taxes, and the boycotting of Israeli products.[1] Leaflets no. 1 to 17 contain an overwhelming majority of appeals for nonviolent measures, including general strikes,[2] local strikes, the raising of Palestinian flags, defiance of school closures, symbolic funerals, the ringing of church bells, and the renaming of streets and schools. Of these appeals, 4.9 percent are bids for throwing stones or using petrol-filled bottles. In other words, of the twenty-seven action methods counseled in the first six months, all but one are explicitly nonviolent, most from a range of recognizable action steps.[3]

Leaflets no. 18 to 39 place more emphasis on economic measures, with ninety-nine appeals classifiable as economic—an effort to raise the financial costs of the military occupation to Israel. Noncooperation methods comprise the bulk of the remaining appeals.[4] Protest activities called for by the fliers include the cancellation of holiday celebrations, the applying of pressure for prisoner releases, appeals for family reunion, and fasting and prayers. That is, 90.4 percent of Leaflets no. 18 to 39 entail specifically nonviolent measures, versus 9.6 percent of the appeals that call for violent actions, such as throwing stones or petrol bottles, and measures against collaborators.[5] Of the fifteen categories of methods employed by Gandhi, as analyzed by scholar Johan Galtung, the Palestinians employed fourteen—the exception being *hijra* (migration).[6]

A predisposal of Palestinian communities to essentially nonviolent struggle can be seen in their restraint despite the thousands of Israeli soldiers in their midst.[7] In 1989, Gene Sharp observed,

> [G]iven the severity of Israeli repression in the form of beatings, shootings, killings, house demolitions, uprooting of trees, deportations, extended imprisonments and detention without trial . . . the Palestinians during the intifadah have shown impressive restraint. Specific instructions . . . [were] issued by the . . . [PLO] and the leadership in the territories *not* to use firearms; with few exceptions, the order has been respected. The 15 percent or so of the uprising that is constituted by low-level violence involves chiefly stone throwing.[8]

Self-control was evident in the action methods, some as modest as families wanting to visit their loved ones detained in Ansar 3 going through the Red Cross—as the Command asked—rather than cooperate with Israeli authorities,[9] and the numbers traveling to the infamous detention center in the Negev declined. On the eve of Yom Kippur in 1988, no violence resulted when youths from the Qalandia camp stopped traffic on the main north-south highway connecting Jerusalem with Ramallah and Nablus. For thirty minutes, beginning at 8:15 P.M., the youths used large boulders and burning tires to block the road. When an outside light went on at a nearby house, "a member of the Palestinian team approached the family and politely asked if they could turn the light off"; Daoud Kuttab reports the action was "well planned" and "disciplined and organised."[10]

The evidence shows conspicuous control of violence for the initial two years of the intifada, and well into the third, and even after that, the uprising did not exhibit organized violence. Yet Hillel Frisch labels the uprising as "prolonged violence," and interprets the "proliferation of diffuse, small-scale organizations" as necessary support for this intended battery.[11] Since Israeli political leaders often found it expedient to underscore what they regarded as the "violent nature" of the Palestinians, Edward Kaufman explains, the stones reinforced the "already acute perceptions of fear in large sections of the population."[12] Sharp concedes the throwing of stones was mild compared to the beatings and shootings of Palestinians by Israeli soldiers (Israeli settlers in the West Bank and Gaza would later take license and be provided with guns to use against the Palestinians), yet he agrees with Kaufman in that rocks had killed Israelis: "Israelis can almost never see a stone thrown at them as a relatively nonviolent expression of rage and a cry for justice," because it invokes memories of the Nazi Holocaust, "triggering highly disproportionate and irrational responses."[13] Thrown stones guaranteed high Palestinian casualties, Sharp cautioned, making it "extremely difficult to find a Palestinian justification of this heavy price in terms of the *instrumental effectiveness of that form of action*."[14] Haj Abd Abu-Diab regretted, "With Mubarak Awad's way, we did not lose people. . . [In] the intifada, we lost people, because of the stones."[15]

Throwing of Stones

Residents of the West Bank and Gaza say that the use of stones is traditional and at the outbreak of the intifada was spontaneous. Stones appear in biblical narratives as punitive actions. They had been thrown at times during the 1920s and 1930s Palestinian opposition to the Balfour Declaration. During the 1987 uprising, the throwing of stones was part of almost any demonstration—impromptu or planned—and could be provoked by Israeli soldiers closing the entrance to a camp or an Israeli-inflicted injury. Fateh, the DFLP, and the PFLP never repudiated their use.[16] Rarely was the throwing of stones isolated. It was usually organized and undertaken by a large group including children, youths, women, and men.[17]

Most Palestinians interviewed here see the practice as hard evidence that they were not using weapons. Stones may have been weapons during the Stone Age, Azmy Bishara observed, but in the intifada concretely manifested the absence of weaponry: "This is neither a weapon nor a guerrilla strike. . . . It symbolizes nakedness against an occupier. . . . [and] the nonaccessability—no presence—of weapons in the hands of the people."[18] International law authorities Richard Falk and Burns Weston view the stones as symbolic, in

light of the "scale and character of the weaponry relied on by the Israeli army.
. . . [in which] Israel has reacted to Palestinian resistance with the excessive
and disproportionate use of lethal force, including the apparent targeting of
civilians and children, . . . repeated and fundamental violations of the Fourth
Geneva Convention, violations that amount to war crimes and crimes against
humanity."[19]

Daoud Kuttab ascribed two aims to the stones:

> One, it was a weapon that was widely available everywhere, and it left no
> traces. Two, it was influenced by the Israeli settlements process. Every-
> where, [Israeli settlers] were driving daily from their houses, commuting;
> therefore, the roads through Palestinian land became very important. In
> other words, the people were there, and the non-lethal weapon was there.
> The intifada was a protest against the occupation, not against Israel. What
> it said was "this is our land; if you trespass without a visa or permission,
> you will be harassed."[20]

The centers from which stones were thrown were adjacent to the main
roads, where friction between Palestinians and Israeli settlers is most
intense.[21] Middle East human rights analyst Joe Stork saw a paradox,
because the same stones thrown by Palestinians were being quarried to build
"fortress suburbs" for Israeli settlements.[22]

To Chaim Bermant, the stones showed that military occupation has its
price.[23] The 1967 boundaries were redrawn by the stones, as, apart from
armed settlers, Israelis increasingly choose not to venture beyond the Green
Line, Israel's 1948 border.[24] Bermant saw arguments taking place in the
Knesset between the Labor and Likud parties on territorial concessions in
return for peace over the heads of the Palestinians, as if they were not
involved; "The Arabs have now shown that it is very much their business
and, in the absence of a ballot, they have voted with stones."[25]

Little hard evidence can be found that the stones were intended to be
murderous.[26] Yet Rabbi David Hartman, who on the Israeli spectrum falls
in the binational tradition of Martin Buber and Judah Magnes, was hit in
the face by a stone that could have killed him. Not surprisingly, he considers the stones not as symbolic instruments of protest, but of homi-
cide.[27] Mubarak Awad viewed the throwing of stones similarly. Nancy
Nye explained:

It upset many Palestinians who attended Mubarak's workshops in the autumn of 1983 that he declared stone throwing to be violence. He also said that the children were courageous. In their own small way, he maintained—then, and during the *intifada*—the children were doing something about the occupation, while their elders were often doing nothing. . . [H]e always classified stone-throwing as violent.[28]

To many Palestinians, the hurled stones were meant to impede and harass—not to kill—the occupying Israeli military forces and the Israeli settlers in the West Bank and Gaza. Ramallah newspaper editor Hafid Barghouti shared this viewpoint, "No Israeli was killed by stones," and there were no lethal injuries from "stones in the face."[29] A hunger striker commented, "It is not a hobby for us to throw stones or Molotov cocktails. We are normal people," but oppression "will express itself."[30] According to a strategic studies institute in Tel Aviv,

Not even the most brilliant public relations campaign could have nullified or even moderated the powerful message generated worldwide by television images of the disturbances, and primarily violent behavior by IDF soldiers against stone-throwing youths and against women and children. The result was to drive home the point that the IDF was an occupation army facing a civilian population fighting for its political right of self-determination.[31]

The throwing of stones broke the stigma of narrowly defined patriarchal gender roles, as grandmothers cracked rocks and mothers stood sentry.[32] In addition, class status had little or no bearing, as shown when two hundred Palestinian lawyers joined a Gaza protest early in the intifada. "Hoary heads and dozens of men in suits, ties, and polished shoes" appeared in the ranks within minutes of arriving at a hospital where, surrounded by soldiers, they were reported as throwing stones.[33]

The stones contributed to an image of "stone-throwing children in the role of 'David' confronting the gigantic military might of the Israeli 'Goliath.'"[34] The fearlessness of the young caught the eye of some Israelis, as suggested by Israeli Brigadier General (Res.) Giora Forman: "Some top IDF officers admire the bravery shown by the Palestinian youth . . . [who] have demonstrated unusual courage. Their actions aren't terrorism—but rather the actions of a national movement."[35] Palestinian cars were often hit with stones, sometimes deliberately, as when Palestinians were out during "strike days," when all were supposed to be home. One writer notes the substantial discretion employed:

> On days of total strike, when transportation was also supposed to halt, even cars bearing Gaza's distinctive grey license plates might come under a hail of stones. Yet there were no attacks on any of a dozen Israeli resort settlements and no Israeli fatalities or even serious injuries from the several million stones that must have been tossed.[36]

Israeli officials claimed that any nonuse of weaponry by Palestinians was due to the success of the Israeli policy of preventing arms from reaching them, but circumstantial evidence supports the Palestinian claim that Palestinians had elected not to use the few weapons they possessed.[37] By early February 1988, as fifty-one Arabs had died, "most shot dead by Israeli soldiers," Israeli military sources confirmed the presence of weaponry when they were reportedly concerned that "the rising death toll was now putting pressure on Palestinians with access to firearms to open up their weapons caches." Sixty days after the start of the uprising, the *Jerusalem Post* and Reuters validated from Gaza the conscious repudiation of weaponry: "In two months of unrest, Palestinian protesters have not fired a single bullet or used explosives other than petrol bombs."[38] Restraint was intentional, as "protesters have relied on slingshots, catapults, stones, ballbearings, bottles and primitive petrol bombs in confronting armed Israeli soldiers. . . . Since the unrest flared on December 9, security forces had found Soviet-made AK-47 rifles, explosives and hand grenades in the territories."[39] Stockpiles of guns in the West Bank and Gaza remained unused.[40]

Israeli journalist and coeditor of the *Palestine-Israel Journal* Hillel Schenker, writing in 1993, considered the uprising a model:

> [I]n the context of the Middle East the nonlethal intifada, as it was carried out during most of the three years of the struggle (a combination of rock throwing and gasoline bombs, nonviolent civil disobedience and infrastructure building), was as close as one could get to the ideal. Unfortunately, the rock is today being replaced by the knife. After three years of struggle and no significant movement toward ending the occupation, the Palestinians are frustrated and hurting.[41]

Even three years into the uprising, London's International Institute for Strategic Studies reported the intifada "continues unabated but without the anticipated rise in the use by the Palestinians of fire-arms and explosives which remains at a very low level."[42] Crude homemade handguns were found in refugee camps, and demonstrators seized handguns from Israeli police or settlers during confrontations, yet the *Jerusalem Post* concludes "all the weapons were later returned or found during searches." Restraint was intentional, Palestinians told the reporter, to avoid escalation of the conflict, and common sense since the success of the uprising depended on mobilizing civilians.[43] To Salim Tamari,

> The side that has always been known about Palestinian resistance is the military side, but during the *intifada*, another form of resistance emerged with the formation of popular committees, strikes, and civil disobedience. This is significant . . . , it gave the Palestinian individual faith in his ability to stand against one of the most important military authorities in the world. The Palestinian individual stood against this force with his body unarmed.[44]

Opposition to the use of weaponry sprang from the "power and popular nature of the unarmed uprising," as well as realization that Palestinians faced "huge human loss if they started shooting instead of throwing stones."[45]

"Paralyzing fear, which led Palestinians to regulate and censor themselves, was shattered by the children in the streets," who neutralized the military might of Israel by "showing that they were ready to die. They so radically turned the tables that the soldiers became afraid of them."[46] Overcoming fear is often an essential point of embarkation for nonviolent struggles, particularly where civilian protagonists face adversaries in possession of an immeasurably superior military apparatus.[47] "Fear is the greatest weapon in the hands of the authorities," Deena Hurwitz observes, while nonviolent action "engenders a high degree of self-empowerment."[48] "For twenty years, the Israeli army was able to control the occupied territories using only 600 soldiers," Daoud Kuttab explains: "The population was kept under control because they feared the army. Since the beginning of the intifada, this fear has evaporated, and even with ten times as many soldiers, Palestinians have not shown any sign of fear."[49] "The very act of resistance transformed the resistors," Souad Dajani notes.[50]

Perceiving what they termed "Arafat's 'children of the stones'" as having picked a "no-choice optional weapon, given that they lacked access to other weapons, such as firearms," Edward Kaufman emphasizes, Israelis were bound by "the legacy of the past," their attitudes profoundly influenced by "the Jewish experience as a persecuted nation, . . . their lives in the Diaspora as victims of the Inquisition, pogroms, ghettos, and in particular the Holocaust." These factors resulted in "self perceptions of themselves as powerless."[51]

The leaflets differentiate between Jews, individual Israelis, and the Israeli military occupation or policies. They express hope that a people who had suffered, as had the Jews, would understand the Palestinian *cri de coeur* and acknowledge their own aspirations to self-determination. Israeli political scientist Yaron Ezrahi concludes the "most significant fact" about the uprising was a "Palestinian discovery that stones can be much more eloquent than bullets."[52] As he sees it, the stones affected Israeli self-perceptions:

By eschewing firearms in favour of stones and broken bottles, the demonstrating Palestinians defined the use of firearms by Israeli soldiers as illegitimate surplus force. . . . The Intifada dramatized the ambiguities between the roles of Israeli military force as an instrument of defense and as a means of domination. As such, the Intifada was a powerful attack on the Israeli defense ethos. . . . [It] reminded all concerned that incorporating the occupied territories would in fact commit Israel to the perpetual use of its military to control and repress not "Arab refugees" but the whole Palestinian nation living on these lands.[53]

Yet from a context of instrumental effectiveness, if seeking to set in motion new policies within Israel, it would have been essential to choose methods that could stimulate changes in Israeli perceptions concerning the injustices of the Palestinians' plight. Nonviolent mobilizations generally seek institutional or behavioral change, rather than ephemeral alterations or attitudinal change. No matter their availability in the rocky soil, and irregardless of their symbolism to a disarmed people, the stones fed Israeli fear and let antagonists criticize the uprising as inherently violent, thus diminishing its political results.

Islamic Groups Flout Nonviolent Resistance

Five days after Gazan funerals exploded into the intifada, the Islamic Resistance Movement (Hamas) was officially established on December 14, 1987, and issued its first leaflet.[54] Hamas demonstrators in Gaza lived in the refugee camps. Israeli military chiefs observed that Islamic "fundamentalists" were "inciting more intensively and more effectively than the PLO activists."[55] While the Muslim Brotherhood, of which Hamas is an offshoot, remained outside the nationalist consensus that identified with the PLO,[56] in choosing the name Islamic Resistance Movement, Hamas was seeking a more militant stance capable of resuscitating the brotherhood in the supercharged atmosphere of the uprising.[57] On August 18, 1988, Hamas circulated a "covenant" on the West Bank laying out its rejection of compromise on the question of Palestine.[58] Before the covenant's issuance, Hamas had all but stopped dissemination of its own separate leaflets, as a result of informal coordination between Islamic revivalists and the Command.[59] The first-time use by a Palestinian Islamic movement of the term *mithaq* (covenant), as employed in the PLO's 1968 charter, was seen as a turning point.[60] In this avowedly political document, Hamas calls itself for the first time a part of the Palestinian nationalist movement, having traced its origins to Sheikh Izz al-Din al-Qassam, whom it claims as a member of the Muslim Brotherhood. It speaks mollifyingly about the national movement and the PLO.[61]

In its covenant, Hamas views all of historic Palestine as *waqf* (Islamic trust), no portion of which may be relinquished, as it "should be consecrated to Muslim generations" until Judgment Day.[62] Inherent in this position is rejection of a Palestinian state based on territorial compromise. Article Thirteen claims "there is no solution for the Palestinian question except through Jihad"; hence "initiatives, and so-called peaceful solutions and international conferences" are not "capable of realising the demands, restoring the rights or doing justice to the oppressed."[63] It was a bid to control the uprising. Beverley Milton-Edwards explains,

> The application of the concept [of *jihad*] to the Palestinian context and to the popular and non-violent campaign of the uprising is a reflection of the Hamas agenda for political control of the *intifada* and its competition with the nationalist movement. In essence, the organization appears to be striving to straddle . . . nationalist and Islamic approaches to the nature of the Palestinian uprising.[64]

The Hamas view of jihad was both "fluid" and "prosaic," and nationalism was declared to be "part of the religious creed."[65] *Jihad* represents serious personal dedication and commitment to Islam as a faith, a struggle against immoral intentions, and quest to better society, according to professor Barbara Stowasser. Only at the very end does Qur'anic revelation denote armed struggle, and this "jihad of the sword" is often referred to as "the smaller jihad." Popular views of jihad, often erroneously interpreted, would more accurately be cited as *qital* (armed struggle by warriors on the field of battle). Muslims are summoned to engage only in defensive war. Islamic rules for war carry the tradition of tribal warfare before Islam, which included ideas of chivalry, forbade the killing of noncombatants, and, according to some legal manuals, prohibited the destruction of property.[66] Although from its inception Hamas rejected the underlying principles of the intifada, it saw fit to cooperate with its leaders. Hamas was not formally part of the Command, yet maintained personal contact with the leadership cooperative. When large demonstrations were planned for Jerusalem and the West Bank, "we asked Hamas to cooperate with us," Eid recalled.[67]

After the massive Gazan funerals that signaled the start of the intifada, one of the earliest contacts by Sheikh Ahmad Yassin, symbolic spiritual leader of the Muslim Brotherhood and founder of Hamas, was with Sheikh Jamil Hamami. An earnest young Jerusalem preacher at al-Aqsa mosque, Sheikh Jamil would become Sheikh Ahmad's key contact with the West Bank, and the main link between the West Bank and Gaza Brotherhoods.[68] Eventually, he became the senior Hamas official in the West Bank and "liaison officer" between Hamas and the Command. According to Sheikh Jamil:

> There was no formal connection between the Command and Hamas, but there was communication under the table. When speaking of the leadership of Hamas in the West Bank, Hamas was a part of the Muslim Brotherhood, but it became independent after one year of the intifada, although the Muslim Brotherhood continued to help Hamas with the news media.[69]

Relations between the Command and Hamas were "very easy," Eid recalled; "but not so with Islamic Jihad."[70] Al-Jihad al-Islami (Islamic Jihad), an organization distinguishing itself from Hamas by its more revolutionary style, emphasized Palestine rather than a broad Muslim vision with transnational aspirations, expressed indifference to Arab regimes, and sympathized with the Iranian Revolution.[71] Islamic Jihad is still persuaded that their exploits fourteen months prior to the start of the intifada ignited the 1987 uprising.[72] For example, on October 15, 1986, Jihad mounted a grenade attack on the elite Israeli Givati Brigade during a graduation ceremony in front of the Western Wall of the Temple Mount (al-Haram al-Sharif), in which seventy soldiers were wounded and the father of a conscript killed. The actions of Jihad were never more than nuisances to Israel, but their horrific tactics provoked feelings of self-reproach among Palestinians who had taken no action against the worsening conditions of military occupation: "More than any other political group, Jihad was responsible for breaking the cognitive barrier of fatalism and demonstrating that Palestinian empowerment against Israel was possible."[73]

Jihad's leaflets and graffiti avoided open confrontation with the nationalist groups and did not preclude allusions to a Palestinian state—despite its bid for a jihad to liberate all of Palestine.[74] Its efforts to destabilize the Israeli military apparatus and its paramilitary operations during the otherwise nonviolent intifada involved individual isolated attacks.[75] While the Command had no formal representation from Islamic Jihad, political scientist Lisa Taraki says a reciprocal relationship between Islamic Jihad and the Command became evident soon after the Command developed a structure.[76] Islamic Jihad was more compatible than Hamas with the secular orientation of the four groups on the Command and more inclined to action than Hamas.[77] In addition, many of the small local committees (the wellspring of the popular committees) had representatives from Jihad, as well as from Hamas, despite the eventual policy of opposition to both the strategies and the goals—the means and ends—of the intifada by Hamas.[78] Still, the uprising resulted in a serious blow to Islamic Jihad, whose leaders were killed or arrested. Without "bench players," Michal Sela notes in the *Jerusalem Post*, for a while Jihad almost disappeared from the political map.[79]

Fateh and Hamas together were thought to have the support of approximately two-thirds of the Palestinian population at this time, but they had also clashed with each other more often than other Palestinian political entities in the territories.[80] In 1988, when the Command proffered the possibility of a formal seat for a Hamas representative, Hamas leaders made acceptance contingent on the expulsion of the communist PCP, a proposal instantly rejected by the Command.[81] Tension rose two years later, when in 1990 the PLO rejected the demands of Hamas that 40 or 50 percent of the seats in the parliamentary Palestinian legislative council (the PNC) be allocated to Hamas.[82] Hamas also wanted endorsement of armed struggle and a refusal to recognize

Israel, two principles that had already been repudiated. Not for the last time, armed clashes occurred between Hamas and Fateh in Tulkarem and Gaza in September 1990. Yet shared opposition to a foreign presence in the Persian Gulf, a result of Iraq's invasion of Kuwait, brought Fateh and Hamas together, and their respective leaders met outside the occupied territories. A thirteen-point "Charter of Honor" between Fateh and Hamas resulted and was jointly signed on September 18, 1990. Sheikh Jamil Hamami explained:

> There were primary differences between the Command and Hamas—we never agreed on any issue. This continued for two or three years with no formal coordination. After three years, the situation made it imperative to develop new mechanisms. At the time, the Israeli occupation had started playing on the differences between the various groups.[83] This led to the "pact of honor." Feisel Husseini signed for Fateh, and I signed for Hamas.[84]

The pact calls for cooperation based on "mutual respect." Soon after, joint parades and demonstrations followed in Nablus.[85] This accommodation was broken when in late 1991, forty persons were wounded in clashes between Hamas and Fateh supporters in Gaza.[86]

In December 1992, Qassamites from Hamas stepped up armed forays against Israeli security forces. Hamas members ambushed an Israeli military patrol, raking it with machine-gun fire and killing three soldiers in what was considered an unprecedented and calamitous blow to the record of unarmed struggle during the previous five years of the intifada.[87] Prior to the attack, fewer than twenty Israeli soldiers had died in the 1987 uprising.[88] Prime Minister Yitzhak Rabin reacted by ordering the arrest of 1,200 Palestinians and the deportation of 416 members of Hamas and Islamic Jihad.[89] As rioting broke out in the curfewed West Bank and Gaza, Israel bused 415 hooded and handcuffed faithful and political Islamists to the "no-man's-land" between Lebanon proper and the Israeli self-declared "security zone" in southern Lebanon. The action had the stunning, immediate, and unanticipated effect of unifying the Palestinian nationalist factions and the Islamic revivalists.[90] Television coverage of freezing but defiant Palestinian professionals, physicians, academicians, and scholars in green parkas in a snow-bound encampment resulted in worldwide condemnation of Israel.[91] "Intended to curb the rising influence of Hamas," Avi Shlaim laments, Rabin's action "had the opposite effect. It discredited the peace talks [just begun], strengthened the extremists, and weakened the moderates. Worse than a crime, it was a mistake."[92]

Near Rabin's residence in Jerusalem on December 17, fifty demonstrators from the Israeli selective refusal movement Yesh Gvul protested the deportations.[93] In an unprecedented development, for the first time Fateh and Hamas united themselves in the issuance of a joint leaflet, coauthored by Sari Nusseibeh and Sheikh Jamil Hamami.[94] It read, "We are coordinating together to escalate the *jihad* in all its forms in order to bring back the deportees and resist the occupation. . . . We call on the striking forces of both Hamas and the unified Command to coordinate in the field and burn the ground from under the feet of the occupiers." The combined leaflet also called for commercial strikes, a sit-in, and marches in front of the International Committee of the Red Cross in East Jerusalem.[95] Nusseibeh's ire at the sight of his fellow pedagogues being cast into the snow apparently led him to suspend his customary strategic thinking, as the handout called for "all forms of struggle." He was reported as being in shock and observing that the deportations would only strengthen the position of Hamas in the territories.[96] Meanwhile, Israeli officials, having purposely helped to enhance the Islamic trend, another name for Hamas, now harbored hopes that their negotiations with the Palestinians might be accelerated by the removal of Hamas and Jihad as rivals to the PLO.[97] Collusion between the government of Israel and Hamas was, at least by 1994, openly acknowledged by Israeli foreign ministry officials, who admitted that the government of Israel had helped the Muslim Brotherhood of Egypt to develop a Palestinian arm in the territories: "The Israeli government was anti-PLO. We tried ten to fifteen years ago to encourage the Islamic movements. . . . We *helped* this reaction to establish a power base in the West Bank and Gaza. In retrospect, we should have talked to the PLO in 1964, when it was first established, but fifteen years ago, we were trying to destroy the power base of the PLO."[98] To Susan Hattis Rolef, this policy was one of Israel's "gravest mistakes."[99] Michal Sela reports, "Israel even went so far as to arm the Islamic organizations."[100]

The intifada allowed the bureaucratic and calcified Muslim Brotherhood, through Hamas, to substantiate its nationalist credentials, which had been questionable until the uprising.[101] While rejecting in theory the loss of any Palestinian land, a softening of its position became perceptible. The goal of Hamas was slowly being redefined to that of lifting the occupation, rather than reversing the partition of Palestine, or, for that matter, restoring the caliphate in Muslim countries.[102] Sheikh Jamil Hamami later stated, "It is the duty of Hamas and duty of the people of Palestine to go against the occupation—not against Jewishness or Judaism—but against the military occupation."[103] Such reassessment accompanied reconsideration of violence, as within Hamas splits and counter-splits occurred with regularity. In 1989, Sheikh Ahmad Yassin told Michal Sela that he rejected the use of violence as a means of pursuing goals: "There is no point. . . . Persuasion is the way," he said, utilizing Qur'anic verses as substantiation, although he allowed that other options were at the individual's initiative.[104] Sheikh Jamil would ultimately leave Hamas because of his disagreement with both its ends and its means.[105]

The evidence suggests that interest in the technique of nonviolent struggle was making inroads into the Islamic trend, although not supplanting a jumbled mass of "everything goes" thinking nor replacing the obstinance of tendencies that engaged in individualistic paramilitary operations. In a strand that runs through this entire chronicle, little if any evidence can be found, then or now, of Israeli efforts to embolden those who were trying to repudiate the mythology of violence, or even wavering from a hard line.

Major differences between the Islamist blocs and the nationalists guiding the intifada thus involved the ends and the means.[106] The uprising was built on three political aims involving post-1967 reality: acceptance of Israel in its pre-1967 borders, removal of Israeli authority from the occupied territories, and establishment of a Palestinian state. Both Hamas and the more purist Islamic Jihad refused to accept the events of 1948 and 1949, yet survival in the euphoria of a mass uprising meant the two groups needed to assert their influence in a political context that was incompatible with their fundamental rejection of accommodation with Israel.[107] This included standing for election, even when drastically outnumbered: "We're not running to win," an Islamic Jihad member told a reporter, describing participation in Bir Zeit University elections, "we're running to show that we exist."[108] The leadership of the intifada surpassed Hamas in its political vision and the solidity of its aims, Lisa Taraki contends. Thus Hamas joined the uprising "to shore up its image in preparation for carving itself a niche in the very state for whose establishment it is not prepared to struggle," in order not to sustain a total loss.[109]

Knowing that it could not then impede a political settlement once underway, the Islamic trend preserved a presence as the process built toward

an agreement. Hamas's participation in the intifada should thus be interpreted as a bid of an Islamist party in a future Palestinian state. By 1994,
Hamas spokespersons had begun to mention Israeli withdrawal from the
occupied territories and the establishment there of an independent Palestinian state, a departure from previous proposals for a unified Muslim state.
A "truce" with Israel was remarked upon. Such moves indicate a desire to
be "a future moderate political partner, rather than a fundamentalist rejectionist group."[110]

Gene Sharp: Power against Those that Cannot Be Defeated by Violence

A "Workshop" for the Tunis-Based PLO and an Israeli Seminar

The Quakers, originally the Society of the Friends of Truth, have a service
organization working in different parts of the world to promote peace and
assist those affected by war. The American Friends Service Committee
(AFSC), founded in 1917 after the United States entered World War I, is
based in Philadelphia. Both a direct service agency and a peace education
organization, the AFSC in the Middle East assists the formation of independent local civil society institutions and strengthens preexisting groups
and charities. In 1986, with the eruption of the intifada still a year away, Gail
Pressburg, director of the AFSC Middle East program, visited the Palestinian
Center for the Study of Nonviolence in East Jerusalem. Expressing interest
in its activities, she asked of Mubarak Awad permission to take photographs.
Awad let Pressburg take snapshots. Although he safeguarded his independence from the PLO, he said she was free to show them to anyone, including
the PLO in Tunis. Pressburg was using photography to spread word about
the growth of "a new politics in Israel, and an emerging civil society among the
Palestinians." The Palestinians, she would explain to analysts and observers,
"had become very realistic about Israel and the fact that they would live next
to Israel, and not replace it."[111] In Tunis, however, Pressburg found PLO
officials badly out of touch with the developments that had been prodded by
the civilian movements after 1969:

> Some in the Palestinian leadership knew about the civil society sector in the
> occupied territories—including vaguely about the work of the Palestinian
> Center for the Study of Nonviolence—but many knew nothing. . . . Khaled

al-Hassan and Abu Ammar [Yasir Arafat] . . . didn't really know about the work of the medical relief committees, the professional associations, or the women's organizations. They knew about al-Haq, but didn't understand the emergence of political people who were not involved in the factions familiar to them. Abu Jihad was intrigued about the center for the study of nonviolence, probably because this was another arena in which he could play.[112]

Awad's desire for independence had led him to spurn Abu Jihad's emissaries, who sometimes appeared at the center with envelopes containing money, and reject offers of staff, with the exception of two low-level volunteers who said they had come with Abu Jihad's blessings.[113] Awad believed that any PLO assent to nonviolent resistance would be superficial and tactical.[114] Raja Shehadeh was coolly aware that the Palestinian political establishment in the diaspora "showed little interest" in al-Haq's approach.[115]

The Difficult Task of Explaining Nonviolent Struggle to the Tunis-Based PLO

In March 1989, after Abu Jihad's assassination and Awad's deportation from Israel, Awad assembled a delegation to go to North Africa to introduce the PLO formally to nonviolent resistance—in effect, another of his workshops. In addition to Awad, the delegation was composed of Gene Sharp and his assistant at the time, Bruce Jenkins; London-based Iraqi scholar Khalid Kishtainy; Abd al-Aziz Said, professor in the school of international service and head of the American University Center for Global Peace in Washington, D.C.; Father Dennis Madden, representative of the Vatican in Jerusalem; Jack O'Dell, policy advisor to the Reverend Jesse Jackson; and Nancy Nye.[116] In Tunis for one week, they discussed nonviolent struggle with PLO officials and others. In Awad's account, he told them that what the PLO was doing was meaningless, it was not organizing in the villages, and the military occupation was worsening.[117] Professor Said recalled, "In each session we explained the strategy and tactics of nonviolent struggle, underscoring the distinction between strategic nonviolent action and pacifism."[118] Meetings took place with Yasir Arafat; second in command of the PLO Salah Khalaf (nom de guerre Abu Iyad); Mahmoud Abbas (nom de guerre Abu Mazen), later elected president; Farouk Khadoumi; Khaled al-Hassan; Bassam Abu-Sharif; Abu Jihad's widow (nom de guerre Umm Jihad), Sami Musallam, Arafat's administrator; Ahmad Qurei (nom de guerre Abu Ala), later a negotiator in Oslo and speaker of the parliamentary PNC; members of the security forces, and Palestinians who had been deported from the territories.

Sharp explained how nonviolent struggle is a technique for wielding nonviolent war—power "designed for use against opponents who cannot be defeated by violence." He suggested the Palestinians could pursue six strategic objectives in the intifada, in order of priority: (1) continue development of parallel institutions, that is, work for "*de facto* independence"; (2) continue the nonviolent action steps of protests, noncooperation, and nonviolent intervention, so that the people become unrulable by the occupying forces; (3) split Israeli public opinion on issues such as the military occupation, continuance of repression, and recognition of an independent Palestinian state, including finding ways of dealing with the extremist Israeli settlers; (4) contribute to divisions of opinion in the Israeli establishment, so as to undermine the reliability of an army's repression; (5) contribute to a split between the United States and Israel on the so-called problem of the Palestinians; (6) encourage world opinion and diplomacy to settle the conflict and assist in *de jure* recognition of Palestinian independence. Alluding to nonviolent struggles underway elsewhere in the world, Sharp explained how the systematic and strategic employment of nonviolent action methods could produce a situation in which no alternative remained for an opponent but to capitulate. Repression exerted against a movement of nonviolent resistance, he put in plain words, is evidence of its power, not reason for its abandonment. He spelled out how episodes of violence—even if limited and only by a minority, as in the intifada—when mixed with nonviolent strategies could be "catastrophic."[119]

When Arafat raised the matter of scant resources, suggesting limitations on PLO funds due to support for services and the families of martyrs, the delegation pointed out that nonviolent struggle provides for the mobilization of all persons, because people are the resource.[120] On one issue there was agreement between the visitors and the PLO: the intifada had succeeded where Arab diplomacy had failed in communicating the reality of Israeli military occupation. Mention of linking the intifada with the struggle of Israeli Arab citizens for their civil rights, raised by Jack O'Dell, was flatly rejected by the PLO officers, who said they wished to avoid any suggestion that the uprising would be carried directly into the state of Israel.[121] Abd al-Aziz Said recalled discussing the possibility that if stones and petrol bombs had *not* been used by Palestinians, the mechanism of disintegration might have ensued, due to political jujitsu.[122] Abu Iyad was particularly intrigued, according to four of the visitors, who also recall that Abu Mazen, Hassan, and Abu-Sharif responded positively.[123] Arafat and Sharp debated whether nonviolent sanctions could be effective against Israeli settlers.[124] The visitors were told that before his death Abu Jihad had possessed a copy of Sharp's 1973 trilogy, *The Politics of Nonviolent Action*.[125]

On the whole the visitors do not remember the encounter as successful or likely to lead to revised policies. A deep gulf in perceptions made the conversations difficult. Bruce Jenkins wrote,

> There is much skepticism, it appears, in the PLO ranks about the utility of nonviolent methods. Arafat stated that his military staff was encouraging military actions. Also, several leaders spoke of the necessity of continuing the struggle "at all levels." Another top official declared that armed struggle could not be dropped until material gains were achieved through the Intifada.[126]

On March 23, 1989, having the day before opened the second round of the U.S.-PLO dialogue, American ambassador to Tunis Robert Pellitreau met with the delegation at the embassy. The next day, the visitors were invited to meet with fourteen Foreign Service officers involved in the dialogue. The discussions pertained to the importance of the Palestinians' using strictly nonviolent means in the intifada.[127] "This was new to the Foreign Service officers," said Richard Undeland, director of the U.S. Information Service for Tunisia, who set up the meeting. He recollected, "Mubarak Awad made a very strong case that the only way the intifada could succeed was through nonviolent strategies, which could move both Israelis and Palestinians—because in any question involving brute force, Israel had all the cards. . . . With the exception of Robert Pellitreau and Edmund Hull, the Foreign Service officers were less interested than I had expected. I was disappointed. Some could not figure out why they were there, including the political officers, but Pellitreau and I were very taken with the discussions."[128] From the reports, it is hard to escape the conclusion that the U.S. diplomats may have understood less about nonviolent strategic action than did the PLO and the Israeli establishment.[129]

Advice for a "Dramatic Shift of Strategy"

Three months later, Gene Sharp returned to Israel and the occupied territories. He spent time with Israelis and Palestinians during his visit and found that the situation had deteriorated. The few fatalities on the Israeli side contrasted with the high ratio of Palestinian deaths. His written notes of July 1989 express chagrin that what had been one Palestinian killed a day was now four or five dead; whereas five might have been injured earlier, forty would be wounded. He was apprehensive that increased Israeli repression would lead the Palestinians to abandon nonviolent methods.[130] He perceived disarray in the Israeli peace camp, along with increased fear and hatred toward Arabs by Israelis in general, often accompanied by the belief that greater repression should be used against the Palestinians. Sharp realized the danger and instability in the situation.

Along with lack of concrete gains from the uprising went increasing calls for violence in the leaflets, especially after the release of no. 40, of May 22, 1989. Worse, the uprising was being undermined by actions ostensibly to "help" the intifada, or in other words to sabotage the nonviolent struggle.[131]

In public lectures and conversations, Sharp noted the imponderabilities for an outsider in discussing another people's struggle, yet he urged that the Palestinians consider a "dramatic shift of strategy."[132] He suggested that a new approach might be publicly announced, in which a different direction of the uprising would be explained, one less likely to ignite Israeli fear, and thus brutality. He recommended appealing to the human sensibilities of the Israelis, "which Jews have often demonstrated elsewhere and in which they have believed."[133] This approach could "make it more possible for sympathetic Israelis both to oppose the repression of nonviolent Palestinians and support the Palestinians' right to independence."[134] Pointing to the Chinese students' hunger strikes prior to Tiananmen Square earlier that same year, and citing hunger strikes by Palestinians during 1936-39, Sharp suggested that such a phase start with fasting, during which time no stones would be thrown. Large numbers of people undertaking twenty-one-day hunger strikes could produce a "significant impact without bringing death" and return the Palestinians to the front pages of the world's newspapers.[135] This second phase of the intifada should be "strictly nonviolent," he cautioned. It should be declared that the Palestinians were strong enough to dispense with throwing stones. Commercial strikes could cease, to allow economic recovery and to "diffuse the responsibility and price of resistance."[136] Voluntary curfews by

Palestinians and other methods should emphasize "a disciplined quiet transition" to the building of institutions and development of self-reliance, with a goal of living in peace alongside Israel.[137]

For nonviolent collective action to be effective, Sharp regarded as fundamental for the Palestinians a shift to a more balanced power relationship with the Israelis and believed this to be dependent on a strategy of building institutions and nonviolent struggle. He suggested that any effort to "cool down" or "settle" the conflict before needed changes took place in the power relationships would be premature and ultimately counterproductive to a lasting peaceful settlement. He reported having heard that the Israelis had taken steps to provoke the Palestinians to use violence, which he regarded as further rationale for the Palestinians to resist all provocations to violence.[138] In discussions, Sharp repeated a point made in writing, "A shift to violence would alter the conflict from an asymmetrical one of nonviolent against violent weapons (which has great advantages for the civilian defenders) to a symmetrical one in which both sides are using violent weapons (which generally accords greater advantage to the better-equipped attackers)."[139]

1990 Hunger Strike: "Last Chance to Keep the Intifada Nonviolent"

Although consternation regarding the mixing of political aims with military methods would remain a gnawing internal fissure, among growing numbers of Palestinian academicians, activist intellectuals, journalists, professionals, and publishers, an appreciation was growing that the asymmetry between Israel and the Palestinians could actually throw international sympathies in their favor, potentially causing Israeli citizenry to identify with their dilemma, and that nonmilitary strategies had a better chance of allowing them to press their case.

In January 1990, responding to a call from Feisel Husseini to reach out to Israelis, Radwan Abu Ayyash, Ziad Abu Zayyad, Ghassan Khatib, and Hanan Mikhail Ashrawi exchanged views with sixteen members of the Knesset. Among them were Dedi Zucker of Citizens' Rights, Arie Lova Eliav and Avraham Burg of Labor, Yair Tsaban of Mapam, and Amnon Rubinstein of Shinui. As a result, in April, all sixteen MKs agreed to work for peace with Palestinians who openly supported the PLO, the furthest any group of elected Israeli officials had trod toward recognition of the PLO.[140] Khatib clarified, "We have concentrated on the American position long enough when the decision will be made in Israel."[141] The Palestinian activist intellectuals said they wanted to persuade Israeli voters to press their own leaders to enter talks with the PLO. Husseini, banned from leaving Israel or entering the occupied West Bank and Gaza Strip, set an example by visiting in the hospital an Israeli crippled by a lone Palestinian's attack on an Israeli bus in June 1990, in which sixteen Jews died. In addition to addressing rallies of Peace Now, Husseini held discussions with a Jewish rabbi who had joined a settlement and was living on the West Bank.[142] Such dialogue reinforced the convictions of those involved, but had little impact on Israelis who believed that they had a God-given right to acquire Palestinian lands by force, if need be, or on Palestinians who considered it their duty to try to retrieve all of Mandate Palestine through any means necessary. Even if the greatly disproportionate deaths of Palestinians to Israelis seemed not to penetrate the psychological defense mechanisms of the majority of Israelis, suggestive evidence implies that Israeli sensitivities were affected by a 1990 Palestinian hunger strike.

On May 20, 1990, a reportedly deranged lone Israeli gunman, Ami Popper, murdered seven Palestinian laborers waiting for a bus and wounded scores of others near the Tel Aviv suburb of Iyun Faraa (Rishon Le Zion).[143] At least fifteen Palestinians were subsequently killed by Israeli security forces, who opened fire on Israeli Arabs and on Palestinians in Gaza that were protesting the Popper "massacre."[144] The occurrence sparked a two-week hunger strike by forty-four Palestinians who were among the broad leadership group guiding the uprising.[145] Committees rapidly organized for drafting statements, handling the news media, making diplomatic contacts, arranging security, and procuring supplies.[146] The hunger strike had brought the hitherto generally anonymous leadership into the open. It had a "profound impact on Israeli sensibilities," Edward Kaufman recalled; "I went there myself, and fasted with them for twenty-four hours."[147] As Jonathan Kuttab, one of the original eight hunger strikers, remembered,

> We had to fax Mubarak Awad to ask him for the guidelines on conducting hunger strikes. We were taking no food, and only water. It was a turning point. Feisel Husseini prophetically said, "This is the last chance to keep the intifada nonviolent." He felt people were beginning to lose faith in the nonviolent message, and it is true that, after that, we started seeing knifings. Until then, there were no knifings.[148]

Inside a fluttering green tent on the grounds of the International Red Cross in Jerusalem, the well-disciplined action brought some fasters to the point of collapse. Meanwhile, Abu Ayyash, Abd al-Hadi, and Ashrawi spoke with reporters and called for an emergency session of the UN General Assembly to discuss the killings. U.S. secretary of state James Baker indicated that the United States would be willing to discuss at a Security Council meeting the placement of UN observers in the occupied territories to help protect Palestinians.[149]

The full dimension of the intifada as a struggle within a struggle was soon revealed. In the midst of the hunger strike, a bomb exploded in Jerusalem, killing a seventy-two-year-old Israeli man and wounding nine others.[150] Two days later, PLO Executive Committee member Muhammad Abul Abbas led an abortive raid on a Tel Aviv beach.[151] This led the United States to suspend its fledgling dialogue with the PLO and to veto a Security Council resolution calling for a delegation to be sent to observe conditions in the occupied territories—a key demand of the strikers.[152] Sitting on his mattress under the tent shaded by pine trees and weakened from fasting, Husseini told a reporter that the veto of the United States, instead of reinforcing nonviolent approaches, had punished its advocates. Overwhelmed by the bad publicity resulting from the Abul Abbas operation, the strikers called off their thirteen-day fast. "Just 12 days before, when the hunger strike began," Timothy M. Phelps wrote, "Israel had been on the defensive, not just for the massacre itself, but for its handling of the unrest that followed, in which more than 15 Palestinians were killed."[153] With complete predictability, the Abul Abbas maneuver had the effect of unifying the Israelis against the Palestinians and dissipating international support for a delegation of observers. Husseini said the Abul Abbas group's attempted armed attack against Israelis was a stab in the back more painful than the frontal wounds delivered by enemy arrows.[154]

The Unraveling of the Intifada, Rejection of "White Revolution"

The same factors that explain the Palestinians' adoption of nonviolent struggle also help to account for the collapse of the strategy. Additionally, forces within Israel, the PLO, and the Palestinian factions were opposed to the nonviolent strategy and wanted it to end.[155] The view from East Jerusalem was not shared among all in the West Bank and Gaza Strip. Some held to the old ideologies of armed struggle and liberation while others, such as the revivalist Islamic blocs of Hamas and Jihad, adamantly opposed new concepts of struggle taking hold. Moreover, as the activist intellectuals were developing new, nonviolent, and exclusively political ways for fighting military occupation in the mid-1980s, official diasporan Fateh ideology continued to aggregate all approaches in a contradictory manner.

In 1986, the year that Nusseibeh proffered the South African prototype as more realistic than the Algerian model, the debate on nonviolent resistance inside the territories had echoed on the periphery of the PLO. On June 12-13, the Palestine National Fund's thirty-person board of directors, meeting in Casablanca, urged Arafat to take inspiration from South Africa's antiapartheid movement.[156] The fund suggested that the PLO undertake the boycotting of Israeli products, abandonment of jobs inside Israel, and civil disobedience. Jaweed al-Ghussein, spokesperson for the PLO's fund-raising arm, told Patrick Seale the fund insisted on a "radical change of direction" and pressed the PLO leadership to accept civil disobedience.[157] Seale's story in London's *Observer* was picked up by *al-Fajr* in East Jerusalem, although it may be noted that a bizarre interpretation was added by the Palestinian weekly that measures such as civil disobedience reflected PLO weakness and crisis.[158] Quite the opposite; it would have been a sign of strength. Even if the diasporan donors grasped the power of nonviolent strategies, there is no evidence of clarity in the Tunis-based PLO concerning the required preparation, discipline, or strategic planning that is mandatory for their effectiveness.

Although the activist intellectuals who were officially or unofficially affiliated with Fateh around East Jerusalem kept up their attempts to influence Tunis, coordinating first with Abu Jihad, and later Arafat, through their Paris intermediary, the continuing reliance of the PLO on the mystique of military cadres and a fusion of incompatible approaches into an ideological hodgepodge "all means of struggle" prevented systematic applications of nonviolent sanctions from bearing fruit, even after the Jerusalem Paper won Abu Jihad's stamp of approval. Those who had forsworn violence were impaired by such ambiguity. Their understanding of the power of nonviolent action was still green. Even Abd al-Fatth Hamayl, one of the Fateh representatives on the Command, who had spent seventeen years in Israeli prisons, where, incarcerated and held with others, he became an advocate of nonviolent struggle, declared, "We, in Fateh . . . believe that the *kind* of struggle is of our choice."[159] Fateh's conservative nature also held it back from endorsing the mobilization of the entire society. Rather, Amal Jamal notes, Fateh's aim was "measured protest that would support its goal: to be recognized as a negotiating partner by Israel," while the leadership of Fateh in exile wanted to "construct its own social frameworks for the exercise of political power that could challenge Israeli authority while preserving existing social relationships."[160]

Fateh's objective had been described in 1970 as being "to politicize the military struggle and militarize the political struggle."[161] In 1974, Arafat had declared political struggle to be the handmaiden to armed struggle. Husseini in 1989 sought to turn Arafat's contrivance on its head and downgrade military resistance under political striving:

> When there is an occupation, people have the right to fight it by any means they can, including the armed struggle. But it is not a must. If it is necessary, it can be used at a certain period, but it is not an end in itself. I believe that at this stage, other means will work better. I am not saying that we should renounce the armed struggle, but now we are not using it. The armed struggle is only part of the political struggle.[162]

Yet by the middle of that same year, Fateh's political program still called for "continuing to intensify and escalate armed action and all forms of struggle to liquidate the Israeli-Zionist occupation of our occupied Palestinian land."[163] Within Fateh, armed struggle remained the canon, with no criticism for mixing conflicting strategies. Such laxity bore resemblance to the time prior to the great revolt of 1936-39, when reactive violent resistance was gratuitously mixed with carefully planned nonviolent campaigns. Nusseibeh explained,

> [In] Fateh classical doctrine, there was never any inconsistency between unarmed and armed forms of struggle, because it was always assumed in the classical doctrine that you have to use a little armed struggle in order to mobilize the masses into an unarmed struggle, as the second stage, that can then develop into a third stage of a popular armed revolution. This was the classical three-stage theory of the revolutionary ideologues.[164]

Among exiles the view stubbornly persisted that it was only after the Palestinians opted for armed struggle that the national identity of the Palestinian people was rescued from oblivion.[165] Although many in the territories regretted the heavy diasporan emphasis on military means in the early years after occupation, armed struggle was never allowed to die of its own ineffectuality.[166] Average Palestinians were often confused and bewildered, not knowing whether such pipedreams were still the goal and, if so, whether they were to be accomplished "through protracted warfare or by stages in which peaceful and violent means would be used alternately."[167]

The PLO's military actions, particularly after 1974 and before 1982, contradicted its political goals of obtaining recognition from the United States and mobilizing international pressure on Israel to lift the occupation. Bombings, shellings, cross-border raids from Lebanon, the taking of hostages, and suicide missions detracted from Palestinian political objectives.[168] At most, clandestine operations "enabled the PLO to 'spoil' diplomatic initiatives that excluded it."[169] The pattern was evident in the initial year of the intifada when, on March 7, 1988, Palestinian guerrillas hijacked a bus carrying unarmed employees to the Dimona nuclear research center in the Negev desert. Three Israelis—a man and two women, and three Palestinians were killed when the bus was attacked, all of them civilians. Inside the occupied territories, Palestinians asserted that it was planned, executed, and celebrated by the diasporan PLO exiles. They were dismayed: "When the Fateh people came from outside, they brought the violence. They had no discipline."[170] Nusseibeh publicly deplored this first guerrilla action against civilians since the start of the uprising, done without the knowledge of Fateh's local leaders: "It's very worrying, because the whole point . . . is to have a so-called white revolution in which people don't use any arms." He called the cold-blooded shooting of passengers a "deplorable act" in which the only purpose served was to "de-legitimize the Palestinian people's struggle against occupation."[171] Prime Minister Shamir insisted that those who had carried out the attack were the same persons who are "igniting the disturbances in the territories."[172]

Shamir's utterance to the contrary, Fateh-linked persons in the territories such as Husseini, Nusseibeh, Abu Zayyad, and Abu Ayyash had been pushing boulders uphill since the mid-1980s, promoting nonviolent struggle as a more realistic alternative to guerrilla sorties.[173] Eqbal Ahmad had observed in 1983 that the Palestinian support of armed struggle had isolated itself rather than the enemy.[174] Persuasion was required. Nusseibeh argued,

We should address ourselves to the Israeli man in the street and tell him that we do not want to throw him into the sea, but that we don't want to be expelled into the desert either. That we do not seek to destroy his state, but that we want to establish our own, alongside Israel. That we don't want him to die, but that we, too, want to live. It is a legitimate message which must be delivered in clear, unambiguous language.[175]

Even internally, some Palestinians persisted in seeing nonviolent resistance as a prelude to armed struggle and wanted reversion to commando operations and bombings.[176] Others thought successes in the political realm could be used to score advantages in the military sphere.[177] Not grasping the singular potential for nonviolent struggle to induce change from within a target group, they seem not to have recognized that the Israelis would remain unified so long as paramilitary operations were simultaneously being directed against them.

The unity achieved in the intifada had never been easy, and the question of the use of arms was sharpened in March 1988, making even more exceptional the subsequent fundamental adherence of the mass movement to an overall strategy for the use of nonviolent sanctions. Four months into the uprising, small incidents were reported that included shots fired at a jeep, detonation of a grenade in Israel, gunshots from the Askar refugee camp near Nablus, and a bus hijacking. Israeli reaction to these events was recorded by human rights monitoring groups as particularly brutal.[178] Even though demonstrations were reaching remote villages that had never before witnessed any form of protest activity, and Palestinians in West Bank villages were exhibiting remarkable persistence, yet some departed from the uprising's discipline. Conviction on the need for civilian action, as opposed to armed struggle, was more strongly and deeply rooted in rural areas than it was in refugee camps and cities, or in Gaza. Ziad Abu Zayyad evaluated Palestinian consciousness of gains from the disavowal of violence as "very deep," rooted in belief that achievements resulted "because we did not use arms."[179] Yet there was also concern about whether the disposition of the intifada as popular, unarmed resistance could continue, when two or three Palestinians were being killed daily. Daoud Kuttab said the Command showed "pragmatism and maturity" in making needed adjustments.[180] Meanwhile Feisel Husseini continued his exertions, including a speech to a Peace Now rally calling for a two-state solution, which evoked the "official wrath" of the Israeli government.[181] He persistently explained to Israeli audiences "the *intifada* is not a military operation, it is a new movement which aspires to liberate thought and consciousness."[182]

The political statement of the November 1988 nineteenth PNC in Algiers said the Palestinian people, through the popular committees, were in charge.[183] Yet following celebrations associated with the issuance of the Declaration of Independence, begotten in the Husseini Document, and amplified by the Palestinian poet Mahmud Darwish, by late autumn an anticlimactic slough ensued, and the question of introducing violence was again raised. So anxiously had residents of the territories awaited the declaration that few focused on what would happen next. Daoud Kuttab warns,

> The success of the right-wing parties in the [autumn 1988] Israeli elections has given some radical Palestinian groups the idea of re-emphasizing the need to go back to the armed struggle. Supporters of the Islamic Fundamentalists also joined the [PFLP] in repeating slogans about using arms against Israel. . . . [T]he armed struggle is not a viable option, . . . if carried out arbitrarily it could spell the end of the intifada . . . a white unarmed popular struggle.[184]

While Husseini and other Palestinians in the territories "tirelessly" sought in the next few months to "dispel deeply entrenched Israeli fears of the PLO and Palestinian national demands," among the exiles outside the territories the old patterns persisted. The Fifth Fateh Congress, meeting in Tunis in August 1989, instead of building on the political gains being made by the intifada, reverted to the theories of the past in calling for "armed action and all forms of struggle."[185] Despite this and alluding to opposition by the Command and the PLO to the use of arms, Abu Iyad stated that the intifada "developed its own particular methods for confronting the occupation"; "we have been very clear about the need to adhere to a no-arms policy within the context of the *intifada*."[186] Still the factions oscillated over the use of weapons against Israeli soldiers and settlers.[187] Arafat came under heat for maintaining a policy of restraint within the PLO. Local Fateh leaders—embroiled in debate—splintered, as radical tendencies and Hamas gained adherents.

Since the Israeli army was the single largest sector of Israeli society in constant contact with the Palestinians, any civilian resistance needed to influence the morale of the soldiers and their willingness to obey orders.[188] The PLO's equivocal posture held little potential for sowing discord in Israeli public opinion or invalidating the Israeli popular support for military suppression of the uprising. The PLO may have vaguely accepted the insiders' suspension of armed actions for the first two years, but the nonviolent discipline in the uprising came under attack as the third anniversary approached.[189] Instead of focusing on how to affect the resoluteness or spirits of the Israeli soldiers, cause defections, or split their ranks, from outside the territories in 1990 came calls that could only solidify Israeli adamancy. The PFLP's George Habash counseled "supporting" the intifada "with fire," and Muhammad Abul Abbas now called for putting "a rifle in the hand of every Palestinian in the occupied territories."[190] By Leaflet no. 65, in late 1990, the Command itself refers to "all forms of struggle."[191]

Civilian Mobilization Opens a Pandora's Box

The nonmilitary movements of the 1980s that brought thousands of micro-organizations into existence permitted an infrastructure of popular committees to spring rapidly into place in December 1987 to cope with Israeli curfews. This same mobilization also opened doors to those who espoused violence, including Hamas. They, in turn, "tended to blame Palestinian defeats on the departure from tradition and religion."[192] Islamic Jihad in particular disavowed any cooperation with Israel. "By the third, fourth, fifth year," Sari Nusseibeh rued, with "acts of violence . . . ongoing in the intifada, Hamas might even argue . . . that attacks on Jews were an inseparable and integral part of the intifada.[193] Israeli collective punishments may have reinforced self-reliance in the popular committees, but they kept their members under duress. Food shortages, restricted movements, and controls on the passage of travelers from one village or town to another through roadblocks and checkpoints were circumvented by the committees, but the incidents of trauma continued to rise steeply, along with deportations, mass arrests, and detentions. Economic constraints were severe, as Palestinian laborers were forbidden to travel to Israel for day jobs where they were paid half as much as their Jewish fellow workers, or, if female, even less. Some one-third of Palestinian revenues came from day laborers. The potency of the popular committees was in one sense validated by Israel's retaliation in outlawing membership in them, yet the committees were also enervated by such measures. Within the Command, the long incarcerations had an extremely chilling effect, particularly on the stamina of those running the popular committees, disproportionately affecting women.[194] Although the ability to resist breaking down or revealing the names of colleagues under torture became a rite of passage and badge of honor, Palestinian clinicians say they will be forced to treat the sequelae from torture in Israeli prisons for years to come.[195] Prohibitions against access by the news media limited full international airing of the harsh reprisals.

By mid-1990, the cry that an independent state was around the corner was replaced by disquiet over the rising physical and economic losses. Criticism was openly expressed of the PLO in exile and the local leadership. Rumors spread that the PLO had taken over the intifada, creating a state of paralysis in which residents of the West Bank and Gaza were again waiting passively for outside developments.[196] The hoped-for apportionment of responsibility had not materialized, in which Palestinians in the territories would commence actions, organize demonstrations, and maintain communications, while the PLO would articulate their grievances in the international corridors of power. Three and a half years after its start, Husseini called for a reassessment and a retooling of the intifada. Instead, the balance of power reverted to the governing elite in exile, whose foremost concern was to preserve its supremacy from the PLO's base in Tunis.

The Killing of Collaborators

The same fragmentation of authority and diffusion of power that had produced the capacity for mass mobilization was also implicated in the license taken to kill collaborators. On February 24, 1988, in Qabatiya, a town of seven thousand, a fortune-teller named Muhammad Ayed was lynched on suspicion of collaborating with the Israeli authorities. During a protest march, youths had thrown stones at his house, and Ayed had opened fire, killing a four-year-old boy and wounding eighteen. The crowd burned Ayed's house, killing him, and hanging his corpse below a Palestinian flag on a telephone pole. The IDF physically closed off the village and cut electricity, telephone, and water services.[197] In Qabatiya, journalist Glenn Frankel recorded, everyone viewed Ayed as an informer under the protection of two Israeli "sheriffs"—operatives of the Shin Bet internal security service in charge of overseeing police matters in the town.[198]

Israel's intelligence-gathering apparatus in the occupied territories at its peak during the first intifada may have involved 18,000 informers.[199] The level of cooperation confounded an Israeli soldier:

> We could not understand how these people were still alive. As Israeli soldiers, we had to deal with these collaborators. We had to work alongside these collaborators, and we could not understand how the people in the

village did not beat their brains out. That would be justified in my opinion.[200]

Shin Bet used sexual entrapment, blackmail, drugs, and money to enlist collaborators, while developing procedures for exploiting them.[201] Leaflet no. 15, of April 1988, calls for "cruel punishment to those who work for the police, the municipalities, and the appointed village committees, who willfully disregard the wishes of the people."[202]

It would have been impossible for the Palestinians to "disengage" from the military occupation without eventually weakening or eliminating the network of Palestinian collaborators utilized by the Israeli military-intelligence complex to support its administration. The Palestinians knew that Israel was dependent on collusion by members of their own society for information. Ironically, the comeuppance for collaborators proves beyond doubt that firearms had been consciously proscribed in the uprising. When shootings of Palestinians by Palestinians began, it provided evidence of weapons in Palestinian communities, which had deliberately elected not to use them in the intifada. Palestinian collaborators repented publicly in the mosques, yet by 1991 more than 450 persons suspected of such cooperation had been killed.[203] The Fateh Hawks, described by Ian Black as "young desperadoes," had killed more Palestinian collaborators than they had Israelis.[204] The Associated Press in August 1993 tallied 755 suspected collaborators slain.[205] By 1994, the Israeli army estimated that 964 collaborators had been killed.[206]

On June 7, 1992, at the instigation of Feisel Husseini, Hamas and Fateh signed a "covenant of honor" intended to regulate the killing of alleged informers and decrease the fighting between supporters of the two groups. The statement called for "thinking deeply" about "liquidating collaborators." It did not urge an end to the punitive killings, but stated "orders for killing collaborators must come from a high, joint leadership," and announced a broad steering committee "to unite efforts against the occupation forces."[207] In February 1994, it was reported that Hamas was offering amnesty to any informer who killed his or her Israeli handler.[208] Interpretations of retributory killing as related to political rivalry are outrightly rejected by Joost Hiltermann. In his view, Israeli issuances slanted reportage, spinning the murders into political competition, rather than accepting a "Palestinian definition of collaborators as those who work for the enemy against their own people, and have therefore forfeited their right to membership in the Palestinian community."[209] Regardless, the Israeli view of the uprising as predictably violent found easy validation in the slaying of Palestinian collaborators.

The Influence of the Activist Intellectuals Wanes

Security had been Israel's stated goal in its efforts to suppress the intifada, but the methods it used to crush what it never officially acknowledged as nonviolent struggle destroyed the very leadership that had advanced nonviolent sanctions to supplant armed struggle. With the leadership of the uprising regularly decimated, after two years none remained on the Command who had worked as volunteers in Feisel Husseini and Gideon Spiro's committees or the Arab Studies Society, participated in Mubarak Awad's workshops or read his *samizdat,* heard Gene Sharp's lectures, been prodded by Sari Nusseibeh's critical questioning and writings, or closely followed the opinions of Ziad Abu Zayyad or Radwan Abu Ayyash. As new factional representatives took the place of imprisoned leaders on the Command, the old vagaries of armed struggle returned. No one subscribing to a strategy of nonviolent resistance would survive on the Command past March 1990. The leaflet writers of the first two years were either in prison, deported, or demoralized. No longer able to maintain a coherent program, violence and decentralization replaced unity.[210]

With the PLO now driving the intifada, its preference for general strikes—the sole method of civil resistance with which it seemed to be familiar—wearied the population, as each faction urged its own strike day. As but one action step in nonviolent struggle, general strikes must be used with extreme caution, because they cannot be targeted with precision, unlike limited strikes that aim at specific grievances. Human resources are wasted by mounting general strikes aimed at complex purposes. Yet a general strike is easy to call, especially for those without knowledge of nonviolent collective action. In 1983, Mubarak Awad had warned against indiscriminate strikes by Palestinians, terming it a "grievous error" to declare an open strike calling for the end of military occupation.[211] Besides, as the identities of the representatives on the Command became revealed, the leadership collective lost its iconic authority. When anonymous, it was captivating, but as names trickled out, its requests for sacrifice and suffering no longer enthralled.[212] Furthermore, Israeli goods were back on the shelves of Palestinian shops.[213]

Internal dissension, old ideologies, lack of support from Tunis, and subversion of the nonviolent strategy meant that excessive Israeli force—instead of being interpreted as evidence of the strategy's effectiveness—became the logic for reviving the failed strategies of the past. Initiatives by local leaders who were meeting with Israelis were, by 1989, being repudiated by the PLO.[214] The intifada was being chronically subjected to calls for a return to armed struggle.[215] The activist intellectuals who had fought for a new consensus in the territories were unable to sustain the upper hand over the tendencies that had for decades fetishized armed struggle. Abu Ayyash appealed, "Internationally, we have made many gains with the intifada that we would lose with armed struggle. . . . If we use guns it will not be an intifada but a war. The Israelis want war. To take this decision would be to play into their hands."[216] Yet the voices of the activist intellectuals could not be heard above the din.

From the beginning, the PFLP had been "dead-set" against the nonviolent strategies.[217] It had divorced PFLP positions from those of the Command numerous times, but eventually the disagreement became fixed. A "war of leaflets" broke out in the spring of 1990, with rival strike bids disrupting life and perplexing the residents of the territories. "The PFLP had tolerated the nonviolent strategy because its overwhelming public support," Hanna Siniora commented; "but as they took hold of the reins, they started shifting to more confrontational approaches. . . . Especially after the Israelis cracked down on Beit Sahour's civil disobedience and tax resistance, the PFLP became convinced that they should return to their traditional military approach."[218] Discord and fatigue showed, as divisions between the PLO factions and Hamas "widened over basic issues, such as whether to escalate the uprising by using firearms, how to deal with alleged collaborators, and whether to give diplomacy a chance."[219]

Rife with internal divisions, the shadow cast by the Iraqi invasion of Kuwait in the summer of 1990 further vitiated the uprising. After the invasion, the rows created by double leaflets, issued four or five times during the first two years of the intifada, intensified. In an ironic twist, the 1991 Gulf War did not intensify the intifada but advanced its disintegration, and sundry Palestinian and PLO avowals of support for Saddam Hussein weakened it still further.

Israeli officials placed the occupied territories under extended curfews in reaction to the declared sympathy for Saddam Hussein.[220] Commiseration from the international community vanished, along with the sympathies of the Israeli peace camp and portions of the Arab world.[221] Association with Saddam Hussein collided with the goals of the intifada, Edward Kaufman reflected: "Much of the longer-term impact was lost, and the United States stopped the incipient negotiations with the PLO, because of the bad experience of Arafat supporting Saddam Hussein in the war against the coalition put together to liberate Kuwait, as well as some isolated failed terrorist acts instigated by exiled Palestinian organizations."[222] As Kuwait expelled Palestinian exiles following the emirate's restoration in the Gulf War, another wave of Palestinian refugees swept into Jordan for the third time since 1948. Remittances sent home to the occupied territories by Palestinians working in the Gulf dropped, poverty increased, and opportunities for day work in Israel all but ceased.[223] PLO funds for the territories fell from $350 million at the height of the intifada in 1988 to $120 million after Iraq's invasion of Kuwait in 1990, according to Palestinian economist Samir Huleileh.[224]

Disenchanted by the PLO's allying itself with Iraq, the activist intellectuals in the occupied territories distanced themselves from Tunis. The need for reform within the PLO was no longer a subject kept private. Ziad Abu-Amr proposed that the PLO revise its position to avoid being undercut by U.S., Arab, and Israeli hostility and suggested three steps: an overhaul of the PLO leadership, narrowing the number of factions within the PLO to three or four, and a shift in focus within the PLO from the diaspora to the occupied territories.[225] Husseini's East Jerusalem family home, Orient House, had become a surrogate government-in-waiting from 1989 onward, as, from his stone mansion, the activist intellectuals maintained contact and communications with international diplomats, the U.S. State Department, Israeli MKs, and the Israeli peace camp. Husseini criticized Iraqi missile attacks on Israel: "I am not happy about bombing Tel Aviv or Baghdad or any city."[226] Yet the decline of the intifada meant that he and other local leaders had less muscle with which to challenge Arafat than before the war.[227]

The PLO Used the First Intifada, and the Intifada Used the PLO

The PLO's lack of understanding of the theories and methods of the uprising meant that it remained wedded to its postulates of *thawra*, and locked in a pact with the Israelis in which both parties agreed fundamentally on the use of violence. Senior PLO officials in Tunis had been well aware that political decision making was by local leaders inside the territories, and they were "driving the bus."[228] The Palestinians in the territories were more pragmatic and willing to compromise with Israel than was the PLO in Tunis. Daoud Kuttab describes the arrangement:

> Leaders of the various PLO factions were able to fend off criticism by saying "this is the wish of the uprising leadership." . . . The intifada thus gave the PLO a new and more powerful [ability] to make concessions—not from a position of weakness—but from that of strength. . . . If anyone came to the PLO and said why are you accepting 242 or recognizing Israel, Arafat would say, this is what my people, who are fighting the Israelis daily, want.[229]

Arafat would invoke the names of Feisel Husseini and Sari Nusseibeh in his internal struggles with those around him who rejected compromise with Israel. Glenn Frankel reports, "Arafat needed Husseini and the insiders to validate his diplomatic moves to ward off the radicals. But Husseini and the pragmatists needed Arafat to grant them political protection and credibility."[230]

When secretary of state James Baker visited Jerusalem in March 1991—the first of numerous trips to the region leading to an international conference in Madrid—Husseini and others claimed to be emissaries from Arafat, who had given approval for the session, "but in fact, they were, for the first time, calling some of the shots themselves."[231] The PLO had, under pressure from the local leaders in the intifada, adopted a more sensible political platform. In Joel Greenberg's view, the "PLO leadership has finally adopted the realism of local Palestinians."[232] Demurring that neither international law nor diplomacy were their métier, no one in the occupied territories thought that the intifada could, on its own, win independence, Abu Zayyad said.[233] As Nusseibeh put it, "We, under occupation, neither have the facts nor the means to assess in a comprehensive manner the true value or significance of a statement or move made in the arena of high politics."[234] Many local leaders wanted to be tied to the broad front that had sustained their identity and did not wish to be alienated from the traditional leadership. Muhammad Jadallah explained,

> We were ready to die so as to keep the PLO leaders as our leaders and as our representatives. We used to go to prison, to be under pressure, to be tortured, because we said yes to the PLO. The PLO was our representative, and people would die for the PLO. So it never crossed our minds that we would want to replace the PLO. It was the other way around. We wanted to do the job and we wanted them to come and get the benefits of the job we were doing. They were like gods for us.[235]

Husseini envisaged a division of labor between the local leadership inside the territories and those outside. He said that he was willing to talk to any Israeli who was ready to listen, but he was unwilling to negotiate, because that was the job of the PLO.[236]

Although, by the end of the second year of the uprising, the Yitzhak Shamir government had conceded a certain willingness to interact with the Palestinians in the territories, it still refused to acknowledge the Palestinians as a people. The refusal of Israeli officials to talk formally to the PLO undermined the arguments of those who wanted an uprising independent from the PLO, even as Israeli focus on who spoke for the Palestinians made it harder for local leaders to adopt a course unrelated to defending the PLO and its ability to represent them.[237]

Preoccupied with curtailing any alternative leadership that might challenge its supremacy, and lacking genuine Arab allies, the PLO actually needed the authenticity and originality of the intifada, with its depth of support. Abu Iyad conceded that the uprising was the PLO's last hope.[238] When Nusseibeh describes the uprising as a "tremendous act of collective will against all odds," the odds include encumbrance by the distant PLO, whose regressive reliance on armed struggle had damaged possibilities for appeals to be made by Palestinians on the grounds of injustice and rectification of historic losses.[239]

PLO wording tended to be threatening in tone, rather than logically appealing.[240] This, despite the fact that more was attained "in fourteen months of relatively restrained *intifada* than in fourteen years of terrorist attacks."[241] Not until 1998 would Arafat admit, "There is now agreement that some armed operations carried out in the past have resulted in delaying [Israel's] turnover of land."[242]

As the uprising resumed after curfews were lifted in the occupied territories, anarchic tendencies that the Command had restrained broke free.[243] The period after the Gulf War was accompanied by the rise of undisciplined "masked youths."[244] Maverick actions by Palestinian splinter groups sabotaged the strategy of nonviolent resistance. Reversion to armed struggle is what precisely any opponent wants in nonviolent resistance, Sharp had warned the Palestinians in 1986. Any use of guns weakens the nonviolent challengers, because it produces support for repression in the target group, breeds revulsion, and unites the opponent's citzenry instead of splitting its ranks.[245] Worse, driven by a fear of independent thinking in the occupied territories, the PLO in Tunis itself instigated dissension and discord among leading figures in the territories. West Bankers say that the PLO split the ranks, particularly of Fateh, through unfulfilled pledges, insinuations that turned one person against another, and by letting some individuals go into financial debt based on false promises and with no help when the bills came due.[246]

Breakdown of the Intifada

A foremost reason for the collapse of the uprising is that the proponents of the nonviolent strategies were inadequately supported by the PLO. "The Palestinians in the territories knew that violence would be counterproductive and used conscious restraint—they wanted to keep it a 'white revolution,'" as Lucy Nusseibeh detailed:

> They were not paying taxes, they were boycotting Israeli products, and they were burning their identity cards. They attacked the Israeli policy of car number tags; they didn't pay taxes and also didn't change the number tags as required. The Israelis simply retaliated by changing the tags—by a certain date all cars needed new tags—and these you could only get by paying the taxes. If they had been better supported from the outside, the uprising would have gone further and quicker. This might have meant that those on the outside would have organized the manufacture of counterfeit car number tags, for example.[247]

Not only did the PLO fail to heed the advice of Sharp to rely on the "weapons" at hand of noncooperation and self-reliance, it also failed to begin preparations for self-governance. Educational institutions in the Arab states might have provided accreditation of the alternative education programs in the intifada by holding academic examinations, for example through Tunisian universities. Not only did the PLO fail to support the intifada strategy, but by putting first the taking over of the uprising, it placed organizational supremacy ahead of its stated goals.[248]

The Israelis, in mimicking the reaction of the British during the 1920s and 1930s and failing to distinguish violent from nonviolent resistance, hastened reversion to a mentality of violent retaliation. Had the nonviolent protagonists in the territories received an Israeli response that differentiated them from their colleagues who were sponsoring paramilitary operations and bombings, their fealty to the PLO might have wavered still further. The failure to keep the intifada independent abetted factionalism, which by the third year was undermining its cohesion.[249] Ironically, the Fateh-affiliated activist intellectuals, such as Abu Ayyash, Abu Zayyad, Husseini, Nusseibeh, and Siniora, in their desire to influence and change the thinking in Tunis, also made easier the ultimate takeover of the intifada by the PLO. Years of dutiful allocation to the PLO are now deeply regretted by many of the Palestinian progenitors of the uprising.[250]

In some cases gaining leverage from their family connections in the fight against worn-out dogma, and waging brilliant cognitive warfare against traditional thinking, the East Jerusalem activist intellectuals eventually lost out to the bankrupt ideas of those who were advocating old, desiccated theories of resistance, and the ideas of these generative figures were never institutionalized. Two schools of thought—one of which saw nonviolent resistance as a predecessor to future armed actions, the other of which believed that nonviolent strategies would produce the best results at negotiations and was the prerequisite for a durable settlement—negated each other. In this internal struggle, activist intellectuals played a seminal role, yet their impact was inhibited as other social realities prevailed. Resistance became all things to all persons. A coherent program could not be sustained. The strict prohibition against the use of weaponry was eventually ignored, and the intifada, which had managed to contain within its circumference contradictory polarities on the question of arms, came to an end. Although the nonviolent consensus was lost, it is significant that the uprising never became in any sense an armed rebellion, and a fundamental determination to limit violent acts and keep a popular civilian character remained in view.

Chapter 12
The Legacy

Achievements of the Uprising Coincide
with Its Most Nonviolent Phase

The first intifada proceeded in roughly four phases. The first started with the spontaneous actions after December 9, 1987. The second stage began a month later, as the Unified National Leadership Command was organized and a relatively coherent program of essentially nonviolent resistance got underway. The zenith, this phase produced the greatest and most enduring results of the uprising and lasted for more than two years, from January 1988 until March 1990, when the leading figures were incarcerated. The third period coincided with Iraq's invasion of Kuwait in August 1990 and the ensuing Gulf War in 1991. As a "war of the leaflets" erupted, the PFLP breached the nonviolent program of the intifada, and Hamas gained ascendancy with its justifications for violence. This juncture saw a surge in violent operations supposed to "help" the uprising (or sabotage the nonviolent strategy), as factions outside the occupied territories urged the arming of Palestinians inside the territories. The fourth segment began as, outside the territories, strides were taken toward an international peace conference in Madrid, held in October 1991. This final period would also see the continued breakdown of discipline, loss of political clarity and purpose, failure to press for goals as a united front, and rising internecine conflict, killing of collaborators, and violence toward Israeli civilians. The extended intifada effectively ended shortly before 1992, five years after it began, by which time armed "strike forces" had appointed themselves or been propelled into action by competing factions that rejected the nonviolent strategy of the uprising.[1]

This book has plumbed the forces that gave rise to the second, most productive phase, which lasted from December 1987 through March 1990, and explores how it was that the nonviolent discipline of that period was established and remained remarkably firm. Inside the territories the perception was that within six months of its start, the uprising had realized its main objectives. Daoud Kuttab, writing at the time, states,

> It has reversed the trend of creeping annexation by directing Palestinians to build their own economic infrastructure, . . . stopped the attempts by Jordan to toy with the idea of representing Palestinians, . . . consolidated the role of the PLO, . . . made Palestinians . . . more self-reliant, and . . . united than in the past. Unarmed Palestinians have succeeded in exposing Israeli brutality, transform[ing] the image of the Palestinians in the international community.[2]

Veteran Israeli journalist Uri Avnery concurs: "The intifada has already won. And its achievements are immense. A Palestinian state already exists today for all practical purposes. A system of self-government is functioning in the occupied territories; national decisions are made by a leadership which enjoys the total support of the people; tremendous sacrifices are willingly incurred, . . . a system of mutual help has come into being and beleaguered committees have held out under awesome pressure."[3] The Palestinian declaration of independence—recognizable as the Husseini Document and with Sari Nusseibeh's voice—had been issued after less than a year, just prior to the nineteenth PNC, or "intifada PNC," held in Algiers on 15 November 1988. Instead of an interim government-in-exile as condoned by Arab leaders in the past, implying a center located outside the territories, the document speaks of the establishment of a Palestinian state in Palestinian territory and accepts the 1947 UN partition boundaries of Resolution 181.[4] The term *armed struggle* was vanishing from the official lexicon of mainstream Palestinian political discourse.[5] Both this phrase and all references to the 1964 Palestinian National Charter were gone from the resolutions of the PNC within one year of the start of the uprising.[6]

Ignored or misread by the media and rebutted by Yitzhak Shamir's government, the Algiers session was a watershed. Susan Hattis Rolef would later observe that professional Israeli PLO watchers had started noticing changes in PLO positions after the twelfth PNC in Cairo in 1974, but academicians and politicians became persuaded of significant alterations only after the nineteenth PNC.[7] Its resolutions made explicit what for fourteen years had been a trend in Palestinian political thought. The 1974 call for a "national authority" had implied two states existing side by side, a concept that grew until, in 1987, at the PNC in Algiers before the outbreak of the first intifada, an international conference and negotiations with Israel were added to the resolutions.[8]

Ironically, with the uproar of support for the declaration of a state at the intifada PNC, the distinctive ability of the uprising to contain within it both secular protagonists and those cultivating political gains through religious organizing came to an end. The 1988 Palestinian Declaration of Independence calls Palestine "the land of the three monotheistic faiths" and refers to "temple, church, and mosque."[9] It was also the first document to refer explicitly to the principle of equality of men and women in the future state, a byproduct of the critical contributions of women in the uprising. Neither of these stances meshed with the creeds of the Islamic revivalists. After the Algiers meeting, the schism between Hamas and the rest of the intifada was clearly visible.

The nineteenth PNC stands out as evidence of the repudiation within the PLO of the doctrine of armed struggle as the "only way to liberate Palestine," and passages of its controversial 1964 Charter are "flatly contradicted" by its resolutions.[10] Its declarations stand out for their hopefulness for reconciliation with Israelis. In March 1989, former U.S. secretary of state Henry Kissinger suggested, "Israel's best hope is with Arab leaders living on the West Bank."[11] However, the Israeli response to the changes in Algiers—including the affirmation of Israel's right to "secure and recognized" borders implicit in the PNC's acceptance of Resolution 242—was to reject them and castigate the international community for being fooled.[12]

The intifada allowed the PLO to pursue a more flexible line of thinking and begin active pursuit of territorial compromise with Israel.[13] Alterations to the Palestinian political terrain in the second stage of the uprising would have been considered villainous earlier. Acceptance of UN Security Council Resolution 242, which treats the Palestinians solely as refugees and implies Palestinian recognition of Israel prior to negotiations in its precept of land for peace, was anathema until the intifada. Sari Nusseibeh reflected, "Just before the nineteenth PNC in Algiers [November 1988] . . . a leaflet mentioned 242 and 338 in one sentence, by themselves, not dressed up, just straightforward, very normal. Many of the things that later were formalized appeared first, undressed, in the various leaflets. Three or four years before, Palestinian headlines would have called 242 the worst thing on earth."[14] Arafat had previously drawn the line at recognizing Israel, but the intifada altered the situation.[15] Within the territories, as a result of the intifada, the ability to compromise had become viewed as strength rather than weakness and had given Palestinians the confidence to make concessions without a feeling of surrender.[16]

By increasing the price of military occupation to Israel, the intifada had made occupation unattractive and unsustainable.[17] "The myth of improving the quality of life" had been destroyed by six months of uprising, Hanan Mikhail Ashrawi said: "Life has no quality under occupation. . . . We have proved that we can exercise a large degree of autonomy ourselves without the Israelis making that as a political condition for the settlement. . . . Palestinians have shown that they are not immature people needing the guardianship of another country."[18] Eleven months after the kindling of the uprising, Kuttab wrote, the Palestinian state "had become a reality recognized by nearly one hundred countries. . . . After forty years of exile and twenty-one years of occupation Palestinians now stand on the threshold of a new dawn, . . . [the result of] the active decision by the Palestinians to take the initiative rather than to wait for others to accomplish their goals."[19]

While the commandos' cross-border sorties, raids, and bombings had the predictable effect of unifying Israelis in opposition to Palestinian claims and had lessened international sympathy for rectification of Palestinian losses, the intifada had done what no armed mission had ever accomplished: it had shown the limits of military means and security measures. "When the Israelis realized the political aims of the uprising," said Reuven Gal, "they began to recognize, that they, the Israelis, 'could not win' militarily."[20]

A 1991 International Conference in Madrid, and the 1993 Oslo Accords

After the intifada PNC in November 1988, news reports of countries around the globe recognizing the newly declared Palestinian state were monitored intently by the populace of the occupied territories, as attention shifted from the uprising to the PLO's diplomatic initiatives.[21] Soon after the November meeting of the nineteenth PNC came the "great events" of December 1988.[22] Arafat met in Stockholm, on December 7, with five American Jewish peace activists, led by lawyer Rita Hauser, and he reiterated the PNC's recognition of Israel. On the thirteenth, he addressed the UN General Assembly in Geneva.[23] There, Arafat again declared Israel's right to exist and repudiated terrorism, and he did so once more the following day in Stockholm, traveling with the same delegation of American Jews.[24] Finally, his words met the dicta established by Kissinger in 1975, and the way was cleared for the United States formally to enter discussions with the PLO.[25] Israeli defense minister Yitzhak Rabin, protesting that it was a grave error for the United States to talk to the PLO, claimed the Americans had legitimized the uprising in the territories.[26] Conversely, the reluctant U.S. agreement to take up a remote diplomatic exchange with the PLO in Tunis was denounced in the Israeli peace camp as insufficient, as Avnery notes: "Significant resolutions of the PLO—such as its recognition of Israel—which were made possible by the intifada and the regaining of national dignity, have not led to a political breakthrough. After two years of the intifada, the only game in town is a ridiculous dialogue between the PLO and an American ambassador."[27] On January 12, 1989, the UN Security Council granted the PLO the right to speak directly to the council as "Palestine," the same as any member state.

Arafat's statements in Geneva and Stockholm in December 1988 arose directly from the uprising and reflected the outlook of the popular leadership in the occupied territories.[28] The momentum continued, and these events led to the revival of proposals for an internationally sponsored conference that could camouflage direct talks between the Israelis and Palestinians. At the end of the Gulf War in 1991, a conference was organized in Madrid to address the Palestinian question under U.S. and USSR sponsorship. Secretary of State Baker held multiple meetings with Feisel Husseini, Hanan Mikhail Ashrawi, and other of the East Jerusalem activist intellectuals in the period leading up to the Madrid meeting.[29] When a Palestinian delegation was assembled to go to Spain for the ceremonies that began on October 30, intended to lead to direct negotiations between Israel and the Palestinians, at its helm was Haidar Abd al-Shafi, the physician in whose Gaza home initial planning meetings for the 1987 uprising had been held. The Palestinians were embedded in the joint Jordanian-Palestinian team, created as a cover to assuage Israeli sensibilities about talking with the PLO, and the PLO was not invited. A separate guidance committee was set up with Feisel Husseini as coordinator, and Hanan Mikhail Ashrawi as spokesperson. They, and the others—mostly physicians, university professors, or with doctorates in various fields—were considered persona non grata as interlocutors by the Israelis and were segregated from the other conference delegates representing forty countries as "advisers," despite having sat down with the U.S. secretary of state at least eight times en route to Madrid.[30] Dr. Abd al-Shafi's

speech stressed a Palestinian right to self-determination, and the commitment to statehood exemplified by the intifada, in which the institutions
and infrastructure of the new state had already begun to be built. His
remarks, in Avi Shlaim's words, "contained more evidence of the new
thinking than all the other speeches, Arab and Israeli, put together," and
were "the most moderate presentation of the Palestinian case ever made
by an official Palestinian spokesman since the beginning of the conflict at
the end of the nineteenth century."[31] For the first time in the international news media, of which perhaps five thousand reporters were in
attendance in Madrid, the Palestinian quandary had a human face, in the
visages of Husseini, Ashrawi, and Abd al-Shafi. The downgrading of the
role of the East Jerusalemites at the behest of Prime Minister Shamir
suited Arafat's fear of loss of control as much as it did the Israeli aversion
to direct negotiations.[32] The Palestinians, after long having been asked to
accept UN Security Council Resolution 242 passed in 1967, and finally
having done so, due to the changes won by the intifada, found in Madrid
that the Israeli delegation would not recognize the applicability of 242,
because it defines the territories as occupied.[33]

Sari Nusseibeh remained in East Jerusalem, and between Madrid and
the signing of the Oslo accord that lay ahead in 1993, headed the organizing
of technical and political committees.[34] With Arafat's support, he organized
two hundred experts divided into thirty-nine teams, to aid the Palestinians'
transition to self-governance.[35] Envisaging live primaries, similar to U.S.
accessible caucuses or elections in which candidates are openly chosen or
slates of delegates prepared, he laid groundwork for the development of
future Palestinian political parties. Nusseibeh described the committees:

> You had to create a party in order to create a government. We needed . . .
> both. The technical committees were to be a professional backbone for
> government—archaeology, transportation, education, electricity. Haj Abd
> Abu-Diab was the coordinator for the electricity committee. Manuel Has-
> sassian [Bethlehem University political scientist] was to coordinate the
> elections committee. If each professional committee were to think collec-
> tively, we could come up with guidelines for negotiating positions. (We
> needed technical visions, not slogans. . . .) Multilateral negotiations would
> be the destination. . . . The major plan in effect with the World Bank was
> done by these committees.[36]

Hanna Siniora judged these committees and teams more consequential than even Nusseibeh's supervision of the uprising, because they "brought the Fateh underground above ground."[37] The extensive planning took years, as teams sketched the dimensions of governance and life for their future state. Yet the plans were about to be disregarded, and along with growth of civil society brought about by the intifada and the formative years preceding it, would be overshadowed by the forthcoming Oslo process and its subsequent failures.

After the Madrid peace conference in October 1991, the PFLP, with its Syrian backing, and Hamas, with its Iranian support, joined forces to oppose the peace process.[38] The PFLP and DFLP opposed the planning by such technical committees. Riad al-Malki attacked the plans as an effort to establish a political party with the "connivance" of the United States and independent of the PLO.[39] Although unable to implement their own notions of armed struggle, the PFLP and DFLP decided to undermine the adherence to the nonviolent template. Leaflet no. 84 of July 1992 "glorified stabbers" and condemned newly elected prime minister Yitzhak Rabin. The leaflet bore the "hallmarks" of the PFLP, the *Jerusalem Post* observed.[40] Meanwhile, Hamas was impatiently asserting itself. With the start of peace talks, Hamas had a chance to promote its strategy against occupation, and its military wing Izz al-Din al-Qassam showed its determination to advertise itself as an "alternative to the timid realism" of Fateh. "The difficulties in the peace negotiations and hardships arising as a result of Israeli policies in the occupied territories worked in favor of Hamas," according to Amal Jamal.[41]

The Madrid conference was followed by ten rounds of bilateral talks in Washington, D.C., starting in December 1991. In the ninth round in April 1993, the Israelis conceded that Feisel Husseini could join the talks as a negotiator, despite residing in East Jerusalem, and approved the principle of a Palestinian police force in the territories. While Arafat's main preoccupation was institutionalization of the PLO as the negotiating partner, the Clinton administration reversed twenty-six years of U.S. policy and, in the words of Avi Shlaim, "accepted the Israeli claim that East Jerusalem and the rest of the West Bank and Gaza were disputed—not occupied—territories. . . . The even-handed approach of the [George H. W.] Bush administration was replaced by an 'Israel first' approach, . . . [as] Clinton refused to put pressure on Israel and adopted a hands-off attitude to the peace process."[42] Caught between the delaying tactics of the Israelis and the resistance of the PLO to their leadership, and undermined by the United States, the estrangement of the activist intellectuals from the political process deepened, as it became clear that the Madrid approach would not be effective.[43]

Subsequent revelation of months of secret PLO-Israeli negotiations leading to the 1993 signing of accords called Oslo I—bartered without interaction or advice from the epistemic community that had produced and guided the intifada—further alienated the activist intellectuals. The Oslo process had originated with Israelis on the political Left, chiefly through the ministrations of the young deputy foreign minister, Yossi Beilin. The key actors were leaders in Labor's peace flank, whose mandate was to reach past the party's customary positions and search for an agreement with the PLO that would suit the Zionist parties to the left of Labor.[44] Certain designated Israelis and Palestinians were able to meet in Oslo without overt acknowledgment.[45] "The fact that Norway had been proposed indicated a serious desire to keep the dialogue away from the eyes and ears of the media," states Mahmoud Abbas (Abu Mazen).[46]

By April 1993, the new Norwegian Foreign Minister Johan Jørgen Holst,[47] and his wife Marianne Heiberg, a social scientist who had studied conditions in the West Bank and Gaza, and social scientist Terge Rød Larsen were providing auspices for the talks. The Israeli negotiators received disproportionate assistance from the Norwegian hosts.[48] Hilde Henriksen Waage, deputy director and senior researcher at Oslo's International Peace Research Institute (PRIO), explains that the Norwegians set up the negotiations "in the way Israel wanted. Basically, the Palestinians were confronted with a fait accompli," in which, after months of talks, "delicate final questions were solved during eight hours of phone calls" on August 18. Two days later in the middle of the night, the Israelis, Norwegians, and Palestinians initialed the declaration of principles in secret in Oslo.[49] The PLO representatives were outmaneuvered.

Having vested in the PLO the political currency achieved by the uprising, the activist intellectuals were disconsolate to learn that major, potentially irremediable concessions had been made in Oslo that neglected the view from the territories.[50] Nor was the content or process from the fourteen negotiating sessions in Olso, held over an eight-month period, shared with what had become an experienced negotiating team in Washington.[51] "The Oslo negotiations were a clear attempt to bypass the local leaders of the West Bank and Gaza and to restore the status of the PLO leaders in Tunis," Amal Jamal determines.[52]

Even more serious, the expectation among residents of the occupied territories that a Palestinian state would exist alongside Israel was not included in the declaration of principles developed in Oslo, but postponed for final negotiations. Nevertheless, in the international community and among many Palestinians the sequence and progression was infused with the anticipation that the Palestinians "would have a state in which, however modest and disarmed, they could live their own lives free of Israeli dictation."[53] Although the Palestinian negotiating team in Oslo had not included the pathfinders who had shaped and guided the intifada during its most productive phase, the PLO representatives based their positions on PNC resolutions that had accepted the principle of partition as the starting point for a solution to the conflict, thus reflecting the concurrence that had been achieved in the intifada. The acceptance of the principle of partition—dating to the Peel Commission's report of 1937, and the 1947 UN General Assembly Resolution 181—went to the heart of the Olso process and was at last accepted by the contenders, with the increasingly significant exception of the Islamic revivalists. While the PLO delegates in Oslo stuck to the tenets of a Palestinian refugee right to return and commitment to an independent Palestinian state with Jerusalem as its capital, free of Israeli settlements, they now considered these positions negotiable. These altered stands rested on the success achieved through the intifada, powered by its self-discipline in the use of nonviolent strategies and belief that negotiations could be beneficial.

Other factors also contributed to a new realism, including the collapse of the Soviet Union, whose patronage and romanticizing of violence had for years artificially inflated the bravado of the PLO; the lessened Saudi financial support in the wake of the PLO stance in the Gulf War; and the generally diminishing footing of the organization in the Arab world. Most important, the Israeli elections of June 1992 had brought to office a government headed by Yitzhak Rabin that considered the time had come to negotiate an end to the conflict, along with willingness to depart from some occupied land. Newfound Israeli readiness to compromise, and a recent PLO disposition toward negotiations wrought by the intifada had come together in the decision to start conferencing. Rabin's appointment of Shimon Peres as foreign minister brought to bear a vision of the Middle East inspired by the European Union.[54] In December of the electoral year, the Rabin government repealed the six-year-old legislation that forbade contact between Israelis and the PLO. This meant that individuals such as Uri Avnery, Amos

Gvirtz, Gideon Spiro, and Michel Warschawski—key Israeli interlocutors for the Palestinian activist intellectuals—who had dared to break Israeli law by their noncooperation in maintaining contact and walking side by side in joint demonstrations with the Palestinians (assumed to be PLO whether independent or not), were no longer in breach of the law when working together. Ironically and just when Israeli-Palestinian communications became feasible, Avi Shlaim describes Rabin's conversion to the idea of dealing with the PLO as being sealed by evaluations reaching him that "the local Palestinian leadership had finally been neutralized."[55]

The Declaration of Principles of the Oslo accords, signed on the U.S. White House lawn on September 13, 1993, signified Israeli recognition of the PLO for the first time, yet fell far short of the November 1988 declaration of independence and its progenitor, the Husseini Document. In an exchange of letters between Yasir Arafat and Yitzhak Rabin without which the signing would not have occurred, the PLO letter recognizes the state of Israel, yet Israel's missive does not recognize the right of the Palestinians to establish their own nation-state. As these principles were structured, in recognizing Israel the Palestinians accepted that nearly four-fifths of historic Israel (the lands within the boundaries of Israel prior to the 1967 war) was no longer a topic for discussion or negotiations. Any and all future territorial parleys would concern adjustments from the West Bank and Gaza Strip, meaning that the Palestinians' land would shrink still more, while the Israelis' territory would grow.

The declaration was an agenda for talks, with a schedule, rather than an agreement. Article 5, clause 3, of the declaration elaborated three matters for future negotiations, after successful implementation of an interim agreement between the two parties: the question of Jerusalem, the subject of the Palestinian refugees, and the predicament of Israeli settlements in the occupied territories. Either side was also allowed to bring additional topics for discussion, contingent on acceptance by the other. The Palestinians accepted the severe limitations, because the article and clause in question would provide later aegis for resolving the matter of statehood, their central goal. Indeed, endorsement of future statehood for the Palestinians, if couched in ambiguities, had been accepted by large proportions of Israelis and in the court of world opinion. Despite the flaws and omissions in the Oslo accords—concerning the settlements, refugees, and status of Jerusalem—Barton Gellman expressed prevalent views in writing, "What validates the pact's grand claim to historic reconciliation between two peoples is the groundwork it lays for a sovereign Palestinian state."[56] A month later, Daniel Rubinstein, columnist for *Haaretz*, told members of American Friends of Peace Now, "Ninety percent of Israelis know that there will be a Palestinian state."[57]

The declaration of principles emphasized process over content. The major PLO concession was the linking of subsequent successful implementation of an interim agreement with negotiations on the final status of the occupied territories and the three topics of settlements, refugees, and Jerusalem. The declaration of principles specified processes in the interim period, namely, an Israeli withdrawal from Gaza and Jericho, thereafter gradual transfer of civil functions from Israel to the PLO, and eventual Israeli withdrawal from Palestinian population centers and towns. Israeli participation in final negotiations was made conditional on successful, peaceful implementation of the interim agreement. The term *peaceful*, explains Ilan Pappé, was "effectively an Israeli veto," because it was "meant in a way that would satisfy the Israeli concept of security, so the implementation of that phase was to be monitored and executed by Israel generals."[58] Thus, says Pappé, the interim agreement

> was dictated by the Israelis, and tailored according to their perceptions of security. Moreover, it represented the Israeli conception of the conflict's nature and substance. The agreement dealt only with problems emanating from the 1967 war, as if that were the basis of the situation, and everything preceding it was irrelevant to a peaceful resolution of the conflict. While the agreed interim phase contributed to ending Israeli control over the lives of large numbers of Palestinians, it did not take the Palestinian perception of the conflict into account, or advance any solutions for the uprooted Palestinians who lost their homeland in 1948.[59]

As it became clear how little of the Palestinian November 1988 declaration of independence and principles in the Husseini Document were reflected in Oslo I, where full statehood was nowhere discussed, the deferential posture of the activists intellectuals toward the PLO began to seem inappropriate, if not farcical. Muhammad Jadallah recalled, "I started to feel, through meetings and dialogues, two things: one, the PLO in Tunis was weak, and they did not know the Israelis, and, two, they were dying to get together with the Israelis."[60]

Eventually Nusseibeh, in an interview headlined "Palestinians Wrong to Rely on America," said he was disillusioned with the course of affairs and the return to violence that was, in his phrase, strictly a deviation from the intifada.[61] He and others—including Ghassan Khatib in the West Bank and Haidar Abd al-Shafi in Gaza—withdrew from political activity.[62]

Civil Society, Noncooperation, the First Intifada, and Statehood

When Lord Balfour in 1919 said he did "not propose even to go through the form of consulting the wishes of the present inhabitants of the country,"[63] it reflected a belief that the Arabs could not govern themselves, and seventy years later such perceptional issues remained. Thus one final look is reasonable on how the values of civil society came to predominate and the methods of civil society were utilized in the intifada from 1987 to 1990, while at the same time the rights required for such a domain had still to be secured through the same techniques. These developments have long-term implications for all the peoples in the region, and elsewhere.

Reading Antonio Gramsci

"The Palestinian professionals who were developing the medical relief committees, teachers' associations, and women's organizations in the late 1970s and 1980s were all reading Antonio Gramsci," recalled Gail Pressburg, whose responsibilities with the American Friends Service Committee had brought her into contact with an extensive range of the civilian nonmilitary groups.[64] Gramsci was delving into how forces that were opposed to a regime—Mussolini's fascism—could effectively and nonviolently promote deep and lasting social and political change. In his view, resistance movements could be successful only if the struggle possessed broad popular backing and permeated the structures of civil society *before* attempting to wrench control of state power. This requires forming alliances among those striving in popular and democratic efforts that are not necessarily related to class, such as movements on behalf of women, students, peace, or civil liberties. For Gramsci, as noted, achieving *egemonia* (hegemony), also *direzione* (direction, or leadership), requires what he calls a "war of position," which entails building blocs of varied and influential forces linked by a common denominator.[65] Gramsci's notion of hegemony suggests that major change through nonviolent action becomes a practical possibility only when groups opposing a state apparatus gain widespread consent within civil society.

In Gramscian terms, the 45,000 Palestinian committees that existed by 1987 were contending in order to achieve hegemony over the ideologies of military liberation and armed struggle. These networks were the essential components to what would become the intifada. The antecedent movements—voluntary work committees, women's movement, and student organizing against Israeli Military Orders 854 and 947—had made concrete such consent by encouraging broad sectors to participate in the opposition. A new political culture, located in civil society, benefited from the capacity of nonviolent resistance to give rise to a democratic ethos in the sense that no one can decide for another to take the risks involved, and persons cannot be conscripted into paying the penalties incurred from, say, civil disobedience. Although the ideological generators for Palestinian nationalism were by the early 1980s located in the territories, it was not solely the intellectuals, academicians, professionals, and journalists who sought a practical alternative to armed struggle and realized that they would have to live alongside Israel. The consensus included refugees living in camps, some of them twice or three times displaced. Sometimes unschooled and unsophisticated, they were among the first to accept the idea of a two-state solution.

Gramsci took from Benedetto Croce the notion of human beings as protagonists in history with the ability to turn thought into action.[66] He considers the role of intellectuals at length in his *Prison Notebooks*.[67] In thirty-three notebooks—written between 1929 and 1935 during a decade spent in Mussolini's prisons, and in six volumes published from 1948 to 1951—Gramsci includes in his concept of hegemony "cultural leadership." Of particular relevance in the Palestinian context is Gramsci's perception of the need to eliminate the division between the intellectual and manual laborer.[68] The Palestinian voluntary work committees, starting in 1972, had the elimination of this separation as one of their objectives. Gramsci is also concerned with knowledge and power, and sees power as a relationship, consistent with the viewpoint in Gene Sharp's writings. Power for Gramsci must be dispersed throughout civil society and embodied in networks of organizations.[69]

Peculiarly compatible with the emerging role of the Palestinian activist intellectuals is Gramsci's extension of the definition of intellectuals to embrace political leaders, artists, literary figures, entrepreneurs, engineers, managers, technicians, and journalists.[70] It is not simply the *thinking* of "organizer intellectuals" that counts with Gramsci, but the function they perform. The connection between thinking and doing also resonates in collective nonviolent action, where it is tacitly understood that one cannot achieve positive ends by violent subjugation.

The Palestinian professionals and intellectuals were ruminating in their lively study and discussions of Gramsci a model in which coercive forms of resistance that injure life and limb are rejected in favor of a search for political mediation and change led by academic, cultural, political, student, youth, and women organizers who rely on nonviolent means. The force exerted by such intellectual engagés and the "hegemonic" consent that they attain, in Gramsci's view, are situated in an autonomous civil society in which intellectuals are the primary historical impetus.

The Palestinians' saga is invariably analyzed through a geographic aperture so narrow and constricted that no sense of perspective is possible regarding the conjunction between the methods of the Palestinians and other peoples elsewhere who have fought for their rights through collective nonviolent action. Nonviolent measures, employed with civil behavior, had been the dominant means employed by the Palestinians earlier in the twentieth century, as they struggled for the revocation of the Balfour Declaration, limits on Jewish immigration, and the achievement of independence. The intifada reflected the reassertion of deep-seated Palestinian values held by the majority and displayed in their quest for recognition of civil and political rights during the 1920s and 1930s. Depth and ingenuity had often typified the Palestinian employment of nonviolent struggle, yet the record has been ignored, mischaracterized, and subjected to a class analysis in which the elite are condemned, or, with some justification, denounced as ineffective. Then too, this predominant narrative has been eclipsed by periodic eruptions of violence, and, again with reason, intermittently obliterated by shock and horror from acts of terrorism. From the first large peaceful demonstration against the Balfour Declaration in Jerusalem on February 27, 1920, to the 174-day general strike of 1936—perhaps the longest in history—through more than two years of the intifada, the Palestinians had employed archetypal methods of nonviolent struggle. Yet little reinforcement had greeted Palestinian attempts to make their case through nonviolent sanctions, and episodic outbreaks of violence and terror operations came to overshadow the more indicative pattern. Disregard for the Palestinian perspective was reflected in Israeli policies backed by London and then by Washington—that is, until the intifada.

The work of the Committee Confronting the Iron Fist was based on an imagined, shared community in which Israelis and Palestinians would together seek a way out of the mutual degradation of military occupation. This imagining of solidarity created the possibility for an appeal to Israeli sensibilities and was equally manifested in the restraint against arms in the uprising. Driven by a need to replace what they regarded as the exhausted covert military ideologies of the 1950s and 1960s, through forming alliances with sympathetic Israelis and envisioning direct negotiations, Feisel Husseini and Sari Nusseibeh's vision of an imagined commonality strengthened the girders of a sphere for political activity that was not coercive and within which the individual could act as an agent of change, while rejecting a guerrilla stance because it would negatively affect the result. Combined with the principle of openness and functioning without secrecy, the fight for Palestinian political and civil rights could accordingly be fastened onto a larger, contemporary framework of respect for the rule of law and human rights. The 1987 uprising and its antecedent movements correspond with Keith Tester's view of civil society as a dialectic of imagination: "On the one hand, civil society is imagined as that which has been achieved. On the other hand, civil society is imagined as that which stands in need of achievement. . . . Civil society was always imagined as a difficult achievement. But, of course, it was precisely the difficulty which made it an attractive destiny in the first place. . . . The point was not so much that civil society was possible, but rather that it needed to be possible."[71]

Civil Disobedience and Civil Society

The twin cardinal virtues of tolerance and nonviolent interaction that in modern political thought constitute civil society displayed themselves during the second phase of the early intifada. For example, frequent allusions were made to the three great revealed religions and injunctions to a "white revolution." Yet civil society also relies on confrontational collective action.

Civil disobedience moves between the "boundaries of insurrection and institutionalized political activity," and to Jean L. Cohen and Andrew Arato is a critical form in modern civil societies, because it keeps alive the vision of a just and democratic civil society. They maintain that civil disobedience may actually constitute civil society.[72] Although Cohen and Arato are concerned chiefly with constitutional democracies where entitlements, the rule of law, and democratic institutions are already established, we may deduce that the use of noncooperation for purposes of establishing rights under authoritarian and nondemocratic circumstances, such as military occupation, can be part of a normative process leading to the formation of such institutions.[73] This is the perspective offered by Adrien Katherine Wing's assessment that the intifada represented an attempt to wrest control over legal decision making, which had customarily been in the hands of outsiders in the West Bank and Gaza Strip—whether Ottoman, British, Jordanian, Egyptian, or Israeli. She cites, in particular, the voluntary compliance of the populace with the new rules of the uprising, the result of the "rulemakers' legitimacy" rather than coercion.[74]

The idea that persons can refuse to be governed by those who dominate them developed as a quiet revolution of thought during the 1980s and became the philosophy prevailing in the intifada. This is not to speak of a Lockean insistence on the right of individuals to withdraw from any contract that does not protect life, liberty, and property—the Palestinians in the West Bank and Gaza had not voluntarily contracted for the imposition of a belligerent occupation. Regardless, full measure was taken of Étienne de la Boétie's proposition—decoded by Mubarak Awad, transmitted in Gene Sharp's writings and lectures, politically interpreted by Feisel Husseini and Sari Nusseibeh, and rendered actionable by an epistemic community around East Jerusalem—that it was *Palestinian* cooperation with the occupation that sustained it.

Moreover, the uprising, and equally important, the years preceding it, represent a transition in which Palestinians—both those affiliated and not affiliated with factions—were learning to work together, exemplifying the norms of civil society and utilizing democratic procedures. By 1991, the popular committees "had transmogrified into professionally based, foreign-funded, and development-oriented centers," anthropologist Rema Hammami notes; "dozens of donor-supported research centers emerged during this period, many founded by academics during the long years of Israeli-imposed university closures."[75] Present-day Palestinian civil society groups trace their lineage to the civilian mobilization of the 1980s, and the leadership that emerged from such networks is among the most ideologically committed to democracy anywhere in the Arab world.[76]

To argue that a hardy, if tempestuous, civil society for the Palestinians is a prerequisite for the evolution of coexistence and peace in the eastern Mediterranean is not to assert that the Palestinians are responsible for a state without actually having one. Where no state exists, it cannot be argued that entities of civil society have the capacity to balance or contest the powers of government. Under occupation, the popular committees of the intifada—

with their divisions of labor and layers of elected leaders ready to replace the incarcerated—became a shadow governance, reflecting a commonality of interest shared by Palestinians from competing nationalist movements and parties who were working together, much as Charles Tilly indicates, as a feature of civil society.[77] As the centers of power diffused, the committees manifested how the structures of civil society can protect popular participation. Mubarak Awad had spread rudimentary knowledge of Gandhi's constructive program into West Bank villages. Just as its small institutions made it possible for the poorest Indians to participate in the national struggles for independence, the popular committees of the Palestinian uprising—alternative institutions, or parallel institutions, whose nonviolent interventions are intended to disrupt established behavior patterns and remove the subjects from the ruler—enabled the young, old, women, refugees, professionals, intellectuals, and others with an aversion to participating in guerrilla operations actively to take part in a national struggle.

Standards of political behavior changed, as the repertoire of nonviolent sanctions steadily expanded. While not necessarily equating democracy with civil society, Edward Kaufman and Shukri Abed consider self-assertion and behaving collectively to be characteristic democratic behaviors.[78] Such qualities were abundant in the early years of the intifada. The building of coalitional arrangements became a staple. Even Hamas and Fateh found common ground. The civic order that evolved was a far cry from the riots and chaos enunciated in the stock phrases of Israeli officials.

Instead of invoking retaliation from Arab states, the fruitful years of the intifada were distinguished by an assumption of responsibility by the occupied. Nowhere was this revealed more clearly than in the significant, often meandering discourse on civil disobedience, conducted through the leaflets. There, the utensils for civil disobedience were identified as the spirit of cooperation, cooperatives, and the strengthening of the local committees that were utterly independent of the occupation. Much as Gramsci had defined the work of the intellectuals in a "war of position"—or transformation of culture—new organizer leaders arose from the voluntary work committees and the women's, youth, student, and prisoners' movements of the 1970s and 1980s. From these, what Guillermo O'Donnell and Philippe Schmitter term "popular upsurge" against authoritarian rule[79] and leadership emerged, tried and tested on the West Bank and in the Gaza Strip, often having scant connection if any to PLO military cadres. The new spokespersons earned their standing through their willingness to provide assistance and accept responsibility that often carried life-and-death consequences.

Information played a significant role and constitutes an adjunct to Palestinian civil society. Facility in issuing reliable news releases and credible reports became a valued skill. The new spokespersons were adept at informational methods, including the use of archives, documentation, and denunciation, as pioneered by Raja Shehadeh and al-Haq. As journalists from around the world gathered to cover the uprising, they were accompanied by Daoud Kuttab, members of the FACTS Information Committee, Radwan Abu Ayyash, Mubarak Awad, Ghassan Khatib, and others as they entered into villages and refugee camps, where they met scores of the women, men, and youths who were running the popular committees.[80] Reporters became the "darlings of the Palestinians, and bane of the soldiers," perceived, Joel Greenberg writes, as a complementary channel to the Palestinians' own efforts at combating a great injustice on the world stage. Ushered into lowly refugee abodes, journalists were urged to take photographs and "write and tell Israelis and the world what the soldiers are doing," which, according to Greenberg, often seemed like "pointless thuggery."[81] The sight of unarmed youths dying daily from the bullets of a vastly superior military, armed by a superpower, touched the sensibilities of viewers, who were at the same time seeing reports of the mighty Soviet Union imploding, abetted by similarly popular and unarmed civil resistance in Poland, East Germany, and the Czech and Slovak republics.

Imprisoned Palestinians were exposed to the intricacies of elections, elaborately employed in the prisoners' movement, and ideas about political struggle as they studied together. Palestinian civil society may have been helped by the incarceration of an estimated 120,000 Palestinians between the start of the intifada and 1995.[82] For the first time, Palestinians from the West Bank met their countrymen and women from Gaza, and vice versa, during confinement in Israeli jails.[83] Such encounters were otherwise impossible, since the occupied Palestinians were not allowed to travel in the territories, hold joint meetings, or convene seminars, party congresses, and national conventions.

Alternative symbols of authority arose, such as invisibly coordinated hunger strikes. Such exposure to ideas and symbols is significant, because nonviolent struggle requires supremacy of thought and discipline in order to restrain reflexive retaliation. Yet, partly because of the lack of support from the PLO, the Palestinians in the territories never undertook training on the scale that would have been necessary for the "total civil disobedience" envisaged by the Jerusalem Paper and the Command's issuances. The Israeli authorities would probably not have allowed mass training programs, no matter their impact on the repudiation of violence. The Palestinians broadened civil disobedience beyond its customary deliberate defiance of laws or military orders regarded as illegitimate, unethical, or immoral, when they proved the "nongovernability" of the territories.[84]

A glance at the 1983 booklet circulated by Mubarak Awad confirms that the methods of nonviolent struggle as adopted in the intifada worked effectively in moving toward seven of the eight aims set forth in the publication. The maximum potential and resources of the Palestinians inside the occupied territories were utilized. Instead of passive activities, the society unified itself in action and enlisted significant sectors of Israeli society in the struggle to lift the occupation. International public opinion became focused on the Palestinians. "Security" arguments used to justify Israeli policies proved of pyrrhic value, as much of Israeli society became persuaded that security lay in giving up land, not seizing more of it.[85] The full destructive potential of the Israeli military apparatus was never unleashed, as brakes were applied by the international and Jewish censure of the break-their-bones reprisals. Israel's own actions had some effects in isolating itself politically and morally, an objective cited in the booklet. Yet one of the original eight goals was regrettably never reached: removal of "the irrational fear of 'Arab violence' [that] acts like a glue which cements Israeli society together."[86] In failing to neutralize Israeli dread and fright, which might have required cessation of all throwing of stones, not only did the unrest not produce political jujitsu in Israeli soldiers or society, much less conversion, it diminished the accomplishments of the uprising. Research offered by Edward Kaufman to a meeting of Palestinians and Israelis in Bethlehem, in 2005, shows that Israelis in large numbers continued to view the nonviolent action of the Palestinians as a ruse, a deception meant to lull them into complacency so that the Palestinians' "real" goal of violent retaliation could begin anew.[87]

The intifada represented a search for methods of fighting for entitlements that could balance the power between the militarily preeminent Israel and the disarmed, dispossessed Palestinians. The Palestinians in the territories chose action methods that fit a world in which norms of universal human rights and concern for democracy were becoming incorporated into statecraft and diplomacy, among them protections for autonomous social action. Their open conveyance of information could compete with Israel's public information systems, bringing Palestinian aspirations into harmony with an era in which information has become a potent tool for reform, empowerment, and even state formation.

Nation building for the Palestinians has had little in common with the Arab and third-world post-colonial settings that comprise the background to Yezid Sayigh's claim that the Palestinians' armed struggle was the unifying element in the construction of a state.[88] Monopolistic assumptions of armed struggle had left the Palestinians beholden to Arab state sponsorship and kept them divided, while the PLO imposed its self-serving coercive authority, ill preparing the Palestinians for the very independence they sought. The Palestinians' quest for a state arose not out of international distributions of power, nor from the aggrandizement of the PLO and its interactions within a system of states, but from a civil society that was able to produce an uprising of historical specificity.

The concept of a Palestinian state, in an age marked by the proliferation of nation-states, is no less a creature of its times than was the Jewish state. The late twentieth century was marked by the rebirth of nations rather than their demise.[89] Initiation of social and political change is increasingly coming from within civil societies.[90] The Zionist claim to Palestine was advanced during an era in which the British empire ruled a quarter of the earth's landmass, and in which belief in the rectitude of European colonialism and conviction in the powers of the nation-state predominated. In the intervening decades, it became fashionable to argue that the Palestinians were responsible for their own fate by virtue of their failure to accept defeat and their predilection for missing opportunities.[91] Yet Israeli historian Yehoshua Porath disputes this point of view:

> It is too easy to simply accuse [the Palestinians] of making continuous blunders. In truth, we are talking about a tragedy. They acted all the time out of a deep sense of justice, not out of [realism]. They couldn't agree to the various compromises offered [in the 1920s to the 1940s] because they couldn't understand them, they didn't conform to their sense of justice. In 1947, . . . how could they have agreed to the UN partition resolution, which allotted the Jews, who were 30 per cent of Palestine's population, 60 per cent of the country? One cannot today expect them to

have understood. . . . The Palestinians' "mistakes" and unwillingness to compromise were inevitable. They couldn't avoid the "mistakes."[92]

Gene Sharp had, in 1989, suggested that realignment in the power relationship between Israel and the Palestinians was a necessity, a shift that he saw as dependent upon the building of institutions and nonviolent struggle.[93] His viewpoint is strikingly similar to Gramsci's contention that power must be dispersed throughout civil society and incorporated into organizational networks before wrenching control of state power. What tipped the balance of power between Israel and the Palestinians for those few years was the capacity of the intifada to compromise Israel's seemingly unassailable supremacy and make the military occupation untenable, to expose factually the real nature of Israel's occupation, to place the Israeli armed services at a disadvantage, to pierce the psychological indifference of segments of the public in Israel, and to arouse sympathies among discerning Israelis and a global community. Once started, the uprising shifted the balance of power away from the PLO in Tunis, weighting the scales in favor of those inside the territories—where leadership networks questioned monopolies of power and Truth based on armed struggle and where symbols and ideas rested on pluralistic popular dissent. Had the Israelis finally reached their limit, Sari Nusseibeh asked—what was left were "mass expulsions and mass murders, because they've tried everything else."[94] Concrete formation of a state for the Palestinians necessitated a limiting of Israeli coercion of the Palestinians.

"Something Revolutionary": The First Intifada through a Prism of Other Struggles

Concurrently with the intifada a number of nonviolent movements encircled the globe in the late 1980s, several in Eastern Europe. In the East German and the Czech and Slovak struggles, as in the case of Poland earlier in the decade, the essential goal was one of independence from the occupation accompanying the end of World War II. The Palestinian uprising sought independence from occupation, which, although dating to 1967, followed upon the losses sustained in 1948. In both their ends and their means, the Eastern European and Palestinian struggles have similarities.

The populations of Eastern Europe and those residing in the lands reserved for the Arabs after the partition of Palestine had been disarmed. The quiescence of the 1950s and 1960s in Central and Eastern Europe yielded to a period in which small epistemic communities of activist intellectuals—academicians, artists, clergy, playwrights, and poets—with their words and writings prepared the way for movements germinated from the circulation of ideas, much as in East Jerusalem. The central political concept in Eastern Europe in the 1970s and 1980s was civil society, a space independent of official life where political dissent could emerge.[95] Opposition pulsed with seminars at "flying" universities in private flats, irreverent cabarets and theatrical troupes, ecological groups, and trade unions, thus allowing Eastern Europeans to reimagine life without occupation and in which civil society was both a tactic and a "prefiguring of 'society-to-be.'"[96] In both the Eastern European and Palestinian settings, for some twenty years prior to noticeable coalescence in a popular uprising, the dissemination of ideas was taking place. During this phase, individuals led workshops, translated, and clandestinely published writings—and in both settings these included Mohandas K. Gandhi, Martin Luther King, Jr., and Gene Sharp—and set up networks of committees that covertly studied such materials years before a coherent movement became visible.[97] In the Czechs' and Slovaks' Velvet Revolution, the Pastors' Movement of East Germany, and the Palestinian intifada, there was little disjuncture between the intellectual elite and the broad sectors of their societies. These efforts offered clear political objectives, spurned fanaticism, and established limited dockets of objectives rather than universalistic delusions.[98] As Michael Walzer suggests, the new social movements of the East and West did not necessarily aim for the taking of power, "reflecting a new valuation of parts over wholes and a new willingness to settle for something less than total victory."[99]

Such movements can be dismissed if attributed to the end of the Brezhnev Doctrine and collapsing levels of support by the Soviet Union for Eastern Europe, or, in the case of the Palestinians, by allocating the phenomenon of the first intifada to the military ineptitude of the PLO, also within the Soviet sphere of influence. It would be equally facile to conclude that the Palestinian turn away from armed struggle represented nothing more than a belated recognition that Palestinians could expect no help from other Arab quarters. These factors may comprise part of the backdrop to the Palestinian uprising, but they do not explain it. In neither Eastern Europe nor the eastern Mediterranean was the sharing of power an option; any potent opposition was considered a threat. The communist regimes of Eastern Europe would not have considered sharing power with dissidents and human rights activists, and the State of Israel would not have contemplated sharing power with the Palestinians.

The first intifada has been classified as a failure, labeled a "mixed struggle," and deemed ineffective. "[I]t strains credulity to define the Palestinian struggle of the late 1980s strictly as a nonviolent conflict," according to Peter Ackerman and Christopher Kruegler.[100] Popular nonviolent movements are never pristine, and the throwing of stones and use of barricades appear in other such struggles. The 1986 movement in the Philippines—which in contrast offers an example of political jujitsu, as soldiers abandoned their army tanks and crossed to the side of the nonviolent challengers of the Ferdinand Marcos regime—employed obstructive barricades of tropical pine trees, lampposts, and drainage grills; it placed sandbags in the path of the army, and used "human sandbags."[101]

In Poland, on August 14, 1980, workers at the Lenin Shipyard in Gdansk went on strike. While the shipyard's former master electrician, Lech Walesa, urged strict adherence to Gandhian injunctions for maintaining contact with the adversary, in this case the communist party, many within Solidarity acted as if it had already disappeared. Chaos followed the initial success of the strike, as some laborers extracted revenge for their own suffering and lost comrades. Z. A. Pelczynski cites former Solidarity activists who considered the upheaval "incoherent," a kind of social avalanche that could not be meaningfully controlled or guided."[102] Workers chronically went on strike without a rational strategy. Walesa, recipient of the 1983 Nobel Peace Prize, was called "the Fireman," for his racing across Poland to put out "blazes."[103]

Rigoberta Menchú Tum, winner of the 1992 Nobel Peace Prize, writes of stones thrown by Mayan villagers in their struggle against the U.S.-backed army in her native Guatemala:

> We knew how to throw stones, we knew how to throw salt in someone's face. . . . You can blind a policeman by throwing lime in his face. And with stones for instance, you have to throw it at the enemy's head, at his face. If you throw it at his back, it will be effective but not as much as at other parts of his body.[104]

Menchú justifies Guatemalan barricades to impede armies, similar to the burning tires used by Palestinians, because the violence originated with the army, exculpating the Maya for using whatever they could to deter the soldiers from further massacres and razing of villages.[105]

In the Burmese prodemocracy movement, elevated to attention by Aung San Suu Kyi's receipt of the 1991 Nobel Peace Prize, violence against security police has often occurred in provincial areas, including stones, poison darts, and beheadings.[106]

Complexities of an essentially nonviolent movement coping with violent tendencies are nowhere better illuminated than by comparing South Africa and the first intifada. Sari Nusseibeh had advocated citizenship in a Palestinian state as a substitute for lost land, what he called the South African model, since the indigenous peoples of South Africa had lost their familial lands to colonists, been dispersed, and were living in "townships" and Bantustans akin to refugee camps. He said the Palestinians should do as the South Africans had done and fight not to return to their ancestral holdings, but to assert their civil and political rights within the institutions and economies of the country. The period from the founding of the African National Congress (ANC) in 1912 to South Africa's 1994 elections represents a time span analogous to that between the Balfour Declaration of 1917 and the Oslo accords in 1993. Options for nonviolently contesting apartheid collapsed in the late 1950s, after the 1960 Sharpeville massacre, when the antiapartheid movement was banned and driven underground that same year. The ANC turned to armed struggle, as its armed wing, Umkhonto we Sizwe (MK), was launched in 1961. In 1985, ANC exiles in Lusaka called for the townships to be made "ungovernable." The "lost generation" of South Africa's youths—whose chaos made the townships impervious to the reach of the Nationalist government—was not unlike the Palestinian "intifada generation." Nelson Mandela was among those who propounded a shift away from half a century of strict adherence to nonviolent strategies, in 1961: "I and some of my colleagues came to the conclusion that as violence in this country was inevitable, it would be wrong and unrealistic for African leaders to continue preaching peace and non-violence at a time when the government met our demands with force. . . . For a long time the people had been talking of violence . . . we, the leaders of the ANC, had nevertheless always prevailed upon them to avoid violence and pursue peaceful methods."[107] The ANC and other antiapartheid groups abandoned their earlier insistence on nonviolent methods decades prior to negotiating a settlement.

In South Africa and the Palestinian areas, a separate armed wing existed (MK and the PLO), neither of which posed a threat to either the South African or Israeli governments, but both of which had symbolic standing with the populace. In both situations, Kurt Schock explains, the mass mobilizations of the 1980s in both areas had emerged with relative independence from the internationally active ANC and PLO, respectively, and in neither case from an armed vanguard as projected by the ideologists of armed struggle. Rather, local leaders shaped by the daily repression of the townships, or the severities of military occupation, led both movements. Much as the Palestinian activist intellectuals sought to channel the energies of militant students, faculty, and youth into actions with potential political efficacy, in South Africa the United Democratic Front (UDF) launched itself for similar purposes in 1983, the year that Mubarak Awad started his workshops. The UDF initially coordinated 565 organizations, including religious organizations, professional associations, student organizations, trade unions, women's groups, and youth groups; at its peak seven hundred affiliates were under its umbrella.[108] The decentralized structures of the UDF were intentionally difficult for the state to repress, as the front reined in the energy of enraged youths and funneled their activities into collective nonviolent action. The UDF's nonviolent resistance was meant to build autonomous institutions. Activist and historian Janet Cherry recalled, "Inside South Africa, the vast majority of leaders and members supported the ANC and its armed struggle—or its moral right to take up arms in a 'just war'—however, we understood that we could be much more effective in mobilising people against the state through mass action, and that use of violence would undermine our organisations and render them vulnerable."[109] Campaigns of noncooperation, including rent and consumer boycotts, proved so effective that a partial state of emergency was imposed in 1985. Despite UDF efforts to channel the fury and wrath of alienated youths into realistic nonviolent methods, it was often the case that they threw bricks, stones, and Molotov cocktails at police and military personnel. Beset by collaborators, as were the Palestinians, hundreds of lives were lost during the mid-1980s to the "necklacing" of alleged traitors with burning rubber tires.

A South Africa–wide state of emergency was imposed in 1986 that limited the use of publicly assertive methods of protest and persuasion (vigils, marches, or parades). Mass demonstrations disappeared, although funerals provided occasions for processional mourning in the thousands. Meanwhile, the UDF-affiliated networks of neighborhood organizations continued to employ the less visible methods of noncooperation and nonviolent intervention (consumer and rent boycotts, and tax resistance) through an infrastructure of street committees led by unknown local persons, as in the Palestinian popular committees. Noncooperation became commonplace and sophisticated, but was hard to make illegal. By 1989, an opening occurred that allowed the Mass Democratic Movement to take over from the UDF and organize a Defiance Campaign of once again visible mass marches. That same year, a campaign of coordinated hunger strikes was instituted to press for release of political prisoners, yet its scale never reached the order of magnitude of the coordinated and disciplined fasting of fifteen thousand in the Palestinian prisoners' movement. With no military bases inside the country, MK was never a menace to the state, and the same was true of the PLO. In 1990, the ANC was unbanned and armed struggle was suspended. Despite this turn of events, levels of street violence escalated in the 1990-94 period, even while negotiations were underway.

For three years prior to the 1994 South African elections, however, the ANC sponsored broad consultations to develop a reconstruction and development plan (RDP). In contrast to the failure of the PLO to prepare for self-governance or give decent support to those trying to do so within the territories, preparation of the RDP built on an extended process, as Walter Sisulu recalled: "In the political schools we ran on Robben Island and in other prisons, long sessions were held to analyze every issue. . . . As we developed intellectually, we were able to see problems in a way that we might otherwise not have seen. . . . While Nelson Mandela dealt with the negotiations, we were able to deal with the future. . . . Both sides became convinced that there was no alternative to negotiations. . . . Violence would only have made our economy worse. . . . Basically, it was our *analysis* that took precedence."[110]

"The ANC recognized that the noncooperation of the people was critical," Stephen Zunes contends, and "the ungovernability of the country by the apartheid regime, and not its physical overthrow, . . . would end apartheid."[111] The practical results of the two struggles, South African and Palestinian, were, however, poles apart. The critical difference, Kurt Schock concludes, was

> the anti-apartheid movement exploited the South African state's dependence relations to exert leverage against the regime, whereas the Intifada . . . . failed to mobilize the support of crucial third parties, such as the Israeli citizens or the U.S. government. . . . [I]t was the ability of the anti-apartheid struggle to exploit the state's dependence relations and mobilize the support of third parties—largely through methods of nonviolent action rather than through violence—that promoted a political transition.[112]

This brief review is not to exhibit approval for any instances of digression from nonviolent discipline, because any deviation and mixing of violence instrumentally limits the potential for what can be accomplished, but to say that judgments against the first intifada for its lack of scrupulosity and inability to hold unanimity after 1990 should also note that nonviolent mobilizations without any acts of violence are historically rare, although, with greater than ever knowledge, increasing. Expediency was involved in the decision to choose nonviolent struggle in each of these struggles, not idealism. Principled nonviolence versus pragmatism, two polarities of thinking in the U.S. civil rights encounter, were not cause for debate in the movements of the 1980s, apart from the Philippines. Against opposition such as Israel's, Daoud Kuttab insists, "nonviolence is more effective than force," as "it tore off all the Israeli arguments. Use of nonviolent struggle for the Palestinians was not ideological—it was a necessity—and there was no alternative."[113] Nusseibeh concurred:

> [Nonviolent struggle] was the next best thing for someone who hesitated at military acts. . . . It was not so much that people preferred nonviolence to violence that made them take up nonviolence, as much as the fact that they couldn't do anything else. When they were convinced, finally, that there was something they could do failing violence, they went ahead and did it.[114]

An argument here that the proponents of nonviolent struggle were substantially able to define the parameters of the intifada for more than two years and into a third is not disqualified by the presence of episodic violence or the eventual collapse of the uprising by 1992 due to violent factions.[115] The erroneous view that nonviolent resistance is the absolute opposite of violence or an exact substitute for it overlooks the fact that both violent and nonviolent struggle are means of contention. The simple dualism of violence as the opposite of nonviolent resistance is a gross distortion of reality, Gene Sharp contends, because responses to conflict more properly fall into categories of action or inaction. Nonviolent action is one type of active response, which, by definition, cannot take place without replacing submissiveness with struggle.[116] Disruption or constriction of the sources of power of the target group, rather than violence, is most likely to create success.

In point of fact, the success of a nonviolent struggle often hinges on the ability to continue functioning and remain flexible despite setbacks and repression, and the capacity to increase its power relative to the target group, either by interrupting its sources of power or by activating third-party sanctions that can exert leverage against the opponent. Efficacy with nonviolent sanctions is often contingent on maintaining discipline *despite* repressive countermeasures; reprisals can indicate that a nonviolent movement is posing a serious challenge to the existing power relationships implicated in the fundamental grievances. Designed "to prevail in an intensely conflictual exchange," nonviolent struggle can elicit concessions and force the side being challenged to do the work of bringing about change. Effectively implemented, the responsibility for what occurs shifts to the adversary. In other words, it falls to the target group to decide whether to give in to the demands of the nonviolent protagonists, whose "irrevocable commitment" includes a foregone binding dedication to accept penalties, consequences, and reprisals.[117] Nonviolent resistance is nothing if not contentious.

What the Palestinian people wanted, Riad al-Malki emphasized, "was not so much nonviolence as something revolutionary."[118] In the Palestinian context of a policy of armed struggle established by exiles in 1968, commando actions could no longer be deemed "revolutionary" by the late 1980s. Václav Havel alludes to this paradox when writing that dissident movements of the Soviet bloc "do not shy away from the idea of violent political overthrow because the idea seems too radical, but on the contrary, because it does not seem radical enough."[119] The intifada, had it secured uncompromising nonviolent discipline, might have changed the face of the Middle East. One must acknowledge, however, that it would have been difficult to have a mass movement of such consistency.[120]

Epilogue

THE SKILL AND SHREWDNESS of nonviolent challengers is not necessarily the biggest determinant of the outcome of civil resistance. At both ends of the twentieth century, great powers were the underwriters of the structures within which the Palestinians struggled to authenticate their heritage. The failure of the Palestinians to earn independence under British colonialism in the 1920s and 1930s is not due to a lack of Palestinian resilience. Similarly, the willingness and capability of Israel to interrupt the protagonists of the intifada and administer violence was probably the major determinant of the road taken by the uprising. In 1989, Joel Greenberg predicted, "any move to end the uprising . . . must provide the intifada leadership with a means to translate their struggle into political gains." He recommended free, nonviolent political expression and organization, and political meetings for the Palestinians with Israelis to enable the uprising's political course. "With a reduction in political repression, the need for violent confrontation would decline. Palestinians would be able to pursue their struggle through more normal, nonviolent means, and devote their energies to political initiatives."[1] Greenberg's proposal fell on deaf ears.

By responding positively to the restraint and discipline manifested in the uprising, and by seizing benefits from the alterations that it represented for accession to peace and security, for decades professed as Israel's goal, Israel could have neutralized the regression to bankrupt ideologies of armed struggle, and in so doing lessen the allure of the Palestinian commando units and Qassamite cells of Islamic resistance. By 1988 and with policy implications for Israel, the vocabulary of armed struggle had all but disappeared from the leaflets of the intifada. The vigorous debate on civil disobedience disclosed the fact that Israel was facing a nonviolent, political, and information-based struggle, against which military suppression would not work.

Instead of profiting from this dramatic development, Israel gave preference to perpetuating the status quo, characterized by harsh suppression of the uprising and its protection and favored status then accorded to the Qassamite groups. Official Israel's refusal to recognize the intifada as an effort to lift the occupation through nonviolent action, not an attempt to defeat Israel with armed struggle, had the effect of weakening the very Palestinians who were working to substitute nonviolent means of contention for organized violence on a permanent basis.

The creators and exhorters of the new political lexicon, who had been rewriting the orthodoxies of *thawra* during the 1970s and 1980s—Radwan Abu Ayyash, Ziad Abu Zayyad, Feisel Husseini, Muhammad Jadallah, Zahira Kamal, Ghassan Khatib, and Sari Nusseibeh—were locked up, despite Israel's longstanding claim that it lacked suitable negotiating partners. An unfettered intifada would have been the most potent countervailing force to the PLO, a known Israeli objective. Yet Israel compromised those who were pressing for dissociation from the PLO and expelled Mubarak Awad—among the keenest advocates for nonviolent struggle not dependent of the PLO. Old assumptions rebounded as Israeli authorities jailed the representatives on the Command one by one so that none remained whose thinking had been honed by the Committee Confronting the Iron Fist, the Arab Studies Society, the writings of the activist intellectuals, or the Palestinian Center for the Study of Nonviolence. Impaired by "interference" from Tunis, and vitiated by the lack of PLO support, the Palestinians in the occupied territories were unable to sustain their increased power in the equation with Israel, which was necessary for compromise and negotiations. Meanwhile, forces on the Israeli landscape marginalized the efforts of diverse and numerous Israeli groups that wanted accommodation with the Palestinians.

Even so, Zeev Schiff called the first intifada "a deluxe uprising," referring to its gains in international public opinion.[2] Over a span of seven decades the only alterations in the pattern of alienation of the Palestinians from their land resulted from the first intifada. "Forty years of violence have got us nowhere," Hanan Mikhail Ashrawi stated in Madrid in 1991.[3] The uprising, Chris Hedges notes, "finally drove the Israelis to negotiate a peace accord."[4] In this sense it had succeeded as had nothing else. It was also territorial, that is, about land, and without understanding its lessons and securing a durable settlement based on justice Nusseibeh predicted, the conflict could become one of race and religion and, therefore, much worse.[5]

The first Israeli military forces to leave the territories occupied in 1967 departed from Jenin, in the northernmost portion of the West Bank, on November 13, 1995. They left the day after the assassination of Prime Minister Yitzhak Rabin and one week ahead of schedule in the opening wave of planned withdrawals called for by the 1993 Oslo I accords.[6] A year earlier, in May 1994, an infant self-government, the Palestinian Authority (PA), had been installed in Gaza and nominally in Jericho, also under the provisions of the accords. Palestinians living in the West Bank and Gaza were soon able to apply for passports and car license plates. When Israel continued to reject as insufficient the 1996 verbal nullification of the offending articles of the 1964 charter, on December 14, 1998, U.S. president Bill Clinton traveled to Gaza to witness the PNC vote with a show of hands to amend the Palestinian National Charter. Israel accepted this action, which implied further impetus for statehood.

Despite a series of bloody attacks by Hamas and Islamic Jihad meant to subvert the process, Israel and the PLO signed the Interim Palestinian-Israel Agreement regarding the West Bank and Gaza Strip, or Oslo II, on September 28, 1995, again, as with Oslo I, with fanfare at the White House. Heads of state Hosni Mubarak of Egypt and King Hussein of Jordan were present that day to mark the completion of the first stage in the agenda for negotiations between Israel and the PLO. In some three hundred pages, it provided for elections of a Palestinian council, transfer of legislative authority to it, withdrawal of Israeli forces from Palestinian population centers, and division of the West Bank into three areas: Area A consisting of Palestinian towns and urban centers to be under Palestinian control, area B made up of Palestinian villages and less dense populations, and area C under Israeli jurisdiction. The Knesset barely approved the Oslo II agreement. The chief material result of the intifada, the declaration of principles of the Oslo accords provided a process for concluding Israeli rule over more than two million Palestinians, and it recognized the political rights of the Palestinians for the first time since Balfour penned that he did not propose to consult the inhabitants of Palestine.

After Madrid, most Palestinians assumed that the passage of time would bring statehood, secured through negotiations. "Nothing of the kind was happening," Rashid Khalidi counters; "Israel was allowed by the United States, in spite of solemn pledges to the Palestinians by the first Bush administration, to help itself to huge bites of the pie that the two sides were supposed to be negotiating."[7] Frequent boundary closures led to declining standards of living in the West Bank and Gaza and rising poverty. Both Israel and the PA savaged human rights and entitlements in the name of security. In the Gaza Strip, where five thousand Israeli settlers lived, Israel controlled one-third of the land and much of the water resources needed by a million Palestinians in an area that demographers consider among the most densely populated on earth. In the West Bank, Israel retained control over water and three-quarters of the land. The building of settlements continued unabated.

"The accord was based on the assumption that the enmity between the two warring tribes would subside during the transition period," Avi Shlaim laments; "On the contrary, the extremists on both sides did everything in their power to undermine the agreement."[8] Shimon Peres formed a government following Yitzkah Rabin's assassination, but was defeated by Benjamin Netanyahu in 1996 elections, in large part in reaction to Hamas suicide bombs in major Israeli cities.[9] The temper of the territories hardened, as a series of upheavals, errors, and setbacks transpired. The sun did not rise on the new dawn about which Daoud Kuttab had mused. The timetable for the accords passed without implementation. Virtually no one heralded its accomplishments. "The entire Oslo process began to unravel under the heavy-handed pressure applied by the Likud government," Shlaim rues, and the balance of power tilted in favor of Israel, determining how the principles would be translated into actuality.[10]

A force of thirty thousand Palestinian police entered the Gaza Strip from Egypt in May 1994, to assume the reins of security as the Israelis departed. The return of approximately 100,000 Palestinian exiles from their foreign base in Tunis brought tension and predicaments, as the locally grown leadership that had led the intifada found themselves deliberately pushed to the side. The concepts, symbols, and methods that had evolved in the occupied territories clashed with the values of the returning exiles. The popular sovereignty of the civil society organizations that had tilled a culture of democratic decision making and elections was shaken by a "multipronged strategy of silencing, co-opting, or marginalizing" their work.[11] The Palestinians who reappeared, some after years in military training camps, had lived under one-party systems of their host governments and were trained in hierarchical command structures. They had typically been penalized for taking initiative. Steeped in retaliatory thinking, they had not participated in the building of Gramsci's "hegemonic consent" for nonviolent change, nor had they been part of the quest for self-sufficient resistance in two decades of civilian nonmilitary movements. After establishment of the PA, myriad Palestinian institutions that had been developing since 1969 began to compete against it—or with each other, particularly after the PA let it be known that it viewed with disfavor these free-standing community organizations.[12] The main political exploit of the returning exiles became that of neutralizing the potency of such groups, even while lauding their accomplishments, because they stood as the sole force capable of jeopardizing the consolidation of power by the new regime. The PA structure absorbed some of their members, usually at mid to lower levels, but in general attacked Palestinian NGOs, the institutional manifestation of the intifada.

Not all groups that had burgeoned in opposition to or in compensation for the occupation were outriders for political liberalization and democratization. Some were marred by what Sara Roy calls "political factionalism, tribalism, classism, and parochialism."[13] To Roy's list could be added patriarchalism.

As the PA dismantled autonomous societies and institutions large and small, it also censored self-regulating news outlets and threw a labyrinthine net of nine different security and police agencies over the populace. This dragnet went to the core of the deal struck by the Oslo process: the PLO could return to the territories, but for purposes of taking over the "security" apparatus. Arafat was to control any inchoate violence; if he could not, or would not, it would be he who had invalidated the accords.

The Palestinian exiles returning from Tunis could not fathom what produced the intifada or its provenance in the 1970s and 1980s. They had not participated in the formation of civilian networks and were not conversant with the discourses of the activist intellectuals and their Israeli counterparts. They had not read the *samizdat* of Awad, attended workshops, heard Sharp's lectures, followed the dialectics of Husseini and Nusseibeh, grappled with the concept of disengagement, nor seen the historically proved action methods of nonviolent struggle applied by Palestinians. They were unexposed to the idea of assuming responsibility and the experience of self-governing popular committees once the intifada was under way, and had not shared in the popularly generated sense of confidence. They had not debated the connection between the ends and means. Nor had they pitched their views on civil disobedience. With their return, the use of threatening language—assiduously rejected inside the territories, in part to reassure Israelis of the Palestinians' readiness for self-governance—also came back, as well as menacing behavior that had in the territories been repudiated along with ideologies of armed struggle.[14]

By July 2000, with the Oslo process run aground, President Clinton hurriedly invited Israeli prime minister Ehud Barak and Yasir Arafat to Camp David in Maryland. Experienced leaders from the occupied territories such as Dr. Abd al-Shafi, Feisel Husseini,[15] or Hanan Mikhail Ashrawi were rejected in favor of PLO officials who had negotiated the Oslo accords, in what Rashid Khalidi calls "the steady decline in the competence of its leadership."[16] Barak offered a nonnegotiable package and immediately dubbed it an extraordinarily generous offer. "Given the choice of taking it or leaving it, Arafat left it," historian James L. Gelvin concludes, "Palestinian negotiators noted that Israel had not lived up to its previous commitments to redeploy its forces or halt settlement growth. Now Palestinians were asked to set aside what they had already negotiated and accept Israeli assurances of good faith. And Barak's refusal to put his offer on paper (lest it give ammunition to his opponents at home) certainly did little to reassure Palestinians. Rightly or wrongly, Palestinians smelled a rat."[17]

The second intifada began on September 28, 2000, when the leader of the Israeli opposition Ariel Sharon unilaterally took more than one thousand security guards and border police onto a site in the Old City of Jerusalem called by Jews the Temple Mount and by Muslims Haram al-Sharif (august sanctuary). As noted, the Temple Mount is sacred to Jews, the vestige of their national grandeur, while Muslims regard the Haram al-Sharif as hallowed ground, because of the al-Aqsa Mosque, built where tradition holds the Prophet's winged horse Buraq carried Muhammad as he ascended into the heavens. A U.S. government study, the Mitchell Report, judges that Sharon's provocative action was undertaken solely to improve his political standing with the Israeli electorate. Sharon would have known about the "Buraq Revolt" that led to the uprisings of 1929. Regardless, the day after Sharon's visit, Palestinians held a nonviolent demonstration. Israeli police reacted by using live ammunition, killing four young protesters. In response, across the territories, turmoil flared. An Israeli journalist reported that the army used more than one million pieces of ammunition against the unarmed demonstrators during the first few days.[18] The early weeks of the second intifada, also called al-Aqsa intifada, were essentially another popular nonviolent upsurge. "We cannot emphasize the fact enough," Israeli peace activist Michel Warschawski stresses, "Palestinian soldiers joined in the confrontations with the Israeli army only after Israeli soldiers armed to the teeth, often with rifles with telescopic sights, had killed several dozen young demonstrators."[19]

Under the terms of the Oslo accords, the Palestinian police were now under arms and in possession of limited weapons for security purposes. Their presence offered justification for Israeli displays of military force, even though the official Palestinian security forces were implicated in clashes in very few cases.

Observers and commentators who for so long had denounced the first intifada as violent and scorned its nonviolent actions as deception and trickery could now claim to behold anarchic disorder. The police and security organs led by the returning exiles played almost no role in the early weeks of the second intifada, neither partaking in it nor trying to end it, as enraged youths hurled rocks at Israeli soldiers. A decade after the fruitful phases of the first intifada, the young had been watching year by year in dismay, as Israeli settlements condemned by the international community grew in number and size following the signing of the Oslo accords. By early 2000 in an "innovation of the Oslo era," Israel built 250 miles of restricted access Israeli-only multilane bypass roads on confiscated land to connect to the settlements, further isolating Palestinian communities and market towns.[20] The encircled Palestinian communities became, effectively, imprisoned in small cantons, subject to Israeli closures, and economically affected by impeded admittance to Israel proper and Arab East Jerusalem. With no territory fully under the absolute control and jurisdiction of the PA, even the 17 percent of the West Bank that it nominally controlled, the new bypass roads from which Palestinians are barred resulted in "seizure of yet more Palestinian land."[21] Although settlements were to be among the final status issues under the Oslo accords, the Rabin government inaugurated a massive expansion of settlements, using economic incentives to lure settlers to relocate. The number of Israeli settlers residing in the West Bank (nearly 200,000 in 2000) and Gaza Strip rose by 70 percent between 1994 and 2000, as both Labor and Likud governments alike continued to implant settlements.[22]

Some of the young had been active in the first intifada, but were unable to see tangible changes in return for the rigors of nonviolent discipline in the first instance and the penalties extracted by their noncooperation in the second. They were now vulnerable to reverberating retaliatory arguments from those who had never fully disaffirmed armed struggle and the emboldened claims of the Islamic revivalists. Others became newly engaged in the Fateh *tanzim* (organization), a vaguely-named militia with political justifications that included street cadres and portions of the preventive security forces, and which undertook most of the armed actions that had begun. With the *tanzim,* for the first time, Israeli settlements came under attack, having dramatically increased in size and number, now abutting Palestinian urban settings, their proximity kindling clashes with the armed settlers. Any contact with the settlements had been scrupulously avoided during the 1987 uprising. "The Palestinians' use of firearms, especially against settlers and settlements near populated Palestinian communities," Daoud Kuttab contends, is a key difference between the two uprisings; moreover, "not since the 1967 war has Israel used such heavy weapons against Palestinians."[23] Another dissimilarity was a rupture between Israeli Arabs who had lived since 1948 within Israel, and Israeli Jews, the result of Palestinian protests within Israel, such that the Israeli Arabs became accused of being a fifth column. The first intifada had assiduously limited itself to the territories occupied in 1967.

Fateh's secretary-general in the West Bank, Marwan Bargouti, led the *tanzim* in the second, al-Aqsa intifada. Bargouti had learned Hebrew during four years in prison as a teenager. After his expulsion during the first intifada, he was allowed to return to the West Bank from exile in September 1994 and was elected as a parliamentarian in 1996. As the number of Palestinian deaths rose after Sharon's Temple Mount provocation, Barghouti directed the *tanzim* to attack Israeli soldiers and settlers who were inside the West Bank and Gaza.[24]

A new wave of suicide bombings in Israel began three months after Sharon's incendiary visit, by which time Warschawski underscores, several hundred Palestinians had died. In December 2000, Hamas undertook its first suicide attack specifically of the al-Aqsa intifada. In May of the following spring, a suicide bomber killed ten Israelis and wounded scores of others at a shopping mall. In August, a similar attack killed eighteen Israelis, six of them children, at a pizza parlor in Jerusalem. On September 5, five bombs detonated in Jerusalem. Due to "the limited vision and organization of other political groups and the relentless Israeli violence," Rema Hammami and Salim Tamari declare, "Hamas was able to become the central player by the end of 2001," and steered the second intifada toward its own goals, while putting the PA at risk.[25] Units from the PLO factions that did not want to be outdone in militancy by the Islamic revivalists soon joined the Qassamite suicide cells of Hamas and Islamic Jihad. Bent on ending the occupation, they unified with murderous intent. Although Palestinian intellectuals in large numbers spoke out against turning a national political struggle into a Muslim-Jewish conflagration, Arafat's standoffish demurral provided indirect support for the insurgence. In Glenn Robinson's judgment, "Arafat neither purposively unleashed the uprising (as Thomas Friedman and other [commentators] suggest) nor did he have great incentive to try to crush it. The al-Aqsa intifada is the predictable expression of anger by a people for whom negotiations to end a military occupation and restore legitimate rights failed. Had Arafat tried to crack down on the [second] intifada, it likely would have led to a Palestinian civil war."[26]

Sir Michael Howard, an historian who has studied terrorism since revolutionaries used it in czarist Russia in the 1870s, detects three principal objectives to terrorism: "One was self-advertisement, what was called 'Propaganda of the Deed,' to show the world that the group existed and was ruthless in its determination to achieve its ends. The second was to demoralise the government and its supporters. The third was to provoke the government into such savage acts of suppression that it forfeited public support and awoke popular and international sympathy for the revolutionary cause. This was known as a 'strategy of provocation.'"[27] Whether the strategy of Hamas and the second intifada was designed for purposes of provoking a reaction worse than the original grievance, this was the effect, as the Israeli government ordered extra-judicial assassinations of those they considered culpable, launched reprisals raids, bulldozed homes and orchards of families of presumed suicide bombers, imposed checkpoints next to every population center or refugee camp throughout the territories, and levied crushing economic blockades that have lasted for years. The suicide attacks in Israel, which came to characterize the Palestinians' second intifada, combined with the remote stance of U.S. president George W. Bush, allowed Ariel Sharon to mount reprisals more ruthless than in the past. In 2001, al Qaeda leader Osama bin Laden otherwise focused President Bush's attention with his organization's fearsome attacks on U.S. cities. Soon floundering in a war of choice in Iraq, the United States was, in Michael Howard's words, provoked into savage acts of suppression that forfeited public support. It was obligatory for the U.S. administration to respond, but it chose to do so without addressing the chronic historical failure to tackle the issues of Palestinian refugees and the military occupation of Palestinians lands, often the crux of the justifications of al Qaeda and similar or linked terror organizations stretching from the Atlantic to South East Asia.

Between September 11, 2001, and March of the following year, Sharon pursued his war of attrition on the PA, despite a few inconsequential interventions from the United States, and notwithstanding a month-long cease-fire by the Palestinians. A renewed round of Israeli invasions brought closures, curfews, and economic blockades, and also led to a sharp rise in emigration by those who were able, often the Christians. "Sharon consistently provoked the increasingly vengeance-driven Palestinian resistance to provide him with a pretext to exit unwanted cease-fires and overcome diplomatic moves to protect Arafat and keep the [PA] alive."[28] B'Tselem reported in 2002 that since 1967 Israel had taken control of 42 percent of the West Bank territory for the use of settlements and their future growth.[29]

In March 2002, Saudi crown prince Abdullah offered a peace plan, based on the Arab world offering full recognition of Israel in return for a full withdrawal from the occupied lands, back to the 1967 borders. The offer was well received in European, UN, and U.S. quarters, and adopted as UN Security Council Resolution 1397. The concept gained enthusiasm from the United States because the administration was considering a military strike on Iraq and would need Saudi support for any such assault, and the Arab League adopted the plan at its subsequent summit meeting in Beirut. On March 27, however, at a Passover meal in Netanya, Hamas carried out a revenge attack, killing thirty Jews. This assault lent justification for the Israeli forces to mount Operation Defensive Shield. The next day began the military reoccupation of all major West Bank towns in areas A, B, and C, but for Hebron and Jericho and some villages.[30] Up until that point, Israeli damage to PA institutions had been targeted at security installations and emblems of future self-governance, such as the Gaza airport and deep-water seaport. Now Ramallah, Nablus, and Jenin experienced systematic destruction caused by the blowing up of homes and bulldozing of whole city blocks, including the sacking of the PA's modest civilian infrastructure and ransacking of governmental ministries. Scores of Palestinian deaths occurred in Nablus and Jenin, where the refugee camp was destroyed, a place from which a number of the suicide bombers had emerged in close proximity to Israeli cities. On April 4, the United States, having procrastinated in its response, asked that Israel withdraw. In the third week of April, Israeli tanks departed the cities they had reoccupied, but for Arafat's compound in Ramallah and the Church of the Nativity in Bethlehem, where *tanzim* and Bethlehem citizens had taken refuge, near the cave within the church that marks the site of Christ's birth. "The siege of Arafat was a symbol of Sharon's power to impose house arrest in full view of the international community," Hammami and Tamari conclude.[31]

The fabric of Palestinian society was rent by the retaliation, while Israelis descended into fear, thereby encouraging more extreme political profiles. In the winter of 2002/2003, the United States after two years of calculated distance proposed a road map—a step-by-step strategy nominally underwritten by the United States, United Nations, European Union, and Russia. It laid out a series of steps progressing to the establishment of an independent Palestinian state in the territories by 2005, without specifying borders, in return for a Palestinian promise to cease the attacks on Israel. The road map was nonspecific, offered little that would alter the reality on the ground, and suffered from the inadequacies of previous efforts to resolve the conflict.[32] Never a priority for the Bush administration, it sidelined the road map with its growing preoccupation with a "war on terrorism."

Unofficial endeavors sought to fill the breach. The People's Voice Initiative was undertaken by Sari Nusseibeh and retired Israeli Admiral and former Shin Bet (internal security) chief Ami Ayalon in March 2002, just before the Israeli incursions. Pessimistic about governmental ability to move forward, they sought approval directly from the two populations, and had reported 94,000 Israeli and 70,000 Palestinian signatures by November 2003.[33] With Swiss backing, the Geneva Accord was spearheaded by Israeli Yossi Beilin, and Palestinian Yasir Abd Rabbo, a champion of coexistence within the PLO, its announcement bolstered by support from former U.S. president Jimmy Carter.

In April 2002, the Israeli government announced the construction of a "separation barrier," a twenty-five-foot high concrete wall, to prevent infiltration by suicide bombers into Israel that is in some places twice the height of the Berlin Wall, and is elsewhere barbed wire or trenches. Armed sniper towers rise every 300 meters in some sections. B'Tselem reports,

> Officially, the purpose of the barrier is to prevent attacks, by means of a physical separation between the West Bank and Israel. However, only some twenty percent of the barrier's route will run along the border between them, the Green Line. As a result, more than 530,000 dunums [approximately 132,500 acres], which represents 9.5 percent of the West Bank (including East Jerusalem), will ultimately be situated between the barrier and the Green Line. This area contains twenty-one Palestinian villages, which are home to more than 30,000 residents, and some 200,000 Palestinians who hold Israeli identity cards and live in East Jerusalem. After the

barrier is constructed, all of these people will be separated from the West Bank. In addition, as a result of its winding route, the barrier will surround on at least three sides fifty more Palestinian villages, in which 244,000 persons live, that lie on the 'Palestinian' side of the barrier.[34]

The impact of the separation wall is to confiscate Palestinian land, isolate Palestinian communities one from another, and weaken their viability; "in places, the barrier dips several miles into the West Bank, leaving settlements, fertile Palestinian land, and valuable water resources on the Israeli side."[35] B'Tselem insists the route of the barrier "defies all security logic and appears politically motivated."[36] On 30 June 2004, Israel's supreme court ordered changes to the West Bank wall, saying its route was causing harm to the local Palestinian population. Scantily reported outside Israel, the court ruled "the route disrupts the delicate balance between the obligation of the military commander to preserve security and his obligation to provide for the needs of the local inhabitants." Such impairment must be minimized, the court held, even if it results in less security for Israel.[37] On July 9, the International Court of Justice in The Hague urged the United Nations to enforce the court's ruling that Israel should tear down its 450-mile separation barrier and compensate the Palestinians for the hardship it had caused.[38]

• • • •

An infernal situation, with the great powers past and present mute, raises the question whether the Palestinian uprising in the period from 1987 to 1990 has been scrutinized for naught? Was it eccentric? Did it fulfill whatever potential it possessed in unusual circumstances? Was the first intifada the result of a peculiar historical condition in which the PLO was in absentia in Tunis? What is the meaning of the intifada for the future of the Israelis and Palestinians, and the region? What are the lessons for those suffering under domination in other climes?

Retrospectively, the first intifada represented a missed historical opportunity for consolidating serious nonviolent social transformation of the relationships for both peoples. The Likud and Labor parties alike bear responsibility for ignoring the opportunities presented by the intifada to hasten an end to violent struggle by Palestinians, including solidifying the common ground that had been achieved in 1990 with the Islamic revivalists.

Yet this tale holds clues for a shared future. In writing of the 2005 Israeli withdrawal from the Gaza Strip, in which 21 settlements and approximately 8,500 settlers were evacuated, Tel Aviv University professor Tanya Reinhart asserts, "There is no doubt that Sharon openly used the Gaza disengagement plan to expand and strengthen Israel's grip of the West Bank."[39] Even so, it is also true that Israeli clinical psychologists Nahi Alon and Haim Omer had worked for one year with military and police in preparation for the Gaza withdrawal, in order to minimize outbreaks of settler violence, explicitly based on detailed study of nonviolent resistance and Sharp's writings. Alon and Omer are attempting to form a coalition of nonviolent activists to offer "alternatives to current normative attitudes" in Israel, and to bring insights from their investigations into the larger discourse on security in Israel, while teaching courses in what they term *constructive fighting*.[40]

Far broader than was visible at the time were the consequences of the Palestinians' secession from the cycle of violence. The moment was not unique in the sense that the Palestinians had historically employed nonviolent struggle as their dominant technique in the 1920s and 1930s for pleading their case before the British and asking them to honor their promises to the Arabs as they had to world Jewry. Yet what it represented within Palestinian polity half a century later was as singular and significant as what it offered to Israel: the repudiation of armed struggle as the means to a limited end, based on compromise.

A lost opportunity implies that other junctures could open and that enough of the improvised structures of civil society remain to offer reasonable hope for the future. Although apparently not considered newsworthy for media reports, the Palestinians are currently engaged in a robust, extensive strategic debate on the substance of the first intifada and its relevance.

Honeycombed across the West Bank are small nonviolent movements that are attempting to minimize the destructiveness of the separation barrier to their communities. Since February 2005, the villagers of Bilin have led a nonviolent struggle against the wall, demonstrating each Friday in the company of Israeli peace activists and international volunteers, in front of Israeli bulldozers and soldiers. Other villages—including Jayyus, Biddu, Deir Ballut, and Budrus—have for more than four years, all but unknown to the outside world, been organizing collective nonviolent action against the barrier, coordinated by local popular committees. Some entitle this "the intifada of the wall." Their successes have been modest but noteworthy, as they have altered the route or slowed the progression of the wall that takes still more land and encircles them in enclaves—although they could not halt it outright.[41]

Any effort to forge a lasting compromise over land between the Israelis and the Palestinians depends on the evolution of new political thinking on both sides. The philosophies manifested by the first intifada engaged all sectors of Palestinian society, which had come together in newfound readiness to accept two states side by side, to be achieved by a unification of means and ends. Exploring this pivotal moment reveals how nonviolent action can improve the chances for reaching negotiations, have a potentially transformative effect on acute conflicts, and lay the groundwork for eventual coexistence. Feisel Husseini's assertion that forgetting is as important as remembering—introduced by him as a dynamic for dealing with the trauma of the Palestinians' sequential losses—hints at eventual imagined reconciliation. Were he alive today, he might also say that memory is important so as not to forget that the accomplishments of the 1987 uprising overlap with its most nonviolent phase.

Ideas were developed on fighting for what was left of one's way of life without debilitating violence. Concepts spread. The new thinking could not be confined or appropriated, as accepted wisdom changed. Despite the common perception of the Palestinians as predisposed to violence, their predominantly nonviolent struggle produced political results toward a negotiated settlement, through massive nonadversarial social mobilization rooted in popular committees, often steered by women.

The intriguing issue remains of how nonviolent struggle can act as an equalizer when unarmed challengers face a hugely lopsided power relationship. The balance of forces between the State of Israel and the Palestinians was altered, as the Palestinians were for more than two years able to wedge open new political space and achieve a more balanced power relationship with the State of Israel. The most substantial equalization of power between the Palestinians and the Israelis across the decades came not through guerrilla warfare or paramilitary operations, but from nonviolent strategies in the first intifada. Albeit squandered on both sides, the basic political accomplishment stands.

The strategic dilemma for the Palestinians is not unlike that for other groups and societies. Any encounter with arms or use of violence by them alters the conflict from an asymmetrical one of nonviolent contestation against violent subjugation, in which the unarmed challengers have the advantage, to a symmetrical affray in which both sides are using violent weapons, thus according justification and greater gains to the better-equipped attackers. The predicament of the Palestinians in the uprising was made more complex not only because of their own shaky grasp of such strategic thinking, although that played a part, but because Israel and the PLO did not comprehend the nature of the uprising, compounded by the failure of the great powers to grasp the passkey that had been wrought.

Since the dynamics of what takes place inside nonviolent mobilizations is poorly understood, any such struggle should be critically examined because of the need to expand knowledge and improve strategy for the technique. In addition, standard conflict resolution strategies can fail when the cause of distress is so deep or egregious that it requires shifts in the positions of the opposing sides in order to create an opening for consideration of solutions. The disappointment of the Oslo process brings up Sharp's cautionary warning that efforts to settle the conflict before needed changes take place in the power relationships could be premature and ultimately counterproductive to a lasting peaceful settlement.

The pragmatic line of reasoning that assumes a more favorable result with regard to one's opponent from the use of nonviolent techniques was unevenly applied, thus preventing the splitting of opinion in Israel or political jujitsu that might have resulted in the lifting of the occupation. Although the Palestinian people exhibited monumental mass discipline, a minority of the population threw stones and Molotov cocktails. The Palestinians can be analytically criticized for not constructing a "strictly" nonviolent mobilization. Yet this charge would be true in most such mobilizations, when studied in depth, to greater or lesser degree. Nonetheless, the struggle within a struggle of the first intifada is an important project for study by peoples bowed down by nonresponsive rulers, adamantine bureaucracies, tyrannical regimes, or even pillaging by armed rebel militias, because popular nonviolent action accomplished what decades of liturgical and actual adherence to armed struggle had not.

Furthermore, earnest soul-searching in Israel was a genuine consequence of the 1987 uprising, a counteractant to the boastful triumphalism that had followed the 1967 military occupation and an element in laying groundwork for enduring change.

When the Palestinians shifted into violent strategies with the second intifada, they lost the potential for causing divisions in Israeli polity that might have altered policies. The post-Oslo suicide bombs had the effect of consolidating Israeli society against the Palestinians. Revulsion generated by attacks on civilians nullified the external pressure for justice worldwide. "Violence is a complete disaster for the Palestinians; it should never have been pursued," historian Beshara Doumani stated; "the only weapon we have is the moral high ground—it was a strategic blunder to turn to violence in the second intifada."[42]

The Palestinians in the first intifada had shown sophistication in appreciating that the best way to equalize the power relationship with Israel was through small institutions, employing the theories and methods of nonviolent struggle with their potential for improving the odds for negotiations and reconciliation, and by open use of information to explain their new thinking. Yet the European and North American universities and research centers that could have helped the activist intellectuals by offering them visiting lectureships and fellowships did not, leaving them to jail or deportation. Their problem was compounded when returning exiles, called "the Tunisians," did not share their experience or insights. The first intifada begs for comparative analysis alongside the similarly protracted multidecade South African conflict, specifically the antiapartheid movement's utilization of the state's dependency relationships and third-party solidarity for leverage against a militarily superior regime.

The Islamic revivalists had capitalized on the diversification of power centers resulting from the social mobilization of the 1970s and 1980s, which created room for divergent points of view and oppositional organizing. Grasping well the huge deficits in basic services and welfare programs created by the military occupation, they addressed these needs, while replying to the yearning for lost access to Muslim holy places and touching the aspirations of the marginalized, including women bereft by relentless losses. They had never wholeheartedly accepted the noncooperation logic propounded in the 1987 uprising, although they had reached an accommodation with it. They chose instead to move in a trajectory that would steadily diverge, leading to a radically contrary path as the two-state solution proposed during the first initfada continually failed to materialize. Nusseibeh's prophecy could still come true, that a conflict over land might become one of race and religion, and consequently much worse. The Qassamite groups will continue to profit politically from the absence of tangible improvements in the lives of the Palestinians.

From the vantage point of the January 25, 2006, parliamentary elections in which Hamas won the majority of seats, it can be seen that the cause of the Islamic revivalists has been helped by Israel in more ways than one, particularly the refusal of Israeli officials to provide positive reinforcement to the Palestinian leaders who were leading efforts to spurn violence and were ready to compromise. Among the lessons of the first intifada that can lead away from the futilities of the past is the fundamental, indeed supreme, value of maintaining communications. A conflict as impacted as that of the Israelis and Palestinians will not be simplistically "ended." Conflicts must continuously be addressed, and they require continuous management. Policies that rely on severing relations and halting discussion cut short the possibility of influencing and changing the perspective of the opponent. Although public servants have limited paths to choose, hence the proclivity for cutting off relations, in this case a relationship with discord is preferable to none.

The germination of a strong Palestinian civil society is of inestimable significance for the region. Although important not to exaggerate the attributes of this nongovernmental domain—cells for terror suicide bombs, or "martyrdom operations," also form within civil society—it is a sector that deserves to be recognized for its intrinsic value in contemporary democratic societies. The 1980s strategies of building institutions and nonviolent struggle of the early stages of the first intifada created structures for a lasting settlement, and enhance a capacity for self-criticism and reform. Political scientist Nathan Brown discerns the worth of this development:

> Palestinian society, both during the first intifada and during the Oslo period, saw the emergence of impressive organizations arising on a local level and, especially during the Oslo period, on a national level. There was a real professionalization of civil society, especially during the Oslo period, and especially within some organizations, which . . . demonstrated to the Arab World a different kind of way of organizing a society. If Palestine were a virtual country, existing only on the Internet, it would probably be the most impressive member of the Arab League, because of the existence of very capable and fairly sophisticated civil society organizations.[43]

One of the least-studied aspects of nonviolent struggle is its ability to serve as a forerunner and predictor for the development of democratic governance and institutions. The 1987 intifada and the years of constructing the movements of committees that produced it have done more for coining a model of authentic democratic governance in the Arab world than any other intervention by any force. Beside their inability to protect Palestinian communities from the repressive violence of military occupation, the military command structures of the guerrilla units did not generate democratic leadership. Few democracies if any have resulted from militarized national liberation struggles. Yet, as a consequence of the 1987 uprising, Adrien Katherine Wing suggests, the Palestinians could construct the first genuine democracy in the Arab world, an integral aspect of which would be institutionalizing the rule of law.[44]

Were a Palestinian state to be established, the residual knowledge of nonviolent struggle from the early first intifada would be an asset for its governance, and that of the entire region, in spreading knowledge of how to fight for justice, entitlements, and human rights without violence—a capacity possibly more important for democracies than for nondemocracies, because of the tendency for majorities presumptuously to ignore minorities. The return of the PLO as part of a formal peace agreement, combined with the claims of Hamas as it has steadily evolved, mean that collective nonviolent action, less needful of creating space, would relocate in a different sociopolitical place. The nonviolent prospectus would become a residual capacity within the society, acting as a brake against overweening aggregations of power, and serving as a check for the Law, lest it enshrine injustices. Moreover, nonviolent resistance as national defense, or a civilian form of military strategy, would be appropriate to a future Palestinian state, most likely not to have an army.[45] Both the disengagement policy of the activist intellectuals and a robust Palestinian civil society are compatible with the basic theories of civilian-based defense. Much as the defense ministries of the Baltic States in the late 1980s prepared extensive guidelines in collaboration with civil society organizations, Palestinian civilian-based defense would require that a large percent of the population have advance training in coordinated and disciplined efforts for self-defense.

Nonviolent struggle tends to favor democratic principles and practices, in part because the technique involves joint collaborative participation of organizations and institutions throughout society. The decentralization of such popular movements is complementary to the necessity for the individuals involved to make personal, voluntary decisions to participate. Persons cannot be commanded to incur the penalties that may result from embarking on nonviolent action. The diffused and pluralistic societal power of mass mobilization can be democratically potentiating once tapped. At issue is whether the intifada leadership considered here, predisposed to democratic governance and tolerance if not cooperation with Israel, will be able to take its rightful place.

Among the most consequential long-term effects of the first intifada has been the modification of Israeli historiography. An intifada of scholars occurred, when Israeli and Palestinian historians and social scientists began meeting together for the first time, shaking off mutual exclusions and presuppositions of the past. Ilan Pappé explains:

> The intifada opened a new chapter in the Israeli-Palestinian dialogue, conducted mainly by scholars. . . . [acquainting] most of the Israeli scholars writing about their country's past who were not connected to radical political groups with the historical version of their Palestinian academic counterparts for the first time. . . . [and bringing] the first recognition of the scholarly merit of what hitherto had been regarded as sheer propaganda. Unpleasant and at times shocking chapters in the Israeli historical narrative were exposed. Above all, Israeli scholars became aware of the basic contradiction between Zionist national ambitions and their implementation at the expense of the local population in Palestine.[46]

Israel, writes Yaron Ezrahi, was paralyzed by its "alternative narratives" of power, with a "hidden narrative of murder beneath the higher narrative of liberation" and a vision of the military that had blinded many to the "counter-narratives of colonization and subordination."[47] Whether or not one agrees with Ezrahi's exact words, no one can dispute an upsurge in the number of Israeli critical social scientists and new historians, whose work is increasingly influential. Maps in future textbooks of Israeli public schools are to show the Green Line, the boundaries of Israel with the West Bank prior to the June 1967 war and as accepted in the 1949 armistice.[48] Fewer and fewer advocate the view (more common outside Israel than within) that everything done for the creation of Israel was correct, and conversely that whatever was done in the alienation of the Palestinians was thus justified.

The boy-who-cried-wolf reaction to the Palestinians' restrained collective nonviolent action, terming the first intifada relentless war and unending violence, was only the first misjudgment. Consistent failures to discern the growth of a new mentality existed well beyond the Israeli government. Formal study of the field of nonviolent struggle is missing from the preparation of diplomats, members of the news media, and public administrators. The U.S. political officers in Tunis in 1989 did not understand why they had been asked to take part in a briefing on nonviolent resistance. Study of the subject is often absent from academic inquiry in international relations and political science, indeed all of the social sciences, often including, most astonishingly, in peace and conflict studies.

Nondemocratic governments may welcome the eruption of violent struggle, because it creates justification for their own brutal repression. Military occupation is a form of dictatorship, and threaded through this narrative is the pattern noted by Captain Sir Basil Liddell Hart in which military generals experience "relief" when resistance becomes violent, or when nonviolent action is mixed with guerrilla attacks, because it is easier to mount "drastic suppressive action" against both at the same time. It is also the case that the capabilities of collective nonviolent action have been ignored and underrated for their potential in transforming acute conflicts, in nation building, and for certain kinds of national defense. The study of history has generally disregarded this form of engagement, and what has been chronicled is often ignored. Many Palestinians still do not understand how part of the potency of nonviolent action lies in its challenge through a technique that deliberately chooses not to use the expected violence.

Jon Immanuel interviewed Sari Nusseibeh for the *Jerusalem Post* in 1990 and reported Nusseibeh's view of the Palestinians as bound together in an embrace with Israel that cannot be pried apart. Nusseibeh said,

> Our own road to statehood is through Israel, through Israeli public opinion. Those who think the U.S. can or would impose a solution on Israel misinterpret the nature of the U.S. political system. It is still our responsibility as Palestinians to emphasize to the Israelis that it is peace that we seek and coexistence, and not the destruction of Israel . . . not for Israel's sake but for our sake. Israel has to come and see the sense for it of accepting a settlement with the Palestinians which is satisfactory to the Palestinians.[49]

In the first intifada, the Palestinians conceptualized new ways of waging struggle for basic civil and political rights and in so doing reshaped the sources of power within Palestinian society, causing shifts away from adherence to the dogma of military means, building leadership structures that emerged from the organizing of a civil society, and expressing readiness to compromise with Israel. They were probing at a profound level the nature of power and the role of their own consent in the shared degradation of two suffering peoples by military occupation. They made common cause with Israelis who were concerned that their own fellow citizens were becoming, in Gideon Spiro's phrase, "victims of blind obedience." Their insights, rather than continued military responses devoid of diplomacy and negotiations, provide platforms for Israelis and Palestinians to search for compromise. As Nusseibeh stated, the road for the Palestinians leads through Israel.

Israel exists as an attempted corrective to one of the cruelest atrocities of history, as remorse and guilt for the silence of Western Christendom in the face of the unconscionable crimes of the Holocaust persuaded the international community that it must help the Jews to establish their own safe haven in their own nation-state. A project of such noble intention, however, not only resulted in the statelessness of the Palestinians, it would continue to be vexed by two dilemmas: it rescued one people at the expense of the other, without acknowledging the correlation, which entailed taking possession of land that was Arab, and it would result in an ethnic theocracy, with the exclusions and hierarchies implied therein. Finding a durable solution for the conflict in the Middle East will require three adjustments: 1) all parties must recognize the repercussions of the failures from Balfour onward to recognize that the Palestinians are stakeholders with rights in Palestine; 2) the Arab world must clearly and unambiguously accept Israel; and 3) the Israelis must plainly and unmistakably come to see themselves as part of the Middle East. Veteran IDF officer Avi Azrieli stresses, "While Israel has flourished economically and technologically by modeling itself on the Western European culture of its early Ashkenazi pioneers, the cultural alienation from its neighbors has intensified Israel's pariah status."[50] He suggests, for example, that teaching Arabic as a national language alongside Hebrew would send a message to its neighbors indicating respect for them and Israel's intention to stay. The generation that guided the Palestinian intifada in its early years not only had largely learned Hebrew, but had taken the greatest strides to date toward unequivocal acceptance of Israel. Had the Palestinian leaders who accepted coexistence with Israel been offered reinforcement rather than jail and deportation, especially when they had reached comity with the Islamic revivalists, they could have formed the crux for acceptance of permanent citizenship for Israelis in the region. Israeli policies instead undermined those who forged the new systems of thought that led to the first intifada and its enunciation of acceptance of a two-state solution. The Palestinians could be Israel's best neighbors—if, as Azrieli phrases it, "Israel accepts its identity as a Middle Eastern country." The Israeli road to thorough acceptance runs through Palestinian statehood.

Acknowledgments

James Piscatori of the faculty of politics at the University of Oxford, and Michael O. Foley of the department of international politics at the University of Wales at Aberystwyth, have earned my deepest respect and esteem for the quality of their advice and guidance, without which this book would not have been possible.

The main research for the book was made possible by two fellowships granted to me in the 1990s by the Albert Einstein Institution in Boston, enabling my field work. Special gratitude goes to sociologist Ronald M. McCarthy, then in charge of the Einstein fellows program, and to Bruce Jenkins, both of whom were persuaded of the worth of this effort and gave crucial early support. The institution's senior scholar Gene Sharp generously granted me full access to his reports from his trips to Israel/Palestine. My association with him and the institution for many years has had a formative effect on my work.

During two years at Oxford, portions of my study of the British colonial period were undertaken as Senior Fellow at the Rothermere American Institute (RAI). The RAI, where I now have a visiting fellowship, threw open the riches of the University of Oxford and archives elsewhere in the United Kingdom for my research on this and other projects. A volume ordered one day would arrive the next at the Vere Harmsworth Library (VHL). Several individuals at the RAI, VHL, and Rhodes House were exceptionally helpful, and I would like to thank them, in particular Eileen Auden, Andrea Beighton, Laura Lauer, Paul Giles, Ruth E. Parr, and especially John Pinfold.

Colleagues of more than two decades on the board of directors of the Arca Foundation, a private philanthropy, were present with me for the meetings of 1988 and 1989 in Israel/Palestine that ignited this study. In sharing their insights with me, they are part of its germinal process. I refer to Smith W. Bagley, Margery Tabankin, Janet Shenk, Nicole Bagley, Nancy Bagley, and especially the late Ellsworth Culver, who was keenly interested in this undertaking before his much lamented death. Historain Frank Peters transformed the two trips into traveling seminars. Rabbi Sandy Ragins of Leo Baeck Temple, Los Angeles, accompanied us on one trip, enriching our deliberations.

A number of authors and thinkers have encouraged this effort, and I am grateful for their assistance. Journalist and historian Milton Viorst has for twenty years encouraged me in this research; indeed he and his author wife Judith Viorst accompanied the Arca Foundation for the seminal meetings. Marcus Raskin of George Washington University, a friend since the civil rights movement, gave me singular encouragement, for which I express deep thanks. I am most grateful to political ideologies expert Michael Freeden, faculty of politics at Oxford and fellow of Mansfield College, where I have a continuing relationship, for his close review of the manuscript.

Others gave assistance of inestimable value. Reuven Gal of the Carmel Institute for Social Sciences, near Haifa, went beyond the call of duty of one scholar helping another. Edward Kaufman, then at the Hebrew University of Jerusalem, has over the years shown great generosity of spirit. I would like to thank Gideon Spiro in Tel Aviv for his kindness, which seems to have no bounds. Mahdi Abd al-Hadi, head of the Palestinian Academic Society for the Study of International Affairs in East Jerusalem, generously gave me access to the PASSIA files. Graham Leonard's help at the earliest stages of my inquiry was most productive. Mary Kathryn Lundregan accompanied me for many interviews and provided scrupulous research back up, for which I am indebted. Christopher A. Miller assisted me in researching Jerusalem newspapers of the 1920s and 1930s and historic archives, in Britain. He has my appreciation, as does Robin O. Surratt for her editorial assistance. I am also grateful for their encouragement to Odeh F. Aburdene, Walid and Helen Kattan, Hasib Sabbagh, Sana Sabbagh, and the late Abdul Majid Shoman.

I would like personally to express thanks to the editor for the book, Ruth Baldwin, whose judgment I came unfailingly to trust.

It is not possible to list the individuals interviewed in Israel and the occupied Palestinian territories, who, in 150 or more interviews, generously submitted to my interrogations—usually with the encumbrance of two running tape recorders, in case one failed, while I simultaneously took notes. To them I offer my most sincere, humble, and warm appreciation, because this book rests upon their consideration and the distinctive charity that is required when asked probing and perhaps ignorant questions. At the time I started taking notes and recording interviews, the material we were discussing was often dangerous, and some were taking great risks in communicating with me on what was illegal. I can never sufficiently thank them.

Mary Elizabeth King
Washington, D.C.
May 8, 2007

Appendix 1: Excerpts, 1977 letter of Aziz Shehadeh to U.S. Secretary of State Cyrus Vance

His Excellency Cyrus Vance
U.S. Secretary of State
Jerusalem

Your Excellency,

I the undersigned, a Palestinian Arab, take the opportunity on the occasion of your visit to this area to submit to you the following Framework for Peace, which I believe represents the view-point of the majority of the Palestinian Arabs in the Occupied Areas and abroad. . . .

We Palestinians must not be ignored in the search for peace. We must play a part in working out our own future.

Furthermore, Israelis and Palestinians should recognize the mutual legitimate rights of both peoples to sovereign, national statehood in the land which both claim as their homeland.

The Israelis have already materialized their rights to national sovereignty. What remains then is for the Palestinian people to implement this very right by establishing their own independent state, within boundaries which will be the result of an agreement reached by both parties and not the product of warfare and military conquest . . . also [taking] into consideration benefits for both sides provided for by UN Resolutions. . . .

[W]e see that we have got to live with the fact of Israel, and we want to work out this relationship with the Israelis themselves. . . . We, for our part, can understand the Israeli need for security, but it must be considered side by side with our right to recover occupied territory and to have a homeland of our own with the recognition of our dignity and worth. . . .

Israel and the emerging [democratic] Palestine State would be in a position to sign a non-aggression pact. . . . [A] prosperous, independent Palestinian State will be a bridge towards lasting peace and cooperation between the Arab nation and Israel. . . .

[A]s Jerusalem is rightly claimed by both nations, it should also belong to both . . . [with] shared sovereignty. I suggest separate municipalities, . . . with a joint commission to control and coordinate public services. Thus Jerusalem will again become the city of peace, holy to three religions and of free access to all. . . .

To compensate or rehabilitate two million refugees will be a task of great magnitude, involving great finance, and I believe that, given a fair settlement, many nations would contribute generously, both those in the Middle East and outside. . . .

Yours faithfully,

Aziz Shehadeh
August 10, 1977

Appendix 2: Excerpts, October 13–15, 1983, Workshop Program

Workshop, "Palestinian Resistance and Nonviolent Ways"

Goals: Our goals are to achieve social justice and self-determination for the Palestinians. . . .

Who Can Join This Citizens' Action? Anyone seeking justice through law and action who wants to liberate him/herself from the Israeli military rule and who wants to work *now* is welcome to join us in accepting nonviolent goals and methods. . . .

Resolving Conflict in Nonviolent Ways:
1. Affirmation—We must affirm that each individual has good in him/her

and has the ability to do good. If we feel good about ourselves, we will see good in others. If we feel confident about ourselves,

    a. we can do the things we want,

    b. we can learn new things,

    c. we can achieve,

    d. we can be free from the Israeli military—we *chose to accept occupation*. . . .

2. Supporting Group—The supporting group fulfills an important role by participating in the following:

    a. negotiation and arbitration;

    b. preparation of the group for direct action; . . .

    e. economic boycotts and forms of strike, i.e., picketing, . . . holding sit-ins, labor strikes;

    f. noncooperation, i.e., nonpayment of taxes;

    g. civil disobedience, i.e., disobeying unjust laws to change them and taking the consequences;

    h. parallel government, i.e., local government to carry out parallel functions.

3. Problem Solving—

    a. Be clear about your objectives. . . .

    b. Do not be frightened. . . . Talk slowly, breathe deeply, maintain eye contact.

    c. Do not be frightening. Someone who wants to commit an act of violence is likely to be more full of fear than the person who is being attacked. . . .

Nonviolent action is the way people can act on the problems and challenges around them without *emotionally* or *physically* damaging anyone. . . .

Problems that Face Us as Palestinians

1. We would like one "quick shot in the arm," i.e., resist one day or one hour, duty is done. . . .

2. We have not anticipated the reaction of the Israelis in the past. . . .

4. We need to use the international press, the Arab press, as well as the Israeli press.

5. Many of us are afraid of physical violence and financial punishment for our actions. We need to overcome these fears.

6. In the past, we have had little reward from nonviolent resistance. If nonviolent resistance is organized well, prepared well, and with masses of people, then it can be a viable tool. . . .

—by Mubarak Awad and Jonathan Kuttab

Appendix 3: Excerpts, 1983 booklet "Nonviolence in the Occupied Territories"

"Nonviolence in the Occupied Territories"

. . . [F]or the [1.3 million] Palestinians who are living in the West Bank and Gaza during this particular time period, the most effective method of struggling is the strategy of nonviolence. . . . Nonviolent struggle is not a negative or passive method. It is an active affirmative operation. . . . Most nonviolent activities will be illegal according to the laws and military orders presently imposed on the population.

The Israeli soldier is an ordinary human being. He is not a frightening beast, nor an animal devoid of conscience and feeling. He has a conscience and an understanding of right and wrong to which it is possible to appeal. Similarly, he can be demoralized because he constantly needs a reasonable justification for his activities. . . .

Israel cannot govern the West Bank and the Gaza Strip without the agreement, approval, and cooperation of the subject people. This approval and cooperation is usually obtained by force, threats, violence, and punishments (individual and collective). Yet in spite of all this, the oppressed people always have the option of rejecting the oppression and refusing to cooperate with it if they are willing to pay the price. . . .

Perhaps one of the most important methods of nonviolent resistance to the occupation is the creation and building of alternative institutions and methods to replace the present unjust institutions of the occupation. . . . The building of an entire infrastructure independently of Israel (universities, factories, institutions, libraries, hospitals, schools . . . [comprises] the necessary nucleus for the coming Palestinian state). . . .

Civil disobedience usually comes at a much later and developed point in the nonviolence struggle. It involves a conscious and deliberate commission of illegal acts and violation of known military orders and laws. This form of direct action must be carefully contemplated. A nonviolent person utilizing this method must be willing to take the full legal consequences of his actions. . . . The Palestinians would be voluntarily accepting . . . suffering inflicted on them. To bravely and steadfastly accept persecution for one's belief brings one very close to the power of nonviolence. It neutralizes the effectiveness of the instruments of repression and improves the internal steadfastness and power of the resister. The greatest enemy to the people and the most powerful weapon in the hands of the authorities is fear. . . .

> —by Mubarak E. Awad, 1983 English translation in PASSIA archives, East Jerusalem (minor syntactical and grammatical errors in original)

Appendix 4, Excerpts, "Fourteen Talking Points of West Bank–Gaza Palestinians"

14 January 1988

. . . The present state of affairs in the Palestinian occupied territories is unnatural and . . . Israeli occupation cannot continue forever. Real peace cannot be achieved except through the recognition of the Palestinian national rights, including the right of self-determination and the establishment of an independent Palestinian state on Palestinian national soil. Should these rights not be recognized, then the continuation of Israeli occupation will lead to further violence and bloodshed and the further deepening of hatred. The opportunity for achieving peace will also move further away.

The only way to extricate ourselves from this scenario is through the convening of an international conference with the participation of representative [*sic*] of the Palestinian people, as an equal partner, as well as the five permanent members of the Security Council, under the supervision of the two Super Powers.

On this basis we call upon the Israeli authorities to comply with the following list of demands as a means to prepare the atmosphere for the convening of the suggested international peace conference . . . [to] achieve a just and lasting settlement of the Palestinian problem in all its aspects. . . . :

1. To abide by the Fourth Geneva Convention and all other international agreements pertaining to the protection of civilians . . . under . . . military occupation; to declare the Emergency Regulations of the British mandate null and void, and to stop applying the iron fist policy.

2. The immediate compliance with Security Council Resolutions 605 and 607, which call upon Israel to abide by the Geneva convention of 1949 and the Declaration of Human Rights. . . .

3. The release of all prisoners who were arrested during the recent uprising. . . .

4. The cancellation of the policy of expulsion and allowing all exiled Palestinians . . . to return to their homes and families. Also the release of all administrative detainees and the cancellation of the hundreds of house arrest orders . . .

5. The immediate lifting of the siege of all Palestinian refugee camps in the West Bank and Gaza, and the withdrawal of the Israeli army from all population centres.

6. Carrying out a formal inquiry into the behaviour of soldiers and settlers in the West Bank and Gaza, . . .

7. A cessation of all settlement activity and land confiscation. . . .

—by Sari Nusseibeh. On January 27, 1988, the "Fourteen Points" were submitted to U.S. Secretary of State George P. Shultz, in Washington, by Hanna Siniora and Fayez Abu Rahme

Appendix 5: Excerpts, the "Jerusalem Paper"

A Working Paper

Jerusalem, 8 February 1988

. . . The relationship of the Palestinian people to the occupation consists of a vast network. The majority of this network includes procedures, transactions, and regulations requiring tacit consent from the Palestinian side, whereas the remaining part of it forms an Israeli, one-sided coercive relationship. . . . [E]nding the occupation necessitates [our] national will to break off all of the relationship's ties to the occupation system, whose existence depends on our tacit consent, so that nothing remains of the occupation except the part only relying on coercion and violence by the other side. . . .

[T]he followings steps are required . . . :

1. Continuing partial strikes while calling on all sectors of the society . . . to adhere to them.

2. Continuing demonstrations. . . .

3. Boycotting bureaus which connect authorities with the Palestinian people:
    a. Resigning from all city and village councils. . . .
    b. Calling on all workers in the police offices to resign. . . .
    c. Calling on all . . . Civil Administration [workers], except the educational and health sectors, collectively to resign. . . .

4. Non-compliance with . . . orders issued from the Israeli authorities. . . :
    a. Refusing to comply with house-arrest orders.
    b. Refusing . . . orders concerning appearing before the police.
    c. Refusing . . . to close establishments, including the educational establishments and universities—except when authorities use force. . . .
    e. Refusing . . . Israeli orders concerning professional licences, registration of associations, motor vehicle registration, and driving.
    f. During later stages of disobedience, refusing to be restricted by press censorship, . . which will inevitably lead to . . . replacement by the underground press.
    g. [B]urning all Israeli identification cards.

5. . . .
    a. Refraining from paying taxes in all forms. . . .
    b. Boycotting all Israeli products for which an alternative may be found.
    c. Calling on merchants to reduce their various imports from Israel. . . .

In the final stages, refraining from paying water, telephone, and electricity bills while considering the possibility of these services being cut off and living without all or most of them for several weeks. . . .

—by Sari Nusseibeh. Tr. comm. Mohssen Esseesy. (Document appears in Arabic with typographic errors as Appendix 1 in Ziad Abu-Amr, *The Intifada: Causes and Factors of Continuity*, 2nd edn [East Jerusalem, PASSIA, 1994], pp. 46–52. Excerpts here correct errors.)

Appendix 6: Excerpts, the "Husseini Document"

Text of Proposal for Palestinian State

The announcement in Jerusalem of the independence document will herald the establishment of an independent Palestinian state within the partition boundaries, as determined in 1947 and by the (UN) Security Council in Resolution 181. Its capital will be Jerusalem and its interim government will consist of two parts: Those who are in exile and those who reside on Palestinian soil. . . .

[T]he issue for debate both in the international and Israeli arenas will change from a demand that the PLO recognize Israel as a precondition for negotiations to a demand that the international community recognize the state established by the efforts of the Palestinian people, whose lands were occupied by the Hebrew state. . . .

The popular committees . . . will gain official status as branches of the new state, helping to continue the growth and development of the state. . . .

[T]he nature of the new state will confirm that it is not aggressive, and that the Palestinian people do not desire the annihilation of the state of Israel. Rather, they wish to live peacefully as its neighbour.

The announcement of the Declaration of Independence . . . does not necessarily mean the creation of an interim Palestinian government-in-exile, as has been suggested by Arab leaders in the past. Instead, it will mean the birth of a Palestinian state in the homeland. In order to reach this objective, the Unified National Leadership of the Uprising [the Command] . . . will take the responsibility of carrying out this objective. Our people will thus hold the reins of the initiative even as they are setting up their state on their national land, instead of persistently demanding that other parties—especially the international conference and the United States—establish such a state. . . .

The nature of the independent Palestinian state will be a republic—elected president, ministerial council made up of elected parties. The state will allow multiple political parties and religions, and the freedom of all believers to worship. It will guarantee the human, economic and political rights of individuals and the community, . . . for the citizen to live in freedom and in dignity, . . . [with] rights stated in the United Nations Declaration of Human Rights. . . .

—by Sari Nusseibeh. Document seized July 31, 1988,
by Israeli authorities from Feisel Husseini's papers.
Excerpted from version in the *Jerusalem Post*,
August 12, 1988

Notes

Preface

1   The author's book on that experience, including an account of Christmas in jail in Atlanta in 1963—*Freedom Song: A Personal Story of the 1960s Civil Rights Movement*—won her a Robert F. Kennedy Memorial Book Award in 1988.

2   Yehoshua Porath, "The Political Organization of the Palestinian Arabs under the British Mandate," in *Palestinian Arab Politics*, ed. Moshe Maoz (Jerusalem: Harry S. Truman Research Institute, Hebrew University, 1975), 19.

3   Helena Cobban, *The Palestinian Liberation Organisation: People, Power and Politics* (Cambridge: Cambridge University Press, 1984), 24.

4   "Palestinian National Charter, Revised by the Fourth Palestine National Congress, July 1968," in *Basic Political Documents of the Armed Palestinian Resistance Movement*, ed. Leila S. Kadi (Beirut: PLO Research Center, 1969), Article 9; "The Palestinian National Covenant, 1968," in *The Israeli-Palestinian Conflict: A Documentary Record, 1967-1990*, ed.Yehuda Lukacs (Cambridge: Cambridge University Press, 1992), 291-95.

5   Anders Boserup and Andrew Mack, *War without Weapons: Non-Violence in National Defense* (New York: Schocken Books, 1975), 11.

6   Barry Rubin, *Revolution until Victory? The Politics and History of the PLO* (Cambridge, Massachusetts; London: Harvard University Press, 1994), 10; "Declaration of Yasir Arafat on Terrorism, Cairo, November 7, 1985," in Lukacs, *Israeli-Palestinian Conflict*, 371.

7   Daoud Kuttab, "Will Guns Be Used?" Unpublished paper, East Jerusalem, May 1988. Kuttab private papers.

8   Walter Lippman, "The Political Equivalent of War," *Atlantic Monthly* 142 (August 1928): 181-82, as cited in Gene Sharp, *"The Political Equivalent of War"—Civilian Defense* (New York: Carnegie Endowment for International Peace, 1965), 6.

9   Ibrahim Abu-Lughod, "On Achieving Independence," *Intifada: Palestine at the Crossroads*, ed. Jamal R. Nassar and Roger Heacock (Westport, Connecticut: Praeger, 1990), 7.

Chapter 1

1   See, for example, David Landau, "PLO behind the Unrest," *Jerusalem Post*, December 18, 1987, 7.

2   Abu-Lughod, "On Achieving Independence," 3.

3   Michael S. Serrill, "Days of Rage in the Territories," *Time*, December 28, 1987, 33.

4   Daoud Kuttab, "Bloody Confrontation," *Middle East International*, December 19, 1987, 3.

5   Syrian poet Nizar Qabbani published an ode to "Atfal al-Kajarah" (Children Bearing Rocks) in *al-Qabas*, December 20, 1987. See the translation by Sharif S. Elmusa, *MERIP Reports, Middle East Research and Information Project* (May-June 1988), 34.

6   Makram Khoury Machool, "This Isn't Rebellion, This Is War," reprint, original of which appeared December 18, 1987, in the Tel Aviv weekly *Hair*, where the article became a media event. On the latter, see *New Outlook*, February 1988, 12-13.

7   John P. Wallach, "Battles Lines: The America Media and the Intifada," book review, *Washington Monthly*, April 1992. On Israeli censorship of television coverage of the uprising, see James V. D'Amato, "How Regimes Profit by Curbing U.S. Television News," *Orbis* 35 (Summer 1991): 351-56.

Israeli photographer Amir Weinberg of *Yediot Aharonot* was dragged along a pavement and kicked by Israeli soldiers. Bradley Burston, "Photographer Said Beaten by IDF," *Jerusalem Post*, January 10, 1988, 2. Former U.S. secretary of state Henry Kissinger recommended at an off-the-record breakfast with American Jewish leaders, "Israel should bar the media from entry into the territories involved . . . , accept the short-term criticism of the world press for such conduct, and put down the insurrection as quickly as possible—overwhelmingly, brutally . . . . Under no circumstances should Israel make any concessions during the present insurrection." Julius Berman, "Behind Closed Doors," *Harper's*, June 1988. On March 4, Israel attempted for the first time to close the entire West Bank to journalists. Alan Cowell, "Israel Curbs Coverage of the West Bank," *New York Times*, March 5, 1988, 5.

8   See Khalil Jahshan, "U.S. Media Treatment of the Palestinians since the *Intifada*," *American-Arab Affairs* 28, 81-8; Hal Wyner, "Israeli Brutality, Press Timidity," *New York Times*, October 8, 1989, 21.

9   Eytan Gilboa, "American Media, Public Opinion, and the *Intifada*," *Framing the Intifada: People and Media*, ed. Akiba A. Cohen and Gadi Wolfsted (Norwood, New Jersey: Ablex Publishing Corporation, 1993), 93, 112.

10   According to a former IDF officer, Israel's first use of tanks in any Palestinian turbulence would not occur until September 1996 in Jerusalem, after Israel opened a tunnel in Jerusalem that runs alongside the Temple Mount and Haram al-Sharif, and street demonstrations in protest were followed by altercations. Reuven Gal, one-hour interview (Jerusalem, March 12, 1997). In China, a student-led nonviolent movement sought to pressure the Chinese communist party for democratic liberties through hunger strikes, sit-ins, boycotts of classes, and, eventually, the disastrous occupation of Tiananmen Square occurred, in which approximately 2,600 persons were killed and more than 7,000 wounded, including both civilians and soldiers. Joshua Paulson, "Uprising and Repression in China-1989," in Gene Sharp, ed., *Waging Nonviolent Struggle, 20th Century Practice and 21st Century Potential* (Boston: Porter Sargent Publishers, 2005), 266.

11   This prompted one of four UN resolutions in four weeks reminding Israel that the West Bank, Gaza Strip, and Jerusalem were occupied areas and calling upon Israel to adhere to the Geneva Convention relative to the Protection of Civilian Persons in Times of War, August 12, 1949. The convention was drafted to formulate internationally recognized civil and moral codes of behavior for an occupying power in a particular territory. Middle Eastern signatories include Egypt, Israel, Jordan, Lebanon, and Syria. After Israel's announcement of the nine deportations, despite U.S. protestations, for the first time since 1981 the United States voted against Israel in the Security Council. Jules Kagian, "The Four Resolutions," *Middle East International*, January 23, 1988, 10. Israel, in response, claimed the convention applied only to mass expulsions. George D. Moffett III, "Palestinians Say Expulsions Were Expected and Won't Work," *Christian Science Monitor*, April 13, 1988.

12   Hirsh Goodman, "Army Meets a New Palestinian: They Are Different from the Clearly Defined Terrorist of 20 Years Ago," *Jerusalem Post*, January 15, 1988, 5.

13   Scott Atran, "Stones against the Iron Fist, Terror within the Nation: Alternating Structures of Violence and Cultural Identity in the Israeli-Palestinian Conflict," *Politics and Society* 18, no. 4 (1990): 484.

14   Peretz Kidron, "Labour's Ideological Supermarket," *Middle East International*, December 19, 1987, 5.

15   Middle East Watch, *A License to Kill: Israeli Undercover Operations against "Wanted" and Masked Palestinians* (New York: Human Rights Watch, 1993), 29.

16   Hirsh Goodman, "Defense Establishment at a Loss to Deal with Unrest," *Jerusalem Post*, January 11, 1988, 1.

17   "The Reluctant Occupiers," *Jerusalem Post*, January 1, 1988, 6.

18   John Bierman and Eric Silver, "Confronting an Uprising," *Maclean's*, January 11, 1988, 20.

19   Chris Wood, "Where Will the Revolt End?" *Maclean's*, April 18, 1988, 23.

20   Edward Cody, "Palestinian Uprising: A Rage Unleashed: "Tired of Living Like This," *Washington Post*, February 28, 1988, 28.

21   Jonathan Frankel, "Palestinian Revolt—and the Israeli Response," *Dissent* (Spring 1988), 151.

22   Russell Watson and Milan J. Kubic, "Why Beat the Rioters? Israel's Painful Dilemma," *Time*, February 8, 1988, 39.

23   Wolf Blitzer, "Senior U.S. Officials, Jews Warning Israel to Stop Beatings Immediately," *Jerusalem Post*, January 24, 1988, 4. "The policy of beatings has reached monstrous dimensions," Citizens' Rights Movement members of the Knesset Yossi Sarid and Dedi Zucker said, after touring Gaza on January 21, 1988, and compiling testimony to produce a report. "The results of the defense minister's policy can be seen on the hands, backs, and heads of hundreds of youths and old people in the Gaza Strip." Yossi Sarid and Dedi Zucker, "Special Report: The Occupied Territories," *New Outlook*, March-April 1988, 16. Not until February 1989 were the first Israeli soldiers brought to trial for

beating Palestinians to death, when four soldiers from the elite Givati brigade, three privates and a corporal, were charged by army prosecutors with manslaughter for the killing of Hani al-Shami. George D. Moffett III, "Do Israeli Officers Order Beatings? Four Soldiers Accused in Palestinian's Death Say Higher Echelons Urge Use of Force; ARMY ON TRIAL," *Christian Science Monitor*, February 15, 1989.

24 John Kifner, "Arabs Recount Israeli Beatings, The New Policy," *New York Times*, January 23, 1988, 1; Susan Sappir, "Israeli Police Minister Denies Army Beating Palestinians," *Reuter Library Report*, January 24, 1988. In June 1988, at four hospitals in Gaza and the West Bank, physicians showed the author deliberately inflicted mid-limb fractures, which heal more slowly than breaks at joints, and crushed hands considered beyond rehabilitation. Surgeons produced glass bullets removed in operations, designed, they said, to evade detection by X-rays, resulting in increased surgical intrusion. Excised "rubber bullets" were made of ballistic metal coated with a thin veneer of rubber.

25 Ann Mosely Lesch, "Uprising for Palestine: Editorial Commentary," *Journal for South Asian and Middle Eastern Studies* 11, no. 4 (Summer 1988): 5; Joel Greenberg, "Soldiers Arrested for Burying Youths," *Jerusalem Post*, January 1, 1988, 1.

26 Lesch, "Uprising for Palestine," 5; Glenn Frankel, "Beating Victims' Anger Festers; Wounded at Gaza Hospital Are Measure of Outrage against Israel," *Washington Post*, February 14, 1988, A1. In late February 1988, the Columbia Broadcasting System (CBS) aired a forty-minute sequence, in which Israeli soldiers beat two Palestinians detained for throwing stones. David Horovitz, "British TV Viewers 'Shocked' by Documentary on 'Beatings to Death,'" *Jerusalem Post*, March 6, 1988, 2; Philip Gillon, "The Threats to TV Freedom," *Jerusalem Post*, March 6, 1988.

27 Editorial, "The Latest on the West Bank," *Washington Post*, February 17, 1988, A18; Lesch, "Uprising for Palestine," 5.

28 Peter Smerdon, "Israeli Army Fears Palestinian Rioters May Turn to Guns," *Jerusalem Post: Reuter Library Report*, February 9, 1988; Ronald R. Stockton, "The Pattern of *Intifada* Deaths," *Middle East International*, June 11, 1988, 15.

29 John Bierman and Eric Silver, "Running Out of Answers: Israeli Tactics Fail to Stem the Intifadeh," *Maclean's*, February 6, 1989, 24.

30 David Makovsky, "Meridor: Collective Punishment Justified to Suppress Intifada," *Jerusalem Post*, September 26, 1989, 2.

31 U.S. Department of State, "Israel and the Occupied Territories," *Country Reports on Human Rights Practices for 1988* (Washington, D.C.: Government Printing Office, 1989), 1376-87.

32 Reuven Gal, two-hour interview (Zichron Yaakov, Mt. Carmel, near Haifa, March 16, 1997). Until 1982, Gal was chief psychologist for the IDF and is a reserve colonel. In 1985, he founded the Israeli Institute for Military Studies in Zichron Yaakov, Mt. Carmel, now the Carmel Institute for Social Studies.

33 "Three Young Men Thrown from Helicopter, February 8, 1988, Jamain Village, Tulkarem Region," *Uprising in Palestine, The First Year: Documentation on Human Rights and the Palestinian Uprising*, ed. Louise Cainkar and Beth Goldring (Chicago and East Jerusalem: Palestine Human Rights Information Center and Database Project on Palestinian Human Rights, 1990), 89-90.

34 Joel Greenberg, "Italian Parliamentarian Chains Self in Ramallah," *Jerusalem Post*, March 3, 1988.

35 Goodman, "Army Meets a New Palestinian," 5.

36 Frank Collins, "How Stones Can Beat Guns," *Middle East International*, March 19, 1988, 16. A criminologist at The Hebrew University of Jerusalem describes the actions of Israeli soldiers in the first nine months of the uprising: "They have killed more than two hundred Palestinians, seriously wounded (by beating, tear-gassing and shooting) many thousands more, locked up some seven thousand people with hardly a semblance of judicial procedure (including nearly two thousand under "administrative detention") . . . blown up houses, and enforced prolonged curfews on hundreds of thousands of people in villages and refugee camps. . . . Beating up people in their homes, breaking their limbs, clubbing them unconscious, shooting unarmed demonstrators in the back. . . . By most standards of national and international law, these are actual crimes. Israel is not involved in an official state of war—the enemy is made up not of armed soldiers but of a million and a half people for whom Israel is responsible." Stanley Cohen, "Criminology and the Uprising," *Tikkun*, September-October 1988, 60.

37 Shyam Bhatia, "Uprising Comes of Age," *Observer*, December 11, 1988, 27.

38 Daoud Kuttab, "Shooting at Demonstrators: What Is the Israeli Policy?" dispatch filed with news media, East Jerusalem, mid-1988, Kuttab private papers; idem, "Will Guns Be Used?" unpublished paper, East Jerusalem, 1988, Kuttab private papers. Kuttab contributed two file folders of computer printouts for this research. When the uprising erupted, none of its progenitors was known, and authoritative journalists on the subject were equally few. Kuttab had been managing

editor of *al-Fajr* (the Dawn), an English-language Palestinian weekly, since 1986. Later a correspondent for *Middle East Mirror* and *Middle East International*, and political advisor to Reuters, in 1997 he was given the International Press Freedom Award by the Committee to Protect Journalists. He is founder and director of Ammannet, the Arab world's first Internet radio station.

39   Uri Avnery, "The Intifada: Substance and Illusion," *New Outlook*, November-December 1989, 12.

40   Al-Haq: Law in the Service of Man, *Punishing a Nation: Human Rights Violations during the Palestinian Uprising, December 1987-December 1988* (Boston: South End Press, 1990), 4.

41   Lieutenant Colonel Yehuda Weinraub, IDF spokesperson and head of information, Tel Aviv, records pursuant to a telephone request of March 18, 1997, trans. Reuven Gal.

42   Rubin, *Revolution until Victory?* 24, 26.

43   CIA Directorate of Intelligence, *Anti-Israel Arab Terrorist Organizations*, Special Report, October 4, 1968, 8, as cited in ibid., 18, 211 n. 29.

44   Rubin, *Revolution until Victory?* 25.

45   Ariel Merari and Shlomi Elad, *The International Dimension of Palestinian Terrorism*, Jaffee Center for Strategic Studies, Tel Aviv University (Jerusalem and Boulder, Colorado: Jerusalem Post Press and Westview Press, 1986), 5.

46   Glenn Frankel, "PLO Asserting Control of Palestinian Uprising: Violence Shifts to Organized Campaign," *Washington Post*, February 20, 1988.

Chapter 2

1   Martin Luther King, Jr., "Letter from Birmingham City Jail" (written April 16, 1963), in *Nonviolence in America: A Documentary History*, ed. Staughton Lynd and Alice Lynd (Maryknoll, New York: Orbis Books, 1995), 254.

2   Gene Sharp, *The Politics of Nonviolent Action*, 3 vols. (Boston: Porter Sargent Publishers, 1973).

3   See ibid.; *Civilian Resistance as a National Defense*, Adam Roberts, ed. (Harrisburg, Pennsylvania: Stackpole Books, 1968); Boserup and Mack, *War without Weapons*; Peter Ackerman and Jack DuVall, *A Force More Powerful* (New York: St. Martin's Press, 2000).

4   Joyce Marlow, *Captain Boycott and the Irish* (New York: Saturday Review Press/E.P. Dutton and Company, 1973), 136-42.

5   Carleton Mabee, *Black Freedom: The Nonviolent Abolitionists from 1830 through the Civil War* (New York: Macmillan, 1970), 115.

6   Fred Halliday, "Hidden from International Relations: Women and the International Arena," in Rebecca Grant and Kathleen Newland, ed., *Gender and International Relations* (Buckingham, UK: Open University Press, 1991), 162.

7   Geir Lundestad, personal communication (Oslo, Norway, December 9, 2002). "Not a single shot was fired," said Torkel Jansson, historian at Uppsala University, in Ivar Ekman, "Where Rejection Is Not a Dirty Word: Norway and Sweden Fête Century-Old Split," *International Herald Tribune* (June 7, 2005), 3.

8   Jacques Semelin, *Unarmed against Hitler: Civilian Resistance in Europe, 1939-1943*, trans. Suzan Husserl-Kapit (Westport, Connecticut: Praeger, 1993).

9   Hannah Arendt, *Eichmann in Jerusalem: A Report on the Banality of Evil* (New York: Viking Press, 1963), 175. See esp. pp. 171-175.

10   Ibid., 175.

11   Ronald M. McCarthy, "Resistance Politics and the Growth of Parallel Governments in America, 1765-1775," 482; and David J. Toscano, "Sullen Silence or Prelude to Resistance: Background to the Continental Association, 1771 to May 1774, 221, in *Resistance, Politics, and the American Struggle for Independence, 1765-1775*, ed. Walter H. Conser, Ronald M. McCarthy, David J. Toscano, Gene Sharp (Boulder, Colorado: Lynne Rienner Publishers, 1986), 482.

12   Walter H. Conser, "The Stamp Act of Resistance," in Conser et al., *Resistance, Politics, and the American Struggle for Independence*, 22, 28.

13   McCarthy, "Resistance Politics and the Growth of Parallel Governments," in ibid., 492.

14   See Conser et al., *Resistance, Politics, and the American Struggle for Independence*, 3-524.

15   April Carter, *Direct Action and Democracy Today* (Cambridge: Polity Press, 2005), 2.

16   Michael Randle, *Civil Resistance* (London: Fontana Press, 1994), 183.

17   Molly Moore, "Millions in France Protest Law, Leadership: Opposition to Labor Bill Widens into Protest of Government Deemed Out of Touch," *Washington Post*, April 5, 2006, A17.

18   Alan Sipress, "Thai Premier Abruptly Gives Up Power: A Day after Pledging to Resign within Weeks, Thaksin Turns Job over to Deputy," *Washington Post*, April 6, 2006, A23.

19   Sonya Geis and Michael Powell, "Hundreds of Thousands Rally in Cities Large and Small," *Washington Post*, April 11, 2006, A8-9.

20   Roland Bleiker, *Popular Dissent, Human Agency and Global Politics* (Cambridge: Cambridge University Press, 2000), 2.

21   Judith M. Brown, *Nehru* (London and New York: Longman, 1999), 35, 47.

22   Balram R. Nanda, fax to author (New Delhi, October 6, 1995).

23   Gene Sharp, "Nonviolence: Moral Principle or Political Technique? Clues from Gandhi's Thought and Experience," in *Gandhi as a Political Strategist, with Essays on Ethics and Politics* (Boston: Porter Sargent Publishers, 1979), 296, 297.

24   On the intellectual journey of Martin Luther King, Jr., see Mary King, "Standing Face to Face with Power: Martin Luther King and the American Civil Rights Movement," *Mahatma Gandhi and Martin Luther King, Jr: The Power of Nonviolent Action* (Paris: UNESCO, 1999; 2nd ed. New Delhi: Indian Council for Cultural Relations and Mehta Publishers, 2002), 85-172.

25   Martin Luther King, Jr., *Stride toward Freedom: The Montgomery Story* (New York: HarperSanFrancisco, 1958), 141; Glenn E. Smiley to John Swomley and Alfred Hassler, February 29, 1956, as cited in *The Papers of Martin Luther King, Jr.*, vol. 3: *Birth of a New Age, December 1955-December 1956*, ed. Clayborne Carson, Ralph E. Luker, Penny A. Russell, and Peter Holloran (Berkeley: University of California Press, 1997), 14 n. 60.

26   Bayard Rustin, interview with T. H. Baker, June 17, 1969, Lyndon Baines Johnson Library, Austin, Texas, as cited in *Birth of a New Age*, ibid.; idem, interview, in Howell Raines, ed., *My Soul Is Rested: Movement Days in the Deep South Remembered* (New York: G. P. Putnam's Sons, 1977), 53.

27   Kurt Schock, *Unarmed Insurrections: People Power Movements in Nondemocracies* (Minneapolis and London: University of Minnesota Press, 2005), 170, 171.

28   Pyarelal, *Mahatma Gandhi: The Early Phase* (Ahmedabad: Navajivan Publishing House, 1965) vol. 1, 5. Pyarelal's figures reflect the government estimate.

29   David Chainawa, "Southern Africa since 1945," in *General History of Africa*, vol. 8 *Africa since 1935*, ed. Ali Alamin Mazrui and C. Wondji (California: Heinemann/UNESCO, 1993), 260.

30   Bill Sutherland and Matt Meyer, *Guns and Gandhi in Africa: Pan African Insights on Nonviolence, Armed Struggle, and Liberation in Africa* (Trenton, New Jersey; and Asmara, Eritrea: Africa World Press, 2000), 152.

31   Walter Wink, *Violence and Nonviolence in South Africa: Jesus' Third Way* (Philadelphia: New Society Publishers, 1987), 4.

32   Ibid.

33   Ibid.

34   Adam Roberts, *Civil Resistance in the East European and Soviet Revolutions*, Monograph Series no. 4 (Cambridge, Massachusetts: Albert Einstein Institution, 1991) 5.

35   B. H. Liddell Hart, "Lessons from Resistance Movements—Guerrilla and Non-violent," in Roberts, *Civilian Resistance*, 205.

36   Mohandas K. Gandhi, "The Doctrine of the Sword," *Young India*, November 8, 1920, vol. 21, *Collected Works of Mahatma Gandhi* [hereafter CWMG], 100 vols., ed. K. Swaminathan (New Delhi: Ministry of Information and Broadcasting, Government of India, 1958-1984), 133, 134.

37   Richard Gregg, *The Power of Nonviolence*, 2nd ed., rev. (London: James Clarke and Company, 1960), 100.

38   David Hardiman, *Gandhi in His Time and Ours: The Global Legacy of His Ideas* (New York: Columbia University Press, 2003). See esp. 39-65.

39   Gene Sharp, "Origins of Gandhi's Use of Nonviolent Struggle: A Review–Essay on Erik Erikson's *Gandhi's Truth*," in *Gandhi as a Political Strategist*, 26.

40   Sudarshan Kapur, *Raising up a Prophet: The African-American Encounter with Gandhi* (Boston: Beacon Press, 1992).

41   Krishnalal Shridharani, *War without Violence* (New York: Harcourt Brace and Company, 1939, 1st ed.; expanded version paperback, Chowpatty, Bombay: Bharatiya Vidya Bhavan, 1962). Limited reprint edition available from Greenleaf Books, Arthur Harvey, 1197 Main Street, Hartford, Maine 04220.

42   See Robert L. Helvey, *On Strategic Nonviolent Conflict: Thinking about the Fundamentals* (Boston: Albert Einstein Institution, 2004), available on http://www.aeinstein.org/organizations/org/OSNC.pdf.

Chapter 3

1   Gershon Shafir, *Land, Labour and the Origins of the Israeli-Palestinian Conflict, 1882-1914* (Cambridge: Cambridge University Press, 1989), 148.

2 Neville J. Mandel, *The Arabs and Zionism before World War I* (Berkeley: University of California Press, 1976), 35-37.

3 David McDowall, *Palestine and Israel: The Uprising and Beyond* (Berkeley: University of California Press, 1989), 17.

4 Leonard Stein, *The Balfour Declaration*, repr. 1961 ed., London: Vallentine, Mitchell and Co. (Jerusalem: Magnes Press, Hebrew University, 1983), 92-94.

5 Shafir, *Land, Labour*, xi–xii, 82–82; Benny Morris, *Righteous Victims: A History of the Zionist-Arab Conflict, 1881-1991* (London: John Murray, 1999), 49.

6 The Turks retreated on the night of December 8, ending four centuries of Ottoman rule. Field Marshal Sir Archibald Percival Wavell, *The Palestine Campaigns*, 3rd ed. (London: Constable and Co., n.d., ca. 1935), 166; W. T. Massey, *How Jerusalem Was Won: Being the Record of Allenby's Campaign in Palestine* (London: Constable and Co., 1919), 202-3. Allenby's proclamation of martial law, telegraphed from London, was greeted by the city's notables without enthusiasm. George MacMunn and Cyril Falls, *Military Operations, Egypt and Palestine: From the Outbreak of War with Germany to June 1917 (History of the Great War)* (London: H. M. Stationery Office, 1928), Imperial War Museum Library, 260-61.

7 "Non-Jewish communities" then comprised 92 percent of the population. Richard P. Stevens, "Zionism as a Phase of Western Imperialism," in *The Transformation of Palestine: Essays on the Origin and Development of the Arab-Israeli Conflict*, ed. Ibrahim Abu-Lughod (Evanston: Northwestern University Press, 1971), 48.

8 Leonard Stein, *Balfour Declaration*, facsimile frontispiece.

9 W. T. Mallison Jr., "The Balfour Declaration: An Appraisal in International Law," in Abu-Lughod, *Transformation of Palestine*, 66-83.

10 Chaim Weizmann, *Trial and Error: The Autobiography of Chaim Weizmann* (New York: Harper and Brothers, 1949), 109-11; Blanche E. C. Dugdale, *Arthur James Balfour: First Earl of Balfour, K.G., O.M., F.R.S.*, vol. 1, *1848-1906* (London: Hutchinson and Co., 1936), 432-36; Ronald Storrs, *Orientations* (London: Nicholson and Watson, 1943), 343.

11 Norman Bentwich, *Palestine* (London: Ernest Benn Ltd., 1934), 66-68; Weizmann, *Trial and Error*, 43-47.

12 "The Basle Programme, August 30, 1897," *From Haven to Conquest: Readings in Zionism and the Palestine Problem until 1948*, ed. Walid Khalidi (Beirut: Institute for Palestine Studies, 1971), 89.

13 "Regardless of the diplomatic egg dance . . . around any mention of the word 'state,' there was no question in anybody's mind that this is what was eventually contemplated." Barbara W. Tuchman, *Bible and Sword: How the British Came to Palestine* (New York: Macmillan, 1984), 306, 346.

14 Nevill Barbour, *Nisi Dominus: A Survey of the Palestine Controversy* (Beirut: Institute for Palestine Studies, 1969; repr. 1946, London: George G. Harrap and Co.), 41-52; Alan R. Taylor, *Prelude to Israel: An Analysis of Zionist Diplomacy, 1897-1947* (Beirut: Institute for Palestine Studies, 1970), 7-8. Herzl's vision of *Eretz Israel* (Greater Israel), extended to the Euphrates. Idem, "Vision and Intent in Zionist Thought," in Abu-Lughod, *Transformation of Palestine*, 20.

15 Acquiescence by Jews in the prevailing fact of their separateness worked against the possibility for Arab-Jewish reconciliation in Palestine. Bernard Wasserstein, *The British in Palestine: The Mandatory Government and the Arab-Jewish Conflict, 1917-1929*, 1st ed. (London, Royal Historical Society, 1978), 4.

16 Barbour, *Nisi Dominus*, 50. See Oskar K. Rabinowicz, *Winston Churchill on Jewish Problems* (New York and London: Thomas Yoseloff, 1960), 46-50, 64-72, 78-80, 164-67, as reprinted in "The Aliens Bill and Jewish Immigration to Britain, 1902-1905," in Khalidi, *Haven to Conquest*, 97-114. Balfour, then prime minister, supported the 1905 bill. Stein, *Balfour Declaration*, 164. In 1914, Balfour told Weizmann that he shared some "anti-Semitic postulates." Ibid., 154, 163. "[A]nti-Semitism was an objective of considerable importance along with expressed concern for British national interests." Mallison Jr., "Balfour Declaration," 69.

17 British support for resettlement of the Jews in Palestine dates to the seventeenth century and was fully developed by the nineteenth century. British representations to the Ottoman Empire on behalf of Jews who wished to settle under Turkish rule rested on precedents established by Henry VIII and Queen Elizabeth I. Albert M. Hyamson, *Palestine under the Mandate, 1920-1948* (London: Methuen and Co., 1950), 1-12, 22.

18 David Gilmour, "The Unregarded Prophet: Lord Curzon and the Palestine Question," *Journal of Palestine Studies* 25, no. 3 (Spring 1996): 63.

19 In John Bowle, *Viscount Samuel: A Biography* (London: Victor Gallancz, 1957), 177.

20 Ann Mosely Lesch, *Arab Politics in Palestine, 1917-1939: The Frustration of a Nationalist Movement* (Ithaca, New York, and London: Cornell University Press, 1979), 41.

21 Wasserstein, *British in Palestine*, 1st ed., 7. See George Antonius, *The Arab Awakening: The Story of the Arab National Movement*, 1938 rev. ed. (London: Hamish Hamilton, 1945), 261-62, 396.

22 Stein, *Balfour Declaration*, 126.

23 Arnold J. Toynbee, Foreword, in Robert John and Sami Hadawi, *The Palestine Diary: 1914–1945* (New York: New World Press, 1970), xiii, xv; Balfour's letter was "a war measure," whose purpose was to enlist sympathy for the Allied side from powerful Jewish interests around the world, said a 1917 cabinet paper circulated by the Duke of Devonshire (Lord Victor Christian William Cavendish) upon becoming secretary of state for the colonies in 1923. Doreen Ingrams, *Palestine Papers, 1917-1922: Seeds of Conflict* (London: John Murray, 1972), 173. Real reasons, George Lenczowski says, were the leverage that American Jews could provide in producing maximum help from the United States in the war effort, and winning over German Jewry to the Allied cause, thereby "producing internal disaffection in the Central powers." George Lenczowski, *The Middle East in World Affairs*, 4th ed., London: Cornell University Press, 1980), 83.

24 John Marlowe, *The Seat of Pilate: An Account of the Palestine Mandate* (London: Cresset Press, 1959), 21, 28, 29.

25 Susan Lee Hattis, "The Bi-National Idea in Palestine during Mandatory Times" (Ph.D. diss., L'Université de Genéve, Institut Universitaire de Hautes Etudes Internationales, Geneva, 1970), 24-34.

26 David Omissi, "The Mediterranean and the Middle East in British Global Strategy, 1935-39," Michael J. Cohen and Martin Kolinsky, *Britain and the Middle East in the 1930s* (New York: St. Martin's Press, 1992), 15; Michael J. Cohen, "British Strategy in the Middle East in the Wake of the Abyssinian Crisis, 1936-39," in ibid., 23.

27 Antonius, *Arab Awakening*, 413-36. Also see Aaron S. Klieman, *Foundations of British Policy in the Arab World: The Cairo Conference of 1921* (Baltimore: Johns Hopkins University Press, 1970), 1-18. At least three contradictory pledges were embodied in the 1916 Sykes-Picot agreement, the correspondence of 1915-16 between Colonel Sir Henry McMahon, high commissioner for Egypt, and Hussein ibn Ali, sharif of Mecca, and Lord Balfour's letter to Lord Rothschild. Although Britain maintained its claim that Palestine (the excluded districts of McMahon's note) was not included in the McMahon-Hussein letters, Balfour's language conditioned Britain's help for a Jewish national home on not prejudicing the "civil and political rights of existing non-Jewish communities of Palestine."

28 Arthur James Balfour, "11 August 1919 Memorandum Respecting Syria, Palestine, and Mesopotamia," 132187/2117/44A, *Documents on British Foreign Policy 1919-1939*, ed. E. L. Woodward and Rohan Butler, vol. 4, 1919 (London: H. M. Stationery Office, 1952), 345. In memoirs, Sir Ronald Storrs, British governor of Jerusalem at the start of the mandate in 1920, notes Arab lack of access to British society: "Politically, all the Arabs in the world would not have turned at the Polls one single vote," whereas Jewry was prominent and influential at all levels of British society. Storrs, *Orientations*, 358-59.

29 Hattis, "Bi-National Idea in Palestine," 20; Neil Caplan, "The Yishuv, Sir Herbert Samuel, and the Arab Question," *Zionism and Arabism in Palestine and Israel*, ed. Elie Kedourie and Sylvia G. Haim (London: Frank Cass, 1982), 1.

30 Lenczowski, *Middle East in World Affairs*, 85. The Zionists "were allowed to communicate with each other . . . abroad, by sending telegrams through the Foreign Office, which transmitted them in code." Dugdale, *Arthur James Balfour*, vol. 2, *1906-1930*, 228.

31 *Great Britain and Palestine, 1915-1939*, Information Department Papers no. 20A, rev. ed. (London: Royal Institute of International Affairs, 1939), 22.

32 Rashid Khalidi, *Palestinian Identity: The Construction of Modern National Consciousness* (New York: Columbia University Press, 1997), 122-41, 141.

33 Bernard Wasserstein, in *British in Palestine*, 1st ed., notes them as follows: pp. 57 (first, Haifa), 60 (second, Damascus), 94-95 (third, Haifa), 106 (fourth, Jerusalem), 120 (fifth, Nablus), 125 (sixth, Jaffa). See also A. W. Kayyali, *Palestine: A Modern History* (London: Third World Centre for Research and Publishing, n.d., ca. 1971), 60, 88, 99, 113, 119. The second congress was not held. Muhammad Y. Muslih, *The Origins of Palestinian Nationalism* (New York: Columbia University Press, 1988), 204-5. The Palestinian Arabs held a series of large meetings to plan opposition to the Balfour Declaration.

34 Field Marshall Edmund Henry Hynman Allenby decided against making the declaration public, as he "had received no guidance from the British Government about their precise intentions regarding the implementation of the Balfour Declaration. In fact they had no precise intentions. As always, the initiative was left to the Zionist Organization." Marlowe, *Seat of Pilate*, 27-28. Bernard Wasserstein judges the Foreign Office had planned not to announce the declaration in Jerusalem, and, when it was published there, appears to have been "issued by mistake." Bernard Wasserstein, *The British in Palestine: The Mandatory Government and the Arab-Jewish Conflict, 1917-1929*, 2nd ed. (Oxford: Basil Blackwell

Ltd, 1991), 33. Chaim Weizmann, leader of world Zionism, persuaded Prime Minister Lloyd George to advise then colonial secretary Winston Churchill, "You mustn't give representative Government to Palestine." Richard Meinertzhagen, *Middle East Diary 1917-1956* (London: Cresset Press, 1959), 105.

35 Palin Report, or the Report of the Court of Inquiry convened by order of H. E. the High Commissioner and Commander-in-Chief, Dated the 12th Day of April 1920, Foreign Office (FO) 371/5121/E120/6.31, July 1, 1920, 56, 57.

36 Kayyali, *Palestine*, 75, 84. The outbreaks in Jerusalem caught the attention of the great powers, yet instead of causing a review of proposed policies, the process went forward to nominate Britain for the Mandate. Not until after the nomination was the Balfour policy formally divulged to the notable families of Nablus in April. Ibid., 84.

37 Yehoshua Porath, *The Emergence of the Palestinian-Arab National Movement*, vol. 1, *1918-29* (London: Frank Cass, 1974), 96.

38 Bentwich, *Palestine*, 93; Kayyali, *Palestine*, 76.

39 Palin Report, 62, 63-64. The Palin inquiry found "no evidence of any definite plan on the part of an organised body of rioters and the whole affair has the appearance of spontaneity" in ibid., 58; it uncovered "no preconceived intention to make an attack on the Jews" in ibid., 63.

40 Ibid., 75-76.

41 The declaration was ratified at the San Remo (Italy) Conference of Allied Powers, which awarded the mandate over Palestine to Great Britain. It was subsequently incorporated into the Treaty of Sévres on August 10, 1920, with Articles 22 and 95 making reference to the Balfour Declaration, and was superseded in July 1923 by the Treaty of Lausanne. The mandate (including the Balfour Declaration) was confirmed by the League of Nations on July 24, 1922. "League of Nations Mandate for Palestine," December 1922, Cmd. 1785 (London: H. M. Stationery Office).

42 Peel Commission Report, 50. Officially the Royal Commission of Enquiry, July 1937, *Palestine Royal Commission Report*, Cmd. 5479 (London: H. M. Stationery Office, 1937), still underlies scholarship of subsequent years. Similar opinions are more bluntly stated in the contemporaneous Palin Report, which concludes the "impatience" and "indiscretion" of "official Zionists" were largely responsible for the crisis in 1920. Palin Report, 80-81.

43 Weizmann, *Trial and Error*, 255-57.

44 Debate persists on the role of Amin. Biographer Zvi Elpeleg says he "roused the marchers and turned the celebration into a violent demonstration." Zvi Elpeleg, *The Grand Mufti: Haj Amin al-Husaini, Founder of the Palestinian National Movement*, trans. David Harvey, ed. Shmuel Himelstein (London: Frank Cass, 1993), 6. Revisionist biographer Philip Mattar rejects an interpretation of Haj Amin as a fomenter. Relying chiefly on the Palin Report, Mattar claims that while the speakers were still beyond the city walls on April 4, 1920, a spontaneous disturbance began in the Jewish quarter of the Old City. Philip Mattar, *The Mufti of Jerusalem: Al-Hajj Amin al-Husayni and the Palestinian National Movement* (New York: Columbia University Press, 1988), 17. The Palin Report notes, "We are faced with a native population thoroughly exasperated by a sense of injustice and disappointed hopes, panic stricken as to their future," in ibid., 78.

45 Elpeleg, *Grand Mufti*, 7-10.

46 Wasserstein, *British in Palestine*, 2nd ed., 132.

47 Elpeleg, *Grand Mufti*, 10-11; Mattar, *Mufti of Jerusalem*, 26.

48 See Sharp, *Methods of Nonviolent Action*, vol. 2, *The Politics of Nonviolent Action*, 117-25, 130; idem, *Waging Nonviolent Struggle*, 51-54.

49 For example, see Elpeleg, *Grand Mufti*, 43, 85-93.

50 Wasserstein, *British in Palestine*, 1st ed., 80; *Handbook of Palestine and Trans-Jordan*, ed. Harry Charles Luke and Edward Keith-Roach, 2nd ed. (London: Macmillan and Co., 1930), 34.

51 Kayyali, *Palestine*, 86.

52 May Seikaly, *Haifa: Transformation of a Palestinian Arab Society, 1918-1939* (London: I. B. Taurus and Co., 1995), 163-64.

53 Yehoshua Porath, "The Political Organization of the Palestinian Arabs under the British Mandate," in *Palestinian Arab Politics*, ed. Moshe Maoz (Jerusalem: Harry S. Truman Research Institute, Hebrew University, 1975), 10.

54 Caplan, "Yishuv, Sir Herbert Samuel, and the Arab Question," in Kedourie and Haim, *Zionism and Arabism*, 5, 6.

55 Kayyali, *Palestine*, 89.

56 Klieman, *Foundations of British Policy*, 127-28; Caplan, "Yishuv, Sir Herbert Samuel, and the Arab Question," 6; Lesch, *Arab Politics in Palestine*, 158-59.

57 Appendix C, Churchill's Reply to the Palestine Arab Deputation, Klieman, *Foundations of British Policy*, 270. "It has been the armies of Britain which have liberated these regions," Churchill writes. Ibid.

58 Caplan, "Yishuv, Sir Herbert Samuel, and the Arab Question," 8, 9; Peel Commission Report, 259.

59 Overall immigration of Russian Jews fleeing pogroms averaged two thousand a year from 1880 until World War I. Bentwich, *Palestine*, 66.

60 W. Basil Worsfold, *Palestine of the Mandate* (London: T. Fisher Unwin Ltd., 1925), 14-15; Lesch, *Arab Politics in Palestine*, 204-5.

61 Peel Commission Report, 51; Caplan, "Yishuv, Sir Herbert Samuel, and the Arab Question," 9.

62 Klieman, *Foundations of British Policy*, 174; Peel Commission Report, 51.

63 Comment of Dr. Montague David Eder, psychoanalyst and head of the political department of the Zionist Organization (after 1927, the Jewish Agency), also president of the Zionist Federation of Great Britain and Ireland, 1931-36. Testifying before the commission of inquiry investigating the Jaffa riots of 1921, over which Chief Justice Sir Thomas Haycraft presided, Eder spoke as Acting Chairman of the Zionist Commission and was regarded as representing the "official Zionist creed." Colonial Office (CO), "Palestine. Disturbances in May, 1921: Reports of the Commissioners of Inquiry [Haycraft Commission Report] with Correspondence Relating Thereto," 1921, Cmd. 1540 (London: H. M. Stationery Office), 57. In the Haycraft Report, Eder "was quite clear that the Jews should, and the Arabs should not, have the right to bear arms, and he stated his belief that this discrimination would tend to improve Arab-Jewish relations." Ibid.

64 Seikaly, *Haifa*, 2, 81-97, 173, 180 nn. 64, 65.

65 Worsfold, *Palestine of the Mandate*, 19; Lesch, *Arab Politics in Palestine*, 159-60.

66 Peel Commission Report, 32.

67 Bernard Wasserstein, "Herbert Samuel and the Palestine Problem," *English Historical Review* 91, no. 361 (October 1976): 770. The "Statement of British Policy in Palestine," presented to the Zionist Organization and the Palestine Arab Delegation in London, was later called "Churchill's White Paper." It read, in part, "Unauthorized statements have been made to the effect that the purpose in view is to create a wholly Jewish Palestine. Phrases have been used such as 'Palestine is to become as Jewish as England is English.' His Majesty's Government regard any such expectation as impracticable and have no such aim in view. . . . [T]he terms of the [Balfour] Declaration referred to do not contemplate that Palestine as a whole should be converted into a Jewish National Home, but that such a Home should be founded *in Palestine*." CO "Correspondence with the Palestinian Arab Delegation and the Zionist Organisation" (Churchill White Paper), June 3, 1922, Cmd. 1700 (London: H. M. Stationery Office), as reprinted in appendix 3, *Great Britain and Palestine, 1915-1939*, Information Department Papers no. 20A, rev. ed. (London: Royal Institute of International Affairs, 1939), 123.

68 "League of Nations Mandate for Palestine," December 1922, Cmd. 1785 (London: H. M. Stationery Office). See Peel Commission, 30-32. Twenty years after the issuance of the Balfour Declaration, in 1937 the commission would grant that little had been known about the indigenous population and admit the opposition of its leaders. Peel Commission Report, 32.

69 Martin Kramer, *Islam Assembled: The Advent of the Muslim Congresses* (New York: Columbia University Press, 1986), 83.

70 Naval Intelligence Division, *Palestine and Transjordan*, Geographical Handbook Series, B. R. 514 (Oxford: Oxford University Press, 1943): 171-72.

71 Nels Johnson, *Islam and the Politics of Meaning in Palestinian Nationalism* (London, Boston, and Melbourne: Kegan Paul International, 1982), 24.

72 Monthly Political Report, June 1922, Wyndham Deedes (the first secretary of the civil service, chosen by Samuel) to Churchill, July 7, 1922, in Kayyali, *Palestine*, 113, 128 n. 116.

73 Sharp, *Methods of Nonviolent Action*, 285-356; idem, *Waging Nonviolent Struggle*, 54-61.

74 Porath, *Emergence of the Palestinian-Arab National Movement*, 144-58. The Arabs "still hoped to make a stand against the Balfour Declaration, and [feared] that by accepting the Assembly they would have recognized its legality, which they had always contested. They also feared the preponderating influence of the Jews in a mixed assembly." Mrs. Stewart Erskine, *Palestine of the Arabs* (London: George G. Harrap and Co., 1935), 78.

75 Caplan, "Yishuv, Sir Herbert Samuel, and the Arab Question," 37.

76 "Papers Relating to the Elections for the Palestine Legislative Council 1923," June 1923, Cmd. 1889 (London: H. M. Stationery Office), 9.

77 Wasserstein, "Herbert Samuel and the Palestine Problem," 771.

78 The elections were invalidated in London, on May 4, 1923; ibid.

79 Kayyali, *Palestine*, 117, 119. Successful use of withholding taxes as a nonviolent sanction by the Palestinians would not occur until the first intifada, in the village of Beit Sahour (chapter 9).

80 P. H. H. Massy, *Eastern Mediterranean Lands: Twenty Years of Life, Sport, and Travel* (London: George Routledge and Son, 1928), 70.

81 Philip Jones, *Britain and Palestine 1914-1948: Archival Sources for the History of the British Mandate* (London: Oxford University Press, 1979), 40; Dugdale, *Arthur James Balfour*, vol. 2, *1906-1930*, 1936), 365.

82 Porath, "Political Organization of the Palestinian Arabs," 12. See Philip Graves, "The Palestine Arabs and their Grievances," *Palestine: Land of Three Faiths* (London: Jonathan Cape, 1923), 99-119.

83 Wasserstein, *British in Palestine*, 2nd ed., 226.

84 Porath, *Emergence of the Palestinian-Arab National Movement*, 258-273. Wasserstein views the failure of British authorities here as indicative of their incapacity to solve the problem of Palestine. Wasserstein, *British in Palestine*, 1st ed., 226.

85 A Brief Guide to al-Haram al-Sharif (Jerusalem: Supreme Moslem Council, Moslem Orphanage Press, 1930), 3.

86 Sami Hadawi, *Palestinian Rights and Losses in 1948: A Comprehensive Study* (London: Saqi Books, 1988), 37.

87 Wasserstein, *British in Palestine*, 2nd ed., 227 n. 27. The *waqf* was west of the wall and not part of the Haram al-Sharif. Ibid., n. 31.

88 Peel Commission Report, 67; Mattar, *Mufti of Jerusalem*, 39; Elpeleg, *Grand Mufti*, 20.

89 CO, "Statement of Policy . . . (Wailing Wall)," November 19, 1928, Cmd. 3229 (London: H. M. Stationery Office).

90 Elpeleg, *Grand Mufti*, 18-20.

91 Lesch, *Arab Politics in Palestine*, 209.

92 Kayyali, *Palestine*, 142.

93 Ibid., 143.

94 To Jews, Safed was one of four "holy cities," the others being Jerusalem, Hebron, and Tiberias. Home to some of the oldest continuous Jewish communities of record, Safed reached its pinnacle in the sixteenth century, yet centuries later was still renowned for "learning and piety." Isabel Burton, *The Inner Life of Syria, Palestine, and the Holy Land: From My Private Journal* (London: C. Kegan Paul and Co., 1879), 508-9.

95 Elpeleg, *Grand Mufti*, 21, 22.

96 Weizmann, *Trial and Error*, 335; Kayyali, *Palestine*, 145.

97 On July 2, 1919, such sentiment was expressed in one of the first Arab issuances on record expressing opposition to Jewish immigration to Palestine. While the memorandum calls Zionist migration "a grave peril," the next sentence reads, "Our Jewish compatriots shall enjoy our common rights and assume the common responsibilities." "Memorandum Presented to the King-Crane Commission by the General Syrian Congress," in *The Israel-Arab Reader: A Documentary History of the Middle East Conflict*, ed. Walter Laqueur, 3rd ed. (New York: Bantam Books, 1976), 33.

98 Cited in Peel Commission Report, 68. Although condemnatory of the mandatory government, the term "non-Jewish communities" was still used for the Palestinian Arabs in its recommendations. The Shaw Report, viewed by some as anti-Zionist, publicly aired the issue of Arab landlessness. Kenneth W. Stein, *The Land Question in Palestine, 1917-1939* (Chapel Hill: University of North Carolina Press, 1984), 88-89. The Shaw Commission concluded that the violence of August 23 was spontaneous and not organized; it did not blame Haj Amin. Parliamentary Papers, *Report of the Commission on Palestine Disturbances of August, 1929*, March 1930, Cmd. 3530 (London: H. M. Stationery Office), 78.

99 Sir John Hope Simpson, "Palestine: Report on Immigration, Land Settlement and Development," London, 1930, Cmd. 3686, 131-36, in Peel Commission Report, 72.

100 CO, "Palestine: Statement of Policy by His Majesty's Government in the United Kingdom, Presented by the Secretary of State for the Colonies to Parliament by Command of His Majesty" (Passfield White Paper), October 1930, Cmd. 3692 (London: H. M. Stationery Office), 14.

101 Storrs, *Orientations*, 373, 374. In 1921 Jews comprised 11 percent of the population, and held 25 percent of the administration of the government; by 1929 they constituted 19 percent of the populace, but held 23 percent of administration positions, termed by Wasserstein "*over*-representation" of Jews in the administration. Wasserstein, *British in Palestine*, 2nd ed., 219.

102 Found in Laqueur, *Israel-Arab Reader*, 50-56.

103 By 1919, the activities of a Jewish self-defense group had become visible. Called the Haganah and formed by Zionist revisionist leader Lieutenant Vladimir Yevgenievich Jabotinsky, it was able to

obtain firearms, possibly with the military government's knowledge. Seikaly, *Haifa*, 173. Jabotinsky's Jewish self-defense groups had firearms prior to May 1920. Bentwich, *Palestine*, 93. During the 1930s, the buildup of Jewish armed groups increased. CO, "Palestine: Statement of Information Relating to Acts of Violence," regarding the Haganah, Palmach, Irgun Zvai Leumi, and Stern Group (Gang); "movements of sabotage and violence under the guise of the 'Jewish Resistance Movement,'" July 1946, Cmd. 6873 (London: H. M. Stationery Office).

104 Shai Lachman, "Arab Rebellion and Terrorism in Palestine, 1929-39: The Case of Sheikh Izz al-Din al-Qassam and His Movement," in Kedourie and Haim, *Zionism and Arabism*, 53.

105 Porath, "Political Organization of the Palestinian Arabs," 15-16.

106 Elpeleg, *Grand Mufti*, 30, 31; Kayyali, *Palestine*, 165.

107 The conference was held on July 31 and September 20, 1931. *Al-Jamia al-Arabiyya* (the Arab League), August 2 and September 23, 1931; Central Zionist Archives, S 25/4108; Civil Investigation Department (CID), Daily Intelligence Summary no. 221, September 21, 1931; "Nablus Congress of 20th September, 1931," FO 371/15333, in Lachman, "Arab Rebellion and Terrorism," 52, 56.

108 Lachman, "Arab Rebellion and Terrorism," 57.

109 Kayyali, *Palestine*, 164.

110 Joseph Nevo, "Palestinian-Arab Violent Activity during the 1930s," in Cohen and Kolinsky, *Britain and the Middle East in the 1930s*, 169-71.

111 Elpeleg, *Grand Mufti*, 30. Former Israeli military colonel, Zvi Elpeleg is a senior researcher at the Dayan Center, Tel Aviv University.

112 Lachman, "Arab Rebellion and Terrorism," 54.

113 Peel Commission Report, 87; Lachman, "Arab Rebellion and Terrorism," 52-53.

114 Seikaly, *Haifa*, 226.

115 Lachman, "Arab Rebellion and Terrorism," 53.

116 Peel Commission Report, 81.

117 Porath, "Political Organization of the Palestinian Arabs," 16-17.

118 Lachman, "Arab Rebellion and Terrorism," 54.

119 Kayyali, *Palestine*, 169.

120 Peel Commission Report, 83.

121 Resolutions enclosed in a dispatch from the chief secretary, April 1, 1933, CO 733/239/17356/4, part 1, in Lesch, *Arab Politics in Palestine*, 192 n. 40.

122 Elpeleg, *Grand Mufti*, 31-32; Kayyali, *Palestine*, 169-70.

123 Elpeleg, ibid., 32.

124 Bentwich, *Palestine*, 10, 11.

125 Kayyali, *Palestine*, 171.

126 Peel Commission Report, 79, 82, 279.

127 Elpeleg, *Grand Mufti*, 36. Eight hundred illegal Jewish émigrés were arriving each month, smuggled by sea or eluding police on frontiers, "infuriating the Arabs for very few of the illegal immigrants ever get deported. . . . [Hence] Arabs have been organizing what are practically private armies, patrols, to watch the coast. . . . The Jews have of course replied to that by starting their own patrols to prevent this and to help the Jews who are trying to enter the country." Letter of September 2, 1934, Thomas Hodgkin, *Letters from Palestine, 1932-36*, ed. E. C. Hodgkin (London: Quartet Books, 1986), 86-87.

128 Martin Kolinsky, "The Collapse and Restoration of Public Security," in Cohen and Kolinsky, *Britain and the Middle East in the 1930s*, 147; Peel Commission Report, 279.

129 Elizabeth Monroe, *Britain's Moment in the Middle East, 1914-1956* (London: Chatto and Windus, 1963), 86.

130 Mattar, *Mufti of Jerusalem*, 64.

131 Peel Commission Report, 84.

132 Kayyali, *Palestine*, 173.

133 Ibid.

134 Peel Commission Report, 84.

135 What had been considered the inadequacy of police and troops to put down the uprisings of 1929 had, by 1933, been altered by police reorganization and creation of a permanent garrison composed of two infantry battalions. Kolinsky, "Collapse and Restoration," in Cohen and Kolinsky, *Britain and the Middle East in the 1930s*, 148. Regular battalions in World War I were comprised of one thousand soldiers. Denis Winter, *Death's Men: Soldiers of the Great War* (London: Allen Lane, 1979), 53.

136 Lachman, "Arab Rebellion and Terrorism," 54; Elpeleg, *Grand Mufti*, 40.

137 Storrs, *Orientations*, 374.

138 Lachman, "Arab Rebellion and Terrorism," 55.

139 Kayyali, *Palestine*, 70-72, cites Haganah archives, 83 n. 112.

140 Seikaly, *Haifa*, 163.

141 The Arabic name is not on record, but a branch in Nablus was known as al-Jamiyya al-Rahiba (the Fearful Society), said to have been started by Hilmi Fityani. District Commandant of Police-Samaria to Director of Public Security, CID, July 29, 1922 (ISA 2/166 Pol 12), in eadem, *Haifa*, 163, 177 n. 16.

142 Lachman, "Arab Rebellion and Terrorism," 56.

143 Nevo, "Palestinian-Arab Violent Activity," 171.

144 Seikaly, *Haifa*, 242.

145 Yehoshua Porath, *The Palestinian Arab National Movement: From Riots to Rebellion*, vol. 2, 1929-39 (London: Frank Cass, 1977), 133.

146 *Al-Manar* 17, no. 9 (1914): 707-8, as cited in Mandel, *Arabs and Zionism before World War I*, 214, 48-49. Rida's emphasis on action rather than words may have influenced Qassam.

147 Issa Khalaf, "The Effect of Socioeconomic Change on Arab Societal Collapse in Mandate Palestine," *International Journal of Middle East Studies* 29, no. 1 (February 1997): 95. Rashid Khalidi suggests Zionist settlers of the first *aliya* (going up) to Israel from other lands treated the Palestinian peasants as had former Arab or Turkish landlords—disappropriating their land, but not displacing them. With the second *aliya*, early in the twentieth century, the doctrine of the conquest of labor introduced more exclusive colonization, and Zionists took over not only technical ownership of the land, but its cultivation. Rashid Khalidi, "Palestinian Peasant Resistance to Zionism before World War I," *Blaming the Victims: Spurious Scholarship and the Palestinian Question*, ed. Edward W. Said and Christopher Hitchens (London: Verso, 1988), 215.

148 Kayyali, *Palestine*, 178-9; Johnson, *Islam*, 34.

149 Seikaly, *Haifa*, 240-41.

150 Johnson, *Islam*, 40.

151 Ibid.; Lachman, "Arab Rebellion and Terrorism," 59-78; Kayyali, *Palestine*, 180.

152 "Palestine Arab Nationalist Movement," 33.

153 Lachman, "Arab Rebellion and Terrorism," 80. "New" Israeli historian Ilan Pappé calls these cadres Haj Amin's "own private army" of a few hundred. Ilan Pappé, *The Making of the Arab-Israeli Conflict, 1947-51* (London: I. B. Taurus and Co., Ltd., 1994), 65.

154 Lachman, "Arab Rebellion and Terrorism," 77-78; Nevo, "Palestinian-Arab Violent Activity," 173.

155 Guerrilla activity was spawned in three centers—the Hebron-Jerusalem-Ramallah area, the Nablus-Tulkarem-Qalqilya region, and Haifa along with lower Galilee. Nevo, "Palestinian-Arab Violent Activity," 171.

156 Kayyali, *Palestine*, 183; Johnson, *Islam*, 42; Nevo, "Palestinian-Arab Violent Activity," 175.

157 Nevo, "Palestinian-Arab Violent Activity," 172.

158 Elpeleg, *Grand Mufti*, 38. Mattar concludes Haj Amin did not lead one single act of violence between 1920 and 1936, and judges that the political violence of 1920, 1921, 1929, and 1933 did not constitute revolts, but "localized spontaneous riots." Mattar, *Mufti of Jerusalem*, 149.

159 Johnson, *Islam*, 56-58.

160 Ibid., 44.

161 Ibid.

162 Ibid., 45. Qassam's death "electrified" the Palestinians. S. Abdullah Schleifer, "The Life and Thought of Izz-id-Din al Qassam," *Islamic Quarterly* 23, no. 2 (Second Quarter 1979): 61. In 1935, "the Zionists still continue[d] to speak of Palestine as a deserted, neglected, derelict land." Erskine, *Palestine of the Arabs*, 74.

163 The six main Arab organizations in 1934, "largely concerned with mutual jealousies and recriminations," had, by 1935, melded into five "parties" and united themselves to address the mandatory government—the exception being the Istiqlal party. Peel Commission Report, 87. The National Defense party came into being in December 1934, and was headed by Ragheb Nashashibi. The Palestine Arab party emerged in April 1935, led by Jamal al-Husseini; in May, the Arab Youth Congress was formed. Two other parties had been in existence since 1933: the Reform party (Islah), led by the Khalidis, and the National Bloc, guided by Abdul Latif Salah. Kayyali says, "The personal and selfish motives behind the proliferation of Arab parties were apparent to all Palestinians, and the ceaseless bickering between these parties exposed them to public derision." Kayyali, *Palestine*, 178.

164 High commissioner to colonial secretary, secret, 7.12.1935, CO 733/278/75156, part 2; CID report, 30.10.1935, FO 371/18957, in Lachman, "Arab Rebellion and Terrorism," 73. Lachman says this meeting was the first time the five parties succeeded in putting aside their chronic differences to form a united position on a major issue. They called themselves the United Front.

165 CO, "Proposed New Constitution for Palestine," March 1936, Cmd. 5119 (London: H. M. Stationery Office).

166 Lesch, "Palestine Arab Nationalist Movement," 34.

167 Ziad Abu-Amr, *Islamic Fundamentalism and the West Bank and Gaza: Muslim Brotherhood and Islamic Jihad* (Bloomington: Indiana University Press, 1994), 98; Nevo, "Palestinian-Arab Violent Activity," 173, 186-87 n. 17.

168 Barbara Kalkas, "The Revolt of 1936: A Chronicle of Events," in Abu-Lughod, *Transformation of Palestine*, 238-41. To Kalkas, had recommendations of previous commissions of inquiry been followed, with their limits on immigration, regulation of land sales, and establishment of a government, the strike would probably not have taken place. Had authorities concurred with the recommendation concerning immigration, the Arab Higher Committee would likely have begun negotiations. See esp. pp. 254-45. Besides specific provocations, the main cause of the Arab rebellion was its "chief and simplest cause"—the arithmetic of Jewish immigration. Monroe, *Britain's Moment in the Middle East*, 86. Nels Johnson holds that the start of the revolt was Qassam's death. Johnson, *Islam*, 53.

169 Peel Commission Report, 96.

170 Kalkas, "Revolt of 1936," 244.

171 Johnson, *Islam*, 47; Elpeleg, *Grand Mufti*, 42.

172 Peel Commission Report, 97; Kolinsky, "Collapse and Restoration," 148.

173 Correspondence of Sir Arthur Wauchope, to J. H. Thomas, April 24, 1936, CO 733/310, 3, as cited in Kayyali, *Palestine*, 190, 224 n. 11. Colonial secretary in Stanley Baldwin's government, Thomas proposed yet another new constitution for Palestine on March 12, 1936.

174 *Falastin*, April 27, 1936, in Kayyali, *Palestine*, 190, 224 n. 5. Half a century later, the popular committees of the first intifada would come into being with similar alacrity.

175 Kalkas, "Revolt of 1936," 242, 246.

176 *Falastin*, May 9, 1936, in Kayyali, *Palestine*, 192, 224 n. 19. Palestinian writer Ghassan Kanafani says one hundred fifty of the "feudal-religious leaderships, the urban commercial bourgeoisie and a limited number of intellectuals" attended this meeting in Jerusalem. Ghassan Kanafani, *The 1936-39 Revolt in Palestine* (Washington, D.C.: Committee for Democratic Palestine, n.d. [ca. 1978]), 19-20. Kanafani's class-based analysis does not differentiate between "civil disobedience and armed insurrection."

177 Kalkas, "Revolt of 1936," 248.

178 Peel Commission Report, 97.

179 Kayyali, *Palestine*, 191-92.

180 Hodgkin, *Letters from Palestine*, 197.

181 Kayyali, *Palestine*, 192. Approximately 65 percent of the Palestinian population were agriculturists, who lived in 500 Palestinian villages in historic Palestine. Edward W. Said, et al., "A Profile of the Palestinian People," in Said and Hitchens, *Blaming the Victims*, 236.

182 Elpeleg, *Grand Mufti*, 42.

183 Lesch, "Palestine Arab Nationalist Movement," 34; Kalkas, "Revolt of 1936," 248.

184 Peasants participated minimally. Their losses would have been extreme if they had failed to harvest the spring crops; they were given the right to sell produce during specific morning hours. Porath, *Palestinian Arab National Movement*, 168.

185 Peel Commission Report, 98.

186 A division includes three brigades, each comprised of four battalions. Kolinsky, "Collapse and Restoration," 149, 164 n. 10. Among regular units in World War I, a division under a major-general had approximately 12,000 soldiers, a brigade 4,000, and a battalion, as noted, 1,000. Winter, *Death's Men*, 53. In Palestine, however, the units were not regular.

187 This six-month quota of 4,500—each certificate issued to the Jewish Agency or governmental immigration department permitting a married man to be accompanied by an entire family—was a significant increase over the 3,250 certificates for the preceding six months. Kalkas, "Revolt of 1936," 254.

188 Kayyali, *Palestine*, 193.

189 Johnson, *Islam*, 48.

190 Kalkas, "Revolt of 1936," 248-49.

191 Philip Grant, "Nonviolent Political Struggle in the Occupied Territories," *Arab Nonviolent Struggle in the Middle East*, ed. Ralph E. Crow, Philip Grant, and Saad E. Ibrahim (Boulder: Lynne Rienner Publishers, Inc., 1990), 46.

192 Kalkas, "Revolt of 1936," 249.

193 "Immediately any act of sabotage occurred, such as mines on the road or a railway derailment, the Striking Force of the Battalion was at once sent out and, before any warning could be given, surrounded the village. . . . The Commanding Officer then entered the village and selected the houses to be blown up. . . . When . . . the villagers themselves had been collected at a place of safety, the necessary explosives were placed in position and the demolition carried out. . . . [At Bala] six demolitions were carried out on one afternoon as a punishment." *Second Battalion, Lincolnshire Regiment, on Special Service in Malta and Palestine, 19 September 1935-20 December 1936*, diary (London: n.p., 1937), Imperial War Museum Library, 20.

194 Kalkas, "Revolt of 1936," 249-50. *Parliamentary Debates (Commons)*, 5th ser., vol. 313 (June 19, 1936), col. 1320, as cited in ibid., 250.

195 Matiel E. T. Mogannam, *The Arab Woman and the Palestine Problem* (London: Herbert Joseph Ltd., 1937), 305.

196 Elpeleg, *Grand Mufti*, 43, 44.

197 Lachman, "Arab Rebellion and Terrorism," 78. "Armed bands which a fortnight previously consisted of 15-20 men were now encountered in large parties of 50-70. The bands were not out for loot. They were fighting for what they believed to be a patriotic war in defence of their country against injustice and the threat of Jewish domination." Sir Vice Marshal Peirse to Air Ministry, October 15, 1936, CO 733/317, 15, in Kayyali, *Palestine*, 196-97, 224 n. 10.

198 Peel Commission Report, 98.

199 Porath, *Palestinian Arab National Movement*, 180; Kalkas, "Revolt of 1936," 252-53. House demolitions in large numbers were instituted under Ormsby-Gore to suppress the revolt. Issa Sifri, *Arab Palestine under the Mandate and Zionism*, vol. 2 (Jaffa: New Palestine Bookshop, 1937), 10, as cited in Kanafani, *1936-39 Revolt*, 21. On August 24, 1938, after an assistant district commissioner was assassinated, a battalion reported, "It has been decided to blow up 400 houses in Jenin. The demolition started this morning and will continue for 4 days. The Navy are assisting with depth charges." *First Battalion Irish Guards, Palestine, July 10th to October 1st 1938*, diary (London: n.p., 1938), Imperial War Museum Library, 12.

200 Kayyali, *Palestine*, 196, 224 n. 33.

201 *Haaretz*, June 15, 1936, as cited in Porath, *Palestinian Arab National Movement*, 180, 347 n. 142.

202 Porath, *Palestinian Arab National Movement*, 175-76.

203 "Letter from Haifa," April 23, 1936, Hodgkin, *Letters from Palestine*, 160-61.

204 *Filastin* (Jaffa), July 27, 1936, as cited in Elpeleg, *Grand Mufti*, 47.

205 Kolinsky, "Collapse and Restoration," 152. Some 30,000 soldiers were in Palestine by 1936. Christopher Sykes, *Orde Wingate* (London: Collins, 1959), 107. Marcel Roubiçek studied tombstones in the Ramleh Military Cemetery and suggests 20,000 soldiers may have been involved between 1936 and 1939 in infantry battalions, RAF squadrons, cavalry regiments, a company of light tanks, one horse artillery battery, two companies of engineers, signal detachments, and armored car companies, in addition to navy personnel. Marcel Roubiçek, *Echo of the Bugle: Extinct Military and Constabulary Forces in Palestine and Transjordan, 1915-1967* (Jerusalem: Franciscan Printing Press, n.d., ca. 1974), 30-33.

206 Zachary Lockman, *Comrades and Enemies: Arabs and Jewish Workers in Palestine, 1906-1948* (Berkeley: University of California Press, 1996), 241.

207 Aaron S. Klieman, "The Arab States and Palestine," *Zionism and Arabism*, 119; Pappé, *Making of the Arab-Israeli Conflict*, 60-61; Porath, *Palestinian Arab National Movement*, 199-216.

208 Porath, *Palestinian Arab National Movement*, 212.

209 Elpeleg, *Grand Mufti*, 47.

210 Peel Commission Report, ix, x.

211 Kolinsky, "Collapse and Restoration," 153.

212 Porath cites Subhi Yasin's calculation that the rebels at their peak numbered between 9,000 and 10,000, including 3,000 full-time "members," 1,000 urban rebels, and 6,000 villagers available as needed. Subhi Yasin, *al-Thawrah al-Arabiyyah al-Kubra fi Filastin, 1936-1939* [Great Arab Revolt in Palestine, 1936-1939] (Cairo: Dar al-Hana,1959), 42, as cited in Porath, *Palestinian Arab National Movement*, 247, 367 n. 117.

213 "[T]he Palestine Arabs had obviously gained nothing by peaceful methods," Hodgkin wrote in July 1936, noting that they were also moved toward violence by London's parliamentary debates on the

legislative council proposals: "In these debates, which were fully reported in the Arabic press and closely followed by the Arab public, die-hard imperialist and labour pro-Zionists united to condemn any movement in the direction of giving any measure of independence to the irresponsible Arabs. The subsequent offer of an Arab delegation to London was regarded by many as the Government's first step in a planned graceful retreat from its legislative council proposals." Hodgkin, *Letters from Palestine*, 195-96.

214 Nasser Eddin Nashashibi, *Jerusalem's Other Voice: Ragheb Nashashibi and Moderation in Palestinian Politics, 1920-1949* (Exeter: Ithaca Press, 1990), 98.

215 Andrews was considered the ablest of the Palestine Service, spoke Arabic and Hebrew, and was the seniormost British official slain in Palestine. Sykes, *Wingate*, 136; Lesch, *Arab Politics in Palestine*, 221. The Arabs believed that he was expediting the transfer of Galilee to the Jewish state, as called for in the partition plan. Barbour, *Nisi Dominus*, 188-89.

216 The partition plan of the Peel Commission would have joined the Arab portion of Palestine with Transjordan, placing it under the rule of Abdullah, to which the Mufti was opposed. Hoping to induce abandonment of partition, Haj Amin organized a congress at Bludan, a Syrian summer resort, to rally other Arabs in the predicament in Palestine. On September 8-10, 1937, 411 delegates, 128 of them Palestinian, met. Elie Kedourie, "The Bludan Conference on Palestine, September 1937," *Middle East Studies*, 17, no. 1 (January 1981): 107-25.

217 Elpeleg, *Grand Mufti*, 48-49.

218 Porath, *Palestinian Arab National Movement*, 183. The Qassamites did not have criminal records prior to the revolt and earned reputations as "devout and righteous fighters." Ibid.

219 Ibid., 249.

220 "[I]n imitation of the [British] Military Courts, the rebel leaders set up summary 'Courts' of their own, before which informers and 'traitors' were tried, and, if convicted, punished or reprimanded." John Marlowe, *Rebellion in Palestine* (London: Cresset Press, 1946), 191.

221 CO, "Policy in Palestine: Despatch Dated 23 December, 1937, from the Secretary of State for the Colonies to the High Commissioner for Palestine," W. Ormsby-Gore, January 1938, Cmd. 5634 (London: H. M. Stationery Office).

222 Papers of Sir Charles Tegart, box 2, file 3, Centre of Middle Eastern Studies, St. Antony's College, Oxford, as cited in Kolinsky, "Collapse and Restoration," 155. During 1938, a district commissioner notes, there were 5,700 cases of major crime; 430 assassinations in which 77 British, 255 Jews, and 500 Palestinian Arabs died; and encounters in which between 2,000 and 3,000 members of Arab armed bands were killed or wounded by the military. A thousand attacks were made on police and military, Jewish settlements were attacked 600 times, telephone lines sabotaged on 700 occasions, and roads and railways interrupted 340 times. Edward Keith-Roach, *Pasha of Jerusalem: Memoirs of a District Commissioner under the British Mandate*, ed. Paul Eedle (London: Radcliffe Press, 1994), 192-93.

223 Baruch Kimmerling and Joel S. Migdal, *Palestinians: Making of a People* (Cambridge, Massachusetts: Harvard University Press, 1994), 116.

224 Nashashibi, *Jerusalem's Other Voice*, 98.

225 Porath, *Palestinian Arab National Movement*, 278.

226 Kolinsky, "Collapse and Restoration," 160. Woodhead proposed the Jewish share of Palestine would be approximately 400 square miles around Tel Aviv, where Jews were then the majority. The concept was utterly rejected by the Zionists, and the Palestinians rejected it on principle. CO, "Palestine Partition Commission" (Woodhead Commission Report), October 1938, Cmd. 5854 (London: H. M. Stationery Office).

227 Ibid., 162. Walid Khalidi says 5,000 may have been killed and 14,000 wounded, citing data compiled from official British sources, appendix 4, in Khalidi, *Haven to Conquest*, 846-49.

228 Sykes, *Wingate*, 138-59, 168-81, 197-99; J. C. Hurewitz, *The Struggle for Palestine* (New York: Schocken Books, 1976), 92-93. Among Wingate's commando trainees was Moshe Dayan, architect of the June 1967 war. Peter Watson, "For Sale: A Hero's Secrets: Maverick Chindit Leader Orde Wingate Made Enemies on Both Sides," *Observer*, June 16, 1996, 12. Operations of Field Squads and Special Night Squads had the effect of "driving moderate Arabs into the ranks of the extremists." Yehuda Bauer, *From Diplomacy to Resistance: A History of Jewish Palestine, 1939-1945*, trans. Alton M. Winters (Philadelphia: Jewish Publication Society of America, 1970), 14.

229 Bruce Hoffman, *Failure of British Military Strategy within Palestine 1939-1947* (Jerusalem: Menachem Begin Institute for the Study of Underground and Resistance Movements, Bar-Ilan University Press, 1983), 11.

230 Kolinsky, "Collapse and Restoration," 161; Lachman, "Arab Rebellion and Terrorism," 78-83.

231 CO, "Palestine Statement of Policy" (McDonald White Paper), May 1939, Cmd. 6019 (London: H. M. Stationery Office), 3, 10-11.

232 Kimmerling and Migdal, *Palestinians*, 122.

233 "Though astute, charismatic, uncorruptible, and ascetic in his dedication to his people," Mattar concludes, "the Mufti's policies . . . were a failure and unwittingly contributed to the dispossession of the Palestinians." Mattar, *Mufti of Jerusalem*, 149. Haj Amin's refusal to compromise on the partition of Palestine and spurning of opportunities to bargain with the British has ensured lasting condemnation; he is often blamed for the sequence of events that resulted in what Palestinians call the catastrophe (*nakba*) of 1948. He cooperated with the Nazis, thinking they would help the Arabs drive out the British, if Germany were to defeat Britain in the Middle East. This glaring error has earned him an ignominious position in the history of the Israeli-Palestinian conflict, and allowed the discrediting of legitimate Palestinian grievances. Yet Haj Amin's defiance would, decades later, lend legitimacy to his kinsman, Feisel Husseini, when, in 1968, he began advocating solely nonviolent approaches in the Palestinian occupied territories (chapter 8).

234 Peel Commission Report, 136-40, 362.

235 Pappé, *Making of the Arab-Israeli Conflict*, ix.

236 Israeli "new" or "post-Zionist" historian Benny Morris concludes "it may fairly be said all 700,000 or so who ended up as refugees were compulsorily displaced or 'expelled.'" Benny Morris, *The Birth of the Palestinian Refugee Problem Revisited* (Cambridge: Cambridge University Press, 2004), 588. For the magnitude of the physical losses experienced by the Palestinians after the United Nations decided to partition Palestine, see Hadawi, *Palestinian Rights and Losses*, 85-102, 117-89.

237 Hurewitz, *Struggle*, 93.

Chapter 4

1 General Assembly Resolution 106 of May 15, 1947, created UNSCOP. Figure from UN document A/364; UN document A/AC.25/W.81/Rev. 2, Annex 5, of October 2, 1961, as cited in Hadawi, *Palestinian Rights and Losses in 1948*, 326 n. 13.

2 Haj Amin's organizing of a general strike and political violence, after the UN partition resolution was passed, was unquestionably detrimental to the Palestinians, judges Mattar. Mattar, *Mufti of Jerusalem*, 149.

3 Morris, *Birth of the Palestinian Refugee Problem Revisited*, 68. Upon Israel's fortieth anniversary, four books were brought out by Israeli historians that question the writing of history on the origins of the state of Israel and the 1948 war: Simha Flapan, *The Birth of Israel: Myths and Realities* (Pantheon Books, 1987); Benny Morris, *The Birth of the Palestinian Refugee Problem 1947-1949* (Cambridge: Cambridge University Press, 1987); Ilan Pappé, *Britain and the Arab-Israeli Conflict, 1948-51* (London: Palgrave Macmillan, 1988); and Avi Shlaim, *Collusion across the Jordan: King Abdullah, the Zionist Movement, and the Partition of Palestine* (Oxford: Clarendon Press, 1988). As a group, the authors are called the Israeli revisionist, or new, historians. See Avi Shlaim, "The Debate about 1948," *International Journal of Middle East Studies* 27, no. 3 (August 1995): 285-304. Morris's 2004 book updates his 1987 study, based on archives not available earlier. Gershon Shafir's *Land, Labour and the Origins of the Israeli-Palestinian Conflict,1882-1914* coincided, although rather than examining "myths" about Israel's independence, Shafir focuses on its "ideological substructure." Shafir, *Land, Labour*, x.

4 Morris, *Birth of the Palestinian Refugee Problem Revisited*, 90-99.

5 Pappé, *Making of the Arab-Israeli Conflict*, 65. Apart from facts brought to light by Israeli new historians on fundamental asymmetries between the Zionists and Arabs, it is also a reality that peasantry cannot easily sustain rebellion. "A peasant's work is most often done alone . . . rather than in conjunction with his fellows. . . . The tyranny of work weighs heavily. . . . Past exclusion of the peasant from participation in decision-making . . . deprives him all too often of the knowledge needed to articulate his interests with appropriate forms of action." Eric R. Wolf, "Peasant Rebellion and Revolution," in *National Liberation: Revolution in the Third World*, ed. Norman Miller and Roderick Aya (New York: Free Press, 1971), 49-50.

6 Morris, *Birth of the Palestinian Refugee Problem Revisited*, 164, 163-66. On depopulation and destruction of villages, see ibid., 65-308. A "policy of clearing out Arab communities sitting astride or near vital routes and along some borders was instituted." Ibid, 166-67. In an oft-cited example, the village of Deir Yassin "had taken no part in the war, and had even fought off Arab bands who wanted to use the village as their base"; on April 9, 1948, Israeli "terrorist bands attacked this peaceful village, which was not a military objective in the fighting, killed most of its inhabitants—240 men, women

and children—and kept a few of them alive to parade as captives through the streets of Jerusalem." Isidore Abramowitz, Hannah Arendt, and Albert Einstein, "New Palestine Party; Visit of Manachem Begin and Aims of Political Movement Discussed," *New York Times*, December 4, 1948.

7   In May 1948, 4,000 Palestinian forces were joined by 8,000 mostly irregular Arab soldiers, "no match" for the active Jewish military force of 22,425. Pappé, *Making of the Arab-Israeli Conflict*, 65. At the end of May 1948, the Haganah became the Israel Defense Forces (IDF).

8   CO, "Palestine: Termination of the Mandate," May 15, 1948 (London: H. M. Stationery Office).

9   Morris, *Birth of the Palestinian Refugee Problem Revisited*, 604.

10 Ibid., 342.

11 UN documents S/1264/Rev. 1; S/1296/Rev. 1; S/1302/Rev. 1; and S/1353/Rev. 1; and S/1353/Rev. 1, as cited in Hadawi, *Palestinian Rights and Losses in 1948*, 324 n. 9. The UN had approved partition and recognized the State of Israel, but did not condone the expulsion of the Palestinian population. See Don Peretz, *Palestinian Refugee Compensation*, Information Paper no. 3 (Washington, D.C.: Center for Policy Analysis on Palestine, 1995). Peretz is director of the Middle East Program, State University of New York, Binghamton.

12 Michael R. Fischbach, "Palestinian Refugee Property Claims: Challenges, Historical Precedents and Practical Suggestions, A Transcript of Remarks," *For the Record*, no. 254 (May 16, 2006), Palestine Center, Washington, D.C.

13 Michael R. Fischbach, *The Peace Process and Palestinian Refugee Claims: Addressing Claims for Property Compensation and Restitution* (Washington, D.C.: U.S. Institute of Peace Press, 2006), 10-11. Fischbach writes, based on archival research including hitherto unviewed records, "The extent to which Israeli forces ethnically cleansed areas under their control through the deliberate expulsion of Palestinians continues to be debated hotly. The historical record indicates that refugees fled for a variety of reasons during the confusion of war, including expulsion, but also including massacres, fear, proximity of military operations. . . . A question more germane . . . is, for whatever reasons the refugees fled, why did Israel refuse to allow them to return to their homes thereafter?" Ibid., 12.

14 Kimmerling and Migdal, *Palestinians*, 189-90; Elpeleg, *Grand Mufti*, 95.

15 Kimmerling and Migdal, ibid., 191; Moshe Maoz, *Palestinian Leadership on the West Bank: The Changing Role of the Arab Mayors under Jordan and Israel* (London, Frank Cass, 1984): xi, 8, 10; Amnon Cohen, *Political Parties in the West Bank under the Jordanian Regime, 1949-1967* (Ithaca: Cornell University Press, 1982), 26.

16 Elpeleg, *Grand Mufti*, .100, 114. The Provisional Basic Law, approved by the Palestine National Council that met October 2-3, 1948, established the All-Palestine Government (an eighty-six-member parliament never given real authority by the Egyptians and undermined by the Jordanians). Appendix F, in ibid., 210-13.

17 Maoz, *Palestinian Leadership*, 6.

18 Everett Mendelsohn, *A Compassionate Peace: A Future for Israel, Palestine, and the Middle East* (New York: Hill and Wang, 1989), 74. Among the Palestinian Arabs remaining in the new State of Israel, viewpoints expressed toward the Jews accentuated friendship and avowed hopes for mutual appreciation and interaction. Jacob M. Landau, *The Arabs in Israel: A Political Study* (London: Royal Institute of International Affairs and Oxford University Press, 1969), 58.

19 Palin Report, 3.

20 *Al-Ahram* (Cairo), May 28, 1964, as cited in Ahmad Jamal Dhaher, "Palestine Liberation Organization" (Ph.D. diss., West Virginia University, 1975), 71; Yehoshafat Harkabi, *The Palestinian Covenant and Its Meaning* (London: Valentine, Mitchell and Co., 1979), 10.

21 William B. Quandt, "Political and Military Dimensions of Contemporary Palestinian Nationalism," *The Politics of Palestinian Nationalism*, ed. William B. Quandt, Fuad Jabber, and Ann Mosely Lesch (Berkeley: University of California Press, 1973), 68.

22 Dhaher, "Palestine Liberation Organization," 73.

23 Jamal R. Nassar, *The Palestine Liberation Organization: From Armed Struggle to the Declaration of Independence* (Westport, Connecticut: Praeger, 1991), 208.

24 "The strictly clandestine character of various Palestinian resistance movements until 1967 was due less to the Israeli enemy than to the attitude of the Arab states, where Palestinian militants were often put under house arrest, thrown in jail or even worse." Leila S. Kadi, "Origins of the Armed Resistance," *Palestine: The Arab-Israeli Conflict*, ed. Russell Stetler (San Francisco: Ramparts Press, 1972), 129. Kadi offers an "official" PLO archivist's perspective from unattributed sources.

25 James L. Gelvin, *The Israeli-Palestinian Conflict: One Hundred Years of War* (Cambridge: Cambridge University Press, 2005), 92, 198. Others also made intemperate remarks. After the war, Golda Meir,

Israeli Labor leader and prime minister from 1969 to 1974, stated, "There was no such thing as Palestinians. When was there an independent Palestinian people with a Palestinian state? . . . It was not as though there was a Palestinian people in Palestine considering itself as a Palestinian people and we came and threw them out and took away their country from them. They did not exist." "Golda Meir: Who Can Blame Israel?" interviewed by Frank Giles, *Sunday Times*, June 15, 1969, 12. Two decades later, Likud prime minister Yitzhak Shamir would refer to Palestinians as "grasshoppers": "We say to them from the heights of this mountain and from the perspective of thousands of years of history that they are like grasshoppers compared to us." Adrian Hamilton, "Grasshoppers Ready to Jump on Racist Israel," *Observer Sunday*, April 3, 1988, 27.

26 Fateh, both a palindrome and acronym for Harakat al-Tahrir al-Filistiniyya (Palestinian Liberation Movement) was established in 1956 or 1957. Yasir Arafat, one-hour interview (Gaza City, January 24, 1996). Also see Yezid Sayigh, *Armed Struggle and the Search for State: The Palestinian National Movement, 1949-1993* (Oxford: Oxford University Press, 1997). Abu Iyad, nom de guerre Salah Khalaf, gives the date as 1958. Abu Iyad with Eric Rouleau, *My Home, My Land: A Narrative of the Palestinian Struggle*, trans. Linda Butler Koseoglu (New York: Times Books, 1981), 27, 28, 29. Helena Cobban cites Khaled al-Hassan—a founder and leader of Fateh—as dating Fateh's unification into a movement as 1962. Cobban, *Palestinian Liberation Organisation*, 23, 274.

27 Hisham Sharabi, *Palestine Guerrillas: Their Credibility and Effectiveness*, Monograph Series No. 25 (Beirut: Institute for Palestine Studies, 1970): 33.

28 Rosemary Sayigh, *Palestinians: From Peasants to Revolutionaries* (London: Zed Press, 1979), 145. "Sections of the Palestinian movement [had] ceased to be free agents and virtually became proxies of Arab governments fighting each other as bitterly as—or even more so than—the Israeli enemy." Walter Laqueur, *The Age of Terrorism* (London: Weidenfeld and Nicolson, 1987), 219. Fateh, one member of the front, was perceived by Palestinians as more vital than the umbrella organization because of its radicalism and activism. Laqueur, *Road to War*, 55.

29 William B. Quandt, "Palestinian and Algerian Revolutionary Elites: A Comparative Study of Structures and Strategies," paper presented at the annual meeting of the American Political Science Association (Washington, D.C., September 5-9, 1972), 9-11.

30 Quandt, "Revolutionary Elites," 9; Quandt, "Political and Military Dimensions," 56, 69-71, 75. See esp. pp. 52-78.

31 Laqueur, *Age of Terrorism*, 220.

32 *Filistinuna*, October 1964, 2-3; "A Dialogue with Fateh," *al-Taliah*, June 1969, 11, as cited in Dhaher, "Palestine Liberation Organization," 76.

33 John K. Cooley, *Green March, Black September: The Story of the Palestinian Arabs* (London: Frank Cass, 1973), 94; "PLO Takeover of the Lebanese Media," repr. from *al-Amal* (Beirut), June 29, 1982, *PLO in Lebanon: Selected Documents*, ed. Raphael Israeli (New York: St. Martin's Press, 1983), 283-84. *Filistinuna* slogans were more anti-Arab than anti-Zionist. Dhaher, "Palestine Liberation Organization," 73.

34 Kadi, "Armed Resistance," 130.

35 Ibid., 133. After its first two reconnaissance fatalities, on July 14, 1963, Fateh began sending small teams for sabotage. Cooley, *Green March, Black September*, 92-93.

36 *Filistinuna* translated and carried Fanon's *The Wretched of the Earth*, *The Damned*, and *Black Skins, White Masks*. These works were also serialized in pamphlets, *Revolutionary Lessons and Experiences*, especially nos. 3, 7, and 11. Dhaher, "Palestine Liberation Organization," 75 n. 24.

37 Sayigh, *Peasants to Revolutionaries*, 149; Dhaher, "Palestine Liberation Organization," 77. At the American University of Beirut in 1948, three medical students, George Habash, Wadi Haddad, and Ahmad al-Khatib founded a student nationalist club. In 1950, they formed the Palestinian branch of the ANM. Upon graduation in 1951-52, each went back to his country of residence to promote the ANM. George Habash and Wadi Haddad went to Jordan and set up free clinics for refugees. Khatib returned to Kuwait and became a leader of the opposition. Bassam Abu-Sharif, two-hour interview (Washington, D.C., October 30, 1997).

38 Cooley, *Green March, Black September*, 138; Kadi, "Armed Resistance," 134. Abu-Sharif recalled, "In 1964, the ANM decided to establish an organization called Shabab al-Thar (Youth of Vengeance). It was pure ANM, straightforward, direct, trained by Egyptians. When the PLO was established, together with the PLA—Palestine Liberation Army—we [in the ANM] decided to send five leading members into the PLA, to create a commando operation that would be armed, trained, and financed by PLA, because we didn't have money. Called Abtal al-Awda, or Heroes of the Return, it was known as PLA, but it was ANM." Abu-Sharif, interview (October 30, 1997).

39 Laqueur, *Road to War*, 61. Later, between 1967 and 1970, Fateh grew from a "few hundred" to between

15,000 and 20,000 members. Walter Laqueur, *Guerrilla: A Historical and Critical Study* (London: Weidenfeld and Nicolson, 1977), 303. Palestinian historian Hisham Sharabi estimates the combined factions had by 1970 trained between 30,000 and 50,000 persons, not all of whom became combatants. Sharabi, *Palestine Guerrillas*, 23.

40 Cooley, *Green March, Black September*, 95-96; Rubin, *Revolution until Victory?* 7.

41 Yezid Sayigh, "Palestinian Armed Struggle: Means and Ends," *Journal of Palestine Studies* 16, no. 1 (Autumn 1986): 98, 102. In Fateh's logic, guerrilla activities represented the first stage of struggle, with raids and sorties meant to provoke Israel into retaliatory acts, which would lead to involvement of the regular Arab armies (primarily Egypt and Jordan), thus making war unavoidable. Walter Laqueur, *The Road to War: The Origin and Aftermath of the Arab-Israeli Conflict, 1967-8* (London: Penguin Books, 1969), 95.

42 Yehoshafat Harkabi, *Fadayeen Action and Arab Strategy*, Adelphi Papers no. 53 (London: International Institute for Strategic Studies, 1968; repr. 1969), 9.

43 Cobban, *Palestinian Liberation Organisation*, 24.

44 Sayigh, *Peasants to Revolutionaries*, 146. Fateh's concern was to prevent the Arab regimes from negotiating a compromised end to the Palestinian struggle in return for withdrawal from the territories. Ibid., 145.

45 "Palestinian National Covenant, 1968," in Lukacs, *Documentary Record*, 292.

46 *Al-Fajr*, November 20, 1981, as cited in Atran, "Stones against the Iron Fist," 487, 511 n. 29.

47 Sayigh, *Peasants to Revolutionaries*, 145.

48 Quandt, "Revolutionary Elites," 16.

49 Ilan Pappé, *A History of Modern Palestine: One Land, Two Peoples* (Cambridge: Cambridge University Press, 2004), 149.

50 Hisham Sharabi's study of obituaries in the Israeli daily newspaper *Maariv* questions whether such operations had more impact on Israeli mortalities than officially acknowledged. Sharabi, *Palestine Guerrillas*, 10-13. Regardless, as Kitty Warnock declares, while such operations may have helped Palestinian morale and revealed Israeli vulnerabilities, the result was to increase the vigilance by the Israeli military and raise the antagonism and fear of the Israeli public. Kitty Warnock, *Land before Honour: Palestinian Women in the Occupied Territories* (London: Macmillan, 1990), 16.

51 Pappé, *History of Modern Palestine*, 198.

52 Maoz, *Palestinian Leadership*, 64; Meron Benvenisti, Ziad Abu-Zayed, and Danny Rubinstein, *The West Bank Handbook: A Political Lexicon* (Jerusalem: Jerusalem Post, 1986), 198.

53 Of the 1,668,200 Palestinians living inside what had been Mandatory Palestine—pre-1967 Israel, the West Bank, and Gaza Strip—more than 300,000 who had resided in the West Bank or Gaza were exiled over the next few months, and a sizeable number temporarily abroad were not allowed to return. "Probable Distribution of Palestinians Just before and after the War Began on 5 June 1967," by Janet Abu-Lughod, "Demographic Characteristics of the Palestinian Population," annex 1, part 2, *Palestine Open University Feasibility Study* (Paris: UNESCO, June 30, 1980), 29, repr. in Edward W. Said, et al., "A Profile of the Palestinian People," table 7, in Said and Hitchens, *Blaming the Victims*, 269.

54 Sari Nusseibeh, one-hour interview (Washington, D.C., July 5, 1994).

55 Rashid Khalidi, "Palestinian People: Twenty-Two Years after 1967," in Lockman and Beinin, *Intifada*, 113.

56 Joost R. Hiltermann, *Behind the Intifada: Labor and Women's Movements in the Occupied Territories* (Princeton: Princeton University Press, 1991), 3, 4.

57 Muhammad Muslih, "Palestinian Civil Society," *Middle East Journal* 47 (Spring 1993): 263.

58 Alain Gresh, "Palestinian Communists and the Intifadah," trans. Diane Belle James, *Middle East Report* 19, no. 2 (March-April 1989): 35.

59 Yezid Sayigh, "Turning Defeat into Opportunity: The Palestinian Guerrillas after the June 1967 War," *Middle East Journal* 46, no. 2 (Spring 1992): 246-47.

60 Ibid., 263; Helena Cobban, "The Dilemma of the PLO," *Middle East Report* 13 (November-December 1983): 4. Vitriolic esoteric appeals and Marxist-Leninist vocabularies were repugnant to the middle class and adversely affected popular support for guerrilla violence. Bard E. O'Neill, *Armed Struggle in Palestine: A Political-Military Analysis* (Boulder, Colorado, and Folkestone, England: Westview Press, 1978), 121.

61 Ann Mosely Lesch, *Political Perceptions of the Palestinians on the West Bank and the Gaza Strip* (Washington, D.C.: Middle East Institute, 1980), 42.

62 Zeev Schiff and Ehud Yaari, *Intifada: The Palestinian Uprising—Israel's Third Front*, trans. Ina Friedman (New York: Simon and Schuster, 1990), 41.

63 Pappé, *History of Modern Palestine*, 187-88.
64 Lesch, *Israel's Occupation*, 54. Israeli authorities rejected seventy-eight textbooks outright; the remaining fifty-six were reprinted with deletions. *Jerusalem Post*, August 30, 1967, as cited in ibid., 50.
65 Ibid., 56.
66 Lesch, *Political Perceptions*, 35-37.
67 Hamdi Kanaan, in *New York Times*, February 7, 1969, as cited in Lesch, *Political Perceptions*, 36, 49 n. 12.
68 Fateh's local armed cells, called *tashish* (nesting), carried out "extremely modest" attacks in 1967, but guerrilla press reports exaggerated them "wildly." Sayigh, "Defeat into Opportunity," 250-51.
69 Nusseibeh, interview (July 5, 1994). "People in Fateh began to realize that its military wing would make Fateh lose." Sari Nusseibeh, two-hour interview (East Jerusalem, November 6, 1994).
70 Muhammad Muslih, "Palestinian Civil Society," *Civil Society in the Middle East*, ed. Augustus Richard Norton, vol. 1 (Leiden, Netherlands: E. J. Brill, 1995), 250.
71 "Memorandum Presented to the King-Crane Commission by the General Syrian Congress," July 2, 1919, in Laqueur, *Israel-Arab Reader*, 33.
72 Hattis, "Bi-National Idea in Palestine, 21.
73 Ibid, 25.
74 Magnes resigned from his pulpit at Temple Emanu-el in New York during World War I and moved to Palestine, where he established the Hebrew University of Jerusalem and became its first president until he died in 1948. His plan advocated controlled immigration to allow Jews in the same number as Arabs in Palestine, and equal representation for each group in the government of a binational state. Bartley C. Crum, *Behind the Silken Curtain: A Personal Account of Anglo-American Diplomacy in Palestine and the Middle East* (New York: Simon and Schuster, 1947), 252.
75 I. F. Stone, "The Other Zionism," *Underground to Palestine* (London: Hutchinson, 1979), 240.
76 See Nashashibi, *Jerusalem's Other Voice*.
77 Nusseibeh, interview (July 5, 1994).
78 Joel Beinin, "The Palestine Communist Party, 1919-1948," *MERIP Reports: Middle East Research and Information Project* 55 (March 1977): 12; Lockman, *Comrades and Enemies*, 81.
79 Even after the PCP split, the platform of the Israeli Communist Party in 1946 still emphasized "the first step towards a bi-national state would be the achievement of Jewish-Arab unity." Sondra Miller Rubenstein, *The Communist Movement in Palestine and Israel, 1919-1984* (Boulder, Colorado: Westview Press, 1985), 281.
80 See *The Case for a Bi-National Palestine: Memorandum Prepared by the Hashomer Hatzair Workers' Party*, in Hebrew and English (Tel Aviv: Hashomer Hatzair Workers' Party, 1946).
81 Musa Budeiri, *The Palestine Communist Party, 1919-1948: Arab and Jew in the Struggle for Internationalism* (London: Ithaca Press, 1979), 95.
82 Gresh, "Palestinian Communists," 35.
83 Cohen, *Political Parties*, 28, 57; Maoz, *Palestinian Leadership*, 10.
84 The JCP was alone in attempting to place its message before the public through a publications program, and had its own printing press. Members functioned through secret cells, where contact was managed through circulation of written materials and supported by couriers (*murasil*). Face-to-face sessions were rare. Cohen, *Political Parties*, 43-53.
85 Ibid., 28-29. The fifty participants were arrested, shackled, and made to walk to Amman, where—with the exception of one marcher who died en route—they were jailed for two months. This "was the first time that West Bank communists had openly challenged the authorities; their overt activities up to this time had been restricted primarily to the distribution of leaflets." Ibid.
86 Ibid., 58, 56.
87 Walter Z. Laqueur, *Communism and Nationalism in the Middle East* (London: Routledge and Kegan Paul, 1956), 129.
88 Hiltermann, *Behind the Intifada*, 40.
89 Laqueur, *Communism and Nationalism*, 132-33.
90 Cohen, *Political Parties*, 38; Amman Radio, April 25, 1957, as cited in ibid., 256 n. 41.
91 Hazem Zaki Nuseibeh, "The Israeli Response to U.N. Resolutions (Statement before the Special Political Committee on the Israeli Practices Affecting the Human Rights of the Population of the Occupied Territories, Given 11 December 1976)," *Palestine and the United Nations* (London: Quartet Books, 1981), 52. Until the first intifada, the Palestinians rejected 242 because it spoke solely of the need for a "just settlement of the refugee problem" and did not address their political aspirations.

92   Emile Sahliyeh, *In Search of Leadership: West Bank Politics since 1967* (Washington, D.C., Brookings Institution, 1988), 87-91; Sayigh, "Defeat into Opportunity," 253.

93   Hillel Frisch, "From Armed Struggle over State Borders to Political Mobilization and Intifada within It: The Transformation of the PLO Strategy in the Occupied Territories," *Plural Societies* 19, no. 2-3 (1990): 103, 104.

94   Gresh, "Palestinian Communists," 35.

95   Rosemary Sayigh contends, "Few peoples have been more systematically kept helpless in the face of attack than the Palestinians, and it is not surprising that the symbol of their resurgence after 1967 was the gun." Sayigh, *Peasants to Revolutionaries*, 154.

96   Ibid., 157.

97   Hillel Frisch, "Between Diffusion and Territorial Consolidation in Rebellion: Striking at the Hard Core of the *Intifada*," *Terrorism and Political Violence* 3, no. 4 (Winter 1991): 45.

98   Ghassan Khatib, two-hour interview (East Jerusalem, December 15, 1997).

99   Khatib recalled Barghouti "led this tendency in the party, with its belief in grass-roots activities, belief in popular struggle versus individualistic military struggle. . . . If one person deserves the credit for this kind of thinking, it is he." Khatib, interview (December 15, 1997). Barghouti's influence extends beyond communist circles. To Hanna Siniora, an editor of *al-Fajr* and nonofficial spokesperson for Fateh during the first intifada, "It was through Mr. Barghouti that I learned to accept Resolutions 242 and 338—when 242 and 338 were in the Palestinian dictum synonymous with treason." The communists had "better foresight," Siniora said: "When the 1947 partition plans were announced, . . . only the communist party had the foresight to say we will accept the partition plans, and one of its leaders in Haifa was killed because the party accepted partition." Hanna Siniora, one-hour interview (East Jerusalem, December 16, 1997). Barghouti later became minister of industry for the Palestinian Authority.

100 In 1974, the Arab League declared the PLO as "sole legitimate representative of the Palestinian people"—a rallying cry with support both inside and outside the occupied territories—although suspiciousness remained in the territories about armed struggle and the "liberation" of all of Palestine.

101 In 1977, they proclaimed, "We the communists, members of the Palestinian Communist organization in the West Bank, declare clearly and frankly, that we are struggling for the existence of a Palestinian state in the West Bank and Gaza Strip, following a complete Israeli withdrawal from all the territories conquered in June 1967, for the repatriation of all Palestinian refugees from 1948 to their homes, and for the Palestinian state to have borders, secure from Israeli or other aggression." "Together with the PLO to Create a Palestinian State," repr. from *al-Watan*, clandestine organ of Palestine Communist party, January 31, 1977, as cited in *MERIP Reports: Middle East Research and Information Project* 55 (March 1977): 17.

102 Hawatmeh Nayef, "Jews and Arabs: One Future," repr. from *al-Hurriyah*, January 12, 1970, in Stetler, *Palestine*, 201-4.

103 Hawatmeh told John Cooley in 1971 of his contacts with Matzpen, Rakah (the Israeli Communist Party), and faculty and students at Hebrew University. Cooley, *Green March, Black September*, 143.

104 Laqueur, *Guerrilla*, 366.

105 Palestine National Council, Political Program, Cairo, June 8, 1974, *Palestinian-Israeli Peace Agreement: A Documentary Record* (Washington, D.C.: Institute for Palestine Studies, 1994), 209, 208.

106 "Towards a Democratic State in Palestine," September 1970 statement of Fateh, Second World Congress on Palestine, Amman, General Union of Palestinian Students, repr. from Liberation News Service, October 15, 1970, in Stetler, *Palestine*, 205-18. The fifth through eleventh PNCs, from 1969 through 1973, adopted a series of compromises on a secular democratic state. Muhammad Muslih, *Toward Coexistence: An Analysis of the Resolutions of the Palestine National Council* (Washington, D.C.: Institute for Palestine Studies, 1990), 17-23.

107 Alain Gresh, *The PLO: The Struggle Within: Towards an Independent Palestinian State*, trans. A. M. Berrett (London: Zed Books, 1985), 37. Gresh explains the PLO position of a "secular democratic state" is an interpretation; PLO documents do not use the word "secular." It was to be a state of Muslims, Jews, and Christians, defined in nonsectarian terms. Gresh, *PLO: Struggle Within*, revised ed., 1988, 34-50.

108 Sari Nusseibeh, two-hour interview (East Jerusalem, November 5, 1994).

109 Edward W. Said, "Intifada and Independence," in Lockman and Beinin, *Intifada*, 9.

110 Terrorism intensified from 1968 to 1973. With the July 28, 1968, hijacking of an El Al airliner to Algiers, the PFLP "initiated the era of international Palestinian terrorism," with operations outside

Israel. Merari and Elad, *International Dimension of Palestinian Terrorism*, 5, 14. It was considered more important to prevent the struggle from slipping into oblivion than to attack the adversary, according to Gerard Chaliand, who writes "transnational terrorism was also an admission of powerlessness." Gerard Chaliand, *Terrorism: From Popular Struggle to Media Spectacle* (London: Saqi Books, 1987), 82, 88. Even at their peak (late 1967, and October 1969 to September 1970), the guerrillas were "more of a psychological nuisance than military threat" to Israel. Cooley, *Green March, Black September*, 155.

111 See Galia Golan, *Soviet-PLO Relations and the Creation of a Palestinian State*, Research Paper no. 36 (Jerusalem: Hebrew University, 1979).

112 Sahliyeh, *Leadership*, 93; Helena Cobban, "The PLO and the Intifada," *The Intifada: Its Impact on Israel, the Arab World, and the Superpowers*, ed. Robert O. Freedman (Miami: Florida International University Press, 1991), 82.

113 Frisch, "Transformation," 103; Hillel Frisch, "The Palestinian Movement in the Territories: The Middle Command," *Middle Eastern Studies* 29, no. 2 (April 1993): 265.

114 Sahliyeh, *Leadership*, 118.

115 Ibid., 97.

116 Gresh, "Palestinian Communists," 35.

117 For the text and signatories, see *Journal of Palestine Studies* 9 (Autumn 1973): 187-89.

118 Frisch, "Transformation," 100-101.

119 "The Palestinian National Front," condensed from *Filistin al-Thawra*, December 26, 1973, *MERIP Reports: Middle East Research and Information Project* 25 (February 1974): 22-23.

120 Sami Mussalam, *The PLO: The Palestine Liberation Organization* (Brattleboro, Vermont: Amana Books, 1988), 8.

121 Nusseibeh, interview (November 5, 1994).

122 Lesch, *Political Perceptions*, 55.

123 Abd al-Jawad Saleh, "Abu Ammar's Biggest Mistake Was Gambling on the Americans,'" *MERIP Reports* 119 (November-December 1983): 27.

124 Muslih, "Palestinian Civil Society," 263.

125 See Cooley, *Green March, Black September*, 112-20; Abu Iyad, *My Home, My Land*, 78-91.

126 Cobban, *Palestinian Liberation Organisation*, 48-52.

127 Rubenstein, *Communist Movement in Palestine and Israel*, 262.

128 Abraham Sela, "The PLO, the West Bank, and Gaza Strip," *Jerusalem Quarterly* 8 (Summer 1978): 70, as cited in Shmuel Sandler and Hillel Frisch, *Israel, the Palestinians and the West Bank: A Study in Intercommunal Conflict*, 2nd ed. (Lexington, Massachusetts: Lexington Books, 1985), 85.

129 Muslih, "Palestinian Civil Society," vol. 1, 251. Hiltermann marks 1974 for the "conscious decision" by the PLO to begin mobilizing in the occupied territories through popular organizations. Hiltermann, *Behind the Intifada*, 12.

130 Ibid., 71-75, 79-80, 84; Salim Tamari, "The Intifada: Sociological Perspective," *Faith and the Intifada: Palestinian Christian Voices*, ed. Naim S. Ateek, Marc H. Ellis, and Rosemary Radford Ruether (Maryknoll, New York: Orbis Books, 1992), 16-22.

131 Sahliyeh, *Leadership*, 99.

132 Geoffrey Aronson, *Israel, Palestinians and the Intifada: Creating Facts on the West Bank* (London and Washington, D.C.: Kegan Paul International, in association with the Institute for Palestine Studies, 1990), 179.

133 Avi Shlaim, *The Iron Wall: Israel and the Arab World* (London: Penguin Books, 2001), 364.

134 William B. Quandt, *Camp David: Peacemaking and Politics* (Washington, D.C.: The Brookings Institution, 1986), 187.

135 President Jimmy Carter later acknowledged, "When we negotiated the Camp David accords, . . . we did not give adequate attention to the needs, desires, yearnings, and problems of security relevant to Jordan, Syria, Lebanon, and the Palestinians." Jimmy Carter, "The Middle East Consultation: A Look at the Future," *Middle East Journal* 42, no. 2 (Spring 1988): 191. Regarding the absence of Palestinians from Camp David, the author has heard Carter say, "We did not intend to be presumptuous." Aziz Shehadeh writes, in his August 1977 letter to Secretary Vance, with whom he and three others met on August 10 at the home of Moshe Dyan, "We Palestinians must not be ignored in the search for peace. We must play a part in working out our own future." (See appendices, p. 349.) On September 29, 1978, Shehadeh and other Palestinians, including Anwar Nusseibeh, father of Sari Nusseibeh, met with the State Department's Alfred Atherton and Harold Saunders days after the signing of the Camp David accords. Seeking to explore how to retrieve from the agreements some

form of self-determination, the group was disappointed. Aronson, *Israel, Palestinians and the Intifada*, 170, 182-84; Lesch, *Political Perceptions*, 89-90.

136 William B. Quandt, "The Uprising: Breaking a Ten-Year Deadlock," paper delivered at the December 8, 1988, conference of the Center for Strategic and International Studies, Washington, D.C., *American-Arab Affairs* 27 (Winter 1988-89): 20-24.

137 Rashid Khalidi, "The Palestine Liberation Organization," *The Middle East: Ten Years after Camp David*, ed. William B. Quandt (Washington, D.C.: Brookings Institution, 1988), 265. See esp. pp. 261-78.

138 Lesch, *Political Perceptions*, 12.

139 Ibid., 13. Article 1, Military Proclamation 101, August 27, 1967: 27 n. 35.

140 Lesch, *Political Perceptions*, 13.

141 The balloting was carried out with the consent of Israel, which hoped to identify alternatives to the increasingly popular PLO, and was similar to elections permitted in some cities in 1972.

142 Don Peretz, *Intifada: The Palestinian Uprising* (Boulder, Colorado: Westview Press, 1990), 16.

143 Sahliyeh, *Leadership*, 76.

144 Sameer Y. Abraham, "The Development and Transformation of the Palestine National Movement," *Occupation: Israel over Palestine*, ed. Naseer H. Aruri (Belmont, Massachusetts: Association of Arab-American University Graduates), 620-26; Hiltermann, *Behind the Intifada*, 5.

145 David McDowall, *The Palestinians: The Road to Nationhood* (London: Minority Rights Publications, 1995), 97.

146 Mustafa Barghouti, "Popular/Mass Movement in the Community," *Journal of Palestine Studies* 2, no. 1 (1989): 126, 128.

147 Hiltermann, *Behind the Intifada*, 65.

148 Hillel Schenker, "To Channel this Energy," interview of Azmi Bishara, associate professor of philosophy, Bir Zeit University, *New Outlook*, August 1988, 18.

149 Hiltermann, *Behind the Intifada*, 4.

150 Laurie A. Brand, *Palestinians in the Arab World* (New York: Columbia University Press, 1988), 31.

151 Aronson, *Israel, Palestinians and the Intifada*, 195.

152 Nusseibeh, interview (November 5, 1994).

153 Hiltermann, *Behind the Intifada*, 65.

154 Musa Budeiri, political scientist, al-Quds University, one-hour interview (East Jerusalem, January 28, 1996).

155 Frisch, "Transformation," 98.

156 Laqueur, *Terrorism*, 124.

157 Laqueur says in military bases outside the occupied territories in 1975, the PFLP had 500 combatants, the DFLP 300, while Fateh had "between 10,000 and 15,000 under arms." Ibid., 191.

158 Abraham, "Development and Transformation of the Palestine National Movement," 621.

159 Fateh, *Min Muntalaqat al-Amal al-Fidai* [Starting Points of Guerrilla Action] (Amman: n.p., 1967), 67, as cited in Laqueur, *Guerrilla*, 365, 438 n. 83.

160 Laqueur, *Terrorism*, 193.

161 Laila Khaled, *My People Shall Live: An Autobiography of a Revolutionary* (London: Hodder and Stoughton, 1973), 88.

162 Nusseibeh, interview (November 5, 1994).

163 Cobban, "The PLO and the Intifada," 82.

164 Nusseibeh, interview (November 5, 1994).

165 Yezid Sayigh, "Struggle Within, Struggle Without: The Transformation of PLO Politics since 1982," *International Affairs* 65, no. 2 (1989): 256; Cobban, "The PLO and the Intifada," 83.

166 Bassam Abu Sharif, two-hour interview (Gaza City, January 24, 1996).

167 Frisch, "Transformation," 100.

168 Jonathan Kuttab, thirty-minute interview (East Jerusalem, March 18, 1997). "Aziz is the first person publicly quoted as talking about a separate Palestinian state." Ibid.

169 Lesch, *Political Perceptions*, 40, 48 n. 5, 49 n. 22. Abu Shilbaya published to this effect in *al-Quds*, December 29, 1970, and January 6, 1971; a statement by Faruqi appeared in the *New York Times* on September 19, 1970, as cited in ibid., 49 n. 22. Lesch notes that Abu Shilbaya in 1971 wrote a book *No Peace without a Free Palestinian State*, and cites other advocates, including educator Ibrahim Duaybis, poet Samira Khatib, and journalists Yusif Nasr and Jamil Hamad. Ibid., 41, 49 n. 22.

170 Ibid., 34. In the case of Faruqi, after petitioning for a Palestinian state, in the early hours of the morning a missile was fired through his bedroom wall. Raja Shehadeh, the son of Aziz Shehadeh, thirty-minute personal communication (East Jerusalem, December 12, 1997).

171 Kuttab, interview (March 18, 1997).

172 Ibid.

173 Ibid.

174 Raja Shehadeh, forty-five-minute interview (Ramallah, March 18, 1997). Then sixteen years of age, Raja was present at the meetings. David Kimche and Dan Bawly confirm such meetings on the West Bank immediately after the war and mention Aziz Shehadeh in their book *The Sandstorm: The Arab-Israeli War of 1967: Prelude and Aftermath* (New York: Stein and Day, 1968), 239, 311.

175 Shehadeh, interview (March 18, 1977).

176 Kuttab, interview (March 18, 1997).

177 The lawyers' strike in the autumn of 1967 was prompted by Israel's decision to shift the Court of Appeals from Jerusalem to Ramallah. Many lawyers and judges deemed the move illegal, refused to practice in the courts, and got "strike support" salary from the Jordanian government. Lesch, *Political Perceptions*, 34.

178 Kuttab, interview (March 18, 1997).

179 Ibid.

180 Shehadeh, interview (March 18, 1997).

181 Shlaim, *Collusion across the Jordan*, 489.

182 Avi Plascov, *The Palestinian Refugees in Jordan, 1948-1957* (London: Frank Cass, 1981), 20. See appendices 3 and 4 for the resolutions passed at the General Refugee Congress and the aims and policies of the congress in ibid., 220-23; Shlaim, *Collusion across the Jordan*, 489.

183 Uri Avnery says Aziz Shehadeh "approached the Israeli delegate, Eliahu Sasson, and told him that the Palestinians were ready to make peace with Israel. After consulting his government, Sasson rebuffed them bluntly. The government of Israel was not interested in dealing with people who did not represent any government." Uri Avnery, *My Friend, the Enemy: Conversations with the PLO* (London: Zed Books, 1986), 58.

184 Shehadeh, communication (December 12, 1997). Ilan Pappé notes the encounter. Pappé, *Arab-Israeli Conflict*, 223. Two other delegations, one led by Muhammad Nimer al-Hawari, also claimed to represent the refugees at Lausanne. Shlaim, *Collusion across the Jordan*, 490.

185 Shehadeh, interview (March 18, 1997).

186 Frisch, "Transformation," 99.

187 *Al-Quds*, August 25, 1970, as cited in Frisch, "Transformation," 99. On May 4, 1974, an editorial appeared in *al-Fajr*, the pro-Fateh English-language weekly, attacking Aziz Shehadeh (and others advocating a Palestinian entity), but did not mention his contributions to the weekly. Frisch, "Transformation," 100.

188 Shehadeh, interview (March 18, 1997).

189 Ibid.

190 Frisch, "Transformation," 99 n. 23.

191 Aziz Shehadeh, "The Voice of the Forgotten Palestinian: An Appeal to the Arab Governments and the Government of Israel," *New Middle East*, December 1968, 14-16. See idem, "Why Fatah Does Not Speak for Democratic Palestine," *New Middle East*, March 1969.

192 Kuttab, interview (March 18, 1997).

193 Aziz Shehadeh, "Must History Repeat Itself? The Palestinian Entity and Its Enemies," *New Middle East*, January 1971, 37.

194 Kuttab, interview (March 18, 1997).

195 Aziz Shehadeh, letter to Secretary of State Cyrus Vance (Ramallah, August 10, 1977). See appendices, p. 349. Shehadeh and others broke a Palestinian boycott against contact with U.S. officials, called by the nationalist mayors who had been elected in 1976 in the occupied territories.

196 "One of his mistakes was that he was inexperienced with the news media. . . . He would leave it to editors to edit, and they would edit to suit their own interests. . . . He was willing to speak with journalists at any time, but had no control over what they wrote." Shehadeh, interview (March 18, 1997).

197 Shehadeh, interview (March 18, 1997). Israeli settlements in the occupied territories, according to Yehoshafat Harkabi, major general (ret.), IDF, and former chief of military intelligence (1950-59), were meant to "foil" Israeli loss of the territories. Likud policy was "reified" by settlements; relinquishing them would have constituted "history's condemnation of the role of Jabotinsky's movement in Zionism." Yehoshafat Harkabi, "Arab-Israeli Conflict at the Threshold of Negotiations," *The Struggle for Peace: Israelis and Palestinians*, ed. Elizabeth Warnock Fernea and Mary Evelyn Hocking (Austin: University of Texas Press, 1992), 252.

198 Interviews in East Jerusalem and Ramallah with persons who knew Shehadeh.

199 Jonathan Kuttab explained: "Al-Haq has helped to move the Palestinian population away from its own narrow view of things and into the international arena. Partly in order to avoid the accusation of being a political organization, al-Haq insists on a set of universal objective standards and court-room quality documentation, that is open, available to neutral observers . . . by documenting precisely what happened in cold, clinical terms that lead the reader to conclude that there was injustice. This approach was totally new . . . to this society. People were full of their own feelings ('we are oppressed') and felt that their case was so clear that they didn't have to prove it, or document it—all they had to do was use rhetoric to describe it. They were surprised when the outside world dismissed their claims or seemed psychologically indifferent. Al-Haq's scholarly, legal approach led us to be blamed in the early days. People would say, 'How come this happened and you didn't print a denunciation in the paper?' Denunciations in Arabic newspapers mean nothing. Instead, we painstakingly documented it, prepared affidavits, analyzed it in terms of international law, and produced, months later, a publication that would be viewed seriously by jurists throughout the world, but might not even be quoted in the local Arabic papers." Jonathan Kuttab, two-hour interview (East Jerusalem, December 12, 1997).

200 The nonviolent methods of documentation and denunciation were the principal techniques used under military dictatorship in Argentina by Professor Adolfo Pérez Esquivel, who won the 1980 Nobel Prize for Peace, the result of his work with Madres de la Plaza del Mayo (Mothers of the Disappeared)—a group that documented and protested the preventive detention and killings of tens of thousands who came to be known as *los desaparecidos* (the disappeared). *Argentina: A Country Study*, ed. James D. Rudolph, Area Handbook Series (Washington, D.C.: Foreign Area Studies, American University, 1986); *Amnesty International 1981 Annual Report* (London: Amnesty International, 1982); Lawrence Weschler, *A Miracle, A Universe: Settling Accounts with Torturers* (New York: Pantheon Books, 1990). These methods have since spread to twenty-nine countries in the Western Hemisphere through the work of Servicio Paz y Justicia (SERPAJ), the Latin American movement for peace and justice, founded by Pérez in Buenos Aires. Both al-Haq and Raja Shehadeh have won international recognition for the probity and conscientiousness of their documentation.

Chapter 5

1 Schooling for girls was available in Ottoman Palestine, sometimes run by missionaries, including perhaps the earliest institution in Palestine, established in 1837 in Jerusalem. Under the British Mandate, Rosemary Sayigh asserts, "public education suffered severe financial neglect." Sayigh, "Palestinian Women: A Case of Neglect," in Najjar and Warnock, *Portraits*, 15.

2 Ellen Fleischmann, *Jerusalem Women's Organizations during the British Mandate: 1920s-1930s* (East Jerusalem: Palestinian Academic Society for the Study of International Affairs [hereafter PASSIA], 1995), 21.

3 Researchers on Palestinian women's activism and political mobilization report difficulties in obtaining documentation. See Julie M. Peteet, *Gender in Crisis: Women and the Palestinian Resistance Movement* (New York: Columbia University Press, 1991), 42; Fleischman, *Jerusalem Women's Organizations*, 1. See eadem, *The Nation and Its "New" Women: The Palestinian Women's Movement 1920-1948* (London: University of California Press, Ltd., 2003).

4 "Palestinian Women: A Case of Neglect," in Najjar and Warnock, *Portraits*, 4; Simona Sharoni, *Gender and the Israeli-Palestinian Conflict: The Politics of Women's Resistance* (Syracuse, New York: Syracuse University Studies on Peace and Conflict Resolution, 1995), 58. Initially led by Milia al-Sakakini and Zlikhah Ishaq al-Shahabi, the PWU concerned itself with issues of welfare, and helped women to organize about nationalist issues. The PWU has been cited as the precursor to the General Union of Palestinian Women.

5 Ghada Talhami, "Women in the Movement: Their Long, Uncelebrated History," *al-Fajr*, May 30, 1986, as cited in Hiltermann, *Behind the Intifada*, 231 n. 3. 128.

6 Fleischman, *Jerusalem Women's Organizations*, 22.

7 See Peteet, *Gender in Crisis*, 43-44; Soraya Antonius, "Fighting on Two Fronts: Conversations with Palestinian Women," *Journal of Palestine Studies* 31 (Spring 1979): 26.

8 Peteet, ibid., interview with Matiel E. T. Mogannam, 46.

9 Fleischman, *Jerusalem Women's Organizations*, 23.

10 Matiel E. T. Mogannam, *The Arab Woman and the Palestine Problem* (London: Herbert Joseph Ltd., 1937), 70.

11 Kayyali, *Palestine*, 168; Sharoni, *Gender*, 59; Antonius, "Fighting on Two Fronts," 26-27.

12 Mogannam, *Arab Woman*, 74-75; Fleischman, *Jerusalem Women's Organizations*, 24.

13 Confidential letter, "Palestine Reception of Women at Government House after the Riots," from Sir John Chancellor to Lord Passfield, October 31, 1929, handwritten draft. Papers of Sir John Chancellor, Rhodes House, Oxford, box 21/MF 26 ff 5. The significance of women appearing unveiled before the High Commissioner caused a stir among elite Palestinians who read or heard accounts of the meeting; support for the act came from unlikely sources, including the respected imam Moulvi Farzand Ali, then based in London.

14 Fleischmann, *Jerusalem Women's Organizations*, 3; Peteet, *Gender in Crisis*, 47.

15 Confidential letter, "Palestine Reception of Women," Chancellor to Passfield. See also, Fleischmann, ibid., 4.

16 Mogannam, *Arab Woman*, 69-76; Fleischman, *Jerusalem Women's Organizations*, 26.

17 Mogannam, ibid., 76.

18 Ibid., 79, 83.

19 Letter to the author from Pamela M. Clark, Registrar, the Royal Archives, Windsor Castle, Berkshire, United Kingdom, January 17, 2006.

20 "First Palestine Arab Women Congress Memorandum to the Permanent Mandate Commission on the subject of Arab grievances," January 28, 1932, and "His Majesty's Government Memorandum to the Permanent Mandate Commission on the subject of Arab Grievances as Expressed by the First Palestine Arab Women Congress," June 22, 1932, CO 733/221/9.

21 The intention to boycott and protest the visit of Sir Philip Cunliffe-Lister, first Earl of Swinton and secretary of state for the colonies (1931-35), and Lord Allenby, was publicized in several local newspapers. There, it was reported that several Arab leaders had refused the invitation to meet with Cunliffe-Lister during his visit. Protest meetings were held in various cities, and a local strike was declared in Gaza. None of these acts of protest or noncooperation, however, matched the creativity, organization, or magnitude of the "silent demonstration."

22 Mogannam, *Arab Woman*, 93-100.

23 Antonius, "Fighting on Two Fronts," 27.

24 "Disturbances at Jaffa on October 27th and Events Leading up to It and Following It" (anonymous report, undated), CO 733/239/5.

25 Fleischmann, *Jerusalem Women's Organizations*, 7.

26 Kayyali, *Palestine*, 191-92.

27 Usama Khalid, "A Palestinian History of Woman's Struggle," *al-Fajr*, March 8, 1985, 8, in Ghada Talhami, "Women under Occupation: The Great Transformation," *Image and Reality: Palestinian Women under Occupation and in the Diaspora*, ed. Suha Sabbagh and Ghada Talhami (Washington, D.C.: Institute for Arab Women's Studies, 1990), 19.

28 Soraya Antonius, "Fighting on Two Fronts," 29; Talhami, "Women under Occupation," 21. The organization remained independent of the PLO and still exists.

29 Talhami, "Women under Occupation." 21.

30 Fleischman, *Jerusalem Women's Organizations*, 32.

31 S. R. Bakshi, *Gandhi and Ideology of Non-Violence* (New Delhi: Criterion Publications, 1986), 47.

32 Ted Swedenburg, *Memories of Revolt: The 1936-1939 Rebellion and the Palestinian National Past* (Minneapolis: University of Minnesota Press, 1995), 193.

33 Cooke cites Palestinian women authors such as Sahar Khalifa and Fadwa Tuqan as predicting in their literary writings that resistance would have to be "accomplished from within and by a new cadre—women and children." Miriam Cooke, *Women and the War Story* (Berkeley: University of California Press, 1996), 200. Cooke cites Khalifa's post-1967 novels as showing "the solutions are in the hands of women who have invented a new kind of fighting." Ibid., 217.

34 Ibid., 201. See also pp. 11-12, 178-79, 191, 195-216.

35 Ibid., 217.

36 Chris Mannings and Joost R. Hiltermann, "Strategies of Palestinian Resistance," *Middle East International*, January 9, 1988, 19.

37 Rosemary Sayigh, "Palestinian Women: A Case of Neglect," in Najjar and Warnock, *Portraits*, 4.

38 Sayigh, "Palestinian Women," 6-7.

39 Ibid., 9.

40 "Rima Salah and Ghada Hashem Talhami to *al-Fajr*: The Movement Should Try to Erect Bridges between Palestinian Women," interview by Afif Safieh, *al-Fajr*, July 5, 1987, 15. On Inash al-Usra, founded by Samiha Khalil in 1965, see Phyllis Bennis, *From Stones to Statehood: The Palestinian Uprising* (London: Zed Books, 1990), 31-32.

41 Taraki, "Political Consciousness," 59.

42 Abd al-Jawad Saleh, two-hour interview (Ramallah and al-Bireh, June 16, 1995).
43 Sayigh, "Palestinian Women," 6.
44 Ibid., 10.
45 Ibid., 7.
46 Ibid., 7-8.
47 Ibid., 9.
48 Ibid., 25.
49 Rita Giacaman, "An Interview with Rita Giacaman: Women, Resistance, and the Popular Movement," *Palestine Focus* 24 (July-August 1987): 3. Giacaman was a Palestinian community health organizer, until she became associate professor at Bir Zeit College.
50 From no nurseries or kindergartens in 1980, the women's committees had developed eighty such centers by 1988. Rita Giacaman, "Palestinian Women in the Uprising: From Followers to Leaders," *Journal of Refugee Studies* 2, no. 1 (1989): 145 n. 4.
51 McDowall, *The Palestinians*, 96.
52 Giacaman, "Palestinian Women," 143; Amni Rimawi, "People's Activities and Trade Union Work: A Personal Account," *Palestinian Women: Identity and Experience*, ed. Ebba Augustin (London: Zed Books, 1993), 79-80.
53 At a roundtable discussion on democracy, at the Palestinian Center for Democracy and Elections in East Jerusalem on June 15, 1995, the fact that women were allowed by Jordan to vote for the first time in 1976 was cited as a reason for the success of the nationalist candidates in the elections. Under Jordanian law, women were disenfranchised until 1973; the 1976 elections were their first opportunity to use the ballot.
54 Hiltermann, *Behind the Intifada*, 9-10, 28, 132; Frisch, "Diffusion and Consolidation," 46.
55 Barghuti, "Institution Building," 127; Sayigh, "Palestinian Women," 10. Italics in original.
56 "Institution Building on the West Bank" (Zahira Kamal), in Najjar and Warnock, *Portraits*, 135, 145. Italics in original. See also Rosemary Radford Ruether, "The Women of Palestine; Steadfastness and Self-help in the Occupied Territories," *Christianity and Crisis*, December 14, 1987, 434-36.
57 Kamal, "Institution Building," 141, 143, 144.
58 Hiltermann, *Behind the Intifada*, 134.
59 "Institution Building on the West Bank" (Amal Khreisheh), in Najjar and Warnock, *Portraits*, 150.
60 Daoud Kuttab, "Palestinian Women Unite," East Jerusalem, December 1988, Kuttab private papers.
61 Hiltermann, *Behind the Intifada*, 134; conclusion, in Najjar and Warnock, *Portraits*, 259.
62 Chart entitled "Structure of the Palestinian Federation of Women's Action Committees in the Occupied Territories," in Najjar and Warnock, *Portraits*, 136-37. Succession in the women's committees was similar to that which occurred as leaders of the local national committees were incarcerated by the British during the "great revolt" of 1936-39.
63 Hiltermann, *Behind the Intifada*, 127.
64 On Israeli targeting of emerging women leaders, see Talhami, "Women under Occupation," 22-23; Committee Confronting the Iron Fist, *We Will Be Free in Our Homeland* (Chicago: Palestine Human Rights Campaign, 1986), 72-75; Zahira Kamal, "Under Town Arrest," *Palestine Focus* 13 (July-August 1985): 3.
65 Giacaman, "Women, Resistance, Popular Movement," 3.
66 Ghada Talhami, "Women under Occupation," in Sabbagh and Talhami, *Image and Reality*, 19-20.

Chapter 6

1 Eqbal Ahmad, "Yasser Arafat's Nightmare" *MERIP Reports, Middle East Research and Information Project* 13 (November-December 1983): 21.
2 British-imposed Salt Laws taxed a chemical compound essential for life by prohibiting the making of salt for personal use from seawater, thus penalizing the poor in India. Gandhi announced a 241-mile march from Ahmedabad to Dandi. Its original seventy-nine adherents swelled to thousands, who walked to the sea and violated the statutes. More than sixty thousand Indians were jailed in the nationwide civil-disobedience movement that followed. B. R. Nanda, *Mahatma Gandhi: A Biography* (Delhi: Oxford University Press, 1958), 290-97. Gandhi chose removal of these prohibitions not only because of the fundamental injustice the laws represented, but because they were an emblem of an unpopular and unrepresentative foreign government.
3 Arafat recalled having met Ahmad in 1974. Asked if he had given serious consideration to Ahmad's proposals, he responded "No." Arafat, interview (January 24, 1996). Bassam Abu Sharif, advisor to Arafat, also denied any influence from Ahmad. Abu-Sharif, interview (January 24, 1996).

4 Eqbal Ahmad, "Revolutionary Warfare and Counterinsurgency," *National Liberation: Revolution in the Third World*, ed. Norman Miller and Roderick Aya (New York: Free Press, 1971), 145, 157.

5 Ahmad, "Yasser Arafat's Nightmare," 20.

6 Antonio Gramsci, *Passato e Presente* (Turin: n.p., 1996), 164, as cited in Norbert Bobbio, "Gramsci and the Concept of Civil Society," in Keane, *Civil Society and the State: New European Perspectives*, ed. John Keane (London and New York: Verso, 1988), 84, 97 n. 21.

7 Perry Anderson, "The Antinomies of Antonio Gramsci," *New Left Review* 100 (November 1976-January 1977): 19, 21. On Gramsci's concept of hegemony, see Bobbio, "Gramsci and the Concept of Civil Society," 91-93; Roger D. Simon, *Gramsci's Political Thought: An Introduction* (London: Lawrence and Wishart, 1982), 21-28; and Raymond Williams, *Marxism and Literature* (Oxford: Oxford University Press, 1977), 108-14.

8 Edward Shils, "The Virtue of Civil Society," *Government and Opposition* 26, no. 1 (Winter 1992): 3.

9 Mustapha K. al-Sayyid, "Slow Thaw in the Arab World," *World Policy Journal* 8, no. 4 (Autumn 1991): 717.

10 Bir Zeit College has its origins in the 1920s as a secondary school. Having been a two-year college in the 1960s, after 1967 it became the first Palestinian institution of higher learning in the occupied territories, and after being made into a four-year institution, during the academic year 1975-76 became Bir Zeit University.

11 Khatib, interview (December 15, 1997).

12 Lisa Taraki, "The Development of Political Consciousness among Palestinians in the Occupied Territories, 1967-1987," in Nassar and Heacock, *Intifada: Palestine at the Crossroads*, 59, 60.

13 "Institution Building on the West Bank" (Siham Barghuti), in Najjar and Warnock, *Portraits*, 126-27.

14 Saleh, interview (June 16, 1995). Saleh later became minister of agriculture of the Palestinian Authority.

15 Lisa Taraki, "Mass Organizations in the West Bank," in Aruri, *Occupation: Israel over Palestine*, 452.

16 Barghuti, "Institution Building," 127.

17 Ibid.

18 Saleh, interview (June 16, 1995).

19 Glenn Edward Robinson, *Building a Palestinian State: The Incomplete Revolution* (Bloomington, Indiana University Press, 1997), 30; Saleh, interview (June 16, 1995).

20 Allowed to return from exile in Jordan twenty years later, Saleh became actively involved in the Palestinian Center for the Study of Nonviolence and its offshoot, the Palestinian Center for Democracy and Elections, both in East Jerusalem.

21 Saleh, "'Abu Ammar's Biggest Mistake,'" pp. 26-27.

22 Saleh, interview (June 16, 1995). Frisch's analysis complements Saleh's account and Taraki's analysis. Although Frisch seeks to prove the emergence of a robotic, inbred command in the intifada, subordinated to hierarchical factional controls (an interpretation rejected here), he acknowledges the "insulation from outside influences" of such organizations as the Shabiba committees, voluntary work committees, and four women's groups. Frisch, "Middle Command," 261.

23 Robinson, *Building a Palestinian State*, 30.

24 Ibid., 29. A committee member described the purpose: "providing . . . for residents during strikes, to advise people, and to help them set up popular committees." Daoud Kuttab, "Ramallah and al-Bireh Resident Clean Up," *al-Fajr*, 9-April 15, 1982, 11.

25 Sahliyeh, *Leadership*, 117.

26 Azmy Bishara, one-hour interview (East Jerusalem, June 17, 1995). Bishara heads the Department of Cultural Studies at Bir Zeit. In the Middle East, "the intellgentsia is numerically small, and the weight of the students, frequently the only organized body considering the absence of political parties in the Western sense, is consequently great." Laqueur, *Communism and Nationalism*, 14.

27 "The Intifada Generation: The Legislative Council," special supplement on the intifada, translation commissioned (hereafter trans. comm.), Nermeen Murad, *al-Ayyam*, January 29, 1996, 1. *Al-Ayyam* describes itself as an independent newspaper.

28 Daoud Kuttab, draft of "Stonethrowers," East Jerusalem, Kuttab private papers; idem, "A Profile of the Stonethrowers," *Journal of Palestine Studies* 67 (Spring 1988).

29 Nusseibeh, interview (November 5, 1994).

30 Sahliyeh, *Leadership*, 117.

31 Frisch, "Transformation," 106; Frisch, "Diffusion and Consolidation," 46-47.

32 Nusseibeh, interview (November 5, 1994).

33 Shaul Mishal and Reuben Aharoni; *Speaking Stones: Communiqués from the Intifada Underground*, (Syracuse University Press, 1994), 4.

34 From *Statistical Abstract of Israel*-1985, no. 35, 724, as cited in Frisch, "Transformation," 94.
35 From *Statistical Abstract of Israel*-1971, no. 22, 647; *Statistical Abstract of Israel*-1976, no. 27: 729, as cited in Frisch, ibid., 95.
36 Jim Lederman, "Dateline West Bank: Interpreting the Intifada," *Foreign Policy* 72 (Autumn 1988): 233.
37 Mishal and Aharoni, *Speaking Stones*, 1.
38 Benvenisti, Abu-Zayed, and Rubinstein, *West Bank Handbook*, 213.
39 Raja Shehadeh, *Occupier's Law: Israel and the West Bank* (Washington, D.C.: Institute for Palestine Studies, 1985), 171. In the autumn of 1982, educators were incensed by requirement of a "loyalty oath," whereby all teachers not holding militarily issued identity cards (even if born in the territories) would agree not to provide "direct or indirect" support to the PLO or any other "terrorist" organization. Having refused to sign, more than twenty-five lecturers from al-Najah University and nineteen from Bir Zeit were either barred from teaching or deported. Ibid., 171-72.
40 Sari Nusseibeh, two-hour interview (East Jerusalem, December 13, 1997); idem, two-hour interview (East Jerusalem, January 28, 1996).
41 Glenn E. Robinson, *Palestinian Leadership in Transition?* Information Brief no. 71 (Washington, D.C.: Center for Policy Analysis on Palestine, March 15, 2001).
42 Salim Tamari, "What the Uprising Means," in Lockman and Beinin, *Intifada*, 131.
43 Benvenisti, Abu-Zayed, and Rubinstein, *West Bank Handbook*, 211.
44 Ibid., 212.
45 Nusseibeh, interview (November 5, 1994); Sari Nusseibeh, "The Gathering Palestinian Storm," repr. from *Los Angeles Times*, January 21, 1988, in *Palestine: A State Is Born*, ed. Afif Safieh (The Hague: Palestine Information Office, 1990), 13.
46 Peretz, *Intifada*, 15.
47 In Order 947, the Israeli army is the source of civil and military authority in the territories, delegating to a civilian administration what nonmilitary powers it sees fit, in line with Israeli interpretations of the Camp David accords, which mention the "withdrawal," not the "abolition," of the military government upon inauguration of an autonomy scheme. Aronson, *Israel, Palestinians and the Intifada*, 254-55. Palestinian jurists interpret 947 as a "unilateral declaration of a constitutional change." Jonathan Kuttab and Raja Shehadeh, *Civilian Administration in the Occupied Territories: Analysis of Israeli Military Order no. 947* (Ramallah: Law in the Service of Man, 1982), 8; Shehadeh, *Occupier's Law*, 69-75.
48 Schiff and Yaari, *Intifada*, 21.
49 Benvenisti, Abu-Zayed, and Rubinstein, *West Bank Handbook*, 217.
50 Shehadeh, *Occupier's Law*, 174-76; David Richardson, "Leagues Out of Their Depth," *Jerusalem Post*, March 19, 1982, as cited in ibid, 206 n. 69. Two hundred were armed and trained; the leagues were "a coalition of rural thugs." Robinson, *Building a Palestinian State*, 17.
51 Aronson, *Israel, Palestinians and the Intifada*, 250-51.
52 Ian Black and Benny Morris, *Israel's Secret Wars: A History of Israel's Intelligence Services* (New York: Grove Weidenfeld, 1991), 476.
53 *Yediot Aharonot*, September 24, 1981, as cited in Aronson, *Israel, Palestinians and the Intifada*, 256-57.
54 Peretz, *Intifada*, 16.
55 Nusseibeh, interview (November 5, 1994).
56 Employed by the British to crush the "great revolt," the Israelis have maintained the practice of demolishing homes. See Lynn Welchman, *A Thousand and One Homes: Israel's Demolition and Sealing of Houses in the Occupied Palestinian Territories*, Occasional Paper no. 11 (Ramallah: al-Haq, 1993), 5-49. More than 2,500 Palestinian homes were demolished by Israel between 1967 and 1997, according to witness groups on the West Bank that use the nonviolent method of "accompaniment"; 239 Palestinian homes in East Jerusalem alone were demolished between 1986 and January 1997. Virginia Baron, "After the Bulldozers, the Rebuilding," *Nonviolent Activist* 14, no. 4 (July-August 1997): 4. B'Tselem ("in the image of God," *b'tselem elohim* [Genesis 1:27], in modern Hebrew is a synonym for human dignity, as in Article 1, Universal Declaration of Human Rights, "all human beings were born free and equal in dignity and rights"), the Israeli Information Center for Human Rights in the Occupied Territories, founded in 1989 by MK Dedi Zucker and other Knesset members and academicians, reports that 1,387 homes were demolished from 1967 to the start of the intifada. "Demolishing Peace: Israel's Policy of Mass Demolition of Palestinian Houses in the West Bank" (Jerusalem: B'Tselem, Israeli Information Center for Human Rights in the Occupied Territories, 1997). [Hereafter B'Tselem will be cited without its full name.] During the intifada, Israel upped its use of house demolitions as punishment.

57   Al-Haq, *Punishing a Nation*, 4.

58   Peretz, *Intifada*, 17. Arms were readily available to Israeli armed settler groups from two primary sources: military weapons and ordinance were distributed to soldiers studying at Israeli yeshivas where such armed groups were strong, and firearms were offered under wraps to settler activists by sympathetic army personnel. Aronson, *Israel, Palestinians and the Intifada*, 206.

59   Zeev Schiff, as cited in Aronson, *Israel, Palestinians and the Intifada*, 291.

60   Attempts at assassination—apparently by Israeli groups advocating forcible expulsion of all Arabs from Eretz Israel and with the evident knowledge of the authorities—were made on three mayors: Bassam Shaka, Karim Khalaf, and Ibrahim Attawil. Shaka's legs were amputated after a bomb detonated in his car. Khalaf lost a foot to a bomb and died of gangrene. Attawil found an explosive device in his car and escaped. Mayors Mohammad Milhem and Fahd Qawasmeh were deported. Others were removed in one way or another. Aronson, *Israel, Palestinians and the Intifada*, 166-67, 192-96, 202, 205-11, 225, 240, 278.

61   Don Peretz, "The *Intifada* and Middle East Peace," *Survival* 32, no. 5 (September-October 1990): 388.

62   On nonviolent sanctions in the Middle East, see Khalid Kishtainy, "Violent and Nonviolent Struggle in Arab History," in Crow et al., *Arab Nonviolent Struggle in the Middle East*, 1990), 9-24. On the Golan Druze resistance of 1981-82, see Brad Bennett, "Arab-Muslim Cases of Nonviolent Struggle," in ibid., 50-52; R. Scott Kennedy, "The Golani Druze: A Case of Non-Violent Resistance," *Journal of Palestine Studies* 13, no. 2 (Winter 1984): 48-64; and idem, *The Druze of the Golan: A Case of Nonviolent Resistance*, monograph (Philadelphia: New Society Publishers, 1984).

63   Kennedy, *Druze of the Golan*, 10, 11.

64   Bennett, "Arab-Muslim Cases of Nonviolent Struggle," in Crow, *Arab Nonviolent Struggle*, 51; Kennedy, *Druze of the Golan*, 11.

65   Kennedy, ibid., 11-12.

66   Bennett, "Arab-Muslim Cases of Nonviolent Struggle," in Crow, *Arab Nonviolent Struggle*, 51.

67   Ibid.

68   Shlaim, *Iron Wall*, 396.

69   Pappé, *History of Modern Palestine*, 221.

70   Cheryl A. Rubenberg, *Israel and the American National Interest: A Critical Examination* (Urbana and Chicago: University of Illinois Press, 1986), 254.

71   Michael K. Deaver, *Behind the Scenes* (New York: William Morrow and Company, 1987), 165-66.

72   George W. Ball, *Error and Betrayal in Lebanon: An Analysis of Israel's Invasion of Lebanon and the Implications for U.S.-Israeli Relations* (Washington, D.C.: Foundation for Middle East Peace, 1984), 21.

73   Zeev Schiff, "Most Likely, Begin Was Fooling Himself," *Haaretz*, December 17, 1997, 7, English ed., book review of Mordechai Zippori, *In a Straight Line* (Tel Aviv: Yedioth Ahronoth Books, 1997).

74   Stephen Green, *Living by the Sword: America and Israel in the Middle East 1968-87* (Brattleboro, Vermont: Amana Books, 1988), 171.

75   Schenker, "To Channel This Energy," 18.

76   Jad Isaac, "Agriculture in the West Bank and Gaza," in Ateek, Ellis, and Ruether, *Faith and the Intifada*, 33; Samih K. Farsoun and Jean M. Landis, "The Sociology of an Uprising: The Roots of the Intifada," in Nassar and Heacock, *Intifada*, 20.

77   Amiram Goldblum, former spokesperson for Peace Now, one-hour interview (East Jerusalem, November 5, 1994).

78   Edward W. Said, "Reflections on Twenty Years of Palestinian History," *Journal of Palestine Studies* 80 (Summer 1991): 6. In an interview, Abu Jihad condemned the Arab world for "confiscating our will." He said, "We can overcome the Israeli effects on our will, . . . but will we overcome the Arab renunciation of the Palestinians from 1966 to this day?" Khalil al-Wazir, one-hour interview (Tunis, October 14, 1984).

79   Frisch, "Transformation," 107.

80   Amal Jamal, *The Palestinian National Movement: Politics of Contention: 1967-2005* (Bloomington: Indiana University Press, 2005), 75.

81   Adnan Milhem, "A Picture from Life—The Sacrifice of the Youth," *al-Fajr*, January 25, 1983.

82   Frisch, "Transformation," 106; idem, "Diffusion and Consolidation," 47.

83   Roundtable discussion, Palestinian Center for Democracy and Elections, East Jerusalem (June 15, 1995).

84   Aronson, *Israel, Palestinians and the Intifada*, 330, 321.

85   John Kifner, "Wave of Palestinian Unrest Reaches Once-Quiet Village," *New York Times*, January 24, 1988.

86   "Institutions Closed during the Uprising," in Cainkar and Goldring, *Uprising in Palestine, The First Year*, 403-5.

87 Frisch, "Transformation," 110.

88 "Membership in, contact with, or expressed support for the aims of proscribed organizations (e.g., the Palestine Liberation Organization or its constituent elements) is grounds for arrest." U.S. Department of State, "Israel and the Occupied Territories," *Country Reports on Human Rights Practices for 1982* (Washington, D.C.: Government Publishing Office, 1983), 1159.

89 Throughout history, prisoners who believed they had no other recourse have used the fast until death. Palestinian hunger strikes often appear in oral histories. See Staughton Lynd, Sam Bahour, and Alice Lynd, *Homeland: Oral Histories of Palestine and Palestinians* (New York: Olive Branch Press, 1994), 159-60, 161-63, 165, 168-69. Labor historian Staughton Lynd directed the "freedom schools" in the Mississippi Freedom Summer of 1964, among the alternative, or parallel institutions, of the 1960s U.S. civil rights movement. Sharp classifies hunger strikes in the third, most serious category of methods—nonviolent interventions, methods of disruption—precisely because such actions intervene, and can "disrupt the operation of the established system." Hunger strikes may be used defensively, to thwart, or offensively, to carry the struggle into the target group's camp. Sharp, *Waging Nonviolent Struggle*, 49, 62; idem, *Methods of Nonviolent Action*, 357-78, 363.

90 Jeremy Bennett, "The Resistance against the German Occupation of Denmark, 1940-45," in Roberts, *Civilian Resistance as a National Defense*, 159; Semelin, *Unarmed against Hitler*, 36.

91 A striker recalled, "[Israeli authorities] forced milk into strugglers through the nose. It caused many illnesses, one being ulcers. Tubes were inserted from the mouth into the stomach and were moved up and down, cutting the walls of the stomach." I. Walid, in Lynd, Bahour, and Lynd, *Homeland*, 159.

92 For a firsthand account by an organizer of this hunger strike, see Jabril Rajoub, "Prison Hunger Strikes: The Case of Nafha Prison, 1980," *We Will Be Free in Our Homeland* (East Jerusalem and Chicago: Committee Confronting the Iron Fist and Palestine Human Rights Campaign, 1986), 58-67. A Fateh activist deported in 1988, Rajoub would later be appointed head of security for the Palestinian Authority.

93 See *A Report on the Treatment of Security Prisoners at the West Bank Prison of al-Faraa* (Ramallah: al-Haq, 1984). Incarceration of political prisoners, i.e., those "convicted or detained on suspicion of committing offences against the 'security' laws of the Israeli military government in the occupied West Bank," al-Haq says, is "strictly against Article 76 of the Fourth Geneva Convention." Ibid., 1.

94 "Coping with the Loss of Palestine" (Umm Ibrahim Shawabkeh), in Najjar and Warnock, *Portraits*, 35.

95 Badran Bader Jaber, in Lynd, Bahour, and Lynd, *Homeland*, 161.

96 So potent was the method of fasting until death, in Gandhi's view, that, because of its emotionally coercive effect, one's opponents were essentially forced to change. Gandhi, *Autobiography*, 432. Calling this method an "infallible" weapon, he believed it was acceptable if repression by the opponent had closed all other avenues of protest, or all other methods had failed. M. K. Gandhi, *The Statesman* (Calcutta), September 2, 1947, 10; idem, *CWMG* 89:132.

97 Badran Bader Jaber, in Lynd, Bahour, and Lynd, *Homeland*, 162.

98 A firsthand description of prisoners organizing an "internal apparatus" in Ramleh and "contacting" other prisons is given by Ali Muhammad Jiddah, in Lynd, Bahour, and Lynd, *Homeland*, 165.

99 Qaddourah Faris, two-hour interview (Ramallah, March 18, 1997).

100 Mahmoud Jasser, two-hour interview (Ramallah, March 18, 1997).

101 Faris, interview (March 18, 1997). As of 2006, approximately ten thousand Palestinians were in Israeli jails. Nadia Hijab, "Hamas, Its Neighbors, and the Quartet," Washington, D.C., Palestine Center, *For The Record*, no. 260, Transcript of Remarks, 24 July 2006 http://ent.groundspring.org/EmailNow/pub.php?module=URLTracker&cmd=track&j=87729429&u=812946.

102 Ali Muhammad Jiddah, imprisoned for seventeen years, said, "[W]e had the ability to transform collective cemeteries [the prisons] into the most academic revolutionary schools. Our people who graduated from Israeli jails were well educated. . . . I began learning the Hebrew language which I now speak and write fluently." Lynd, Bahour, and Lynd, *Homeland*, 165.

103 Faris, interview (March 18, 1997); Jasser, interview (March 18, 1997). On March 10, 1997, the author was in adjacent offices as Israeli officials entered the Nuzha Building in East Jerusalem and sealed the headquarters of the "Prisoners' Club." Four similar groups also were closed that day by the Netanyahu government, which alleged that these were offices of the Palestinian Authority. Members of the prisoners' clubs, however, speak with pride of their financial independence from any authority and argue the validity of nonmilitary political methods and democratic procedures.

104 To Frisch, the former prisoners, once released and under surveillance, moved toward political organizations allied with their factional preferences, suggesting a turn to political struggle as a function of eluding further incarceration. Frisch, "Diffusion and Consolidation," 47-48. Doubtless true

for some, the research here discloses a deeper political transformation taking place in prisons. "[I]n full view of their Israeli jailers, Palestinian security prisoners (who are held separate from common criminals) built an independent network whose cohesion, intellectual verve, and rich store of experience would manifest themselves in all their power during the Palestinian uprising. . . . What even the PLO did not know was the degree to which the Palestinians' prison experience was the force transforming the spontaneous outburst of rage into a sustained, organized revolt." Ehud Yaari, "Israel's Prison Academies: The Palestinian Uprising Can Almost Be Called a Product of the Israeli Prison System," *Atlantic*, October 1989, 22. Still, such interpretations neglect the significance of this movement within a movement for adoption of nonviolent resistance.

105 Barghuti, "Institution Building," in Najjar and Warnock, *Portraits*, 132, 131.

106 Analyzing his victory, Faris says, "[T]he resistance background of the imprisoned leaders stayed very much in the minds of the voters, . . . a decisive factor in my success." Interviews with Marwan Barghouti, Qaddourah Faris, Jamal Shoubaki, et al., "Intifada Generation," *al-Ayyam*, 2-3.

107 Faris, interview (March 18, 1997).

108 Gene Sharp, *The Role of Power in Nonviolent Struggle*, Monograph Series no. 3 (Boston, Albert Einstein Institution, 1994): 6-8.

109 Benvenisti, Abu-Zayed, and Rubinstein, *West Bank Handbook*, 162.

110 Nora Kort, director, Catholic Relief Services, one-hour interview (East Jerusalem, November 4, 1994).

111 John Kifner, "Israelis and Palestinians Change Their Tactics but Not Their Goals," *New York Times*, May 15, 1988, 1. The quality of services varied, and the calibre of leadership was uneven, but their existence in great numbers is indisputable. Costa Dabbagh, director, Middle East Council of Churches, one-hour interview (Gaza City, November 8, 1994).

112 Feisel Husseini, one-hour interview (East Jerusalem, June 14, 1995).

113 Faysal Husayni, Interview, *Journal of Palestine Studies* 72 (Summer 1989), 4, 5.

114 Muhammad Muslih identifies four types of organizations in Palestinian civil society during the period after 1967: political shops, voluntary cooperatives, voluntary mass organizations, and Islamist groups. Muslih views them as "penetrated" by the PLO, rather than as presented here, in which broad nonmilitary civilian organizing, much of it only nominally affiliated with factions, shaped a civil society despite the absence of a nation-state, while in effect preparing for massive nonmilitary resistance to belligerent occupation. Muslih credits Fateh for the post-1967 civilian nonmilitary mobilization, despite its instigation by the communists, as shown here, and sees student associations as "political proxies" for mobilization by PLO commando groups. Muslih, "Palestinian Civil Society," 251-52. He says cooperatives developed as a result of the intifada. Ibid., 253. In 1984, the author visited cooperatives for breeding chickens, bee-keeping, and raising rabbits in the territories. Regarding voluntary mass organizations, he erroneously traces these organizations to student voluntary work committees to clean up the Old City of Nablus in the mid-1970s, rather than to 1972 in Ramallah and al-Bireh, as shown here and corroborated by Ghassan Khatib. Khatib, interview (December 15, 1997). Fourth in Muslih's classifications are Islamist groups, about which he says little.

115 Michael S. Serrill, "In the Eye of a Revolt," *Time*, January 25, 1988, 32.

116 Ziad Abu-Amr, *Islamic Fundamentalism and the West Bank and Gaza: Muslim Brotherhood and Islamic Jihad* (Bloomington: Indiana University Press, 1994), 3. Branches were soon established in Haifa, Jaffa, Lydda, Nablus, and Tulkarem. After the 1948 war, branches were set up in Anabta, Bethlehem, Dura, Hebron, Jenin, Jericho, Qalqilya, Sur Bahir, Surif, Tubas, and elsewhere. Cohen, *Political Parties*, 144-45.

117 Thomas Mayer, "The Military Force of Islam: The Society of the Muslim Brethren and the Palestine Question, 1945-48," in Kedourie and Haim, *Zionism and Arabism*, 100-101.

118 Ibid., 109-10.

119 Maoz, *Palestinian Leadership*, 11.

120 Abu-Amr, *Islamic Fundamentalism*, 4.

121 Cohen, *Political Parties*, 146, 149.

122 Ibid., 153.

123 Abu-Amr, *Islamic Fundamentalism*, 7.

124 Shaul Mishal and Avraham Sela, *Hamas: A Behavioural Profile*, monograph (Tel Aviv: Tami Steinmetz Center for Peace Research, 1997), 10; Jean-François Legrain, "Hamas," *Oxford Encyclopedia of the Modern Islamic World*, ed. John L. Esposito (Oxford: Oxford University Press, 1995), 94. In 2004, Yasin was killed by an Israeli targeted assassination.

125 Yvonne Haddad, "Islamists and the 'Problem of Israel': The 1967 Awakening," *Middle East Journal* 4, no. 2 (Spring 1992): 275, 276.

126 Abu-Amr, *Islamic Fundamentalism*, 10.

127 Souad R. Dajani, *Eyes without Country: Searching for a Palestinian Strategy of Liberation* (Philadelphia: Temple University Press, 1994), 55; Cobban, "Gunless in Gaza," 213.

128 Abu-Amr, *Islamic Fundamentalism*, 43-45.

129 Lisa Taraki, "The Islamic Resistance Movement in the Palestinian Uprising," in Lockman and Beinin, *Intifada*, 172-73.

130 Abu-Amr, *Islamic Fundamentalism*, 102, 104, 95, 51, 63-67.

131 Caryle Murphy, "Bombing May Show Split within Hamas Leadership," *Washington Post*, October 20, 1994, A36.

132 Abu-Amr, *Islamic Fundamentalism*, 67.

133 All but verified in a 1989 editorial in the *Jerusalem Post*, "Before the outbreak of the intifada, Jerusalem may even have had reason to believe that the Islamic fundamentalists would usefully drain away Palestinian nationalist sentiment into less harmful channels. Divide the opponents and keep the territories was the rule. But for the past nearly two years there could be no doubt that, politically, Hamas represents the very extremity of violent Palestinian extremism. . . . " "Violent Islam Outlawed," *Jerusalem Post*, October 3, 1989.

134 Steve Sherman, "Gazans and the *Intifada*: United and Steadfast," *Middle East International*, April 13, 1990, 18; Youssef M. Ibrahim, "Deportees Go It Alone," *International Herald Tribune*, December 20, 1992, 1; Tom Masland, et al., "Building an Enemy," *Newsweek*, February 15, 1993, 28. By 1989, due to the large numbers of its adherents arrested, Hamas would shift its decision making to exiled officials in Jordan, Syria, and Iran. Wafa Amr, "Hamas Locked in Dispute over Halting Israel Attacks," Reuters North American Wire, May 20, 1996.

135 Tamari, "What the Uprising Means," 137. In Gaza, Tamari notes, when the Muslim Brotherhood attacked the Red Crescent Society and the communists, they were allowed to do so with no interference from Israeli security forces, and when two liquor stores were burned, there was no intervention.

136 David Shipler, *Arab and Jew: Wounded Spirits in a Promised Land* (New York: Times Publishers, 1986), 176-77. Bassam Abu-Sharif alleges that in 1987, Israel gave Hamas permission to open twenty centers in the territories. Bassam Abu-Sharif and Uzi Mahnaimi, *Tried by Fire: The Searing True Story of Two Men at the Heart of the Struggle between the Arabs and Jews* (London: Little, Brown and Co., 1995), 226.

137 Susan Hattis Rolef, "Israel's Policy toward the PLO: From Rejection to Recognition," in *The PLO and Israel: From Armed Conflict to Political Solution, 1964-1994*, ed. Avraham Sela and Moshe Maoz (New York: St. Martin's Press, 1997), 259.

138 Yigal Caspi, Israeli Foreign Ministry spokesperson in 1994 when Shimon Peres was foreign minister, one-hour interview (Jerusalem, November 10, 1994). "Fifteen years ago, at a time when we should have been talking to the PLO, we were instead trying to destroy its power base," Caspi said.

139 Nusseibeh clarified, "Perhaps three cell members in a faculty union were Fateh, out of 150 who defined themselves as Fateh." Nusseibeh, interview (November 5, 1994).

140 Nusseibeh, interview (November 5, 1994).

141 Frisch, "Diffusion and Consolidation," 48.

142 Hiltermann, *Behind the Intifada*, 5, 6.

143 Sara M. Roy, *The Gaza Strip: The Political Economy of De-Development* (Washington, D.C.: Institute for Palestine Studies, 1995).

144 Frisch, "Middle Command," 263.

145 Ehud Yaari, "Runaway Revolution: PLO Attempts to Control Palestinian Uprising in the Occupied Territories," *Atlantic*, June 1988, 25.

146 Sahliyeh, *Leadership*, 4. See Frisch, "Transformation," 109; Robinson, *Building a Palestinian State*, 1-18.

147 Tamari, "The Intifada," 18, 19.

148 This would be shown later in the first Fateh elections in the occupied territories, on November 4, 1994, in Ramallah. Winners would come from the young underground leadership of the intifada, individuals like Qaddourah Faris, who had spent years in Israeli prisons, and local intifada activists from refugee camps and villages. Most candidates on Arafat's list, from the cadres newly returning from Tunis, would not be elected. Lamia Lahoud, "Younger Fatah Takes over in Ramallah," *Jerusalem Post*, November 7, 1994.

149 Penny Johnson, Lee O'Brien, and Joost R. Hiltermann, "The West Bank Rises Up," in Lockman and Beinin, *Intifada*, 38. Whether the emerging leadership was "new" or not is a matter of debate regarding the first intifada. See, for example, Frisch, "Middle Command."

150 Machool, "This Isn't Rebellion," 14.

151 Peretz, "*Intifada* and Middle East Peace," 389.

152 Between September and December 1987, Israeli authorities "cracked down hard" on the Balata refugee camp, and the Gaza Strip, leading Daoud Kuttab to conclude "the Israeli government had begun to realize that a network of local organizations was taking root in the occupied territories." Kuttab, "Stonethrowers," 20.

153 Ali Jarbawi, one-hour interview (Ramallah, June 16, 1995).

Chapter 7

1 Wesley G. Pippert, "Seeking Justice through Nonviolent Resistance," *Christianity Today*, March 20, 1987.

2 David Richardson, "Confrontation Quest," *Jerusalem Post*, November 25, 1983.

3 George P. Sakalosky, thirty-minute personal communication (Columbus, Ohio, November 11, 1998).

4 Edward Grossman, "Palestinian Pacifist," *Jerusalem Post*, October 17, 1986.

5 Mubarak Awad and John Cavanaugh-O'Keefe, "*Sabr*: Nonviolence in Palestine," unpubl. manuscript (Washington, D.C., 1992), 84.

6 Sarah Peery, "Palestinian Center Advocates Nonviolence," *Post-Standard* (Syracuse, N.Y.), May 23, 1986.

7 Richardson, "Confrontation Quest."

8 Ibid.

9 Mubarak E. Awad, "Compilation of the Opinions of the Majority of the Group," results of a three-page questionnaire (East Jerusalem, Palestinian Counseling Center, May 3, 1983).

10 Jonathan Kuttab, two-hour interview (East Jerusalem, June 17, 1995).

11 Awad, interview (October 19, 1995).

12 David Richardson, "Palestinians Weigh Pros and Cons of Passive Resistance," *Jerusalem Post*, October 16, 1983.

13 Richardson, "Confrontation Quest." The workshops were "actively supported and encouraged" by the Quakers and Mennonites. Idem, "Pros and Cons."

14 Ibid.

15 Richardson, "Pros and Cons." The Israelis knew that Awad was not in conformity with the rigidly politicized social order. Awad was told by one Israeli government official, "We are waiting for the Palestinians to bury you." Peery, "Palestinian Center Advocates Nonviolence"; Grossman, "Palestinian Pacifist."

16 Nancy Nye, memorandum (Washington, D.C., April 20, 1995).

17 Milton Viorst, "Letter from Jerusalem," *Mother Jones*, April 1988, 23. See also Richardson, "Confrontation Quest."

18 Richardson, "Confrontation Quest." Awad told Richardson that the Palestinians were sufficiently politically astute to undertake nonviolent resistance and that villages offered more fertile ground than urban areas, where business and mercantile concerns came first. He also stated his view that women were politically more fervent than men and that the plight of the Palestinian refugees was inherently political.

19 Mubarak Awad and Jonathan Kuttab, "Palestinian Resistance and Nonviolent Ways," program for workshops (East Jerusalem, October 13-15, 1983), 2. Italics in original. (See appendices, p. 350.)

20 Ibid., 1.

21 Ibid.

22 Acceptance of penalties for noncooperation is expressed in the program as follows: "Self-suffering is not as 'martyrs,' yet not harming our opponents even if they harm us." Ibid., 4. The idea of self-sacrifice—the literal meaning of the *fedayeen* (Palestinian guerrillas of the 1950s and 1960s)—is in Mubarak Awad's materials reconstituted as popular self-sacrifice by men, women, and children, but aimed at specific injustices or survival. Instead of invoking martyrdom, in Awad's writings Palestinians of all ages and walks of life could express their grievances, afflictions, and inequities without an intention to harm, injure, or destroy the opponent, since change in the target group can be induced by the ability of the nonviolent protagonist to penetrate the adversary's psychological defenses.

23 Awad, "Palestinian Resistance," 2.

24 Letter from M. K. Gandhi, April 18, 1932, CWMG, vol. 49, 320-21.

25 Martin Luther King, Jr., "Nonviolence and Racial Justice," *Christian Century*, February 6, 1957.

26 King, "Non-Aggression Procedures to Interracial Harmony," address delivered to executives of the Home Mission Societies of Christian Friends, Green Lake, Wisconsin, July 23, 1956, Clayborne Carson et al., *Papers of Martin Luther King, Jr.*, vol. 3, 325.

27 Gandhi, *Harijan*, March 23, 1940.

28   King, "Non-Aggression Procedures," 326. "Nonviolent resistance does not seek to defeat or humiliate the opponent. . . . The nonviolent resister must often express his protest through noncooperation or boycotts, but he realizes that noncooperation and boycotts are not ends themselves; they are merely means to awaken a sense of moral shame in the opponent." King, "Nonviolence and Racial Justice."

29   Gandhi, *Young India*, April 3, 1930.

30   Mohandas K. Gandhi, *An Autobiography: The Story of My Experiments with Truth*. Ahmedabad, India: Navajivan Publishing House, 1940, 337.

31   King, "Nonviolence: The Christian Way in Human Relations," *Presbyterian Life*, February 8, 1958, 12.

32   Gandhi, *Young India*, June 16, 1920.

33   King, question-and-answer session, National Press Club luncheon, August 22, 1962, Washington, D.C., audio transcription, Martin Luther King, Jr., Papers, King Library and Archives, Atlanta, Georgia.

34   King, "His Influence Speaks to World Conscience," *Hindustan Times*, January 30, 1958.

35   King, "Nonviolence and Racial Justice."

36   Ibid.

37   King, "Remaining Awake through a Great Revolution," his last Sunday sermon, National Cathedral, Washington, D.C., March 31, 1968, appendix 2 in Mary King, *Mahatma Gandhi and Martin Luther King, Jr.*

38   Awad, "Palestinian Resistance," 5. Italics in original.

39   Mubarak E. Awad, *Nonviolence in the Occupied Territories*, English trans., PASSIA archives (East Jerusalem: Palestinian Center for the Study of Nonviolence [hereafter PCSN]), 1983. (See appendices, p. 352, for excerpts from the booklet.)

40   The booklet was published in English the following year in Britain and the United States. Mubarak Awad, "Non-Violence in the Occupied Territories," *Race and Class* 25, no. 4 (Spring 1984): 71-83; idem, "Non-Violent Resistance: A Strategy for the Occupied Territories," *Journal of Palestine Studies* 13, no. 4 (Summer 1984), 22-36; idem, *Nonviolent Resistance: A Strategy for the Occupied Territories*, monograph (Philadelphia: New Society Publishers, 1984); idem, "Gandhi in the West Bank," excerpts, *Harper's*, January 1986, 23-24.

41   Diary of Beth Heisey Kuttab.

42   Douglas Brinkley, thirty-minute personal communication (East Jerusalem, January 22, 1996); Brinkley, *The Unfinished Presidency: Jimmy Carter's Journey beyond the White House* (New York, Viking, 1998), 240-41. Also see Jimmy Carter, *The Blood of Abraham* (Boston: Houghton Mifflin, 1985), 116.

43   Mubarak E. Awad, one-hour interview (Boston, October 19, 1995).

44   Awad, *Nonviolence*, 4.

45   Ibid, 5.

46   Ibid, 16.

47   Nye, memorandum (April 20, 1995), 3.

48   For the list, see Gene Sharp, *Methods of Nonviolent Action*, vol. 2, *The Politics of Nonviolent Action* (Boston: Porter Sargent Publishers, 1973): xi-xvi; idem, *Waging Nonviolent Struggle*, 51-64. Available on http://www.aeinstein.org/organizations.php3?orgid=88&typeID=15&action=printContentTypeHome

49   What was distributed in the 1980s in the Palestinian areas was generically entitled by Sharp in English as *Power, Struggle and Defense*, and translated into Arabic as *al-Muqawama bi La-Unf*. A version was brought out in Israel in the mid-1980s by Mifras Publishing House in Hebrew, entitled *Hitnaggedut Lo Alima* (Nonviolent Opposition). The first chapter of Sharp's monograph *National Security through Civilian-Based Defense* (Omaha, Nebraska: Association for Transarmament Studies, 1970) bears closest resemblance to what Awad had translated into Arabic in 1983. Gene Sharp, two-hour interview (Cambridge, Massachusetts, October 19, 1995).

50   Sharp, interview (October 19, 1995); Jonathan Kuttab, two-hour interview, East Jerusalem (December 12, 1997).

51   Josef Jøsten, "Czechoslovakia: From 1968 to Charter 77-A Record of Passive Resistance," *Conflict Studies* 86 (August 1977): 11.

52   Janusz Bugajski, *Czechoslovakia: Charter 77's Decade of Dissent*, Washington Papers 125 (London, Praeger: 1987): 9. Documents were secreted out to an international audience, in hopes that world attention could accelerate reform.

53   Kuttab, interview (December 12, 1997).

54   Grossman, "Palestinian Pacifist."

55   Richardson, "Confrontation Quest"; Yisrael Medad, "Palestinian Pacifist," letter to the editor, *Jerusalem Post*, October 24, 1986.

56   Mubarak Awad, two-hour interview, Washington, D.C. (January 14, 1995); Joel Greenberg, "Awad: Israel Climbed up a Tree," *Jerusalem Post*, November 26, 1987, 2.

57 Grossman, "Palestinian Pacifist."

58 Ibid.

59 Elaine Ruth Fletcher, "Awad: The Crucial Question," *Jerusalem Post*, November 27, 1987.

60 Awad, interview (October 11, 1992); Awad, *Nonviolence*, 3. "One of the most ruinous attitudes is that of *trying out* non-violence, and, if that does not lead to success, *intending* to use violence," Arne Naess writes; "The thought 'I shall first be non-violent, and if it does not succeed I am justified in using violence' is contradictory. There can be no first stage non-violence." Arne Naess, *Gandhi and Group Conflict: An Exploration of* Satyagraha; *Theoretical Background* (Oslo: Universitetsforlaget, 1974), 115.

61 Grossman, "Palestinian Pacifist."

62 Nat Hentoff, "The Olive Trees of Qatanna," *Village Voice*, December 23, 1986, 38.

63 Richardson, "Confrontation Quest"; Shlomo Riskin, "In Sheep's Clothing," *Jerusalem Post*, May 12, 1988; Phil Baum and Raphael Danziger, "This Palestinian Is No Gandhi," letter to the editor from the associate executive director and assistant director of the American Jewish Congress, *New York Times* (January 4, 1988).

64 Diary of Beth Heisey Kuttab. Kuttab is married to Jonathan Kuttab.

65 Hisham B. Sharabi was founding chairman of the Jerusalem Fund and the Palestine Center, cofounder of the Center for Contemporary Arab Studies at Georgetown University, and editor of the English-language quarterly, *Journal of Palestine Studies*. Born in Jaffa in 1927, he died in 2005.

66 Hisham B. Sharabi, one-hour interview (Washington, D.C., February 22, 1995); Awad, interview (February 14, 1995).

67 Awad, interview (February 14, 1995); R. Scott Kennedy, personal communication (East Jerusalem, January 29, 1996).

68 Kuttab, interview (June 17, 1995); Sharabi, interview (February 22, 1995).

69 Sharabi, interview (February 22, 1995); Heidi Shoup, executive director, Jerusalem Fund, twenty-minute personal communication (Washington, D.C., May 24, 1995). On fund-raising, see Margo Nakhoul, "Palestinian Nonviolence," Kuwait News Agency, May 21, 1986, 1; "A U.S. Arab in West Bank Loses Rights," *New York Times*, September 29, 1987, A16.

70 Awad and Nye were married in a Quaker wedding with no clergy; the couple refused to obtain a civil wedding license, because they did not wish to apply to the issuing Israeli Ministry of Religion, believing the requirement to be a politicization of religion. Even in matrimony, Awad evinced resistance, adding to his growing notoriety. Nancy Nye, personal communication (Washington, D.C., July 3, 1995). Awad and Nye worked together on counseling workshops, training, and technical assistance programs. Nancy Nye and Mubarak Awad, *Palestinian Counseling Project Progress Report* (East Jerusalem, July 15, 1985), files of PCSN.

71 Awad, interview (February 14, 1995). Gandhi's relationships with Muslims left indelible imprints. His closest childhood friend, Mehtab, was Muslim. In South Africa, Gandhi practiced with the Muslim legal firm of Dada Abdulla and Co. He read the Qur'an in translation. B. R. Nanda, *Mahatma Gandhi: A Biography* (Delhi: Oxford University Press, 1958), 21, 29, 81, 37, 40, 41; idem, *Gandhi: Pan-Islamism, Imperialism, and Nationalism in India* (Bombay: Oxford University Press, 1989); *Encyclopedia of Religion*, ed. Mircea Eliade, vol. 5 (New York: Macmillan, 1987), 482.

72 Eknath Easwaran, *A Man to Match His Mountains: Badshah Khan, Nonviolent Soldier of Islam* (Petaluma, California: Nilgiri Press, 1984).

73 Mohammad Raqib, "The Muslim Pashtun Movement of the North-West Frontier of India—1930-1934," in Sharp, *Waging Nonviolent Struggle*, 125.

74 Krishnalal Shridharani, *War without Violence: A Study of Gandhi's Method and Its Accomplishments* (New York: Harcourt, Brace and Co., 1939), 213, 289.

75 Mukulika Banerjee, *The Pathan Unarmed: Opposition and Memory in the North West Frontier* (Karachi; New Delhi: Oxford University Press, 2001), 8. Unarmed supporters held Peshawar for four days in April 1930. Ibid., 57-58. The Pashtuns maintained nonviolent discipline despite "severest provocation." Ibid., 58.

76 Charles Allen, *Soldier Sahibs: The Men Who Made the North-West Frontier* (London: Abacus, 2000), 18, 13.

77 "Nonviolent Soldier of Islam Introduced to Palestinians," Newsletter (East Jerusalem: PCSN, April-June 1986).

78 Nye, memorandum (April 20, 1995), 4; Peery, "Palestinian Center Advocates Nonviolence." After three years, the budget of the center was approximately $50,000 a year, with contributions mostly from private nonprofit institutions in the United States, including American Near East Refugee Aid (ANERA), United Palestine Appeal, United Methodist Women, Lutheran Church of America, Church of the Brethren, Mennonite Foundation, and private donors. Letter to Eschaton Foundation, from Mubarak Awad, thanking the foundation for $1,000, August 23, 1986; Peter Gubser, "Letter of Grant Award," $40,000 to PCSN from ANERA, August 26, 1987; Kenneth O. Holderread, "Letter from Church of the Brethren General Board," letter to Nafez Assaily awarding $1,000 grant to PCSN, November 30, 1990, East Jerusalem: PCSN files.

79 Ronita Torcato, "Tranquility amidst Terror," Indian Post (Mombai [Bombay]), May 19, 1987.

80 Nafez Assaily, "The Arabs before Islam" and "Qur'an Verses Advocating Nonviolence in Islam," Newsletter (East Jerusalem, PCSN), October 1989, 14-15.

81 Pappé, History of Modern Palestine, 166.

82 "An Invitation to Palestinians to Visit their Homes in Ramallah and Jaffa," al-Fajr, January 13, 1985.

83 Nadav Haetzni, "A Voice Calls the Palestinians to Visit their Houses in Ramle, Lod, and Jaffa," Hadashot, January 12, 1986, trans. comm. Zoughbi E. Zoughbi.

84 Stephen Franklin, "'Palestinian Gandhi' or Terrorist?" Chicago Tribune, May 18, 1988.

85 "Local Products Day: First Monday of Each Month; Eat and Drink Only Local Products," al-Fajr, May 30, 1986; "Local Products Day," trans., al-Quds, June 2, 1986; Local Products Day, four-page tabloid supplement (East Jerusalem, PCSN, November 1986); "Summary of Actions, Report on Previous Year's Activity," ibid.

86 Awad, interview (October 11, 1992).

87 See Thomas Smerling, "Gandhi's Spirit on the West Bank?" Christian Science Monitor, April 15, 1986, 15.

88 Nanda, Gandhi: Pan-Islamism, Imperialism, and Nationalism, 290.

89 Ben L. Kaufman, "Activist Teaches Lesson of Non-Violence," Cincinnati Enquirer, May 28, 1986.

90 Awad, interview (January 14, 1995).

91 Grossman, "Palestinian Pacifist."

92 Newsletter (East Jerusalem, PCSN), July-September 1986.

93 Awad, interview (January 14, 1995).

94 Husseini acknowledged arranging protection for Awad. Feisel Husseini, one-hour interview, East Jerusalem (January 30, 1996).

95 Sari Nusseibeh, two-hour interview, East Jerusalem (January 28, 1996); Andrew Rigby, Living the Intifada (London: Zed Books Ltd., 1991), 174.

96 Husseini, interview (January 30, 1996).

97 Awad, interview (October 19, 1995).

98 M. K. Gandhi, Constructive Programme: Its Meaning and Place (Ahmedabad, India: Navajivan Publishing House, 1941), 21-22.

99 Sharp, "The Theory of Gandhi's Constructive Program," in Gandhi as a Political Strategist, 77-86.

100 Jayantanuja Bandyopadhyaya, Social and Political Thought of Gandhi (Bombay: Allied Publishers, 1969), 205-6.

101 Sharp, Methods of Nonviolent Action, 398. On alternative institutions extensively developed in Kosovo throughout the 1990s, see Howard Clark, Civil Resistance in Kosovo (London: Pluto Press, 2000), esp. "Parallel Structures," 95-121.

102 Eqbal Ahmad, "Revolutionary Warfare and Counterinsurgency," extracted from Norman Miller and Roderick Aya, National Liberation: Revolution in the Third World (New York: Free Press, 1971), in Chaliand, Terrorism, 248-49.

103 Awad, interview (January 14, 1995).

104 Hafid Barghouti, two-hour interview (Ramallah, January 25, 1996). Barghouti is editor in chief of al-Hayat al-Jadida (New Life), a daily newspaper in Ramallah.

105 "Tqu Villagers Block Settler Expansion," al-Fajr, January 17, 1986. Ibrahim Matar's survey of all Israeli settlements on 54 percent of the West Bank and 30 percent of Gaza confiscated by Israel after 1967 contends, "95 percent of all land taken for Jewish settlements was, in fact, private Palestinian

property, and only five percent could be classified as state land." Ibrahim Matar, "Settlements: Facts and Figures," *Settlements and Peace: The Problem of Jewish Colonization in Palestine*, special report (Washington, D.C., Center for Policy Analysis on Palestine, 1995), 14.

106 Awad and Cavanaugh-O'Keefe, "*Sabr*," 135.

107 Smerling, "Gandhi's Spirit on the West Bank?"

108 Abd Abu-Diab, one-hour interview (Ramallah, December 11, 1997).

109 "Tqu Villagers Block Settler Expansion."

110 Ibid.

111 Robert Hirschfield, "Practicing Nonviolence on the West Bank," *Christian Century*, October 8, 1986, 853.

112 Daoud Kuttab, *Dr. Mubarak Awad and the Palestinian Center for the Study of Nonviolence* (East Jerusalem, no publ., n.d.), 3.

113 Abu-Diab, interview (December 11, 1997).

114 Jonathan Kuttab, one-hour interview (East Jerusalem, November 5, 1994); Abu-Diab, interview (December 11, 1997).

115 "Nature Preservationists Uproot 6,000 Trees," *al-Fajr*, January 10, 1986.

116 Victor Schonfeld, *Courage along the Divide*, seventy-eight-minute documentary film broadcast on ITV, London (September 9, 1986); David Whitfield, "Shopping to Undermine the Israeli Occupation: Civil Disobedience on the West Bank," *Morning Star*, September 9, 1986. Damage was estimated by the villagers at more than 100,000 Jordanian dinars (equivalent to $285,000 USD). "Nature Preservationists Uproot 6,000 Trees."

117 Virginia Tilley, "Israel Authority Breaks a Promise; Uproots New Saplings," *al-Fajr*, January 31, 1986.

118 "Activists Try to Replace Uprooted Trees," *Jerusalem Post*, January 26, 1986.

119 Tilley, "Israel Authority Breaks a Promise."

120 "General Instructions for Participants in Tree Planting Action at Qatanna," one-page flier (East Jerusalem, PCSN, 1986). Participating Israeli peace activists hailed the guidance: "The distribution to all participants of written guidelines, prepared beforehand, and including a clear commitment not to act violently even when provoked, can be very useful." "Summing Up," in *Creative Resistance: Anecdotes of Nonviolent Action by Israeli-Based Groups*, ed. Maxine Kaufman Nunn (Jerusalem: Alternative Information Center, 1993), 85.

121 "Nature Preservationists Uproot 6,000 Trees."

122 Ibid.

123 Amos Gvirtz, "Planting Olive Trees at Qatana-Palestinians and Israelis for Nonviolence," in Kaufman Nunn, *Creative Resistance*, 23-24. Gvirtz lectured Israeli officers at the scene about nonviolent struggle, Gandhi, and King.

124 Tom Keene, "Mubarak Awad: Behind the Intifada," *Peace Media Service*, 1990, as cited in Rigby, *Living the Intifada*, 173, 174.

125 "Press Release on Tree Planting, 'Tu Beshvat' in Qattana," joint PCSN and Arab-Jewish Fellowship of Nonviolence and Peace (East Jerusalem: PCSN, January 24, 1986); Hirschfield, "Practicing Nonviolence on the West Bank," 854.

126 Tilley, "Israel Authority Breaks a Promise."

127 Torcato, "Tranquility amidst Terror."

128 Ibid.

129 Joel Greenberg, "Trespass Charges against Palestinian," *Jerusalem Post*, September 24, 1986; Whitfield, "Shopping to Undermine the Israeli Occupation."

130 "Olive Trees at Root of Land Dispute . . . A Continuing Story," Newsletter (East Jerusalem, PCSN), April-June 1986, 5.

131 Ibrahim Matar, "The Non-violent Struggle to Protect Palestinian Property," in *Jewish Settlements, Palestinian Rights, and Peace*, Information Paper no. 4 (Washington, D.C., Center for Policy Analysis on Palestine, 1996): 13.

132 After 1967, acquisition of Palestinian land by Israelis was not the byproduct of the process of acquiring land that had occurred prior to 1948. Rather, Ibrahim Matar writes, it was "outright seizure of private property," often based on the "pretext of security." Matar, "Settlements: Facts and Figures," 11.

133 Some 6,500 Israeli settlers reportedly lived in and around Hebron, "hundreds" of them armed. George D. Moffett III, "Digging in Their Heels outside Hebron," *Christian Science Monitor*, June 6, 1989.

134 "Summary of Actions," 1986 PCSN report.

135 Torcato, "Tranquility amidst Terror."

136 Victor Schonfeld and Jennifer Millstone, dir., *Shattered Dreams*, British cinema and ITV, 1986.

137 "Summary of Actions," 1986 PCSN report.

138 "IFOR News Release" (East Jerusalem, IFOR in collaboration with PCSN, May 28, 1986).

139 Joel Greenberg, "Peace Group Visits Hebron to Support Arab Shopkeepers," *Jerusalem Post*, May 30, 1986.

140 Campaign of Solidarity with Hebron Merchants, one-page public invitation (East Jerusalem, PCSN, 1986).

141 Barghouti, interview (January 25, 1996).

142 "Public Invitation," flier inviting public to picnic sponsored by the Committee on Family Reunification, garden of the Palestinian (Rockefeller) Museum, East Jerusalem, Friday, June 19, 1987.

143 Joe Franklin, "What Makes Awad Run?" *Jerusalem Post*, December 10, 1987.

144 Saida Hamad, "Families Demand Reunion," *al-Fajr*, June 21, 1987.

145 Kuttab, *Dr. Mubarak Awad*, 2; Asher Wallfish, "Awad Visits Knesset, MKs Scramble to Vent Anger over Deportation Case," *Jerusalem Post*, November 25, 1987, 2.

146 Morris Draper, letter to Mubarak Awad from the American Consul General, response to Awad letter of October 10, 1987, regarding family reunification (East Jerusalem: U.S. Consulate General, October 20, 1987). PCSN archives, East Jerusalem.

147 Gene Sharp, "Considering Policy Options and Consequences for Israel Facing the *Intifada*," paper presented at a seminar of the Israeli Institute of Military Affairs, "Impact of the *Intifada* on Israeli Society: Facts, Assessments, and Predictions," Zichron Yaacov, July 10, 1989, 5. Italics in original.

148 Ephraim Sneh, thirty-minute interview (Jerusalem, March 10, 1997).

149 Edy Kaufman, thirty-minute personal communication (Jerusalem, March 17, 1997).

150 Sharp, interview (October 19, 1995).

151 Two-hour interview of ten youths (Qalandia refugee camp, West Bank, January 22, 1996).

152 Etienne (also Èstienne) de la Boétie, *Discours de la Servitude Volontaire* (orig. 1552), also known as *Contr'un* (Anti-Dictator), in *Oeuvres Complétes d'Etienne de la Boétie* (Paris: J. Rouam et Cie., 1892); or idem, "Discours de la Servitude Volontaire," in *Oeuvres Complétes*, ed. P. Bonnefon (Genéve: Slatkine Reprints, 1967). Tolstoy, whose impact on Gandhi is well documented, was influenced by Boétie. Acknowledged or unacknowledged, Boétie's propositions form the context for writings on civil disobedience, including those of Thoreau, Tolstoy, Gandhi, King, Václav Havel, and Aung San Suu Kyi. See Bleiker, *Popular Dissent*, 51-95, esp. 87-93.

153 The points made by Sharp in his 1986 lectures are reflected in an extensive interview with him that was distributed widely in the occupied territories during 1986 and 1987. See Afif Safieh and Jennifer Bing, "Exclusive Interview: Gene Sharp on Nonviolent Struggle," *al-Fajr*, May 2, 1986, 7, 13. The full text was circulated as a forty-seven-page booklet, "Nonviolent Struggle: An Efficient Technique of Political Action" (East Jerusalem, PCSN, 1987). An edited version appeared as "Gene Sharp: Nonviolent Struggle," Interview by Afif Safieh, *Journal of Palestine Studies* 65 (Autumn 1987): 37-55.

154 Kuttab, interview (December 12, 1997).

155 Abu-Diab, interview (December 11, 1997).

156 Ghassan Khatib, two-hour interview (East Jerusalem, December 15, 1997); "The Popular Movement: The Process of Disengagement," *Towards a State of Independence: The Palestinian Uprising, December 1987-August 1988* (East Jerusalem, FACTS Information Committee, 1988) (hereafter FACTS), 16-19.

157 Awad, *Nonviolence*, 3.

158 Fletcher, "Awad: Crucial Question." The Palestinians had a sit-and-wait attitude—waiting for the United States and the Arab world—Jonathan Kuttab argues: "We even invented a wonderful term for it: *sumud*—steadfastness." Jonathan Kuttab, "The Children's Revolt," *Journal of Palestine Studies* 68 (Summer 1988): 28. *Samud*, clinging to the land, became for some a form of nonviolent resistance. Political scientist Azmy Bishara uses the term to differentiate between civil disobedience on the one hand and, on the other, "steadfast" nonviolent initiatives for preserving a society's defenses, as expressed in the alternative institutions of the intifada. Azmy Bishara, one-hour interview (East Jerusalem, June 17, 1995).

159 Kuttab, interview (November 5, 1994).

160 "A U.S. Arab in West Bank Loses Rights."

161 Awad, interview (February 14, 1995). Gandhi viewed both ethical and practical approaches to nonviolent struggle as indivisible and ultimately the most expeditious avenue. Awad often promoted the distinction made by Gandhi of hating the oppression, but not the oppressor. Awad, interview (October 19, 1995). "The fight should be against the system, against the structure, not against real people." Johan Galtung, *Nonviolence and Israel/Palestine* (Honolulu: University of Hawaii Institute for Peace, 1989), 8.

162 Abu-Diab, interview (December 11, 1997).

163 Ibid.

164 Daniel Eisenstadt, rapporteur, "Nonviolence in the Occupied Territories of the West Bank," on a presentation by Mubarak Awad, April 18, 1984, *Transforming Struggle: Strategy and the Global Experience of Nonviolent Direct Action* (Cambridge, Massachusetts: Program on Nonviolent Sanctions in Conflict and Defense, Center for International Affairs, Harvard University, 1992), 121.

165 "The Palestinian Pacifist," *New Republic*, June 13, 1988, 9. Although Awad and the center were readily accessible and journalists circulated freely through its offices, accounts routinely misconstrued their work. *Intifada*, by Zeev Schiff and Ehud Yaari, contains factual mistakes in virtually every paragraph of chapter nine devoted to Awad, "The Pendulum of Civil Disobedience," in Schiff and Yaari, *Intifada*, 240-66.

166 Grossman, "Palestinian Pacifist."

167 Franklin, "What Makes Awad Run?"

168 Don Peretz, *Intifada: The Palestinian Uprising* (Boulder, Colorado: Westview Press, 1990), 53.

169 Grossman, "Palestinian Pacifist."

170 Awad, interview (October 19, 1995); Wolf Blitzer and Walter Ruby, "Awad Embarks on All-Out News Media Campaign in U.S.," *Jerusalem Post*, June 16, 1988.

171 Elaine Ruth Fletcher, "Hecklers Disturb Awad Talk," *In Jerusalem*, December 4, 1987.

172 "A U.S. Arab in West Bank Loses Rights."

173 Yisrael Medad, "The House on Nablus Road," *Jerusalem Post*, December 29, 1987.

174 Dan Leon, "Mubarak Awad's Friend," *New Outlook*, July 1988, 34-35.

175 Franklin, "'Palestinian Gandhi' or Terrorist?" Awad's reluctance to condemn violent resistance continued to be publicly debated, at least as late as 1993. See Jon Immanuel, response to Joseph Lerner, "Mubarak Awad," letter to the editor, *Jerusalem Post*, September 26, 1993, 6.

176 One explanation for erroneous accounts of Awad was offered by professor Hisham B. Sharabi, who suggested that Israeli electronic intercepts of Sharabi's telephone calls from Washington, D.C., to Tunis, imploring the PLO to let Awad try his strategy, may have distorted Israeli views of Awad's work. Sharabi, interview (February 22, 1995).

177 Fletcher, "Awad: Crucial Question"; Joel Greenberg, "Jerusalem Residence Denied to Palestinian Activist, Awad," *Jerusalem Post*, October 1, 1987.

178 Wolf Blitzer, Andy Court, and Menachem Shalev, "Shultz Urges Shamir to Reconsider on Awad: Court Stays Deportation for Debate on Legal Status," *Jerusalem Post*, May 9, 1988.

179 Blitzer, Court, and Shalev, "Shultz Urges Shamir to Reconsider on Awad." According to the Israeli human rights monitoring organization B'Tselem, "[E]very Palestinian resident of East Jerusalem who cannot prove that he or she . . . has lived [in Jerusalem] continuously in the past permanently loses the right to live in the city of their birth"—"based on the presumption that East Jerusalem Palestinians are immigrants, who live in their homes by virtue of a permanent residency permit which Israel grants them." Tens of thousands of persons born in East Jerusalem risk losing residency. "1987-1997: Ten Years since the Beginning of the Intifada" (Jerusalem: B'Tselem, 1997), 17-18, 21; "A Quiet Deportation," *B'Tselem Human Rights Report* 5, no. 1 (Autumn 1997): 2.

180 "Neither Jewish ethics nor Jewish tradition can disqualify terrorism as a means of combat. We are very far from having any moral qualms as far as our national war goes. . . . Terrorism is for us a part of the political battle . . . and it has a great part to play. . . . [Our terrorism] is not aimed at persons, but rather at representatives, and therefore it is effective. If, in addition, it shakes the Jewish population out of its complacency—so much the better." Yitzhak Shamir, *Hehazit* (the Front; Lehi's underground journal), summer 1943, reprinted from *al-Hamishmar*, December 24, 1987, in *Middle East Report* 18, no. 3 (May-June 1988): 55.

181 Claiborne Pell, telegram to Prime Minister Yitzhak Shamir protesting impending deportation of Mubarak Awad (Washington, D.C., U.S. Senate, May 9, 1988), PCSN files, East Jerusalem.

182 Oz Frankel, "Shamir: 'Awad Is No Gandhi,'" *Jerusalem Post*, May 26, 1988.

183 Franklin, "'Palestinian Gandhi' or Terrorist?"

184 Yossi, "High Court of Justice 282/88," affidavit from a member of the Department of General Security Services (Shin Bet) "responsible for countering subversion and hostile terrorist activity in the area of Jerusalem and Judea and Samaria," trans. from Hebrew (West Jerusalem: Israeli High Court, ca. March or April 1988), 1, on file, law offices of Jonathan Kuttab, East Jerusalem.

185 Mubarak E. Awad, "Statement of Decision Not to Appeal the Deportation Decision of the Israeli Government" (East Jerusalem: law offices of Jonathan Kuttab, May 24, 1988). In December 1987, three days before the outbreak of the intifada, addressing religious Jews at Beit Elisheva, he said, "I

am not for a two-state solution, nor for a one-state solution," adding that he lacked a political formula for solving the conflict. Fletcher, "Hecklers." On January 19, 1988, he told *Tikkun*, "I am for a two-state solution . . . [in] a peace agreement," expressing the hope that if the Palestinians had a state of their own, they could better rein in those who wanted armed struggle than they were able to do when militarily occupied. "Interview of Mubarak Awad, Conducted January 19, 1988," *Tikkun*, March-April 1988. Two years earlier, in 1986, he had accepted the 1969 goal of a "secular democratic state" in all of Palestine. Grossman, "Palestinian Pacifist." Awad's dilemma of trying to teach the technique of nonviolent struggle without its dictating a precise political outcome would finally be relieved by the consensus developed in the intifada on a two-state solution.

186 Joel Brinkley, "Arab-American Appeals Israeli Ouster," *New York Times*, May 9, 1988.

187 Andy Court et al., "Mubarak Awad Faces Midnight Deportation," *Jerusalem Post*, March 8, 1988.

188 Kuttab, interview (June 17, 1995).

189 Leon, "Mubarak Awad's Friend," 35; Edy Kaufman, "Why a Jew Fasted for an Arab," *Jerusalem Post*, May 19, 1988, 8; Sidra DeKoven Ezrahi, "Under Jerusalem's Barren Mulberry Tree: Violent Encounters in the City of Peace," *New Outlook*, July 1988, 32-33.

190 Mubarak Awad, one-hour interview (East Jerusalem, January 23, 1996).

191 "Message to Shamir on Mubarak Awad," cable instructions to American Ambassador in Tel Aviv to deliver message from Secretary of State George P. Shultz asking the rescinding of the High Court's order to deport Mubarak Awad, and text of message, U.S. State Department, Washington, D.C., May 6, 1988.

192 State of Israel, "Minister of Interior Signs Order for Deportation of Mubarak Awad," press bulletin no. 21 (Jerusalem: Ministry of Interior, June 5, 1988). Andy Court, "Landmark High Court Ruling: Awad Deportation Is Legal," *Jerusalem Post*, June 6, 1988.

193 Court, "Landmark High Court Ruling," postscript by reporter Ben Lynfield.

194 "Forced Exile: An Activist Is Deported," *Time*, June 27, 1988: 32.

195 "Silencing a Troublemaker: A Denial of Due Process," *Newsweek*, May 23, 1988, 30; Charles A. Kimball, "The Expulsion of Mubarak Awad," *Christian Century*, July 20-27, 1988, 676.

196 "Silencing a Troublemaker." Awad's case set a precedent. According to B'Tselem, the practice of deportation from the occupied territories ceased to be used as a punitive measure by the end of 1992, yet "quiet deportation" of East Jerusalemites continues apace. By 1995, more than two thousand Palestinians had lost their Jerusalem residency cards based on the Awad case. Asher Felix Landau, "Wife Who Followed Husband Lost Her Way Back Here," *Jerusalem Post*, June 12, 1995, 7. Former Israeli attorney general Yitzhak Zamir concedes that international law forbids the expulsion or transfers of populations, but says expulsion of individuals is "not forbidden," Benny Morris, "Rights and the Man: Interview of Former Attorney General Yitzhak Zamir," *Jerusalem Post*, February 15, 1988, 4.

197 "Statement of Mubarak Awad Released to the Press," May 8, 1988, Jerusalem (East Jerusalem, PCSN files).

198 Blitzer, Court, and Shalev, "Shultz Urges Shamir to Reconsider on Awad." In his statement, Awad says, "My ideas have caught on, and everyone is trying to use them in different forms." Joel Brinkley, "Israel Weighs Appeal by U.S. Arab," *New York Times*, May 24, 1988, 8.

199 Asher Felix Landau, "The Mubarak Awad Judgment," Petition of Mubarak Awad to the High Court, before Justices Aharon Barak, Gavriel Bach, and Shoshana Netanyahu; Judgment given by Justice Aharon Barak, *Jerusalem Post*, June 10, 1988.

200 Mubarak Awad, "Statement," to Israeli High Court, in Cainkar and Goldring, *Uprising in Palestine, the First Year*, 195.

201 Sidra DeKoven Ezrahi, one-hour interview (Jerusalem, November 11, 1994); Wolf Blitzer and Joshua Brilliant, "U.S. Deplores Awad Expulsion," *Jerusalem Post*, June 14, 1988.

202 Blitzer and Ruby, "Awad Embarks." U.S. immigrants to Israel formed an Ad Hoc Committee for Mubarak Awad, to protest the revocation of his Jerusalem residency card. The *Jerusalem Post* opined Israel's moves against Awad had "besmirched" Israel's image. Editorial, "Dubious and Clumsy," *Jerusalem Post*, November 23, 1987. Meron Benvenisti testified on Awad's behalf, saying that Israeli law was not originally intended to infringe on the rights of East Jerusalemites if they left the area. Court, "High Court Ruling Expected." MKs Mattityahu Peled and Mohammed Miari of the Progressive List for Peace and Dedi Zucker of Citizens Rights opposed the deportation. Joel Greenberg, "Palestinian Activist Told to Leave," *Jerusalem Post*, November 18, 1987. Yitzhak Rabin defended the decision to deport Awad, but Ezer Weizman, minister without portfolio and nephew of Chaim Weizmann, publicly disagreed. "Rabin: We're Acting Fairly with Awad," *Jerusalem Post*, May 12, 1988; Joel Greenberg and Joshua Brilliant, "Weizman Disagrees with Awad Expulsion Order," *Jerusalem Post*, November 20, 1987, 1. Shimon Peres issued a four-page defense of the decision. Court, et al., "Mubarak Awad Faces Midnight Deportation."

203 Editorial, "Fabricating a Hero," *Jerusalem Post*, June 13, 1988.

204 Editorial, "Varieties of Violence," *Jerusalem Post*, May 16, 1988.

205 "Tapes Show Prime Minister's Office Used Misleading Awad Quote," *Jerusalem Post*, May 13, 1988; Elyakim Haetzni, "The Differing Documents: The Haetzni Document," *Jerusalem Post*, May 13, 1988; Joel Greenberg, "Awad Detained," *Jerusalem Post*, March 17, 1988.

206 Mubarak Awad, "The Taped Transcript," *Jerusalem Post*, May 13, 1988. Joel Greenberg, a member of the editorial staff of the *Jerusalem Post* and a reporter who followed Awad closely, clarified the contents of Awad's 1983 booklet, in "It Depends on What's 'Non-Violence,'" *Jerusalem Post*, November 27, 1987.

207 Joel Greenberg, "High Court Asks Shamir Why Awad Shouldn't Be Deported," *Jerusalem Post*, March 15, 1988; Franklin, "'Palestinian Gandhi' or Terrorist?"

208 Passed by the Knesset on July 5, 1950, the Law of Return states, "Every Jew has the right to immigrate to the country." Laqueur, *Israel-Arab Reader*, 128.

209 Franklin, "What Makes Awad Run?"

210 Amos Gvirtz, "Difficulties of the Peace Movement and Ways of Overcoming Them," working paper (Kibbutz Shafayim, Israel, ca. early 1988).

211 Name withheld, one-hour interview (East Jerusalem, December 13, 1997).

212 Siniora, interview (December 16, 1997).

213 Ezrahi, "Under Jerusalem's Barren Mulberry Tree," 33.

214 Riad al-Malki, two-hour interview (Washington, D.C., May 3, 1995). Malki said he read all three volumes of Sharp's *Power of Nonviolent Action* in one day. Ibid. Malki emerged as a PFLP spokesperson toward the end of the first year of the uprising. An engineering professor at Bir Zeit University, he also directed the PANORAMA Center for the Dissemination of Alternative Information in East Jerusalem. He is described as a "leading member of the Unified National Command, . . . a key PFLP leader in the territories who helped write the clandestine leaflets." John Wallach and Janet Wallach, "Riad Malki," *The New Palestinians: The Emerging Generation of Leaders* (Rocklin, California: Prima Publishing, 1992), 225.

215 Daoud Kuttab, one-hour interview (East Jerusalem, November 4, 1994).

216 Jonathan Kuttab, interview (June 17, 1995).

Chapter 8

1 Martha Diase, "Profiles of Israelis and Palestinians concerned with Peace," in Fernea and Hocking, *Struggle for Peace*, 206.

2 Gideon Spiro, "Israeli Soldiers Who Say 'There Is a Limit,'" *Middle East International*, September 9, 1988, 18-20.

3 During this period, Husseini was acknowledged as the highest-ranking member of Fateh in the West Bank. In 1995, he was named minister for Jerusalem of the Palestinian Authority. He died on May 31, 2001.

4 Irene Ertugrul, "Working Together for Peace," *Middle East International*, January 9, 1987, 17. More than 200 supporters of CSBZ demonstrated in Ramallah on November 28, 1981, to protest the Israeli government's increasing use of home demolitions and closure of Bir Zeit University during the rebellion against Military Order 947. Truncheon-wielding Israeli forces fired tear-gas grenades, injuring a number of Israeli protesters; six were detained for several days. Aronson, *Israel, Palestinians and the Intifada*, 261; Tamar Berger, "The Committee of Solidarity with Bir Zeit and the Committee against the War in Lebanon," in Kaufman Nunn, *Creative Resistance*, 45-46.

5 David Hall-Cathala, *The Peace Movement in Israel, 1967-87* (New York: St. Martin's Press, 1990), 62.

6 Concerning contacts between Israeli and Palestinian poets and writers, see Yoram Kaniuk, "The Israeli and Palestinian Writers and Artists Committee," *New Outlook*, September-October 1988, 23-26.

7 Feisel Husseini, one-hour interview (East Jerusalem, January 30, 1996). Husseini's use of "direct action" is intentional; such committees were illegal, hence to meet was a form of civil disobedience. The Committee Confronting the Iron Fist (CCIF) also called itself the Committee to Confront the Iron Fist.

8 See Sharp, *Methods of Nonviolent Action*, 117-54; Hall-Cathala, *Peace Movement in Israel*, 62.

9 See Jan Zielonka, *Political Ideas in Contemporary Poland* (Aldershot and Avebury, England: Gower Publishing Company, 1989), 10-18, 22-23, 27, 81, 95; Bugajski, *Czechoslovakia*, 10; Tim D. Whipple, "From 1968 to 1989: A Chronological Commentary," *After the Velvet Revolution: Václav Havel and the Leaders of Czechoslovakia Speak Out*, ed. Tim D. Whipple, (New York: Freedom House, 1991), 7-8; Jøsten, "Czechoslovakia: From 1968 to Charter 77): 1.

10 See Joshua Paulson, "Mothers of the Plaza de Mayo, Argentina-1977-1983," in Sharp, ed., *Waging Nonviolent Struggle*, 217-22.

11 "Arab-Israeli Cooperation against the 'Iron Fist': Husseini and Spiro Speak Out," *al-Awdah*, February 9, 1986, 16.

12　Dan Tschirgi, "High Hope, Bad News on the West Bank," *Los Angeles Times*, June 28, 1987, part 5, 2.

13　"Demonstration Announced to Protest Deportations and Administrative Detentions," press release announcing February 1, 1986, protest before the Israeli military commander, Beit Hanina, to protest practices allegedly violating the Fourth Geneva Convention (East Jerusalem: Committee to Confront the Iron Fist [CCIF], January 29, 1986).

14　Jabril Rajoub had been sentenced to life imprisonment in 1970 for supporting Fateh. The thirty-three-day hunger strike in 1980—described by Rajoub in "Prison Hunger Strikes," noted on p. 389, n. 92—was accompanied by protests from the committee, after which Rajoub was moved to a regular prison cell, where the beatings and psychological harassment of which the committee had accused the authorities came to a stop. "We Can Confront the Iron Fist; Jabril Rajoub's Demands Met! Ends Hunger Strike after 34 Days," flier on administrative detention, torture, house demolitions of families of detainees, and the Prisoner Exchange Agreement of May 20 (East Jerusalem: CCIF, 1985). On January 3, 1988, considered by the Israeli government a dangerous Fateh operative, Rajoub was deported. "Four Expelled Secretly; UN Security Council to Meet on Deportations," *Jerusalem Post*, January 14, 1988, 1; George D. Moffett III, "Israel Sends Four Palestinians Packing, U.S. Laments Expulsion of Activists Accused of Violence to Lebanon," *Christian Science Monitor*, January 14, 1988. After seventeen years in Israeli prisons, Rajoub was in 1993 appointed by Yasir Arafat as chief of two thousand mostly Fateh activists in the Preventive Security Service for the West Bank. Graham Usher, "The Politics of Internal Security in Palestine," *Middle East International*, March 1, 1996, 15-16.

15　"Jews, Arabs Protest 'Iron Fist,'" *al-Fajr*, February 7, 1986.

16　Eventually realizing that the protagonists were primarily Palestinian, the police denied permission for a large march planned for the fifth anniversary of the Sabra and Shatila massacre in September 1987, even though the three applicants were Israeli. Michel Warschawski, "The Committee against the Iron Fist: Prototype for Israeli-Palestinian Cooperation, 1985-1987," in Kaufman Nunn, *Creative Resistance*, 82, 83.

17　"Demonstrators Protest Poor Prison Conditions," *al-Fajr*, March 21, 1986.

18　Steve Hagey, "Violence, Protests Mark Jerusalem Day," UPI, June 5, 1986.

19　"Arab-Israeli Cooperation against the 'Iron Fist,'" 17.

20　"Let Today's March Be a Step in the 'March of the Millions' against Occupation," flier in English with Arabic and Hebrew heading (East Jerusalem: CCIF, June 14, 1987).

21　Gal, interview (March 16, 1997).

22　See Benedict Anderson, *Imagined Communities*, rev. ed. (London: Verso, 1991), 6, 187-206.

23　Husseini, interview (January 30, 1996).

24　*Palestinians in Profile: A Guide to Leading Palestinians in the Occupied Territories*, ed. Matthew W. Petterson, Yvonne M. Ingalls, and Neil Patrick (East Jerusalem: PANORAMA Center for the Dissemination of Alternative Information, 1993), 248; Paul Hunt, "Some Aspects of Law and Practice in the Occupied Territories," *Journal of Refugee Studies* 2, no. 1 (1989): 155.

25　Wallace, "Israeli Security Officials," 18; Joel Greenberg, "Easing Its Stand on Detentions, Israel Frees a Palestinian," *New York Times*, April 16, 1998: A6.

26　Reuven Kaminer, *The Politics of Protest: The Israeli Peace Movement and the Palestinian Intifada* (Brighton: Sussex Academic Press, 1996), 107-8.

27　Daoud Kuttab, "Atmosphere in the Husseini Home," draft dispatch to news media, Kuttab private papers (East Jerusalem: approximately January 31, 1989), 2.

28　Husseini's ability to touch the imagination of both Palestinians and Israelis was linked to his father's death at the mountain village of al-Qastel. On the main road from Tel Aviv to Jerusalem, the town was an outpost for British military forces proceeding to capture Jerusalem in December 1917. Rowlands Coldicott, *London Men in Palestine, and How They Marched to Jerusalem* (New York: Longmans, Green and Co., 1919), 157-89. The town was again a watershed when the Israelis captured it in 1948. Despite a peace agreement between al-Qastel and Jerusalem in the spring of 1948, Operation Nahshon was implemented by the Haganah, villages along certain routes were cleared, and their inhabitants killed or expelled. The operation began with the "unopposed conquest" of al-Qastel, the first village so destroyed, from April 2-3. Arab irregulars retook the village on April 8, when Abd al-Qadir al-Husseini was killed. Morris, *Birth of the Palestinian Refugee Problem Revisited*, 234-35. See Wallach and Wallach, "Faisal Husseini," in *New Palestinians*, 45-48. Forty-one years later, an Israeli soldier who shot at Husseini's father writes of reverberations from his death. Yoram Kaniuk, "Arabs and Israelis Must Forget a Little," *New York Times*, April 25, 1989.

29　Siniora, interview (December 16, 1997).

30 Among Palestinians, Husseini was not harmed by the supposition that Haj Amin had ordered the assassination of King Abdullah, which took place while he was en route to al-Aqsa Mosque on July 20, 1951, and the fact that three members of the Husseini clan were among the defendants. "[E]ven if Haj Amin was not directly involved in the murder itself, there is no doubt that he influenced those who planned and perpetrated it." Elpeleg, *Grand Mufti*, 126.

31 Mahdi Abd al-Hadi, two-hour interview (East Jerusalem, December 13, 1997). Family contacts from Iraq to the Arabian Peninsula to North Africa helped Husseini to tread his own path without suffering the consequences that others had faced for independently pursuing options.

32 Wallach and Wallach, "Faisal Husseini," in *New Palestinians*, 60. On Husseini's disenchantment with armed resistance, see Wallach, "Battles Lines," 41-81, passim.

33 On manufacturing of political symbols by agents of change, see Dale F. Eickelman and James Piscatori, *Muslim Politics* (Princeton: Princeton University Press, 1996), 58.

34 Sarah Helm, "Pragmatist Will Speak for Palestinians," *Independent*, April 26, 1993, 12.

35 Eric Goldstein, *Journalism under Occupation: Israel's Regulation of the Palestinian Press* (New York: Committee to Protect Journalists and Article 19, 1988), 2.

36 Rubinstein, then correspondent for *Davar*, "National Conference on Nonviolent Sanctions," Albert Einstein Institution, Cambridge, Massachusetts, as cited in Robert B. Ashmore, "Nonviolence as an *Intifada* Strategy," *American-Arab Affairs* 32 (1990): 98.

37 Barton Gellman, "Female Arab Prisoners Are Released by Israel," *Washington Post*, February 12, 1997, A25.

38 *Faisal Abdal Husseini v. State of Israel*, unofficial translation from Hebrew, Israel's High Court of Justice decision upholding Husseini's detention and the government's refusal to draw a distinction between PLO "terrorism" and political activity (Tel Aviv, December 6, 1987). Husseini was often incarcerated for his advocacy of nonviolent action. Under house arrest after sunset, and under city arrest by day between 1982 and 1987, the committees continued to meet at his home. Susan Sachs, "The PLO's 'Consensus Maker,'" *Newsday*, May 4, 1993, 17; Husseini, interview (January 30, 1996); Glenn Frankel, "Historic Mansion Becomes Jerusalem Issue, Israel Demands Palestinians Limit Use of Orient House," *Washington Post*, July 14, 1996.

39 Husayni, Interview, 8.

40 Husseini, interview (January 30, 1996).

41 Yizhar Beer, "Faisal Husseini: The Making of a Leader," repr. from *Haaretz*, in *New Outlook*, March 1990, 25.

42 For example, Robinson, *Building a Palestinian State*, 99, 166; Hunter, *Palestinian Uprising*, 156.

43 Gal, interview (March 16, 1997). At the time of the intifada, the Palestinian leaders who are the subject of this chapter were unknown to the Israeli public. Mordechai Bar-On, *In Pursuit of Peace: A History of the Israeli Peace Movement* (Washington, D.C.: U.S. Institute of Peace, 1996), 395 n. 20.

44 Kaminer mistakenly cites the starting date for Husseini's committees as 1986, rather than 1980, and does not explain their derivation. Kaminer, *The Politics of Protest*, 106. See Colin Shindler, *Ploughshares into Swords? Israelis and Jews in the Shadow of the Intifada* (London: I. B. Taurus, 1991), 106, 210; Hall-Cathala, *Peace Movement in Israel*, 62.

45 Hanan Mikhail-Ashrawi, "The Search for Peace: Dynamics and Principles of the Palestinian Intifada," in *From Intifada to Independence*, ed. Afif Safieh (The Hague, PLO Information Office, 1989), 21.

46 "Palestinians Stage Anti-Israel March through Jerusalem," *Jerusalem Post*, June 21, 1987; Saida Hamad, "Palestinians, Israelis March against Occupation," *al-Fajr*, June 21, 1987.

47 Whether to seek government authorization for holding demonstrations or assert a right to protest had been an issue in the 1930s. Lesch, *Arab Politics in Palestine*, 214.

48 Hamad, "Palestinians, Israelis March."

49 "Palestinians Stage Anti-Israel March through Jerusalem."

50 Sari Nusseibeh, "Midwife at the Birth of a State," *Guardian*, December 9, 1989, 23

51 Husseini, interview (January 30, 1996). See also Daniel Williams, "The Death of a Man, the Loss of a Philosophy," *Washington Post*, 10 June 2001, B4.

52 Jamal, *Palestinian National Movement*, 64. The amount received would have been equivalent to approximately $400 million USD.

53 Arafat, 1985 Cairo Declaration on Terrorism, in Lukacs, *Israeli-Palestinian Conflict*, 370-71.

54 See Ackerman and DuVall, *Force More Powerful*, 457-68.

55 Yasir Arafat, speech, UN General Assembly, November 13, 1974, in *Palestinian-Israeli Peace Agreement: A Documentary Record* (Washington, D.C.: Institute for Palestine Studies, 1994), 216, 227.

56 Sari Nusseibeh, "True Justice Could Bring Peace," *Guardian Weekly*, March 10, 1991, 8.

57 Harkabi, *Fadayeen Action and Arab Strategy*, 34, 35.

58 The East Jerusalem activist intellectuals were not without counterparts and recusants in Israel. In 1981, the Ratz faction adopted a position, which called for negotiations to be rooted in the right to self-determination for the Palestinians. The platform specified that Palestinian participation be included, "specifically any group that accepts negotiations as the only way to settle the dispute." Dedi Zucker, *Jerusalem Post*, March 25, 1981, as cited in Hall-Cathala, *Peace Movement in Israel, 1967-87*, 145-46. By mid-1986, Citizens' Rights MK Yossi Sarid had formulated his own program of nonviolent resistance for the occupied territories. "Gandhi on the West Bank?" *Peace Now Newsletter*, Summer 1986. In the same year, Meron Benvenisti (a Ratz MK) conjectured, "Eventually the Palestinians will learn that their real power lies in civil disobedience, not senseless terrorism." Smerling, "Gandhi's Spirit on the West Bank?" 15.

59 Sayigh, "Palestinian Armed Struggle," 104-5.

60 Mark A. Heller and Sari Nusseibeh, *No Trumpets, No Drums: A Two-State Settlement of the Israeli-Palestinian Conflict* (New York: Hill and Wang, 1991), 32.

61 Cooley, *Green March, Black September*, 139.

62 Jon Immanuel and Asher Wallfish, "Nusseibeh's Detention Stuns Left, Annoys U.S.," *Jerusalem Post*, January 31, 1991.

63 Faisal Husseini, "A New Face in the Middle East," *New Outlook*, November-December 1989, 14.

64 Feisel Husseini, as quoted in Ashmore, "Nonviolence as an *Intifada* Strategy," 97.

65 Naseer H. Aruri, "A New Climate of Opportunity for Palestinians," *Middle East International*, December 2, 1988, 18.

66 Chaliand, *Terrorism*, 82; Rubin, *Revolution until Victory?* 25.

67 Siniora, interview (December 16, 1997). Siniora assigned journalists to report on the committees and helped to plan campaigns in the period leading up to the intifada. Elaine Ruth Fletcher and Yehuda Litani, "Palestinians Weigh Their Disobedience Measures," *Jerusalem Post*, January 6, 1988. Siniora publishes the *Jerusalem Times*, an English-language weekly, and the monthly *Palestine Business Report*.

68 Helena Cobban acknowledges the "special role" played by Palestinian intellectuals in East Jerusalem during the first year of the intifada, to build a case for a division of labor between the mass uprising and the intellectuals. The result is to minimize the generative role played by these East Jerusalemites in altering political thinking inside the territories in the years preceding the uprising. Since Cobban does not focus on how changes in political thought paved the way for the intifada, investigate its synthesis with other forces leading to a preponderantly nonviolent movement, nor examine how knowledge spread of nonviolent methods, she does not explain how such cognitive developments would be reflected in the leaflets from the leadership command. Cobban, "The PLO and the Intifada," 84-91.

69 Ziad Abu Zayyad, one-hour interviews (East Jerusalem, June 8, 1988; January 28, 1996).

70 Wallach and Wallach, "Ziad Abu Zayyad," in *New Palestinians*, 131.

71 Ibid., 124. *The West Bank Handbook: A Political Lexicon*, by Benvenisti, Abu-Zayed (Abu Zayyad), and Rubinstein, is the first book jointly authored by Palestinian and Israeli writers. Ibid.

72 Michael Sheridan, "Allies Protest at Israel's Arrest of PLO 'Spy,'" *Independent*, January 31, 1991, 6.

73 "Israel Detiene a Un Líder Palestino Moderado Acusado de Espiar para Irak," *El Pais*, January 31, 1991; Anton La Guardia, "Israelis Arrest Professor," *Daily Telegraph*, January 31, 1991. Within Israel, the action was controversial. Jon Immanuel, "Nusseibeh Detained for 'Spying for Iraq,'" *Jerusalem Post*, January 30, 1991, 1.

74 Three years later, at a January 31, 1991, hearing, two arguments would be presented for Nusseibeh's detention; beside the spying accusation, it was asserted that Nusseibeh was a Fateh leader who drafted the leaflets of the uprising. Isabel Kershner, "Saving Sari from Himself?" *Jerusalem Report*, February 14, 1991, 6. Ephraim Sneh, retired brigadier general, former head of the civil administration in the West Bank, and Labor MK, calls Nusseibeh "the leading Palestinian intellectual in the territories . . . who urges a nonviolent, negotiated resolution of the Arab-Israeli conflict." Ephraim Sneh, "Undue Process," *Jerusalem Report*, February 14, 1991, 45. Nusseibeh was arrested on the day he met with Peace Now representatives at his home and was held for three months without charges.

75 Radwan Abu Ayyash, two-hour interview (Ramallah, January 29, 1996).

76 Diase, "Profiles of Israelis and Palestinians," 233. See Wallach and Wallach, "Radwan Abu Ayyash," in *New Palestinians*, 269-92.

77 Ibid.

78 Abu Ayyash, interview (January 29, 1996).

79 Abu Zayyad, "Palestinian Right of Return," 75.

80 Abu Ayyash, interview (January 29, 1996).

81 Ibid.

82 Israeli officials claimed the arrests were based on evidence that Abu Ayyash and Abu Zayyad had "fomented violence" and played "a key role in terror and incitement." Sami Aboudi, "Angry Palestinians Criticize Israel's Arrest of Leaders," Reuters, November 14, 1990; Miriam Jordan, "One Million Arabs under Israeli Curfew," Reuters, November 14, 1990.

83 Aruri, "New Climate of Opportunity for Palestinians," 18.

84 Anwar Nusseibeh had been named government secretary in the All-Palestine Government of 1948 and to the Arab Higher Committee, was a member of the Trans-Jordanian parliament, and served as Jordan's minister of defense.

85 "Few Ayan [collectively notability, or notables, meaning elite] families managed to remain neutral in the Husseini-Nashashibi struggle." The Nusseibehs were one of the few families viewed as neutral in the 1930s and 1940s alignments of the Husseini and Nashashibi clans. Morris, *Birth of the Palestinian Refugee Problem Revisited*, 21, 37 n. 25.

86 Nusseibeh, interview (December 13, 1997).

87 Ibid.

88 Ibid. Nusseibeh is today president of al-Quds University, East Jerusalem.

89 Meir Litvak, "Inside Versus Outside," in Sela and Maoz, *PLO and Israel*, 178.

90 Nusseibeh, interview (December 13, 1997).

91 Sari Nusseibeh, "Not for Itself," *al-Fajr*, July 26, 1985.

92 Michal Sela, "Nusseibeh: Yes, to Annex; Interview of Sari Nusseibeh," trans. comm. Zoughbi E. Zoughbi, *Koteret Rashit*, November 13, 1985.

93 Sari Nusseibeh, "Living under Shamir Is Better than Living under Hussein," trans. comm. Zoughbi E. Zoughbi, *al-Mawqif*, October 19, 1985.

94 Nusseibeh, interview (July 5, 1994).

95 Journalist Robert Fisk recounts a meeting with Israel's custodian of absentee property, Jacob Manor. Fisk says he asked Manor how much land in Israel has two claimants—an Arab and a Jew holding a British Mandate or Israeli deed to the same property—to which the custodian responded perhaps 70 percent. Fisk, *Pity the Nation*, 45. "If the areas of Israel proper and those in the occupied territories already colonized, requisitioned or annexed are subtracted from the total area of Mandatory Palestine, the Palestinians in occupied territories today [1988] stand on no more than 15 percent of the soil of the country." Walid Khalidi, "Toward Peace in the Holy Land," *Foreign Affairs* 66, no. 4 (Spring 1988): 771.

96 Sari Nusseibeh, "Perhaps a New National Strategy," *al-Fajr*, May 9, 1986.

97 As noted, Benny Morris says approximately 400 villages were depopulated in the course of the 1948 war, yet Palestinian historian Walid Khalidi counts 436 depopulated Palestinian villages, as differentiated from physically destroyed. *All That Remains: The Palestinian Villages Occupied and Depopulated by Israel in 1948*, ed. Walid Khalidi (Washington, D.C.: Institute for Palestine Studies, 1992), xviii.

98 Nusseibeh, interview (July 5, 1994).

99 Ibid.

100 It would be naïve, say Palestinian educators, to think that Palestinian children do not grasp the scale of their loss. Asked where they come from, schoolchildren often name villages that have not existed for more than half a century. Abla Nasir, director, Tamer Institute for Community Education, thirty-minute communication (Ramallah, March 17, 1997). In 1951, Israel signed the 1949 Fourth Geneva Convention. Paragraph 6 of Article 49 addresses the treatment of civilians in time of war, viewed outside Israel as barring settlements on occupied land: "The occupying power shall not deport or transfer parts of its own civilian population into the territory it occupies." What upsets children about the settlements that Israel began establishing in the occupied territories soon after the 1967 war, teachers report, is that their presence signifies still further loss. Ibid. See Adam Roberts, "Prolonged Military Occupation: The Israeli-Occupied Territories, 1967-1988," *International Law and the Administration of the Occupied Territories: Two Decades of Israeli Occupation of the West Bank and Gaza Strip*, ed. Emma Playfair (Oxford: Clarendon Press, 1992), 25-85; Mazen Qupty, "The Application of International Law in the Occupied Territories as Reflected in the Judgments of the High Court of Justice in Israel," in ibid., 87-124; Richard A. Falk and Burns H. Weston, "The Relevance of International Law to Israeli and Palestinian Rights in the West Bank and Gaza," in ibid., 125-49.

101 Such ideas have steadily gained currency, and a literature is developing, complemented by the work of Israel's "new" historians. See as examples, Rashid Khalidi, "Toward a Solution," in *Palestinian Refugees: Their Problem and Future*; Ziad Abu Zayyad, "The Palestinian Right of Return: A Realistic Approach," *Palestine-Israel Journal* 2 (Spring 1994).

102 Sari Nusseibeh, "Kosher Swimming," *al-Fajr*, September 12, 1986.

103 Nusseibeh, interview (July 5, 1994).

104 Sari Nusseibah, "In a Different Time Zone," interview by Hillel Schenker, *New Outlook*, January 1988, 29.

105 Sari Nusseibeh, "Occupied Territories 20 Years Hence: Need to Struggle against Israeli Extremists," *al-Fajr*, November 14, 1986. An Israeli critique with a comparable analogy between South African and Israeli apartheid is found in Israel Shahak, "Israeli Apartheid and the *Intifada*," *Race and Class* 30, no. 1 (July-September 1988): 1-12.

106 Sari Nusseibeh, "The Continuation of the Status Quo," reprinted from *al-Fajr*, August 9, 1987, in Safieh, *Palestine*, 10. Algeria was Fateh's "first patron and model." Rubin, *Revolution until Victory?* 10. Algerian guerrilla methods had been key to Fateh's mid-1960s raids. Laqueur, *Road to War, 1967*, 58; Maoz, *Palestinian Leadership*, 7. In addition to adulation of the war in Algeria, Nusseibeh recalls his students as enthralled by Frantz Fanon, enamored of the Cuban revolution, and drawing inspiration from the French and American perdition in Indochina. He, however, considered that such guerrilla struggles had little relevance for the dilemma faced by the Palestinians, in part because the Palestinians had been disarmed after 1967.

107 Nusseibeh, interview (July 5, 1994).

108 Nusseibeh, "Continuation of the Status Quo," 9.

109 Ibid., 8.

110 Nusseibeh, interviews (November 6, 1994; January 28, 1996; December 13, 1997).

111 Budeiri, interview (January 28, 1996); Nusseibeh, interview (November 6, 1994).

112 Nusseibeh, "Occupied Territories 20 Years Hence," idem, "The Eyes of Palestine: How Arabs See Likud's Victory," *Washington Post*, June 9, 1996, C1.

113 Joel Greenberg and Menachem Shalev, "Siniora to Stand for Jerusalem Elections," *Jerusalem Post*, June 5, 1987, 1.

114 Yehuda Litani, "Major Change," *Jerusalem Post*, June 5, 1987, 1.

115 Ibid., 1. Also see Aryeh Green, "Local Peace Could Find the Way," *Jerusalem Post*, November 13, 1987, 9.

116 Yehuda Litani, "The Morning After," *Jerusalem Post*, November 19, 1987.

117 Siniora, interview (December 16, 1997).

118 Helena Cobban, "Human Rights and NGOs in the Middle East, and the Failure of the Present Arab-Israeli Peace Process to Include a Human-Rights Dimension," remarks prepared for the Helsinki Commission Seminar, "OSCE at 20: Relevance to Other Regions?" (U. S. Senate, November 14, 1995). In Helsinki, Finland, on August 1, 1975, thirty-three European countries (except Albania), the United States, and Canada signed the Helsinki Final Act of what became the Conference on Security and Co-operation in Europe. While not part of a binding treaty, the agreement's human rights principles committed the signatory nations to follow its terms. Cobban sees the Palestinians as having greater readiness to operate in this framework, compared to Eastern Europe a decade earlier.

119 From anthropologist James C. Scott's work on "hidden transcripts," we may infer that the Palestinian activist intellectuals—relying on commercially available information technologies—had less need for the tactical ploys, ambiguity, and disguised discourse of the 1960 and 1970s, or the PLO. James C. Scott, *Domination and the Arts of Resistance: Hidden Transcripts* (New Haven, Connecticut: Yale University Press, 1990).

120 Kuttab, "Atmosphere in the Husseini Home." Years later, Husseini told American Jewish supporters of Israeli peace groups that regional cooperation would become essential, and the peace process would be the gate to regional cooperation. Feisel Husseini to American Friends of Peace Now, residence of Linda Heller Kamm, Washington, D.C., October 11, 1993.

121 Husayni, Interview, 11.

122 Husseini, "New Face in the Middle East," 18. In this speech, published in a Jewish peace advocacy publication, Husseini usurped the Zionist slogan attributed to Israel Zangwill Moshe—give the "country without a people [to] the people without a country."

123 Patrick Seale, *Abu Nidal: A Gun for Hire* (New York: Random House, 1992), 49, 172-76; Mark Tessler, *A History of the Israeli-Palestinian Conflict* (Bloomington: Indiana University Press, 1994), 633. Abu Nidal (Sabri al-Banna) was born in Jaffa in 1937, 56-67. Isam A. Sartawi, letter to Austrian chancellor Bruno Kreisky (Hotel Imperial, Vienna, January 27, 1977), PASSIA archives, 2.

124 Said Hamammi, "Making the First Move towards Peace in Palestine," *The Times*, December 17, 1973. Avnery devotes 169 pages to Sartawi and Hamammi in Avnery, *My Friend, the Enemy*.

125 Avnery, *My Friend, the Enemy*, 1986, 119-64; Mattiyahu Peled, "My Meetings with PLO Representatives"

(in Hebrew) *Maariv*, January 7 and 21, 1977, as cited in Rolef, "Israel's Policy toward the PLO," 260, 270 n. 28. Avnery was the first Zionist figure to meet publicly with Arafat, in Beirut on July 3, 1982. Avnery, ibid., 3-14. Between October 1982 and June 1987, MK Arie Lova Eliav, former secretary-general of the Labor party, held some forty meetings with PLO figures. *Haaretz*, June 21, 1987, as cited in Rolef, ibid., 270 n. 33.

126 Nusseibeh, interview (January 28, 1996).

127 Husseini, interview (January 30, 1996). These contacts coincided with the European Community's passage of the Venice Declaration, on June 13, 1980, in which nine member states called for recognition of the Palestinian right to self-determination and for PLO participation in Middle East negotiations for peace.

128 Nusseibeh, interview (January 28, 1996). Since Nusseibeh was not part of Fateh's "military wing," he was never regarded as a true Fateh activist within military circles. Pinhas Inbari, "PLO Power Struggle Leads to Anti-Arafat Coalition," *Jerusalem Post*, January 5, 1994, 8.

129 Edy Kaufman and Shukri B. Abed, "The Relevance of Democracy to Israeli-Palestinian Peace," *Democracy, Peace, and the Israeli-Palestinian Conflict*, ed. Edy Kaufman, Shukri B. Abed, and Robert L. Rothstein (Boulder, Colorado: Lynne Rienner Publishers, 1993), 233.

130 Joel Greenberg and Menshem Shalev, "Herut Talks with PLO Backers," *Jerusalem Post*, September 20, 1987. Amirav, born in what is now Russia in 1945, served in the elite paratrooper corps, and was considered one of Yitzhak Shamir's closest aides. Of his meetings with Husseini, he says, "Through our talks I found out not only about Palestinian political positions, but that people can change. I saw that Faisal al-Husseini and other Palestinians I now consider my friends were ready to give up ideas about Jaffa and Galilee. . . So I said, 'OK, if you're ready to do that, I'm ready to give up Bethlehem, the Judea mountains and Samaria. . .'" Diase, "Profiles of Israelis and Palestinians," 172. Sarah Helm quotes Amirav's recollection of a 1985 secret meeting with Feisel Husseini: "I was struck by the fact that he had no anger or hatred. He told me there was a time when he could not say the word *Israel*. 'Now I am saying it. . . . I realise we both have to live here,' he said." Helm, "Pragmatist Will Speak for Palestinians," 12.

131 "Peace Talks between Israel and Palestine Shall Proceed on the Basis of Mutual Recognition of the Independence and Self-Determination of Each . . . . ," prenegotiations proposal for talks in Geneva, July 8, 1987, signed by Abba Eban, Hanna Siniora, Wael Fouad Muhammad Ayesh al-Helekaway, and Abd al-Hamid al-Sayegh. PCSN archives, East Jerusalem.

132 Wallach and Wallach, "Faisal Husseini," in *New Palestinians*, 65. Zeev Schiff and Ehud Yaari devote more than six pages to this episode in *Intifada* and include a transcript from one of the secret sessions. Schiff and Yaari, *Intifada*, 273-81.

133 Ibid., 67; Rolef, "Israel's Policy toward the PLO," 265, 272 nn. 55, 56.

134 In 1988, Amirav told of his meetings with Husseini and Nusseibeh, the "package" that was prepared, and how Likud had rejected him as a result. Moshe Amirav, one-hour interview (Jerusalem, June 8, 1988). See Schiff and Yaari, *Intifada*, 274-77; Diase, "Profiles of Israelis and Palestinians," 172.

135 Schiff and Yaari, *Intifada*, 277.

136 Husayni, Interview, 13. Husseini believed that Shamir cynically exploited the initiative to ward off pressures from the Labor party for an international conference and to preempt external influences on Israel to talk directly with the PLO. Wallach and Wallach, "Faisal Husseini," in *New Palestinians*, 68.

137 Husayni, Interview, 13. Husseini mentions subsequently conferring with Amirav, then a member of Shinui, during three days of meetings that covered the Israeli political spectrum from left to right. Ibid.

138 Nusseibeh, interview (January 28, 1996).

139 Husayni, Interview, 13.

140 Gideon Gera calls this process *Israelization*. Gideon Gera, "Israel and the June 1967 War, 25 Years Later," *Middle East Journal* 46, no. 2 (Spring 1992): 237. In late 1985, Israel accepted in principle the appeal of Jordan's King Hussein for an international umbrella under which negotiations could occur. Recognizing that Jordan could not risk direct public talks with Israel after the assassination of Anwar Sadat, Shimon Peres accepted the principle of an international conference as a context for direct negotiations. The PLO privately accepted the concept of negotiations with Israel under such sponsorship, but did not admit so publicly. From the autumn of 1984 to 1993, the author acted as an intermediary for President Jimmy Carter and held discussions on this issue with Yasir Arafat and some associates. Carter consistently encouraged the PLO to endorse the idea of negotiations with Israel, advising presidents Ronald Reagan and George H. W. Bush on his efforts, yet it was only in private during the 1980s that Arafat would acknowledge the necessity for such a commitment.

141 Abu Ayyash, interview (January 29, 1996).

142 "The Palestinians' Fourteen Demands," *Journal of Palestine Studies* 67 (Spring 1988): 63-65; Hanna Siniora and Fayez Abu Rahme, "Appendix J: The Fourteen Talking Points of West Bank-Gaza Palestinians, January 14, 1988," in Quandt, *Middle East: Ten Years after Camp David*, 484-87; "Fourteen Talking Points of West Bank-Gaza Palestinians, 14 January 1988," *Arab-Israeli Peace Process Briefing Book*, ed. Robert Satloff (Washington, D.C.: Washington Institute for Near East Policy, ca. 1991), section 4, 22-26. See excerpts in appendices, p. 353.

143 Sari Nusseibeh, personal communication (East Jerusalem, June 17, 1995).

144 For a concise analysis of this document, whose authorship by Nusseibeh was not generally known, see Khalidi, "Toward Peace in the Holy Land."

145 Nusseibeh, interview (January 28, 1996). Wilson's twelfth point states nationalities other than the Turkish in the Ottoman Empire "should be assured an undoubted security of life and unmolested opportunity of autonomous development."

146 "Palestinians' Fourteen Demands."

147 "27 January 1988 Letter to Secretary of State George Shultz," in Lukacs, *Israeli-Palestinian Conflict*, 435-37. Siniora recalled, "They had put me in prison for twelve hours to [try to] prevent the initial 14 January press conference from taking place. . . . Later, I was invited with Fayez Abu Rahme to [Washington], the first time that a Palestinian from the territories was invited to the State Department. We carried as our demands (reflecting the demands of the intifada), the Fourteen Points." Siniora, interview (December 16, 1997). To interpret this move as nothing more than elites doing what elites normally do, and to view the developments discussed here through a class-based analysis, risks overlooking the potency of alterations in thinking being catalyzed by the activist intellectuals. Social mobilization theoreticians would view the developments here as frame alignment, or especially frame transformation, in which a new set of beliefs takes precedence over previous ones, functioning as a different master frame.

148 Fayez Abu Rahme, head of the Gaza Bar Association, was also the brother-in-law of Abu Jihad. Barry Rubin, "The PLO and the Palestinians: A Revolution Institutionalized," *The Politics of Change in the Middle East*, ed. Robert B. Satloff (Boulder, Colorado: Westview Press, with the Washington Institute for Near East Policy, 1993), 170 n. 25.

149 Ziad Abu-Amr, "Notes on Palestinian Political Leadership: The "Personalities" of the Occupied Territories," *Middle East Report* (September-October 1988), 23-25. Abu-Amr is regarded on the Bir Zeit faculty as independent.

150 Benvenisti, Abu-Zayed, and Rubinstein, *West Bank Handbook*, 66, 67.

151 On June 28, 1967, 71,000 dunums of land, 6,000 of which had been included in the Jordanian-controlled portions of the city, were lodged under the jurisdiction of the Israeli Jerusalem municipality. (A dunum is one thousand square meters, roughly equivalent to one quarter of an acre.) The portions brought into what Israel considered "unified Jerusalem" extended north to Ramallah and south to Bethlehem. Geoffrey Aronson, *Settlements and the Israeli-Palestinian Negotiations: An Overview* (Washington, D.C.: Institute for Palestine Studies, 1996), 17. B'Tselem concurs with the claims of the international community that East Jerusalem is occupied territory whose status should be determined by negotiations, while ensuring protection of the human rights of all involved. *A Policy of Discrimination: Land Expropriation, Planning and Building in East Jerusalem* (Jerusalem: B'Tselem, 1995), 3, 1. See Terry Rempel, "The Significance of Israel's Partial Annexation of East Jerusalem," *Middle East Journal* 51, no. 4 (Autumn 1997): 520-34.

152 When East Jerusalem and nearby villages were annexed in 1967, B'Tselem notes, Israeli law was imposed in contravention of international law, which holds that an occupying country is not allowed to annex conquered territories, except as a result of a peace treaty, because "the question of annexation of a certain place is not contingent . . . on the arbitrary will of each state." Since then, "the Israeli government has adopted a policy of systematic and deliberate discrimination against the Palestinian population . . . in all matters relating to expropriation of land, planning, and building." *Policy of Discrimination*, 3, 1. Between 1967 and 1996, 24,000 of the 71,000 annexed dunums were expropriated for construction of Israeli settlements, and a quota on construction for Palestinians has since held the Arab quotient of the city's inhabitants at 26 percent. Aronson, *Settlements*, 17, 18. A Palestinian economist asserts East Jerusalem has been enlarged by expropriated land since 1967 such that by 1997 it was three times the size when brought under Israeli authority. Ibrahim Matar, *The Transformation of Jerusalem, 1948-1997*, monograph (London: n.p., 1997), 10. Matar says more than 135 homes in the Moroccan (Maghrebi) Muslim quarter of the Old City were destroyed after the 1967 war to make room for a plaza, and reports that five thousand Palestinians were evicted from other Muslim quarters, leading to a Jewish quarter in the Old City then four times the size it

was in 1948. Matar, *Transformation of Jerusalem*, 10. See idem, "From Palestinian to Israeli: Jerusalem, 1948-1982," *Journal of Palestine Studies* 48 (Summer 1983): 57-63.

153 See Goldstein, *Journalism under Occupation*, 18, 19.

154 Daoud Kuttab, "Jerusalem," dispatch filed with news media (East Jerusalem: May 1988), Kuttab private papers.

155 Husayni, Interview, 3.

156 Under town arrest orders, a modified form of house arrest, Husseini could not leave East Jerusalem's city limits, was obliged to remain inside his house from dusk to dawn and to report twice weekly to police. Frankel, "Israelis Detain Arab Activist," A21. Subjected to town arrest from 1982 until April 1987, Husseini was jailed without charge during a security crackdown following protests throughout the occupied territories over the prison conditions of Palestinian prisoners. Ibid.

157 "Update July 28, 1988"; "Arab Studies Society Appeal: Arab Studies Society Closed for One Year; Society Director Placed under Administrative Detention," in Cainkar and Goldring, *Uprising in Palestine, the First Year*, 259, 271. The Database Project on Palestinian Human Rights was housed in the Arab Studies Society; twelve field workers throughout Israel and the Palestinian territories collected information on human rights violations. Rosemary Radford Ruether, "The Database Project on Palestinian Human Rights," *Christianity and Crisis*, December 14, 1987, 436.

158 Document alleged to have been among Feisel Husseini's papers, reprinted from *Jerusalem Post*, August 12, 1988, in Cainkar and Goldring, *Uprising in Palestine, the First Year*, 317-19. See appendices, p. 349.

159 Jonathan Karp, "Shamir Calls Plan for Palestinian State Insane and Dangerous," Reuters, August 8, 1988; Joel Greenberg, "A New Direction for the Uprising," *Jerusalem Post*, August 12, 1988.

160 Thomas L. Friedman, "The King's Move: Hussein Cuts Off the West Bank, Spites Arafat; Stay Tuned," *New York Times*, August 7, 1988; Joel Greenberg, "Nusseibeh Wants Provisional Government Now," *Jerusalem Post*, November 17, 1989.

161 Greenberg, "New Direction."

162 Although the generic concept was not new, Nusseibeh considers that the specific idea for a declaration of independence for a Palestinian state was first "floated" in the contemporary era in 1979 or 1980, in the paper on civil disobedience by Adnan Idris noted earlier. Maher Abukhater, "Towards the Proclamation of the State," interview of Sari Nusseibeh, *al-Fajr*, August 14, 1988; Nusseibeh, interview (December 13, 1997). The impact of Aziz Shehadeh in the late 1960s and 1970s on Feisel Husseini and Jonathan Kuttab in this regard was noted in chapter 4. In May 1988, the Palestinian debate was heightened by publication of a similar suggestion of bringing a state into being without negotiations, when Jerome M. Segal, a U.S. Jewish academician, made an analogy to Israel's proclamation of a state without approval from the Arabs. Jerome M. Segal, "A Radical Plan for Mideast Peace; If Palestinians Really Want a State, They Should Declare One," *Washington Post*, May 22, 1988: C5; Shindler, *Ploughshares into Swords?* 105-6. Segal's piece also appeared in *al-Quds*.

163 Husseini, interview (June 14, 1995).

164 Ibid.

165 Nusseibeh, interview (July 5, 1994).

166 The author has found no reference to this document in the literature except by Ziad Abu-Amr, who incorrectly attributes the text to Abu Jihad. Ziad Abu-Amr, *The Intifada: Causes and Factors of Continuity*, trans. comm. Mohssn Esseesy, 2nd ed. (East Jerusalem: PASSIA, 1994), 26n. As his source for its attribution to Abu Jihad, Abu-Amr cites Lutfi al-Khuli, *The Uprising and the Palestinian State* (Cairo: al-Ahram Centre for Translation and Publishing, 1988), 311. Don Peretz reports that a seventeen-point paper appeared anonymously in the West Bank and Gaza after January 1988, probably a reference to this document, although he does not provide details. Peretz, *Intifada*, 52.

167 References to the paper are from Abu-Amr, *Intifada*, where it is attached as the first appendix, 46-52. Excerpts translater in appendices, p. 354.

168 Some in official Fateh circles may not have been committed, while others probably did not know of the paper. The Popular Front for the Liberation of Palestine (PFLP) was opposed to the full program, including its proposed negotiations with Israel, while the DFLP and communists showed flexibility. Nusseibeh, interview (July 5, 1994). For example, a PFLP leaflet was issued in December 1988, which called for rejection of UN Resolutions 242 and 338 and urging armed struggle. Again, in February 1990, the PFLP would issue a statement in Damascus, urging the use of arms against Israeli troops, despite, as Colin Shindler writes, "the very fact that firearms were not used during the Intifada had made a considerable impression in the West." Atran, "Stones against the Iron Fist," 512 n. 36; Shindler, *Ploughshares into Swords?* 230.

169 "The al-Quds Working Paper was written by a group of people here, more than one person. I think I actually penned it by hand. It cannot be claimed to be written by anybody else. I have it on disk . . . . Ziad Abu Zayyad was involved [and] various people. Then to give it absolute form and coherence, if you like, I think it was I who actually wrote it down." Nusseibeh, interview (January 28, 1996).

170 Ian Black and Benny Morris note, "The facsimile machine became a symbol of the intifada, . . . rarely clandestine activities in the traditional clandestine sense. It involved ideas, money and public relations, not guns and bombs." Black and Morris, *Israel's Secret Wars*, 467.

171 Nusseibeh, interviews (January 28, 1996; December 13, 1997). This arrangement, which persisted during the intifada, is confirmed without details in Paul Taylor, "Palestinian Leaders Rely on Fax and Olive Branch," Reuters, May 8, 1989.

172 Nusseibeh, interview (November 5, 1994); Sari Nusseibeh, "Assessing Two Years of Intifada," reprint of a February 1990 speech at Oxford University, in Safieh, *Palestine*, 50. "We were told, 'Fine. This is excellent as a program. Carry on.' We, therefore, felt that we had backing. A bit later, there was an internal instruction from the Fateh leadership outside, in which, more or less, the same ideas were introduced." Nusseibeh, interview (January 28, 1996).

173 Nusseibeh, "Assessing Two Years of Intifada," 50.

174 Nusseibeh, communication (June 17, 1995).

175 Nusseibeh, interview (November 6, 1994).

176 Ibid. "People involved in drawing up the program were involved directly and indirectly in the representation of Fateh in the Unified National Leadership Command." Nusseibeh, interview (November 6, 1994).

177 Nusseibeh calls this "background literature," in contrast to the "surface literature" being publicly disseminated. Nusseibeh, "Time for Palestinian Offensives," 17. Either way, in view of large gaps in what has been published about the first intifada, the Jerusalem Paper should be considered a primary source. See appendices, p. 354, for excerpts.

178 Sari Nusseibeh, "A Palestinian Moderate's Plea from a Cell in Ramleh Jail," *Guardian*, March 4, 1991. When the author first met Nusseibeh at the King David Hotel, in West Jerusalem in June 1988, he had been arrested by the Israelis en route and questioned for several hours.

Chapter 9

1 Tschirgi, "High Hope, Bad News," 2, part 5. See also Ann Mosely Lesch, "Prelude to the Uprising in the Gaza Strip," *Journal of Palestine Studies* 77 (Autumn 1990): 1-23.

2 Dan Fisher, "Palestinian Student Killed in Clash with Israeli Forces at West Bank University," *Los Angeles Times*, April 14, 1987, 6.

3 Ian Black, "The Prisoners of the Killing Fields," *Guardian*, May 26, 1987.

4 Fisher, "Palestinian Student Killed," 6; "Conflict Increases in Israeli Prisons," *al-Fajr*, July 5, 1987, 2.

5 "Reluctant Occupiers," 6.

6 Bradley Burston, "One Dead, Forty-Two Hurt as Gaza Violence Continues," *Jerusalem Post*, January 11, 1988; Kuttab, "Bloody Confrontation," 3. On "liberation" of Salfit, a village of several thousand, southeast of Nablus, see Joel Greenberg, "Abandoned by the IDF," *Jerusalem Post*, June 16, 1989. Balata refugee camp was declared a "liberated zone" by Palestinian youths. "Frustration and Poverty Ten Years On: Balata Refugee Camp," reprinted from *al-Hayat al-Jadida*, December 7, 1997, trans. Joharah Baker, *Palestine Report*, December 12, 1997, 16.

7 Joel Greenberg, "Summit Disappoints Palestinians," *Jerusalem Post*, November 18, 1987, 5; Yehuda Litani, "The Arab Summit: Final Scoreboard," *Jerusalem Post*, November 13, 1987, 9.

8 Chris Wood, "Where Will the Revolt End?" *MacLean's*, April 18, 1988, 23. Prime Minister Yitzhak Shamir said the hang-gliding episode "shattered the barrier of fear" that maintained order among the Palestinians. Edward Cody, "Palestinian Uprising: A Rage Unleashed: 'Tired of Living Like This,'" *Washington Post*, February 28, 1988, 28.

9 Abu Ayyash, interview (January 29, 1996).

10 An early, relatively accurate comment on the funneling of ideas by the activist intellectuals during the first intifada is found in Zvi Gilat, "The Leadership of the Uprising," *New Outlook*, March-April 1988, 11-13.

11 Gabi Sheffer, "The Palestinians' Endurance," *Jerusalem Post*, March 21, 1988, 8; idem, "The Endurance of the Palestinians," *New Outlook*, May 1988, 20-21.

12 Yehuda Litani, "Protest in Territories Is Led by Local Committees," *Jerusalem Post*, February 3, 1988, 1.

13 Kuttab, "Profile of the Stonethrowers," 21, 22.

14 See Litani, "Protest in Territories," 1. Years later, some Palestinians claim that leaders of West Bank

village support committees are still sought by Israeli officials, including by sharpshooters working from lists that date to 1988. Interviews (West Bank, 1994-97).

15 Jarbawi, interview (June 16, 1995). Hiltermann notes, "What is remarkable is that the entire population could be mobilized simultaneously, and that a support structure needed to sustain the uprising's momentum came into being and functioned efficiently, with a leadership that was promptly accepted as legitimate by the population, in less than a month." Hiltermann, *Behind the Intifada*, 173.

16 Hatem Abd al-Qader Eid, two-hour interview (East Jerusalem, January 28, 1996).

17 Muhammad Jadallah, two-hour interview (East Jerusalem, December 15, 1997). Jadallah, a cardio-vascular surgeon, was the cofounder and chair of the DFLP's Union of Health Care Committees. Hanna Siniora corroborates Jadallah's viewpoint: "The younger generation of leaders from the Democratic Front were the first ones to act, people who later were exiled from the country, and they were the first to come out with the first proclamation. . . . Even Feisel [Husseini] at that time was not part of the intifada because he was in prison. People from Fateh joined in with the DFLP." Siniora, interview (December 16, 1997).

18 Nusseibeh, interview (December 13, 1997).

19 Khatib, interview (December 15, 1997). Born in Nablus in May 1954, Khatib was arrested five times, with his longest prison term four years. Having joined the communist party as a youth, in 1982 he was graduated from Bir Zeit University, where he was elected five times to the student council, often chairing it during student upheavals. He received a master's degree in economic development from the University of Manchester, UK. Upon returning from Britain, he joined the cultural studies faculty at Bir Zeit and established the East Jerusalem Media and Communications Center (JMCC) a few months after the 1987 uprising started. Khatib ran the JMCC for years, even while under arrest, and JMCC, which publishes *Palestine Report*, continued publishing. Along with Yossi Alpher, an Israeli who has served as director of the Jaffee Center for Strategic Studies, Tel Aviv University, Khatib publishes www.bitterlemons.org, a Web site that offers Israeli and Palestinian viewpoints on the Israeli-Palestinian conflict and the peace process. During the intifada, having determined that foreign journalists and fact-finding missions needed help in understanding the complexity of the uprising, he "organized delegations to the depths of our society—Balata refugee camp, meetings with the popular committees." Ibid. A member of the Palestinian delegation to the Madrid peace conference in 1991 and the Washington negotiations that followed, Khatib later accepted a ministerial post in the Palestinian Authority as minister of labor. See "Ghassan Khatib," in Wallach and Wallach (eds.), *New Palestinians*, 246-68.

20 Khatib, interview (December 15, 1997).

21 Shafi would head the delegation of Palestinian negotiators at the 1991 Madrid peace conference.

22 Khatib, interview (December 15, 1997).

23 This factor would contribute to the eventual turn toward violence later in the first intifada.

24 Schiff and Yaari, *Intifada*, 215-17; Frisch, "Diffusion and Consolidation, 49.

25 Nusseibeh, interview (November 5, 1994).

26 Hamayl was on January 20, 1996, elected as an independent from Ramallah to the Palestinian Legislative Council. Hamayl, interview (January 25, 1996).

27 Eid, interview (January 28, 1996).

28 Jadallah, interview (December 15, 1997). On Jadallah, see "The Detention and Torture of Dr. Jadallah: November 15, 1988," in Cainkar and Goldring, *Uprising in Palestine, the First Year*, 447-48; Jon Immanuel, "The Accord: Supporters Unite, Opposition Falters," *Jerusalem Post*, September 10, 1993; Sami Aboudi, "Palestinian Militants Rail against False Democracy," Reuters, January 19, 1996.

29 Sari Nusseibeh, "The Intifada: A Two-Year Perspective," speech given in Washington, D.C., November 1989, in Safieh, *Palestine*, 44. Nusseibeh explained: "You are given a working paper and asked what you think. You read it, and I read it. It circulates. People are communicating, but not directly. I would know you; you would know me; but I wouldn't necessarily speak with you openly about a problem or an idea that actually was being debated between you and me, through the working group." Nusseibeh, interview (July 5, 1994).

30 According to Glenn Frankel, the Shabiba movement at the time consisted of a core group of 150 to 200 dues-paying members, with another thousand who gave it "loose allegiance." Glenn Frankel, "Palestinian Mistrust Mars Shultz Tour," *Washington Post*, February 26, 1988, 1.

31 Mubarak Awad, "Nonviolence: Working Definitions," *International Journal of Nonviolence* 1 (September 1993): 4. Imagery may persist from the ancient past. In the New Testament of the Bible, Mark 6:11, Jesus said to the disciples, "If any place . . . refuse to hear you . . . shake off the dust that is on your feet as a testimony against them" (New Revised Standard Version). See Andrew Rigby, *Living the* Intifada (London: Zed Books, 1991), 2.

32 Bennis, *Stones to Statehood*, 27.

33 Ali Hussein Qleibo, *Before the Mountains Disappear: An Ethnographic Chronicle of the Modern Palestinians* (Jericho, Palestinian areas: Kloreus Books, 1992), 69.

34 The first appearance of *intifada* was not in 1987; the word had been used in the student struggles of the 1980s.

35 Edward W. Said, "Intifada and Independence," *Intifada: The Palestinian Uprising against Israeli Occupation*, ed. Zachary Lockman and Joel Beinin (Boston: South End Press, 1989), 5.

36 Sari Nusseibeh, "A True People's Revolution," *Middle East International*, December 15, 1989, 17.

37 Nusseibeh, interview (July 5, 1994). A probable reference by Salah Khalaf (Abu Iyad) to the "Jerusalem Paper" appeared in the *Washington Post*, in February 1988, the month it was initially faxed from Nusseibeh's office to Tunis. Jonathan Randal reports Abu Iyad "was impressed by a working paper on escalating the disturbances recently sent from inside the occupied territories." Jonathan Randal, "Uprisings Invigorate PLO Leaders; Movement's Future Still Held Uncertain," *Washington Post*, February 25, 1988, A39.

38 Daoud Kuttab, "The Strengths of the *Intifada*'s Unified Command," *Middle East International*, September 9, 1988, 17.

39 Khatib, interview (December 15, 1997). The roots of the PCP were in Israel and the occupied territories. By contrast, Fateh wanted coordination with exiled Palestinian leaders in Tunis. Ziad Abu-Amr, "The Palestinian Uprising in the West Bank and Gaza Strip," *Arab Studies Quarterly* 10, no. 4 (Autumn 1988): 389.

40 Kuttab, "Strengths of the *Intifada*'s Unified Command," 17.

41 Schenker, "Channel this Energy," interview of Azmi Bishara, 18.

42 Kuttab, "Profile of the Stonethrowers," 22.

43 Ten Qalandia youths, interview (January 22, 1996); Nusseibeh, "Two-Year Perspective," 43.

44 Abu-Diab, interview (December 11, 1997); Sari Nusseibeh, personal communication (East Jerusalem, December 16, 1997).

45 Khatib, interview (December 15, 1997). "DFLP officials have claimed responsibility for establishing the UNLU [Command], but were upstaged, they contend. . . . " Hiltermann, *Behind the Uprising*, 237 n. 18.

46 Nusseibeh, "Two-Year Perspective," 44.

47 Nusseibeh, interview (December 13, 1997). Shehadeh (no relation to Raja Shehadeh) was described as a senior Fateh official. Hisham Abdallah, "Fatah Torn between Political Future and Revolutionary Past," Agence France-Presse, December 30, 1993.

48 Nusseibeh, interview (July 5, 1994).

49 Jadallah, interview (December 15, 1997). This third leaflet, which appeared January 10, 1988, is considered by the PCP to be the fourth, but by the Command to be its first. No single account of the leaflets' history would be acceptable to all factions, due to human variations in perspective. More than one causal account is characteristic of clandestine movements. A DFLP activist, Muhammad Abdullah Labadi (nom de guerre Abu Samer), drafted what Zeev Schiff and Ehud Yaari term the first leaflet, but most Palestinians interviewed regard it as the second leaflet. Schiff and Yaari, *Intifada*, 106-10, 192-95. Labadi was deported in 1988. Dan Fisher, "Israel To Deport Ten Palestinian Activists," *Los Angeles Times*, July 9, 1988, 5. Labadi's confessions, upon arrest, are viewed as the basis for what Schiff and Yaari say in *Intifada* about the leaflets. Schiff and Yaari's book is disregarded by Palestinians who claim that it is based on information obtained under duress, particularly material on pp. 106-11, and also pp. 198-219 on the Command. Ghassan Khatib asserted, "The book is biased because those who got arrested first were the representatives of the DFLP—they were arrested first and they confessed first. Schiff and Yaari got their first information from Israeli intelligence, through the confessions of those persons. . . . The others, who were careful enough not to be arrested and strong enough not to confess, did not have the chance to put across their point of view. . . . When Schiff and Yaari's book came out during the intifada, we were really frustrated because we knew that many things in it were incorrect, but we could not say that they were wrong. . . . The authors themselves personally told me, 'the sources are all from the written confessions of mostly Muhammad Labadi and members of the DFLP in Israeli jails.' I myself have copies of such confessions, because lawyers can get copies." Khatib, interview (December 15, 1997). Khatib, whose origins are in the PCP, said that in an effort in Gaza led by Bassam Salhi (later arrested and imprisoned for three years), the communist party took the initiative and issued four communiqués believed by the PCP to lay the basis for the intifada. In this view, the enumerated leaflets began after the fourth Gaza communiqué. Ibid. See Gaza Communiqués of December 16, 1987, January 8 and 12, 1988; and (n.d.) February 1988, in FACTS, 90-96. The FACTS Information Committee compiled

weekly reports from January through September 1988, constituting the single most useful resource on the initial year of the first intifada. A second volume, consolidating these reports and adding the committee's weekly reports through 1989, is Samir Abbed-Rabbo and Doris Safie, *The Palestinian Uprising: FACTS Information Committee* (Belmont, Massachusetts: Association of Arab-American University Graduates, Inc., 1990).

50 Joel Greenberg and Bradley Burston, "Authors of 'Leaflet-11' Arrested," *Jerusalem Post*, March 25, 1988, 1.

51 Aruri, "New Climate of Opportunity," 18. The leaflets were reminiscent in approach to the 1950s activities of the Jordan Communist Party.

52 Khatib, interview (December 15, 1997).

53 Jadallah, interview (December 15, 1997); Khatib, ibid.

54 "Arguments among the leaflet writers went like this: Do you condone the attacking, throwing bombs or Molotov cocktails at civilians, or settlers, or soldiers, in the West Bank or in Israel, or knives, or whatever? Or do you only condone strikes?" Nusseibeh, interview (January 28, 1996). "There was always opposition, people wanting to make things violent, leaflets with two sides to them, and you must remember . . . the mobilization Hamas was making wasn't along these same lines." Nusseibeh, interview (November 5, 1994).

55 Shin Bet at times put out fake communiqués to bewilder and knowingly mislead the populace. Lockman and Beinin, *Intifada*, 327.

56 After Leaflet no. 9 of March 2, 1988, fissures began to show on the question of arms, during a period said by human rights monitoring groups to have been characterized by a particularly brutal response from the occupying forces. Shehadeh, "Occupier's Law," 29. See also al-Haq, *Punishing a Nation*, and *Nation under Siege* (Ramallah, 1990). When differences between Palestinian communists and the rest of the Command arose over a proposed appeal for the use of Molotov cocktails, the communists urged the "taming" of the uprising. Daoud Kuttab, untitled news report, East Jerusalem, ca. March 10, 1988, Kuttab private papers; confirmed by Ghassan Khatib, interview (December 15, 1997).

57 Daoud Kuttab reports, "One of the first decisions of the leadership of the Palestinian uprising when it started was that Palestinians will not use gunfire in their protest activities. The leaders of the uprising insisted on their position even when PLO Chairman Yasser Arafat threatened the possibility of ordering his supporters to use it [gunfire], if the Israelis didn't lessen the oppression." Kuttab, "Will Guns Be Used?" dispatch to news media, East Jerusalem, ca. May 1988, Kuttab private papers. The PLO in Tunis announced a policy proscribing the use of weapons. The *Jerusalem Post* cited defense sources that "early in the unrest Israel intercepted secret orders from Palestine Liberation chief Yasser Arafat to supporters in the occupied territories not to use guns and bombs." Peter Smerdon, "Israeli Army Fears Palestinian Rioters May Turn to Guns," *Jerusalem Post*, February 9, 1988.

58 Acclaim for the Command was high, as shown by an amusing incident at a supermarket in Beit Hanina. "The shops were supposed to close at 1:00 o'clock, but one shop used to stay open an extra thirty minutes. One day, when a woman was lingering towards the close of business, the owner told her to hurry because he had received a threat from the leadership of the intifada. She was excited and wanted to see the threat—the people usually wanted whatever contact they could make with the anonymous Command. When the shop owner showed her the warning, she studied it closely and recognized the handwriting. The 'threat' was from her nine-year-old son, who had written that the proprietor had better stick to the hours set by the intifada." Jonathan Kuttab, interview (November 5, 1994).

59 Malki, interview (May 3, 1995). See Tamari, "Sociological Perspective," in Ateek, Ellis, and Ruether, *Faith and the Intifada*, 20. This fluidity is borne out by Legrain's compendium of the first year's leaflets, e.g., three versions appear for Leaflet no. 10, not counting Israeli counterfeits. Legrain, *Les Voix du Soulévement Palestinien*, 50. The Command gained in legitimacy when it retracted unrealistic calls. Adrien Katherine Wing, "Legal Decision-Making during the Palestinian *Intifada*: Embryonic Self-Rule," *Yale Journal of International Law* 18, no. 1 (Winter 1993): 130.

60 Sari Nusseibeh's secretary, Hanan Gheith, trained in a secretarial school run by his mother, Nuzha, typed leaflets. Nusseibeh, interview (December 13, 1997).

61 Paul Taylor, "Palestinian Moslem Brothers Gain Despite Imprisonment," Reuters, December 1, 1989. On "linguistic transformation," see Hanan Mikhail Ashrawi, *This Side of Peace* (New York: Touchstone/Simon and Schuster, 1995), 133-34.

62 Nusseibeh, interview (January 28, 1996). Izzat Ghazzawi and Radi Jarai were sentenced to more than two years in prison for writing leaflets. "Two Jailed for PLO Activity; Court Finds Nusseibeh Wrote Inciting Leaflets," *Jerusalem Post*, April 20, 1990. The judges' verdict said Nusseibeh had dictated the text.

63 More than one hundred fax machines were in use in the West Bank and Gaza Strip. Telephone links had to go through PLO "stations" in Europe, because there were no direct phone connections to the occupied territories from any Arab country. Mushahid Hussain, "Faith in the Intifada," *Jane's Defense Weekly*, March 24, 1990, 556. Access to telephone lines for journalists and others was rigidly controlled, and a ban on fax machines in the West Bank was introduced in June 1991. Taher Shreiteh, a freelance reporter who worked for Reuters, CBS, and the *New York Times* was jailed for failing to report that he owned a fax. Jonathan Ferziger, "Palestinian Journalist Held on Charges of Hiding Fax Machine," UPI, February 18, 1991; Caroline Moorehead, "Israel's Censors under Scrutiny," *Independent*, October 19, 1992, 11.

64 Nusseibeh, interview (January 28, 1996). Joel Brinkley corroborates this: "The underground leaders—a rotating group of senior activists whose names are a closely held secret—are essentially on their own, too. Before they distribute the latest leaflet, they fax copies to P.L.O. headquarters in Tunis for comment. And though they consult with P.L.O. leaders on 'foreign policy' matters—how to respond to this or that international peace plan, for example—the leaders in the occupied territories are not afraid to ignore the P.L.O.'s advice." Joel Brinkley, "Inside the Intifada," *New York Times*, October 29, 1989, section 6, 6.

65 Mahdi Abd al-Hadi, interview (December 13, 1997).

66 Eid, interview (January 28, 1996).

67 Awad, *Nonviolence*; Sharp, *Methods of Nonviolent Action*: xii-xvi. This is easily discernible by comparing a single section in Awad's booklet, "Refusal to Cooperate," with the first thirty leaflets. Awad, *Nonviolence* (excerpts in appendices, p. 352); Lockman and Beinin, *Intifada*, 327-94; FACTS, 90-136; Jean-François Legrain with Pierre Chenard, *Les Voix du Soulèvement Palestinien, 1987-1988: Edition Critique des Communiqués du Commandement National Unifé du Soulèvement et du Movement de la Résistance Islamique*, trans. Jean-François Legrain with Pierre Chenard (Paris: Centre d'Etudes et de Documentation Économique, Juridiue et Sociale [CEDEJ]), 1991, passim. Awad's urging of refusal to work as laborers in the building of Israeli settlements occurs in Leaflets no. 6, 9, 13, 14, 15, 18, and 19. Refusal to fill out forms, a type of cooperation with Israeli authorities, appears in Leaflets no. 17, 18, 19, and 26. Refusal to carry or produce identity cards is called for in Leaflets no. 18 and 19. Refusal to pay fines is noted in Leaflets no. 6 and 9. Refusal to submit requests for permits and licenses is bade in Leaflets no. 13, 17, and 18. Refusal to appear when summoned by the police or civil administration occurs in Leaflet no. 26. Refusal to work as an employee of the military occupation is urged in Leaflets no. 6, 12, 13, 14, 15, 17, 18, 19, and 20. Refusal to pay income taxes is specified in Leaflets no. 9, 12, 13, 14, 17, 18, 19, 20, and 26. Refusal to pay the value added tax or other taxes is asked in Leaflets no. 6, 9, 12, 13, 14, 17, 18, 19, 20, and 26. Refusal to accept house arrest, restrictions on travel, curfews, orders closing areas, or closed schools appears in Leaflets no. 13, 15, and 17. The booklet's admonitions for self-reliance, limited goals for specific actions, and of preventing Israeli authorities from accomplishing their aims are reflected in the Command's leaflets. The idea of self-sacrifice—the literal meaning of the Palestinian *fedayeen* of the 1950s and 1960s—is redefined in the booklet as a popular form of endurance by men, women, and children, usually aimed at specific injustices or survival.

68 Joel Greenberg, "Israel Battle Moves from the Streets," *Jerusalem Post*, March 18, 1988.

69 Brinkley, "Israel Weighs Appeal by U.S. Arab," 8.

70 Mahdi Abd al-Hadi recalls Feisel Husseini took the term *white revolution* from Abu Jihad, who, he says, first used it pertaining to the Palestinians in the occupied territories. By Hadi's account, Abu Jihad said, "This white revolution will not ask clean hands or dirty hands—it will ask all hands." Hadi, interview (December 13, 1997). Origins of this term are obscure. Gandhi writes in 1939: "[I]f it is possible to train millions in the black art of violence, which is the law of the beast, it is more possible to train them in the white art of non-violence. . . . " M. K. Gandhi, *Harijan*, September 30, 1939.

71 Nusseibeh, interview (January 28, 1996).

72 Eid, interview (January 28, 1996).

73 Daoud Kuttab, "Six-Month Anniversary of the Intifadah," East Jerusalem, May 1988, Kuttab private papers, 8, 9.

74 Ibid. Helena Cobban suggests a "shift in the centre of gravity" was accelerating from 1977 onward and quotes Khaled al-Hassan as saying in 1983, "I think now that the people inside, they have more weight than we have. Their support to us gives us the international legality." Cobban, *Palestinian Liberation Organisation*, 257, 258.

75 George D. Moffett III, "PLO Shows It Can Capitalize on Unrest: Deeper Roots in Occupied Lands Help Build Loyalties," *Christian Science Monitor*, December 31, 1987.

76 Salim Tamari, "It Is Time to Converse Calmly; An Incredible Realization of Talent and Energy that We Did Not Know Was inside Us," trans. comm. Nermeen Murad, *al-Ayyam*, Ramallah, January 29, 1996.

77 Kaminer, *Politics of Protest*, 128.

78 Jadallah, interview (December 15, 1997).

79 Ibid. Numerous interviews rebut Jamal's assertion that the "political entrepreneurship" of this group derived from the support of the PLO. He deems the "façade" of the activist intellectuals a "pure example of patronage politics"—a substantially different causal narrative from that presented here. Jamal, *Palestinian National Movement*, 90-91.

80 Frisch, "Middle Command," 262; Mustafa (Mejdi) Showkat, two-hour interview (Gaza City, January 24, 1996). Showkat worked closely with Arafat.

81 Journalist Ned Temko grasped the equation: "The intellectual direction of the uprising is being provided in large part by West Bankers in their twenties or thirties who, as students in high schools and universities, helped coin a distinctly local brand of Palestinian nationalism. Their avowed aim is to force the establishment of a Palestinian state in the West Bank and Gaza that would be independent both of Israel and of the neighboring Arab states such as Jordan. Their reasoning is that the present uprising—deliberately avoiding the use of gunfire in favor of stones and roadblocks—has offered an unprecedented chance to galvanize world opinion for such an option. But on the front line, the unrest is being spearheaded by Palestinians in their mere teens, or even younger, . . . subject to the discipline of its political strategists. On the crucial decision not to use firearms, the line is holding firm." Ned Temko, "In Israeli-Occupied Lands, Youths Lead Charge; Palestinian Parents and Israeli Army on Defensive as Teen-Agers Lead Unrest," *Christian Science Monitor*, March 15, 1988.

82 Nusseibeh, "Midwife at the Birth of a State," 40.

83 Ashrawi would subsequently, with Feisel Husseini, become a surrogate for the PLO in meetings with U.S. Secretary of State James A. Baker III in the months leading up to the October 1991 Madrid conference, when the government of Israel still proscribed contact with the PLO (see chapter 12).

84 See Wallach and Wallach, "Mamdouh Aker," in *New Palestinians*, 164-84. Aker stated, "We will not allow an Arab leader to make a demand for a Palestinian state in all of Palestine at a time that we Palestinians are asking for a two-state solution, neither will we accept anything less than a Palestinian state and our right to self-determination." Kuttab, "Six-Month Anniversary of the Intifadah."

85 By the time of the intifada, the federation Kamal led, noted in chapter 5, had more than 5,000 members and 107 centers throughout the occupied territories, with generation of income the focus of much of its activities. Warnock, *Land before Honour*, 145; Hiltermann, *Behind the Intifada*, 151.

86 Ashrawi, *This Side of Peace*, 50-51.

87 Jadallah, interview (December 15, 1997).

88 Ashrawi, *This Side of Peace*, 51. Papers were secretly circulated to elaborate different angles, for example, whether a declaration of independence should follow upon or complement the call for total civil disobedience. Nusseibeh, "True People's Revolution," 18.

89 Izzat Ghazzawi, literature professor at Bir Zeit and Ramallah novelist, was head of the Palestinian Writers Union and father of a sixteen-year-old boy who was shot and killed by Israeli troops during a demonstration at his school. On Ghazzawi, see Susan Sachs, "Hamas Slaying Sparks Gaza Riots," *Newsday*, November 26, 1993, 19; Liat Collins, "New Palestinian-Israeli Journal Launched," *Jerusalem Post*, January 12, 1994, 3; Ethan Bronner, "Capital Investment: Town North of Jerusalem Draws Palestinians' Focus," *Boston Globe*, October 11, 1995, 8A. Ghazzawi later published a collection of his letters from prison.

90 Nusseibeh, interview (December 13, 1997). Samir Sbeihat would be elected to chair the Palestinian Union of Students and later become president of the World Council of Palestinian Students. Jon Immanuel, "Closure Tops Palestinians' List of Grievances," *Jerusalem Post*, February 7, 1995, 1.

91 Nusseibeh, interview (December 13, 1997).

92 Siniora, interview (December 16, 1997).

93 Ibid.

94 Siniora noted, "The Fateh organization realigned itself behind Feisel when he was released. There was always competition between Feisel and Radwan Abu Ayyash, [later] deputy minister and in charge of the Palestinian Broadcasting Corporation. Radwan was part of the organized official intifada leadership. Eventually he carried a dual role, and became a public figure as well as having excellent connections with the underground party organizations." Siniora, interview (December 16, 1997). See Jon Immanuel, "Husseini Rival Sets up Group to Promote Alternative Voice," *Jerusalem Post*, June 19, 1992.

95 Siniora, interview (December 16, 1997); Nusseibeh, interview (December 13, 1997).

96 Nusseibeh, interview (December 13, 1997).

97 Nusseibeh and his wife, Lucy Austin Nusseibeh, at times carried hundreds of thousands of dollars

in cash in plastic bags. Nusseibeh, interviews (December 13 and 16, 1997); Joel Greenberg, "Indict-ments Shed Light on Intifada Leadership; 'Salon' Activists Feeling the Heat," *Jerusalem Post*, May 12, 1989; Dvorah Getzler, "Bar-Lev: Nusseibeh Funds Intifada," *Jerusalem Post*, May 25, 1989; Siniora, interview (December 16, 1997). Couriers brought funds from the PLO into the territories to help finance the uprising and meet the income needs of striking municipal workers and government employees, subsidies for the unemployed, and stipends for students and families of martyrs. Israel tried to stanch the flow by limiting the cash that could be brought by visitors to the territories, because numerous returning residents carried intifada money in small quantities. None of these funds were used for weaponry, according to Peretz, in "*Intifada* and Middle East Peace," 391. In Feb-ruary 1988, moves were made to prevent any Palestinian from bringing into Israel or the territories more than $1,000. Joel Greenberg, "Goren: Move to Slash PLO Funds to Areas," *Jerusalem Post*, Feb-ruary 15, 1988, 2; idem, "Screws Turned on West Bank Tax Collection," *Jerusalem Post*, February 18, 1988, 1; Jonathan Randal, "Palestinians See Uprising Losing Momentum, but Vow to Continue," *Washington Post*, May 13, 1988, A30. In March 1988, moneychangers who regularly crossed the Allenby Bridge from Jordan with $36 to $45 million in cash and checks each way were refused passage. Andrew Whitley and Tony Walker, "A Shift from Stones to Sanctions," *Financial Times*, March 28, 1988, 20. Funds declined as Israel restricted the sum that could be repatriated. "In October 1987, incoming funds totaled 3.3 million [Jordanian] dinars [equivalent to $9.7 million USD] and $12 million; in October 1988 this dropped to 1,958,000 dinars [equivalent to roughly 5 million dollars] and $400,000; and in October 1989, the figures were 262,700 dinars [equivalent to $457,000 USD]and $7,700." Aryeh Shalev, "The Second Year of the Intifada," *The Middle East Military Balance, 1989-1990*, ed. Joseph Alpher, with Zeev Eytan and Dov Tamari (Tel Aviv: Jaffee Center for Strategic Studies, 1990), 148.

98 Nusseibeh, interview (January 28, 1996).

99 Siniora, interview (December 16, 1997). Also see Stephen Franklin, "West Bank Prof on the Spot or Off the Hook," *Chicago Tribune*, May 21, 1989, 1; "Arab Philosopher Linked to Uprising," *New York Times*, May 5, 1989, A11.

100 Nusseibeh, interview (December 13, 1997); Nusseibeh, communication (December 16, 1997).

101 Nusseibeh, interview (December 13, 1997).

102 Nusseibeh, interview (January 28, 1996). At the start of the intifada, Nusseibeh established the Holy Land Media Press Center, along with his wife Lucy and Samir Sbeihat, in his late father's private office. "We thought that the time would come when the newspapers would be shut down, so no one would be able to monitor what was happening, so we started doing it ourselves, with reports from stringers," Nusseibeh recalled. "When we became known, we gave ourselves more respectability, called it the *Monday Report*, and brought it out every Monday. All the journalists would come by to ask for it. The authorities closed down the *Monday Report* [in June 1989] because, they said, it did not have a license. I think it was closed down because it gave a good idea of what was happening." Nusseibeh, interview (January 28, 1996). See David Makovsky, "Police Tell Nusseibeh to Stop Newsletter," *Jerusalem Post*, May 30, 1989; idem, "Police Shut Nusseibeh's Office as "Planning Center of Intifada," *Jerusalem Post*, June 16, 1989.

103 Michal Sela, "'Nusseiba Is Paymaster of Intifada,'" *Jerusalem Post*, May 5, 1989, 1; Greenberg, "Indictments Shed Light on Intifada Leadership"; Ian Black, "Israel's Collaborators Find Bleak Welcome," *Guardian*, October 10, 1991, 28. Nusseibeh and Abu Ayyash were branded as terrorist leaders by Ariel Sharon, trade minister, retired general, member of Yitzhak Shamir's govern-ment, and, according to Yaron Ezrahi, the leading figure pressing for the classification of the intifada as war. Yaron Ezrahi, *Rubber Bullets: Power and Conscience in Modern Israel* (Berkeley: University of California Press, 1997), 208. A Palestinian source told Paul Taylor, "[W]ithout the restraining guidance of the moderate East Jerusalem intellectuals, things would turn more vio-lent and anarchic. . . . It would be the end of the 'white,' bloodless intifada." Paul Taylor, "Israel Faces Dilemma with Palestinian Uprising Leaders," Reuters, May 8, 1993.

104 Hadi, interview (December 13, 1997).

105 Siniora, interview (December 16, 1997).

106 Abu-Diab, interview (December 11, 1997).

107 Eid, interview (January 28, 1996).

108 Ibid.

109 Faisal Husseini, "Husseini Speaks Out: The Intifada and Public Opinion," *New Outlook*, March 1990, 26.

110 Hurwitz, "Nonviolence in the Occupied Territories," 23.

111 Barghouti, interview (January 25, 1996).

112 Ibid. As one example, on January 7, 1988, when civil disobedience was proffered by Siniora in

response to the deportation of nine Palestinian activists, factional spokespersons undermined the proposal for boycotting Israeli-made cigarettes and soft drinks. Regardless, Siniora judged the boycott of Israeli products successful, as proved when several Palestinian companies that benefited from the punitive sanctions against Israeli firms went bankrupt as the boycott tapered and Palestinians reverted to purchasing Israeli goods. Siniora, interview (December 16, 1997).

113 Jadallah, interview (December 15, 1997); Nusseibeh, interview (January 28, 1996).

114 Daoud Kuttab, "Who Is behind the Uprising?" *Jerusalem Post*, February 17, 1988, 5. The Palestinians in the occupied territories, were not "subordinated"—the term favored by Helena Cobban, Hillel Frisch, and Meir Litvak. Cobban, "PLO and Intifada," 97; Frisch, "Middle Command," 254, 261; Litvak, "Inside Versus Outside," in Sela and Maoz, *PLO and Israel*, 181. Through the first quarter of the third year of the uprising, they were determinative.

115 To Nusseibeh, meetings with Israelis were "a continuing attempt to break the Israeli government's monopoly over Israeli public opinion." Talks were part of the intifada program, to increase "support in Israel for a peace settlement based on the necessity of ending the occupation, negotiating with the PLO and recognizing the right of the Palestinian people to establish an independent state." Splits in Israel caused by such meetings were tangible evidence of the need to continue them, in Nusseibeh's view. Joel Greenberg, "Husseini and Nusseibeh: 'Our Talks with Israelis Will Shift Public Opinion,'" *Jerusalem Post*, February 22, 1989. In February 1989, in the Notre Dame Hotel at the line dividing East and West Jerusalem, Israelis, including two Peres aides to finance minister Shimon Peres—deputy finance minister Yossi Beilin and Peres advisor Nimrod Novik—met with Palestinians. Also included were Ephraim Sneh, MK Avraham Burg, Yair Hirschfeld of Haifa University, Boaz Carmi, and Arye Ofri, all members of the "Mashov Circle," a left-leaning group within Labor. The Palestinians present were Feisel Husseini, Sari Nusseibeh, Ziad Abu Zayyad, Ghassan Khatib, Mamdouh Aker, Hanan Mikhail Ashrawi, journalist Saman Khouri, and Khalil Mahshi. Joel Greenberg, "Peres Aides Meet Husseini, Nusseibeh," *Jerusalem Post*, February 16, 1989; idem, "Sari Nusseibeh Dismisses Rabin Elections Proposal," *Jerusalem Post*, February 6, 1989.

116 Mubarak E. Awad, communication (Washington, D.C., March 26, 1998). See Mamdouh Aker, "The Correct Diagnosis: A Doctor's View of the Unrest," *Jerusalem Post*, February 10, 1988, 10; idem, "Dialogue Instead of the Cycle of Suffering," *Jerusalem Post*, March 7, 1988, 2.

117 Ziad Abu-Amr, "The *Intifada* Is on a Stoney Road," *Middle East International*, June 11, 1988, 16.

118 See Jonathan C. Randal, "New, Largely Invisible, Force Seen Guiding Anti-Israeli Protests," *Washington Post*, January 28, 1988, A26. A Palestinian told Randal, "The problem is not the PLO, but the future of an independent Palestinian state in the territory. If Israel was ready to negotiate on those terms, we would drop the PLO without hesitation." Ibid.

119 On the disjuncture between the PLO's preoccupations for its own survival versus the potential for progress toward the full negotiated settlement as sought by the activist intellectuals, see Raja Shehadeh, *From Occupation to Interim Accords: Israel and the Palestinian Territories*, Cimel Book Series no. 4 (London and The Hague: Kluwer Law International, 1997), esp. 103-21, 128-29, and 157-61.

120 Letter from Sari Nusseibeh to well wishers, from Nissan jail in Ramleh, February 25, 1991, East Jerusalem, PCSN files.

121 Kuttab, "Will Guns Be Used?" The death of the first Israeli soldier during the intifada was reported in Joel Greenberg, "Reservist Slain on Duty in Bethlehem," *Jerusalem Post*, March 21, 1988, 1. Western diplomats in Jerusalem confided to a U.S. professor of education that the death had occurred at Israeli hands, when a reservist was shot from the top of a building, something no Palestinian in the heavily patrolled city of Bethlehem could have done, as Israeli sharpshooters were deployed on rooftops. When senior Israeli brass were absent from the funeral for the deceased, diplomats deduced that he had been killed by friendly fire. The shooter was eventually convicted for a "crime of passion," when it was realized that the motive was retaliation for an extramarital affair, but only after curfew punishment of Bethlehem. Graham Leonard, personal communication (Ramallah, June 18, 1989).

122 According to Israeli chief-of-staff Dan Shomron, the firebombing was spontaneous, when boys from the Takruri family got bored and chose to launch Molotov cocktails at Israeli vehicles. The young mother froze in fear, huddling over her children and resisting efforts by a soldier to drag them out. Patrick Bishop, "Jericho Walls Tumble Again," *Daily Telegraph*, November 10, 1988, 21; George D. Moffett III, "Israeli Vote May Turn Right in Response to Bus Attack; Palestinian Action Likely to Spur Backlash," *Christian Science Monitor*, November 1, 1988.

123 Weapons seized from Israeli soldiers were often returned. In Nablus, a soldier dropped his rifle while dispersing a demonstration, only to have it handed back by a demonstrator. Yaari, "Runaway Revolution," 28. An Israeli soldier was stripped to his underwear, but allowed to run back to his

post. A Palestinian youth took a soldier's rifle away, broke it in two, and gave it back. Vitullo, "Uprising in Gaza," in Beinin and Lockman, *Intifada*, 47. In Beita, Palestinians returned arms to Israeli authorities after an Israeli was killed by another Israeli, who was later disarmed by the villagers. Rashid Khalidi, "The Uprising and the Palestine Question," *World Policy Journal* 5, no. 3 (Summer 1988): 517 n. 16. When stones were thrown at a group of Israeli youths bicycling from the Eilon Moreh settlement on the West Bank, their armed guards opened fire, killing a fifteen-year-old Israeli girl, Tirza Porat, and two Palestinians. An army review shifted the blame to Roman Aldubi, one of the settlers guarding the Jewish group. Bermant, "The Light that Failed," 14; George D. Moffett III, "Palestinians Say Expulsions Were Expected and Won't Work," *Christian Science Monitor*, April 13, 1988. Porat's death, on April 6, 1988, was the first Israeli civilian death in the 1987 intifada. Kenneth Kaplan, "The IDF's Political War," *Jerusalem Post*, December 8, 1989.

124 Nusseibeh, "*Intifada*: Personal Perspective," 27. See also Jeff Black, "Siniora Tells Peace Now Rally: Uprising Aimed at Occupation—Not against Israel," *Jerusalem Post*, February 14, 1988, 2. In November 1989, Nusseibeh called for a provisional state, with ministers from the PLO executive committee and the bureaucracy assembled from thousands of Palestinian workers in health, education, and social services—a "National Authority." Nusseibeh said Palestinians had been building such an infrastructure for two years through the popular committees, "walls for which a roof can be built by declaring a provisional government." Security forces could block unilateral establishment of such an authority, yet he argued this would advance the process of "state-creation" of the intifada, and it was this activity that should be the focus of Palestinian efforts, not escalation of violence. Joel Greenberg, "Nusseibeh Wants Provisional Government Now," *Jerusalem Post*, November 17, 1989; idem, "West Bank; PLO Victory," November 24, 1989.

125 Nusseibeh, interview (January 28, 1996).

126 Nusseibeh, interview (January 28, 1996).

127 Daoud Kuttab, "Abu Jihad and the Occupied Territories," dispatch to news media, East Jerusalem, April 1988, 2, Kuttab private papers. Ghassan Khatib disputes the view of Abu Jihad as a prophetic figure: "He tried to strengthen Fateh inside, through . . . means that were harmful to the struggle in general. In the 1970s, he . . . caused splits in the trade unions, women's movement, and voluntary work committees. . . . Fateh was not very strong [in the territories] . . . so when it moved to give attention to the 'inside,' he wanted Fateh to be dominant by any means. Whenever Fateh wasn't able to achieve dominance through elections, they would split the organization." Khatib, interview (December 12, 1997). The DFLP's Muhammad Jadallah claimed about Abu Jihad, "His interference was limited to Fateh. . . . He was a man that we were happy to work with—responsible and clean." Jadallah, interview (December 15, 1997).

128 Kuttab, "Abu Jihad and the Occupied Territories." At the time of his death, Abu Jihad was said to have "urged the Palestinian civilians not to use guns in their fights against Israeli soldiers, and he often expressed pride that the Palestinians were fighting the Israelis with stones, not bullets." Elaine Sciolino, "Abu Jihad: A Strong Right Arm to Arafat Who Lived by the Sword," *New York Times*, April 17, 1988.

129 Abu Jihad was assassinated by an Israeli naval sabotage unit called Flotilla 13, dating to 1945 when Zionist commandos sank two British patrol boats in Haifa harbor and Jaffa that were looking for illegal Jewish immigrants. Serge Schmemann, "Raiding Party in Lebanon Belonged to Elite Unit," *New York Times*, September 6, 1997, 8. Mossad planned the mission after three Israeli civilians were killed in a March 1988 Fateh operation at Dimona that distressed local Fateh adherents (chapter 11). Colin Smith, Eric Silver, and Mike Theodoulou, "Hitting Where It Hurts: How the Israeli Secret Service's Audacious Killing of Yasser Arafat's Deputy Repaired the Country's Battered Ego," *Observer Sunday*, April 24, 1988, 21. A reconstruction is found in Abu-Sharif and Mahnaimi, *Tried by Fire*, 236-42.

130 Nusseibeh, interview (November 5, 1994). Palestinians often construe Abu Jihad's assassination as an exploit intended to end the intifada by removing the person in the PLO hierarchy who had the closest daily contact with the uprising. Kuttab, "Children's Revolt," 27.

131 Marwan Barghouti, "Arafat and the Opposition: An Interview with Marwan Barghouti," *Middle East Report* 191, November-December 1994, 22. Barghouti headed the student council at Bir Zeit University from 1983 to 1987, when he was deported. He later became vice president of Fateh Higher Council in the West Bank and was, in January 1996, elected to the Palestinian legislative council from Ramallah. According to Nusseibeh, Marwan Barghouti and Adnan Idris (author of the first document on civil disobedience encountered by Nusseibeh), were instrumental in writing the basic by-laws of the Shabiba movement, and Bhargouti was long "predisposed" to the use of political tools of struggle. Nusseibeh, interviews (December 13, 1997; December 16, 1997). He would later be perceived as the commander of the notoriously violent second intifada that would start in 2000 (see Epilogue).

132 *No Voice Is Louder than the Voice of the Uprising: Calls 1-47 of the United National Leadership of the Uprising in the Occupied Territories/State of Palestine* (Nicosia, Cyprus: Ibal Publishing, Ltd., 1989), 68, 71. See also Leaflet no. 14, "Abu Jihad [Khalil al-Wazir] Appeal," April 22, 1988, trans. comm. Zoughbi E. Zoughbi (East Jerusalem, Unified National Leadership Command of the Uprising), PASSIA archives.

133 Yossi Melman and Dan Raviv, *The Imperfect Spies* (London: Sidgwick and Jackson Ltd., 1989), 29.

134 According to Melman and Raviv's analysis of the Israeli intelligence agencies, Israeli authorities wanted to show the PLO that its "military side" could not gain from the intifada and thought a "show-off" expedition would raise morale for Israelis who were suffering from their government's inability to put down the uprising. Melman and Raviv, *Imperfect Spies*, 26.

135 Ihsan A. Hijazi, "An Aide to Arafat Comes under Fire; Hard-Line Palestinian Groups Criticize the Adviser's Call for Talks with Israel," *New York Times*, June 22, 1988. Bassam Abu-Sharif, writes Patrick Seale, "gave up [George] Habash's extreme rejectionism to become the most ardent dove in Arafat's moderate camp, the front runner of the process that led the PLO formally to renounce terrorism and recognize Israel." Seale, *Abu Nidal*, 41. Asked why Palestinians had embarked on a policy of armed struggle in the 1960s, Abu-Sharif responded, "to light a candle in the darkness of Arab defeat.'" Abu-Sharif, interviews (January 24, 1996; October 30, 1997).

136 "Towards a Solution," FACTS Weekly Review 17, July 3-9, 1988, 261-62. Also see Greenberg, "New Direction for the Uprising."

137 Daoud Kuttab, "Faisal Husseini Arrested Again," East Jerusalem, June 1988, Kuttab private papers.

138 Bassam Abu-Sharif, "Arafat Adviser's 'Direct Negotiations' Document-Israeli and Palestinian Reaction," from *al-Quds* radio, June 20, 1988, in *BBC Summary of World Broadcasts*, June 22, 1988.

139 Nusseibeh, interview (January 28, 1996).

140 Hani al-Hassan, "The Promise of Peace in the Middle East," *Middle East Mirror*, December 12, 1989, 10.

141 In Gaza alone, 200,000 persons were under curfew by mid-January 1988. Joshua Brilliant, "Shomron: Gaza Strip Quiet Only Temporary," *Jerusalem Post*, January 15, 1988, 2; Kenneth Kaplan, "A Battle of Statistics," *Jerusalem Post*, January 27, 1989; Ian Black, "Intifada Enters Year Three under Curfew," *Guardian*, December 9, 1989, 8.

142 F. Robert Hunter, *The Palestinian Uprising: A War by Other Means* (Berkeley, University of California Press, 1993), 96; Aryeh Shalev, *The Intifada: Causes and Effects*, originally published as Study no. 16 by the Jaffee Center for Strategic Studies, Tel Aviv (Boulder, Colorado: Westview Press, 1991), 87. Defense minister Yitzhak Rabin explained the policy: "There will be a curfew where a riot takes place. . . . If they want to strike, at least this is not violence." Israel Radio interview with Rabin by Yoram Ronen, Moshe Shlonsky, and Ehud Yaari, January 13, 1988; FBIS, January 14, 1988, reprinted in *Journal of Palestine Studies* 67 (Spring 1988): 153-54.

143 Sarid and Zucker, "Special Report," 17; Daoud Kuttab, "The Palestinians" Unified Command," *Middle East International*, February 6, 1988, 10.

144 Kuttab, "Profile of the Stonethrowers," 21. Muhammad Jadallah described, "We organized medical teams to break the curfews, to avoid checkpoints, and to go through mountains so as to reach Palestinian communities under siege, under curfew with sick people—whether ill from normal diseases or sick from being injured in the continuous confrontations." Jadallah, interview (December 15, 1997).

145 Johanna McGeary, "Day by Day with the *Intifadeh*; Defying Israel's Rule, Palestinians Become Self-Reliant," *Time*, May 23, 1988.

146 Sherman, "Gazans and the *Intifada*," 18.

147 Muslih, "Palestinian Civil Society," in Norton, *Civil Society*, vol. 1, 252-54. By the mid-1980s, there were 220 cooperatives in the West Bank, with a membership of 26,000, providing agriculture, housing, and services such as electrification and transport. David Lewis, "The Importance of Palestine's Cooperatives," *Middle East International*, June 14, 1985, 15-16.

148 Daoud Kuttab, "Palestinians Decentralize," dispatch to news media, East Jerusalem, April 1988, Kuttab private papers.

149 Joel Brinkley, "Hard Lessons from the Arab Unrest," *New York Times*, May 22, 1988, 3; Moorehead, "Israel's Censors under Scrutiny," 11; Marwan Darweish, "The *Intifada*: Social Change," *Race and Class* 31, no. 2 (October-December 1989): 55. On July 6, 1988, a leaflet ran an item, "School's Out," stating "justifications for these closures were that school children had been demonstrating and abiding by the call of the [Command], to attend classes until 12 noon only." "Aqsa Appeal," 14.

150 Struck, "Palestinian University Is Reopened," 8A. "Israel's closure of the Palestinian universities came under increasing censure from human rights groups and international educators' organizations. The United States also pressured Israel to reopen the schools." Ibid. An Israeli criminologist

at Hebrew University criticized the policy: "Neither respect for law nor sensitivity to international declarations of human rights have disturbed Israeli governments during the last 21 years and certainly not during the intifada." Stanley Cohen, "Education as Crime," *Jerusalem Post*, May 18, 1989, 4.

151 "Education during the Intifada," *Educational Network* (Ramallah) 1 (June 1990): 1. Published quarterly by Khalil Mahshi and educators around Friends School in Ramallah, the periodic report details punitive measures imposed on teachers in the West Bank and the alternative systems they created to compensate for school closures.

152 "Israeli Measures further Deteriorate Education," *Educational Network* (Ramallah), February 1992. Initial reaction to events in the West Bank and Gaza often occurred at Bir Zeit, as students moved off campus to create roadblocks of burning tires to await the Israeli army and demonstrate. Its students and faculty, Izzat Ghazzawi said, "thought they were responsible for ending the occupation. . . . [They] knew how many prisoners there were in Israeli prisons, . . . how much in taxes Israel got from the occupied territories, . . . about al-Haq [and]. . . the Geneva convention[s], . . . The Israelis were afraid of the information." Struck, "Palestinian University Is Reopened," 8A.

153 Hirsh Goodman, "Army Meets a New Palestinian: They Are Different from the Clearly Defined Terrorist of Twenty Years Ago," *Jerusalem Post*, January 15, 1988.

154 See Joel Greenberg, "PLO Urges Rioters to Oust Councils," *Jerusalem Post*, March 2, 1988, 1. One study concludes there was "no evidence that the closure of schools led to a reduction in demonstrations." *Palestinian Education: A Threat to Israel's Security? The Israeli Policy of School Closures in the Occupied West Bank and Gaza Strip, December 1987-January 1989* (East Jerusalem: JMCC, 1989), 37.

155 Bishara, interview (June 17, 1995); Jonathan Kuttab, interview (June 17, 1995).

156 A review of the status of the twenty-six refugee camps in the West Bank and Gaza is found in Ziad Abu-Amr, "An Overview of Social Conditions in the Refugee Camps," *Journal of Refugee Studies* 2, no. 1 (1989): 149-51.

157 Antonio Gramsci, *Selections from the Prison Notebooks of Antonio Gramsci* (1929-1935), ed. and trans. Quintin Hoare and Geoffrey Nowell Smith (New York, London: International Publishers, Lawrence and Wishart, 1985), 5-24, 334.

158 From 20 villages that openly participated in the intifada in December 1987, the number rose to 200 in February 1988, and thence to 232 in March. *Observer*, December 11, 1988, as cited in Sayigh, "Intifadah Continues," 28.

159 Nusseibeh, interviews (November 5, 1994; January 28, 1996).

160 Nusseibeh, interview (November 5, 1994).

161 Nusseibeh, interview (July 5, 1994).

162 Between the popular committees and alternative education, "new and creative ideas" were being tested, Kuttab writes; "in this sense, Israeli policy has, ironically, served the Palestinians." Daoud Kuttab, "The Palestinian Uprising: The Second Phase, Self-Sufficiency," *Journal of Palestine Studies* 68 (Summer 1988): 42, 43.

163 "Education during the Intifada," 1. The Israeli policy banning alternative education was paradoxical, as closures represented Israeli relinquishment of control over Palestinian education, and would give way to "a battle over the 'facts' of the Israeli-Palestinian conflict." Sarah Helm, "Palestinians in a Class of Their Own," *Independent*, September 2, 1994.

164 Shaul Mishal and Reuben Aharoni, *Speaking Stones: Communiqués from the Intifada Underground* (Syracuse University Press, 1994), 121.

165 Daoud Kuttab, "Popular Teaching Begins in the Home," dispatch to news media, East Jerusalem, September 1988, Kuttab private papers.

166 Ann Peters, "Israelis Punish Palestinians with School Closings," UPI, September 4, 1988.

167 "Education during the Intifada," 1.

168 Bishara, interview (June 17, 1995); *Palestinian Education*, 18-20, 37; Daoud Kuttab, "School Year Gets Off to a Slow Start," dispatch to news media, East Jerusalem, September 1988, Kuttab private papers. At an academic conference in East Jerusalem, the headmaster of the Friends Boys School in Ramallah, Khalil Mahshi, said students relished the voluntary and semi-secret educational methods. Kuttab, "Palestinian Uprising: Second Phase, Self-Sufficiency," 42, 43.

169 Daoud Kuttab, "Underground Education," dispatch to news media, East Jerusalem, September 1988, Kuttab private papers.

170 Harriet Lewis and Thea Cygielman, "Only the Intifada Ensures the Political Process," interview of Ziad Abu Zayyad, *New Outlook*, November-December 1989, 28.

171 Hiltermann, *Behind the Intifada*, 205.

172 Elise G. Young, *Keepers of the History: Women and the Israeli-Palestinian Conflict* (New York and

London, Teachers College Press, 1992), 69. See also Joel Greenberg, "Marches Dramatize Role of Palestinian Women in Protest," *Jerusalem Post*, March 9, 1988, 4.

173 Kuttab, "Children's Revolt," 28. The committees' functions were described for street dissemination in May 1988 as follows: (1) *Services*: guard and security committees, popular education; health committees for normal needs and emergencies; food supplies; agriculture; and media and consciousness-raising committees to "defeat rumors." (2) *Support services*: supervision of warehouses, reservation of water supplies, saving paraffin oil, provision of hand-held flashlights. (3) *Direct action*: closing roads, raising the Palestinian flag, marches, and sit-ins. Command, "Civil Disobedience Statement," May 23, 1988, East Jerusalem, PASSIA Archives. Rana Salibi, "Women's Activities in Popular Committees during the Intifada," in Augustin, *Palestinian Women*, 165. In December 1988, the Higher Women's Council formed to unite the four major women's organizations into one forum. Hiltermann, *Behind the Intifada*, 198; Ebba Augustin, "Developments in the Palestinian Women's Movement during the Intifada," in Augustin, *Palestinian Women*, 26-27; Kuttab, "Palestinian Women Unite."

174 Johnson, O'Brien, and Hiltermann, "West Bank Rises Up," in Lockman and Beinin, *Intifada*, 40.

175 Philippa Strum, *The Women Are Marching: The Second Sex and the Palestinian Revolution* (Chicago: Lawrence Hill Books, 1992), 139-40. See Hiltermann, *Behind the Intifada*, 200-207. The greatest quandary of all for women was the cultural-religious predicament in which Muslim widows were to be pleased by "martyrdom" of their husbands. The issue is given poignancy in that more than one thousand Palestinians died in the first three years of the intifada, often husbands. Hans Sande, "Palestinian Martyr Widowhood—Emotional Needs in Conflict with Role Expectations?" *Social Science and Medicine* 34, no. 6 (March 1992): 709-17. Also see Nahla Abdo, "Women of the *Intifada*: Gender, Class, and National Liberation," *Race and Class* 32, no. 4 (April-June 1991): 19-34; Giacaman, "Palestinian Women in the Uprising: 137-46; Darweish, "*Intifada*: Social Change," 58-60.

176 Bennis, *Stones to Statehood*, 34.

177 Said, "Intifada and Independence," in Lockman and Beinin, *Intifada*, 20-21. Giacaman and Johnson, "Palestinian Women," 165, 166, doubt that women expanded their allotment in society due to the uprising. Women are rarely mentioned in the Command's leaflets except in patriarchal images of sexual fertility, as mythic figures, or in nurturing roles. Joseph Massad, "Conceiving the Masculine: Gender and Palestinian Nationalism," *Middle East Journal* 49, no. 3 (Summer 1995): 467-83; Strum, *Women Are Marching*, 139-40. Women were crucial to the grassroots infrastructure of the popular committees, but the circumnavigatory process of writing the leaflets yielded stilted writing that was not sensitive to gender.

178 The role of mosques as anything other than points of distribution is vehemently denied: "It is not true that the mosques are the centers of inflammatory activity. We use their loudspeakers, that's all," a Gaza intifada leader told a Palestinian journalist. Machool, "This Isn't Rebellion," 15.

179 Command, "Aqsa Appeal," Communiqué 21, July 6, 1988, 4, East Jerusalem, PASSIA Archives.

180 Jonathan Kuttab, interview (November 5, 1994). Behind the flow of leaflets, "a new genre of uprising literature" developed. Nusseibeh, "Two-Year Perspective," 44.

181 Frank Collins, "How Stones Can Beat Guns," *Middle East International*, March 19, 1988, 16.

182 Name withheld, interview (East Jerusalem, December 13, 1997).

183 Children from six to fourteen years of age comprised 35 percent of the total population in the West Bank and Gaza. "Appeal to the Director General of UNESCO concerning Education," November 8, 1988, letter from the Association of Women's Committees for Social Work in the Occupied Territories, in Cainkar and Goldring, *Uprising in Palestine, First Year*, 451.

184 Kate Rouhana, "Children and the Intifada," *Journal of Palestine Studies* 72 (Summer 1989).

185 Source affected content. See Kirsten Nakjavani Bookmiller and Robert J. Bookmiller, "Palestinian Radio and the Intifada," *Journal of Palestine Studies* 76 (Summer 1990): 96-105, based on monitored broadcasts in FBIS-Near East and South Asia, from December 1987 through April 1990. The Damascus station sometimes altered the leaflets to make them consistent with Syria's known hostility toward the PLO, whereas the Baghdad broadcasts were as issued by the Command. Lockman and Beinin, *Intifada*, 327. See Louis Toscano, "Clandestine Radio Station Aiding Palestinian Protests," UPI, February 16, 1988.

186 See Saleh Atta, "Israelis Responsible for Forgeries, Claims Arab Magazine: The War of the Leaflets," *Jerusalem Post*, August 2, 1989.

187 Paul Steinberg and A. M. Oliver, *The Graffiti of the Intifada: A Brief Survey* (East Jerusalem, PASSIA, 1990), 3.

188 Infighting between Islamic organizations and the more inclusive factions was traceable through a graffiti war. Steinberg and Oliver, *Graffiti*, 10.

189 Kifner, "Wave of Palestinian Unrest." Despite the Palestinians' boycotts of Israeli goods, alternative factories had not developed, meaning, Nusseibeh notes, "If someone wants to write political graffiti, he has to use Israeli wall paint." Geraldine Brooks, "Israelis and the Arabs of Occupied Regions Share Uneasy Reliance," *Wall Street Journal*, January 22, 1988, 1.

190 Jøsten, "Czechoslovakia: From 1968 to Charter 77," 11.

191 Daoud Kuttab, "Wanted," dispatch to news media, East Jerusalem, 1988, Kuttab private papers.

192 Lockman and Beinin, *Intifada*, 367.

193 Kuttab, "Refugee Camps vs. Villages," 2; idem, "Wanted."

194 Melanie Kaye-Kantrowitz, "Women Play Key Role in Opposing the Occupation," *Utne Reader*, May 1989, 43, excerpt from *Jewish Currents*, May 1989.

195 "Aqsa Appeal," 11.

196 The kaffiyeh, wrapped to the eyes to protect the identification of the wearer from Israeli intelligence cameras, became a symbol of its unity. During the great revolt of 1936-39, the Ottoman tarboosh (fez) identified moderates, whereas the keffiyyeh betokened nationalists.

197 Lockman and Beinin, *Intifada*, 304, 305. Children made hobbies of collecting tape cassettes of local intifada songs. Michal Sela, "'Child's Play' in Gaza," *Jerusalem Post*, October 6, 1989. On Ansar 3, see "Appeal from the 'Camp of Slow Death': Hunger in Ansar 2, Hunger Strike in Ansar 3; Open Letter from Ansar 3," in FACTS, 223-26. Also see account on Salah Taamari, "hero of Ansar," by Israeli journalists Amalia Barnea and Aharon Barnea, in *Mine Enemy*, trans. Chaya Amir (New York: Grove Press, 1986). Taamari is governor of the Bethlehem district.

198 Kuttab, interview (November 5, 1994). Also see Barbara Harlow, "Narrative in Prison: Stories from the Palestinian *Intifada*," *Modern Fiction Studies* 35, no. 1 (Spring 1989): 29-46.

199 Said K. Aburish, *Cry Palestine: Inside the West Bank* (Boulder, Colorado: Westview Press, 1991), 124-26.

200 Daoud Kuttab, "An Inside Look at Palestinian Independence Day Celebrations," dispatch to news media, East Jerusalem, November 1988, Kuttab private papers.

201 Awad, *Nonviolence*, 14, 15. Awad's 1983 booklet envisioned the popular committees as breaking the military occupation: "The creation of these institutions obstructs the process of annexation and Judaization and makes possible a political solution built upon Israeli withdrawal and the creation of an independent Palestinian state." Ibid., 14. Joel Greenberg notes the popular committees implemented ideas in Awad's booklet, where preparation had been advocated for committees to provide for the needs of the populace under reprisals. Greenberg, "Battle Moves from the Streets."

202 See appendices, p. 354, for excerpts.

203 Hadi, interview (December 13, 1997).

204 Little cognizance of such derivations is found in the politics literature. Hillel Frisch, for example, contends that such localized structures were conceived only as far back as the 1970s and the National Guidance Committee. Frisch, "Diffusion and Consolidation," 50.

205 Jadallah, interview (December 15, 1997).

206 Daoud Kuttab, "Local Communities Taking More Initiative," dispatch filed with news media, East Jerusalem, October 1988, Kuttab private papers.

207 Abukhater, "Towards the Proclamation of the State," interview of Nusseibeh.

208 Tamari, "Intifada," 20. These groups were also the chief instruments for coping with retaliations such as the cutting off of electricity or water, often for protracted periods, as when the Jalazoun camp near Ramallah went for forty-two consecutive days without electricity. Daoud Kuttab, "Refugee Camps vs. Villages," dispatch to news media, East Jerusalem, June 1988, Kuttab private papers.

209 Muslih, "Palestinian Civil Society," 266, 267.

210 Jonathan Kuttab, interview (November 5, 1994).

211 "Husseini Document," in Cainkar and Goldring, *Uprising in Palestine, the First Year*, 318.

212 Ibrahim Abu-Lughod, Introduction, in Nassar and Heacock, *Intifada*, 9.

213 Greenberg, "Battle Moves from the Streets."

214 Mishal and Aharoni, *Speaking Stones*, 98. Leaflet no. 18, although not addressed explicitly to Israelis, was the first to direct a call to Israel. It made the following demands: "withdrawal of the Israeli army from the cities, villages, and refugee camps" of the territories, the release of prisoners, and return of deported Palestinians, lifting of the "state of siege" in the territories, cancellation of special military orders and civil regulations issued in response to the intifada, allowance for "democratic and free elections" in the territories, and removal of restrictions on the Palestinian "national economy" to allow the development of industrial, agricultural, and service sectors. It said these steps should be monitored by international observers and would lead to "the right to return to self-determination and the right to establish our independent state." Joel Brinkley, "Ex-Israel Officers

Ask Deal on Peace: Former Military Figures Say the Occupation Is Hurting the Nation's Security," *New York Times*, May 31, 1988.

215 Awad, *Nonviolence*, 14.

216 Robinson, "Creating Space," 151; Mustafa Barghouti, "Popular/Mass Movement in the Community," *Journal of Palestine Studies* 2, no.1 (1989): 128.

217 Robinson, *Building a Palestinian State*, 66.

218 Ibid., 68.

219 *Haaretz*, November 11, 1988, as cited in Frisch, "Diffusion and Consolidation," 50, 60 n. 37.

220 Barghouti, "Popular/Mass Movement," 128.

221 Rita Giacaman and Penny Johnson, "Palestinian Women: Building Barricades and Breaking Barriers," in Lockman and Beinin, *Intifada*, 412 n. 9; Strum, *Women Are Marching*, 203.

222 FACTS, vii, 15.

223 Malki, interview (May 3, 1995).

224 Ibid.

225 "Aqsa Appeal," Communiqué 21, July 6, 1988, 12. By December 1988, according to Cainkar and Goldring, more than 100,000 olive and fruit trees had been uprooted (in contrast to 18,000 during 1987, through December 8). *Uprising in Palestine, the First Year*, table, "Human Rights Violations Summary Data," 9. As destruction of Palestinian harvests and fruit and olive trees by Israeli settlers intensified, groups of Palestinian youths set forest fires among Israeli settlements and parks. Leaflet no. 19 of June 6, 1988, bades "destroying and burning the enemy's industrial and agricultural property" on June 22. Lockman and Beinin, *Intifada*, 363. Daoud Kuttab said sources on the Command indicated this referred to Israeli settlements and was for one day only. Daoud Kuttab, "Are the Fires and Firebombs a New Strategy?" East Jerusalem, June 1988, Kuttab private papers. Mubarak Awad and PCSN volunteers sought out such groups to explain that retaliation against settlements would result in more damage to Palestinian crops. Mubarak E. Awad, one-hour communication (Washington, D.C., April 30, 1998).

226 Kifner, "Israelis and Palestinians Change Their Tactics."

227 McGeary, "Day by Day with the *Intifadeh*," 31; George D. Moffett III, "Palestinian Unrest Plants New Roots; Victory Gardens Form Key Strategy for Sustaining Resistance to Israel," *Christian Science Monitor*, April 8, 1988; Kifner, "Israelis and Palestinians Change Their Tactics," 1

228 Jad Ishaq, one-hour interview (Bethlehem, November 10, 1994).

229 Shyam Bhatia, "Uprising Comes of Age," *Observer*, December 11, 1988, 27.

230 Isaac, "Agriculture in the West Bank and Gaza," 33, 37, 38.

231 Kuttab, "Six-Month Anniversary." What Shaul Mishal and Reuben Aharoni call "communal economic activities," or agricultural self-sufficiency, appear in twelve leaflets issued by the Command, but not at all in Hamas leaflets that had begun to appear. They explain this absence of home-economy or agricultural directives by asserting that the density of Gaza, stronghold of Hamas, precluded the use of space for agriculture. Mishal and Aharoni, *Speaking Stones*, table 5, 288-89. The more likely explanation is the worldview of Hamas, in which religious reclamation ranked foremost. Window box or rooftop gardening can work in squalid urban ghettoes anywhere; rabbit hutches or chicken coops can be set up in the most woeful of refugee camps.

232 Elaine Ruth Fletcher, "Intifada Enters Its Fourth Year," *Sunday San Francisco Examiner and Chronicle*, December 9, 1990, A15.

233 Muhammad Zahaike, *Intifada of the Press*, the chapter "Bread and Salt," trans. comm. Sami Awad (East Jerusalem: privately printed, ca. 1995), 134-35.

234 FACTS Weekly Review 16, June 27-July 2, 1988, 16.

235 "Israel Says It Seized 200 Arabs in Crackdown," *New York Times*, September 10, 1988, 28.

236 Kenneth Kaplan, "Paratrooper's Killers Convicted; Mass Arrest of Intifada Leaders," *Jerusalem Post*, July 5, 1989.

237 Schiff and Yaari, *Intifada*, 146, 147.

238 Michal Sela, "Gaza Curfew Is Only Beginning of Crackdown," *Jerusalem Post*, May 18, 1989. Arrests and punishments did not exempt women, a double hardship as their detention posed severe problems for communities and extended families. Women suffered 20 or 25 percent of all casualties during the first ten months of the uprising. Yezid Sayigh, "The Intifadah Continues: Legacy, Dynamics and Challenges," *Third World Quarterly* 11, no. 3 (July 1989): 27-28.

239 Atran, "Stones against the Iron Fist, 517 n. 61.

240 Martin and Manney, "Tax Strike for Justice," 37; Sari Nusseibeh, "Assessing Two Years of Intifada," in Safieh, *Two Years of Intifada*, 53.

241 Robinson, "Creating Space," 131.

242 Siniora, interview (December 16, 1997); Bhatia, "Uprising Comes of Age," 27. Bhatia says the baker's son was forced by an army patrol to move stones from the road and put them in his father's oven, after which the boy was obliged to turn on the oven so he could be taught how to bake stones instead of bread. Ibid.

243 More than 150 "prolonged sieges" of seven days or more occurred during the initial year of the intifada, according to Cainkar and Goldring, *Uprising in Palestine, the First Year*, table, "Human Rights Violations Summary Data," 9.

244 George Martin and James Manney, "Tax Strike for Justice: Report from Beit Sahour; Building Autonomy," *Commonweal* 117, no. 2 (January 1990): 38.

245 Robinson, "Creating Space," 130-35, 143-83; Ishaq, interview (November 10, 1994). Ishaq directs the Applied Research Institute in Bethlehem.

246 Atran, "Stones against the Iron Fist, 517 n. 61.

247 Shalev, "Second Year of the Intifada," 149. B'Tselem one year later issued a study of tax collection in the occupied territories charging that collection methods violated Israeli civil and military law and had become a form of collective punishment to oppose the intifada. Exorbitant assessments were alleged, and since they were usually not paid, massive attachment of property occurred. B'Tselem as cited in Joel Greenberg, "Rights Body Raps Tax Policy in the Areas," *Jerusalem Post*, February 27, 1990. Israel seemed to have been threatened by the "development of an autonomous Palestinian economic and social fabric." Martin and Manney, "Tax Strike for Justice"; 37.

248 Sidra DeKoven Ezrahi, "Between the Lines: To Beit Sahur and Back," *Tikkun* 5, no. 3 (January-February 1990): 9-12; Abu-Diab, interview (December 11, 1997); Terry Rogers, "Peaceful Tax Resistance in Beit Sahour," *Catholic Worker*, May 1990, 3.

249 Atran, "Stones against the Iron Fist," 517 n. 61.

250 Dajani, *Eyes without Country*, 65.

251 Vogele, "Learning and Nonviolent Struggle," 320.

252 "FACTS Weekly Review 9, 1-7 May 1988," 137; Sarid and Zucker, "Special Report," 17. In one instance, the Israeli army bulldozed a Palestinian olive grove in trying to break compliance with a general strike. Alan Cowell, "Israeli Army Tries New Tactic to Break Strike," *New York Times*, September 18, 1988.

253 Kuttab, interview (November 5, 1994).

254 "FACTS Weekly Review 9, 1-7 May 1988," 138.

255 Ibid. Other FACTS reviews on the merchants' struggle appear on pp. 139-42.

256 Andy Court, "Respite for East Jerusalem Merchants," *Jerusalem Post*, February 3, 1988; Salim Tamari, "Revolt of the Petite Bourgeoisie: Urban Merchants and the Palestinian Uprising," in Nassar and Heacock, *Palestine at the Crossroads*, 161-73. On doing more than is required as a method of nonviolent action, see Danilo Dolci, *Outlaws of Partinico*, trans. R. Munro (London: MacGibbon and Kee, 1960).

257 Lucy Austin Nusseibeh, one-hour interview (East Jerusalem, November 5, 1994). Then director of the Palestinian Center for Democracy and Elections, an offshoot of PCSN, she is the daughter of the Oxford philosopher J. L. Austin, and her mother Jean Austin also taught philosophy at Oxford, both of them close colleagues of Isaiah Berlin, scholar of the history of political thought. She married Sari Nusseibeh, met while they were both studying at Oxford, and is director of MEND (Middle East Nonviolence and Democracy), a nongovernmental organization that has run training programs on active nonviolence in eight major West Bank cities, with more awaiting their turn. See Lucy Nusseibeh, "Breaking the Cycle of Violence," *Forced Migration Review*, no. 26 (August 2006): http://www.fmreview.org/text/FMR/26/21.doc. No merchant would ignore a bid to strike. Alain Frachon and Yves Heller, "Intifada Becomes a Way of Life," repr. from *Le Monde*, in *Guardian Weekly*, December 17, 1989, 13. The Command possessed a "high degree of legitimacy in the eyes of most Palestinians, and also a degree of effective authority that the Israelis resented and feared." Wing, "Embryonic Self-Rule," 131.

258 Sari Nusseibeh, interview (January 28, 1996). A "mini-intifada" of nonviolent direct action in Balata had preceded the December 1987 uprising by months. "The Israeli authorities were so alarmed by [Balata's mid-1987] symptoms of civil disobedience that their crackdown was particularly harsh. . . . Little did anyone know then that the [Israeli] army behaviour in Balata was to become the rule, or that the Balata tremour was to develop into a full-scale eruption." Nusseibeh, "Two-Year Perspective," 43. Glenn Frankel cites Balata's Shabiba organization of youths aged fourteen to seventeen as indicative of the local control exerted in the intifada. Glenn Frankel, "PLO Asserting Control of Palestinian Uprising: Violence Shifts to Organized Campaign," *Washington Post*, February 20, 1988, A1.

259 Whitley and Walker, "From Stones to Sanctions"; see also Cowell, "Israeli Army Tries New Tactic."

260 Greenberg, "Battle Moves from the Streets."

261 Solidarity of merchants was crucial to the early success of the uprising. On the day that Feisel Husseini was released from custody, January 29, 1989, Mustapha Abu Zahra, one of sixteen wholesale merchants who had defied an Israeli military order, was freed from six months of administrative detention. General Amram Mitzna had used 1945 British regulations as the basis of a decree to East Jerusalem shop owners to remain open all day. Abu Zahra and fifteen other merchants not only closed shop instead, but served prison terms rather than pay fines. They told the chief judge of the Israeli High Court, "Yes, we understood the order of the Israeli general, but we don't take orders from him, we only follow orders from our leaders." Daoud Kuttab, "Palestinian Chooses Prison Term Rather Than Paying Fine," dispatch to news media, East Jerusalem, January 31, 1989, Kuttab private papers.

262 Court, "Respite for East Jerusalem Merchants."

263 Mishal and Aharoni, *Speaking Stones*, 62.

264 Hanan Mikhail Ashrawi, "Intifada: Political Analysis," in Ateek et al., *Faith and the Intifada*, 11.

265 Tamari, "Intifada," 19, 4.

266 Daoud Kuttab, "Nablus: The Capital of the Intifada," dispatch filed with news media, East Jerusalem, ca. 1988, Kuttab private papers.

267 Yehoshua Porath, interviewed by Benny Morris, "A United Uprising," *Jerusalem Post Magazine*, March 4, 1988, 7.

268 Tamari, "Time to Converse Calmly."

269 Kuttab, "Children's Revolt," 27, 28.

270 Unified National Leadership Command of the Uprising, "Palestine Appeal," Leaflet no. 16, May 12, 1988 (East Jerusalem), PASSIA Archives.

271 Command, "Civil Disobedience Statement."

272 Ibid.

273 Ian Black, "Confusion Spreads as West Bank Leaders Squabble over Strike," *Guardian*, May 26, 1988, 9; Legrain, *Les Voix du Soulèvement Palestinien*, 102-103. Legrain concurs with Black and suggests the DFLP was internally divided as to alignment with Nayef Hawatmeh or DFLP reformer Yasir Abd Rabbo. Ibid., 102. Daoud Kuttab says Fateh leaders whose viewpoint was expressed in the limited call believed that in order for 100,000 or more Palestinians to cease working in Israel, a jobs alternative would be needed. Their voices would carry, if only because Fateh would have access to sufficient funds to sustain a civil disobedience campaign where thousands of Palestinians resigned from their jobs. Daoud Kuttab, "Next Phase, Civil Disobedience," *Middle East International*, June 11, 1988, 6; Black, "Confusion," 9. PLO officials asserted that $30 to $50 million per month might be needed were Palestinians to stop working in Israel. Randal, "Uprisings Invigorate PLO Leaders," A39.

274 Nusseibeh, "True People's Revolution," 17. See Joel Greenberg, "Wave of Resignations by Arab Policemen in Areas," *Jerusalem Post*, March 13, 1988, 1.

275 Whitley and Walker, "From Stones to Sanctions," 20. Yet Reuven Gal observed that such noncooperation added severe strains on a populace already in need of earnings: "Paradoxically, Palestinians in the tens of thousands kept coming every morning into Israel for jobs. This is not noncooperation; in fact, it is yielding to cooperation. If I were an outsider, it would only add to my admiration that they continued with the intifada on the one hand, but had to keep the bread on the table on the other hand. Perhaps this is one of the hidden, unspoken reasons that kept the intifada nonviolent for such a long time—because every time there was any deviance from nonviolence, the Israeli reaction was to retaliate . . . not just with reprisals, but with closures. . . . That for the Palestinians was the worst sanction—even worse than being fired or shooting." Gal, interview (March 12, 1997).

276 Unified National Leadership Command of the Uprising, Leaflet no. 20, "Jerusalem Appeal," June 22, 1988 (East Jerusalem), PASSIA Archives; Communiqué 20, FACTS Weekly Review 15, June 16-19, 1988, 122-25.

277 Lines were cut ostensibly to stop contacts between local activists and the PLO. Joel Greenberg, "International Phone Links Severed to Areas," *Jerusalem Post*, March 17, 1988, 2. Later, after distribution of a leaflet calling for a five-day strike, stepped-up demonstrations, and civil disobedience, lines were cut for five days. Idem, "Telephone Lines Silenced in Ramallah, Bethlehem," *Jerusalem Post*, October 11, 1989, 2.

278 Whitley and Walker, "From Stones to Sanctions," 20; Moffett, "Uprising's Other Toll." Mubarak Awad said about the Israeli measures, "The cut-off of electricity, phones, fuel and perhaps even water means that Israel is doing the job of separation for us. . . . If we start collecting wood for fuel and build our own water system, we will be working on survival, and resistance will then have a double meaning and purpose: to survive and to achieve our political aims." Greenberg, "Battle Moves from the Streets."

279 "Aqsa Appeal," 4, 13.
280 Daoud Kuttab, "'Two Years of the *Intifada:* The Ups and Downs of the Second Year," *Middle East International,* December 15, 1989, 15-16.
281 Daoud Kuttab, "Beit Sahour Residents Punished for Giving up ID Cards," East Jerusalem, May 1988, Kuttab private papers.
282 Nusseibeh, "Two-Year Perspective," 45.
283 Daoud Kuttab, "Crossing Point," dispatch to news media, East Jerusalem, 1988, 1, Kuttab private papers. Meron Benvenisti told *Financial Times* the economies of the West Bank and Gaza were "mere appendages" of the Israeli economy. The total industrial output of the territories was $80 million, comparable to the annual output for one Israeli factory; the economies of the West Bank and Gaza combined were equivalent to 4.5 percent of Israel's GDP. Whitley and Walker, "From Stones to Sanctions," 20.
284 Abu-Diab, interview (December 11, 1997); Kuttab, "The Strengths of the *Intifada*'s Unified Command," 18; Shalev, "Second Year of the Intifada," 149.
285 Jadallah, interview (December 15, 1997).
286 Notwithstanding evidence to the contrary from dozens of formal tape-recorded interviews with representatives from the four factions, any number of PLO staff who were based in Tunis later took credit for writing the leaflets of the intifada.
287 Robinson, *Building a Palestinian State,* 88-89. The PLO rationale for minimizing civil disobedience is often explained by pleading difficulty in asking further sacrifices from the already-suffering Palestinians in the territories. See for example Walid Ayyad, "The Palestinian Uprising of 1987-1988 and Its Implications for War and Peace in the Middle East," M.A. thesis (Fresno: California State University, 1988), 67. The more plausible explanation would be failure to comprehend this noncooperation method as a means of wielding power.

Chapter 10

1 Pappé, *History of Modern Palestine,* 113.
2 Eugene Weiner, thirty-minute telephone interview (San Francisco, November 4, 1997). Weiner is co-founder of the Abraham Fund, a charitable and educational U.S. organization that promotes coexistence projects among Jewish, Arab, and Druze Israelis, and editor of the *Handbook of Interethnic Coexistence* (New York: Abraham Fund and Continuum, 1998). The handbook, developed with the participation of Gene Sharp, addresses coexistence, and is intended for global use. Ibid.
3 Gal, interview (March 12, 1997).
4 Seven weeks later, General Yariv would state that Israel had less to fear from the creation of a Palestinian state than from a continuation of its efforts to quell the unrest in the territories. Bradley Burston, "Status Quo More Frightening than a Palestinian State—Aharon Yariv," *Jerusalem Post,* March 30, 1988, 1.
5 Sharp, "Considering Policy Options and Consequences for Israel," 15.
6 Ibid., 11-19.
7 Gal, interview (March 16, 1997).
8 Sharp, interview (October 19, 1995); Weiner, interview (November 4, 1997). An Israeli preference for Palestinians to use violent means of contention is often suggested by West Bankers and Gazans—a view that holds that everything the Israelis did in response to the Palestinian intifada was designed to push the Palestinians toward taking violent retaliation, since Israeli authorities felt more comfortable subjugating violence with violence. Mubarak Awad's deportation is held up as evidence for this point of view. Ian Black corroborates this perspective, in "Tension High as Arabs Wait for Security Council Verdict; Israeli Police Vigilant as PLO Debates Resumption of Armed Struggle," *Guardian,* October 12, 1990, 8. Sharp agrees, "Despite Israeli rhetoric against Palestinian violence, there are various signs that the Israeli officials prefer to deal with Palestinian violence rather than with nonviolent struggle." Gene Sharp, "The Intifadah and Nonviolent Struggle," *Journal of Palestine Studies* 73 (Autumn 1989): 12.
9 Weiner, interview (November 4, 1997).
10 Gal, interview (March 16, 1997).
11 Ibid.
12 Ibid.
13 "The Impact of the *Intifada* on Israeli Society: Facts, Assessments, and Predictions" was attended by professor of sociology Elihu Katz of the Gutman Institute for Applied Research; Motti Kirshenbaum, director of Israel Television; social psychologist Ayala Pines of Tel Aviv University; Yoram

Perri of the Center for Strategic Studies, Tel Aviv University; professor of criminology Simha Landau of the Hebrew University; and CISS personnel Reuven Gal and Ofra Maysless. The papers presented in July 1989 appear in *The Seventh War: The Effects of the Intifada on Israeli Society*, Hebrew, ed. Reuven Gal (Hak Hukabutz Hamuhud Publishing House, Ltd., 1990).

14 Gal, interview (March 16, 1997).

15 Weiner, interview (November 4, 1997).

16 Joel Brinkley, "P.L.O. Shift on Violence 'Irrelevant,' Arens Says," *New York Times*, February 4, 1989, 4.

17 Sharp, "Considering Policy Options and Consequences for Israel," 10-11.

18 Weiner, interview (November 4, 1997).

19 Kimmerling and Migdal, *Palestinians*, 224.

20 Efraim Inbar, "Israel's Small War: The Military Response to the *Intifada*," *Armed Forces and Society* 18, no. 1 (Autumn 1991): 35.

21 C. E. Callwell, *Small Wars: Their Principles and Practise*, originally published in 1896, repr. 3rd ed. (Lincoln: University of Nebraska Press, 1996), 26.

22 Stuart A. Cohen and Efraim Inbar, "A Taxonomy of Israel's Use of Force," *Comparative Strategy* 10 (April 1991): 128, 129.

23 Cohen and Inbar, "Taxonomy," 129.

24 Meir Pail, "Intifada Frustrations," *New Outlook*, April 1990, 20. In 1988, Meron Benvenisti said, "Israeli policy is now to harass the Palestinians in any way possible." Peter Smerdon, "Israeli Cash Sweep Is Newest Front for Palestinian Uprising," Reuter Library Report, August 2, 1988.

25 Ziad Abu-Amr, "The *Intifada* Is on a Stoney Road," *Middle East International*, June 11, 1988, 17.

26 "Reluctant Occupiers," 6.

27 Meron Benvenisti, "Israel's 'Apocalypse Now,'" *Newsweek*, January 25, 1988, 33.

28 Gal, interview (March 12, 1997).

29 George D. Moffett III, "Arafat the Ambivalent: PLO Role Puzzles Mideast-Watchers," *Christian Science Monitor*, March 21, 1989, 3. When Israeli military leaders in February 1989 claimed that Fateh had ceased attacks against Israel and Jewish targets abroad in the preceding three months, civilian chiefs denied any change. Brinkley, "P.L.O. Shift on Violence," 4. The *Jerusalem Post* editorialized that the intifada deserved to be labeled "massive Palestinian violence." "After Twenty Months," *Jerusalem Post*, August 22, 1989.

30 See, for example, Yisrael Medad, "Intifada: The Face-Off," *Jerusalem Post*, December 18, 1989.

31 Khalil Jahshan, "U.S. Media Treatment of the Palestinians since the *Intifada*," *American-Arab Affairs* 28 (Spring 1989): 87. Israeli political scientist Susan Hattis Rolef states that from the 1970s onward, Israel essentially dictated the rules to the Americans. Rolef, "Israel's Policy toward the PLO," 268. This meant that Washington would not bring the term *Palestinian state* into usage until well after Israeli nomenclature had changed in response to the intifada.

32 Rubinstein, remarks, National Conference on Nonviolent Sanctions, 1990, as cited in Ashmore, "Nonviolence," 92. A 1990 opinion piece in the *Jerusalem Post* mentions that Gene Sharp's writings were under study in Palestinian circles. It argues that the problems encountered by Israel in applying physical force against the intifada suggest that the government did not understand the basic principles of nonviolent resistance. "Without being facetious, I wish to suggest that the IDF would also be well advised to go to school with Gene Sharp and to inaugurate a branch dedicated to non-violent combat." Frederick M. Schweitzer, "The Power of Non-Violence," *Jerusalem Post*, January 11, 1990.

33 Myra Noveck, "City Lacks Contact with 'True' Leaders of Arab Disturbances," *In Jerusalem*, February 12, 1988, 3

34 Daoud Kuttab, "Mubarak Awad Loses His Case," *Middle East International*, June 11, 1988, 7. Gene Sharp told the Carmel Institute for Social Sciences in 1989, "Despite the Israeli rhetoric against Palestinian violence it is highly significant that the person most effective in urging use of nonviolent means—Mubarak Awad—was deported, and recently two Palestinians were refused exit permits specifically because the conference in Canada at which they were to speak was on 'nonviolence.' They were told, I understand, that had the topic been on anything else they would have been allowed to attend." Sharp, "Considering Policy Options and Consequences for Israel," 8.

35 Shlaim, *Iron Wall*, 453. Shlaim says Rabin later denied having uttered the words "break their bones." Yet the term stuck. Ibid.

36 Sarid and Zucker, "Special Report," 16-17.

37 C. Robert Zelnick, "West Bank and Gaza: An Alternative Policy for the Israelis," *Washington Post*, February 17, 1988, A19.

38   Avi Shlaim, "A Costly Game of Consequences," *Guardian*, October 12, 1990, 23.

39   A majority of Israel's voters, approximately 58 percent, backed parties that favored or were willing to consider giving up parts of the occupied territories, while parties pledging to retain "every inch" of occupied land received slightly more than 42 percent of the total. In the new Knesset, 68 of the 120 seats went to representatives of parties that were willing to consider territorial compromise, while 52 seats went to those whose platforms brooked no compromise on the West Bank and Gaza. Prime Minister Yitzhak Shamir, leader of Likud, became head of a coalition government whose Cabinet was dominated by individuals for whom compromise on land was anathema. Joel Brinkley, "Issues of Faith, More Than Land, Now Preoccupy an Anxious Israel," *New York Times*, November 8, 1988, A1; Asher Wallfish, "Shamir: We Won't Give Arabs an Inch of Our Land," *Jerusalem Post*, May 18, 1989.

40   Naseer H. Aruri, "A New Climate of Opportunity for Palestinians," *Middle East International*, December 1988, 19; Jon D. Hull, "Still Stuck in the Stone Age: As the Palestinian Uprising Enters Its Third Year, Both Sides Have Reason to Mourn," *Time*, December 11, 1989, 59.

41   Scott Atran, "The Surrogate Colonization of Palestine, 1917-1939," *American Ethnologist* 16, no. 4 (1989): 719-44.

42   "The principle of deciding territorial claims on the basis of ancient religious texts is a recipe for insecurity." Anthony Lewis, "Israel's Lethal Mix of Religion and Nationalism," *International Herald Tribune*, January 4-5, 1997, 6.

43   The mechanisms of change have been analyzed by Clarence Marsh Case, George Lakey, Richard Gregg, Gene Sharp, Johan Galtung, and others. See Sharp, *Dynamics of Nonviolent Action*, vol. 3, *Politics of Nonviolent Action*, 707-768; George Lakey, "The Sociological Mechanisms of Nonviolent Action," *Peace Research Review* 2, no. 6 (1968): 1-102; and Clarence Marsh Case, *Nonviolent Coercion: A Study in Methods of Social Pressure* (New York: Century Company, 1923). In addition to indebtedness to the work of Case and Gregg, Sharp's work builds on George Lakey, "The Sociological Mechanisms of Nonviolent Action" (master's degree thesis, sociology, University of Pennsylvania, 1962), substantially the basis of idem, *Nonviolent Action: How It Works* (Wallingford, Pennsylvania: Pendle Hill, 1963).

44   Sidra DeKoven Ezrahi, "Under Jerusalem's Barren Mulberry Tree," *Jerusalem Post*, June 1, 1988; eadem, one-hour interview (Jerusalem, November 11, 1994); Janet Aviad, leader of Shalom Achshav (Peace Now), one-hour interview (East Jerusalem, November 12, 1994); Rafael Moses, Israeli psychiatrist, one-hour interview (East Jerusalem, November 5, 1994).

45   Husseini, interview (January 30, 1996).

46   "The Palestinians cannot now seek a solution that would return the status quo to what it was at the turn of the century, and displace 3.5 million Jews." Nadia Hijab, "The Palestinians Once Had a Land and Still Have Rights," *International Herald Tribune*, 16 March 1988.

47   The responses of the target group to nonviolent struggle are usually mixed, resulting in a continuum of the mechanisms of change, including partial defeats and successes. Sharp, *Dynamics of Nonviolent Action*, 755-56. Subgroups may react differently. Ibid., 706.

48   Vogele, "Learning and Nonviolent Struggle," 332.

49   Sharp, *Dynamics of Nonviolent Action*, 741-55; idem, *Waging Nonviolent Struggle*, 47.

50   "Disintegration" as a mechanism of change could be seen in East Germany in 1989, as the regime and its secret police, the Stasi, and security systems imploded in response to the Pastors' Movement. See Roland Bleiker, *Nonviolent Struggle and the Revolution in East Germany*, Monograph Series no. 6 (Cambridge, Massachusetts: Albert Einstein Institution, 1993); Robert Darnton, *Berlin Journal, 1989-1990* (New York: W. W. Norton, 1991), and Konrad H. Jarausch, *The Rush to German Unity* (Oxford: Oxford University Press, 1994).

51   See Sharp, *Methods of Nonviolent Action*, 113.

52   Hall-Cathala, *Peace Movement in Israel*, 177, 216, 217. The Group of 27 emphasized "preparedness to defend the state [of Israel] in its 1967 boundaries" and declared itself the "first public resistance to Israeli occupation." Toma Shick, "The Price of a Conscience in Israel," *al-Fajr*, April 9-15, 1982, 12. The International Movement for Conscientious War Resisters was founded in Palestine in 1925 and led by Judah Magnes, Martin Buber, and others. Affiliated with War Resisters International (WRI), during the 1948 war it supported conscientious objectors who refused to participate in hostilities. Ibid. On WRI, see Howard Clark, "War Resisters International," in Roger S. Powers et al., *Protest, Power, and Change: An Encyclopedia of Nonviolent Action* (New York and London: Garland Publishing, 1997), 563-65.

53   Kenneth Kaplan, "The Book and the Sword," *Jerusalem Post Magazine*, December 30, 1988, 9.

54   Major General (Ret.) Josef Geva and Major General Monacham Meron, one-hour interview (Jerusalem, June 8, 1988).

55 Gideon Spiro, one-hour telephone interview (Tel Aviv, November 12, 2006).

56 Ibid.

57 Ibid; Shindler, *Ploughshares into Swords?* 193.

58 Paul, "Israel and the Intifadah: Points of Stress," 16.

59 Naomi Chazan, one-hour interview (East Jerusalem, June 6, 1988).

60 Schenker, "To Channel This Energy," 11; Micah Sifry, "Eyeless in Gaza," *Nation*, January 16, 1988, 40. Concerning a four-day march bidding Israeli youths to refuse army service in the occupied territories, see Andy Court, "Red Line March Ends with Call for Youths Not to Serve in Areas," *Jerusalem Post*, March 3, 1988, 2.

61 Mordechai Bar-on, one-hour interview (Jerusalem, June 8, 1988).

62 Peretz Kidron, "'The Right to Say 'No,' ' review of *On Democracy and Obedience*, ed. Ishai Munuchin (Tel Aviv: Yesh Gvul and Siman Kriah, 1990), *New Outlook*, August 1990, 42.

63 Chazan, interview (June 6, 1988); Dajani, *Eyes without Country*, 80-81, 199 n. 75; "Institute Has Pleasant View, Tough Topic," *Security Affairs* (September 1989), 3.

64 Spiro, "Israeli Soldiers Who Say 'There Is a Limit,'" p. 19.

65 Kaminer, *Politics of Protest*, 67.

66 Spiro, interview, November 12, 2006.

67 Shindler, *Ploughshares into Swords?* 193.

68 Ibid; George D. Moffett III, "An Israeli Soldier with Different Sense of Duty," *Christian Science Monitor*, July 25, 1988.

69 Shindler, ibid.

70 Gideon Spiro, one-hour telephone interview (Tel Aviv, November 17, 2006).

71 Edy Kaufman, "The *Intifadah* and the Peace Camp in Israel: A Critical Introspective," *Journal of Palestine Studies* 17, no. 4 (Summer 1988): 67; Bar-on, *In Pursuit of Peace*, 97-102, 319.

72 Goldblum, interview (November 5, 1994).

73 Major General (Ret.) Geva commanded the Central Area and in 1988 became Chairman of the Council for Peace and Security. He and Major General Monacham Meron were two of the Israeli military generals who founded the Council for Peace and Security, in March 1988. Geva and Meron, interview (June 8, 1988). In chapter 8, Moshe Amirav, also a member of the council, had in 1987 as a member of the Likud central committee held discussions on behalf of then prime minister Yitzhak Shamir with Feisel Husseini and Sari Nusseibeh. Amirav, interview (June 8, 1988).

74 Spiro, interview (November 12, 2006).

75 James Paul, "Israel and the Intifadah: Points of Stress," *Middle East Report* 154 (September-October 1988): 14; Sifry, "Eyeless in Gaza," 40. Still active, the nonpartisan council is composed of hundreds of Israeli reserve officers, ranking from major to general, who proclaim, "Peace with the Palestinians is vital for Israel's security." Peretz Kidron, "Chicken-Hearted America: Betrayal of the Forces of Peace," *Middle East International*, April 10, 1998, 3.

76 Glenn Frankel, "Israeli Army Suffers Casualty: Confidence; "We Are Losing, Palestinians Winning," *Washington Post*, January 30, 1989. A senior IDF officer told Yehuda Litani, "It is very bad that we, the IDF, have got into this mess. We trained our soldiers to fight wars, to defend the borders, and now we are doing the work of policemen—or more accurately, we are riot squads." Yehuda Litani, "No Bypassing Palestinians and PLO," *Jerusalem Post*, February 12, 1988, 20.

77 "The Uprising's Hidden Toll," transcript of February 1989 Tel Aviv discussion by Israeli reserve officers, trans. Willis Johnson, *Harper's*, August 1989, 20-21. To Zeev Schiff, the intifada resulted in "brutalization" of a generation of soldiers, eroding the "moral high ground" claimed by Israel. Zeev Schiff, "What Has Happened to the IDF during the Intifada?" *Haaretz*, June 16, 1989, as cited in Ashmore, "Nonviolence as an *Intifada* Strategy," 100-1301. Prime Minister Yitzhak Rabin would later say, "We are paying with blood for ruling another people. . . . Ruling over another people has corrupted us." Anthony Lewis, "The Logic of Peace," *New York Times*, May 20, 1994; idem, "Israel's Next Task: Complete the Peace," *International Herald Tribune*, July 30-31, 1994, 4.

78 Cited in Clyde Haberman, "Israelis Deglamorize the Military," *New York Times*, May 31, 1995, A10.

79 Getzler, "Conference Aims to Sound Alarm," 4. Also, Kenneth Kaplan notes, the Israeli arms industry was "reduced to producing glorified industrial-strength stone throwers and marble shooters," i.e., "monster" gadgets to be used against Palestinians. Kenneth Kaplan, "Going Back to the *Davidka*," *Jerusalem Post*, May 20, 1988, 6.

80 Robert Fisk, "One Small Victory in the Eternal Struggle: Jewish Scholar Hails Peace Settlement as a Step in the Right Direction," *Independent*, September 7, 1993, 10.

81 Abu-Diab, interview (December 11, 1997). On the origins of this joint Israeli-Palestinian human

chain in the work of the Committee against the Iron Fist, see Warschawski, "Committee against the Iron Fist," in Kaufman Nunn, *Creative Resistance*, 84.

82 Sami Aboudi, "Palestinians to Reach Out to Israeli Public for Peace," Reuters, January 17, 1990; Jackson Diehl, "Shamir to Fire Weizman over PLO Contacts; Move May Jeopardize Ruling Coalition," *Washington Post*, January 1, 1990, A21.

83 Mary Curtius, "Israeli Police Attack Marchers at Peace Rally," *Boston Globe*, December 31, 1989, 17.

84 Daniel Williams, "Israeli Police Attack Peace March," *Los Angeles Times*, December 31, 1989, A24; Michal Sela, "Police Are Accused of Using Force without Provocation," *Jerusalem Post*, December 31, 1989.

85 Ian Black, "Water Cannon Swamps Jerusalem Peace Rally," *Guardian*, January 1, 1990, 20; Qleibo, *Before the Mountains Disappear*, 63-64.

86 Galia Golan, one-hour interview (Jerusalem, June 8, 1988). "We need displacement of a whole vengeance theory regarding Arabs.... The vast majority of Israelis are not racist, but afraid." Avi Ravitzki, one-hour interview (Jerusalem, June 8, 1988). Ravitzki was active in Netivot le Shalom (the Pathways to Peace).

87 Gerardus van der Leeuw, *Religion in Essence and Manifestation* (Princeton: Princeton University Press, 1986), 636-640.

88 David Hoffman, "Israel Facing Occupation's Scars," *Washington Post*, May 16, 1994, A1; idem, "Amid Setbacks, Slow Change in Israeli Attitudes," *International Herald Tribune*, July 18, 1994, 1; Bob Hepburn, "Scars of the Intifadeh: Five Years of Uprising Have Permanently Marked the Psyche of an Entire Generation of Israelis," *Toronto Star*, December 26, 1992: H1.

89 Robert Charvin, "The 'Intifada': From Palestinian People's Self-Assertion to Statehood," *Palestine and Law* (Brussels: International Association of Democratic Lawyers, 1988), 14; Herbert Mitgang, "PEN Unit Chides Israel over Censorship," *New York Times*, June 25, 1988; Andy Court, "IDF Closes East Jerusalem News Agency," *Jerusalem Post*, March 30, 1988, 1.

90 Ian Black, "Israel Suspends Ban on Intifada Protest Songs," *Guardian*, December 7, 1989, 8.

91 As cited in John M. Goshko and Nora Boustany, "Congress' First Hearing on Intifada Is a Tense One," *Washington Post*, May 10, 1990, A19.

92 Spiro, "Israeli Soldiers Who Say 'There Is a Limit,'" p. 19. A reliable account of Yesh Gvul is by Peretz Kidron, former spokesperson for the organization. Peretz Kidron, "Selective Refusal," *Palestine-Israel Journal* 3, nos. 3 and 4 (Summer and Autumn 1996): 129-37. See also Hall-Cathala, *Peace Movement in Israel*: 171-78; and Myron J. Aronoff, *Israeli Visions and Divisions: Cultural Change and Political Conflict* (New Brunswick, New Jersey: Transaction Books, 1989), 148-58.

93 Frankel, "Israeli Army Suffers Casualty." In an interview, Shomron told Joel Brinkley, "We as an army cannot change political consciousness. Our job is to reduce the level of violence so that the political leadership can explore various options" for a political settlement. "P.L.O. Shift on Violence," 4.

Chapter 11

1 Part one is Nafez Assaily, "Intifada: Palestinian Nonviolent Protest—An Affirmation of Human Dignity and Freedom" (East Jerusalem, PCSN, May 1988); part two is Hal Gangnath and Nafez Assaily. "Intifada: Palestinian Nonviolent Protest—An Affirmation of Human Dignity and Freedom" (East Jerusalem, PCSN, May 1989).

2 A general strike was called on thirty-two occasions, approximately one-fifth of all bidden methods. Ibid.

3 Of these, seventeen (roughly 10 percent) fall into the category of solidarity, such as visiting the families and graves of martyrs, financially assisting Palestinian institutions, and agricultural or land-reclamation projects. Ibid.

4 Sixty-three calls for strikes, 28 appeals for noncooperation, 13 bids for consumer boycotts, 21 measures pertaining to popular committees, 21 calls for demonstrations, and 8 appeals for the resignation of all Palestinians from jobs in Israeli institutions. Ibid.

5 Of the 263 appeals in the second group of leaflets, 22 ask for stones to be thrown and 6 call for attacks on traitors. Ibid.

6 *Hijra* derives from the Prophet Mohammed's migration from Mecca to Medina in the seventh century. *Hijra* is an extreme form of noncooperation involving mass migration to deny the adversary the ability to accomplish its goals. To emigrate would not thwart the territorial maximization sought by the Israeli right wing. Galtung, *The Way Is the Goal*, 108-23. On *hijra*, see Muhammad Khalid Masud, "The Obligation to Migrate: The Doctrine of *Hijra* in Islamic Law," ed. Dale F. Eickelman and James Piscatori, *Muslim Travellers: Pilgrimage, Migration, and the Religious Imagination* (London: Routledge, 1990), 29-49. *Hijra* was used with definitive effect in East Germany in the 1980s, where it was called "exit." See Ronald Bleiker, *Nonviolent Struggle and the Revolution in East Germany*; idem, *Popular Dissent*, 121-27, 131, 168.

7   Shyam Bhatia cites 70,000 soldiers deployed in the occupied territories in the spring of 1988. Bhatia, "Uprising Comes of Age," 27. By 1989, perhaps 10,000 soldiers were involved in "anti-intifada" military activities in the territories. Alpher, Eytan, and Tamari, *Middle East Military Balance*, 243. By the second year of the intifada, through March 1990, Israeli analyst Aryeh Shalev notes the IDF reduced its numbers stationed in the West Bank and Gaza by one-third from the previous year. Shalev, "Second Year of Intifada," 128. Efraim Inbar gives no supporting data for his estimate that "only 5 percent of Palestinian activity included the use of firearms." Efraim Inbar, "Israel's Small War: The Military Response to the *Intifada*," *Armed Forces and Society* 18, no. 1 (Autumn 1991): 30. Given the depth of popular participation in the uprising by the Palestinians, such a percentage appears grossly high.

8   Sharp, "Intifadah and Nonviolent Struggle," 7.

9   Finding a way to visit loved ones without interaction with the occupation authorities is noted in an essay by a reserve IDF officer who is scathingly critical of Israeli policy—an early description of the intifada published in Hebrew, appearing in the monthly *Monitin*, spring 1988, reprinted in "Gaza Hell-Hole," *Jerusalem Quarterly* 53 (Winter 1990): 62-63.

10 Daoud Kuttab, "Palestinian Youths Block Main Jerusalem-Ramallah Highway," dispatch to news media, East Jerusalem, autumn 1988, Kuttab private papers.

11 Frisch, "Diffusion and Consolidation," 48, 50.

12 Edward Kaufman, one-hour interview (Jerusalem, December 15, 1997); idem, "The Intifada's Limited Violence," *Journal of Arab Affairs* 9, no. 2 (Autumn 1990): 113; idem, "Israeli Perceptions of the Palestinians 'Limited Violence' in the *Intifada*," *Terrorism and Political Violence* 3, no. 4 (Winter 1991): 25.

13 Sharp, "Intifadah and Nonviolent Struggle," 7.

14 Ibid. Italics in original.

15 Abu-Diab, interview (December 11, 1997).

16 Ian Lustick's view of the uprising as a revolt of violence is misleading, but his analysis of "solipsistic" violence may have some truth. He suggests the main purpose of inflicting destruction or death by both Zionists and Palestinians has been to alter the mind set of one's own group—rather than to affect *the other*, i.e., Zionist terrorism and Palestinian armed struggle were to boost internal group psychology. Lustick, "Changing Rationales for Political Violence," 75, 76.

17 "The youngest category . . . 7-10 age group . . . . are seen rolling the tyres to the middle of the road, pouring some gasoline on them and [striking] a match to light them. . . . The burning of the tyre will keep cars from traveling that particular road and . . . attract soldiers. . . . The 11-14 age group is involved in putting up large stones in the road to slow down or stop traffic . . . [or] using home-made slingshots. . . . The 15-19 group are the veteran stone throwers. . . . Speed and knowledge of their turf gives them a big advantage over the soldiers who are loaded with equipment and who have to travel in units so they will not be trapped. Young Palestinians over 19 take key positions in order to lead the entire team." Kuttab, original draft of "Profile of the Stonethrowers," 6.

18 Bishara, interview (June 17, 1995).

19 Richard A. Falk, "International Law and Palestinian Resistance," in *The Struggle for Sovereignty: Palestine and Israel, 1993-2005*, ed. Joel Beinin and Rebecca L. Stein (Stanford, California: Stanford University Press, 2006), 316.

20 Daoud Kuttab, interview (November 4, 1994). Aryeh Shalev confirms Kuttab's depiction, when noting the majority of Israeli civilians injured each month in 1988 and 1989 were in the West Bank, "where the Jewish population is far larger and more dispersed than in the Gaza Strip, and generates far more Israeli traffic on roads that pass through or near Arab population concentrations." Shalev, "Second Year of Intifada," 134-35. By spring 1988, 60,000 Israeli settlers lived in the West Bank. Eric Silver, "Faithful Jewish Hikers to Return in Force," *Observer Sunday*, April 10, 1988, 23. By summer 1989, the number had risen to 70,000. Moffett, "Digging in Their Heels outside Hebron."

21 Allen G. Noble and Elisha Efrat, "Geography of the Intifada," *Geographical Review* 80, no. 3 (July 1990): 302. Palestinian villages were sealed, some "blockaded by earth ramparts built by IDF bulldozers," and IDF roadblocks barred journalists and Palestinians from traveling into or out of the West Bank, but Israeli settlers were "allowed free passage." Joel Greenberg, "Arrests Reinforce Crackdown; Gazans Find Links to Outside World Severed," *Jerusalem Post*, March 30, 1988, 1.

22 Joe Stork, "The Significance of Stones: Notes from the Seventh Month," *Middle East Report* 154 (September-October 1988): 4.

23 Chaim Bermant, "Struggle for Israel's Soul," *Observer Sunday*, October 30, 1988, 25.

24 Bronner, "Intifadah Five Years Later," 2; Nusseibeh, interview (November 5, 1994).

25 Chaim Bermant, "The Light That Failed," *Observer Sunday*, April 17, 1988, 14.

26 By mid-1988, not one Israeli soldier had died from thrown stones. The soldiers were under orders to

shoot only when their lives were in danger, thus Daoud Kuttab contends "in the case of the hundreds of Palestinians killed or badly wounded in the upper parts of the body, soldiers' lives were not in danger." Daoud Kuttab, "Shooting at Demonstrators, What Is the Israeli Policy?" dispatch to news media, East Jerusalem, mid-1988, Kuttab private papers. By mid-January 1988, Israeli soldiers had been given orders to fire low-caliber rifles at the legs of leaders. Goodman, "Army Meets a New Palestinian."

27 Lance Morrow, "An Intifadeh of the Soul," *Time*, July 23, 1990, 8.

28 Nancy Nye, personal communication (Washington, D.C., July 3, 1995).

29 Hafid Barghouti, interview (January 25, 1996).

30 Ali Muhammad Jiddah, in Lynd, Bahour, and Lynd, *Homeland*, 165.

31 Shalev, *Intifada: Causes and Effects*, 41.

32 Daoud Kuttab's original draft "A Profile of the Stonethrowers" notes a triple-team formation including women: "The first team is composed of lookouts, whose job it is from their positions on rooftops to indicate when and from where the army is coming. This team often includes women, who use their own homes as observation points."

33 Machool, "This Isn't Rebellion," 15.

34 The uprising "reversed irrevocably the David and Goliath metaphor that the Israelis had promoted," with themselves as David. Sherna Berger Gluck, *An American Feminist in Palestine* (Philadelphia, Temple University Press, 1994), 7.

35 Peretz, *Intifada*, 87.

36 Anita Vitullo, "Uprising in Gaza," *Middle East Report* 152 (May-June 1988): 22.

37 Although Zeev Schiff and Ehud Yaari come to a false conclusion in asserting that the restraint of arms was "instinctive," they are correct in observing "bona fide weapons were never to be found in the hands of the insurgents" and perceiving a fundamental decision to dispense with armed struggle. Schiff and Yaari, *Intifada*, 120. The earliest Israeli-Palestinian gun battle in the first intifada did not occur until May 19, 1989, seventeen months after the start of the uprising, in a village fifteen miles southwest of Jerusalem. Trapped after a car chase with three military vehicles, a squad of local Palestinians fired with stolen IDF-issued automatic weapons, killing one soldier and wounding seven others. All of the Palestinians were killed. Glenn Frankel, "Clashes Kill Eight Palestinians, Israeli Soldier; Uprising Produces First Major Shootout," *Washington Post*, May 19, 1989, A1. The operation was carried out by the Syrian-backed Abu Musa faction, Fateh-Uprising led by Col. Said Musa, which had tried to unseat Arafat in 1983. Joel Greenberg, "Arafat: No Guns, but Limit to Patience; Armed Clash Not Seen as Intifada 'Turning Point,'" *Jerusalem Post*, May 21, 1989.

38 Smerdon, "Israeli Army Fears."

39 Ibid. "Caches of small arms believed to have been secreted by some PLO factions [were] strictly forbidden by the leaders of the uprising." Peretz, "*Intifada* and Middle East Peace," 392.

40 Yehuda Litani, "PLO's 'Remote Control' Won't Determine Events in Uprising," *Jerusalem Post*, March 21, 1988, 1.

41 Hillel Schenker, "A Nation Living on the Edge; Letter from Israel," *Nation*, January 21, 1993, 45.

42 *Military Balance, 1989-1990* (London: International Institute for Strategic Studies, 1990), 94.

43 Smerdon, "Israeli Army Fears."

44 Tamari, "Time to Converse Calmly."

45 Kuttab, "Crossing Point," 2. Having largely ended cross-border attacks from Lebanon, in late 1988 and early 1989 Fateh created an underground Popular Army—also known as Assault Groups—to carry out armed operations inside Israel and the occupied territories. David B. Ottaway, "Arafat Faction of PLO Linked to Terrorism, Israelis Charge," *Washington Post*, February 2, 1989. This unilateral Fateh decision to set up a clandestine Palestinian force came as a blow inside the diaspora to set up a clandestine Palestinian force came as a blow inside the territories, and was opposed. *Al-Anba*, Kuwait, January 19, 1989, as cited in Frisch, "Diffusion and Consolidation," 51, 61 n. 43.

46 Kuttab, "Children's Revolt," 27.

47 Sharp assisted by Jenkins, *Civilian-Based Defense*, 50.

48 Hurwitz, "Nonviolence in the Occupied Territories," 23. Development of a body of humor substantiates abandonment of fear. Bir Zeit anthropologist Sharif Kanaana's analysis of two hundred jokes from the uprising found the largest category to involve competition with the Israelis. He found no ethnic humor, nor slurs against the Jews. The lampooned were neither Israeli civilians nor even settlers, but solely the Israeli army. In jests, "when Palestinians manage to get hold of an Israeli soldier and overpower him, they never harm him. What they usually do in these stories is to try to humiliate the army to which he belongs." The badinage reflects a mood, in which whenever a Palestinian confronts an Israeli, the Palestinian is depicted as superior, or, at a minimum, equal. Sharif

Kanaana, "Encounters with Folklore: Humor of the Palestinian *Intifada*," *Journal of Folklore Research* 27, no. 3 (1990): 233, 234, 235.

49 Daoud Kuttab, "Israeli Military Campaign to Restore Fear among Palestinians," dispatch to news media, East Jerusalem, August 1988, Kuttab private papers. Ian Lustick rightly notes that overcoming fear was an objective in the intifada, yet nothing uncovered by this research suggests, as does Lustick, that it was through the throwing of stones or Molotov cocktails that this objective was attained. Ian S. Lustick, "Changing Rationales for Political Violence in the Arab-Israeli Conflict," *Journal of Palestine Studies* 77 (Autumn 1990): 75, 76. Palestinian mastery of fear was born of the realization that the Palestinians themselves could withdraw submission to occupation and substitute self-reliance.

50 Souad Dajani, "Nonviolent Resistance in the Occupied Territories: A Critical Reevaluation," in Zunes et al., *Nonviolent Social Movements*, 52.

51 Edward Kaufman, "The Potential Impact of Palestinian Nonviolent Struggle on Israel: Some Preliminary Lessons and Projections for the Future," paper presented at the International Conference on Celebrating Nonviolent Resistance, Bethlehem, December 29, 2005. Paper based on action research jointly undertaken with the Nationwide Nonviolence Network and Communication Channels project of Middle East Nonviolence and Democracy (MEND), and its Israeli partner the Truman Institute, Hebrew University, Jerusalem. Partly supported by the EU, MEND is consolidating a network of active nonviolence at the national Palestinian level, training Palestinian activists in the West Bank (www.mendonline.org).

52 Ezrahi, *Rubber Bullets*, 204.

53 Ibid., 204-5, 275.

54 Jamil Hamami, one-hour interview (East Jerusalem, December 15, 1997). Hamami was a leader of Hamas at the time. Nissim Rejwan, "Hamas: 'From the Sea to the River,'" *Jerusalem Post*, December 19, 1990.

55 Asher Wallfish, "Rabin Says Time Needed to Restore Order," *Jerusalem Post*, January 11, 1988.

56 The PLO never "Islamized" the broad front politically, partly due to prominence of Christians such as George Habash and Nayef Hawatmeh, and historical contributions by Palestinian Christians.

57 Taraki, "Islamic Resistance Movement," 31. Refugee camps in the occupied territories are 99 percent Muslim; approximately 350,000 persons live in the twenty-six camps in the West Bank and Gaza, with other refugees dwelling in poor urban areas. Kimmerling and Migdal, *Palestinians*, 194; Abu-Amr, "Social Conditions in the Refugee Camps," 149. Military occupation intrudes on Muslim religious life by censorship of sermons, arrest of preachers, and blockades preventing worshippers access to the Haram al-Sharif. "Hamas is a sentiment . . . an index to Palestinian frustration." Mushahid Hussain, "America's Quest for an Islam Policy," *Middle East International*, March 3, 1995, 17.

58 Covenant of the Islamic Resistance Movement (Hamas), August 18, 1988, English version issued by Hamas. Cornell University Library, http://www.library.cornell.edu/colldev/mideast/hamas.htm.

59 The Muslim Brotherhood had regularly cooperated with the PLO in offering support for the families of martyrs in the form of an initial sum approximating $850 USD (equivalent to roughly 400 Jordanian dinars), plus monthly stipends on a sliding scale. Sande, "Palestinian Martyr Widowhood," 711. Jonathan Randal says the PLO had provided arms, money, and training for Gazan Islamic blocs since 1986. Randal, "New, Largely Invisible, Force," A26.

60 Michal Sela, "'Resistance Is a Moslem Duty': History of Hamas," *Jerusalem Post*, May 26, 1989, 9.

61 Covenant of Hamas, Article Seven, 7; Article Twenty-seven, 25.

62 Ibid., Article Eleven, 9-10.

63 Ibid., Article Thirteen, 11, 12.

64 Beverley Milton-Edwards, "The Concept of *Jihad* and the Palestinian Islamic Movement: A Comparison of Ideas and Techniques," *British Journal of Middle Eastern Studies* 19, no.1 (1992): 50.

65 Ibid., 52; Covenant of Hamas, Article Twelve, 10.

66 Barbara Stowasser, "Jihad or Qital?" (Washington, D.C.: Center for Contemporary Arab Studies News, Georgetown University, October 2001), 7.

67 Eid, interview (January 28, 1996).

68 Abu-Amr, *Islamic Fundamentalism*, 64; "Israel Seeking Peace Appeal from Hamas Leader," Reuters North American Wire, May 23, 1996; Taylor, "Palestinian Moslem Brothers Gain Despite Imprisonment." Ahmad Yasin would die in 2004 in an extralegal killing by Israel, a "targeted assassination."

69 Hamami, interview (December 15, 1997).

70 Eid, interview (January 28, 1996).

71 Though Sunni, Jihad admired the achievements of the Iranian Revolution, but received no instructions from abroad. Hamas saw the victory of Islam as paramount and the first step in resolution of

the Palestinian problem, but Jihad gave the struggle against Zionism and elimination of Israel priority over religious education. Armed struggle, initially rejected by the Muslim Brotherhood, was part of Jihad's strategy. Michal Sela, "The Islamic Factor," *Jerusalem Post*, October 25, 1989; IDF spokesman, "Jihad's Affinity to Fatah," trans. Denise Ben-Dor, *Jerusalem Post*, February 3, 1988, 5.

72 Abu-Amr, *Islamic Fundamentalism*, 100.

73 Robinson, "Creating Space," 276.

74 Abu-Amr, "Palestinian Uprising," 394.

75 Milton-Edwards, "Concept of *Jihad*," 52.

76 On contacts between the two groups, see Taraki, "Islamic Resistance Movement," 32. Hatem Abd al-Qader Eid doubts whether Islamic Jihad was in close contact with the Command: "I didn't know anyone from Jihad. I had heard about Jihad, but I personally didn't know anybody from Jihad, but [representatives on the Command] knew lots of Hamas people." Eid, interview (January 28, 1996).

77 Islamic Jihad was ideologically close to Fateh. The Abu Jihad "Western Front Command" of Fateh had tried to encourage Jihad as a fighting arm against the occupation as early as 1982. Sela, "Islamic Factor."

78 Some popular committees had both Islamic blocs represented, yet did not include the military tendencies that were resuscitating the thinking of Sheikh Izz al-Din al-Qassam. Hamas and Islamic Jihad each had Qassam Brigades. Graham Usher, "Israel Burns the Palestinian Haystack," *Middle East International*, March 15, 1996, 3-5; David Hoffman, "The Making of a 'Martyr,'" *Washington Post*, March 12, 1996, A1. Hamas created the Qassam Brigades for suicide missions; the number of fighting personnel may not have exceeded one hundred. Ibrahim, "Many Faces of Hamas."

79 The crushing of Jihad by Israeli security forces at the end of 1987 was a factor in mobilizing the entire Gazan populace to take to the streets in mass demonstrations. Sela, "Islamic Factor."

80 Jon Immanuel, "Hamas, Fatah Agree to 'Regulate' Informer Killings," *Jerusalem Post*, June 8, 1992.

81 Frankel, "Hardline Arab Group," 20.

82 Rejwan, "Hamas: 'From the Sea to the River.'"

83 Israeli security forces found tension between Hamas and the Command useful. Sela, "Resistance Is a Moslem Duty," 9.

84 Hamami, interview (December 15, 1997).

85 Daoud Kuttab, "*Intifada* Revived," *Middle East International*, September 28, 1990, 13.

86 Glenn Frankel, "Talks Please Palestinians—So Far; Expectations Remain Low that Israel Will Grant Concessions," *Washington Post*, November 4, 1991, A17.

87 Ethan Bronner, "Intifadah Five Years Later: A Struggle Shows Signs of Fatigue," *Boston Globe*, December 10, 1992, 2.

88 Hugh Carnegy, "A Lull in the Battle for Peace: Middle East Talks Hang in the Balance after the Deportation of Alleged Islamic Militants from Israel," *Financial Times*, December 19, 1992, 6.

89 "Israel Warns Lebanon on Deportees," Press Association Newsfile, December 20, 1992.

90 Christopher Walker, "Rabin Expulsions Drive PLO into the Arms of Militants," *The Times*, December 21, 1992.

91 The deported were theoreticians, fund raisers, and heads of Islamic institutions, "not gunmen." "Israel Expels 400 Palestinians as Threat," *St. Petersburg Times*, December 18, 1992, 1A.

92 Shlaim, *Iron Wall*, 510.

93 Bill Hutman, "Security Tightened after Expulsions," *Jerusalem Post*, December 18, 1992.

94 Hamami, interview (December 15, 1997); Nusseibeh, interview (December 16, 1997); Bill Hutman, "Joint Hamas, PLO Handbill Calls for 'Jihad' against Israel," *Jerusalem Post*, December 21, 1992.

95 Jonathan Ferziger, "Lawyers Demand Israel Bring Back Deportees," UPI, December 20, 1992.

96 Carnegy, "Lull in the Battle for Peace."

97 Michael Parks, "Israel Deports 400 Palestinians," *Los Angeles Times*, December 18, 1992, 1. The growing influence of Hamas may have been a factor in persuading a wavering Prime Minister Rabin to accept the PLO as a negotiating partner. Yossi Klein Halevi, "How Arafat Uses Hamas," *New York Times*, March 14, 1996.

98 Caspi, interview (November 10, 1994). See Hareven, "Eyeless in Gaza," 17; Yehuda Litani, "Militant Islam in the West Bank and Gaza," *New Outlook*, November-December 1989, 42. In 1991, when the U. S. government had no formal dialogue with the PLO, it was revealed that American diplomats had covertly opened dialogue with Hamas in Amman. Douglas Roberts, "U.S.-Palestinians," Voice of America, March 2, 1993. "It was the Americans who approached us," Imad Falouji of Hamas said. Mary Anne Weaver, "The Quandary: Report from Gaza," *New Yorker*, August 19, 1996, 26.

99 Susan Hattis Rolef, "Israel's Policy toward the PLO: From Rejection to Recognition," in Sela and Maoz, *PLO and Israel*, 259.

100 Sela, "The Islamic Factor," *Jerusalem Post*, October 25, 1989.

101 Abu-Amr, "Palestinian Uprising," 400.

102 Hamami, interview (December 15, 1997).

103 Ibid. Despite Shaykh Jamil Hamami's own personal universalism, Don Peretz asserts a key difference between the leaflets of the Command and those of Hamas is that the Command's communiqués did not attack Jews. Peretz, "The *Intifada* and Middle East Peace," 390-91.

104 Sela, "Resistance Is a Moslem Duty," 9.

105 "Islam is a religion of mercy and justice for all people, but what happened after 1967 with the military occupation justifies the resistance of Hamas against the occupation. Hamas did not differ [with the PLO] on methods of resistance until after Oslo. The PLO before Oslo had used armed struggle—which Israel calls terrorism. Hamas continued armed struggle after Oslo, because Oslo did not fulfill the rights of the Palestinians. I personally believe the situation was different after Oslo and had differences with Hamas on this point, and after this I broke away. It is known that I had differences with Hamas on the continuation of armed struggle." Hamami, interview (December 15, 1997). Mustafa Abu Sway, professor of Islamic philosophy at al-Quds University, among whose students was Sheikh Jamil, said Sheikh Jamil severed his connection with Hamas because he believed that the peace process and the Palestinian Authority should be given a chance to succeed. Mustafa Abu Sway, personal communication (East Jerusalem, December 15, 1997). Despite Sheikh Jamil's dissociation from Hamas over the use of violence, Israeli security forces arrested him at his home in Bir Nabala, north of Jerusalem, on February 20, 1995. "Israel Police Wound Arab near Jerusalem Old City," Reuters North American Wire, February 21, 1995.

106 Hamas leaflets appealed directly to the populace, but the Command emphasized popular committees. Comparative analysis of underground leaflets from the Command and Hamas by Shaul Mishal and Reuben Aharoni shows the committees are not mentioned by Hamas. Nor is civil disobedience cited. Sit-ins and resignation from jobs do not appear in the Hamas fliers analyzed. Rallies or demonstrations appear in only two Hamas leaflets studied. Mishal and Aharoni's work is flawed by their pooling of both nonviolent and violent directives into absolute numbers, thus failing to differentiate the disciplined preparation required for collective nonviolent struggle versus reactive and individualistic actions of violent commando tactics. Typically they write, "The population was called on to cooperate in both violent and nonviolent actions." Mishal and Aharoni, *Speaking Stones*, 37. This erroneously misses the back and forth creep to the violent calls, so often contradictory, disclosing internal struggle, and occurring more slowly than these authors discern.

107 Jarbawi, interview (June 16, 1995).

108 "Bit of West Bank's Future in Smooth Campus Vote," *New York Times*, November 14, 1992.

109 Taraki, "Islamic Resistance Movement," 32, 176-177.

110 Wafa Amr, "Hamas Wants In as Israel-PLO Breakthrough Nears," Reuters North American Wire, April 21, 1994.

111 Gail Pressburg, thirty-minute interview (Washington, D.C., June 12, 1998).

112 Ibid. Development during the 1980s of decentralized, non-factionalized organizations and institutions, led by local, professionally trained leaders, is described by Pressburg, in "The Uprising: Causes and Consequences," *Journal of Palestine Studies* 67 (Spring 1988): 38-50.

113 Awad, interview (February 14, 1995).

114 Grossman, "Palestinian Pacifist."

115 Shehadeh, *From Occupation to Interim Accords*, 160.

116 Sharp, interview (October 19, 1995).

117 Mubarak E. Awad, one-hour lecture, international peace and conflict resolution division, American University (Washington, D.C., March 26, 1998).

118 Abd al-Aziz Said, one-hour interview (Washington, D.C., June 19, 1998).

119 Gene Sharp, "Basic Presentation to Palestinian Leaders," Tunis, March 1989, 2-6, notes in archives of the Albert Einstein Institution, Boston.

120 Abd al-Aziz Said recalled Sharp's initial encounter with Arafat, condensing it: Sharp asked if there were examples of when the Americans had listened to the Arabs. During the oil embargo of 1973 and the intifada, Arafat replied. Sharp asked if these two examples had anything in common. Arafat nodded: "nonviolent methods." Arafat acknowledged that the armed option was not working. Said, interview (June 19, 1995).

121 Bruce Jenkins, "Report on Meetings with PLO Representatives," Tunis, March 18-26, 1989, unpublished paper, archives of the Albert Einstein Institution, Boston, 3.

122 Said, interview (June 19, 1995).

123 Awad, interview (February 14, 1995); Nye, communication (October 6, 1992); Said, interview (June 19, 1995); Sharp, interview (October 19, 1995).

124 Arafat criticized Sharp's assessment as failing to address serious violence by extremist Israeli settlers. Sharp, "Basic Presentation to Palestinian Leaders," 6.

125 Jenkins, "Meetings with PLO Representatives," 1. Sharp, *Politics of Nonviolent Action.*

126 Jenkins, ibid., 8.

127 Bruce Jenkins, "Report on Meetings with U.S. Ambassador and Embassy Staff," Tunis, 23-March 24, 1989, unpublished paper, archives of the Albert Einstein Institution, Boston, 1989.

128 Richard E. Undeland, one-hour interview (Washington, D.C., May 27, 1998).

129 Awad, interview (February 14, 1995); Nye, communication (October 6, 1992); Said, interview (June 19, 1995); Sharp, interview (October 19, 1995). Seven years later, Arafat said there was no lasting impact from the delegation's visit. Arafat, interview (January 24, 1996).

130 Gene Sharp, "Notes on Strategic Problems of the Palestinian *Intifada,*" unpublished paper, archives of the Albert Einstein Institution, Boston, July 25, 1989, 10.

131 Barghouti, interview (January 25, 1996). Attempted infiltration, allegedly by Fateh, is described in Joshua Brilliant, "Terrorists Crossed Negev Border Carrying Uzis," *Jerusalem Post,* February 12, 1988, 1. Five months into the intifada, nearly one dozen attempts had been made by armed Palestinian units to infiltrate from Lebanon, resulting in the killing of three Israeli soldiers, according to Israeli sources. Glenn Frankel, "Two Israelis, Three Arabs Die in Gun Battle: Guerrillas Crossed Lebanese Border," *Washington Post,* April 27, 1988; Ian Black, "Israel Kills Group of Armed Palestinian Infiltrators," *Guardian,* March 3, 1989, 12; Seale, "Undermining the *Intifada,*" in *Abu Nidal,* 262-267; Al Venter, "Stopping Infiltrators-On Patrol with the Israeli Navy," *International Defense Review* 22, no. 10 (October 1, 1989): 10.

132 Sharp, "Notes on Strategic Problems," 11.

133 Ibid., 13.

134 Ibid., 16.

135 Ibid., 12, 16.

136 Ibid., 15.

137 Ibid., 12-13; Sharp, "Intifadah and Nonviolent Struggle," 8-11.

138 Gene Sharp, "The *Intifada* and Nonviolent Struggle: An Assessment and Notes on Strategic Problems," unpublished paper, Cambridge, Massachusetts: Albert Einstein Institution, March 1989, 7.

139 Sharp, *Civilian-Based Defense,* 95.

140 Sharmine Narwani, "Israeli Legislators Enter Talks with Pro-PLO Palestinians," Reuters, April 5, 1990; Aboudi, "Palestinians to Reach Out."

141 As cited in Aboudi, "Palestinians to Reach Out."

142 Ibid.

143 Ian Black, "Consumed by the Lava of Hatred," *Guardian,* May 26, 1990, 23; Edward Cody, "Arafat Urges UN to Shield Palestinians," *International Herald Tribune,* May 26-27, 1990, 1; "Arab Massacre Evokes Little Israeli Remorse," *Atlanta Journal and Constitution,* May 28, 1990, 12.

144 Ian Black, David Hirst, and Wafa Amr, "Arabs Die in Protests at Massacre," *Guardian,* May 22, 1990, 1; Ian Black, "Killings Stir Israeli Arabs to Unaccustomed Anger," *Guardian,* May 23, 1990, 8; "Israeli Group Faults Army for Shooting," *Boston Globe,* June 4, 1990, 16.

145 Ashrawi, *This Side of Peace,* 64-68.

146 Ibid., 66.

147 Kaufman, communication (March 17, 1997).

148 Kuttab, interview (March 18, 1997).

149 Cody, "Arafat Urges UN"; George D. Moffett III, "Palestinian Hunger Strike Prompts Discussion at UN of Shooting Incident," *Christian Science Monitor,* May 25, 1990.

150 Timothy M. Phelps, "Betrayed in Their Hunger for Peace," *Newsday,* June 3, 1990, 13.

151 Abul Abbas was infamous as head of the Iraqi-backed extremist splinter group, the Palestine Liberation Front (PLF), which was responsible for the October 1985 *Achille Lauro* cruise ship hijacking and murder of Leon Klinghoffer, a sixty-nine-year-old disabled American Jew on board, whose crippled body was thrown into the sea. Patrick Seale maintains that Arafat could not control the Abul Abbas group. Seale, *Abu Nidal,* 50, 77, 238.

152 Phelps, "Betrayed in Their Hunger for Peace," 13.

153 Ibid.

154 As cited in Ashrawi, *This Side of Peace,* 67.

155 The first call to violence appears in Leaflet no. 6 of February 2, 1988. Mishal and Aharoni, *Speaking*

Stones, 288. Leaflet no. 6 contains a list of calls to strike, refrain from working in Israeli settlements, resign from jobs with occupation authorities, form merchants' committees, abstain from paying taxes, and promote local industry and home economy. Last on the list is the following: "Respond in a revolutionary manner to the [Israeli] policy of beating and breaking [bones] by escalating the war of Molotov cocktails and stones." Lockman and Beinin, *Intifada*, 335. This seventh and last point does not appear in the version published in Nicosia by Ibal Publishing, an organ associated with the PLO. *No Voice Is Louder*, 30-33.

156 The Palestine National Fund was established by the same May 28, 1964, Palestine National Congress that set up the PLO. Its purpose was to finance the organization through annual subscriptions paid by each Palestinian over eighteen years of age, loans, contributions, and bonds. Kadi, "Armed Resistance," 132.

157 Patrick Seale, "Paymasters Desert Beleaguered Arafat," *Observer*, June 22, 1986, 13. For an account of Jaweed al-Ghussein, see Shawn Tully, "The Big Moneymen of Palestine, Inc.," *Fortune*, July 31, 1989, 113-14.

158 "PLO to Advocate Civil Disobedience in Occupied Territories," *al-Fajr*, June 23, 1986.

159 Abd al-Fatth Hamayl, two-hour interview (Ramallah, January 25, 1996).

160 Jamal, *Palestinian National Movement*, 69, 62.

161 Words of a Fateh leader in Oslo, as cited in Jabber, "Palestinian Resistance and Inter-Arab Politics," in Quandt, Jabber, and Lesch, *Politics of Palestinian Nationalism*, 197 n. 18.

162 Husayni, Interview, 8.

163 Fatah Political Platform, Fifth General Congress, Tunis, August 8, 1989, in Lukacs, *Israeli- Palestinian Conflict*, 441.

164 Nusseibeh, interview (January 28, 1996).

165 Afif Safieh, "The PLO: The Challenge and the Response," reprint of a paper presented in Colombo, Sri Lanka, August 1981, in *One People Too Many?* ed. Afif Safieh (The Hague: PLO Office, 1988), 7; idem, "Dead Ends?" reprint, lecture offered at MIT, January 1986, in ibid., 31.

166 Mannings and Hiltermann, "Strategies of Palestinian Resistance," 19; Manuel Hassassian, "From Armed Struggle to Negotiation," *Palestine-Israel Journal* 1 (Winter 1994): 273.

167 Sayigh, "Palestinian Armed Struggle," 103.

168 Sayigh, ibid., 104-5; idem, "Armed Struggle and Palestinian Nationalism," in Sela and Maoz, *PLO and Israel*, 31

169 Published self-criticism was exceedingly uncommon, yet a rare instance was the admission by Abu Iyad: "the main cause of our failure has been our ignorance of western society and of the complex democratic mechanisms that operate there." Abu Iyad (Salah Khalaf), "Al-Fatah's Autocriticism," reprinted from Abu Iyad, *Palestinien sans Patrie* (Paris: Editions Fayolle, 1979), *Guerrilla Strategies: An Historical Anthology from the Long March to Afghanistan*, ed. Gérard Chaliand (Berkeley: University of California Press, 1982), 326.

170 Name withheld, interview (West Bank, 1996).

171 Dan Fisher, "Six Killed in Hijacking of Israeli Bus; Three Civilians Slain; Three Arab Gunmen Die in Assault by Police," *Los Angeles Times*, March 8, 1988, 1. The phrase *white revolution*, in wide use in the territories, was intended to evoke a clean image of innocent civilians rising up. Nusseibeh explains, "It is white in the sense that its value lies in the fact that it is unarmed." Jeffrey Bartholet, "Hijacking Blackens Palestinian 'White Revolution,'" Reuters, March 8, 1988. Fateh took responsibility for the Dimona action. Ibid.; Andrew Whitley, "PLO Raid In Israel Leaves Six Dead," *Financial Times*, March 8, 1988, 44.

172 Yoram Kessel, "'Attack Was PLO Bid to Get Back in Picture'; Rabin after Three Hostages Die in Negev Bus Hijacking," *Jerusalem Post*, March 8, 1988, 1.

173 Reports from a 1986 conference in Amman on Arab nonviolent struggle circulated inside the territories, yet it is doubtful that they had any impact on the PLO in Tunis. Lamis K. Andoni and Fred Donovan, "Scholars, Activists Hold Lively Discussions on Aspects of Nonviolent Political Struggle," *Jordan Times*, November 16, 1986; Lamis K. Andoni and Fred Donovan, "Conference on Nonviolent Political Struggle Continues with Case Studies of Civil Resistance," *Jordan Times*, November 17, 1986; Jonathan Kuttab, interview (November 5, 1994). At the session, Iraqi political scientist Khalid Kishtaini presented ten arguments against the supposition that Islamic and Arab culture is based on a history of wars and conquests. Lamis K. Andoni and Fred Donovan, "ATF [Arab Thought Forum] Conference on Nonviolent Political Struggle Concludes," *Jordan Times*, November 18, 1986. There, Gene Sharp presented a paper on the dispersal of the loci of power. Sharp, *Role of Power in Nonviolent Struggle*. The East Jerusalem activist intellectuals drew reinforcement from reports of the conference. Kuttab, interview (November 5, 1994).

174 Ahmad, "Arafat's Nightmare," 22.

175 Sari Nusseibeh, "How to Influence Israel," *Newsweek*, March 28, 1988.

176 Several representatives on the various iterations of the Command looked upon the intifada as a step toward armed struggle. "There was always a problem about how to view it," Sari Nusseibeh recalled; "If you ask the question, what was the intifada? I don't think you'll find an answer, because it was different for different people. This reflected itself in the fights that took place between the various leaflet writers—to introduce this word, not this word." Nusseibeh, interview (January 28, 1996).

177 In December 1988 in the territories, the PFLP issued a pamphlet calling for the resumption of armed struggle. In a handout that contradicted Leaflet no. 29 from the Command, it stated its opposition to the PNC's acceptance of UN Security Council Resolutions 242 and 338. By February 1990, the Damascus-based leadership was issuing a call for Palestinians to take up arms against Israeli soldiers, despite the significant gains that had been made in Western sympathy by the restraint of the intifada. Daoud Kuttab, "The Loser and Winners after the Declaration of Independence," dispatch filed with news media, East Jerusalem, November 1988, Kuttab private papers; Shindler, *Ploughshares into Swords?* 230; Tony Walker, "After the Violence Comes Civil Disobedience," *Financial Times*, February 26, 1988, 3. When other anti-Arafat Damascus-based factions, such as Ahmad Jabril's PFLP-GC, intensified attempts at cross-border operations, Arafat stated that he opposed guerrilla raids from southern Lebanon; a few days later, he said they were a justifiable form of resistance. DFLP members also reportedly agitated for armed struggle. Moffett, "Arafat the Ambivalent," 3.

178 Raja Shehadeh, "Occupier's Law and the Uprising," *Journal of Palestine Studies* 67 (Spring 1988): 29. See also al-Haq, *Punishing a Nation; Nation under Siege* (Ramallah: al-Haq, 1990).

179 As cited in Lewis and Cygielman, "Only the Intifada Ensures the Political Process," 29. A visit to West Bank villages by 2,500 Israelis on May 27, 1989, showed the adherence by most Palestinians to nonviolent discipline. "Peace meetings" organized by Peace Now, and arranged in cooperation with local Palestinian activists, were held at Nahalin, south of Bethlehem (where five men had been killed in a bloody pre-dawn raid by Israeli border police a month earlier); Ein Yabrud and Turmus Aiya, north of Ramallah, and at Jabel Mukaber, in East Jerusalem. "Car convoys of activists, displaying Peace Now signs in Hebrew and Arabic, were greeted with waves and V-signs by Palestinian onlookers." Joel Greenberg and Larry Derfner, "Peace Now Convoys Warmly Greeted by Palestinians: Bitter Memories and Open Arms," *Jerusalem Post*, May 28, 1989. Dozens of Israeli peace activists drove into hamlets that had been witnessing violent retaliation from their own army, as the villagers embraced the Israelis. Glenn Frankel, "Palestinians Divide on Use of Arms and Israeli Vote Initiative," *Washington Post*, June 15, 1989, A29.

180 Daoud Kuttab, untitled dispatch to news media, East Jerusalem, approximately March 10, 1988, Kuttab private papers.

181 *Independent*, May 12 and 23, 1988, as cited in David McDowall, *Palestine and Israel: The Uprising and Beyond* (Berkeley: University of California Press, 1989), 15, 270 n. 57.

182 Husseini, "Husseini Speaks Out: The Intifada and Public Opinion," 25.

183 "Political Communiqué," Nineteenth Palestine National Council, November 15, 1988, *Journal of Palestine Studies* 70 (Winter 1989): 219.

184 Kuttab, untitled two-page dispatch filed with news media, East Jerusalem, November 1988, Kuttab private papers.

185 Victor Cygielman, "Obsolete Slogans Block Understanding," *New Outlook*, March 1990, 38, 39. Cygielman was Israeli correspondent to *Le Nouvel Observateur*. See "Fatah Calls for More Armed Action, Says Pullback Must Come before Poll," *Jerusalem Post*, August 9, 1988. "Fatah Political Platform," Fifth General Congress, Tunis, August 8, 1989 (excerpts), in Lukacs, *Israeli-Palestinian Conflict*, 441.

186 Khalaf, "Lowering the Sword," 104.

187 In an interview, the PFLP's leader, George Habash, was asked why the Palestinians did not differentiate between military and civilian targets as had armed postcolonial revolutionary insurgencies in other parts of the world. His response shows the unmethodical agglomeration of oppositional strategies: "Between 1945 and 1965, the Palestinians tried to fight by all means. Now the PLO in general concentrates on diplomatic struggle, political struggle, and armed struggle *inside* Palestine, not in Europe." George Habash, two-hour interview (Damascus, June 12, 1988).

188 Dajani, "Formulation of a Strategy of Nonviolent Civilian Resistance," 42.

189 Two Israeli soldiers were killed in an ambush in Gaza in November 1989, the first operation of its kind; Palestinian sources did not deny Israel's claim that the attack had been carried out by Fateh, signifying a breakdown in adherence to the intifada strategy. Assad Saftawi, a Fateh leader in Gaza, told Timothy Phelps, "The more extremist organizations gave us a chance two years ago to achieve

something for the Palestinian people. . . . [T]he moderate Palestinian line didn't achieve anything and this creates danger for this line and opens a big gate for the extremists." Timothy M. Phelps, "Grim Forecast on Uprising; As Intifada Enters Third Year, Fears that Guns Will Replace Stones," *Newsday*, December 9, 1989, 7.

190 Jonathan Wright, "Radical Palestinians Recommend Military Action against Israel," Reuters, October 12, 1990; Frankel, "Palestinians Divide," A29. By late 1990, Fateh, the PCP, and the DFLP maintained they wanted the intifada to remain a mass movement and feared harsher repression if Palestinians started shooting Israelis; the Command sanctioned the killing of Israeli soldiers in the territories, although not specifically recommending shooting them. This came in response to the October 8, 1990, shooting and deaths of twenty-one Palestinians by Israeli police on Jerusalem's Temple Mount and Haram al-Sharif. The UN Security Council on October 12 adopted U.S.-backed Resolution 672 criticizing Israel for the killings. Reuters, "Security Council Disregards Attack on Jewish Worshippers," *Jerusalem Post*, October 15, 1990.

191 Ian Black, "Signs of Intifada Turning to Arms," *Guardian*, December 4, 1990, 13. Such moves were led by the PFLP, Hamas, and a minority in Fateh, and were opposed by the communists, the DFLP, and some in Fateh.

192 Souad Dajani, "Nonviolent Resistance in the Occupied Territories: A Critical Reevaluation," in *Nonviolent Social Movements: A Geographical Perspective*, ed. Stephen Zunes, Lester R. Kurtz, and Sarah Beth Asher (Oxford: Blackwell Publishers, 1999), 57.

193 Nusseibeh, interview (January 28, 1996).

194 Malki, interview (May 3, 1995).

195 Eyad Sarraj, "Torture and Mental Health: The Experience of Palestinians in Israeli Prisons" (Gaza City, Gaza Community Mental Health Program, 1993); idem, "Rehabilitation of Ex-Political Prisoners" (Gaza City, Gaza Community Mental Health Program, April 17-18, 1994); Samir Quta, Raija-Leena Punamäki, and Eyad Sarraj, "House Demolitions and Mental Health: Victims and the Witnesses" (Gaza City, Gaza Community Mental Health Program, 1993); Eyad Sarraj and Samir Quta, "Relations between Traumatic Experiences, Activity, and Cognitive and Emotional Responses among Palestinian Children" (Gaza City, Gaza Community Mental Health Program, 1993). In July 1995, Israeli prime minister and defense minister Yitzhak Rabin granted that eight thousand Palestinians had been subjected to "violent shaking" during interrogations by Israel's General Security Services. Serge Schmemann, "In Israel, Coercing Prisoners Is Becoming Law of the Land," *New York Times*, May 8, 1997, 10. B'Tselem emphasizes the banal character of torture as used on approximately 850 Palestinians annually. Yuval Ginbar, *Routine Torture: Interrogation Methods of the General Security Service* (Jerusalem: B'Tselem, 1998). See Allegra Pacheco, "Israeli Justice on Torture: A Shining Light unto the Nations?" *Notes from Within* 12 (December 1996): 11.

196 Daniel Williams, "Intifada Showing Signs of Failure, Discontent; Israel: Arabs Display Unhappiness at Mounting Physical and Economic Losses," *Los Angeles Times*, July 22, 1990, A1. Palestinian journalist Hamdi Farraj said, "When the *intifada* began, the slogan was 'No voice speaks louder than the *intifada*.' But as [time] went on . . . the PLO did not give local leaders the freedom to do what we wanted. Now, we are in a state of waiting." Ibid.

197 Greenberg, "After a Month of Siege, Kabatiya Faces a Grim Life."

198 Glenn Frankel, "Collaborator's Death Jolts Arabs and Israelis; Attack May Signal End of Arrangements Used to Control Occupied Territories," *Washington Post*, March 1, 1988, A1.

199 David Hoffman, "Collaborators Terrified of Palestinian Rule: Israeli-Protected Village of Informers Fears It Will Be Left to Fend for Itself," *Washington Post*, September 27, 1993, A13. Based on studies of occupied Europe in World War II, Andrew Rigby makes a comparison: "It is impossible to live under occupation without some form of collaboration with the occupier. . . . In Belgium, with a population of 8 million, 300,000 were investigated for collaboration. In Holland, with a population of 9.2 million, over 250,000 people were investigated. In each occupied country hundreds of thousands were suspected of collaboration." Andrew Rigby, "The Phenomenon of Collaborators," in *The Phenomenon of Collaborators in Palestine* (East Jerusalem: PASSIA, 2001), 9.

200 Kathy Bergen, David Neuhaus, and Ghassan Rubeiz, *Justice and the Intifada: Palestinians and Israelis Speak Out* (New York: Friendship Press, 1991), 31.

201 Black and Morris, *Israel's Secret Wars*, 253-55, 395, 398, 475-79.

202 Jeffrey Goldberg, "Stranger in a Strange Land," *Jerusalem Post*, December 27, 1991.

203 Ian Black, "Sari Nusseibeh," *Guardian*, March 4, 1991.

204 Ian Black, "PLO Fights Islamic Rivals in Gaza's Uncivil Little War," *Guardian*, July 9, 1992, 24.

205 Hoffman, "Collaborators Terrified of Palestinian Rule," A13.

206 David Hoffman, "'Collaborator' Deaths Blamed on Both Sides," *Washington Post*, December 1, 1994, A12.

207 Immanuel, "Hamas, Fatah Agree to 'Regulate' Informer Killings"; Beer and Abdel-Jawad, *Collaborators*, 167. Feisel Husseini states "mistakes" were made and the Command's reluctance to declare itself clearly led to increased killings in appendices, ibid., 213-15.

208 Neil MacFarquhar, "Palestinian Self-Rule Drives Informers from Homes," *Washington Times*, February 20, 1994, A6.

209 Hiltermann, "Enemy Inside," 230.

210 Nusseibeh, interview (November 5, 1994); Immanuel, "Sari Nusseibeh: Palestinians Wrong."

211 Awad, *Nonviolence*. General strikes could also backfire, as in the Old City of Jerusalem, when some Israelis used strike days to take over Palestinian shops and property.

212 Nusseibeh, interview (July 5, 1994).

213 Clyde Haberman, "Strike! Strike! Strike! Some Arabs Feel Cudgeled," *New York Times*, June 4, 1993.

214 Yehuda Litani, "Fear Stalks the Streets," *Jerusalem Post*, September 8, 1989.

215 Black, "Signs of Intifada Turning to Arms," 13; idem, "War of Stones Becomes a War of Guns," 10.

216 Idem, "Tension High," 8.

217 Nusseibeh, interview (January 28, 1996). Paul Taylor, "Rifts Emerge among Palestinians as Uprising Stagnates," Reuters, April 1, 1990. The PFLP began publishing its own leaflets saying that Palestinians should form a new "national front" to oppose peace talks and initiate new civil disobedience drives to force Israel out of the territories. They attacked the idea that a united Jerusalem should be the capital for both Israel and a Palestinian state—suggested by Feisel Husseini and Sari Nusseibeh—and called upon Israel's 650,000 Arab citizens to join the intifada, something the PLO had taken pains not to do. Jackson Diehl, "Palestinians Split on U.S. Plan for Talks with Israel," *Washington Post*, April 14, 1990, A10; Taylor, "Rifts Emerge."

218 Siniora, interview (December 16, 1997).

219 George D. Moffett III, "After Two Years, Palestinians Dig In for War of Attrition," *Christian Science Monitor*, December 8, 1989; Michel G. Jubran, "The PLO's Inner Struggle," *Christian Science Monitor*, May 5, 1992, 18. By 1992, Sari Nusseibeh would warn that the intifada no longer had a general strategy as in the first two years, a judgment made at the very moment, Ian Black notes, that Israelis had accepted the "permanence" of Palestinian resistance and half the Israeli populace conceded that there was no military solution. Bronner, "Intifadah Five Years Later," 2; Ian Black, "Five Years On, the Intifada Is Losing Its Way," *Guardian*, December 10, 1992, 10.

220 Jon Immanuel, "Curfew Taking Toll on Areas' Economy," *Jerusalem Post*, January 14, 1991; Jonathan Ferziger, "Palestinians Still under Wartime Curfew," UPI, March 4, 1991.

221 Jon Immanuel, "Post-War Palestinian Problematics," *Jerusalem Post*, January 25, 1991. In September 1991, Khaled al-Hassan, who chaired the PNC's foreign relations committee, told a Saudi newspaper, "Our policy in the Gulf War had destructive results, most prominently being . . . deadly isolation, especially in Europe." Immanuel, "Kill Sellers of Jerusalem Property."

222 Kaufman, "Potential Impact of Palestinian Nonviolent Struggle on Israel."

223 Don Peretz, "The Impact of the Gulf War on Israeli and Palestinian Political Attitudes," *Journal of Palestine Studies* (Autumn 1991): 18.

224 Jon Immanuel, "Abdel-Shafi—From Chief Pessimist to Chief Executive?" *Jerusalem Post*, August 25, 1993.

225 Tony Walker and Hugh Carnegy, "The Middle East; Baker Hears All the Old Tunes on Peace Merry-Go-Round," *Financial Times*, March 14, 1991.

226 Ibid.

227 Jackson Diehl, "Mideast Peace Bid By Baker Faces Tough Obstacles," *Washington Post*, March 5, 1991, A12.

228 Glenn Frankel, "PLO Asserting Control of Palestinian Uprising: Violence Shifts to Organized Campaign," *Washington Post*, February 20, 1988, A1; Jonathan Randal, "Uprisings Invigorate PLO Leaders; Movement's Future Still Held Uncertain," *Washington Post*, February 25, 1988, A39.

229 Kuttab, "Confidence to Make Concessions."

230 Glenn Frankel, "Divided They Stand," *Washington Post Magazine*, October 30, 1994. When Leaflet no. 40 of May 22, 1989, called for an Israeli settler or soldier to be killed for each dead Palestinian, the appeal was retracted the following day in a PLO statement from Tunis, after a telephone call from a group meeting at Husseini's home expressed the dismay of local Fateh leaders. Idem, "Palestinians Divide on Use of Arms and Israeli Vote Initiative," *Washington Post*, June 15, 1989, A29.

231 Frankel, "Divided They Stand."

232 Joel Greenberg, "Where Is the *Intifada* Heading?" *Moment* (Washington, D.C.), June 1989, 41-42.

233 Harriet Lewis and Thea Cygielman, "Only the Intifada Ensures the Political Process," interview of Ziad Abu Zayyad, *New Outlook*, November-December 1989, 29.

234 Nusseibeh, "True People's Revolution," 18.

235 Jadallah, interview (December 15, 1997).

236 Husayni, Interview, 13.

237 Although the right to representation by the PLO was first acknowledged by the Arab states at the Rabat, Morocco, summit in 1974, Jordanian acquiescence to the PLO as the sole legitimate representative of the Palestinian people was not fully accepted until the intifada impressed upon King Hussein the prudence of cutting ties between Jordan and the West Bank, which he did on July 31, 1988. Rashid Khalidi, "The Palestinian People: Twenty-Two Years after 1967," in Lockman and Beinin, *Intifada*, 114.

238 Soon after the intifada PNC, Abu Iyad said, "We Arabs have nothing other than this *intifada* in our hands. Through it we reactivate political action." Salah Khalaf, *Ukaz* (Jeddah), November 12, 1989, FBIS-NES, November 27, 1989, 5.

239 Sari Nusseibeh, "Freedom, the Person and the Nation," paper presented at the University of Pavia, Italy, May 1988, in Safieh, *Palestine*.

240 Arafat in March 1988 told an Egyptian newspaper that in the intifada, "We are acting in two stages: . . . half a civil rebellion, and finally a full civil rebellion." He menaced, "If afterwards, whatever we want to achieve won't be achieved, we will think of using arms also in the territories." Arafat was speaking to *al-Wafd* (the Delegation), named for the Wafd political party, as cited in Yehuda Litani, "PLO's 'Remote Control' Won't Determine Events in Uprising," *Jerusalem Post*, March 21, 1988, 1.

241 David Fairhall, "The Stone that Stunned David," *Guardian*, February 27, 1989, 23.

242 Imad al-Din Adeeb, interview of Yasir Arafat, from *al-Quds*, April 19, 1998, Orbit Satellite Television, trans. Joharah Baker, *Palestine Report* 4, no. 42 (April 24, 1998): 18.

243 Islamic Jihad threatened to kill the Palestinian activist intellectuals who met with Secretary of State Baker and singled out Feisel Husseini in particular. "Jihad Threatens to Kill Husseini," *Jerusalem Post*, August 5, 1991.

244 The masked youths (*mulathamin*), belonged to Fahd al-Aswad (the Black Panthers), a group founded in Nablus in 1989, reportedly an armed wing of Fateh, and the Red Eagles of the PFLP. The emergence of such gangs as a "freelance arm" of the intifada indicated loss of unity and cohesion, as chagrin with the meager fruits spread. "Fatah Calls West Bank Strike over Israeli Arrests," Reuters; George D. Moffett III, "Resistance Is a Way of Life in Battle-Scarred West Bank City of Nablus," *Christian Science Monitor*, December 10, 1989: A8; Ian Black, "Israelis Shoot Dead Four Black Panthers," *Guardian*, December 2, 1989, 9. Daoud Kuttab reports that when Black Panthers in Nablus killed nineteen collaborators, Arafat privately attempted to persuade them to disarm and appealed to them personally through the PLO's Baghdad-based radio, but they refused. Daoud Kuttab, "Beit Sahur Battles On," *Middle East International*, November 3, 1989, 10.

245 "Sharp: Nonviolent Struggle," interview by Afif Safieh, 45, 46.

246 Interviews (West Bank, December 1997).

247 Lucy Nusseibeh, interview (November 5, 1994).

248 Feisel Husseini called for Fateh to turn itself into a political party. Abdallah, "Fatah Torn."

249 Kuttab, "Two Years of *Intifada*," 15.

250 Jadallah, interview (December 15, 1997); Abd al-Hadi, interview (December 13, 1997).

Chapter 12

1 Where the first intifada is misperceived as a fundamentally violent phenomenon, or seen as but a phase of unending war against Israel, it is often considered to have ended in September 1993 with the signing of Oslo I.

2 Kuttab, "Second Phase, Self-Sufficiency," 43.

3 Avnery, "Intifada: Substance and Illusion," 12.

4 Nusseibeh, "Time for Palestinian Offensives," 17. See also George D. Moffett III, "Palestinians Set to Declare Territories Independent: Their Own State," *Christian Science Monitor*, November 10, 1988. The activist intellectuals had no interest in an exiled government and wanted a provisional government located in the territories, with the diasporan leadership as the titular heads outside. Sari Nusseibeh, as quoted in Greenberg, "Nusseibeh Wants Provisional Government Now." Regardless, a provisional government was never formed.

5 Changes were also occurring in Israeli discourse. "I knew the intifada was creating a transformation

on the Israeli side because, right up to the intifada, the words 'Palestinian state' were taboo on Israeli television," Nusseibeh recalled; "once the intifada began, suddenly 'Palestinian state' and 'Palestinian people' came into use." Nusseibeh, interview (July 5, 1994).

6 Said, "Intifada and Independence," in Lockman and Beinin, *Intifada*, 18; Khalidi, "Political Implications of the Uprising," 17; "Political Communiqué," Nineteenth Palestine National Council, 216-23.

7 Rolef, "Israel's Policy toward the PLO," in Sela and Maoz, *PLO and Israel*, 257.

8 Recognition of Israel was again avoided in Algiers in 1988 at the intifada PNC, to provide an umbrella broad enough to encompass George Habash, leader of the PFLP. The PFLP was opposed to the nonviolent strategies of the intifada but subsequently adhered to the PLO's decision to work for a two-state solution encompassing only part of historic Palestine, until 1990 when it again called for arms. At the 1991 PNC in Algiers, Arafat sought to bring Habash and Nayef Hawatmeh of the DFLP into agreement on participating in the international conference in Madrid. Feisel Husseini and Hanan Mikhail Ashrawi, forbidden by Israel to travel to Algeria for the PNC, did so secretly and reported on their numerous sessions with Secretary of State James Baker, part of the effort to bring along the PFLP and DFLP.

9 "Palestinian Declaration of Independence," Nineteenth Palestine National Council, November 15, 1988, *Journal of Palestine Studies* 70 (Winter 1989): 213.

10 Said, "Intifada and Independence," in Lockman and Beinin, *Intifada*, 18. Ziad Abu-Amr asserts that acceptance of Resolutions 242 and 338 showed the obsolescence of the 1964 document. "The uprising bailed the PLO out of an already faltering armed struggle." Ziad Abu-Amr, "The Politics of the Intifada," in Hudson, *Palestinians: New Directions*, 5, 6.

11 Henry Kissinger, "Israel and the PLO—Wishes and Reality," *Washington Post*, March 11, 1989, A19.

12 Joel Brinkley, "Peres Denounces Palestinian Move as a False Display of Moderation," *New York Times*, November 18, 1988, A14.

13 Bernard Mills, "The Uprising of Youth that Has Shaken Attitudes towards Israel," *Independent*, April 13, 1989, 26. Mills was formerly director of UNRWA in Gaza.

14 Nusseibeh, interview (November 5, 1994). On 242, also see Nusseibeh, "Personal Perspective."

15 "Survivor Plays His Last Card," *Observer Sunday*, December 18, 1988, 13.

16 Daoud Kuttab, "The Confidence to Make Concessions," dispatch to news media, East Jerusalem, November 1988, Kuttab private papers. See also idem, "A Palestinian Critique of Rabin's Peace Plan," *Christian Science Monitor*, March 2, 1989.

17 In 1988, Israel earned $850 million yearly from exports to a captive Palestinian market, plus $200 million from indirect taxes, Hanna Siniora writes in "An Analysis of the Current Revolt," *Journal of Palestine Studies* 67 (Spring 1988): 6. Israeli economic minister Gad Yaacobi put the cost of the first intifada to Israel during its initial quarter at $320 million. Whitley and Walker, "Shift from Stones to Sanctions," 20. By July 1988, Yaacobi estimated overall losses at more than $500 million. Glenn Frankel, "Uprising Casualty: The Quality of Life," *Washington Post*, July 25, 1988, A1. See also Ian Black, "Arab Unrest Takes Economic Toll," *Guardian*, March 4, 1988; George D. Moffett III, "Arab Uprising's Other Toll: To Fight Unrest, Israel Makes Palestinians Pay New and Higher Taxes," *Christian Science Monitor*, July 19, 1989.

18 As cited in Daoud Kuttab, "Six-Month Anniversary of the Intifadah," draft essay, East Jerusalem, May 1988, Kuttab private papers.

19 Kuttab, "Popular Teaching Begins in the Home," handwritten attachment.

20 Gal, interview (March 12, 1997).

21 By 1990, more states would recognize the Palestinian Declaration of Independence than had recognized Israel's. Ian J. Bickerton and Carla L. Klausner, *A Concise History of the Arab-Israeli Conflict* (Englewood Cliffs, N.J.: Prentice-Hall, 1991), 238.

22 Said, "Intifada and Independence," in Lockman and Beinin, *Intifada*, 17.

23 David Hirst, "A Passport to the World," *Guardian*, December 16, 1988. The meeting was held in Switzerland because the United States would not allow Arafat to travel to New York to deliver his remarks.

24 Yasir Arafat, speech to UN General Assembly, Geneva, December 13, 1988, in *Palestinian-Israeli Peace Agreement: A Documentary Record* (Washington, D.C., Institute for Palestine Studies, 1994), 283-97; Reuters, "Text of Statement by Arafat," *Washington Post*, December 15, 1988.

25 Leaflet no. 31 of December 22, 1988, welcomed the U.S. decision to talk to the PLO and declared it an "achievement of the *intifada*." Legrain, *Les Voix du Soulèvement Palestinien*, 241.

26 Roy Isacowitz, "Turmoil as Israel Seeks Response," *Sunday Times*, December 18, 1988, A17.

27 Avnery, "Intifada," 13. A Palestinian journalist argues the events in Geneva ignored the moral issue involved: "[T]the Palestinians are urged to recognize Israel's 'right to exist' before they are allowed

even to negotiate. Everyone has a right to exist. What the Palestinians challenge is Israel's right to Palestine." Hijab, "Palestinians Once Had a Land and Still Have Rights."

28 Rashid Khalidi, "The Resolutions of the 19th Palestine National Council," *Journal of Palestine Studies* 74 (Winter 1990): 33. Arafat himself revealed this point by acknowledging, "Neither Arafat, nor any [one else] for that matter, can stop the intifadah. . . . The intifadah will come to an end only when practical and tangible steps have been taken toward . . . establishment of our independent Palestinian state." Yasir Arafat, press conference statement, Geneva, December 14, 1988, in *Palestinian-Israeli Peace Agreement*, 298. Publicly, however, Arafat claimed participants in the intifada were merely obeying instructions, e.g., in their refusal to use weaponry: "This is a decision taken by myself and accepted in our leadership and . . . followed strictly by our masses and our people. We said no using arms in our intifada." Yasir Arafat, *MacNeil-Lehrer Newshour*, Public Broadcasting System, April 20, 1989, interview transcript of broadcast no. 3414, 3. In fact, the directional circuitry was the reverse.

29 For a firsthand account of these meetings, see Ashrawi, *This Side of Peace*, 81-94.

30 On Israel's barring Husseini from official membership on the Palestinian team, see Helm, "Pragmatist Will Speak for Palestinians," 12. Also see Michael Sheridan, "Middle East Conference: New Breed Who Will Plead Palestinian Case; The Collapse of Armed Struggle against Israel Has Shifted Influence towards a More Bourgeois Western-Educated Selection of Representatives," *Independent*, October 30, 1991, 10.

31 Shlaim, *Iron Wall*, 485, 488.

32 Said K. Aburish, *Arafat: From Defender to Dictator* (London, Bloomsbury, 1998), 233-42.

33 Sari Nuseibeh, "Palestinian Attitudes toward the Peace Process," *The Arab-Israeli Negotiations: Political Positions and Conceptual Framework*, ed. Robin Twite and Tamar Hermann (Tel Aviv: Papyrus Publishing House, 1993), 84-85.

34 Joel Greenberg, "Sticks and Stones Yield to War of Words," *Jerusalem Post*, November 15, 1991.

35 Ian Black, "Race on for Palestinian Autonomy; The Arabs Have Swapped Bullets for Paper in the Final Battle for Their Land," *Guardian*, August 1, 1992, 9. Established by Nuseibeh and Ziad Abu Zayyad, the political committees (separate from the technical committees), carried the "seeds of a Palestinian political structure and blueprints for autonomy." Jon Immanuel, "The Palestinians' 'Mainstream' Philosophy," *Jerusalem Post*, November 29, 1991; idem, "Nuseibeh to Replace Husseini in Talks," *Jerusalem Post*, December 29, 1991. See also Simon Edge, "Palestinians Plan for Self-Rule," *MEED Middle East Business Weekly*, November 20, 1992, 2.

36 Nuseibeh, communication (December 16, 1997). Yezid Sayigh says the purpose of the committees, under Arafat's sponsorship, was to limit the emergence of an autonomous power base and especially to circumscribe the influence of Feisel Husseini. Sayigh, *Armed Struggle and the Search for State*, 654. Arafat's contradictory instructions turned Nuseibeh and Husseini against each other. Aburish, *Arafat*, 236. The committees would later be disbanded. The only one not disbanded was the Women's Affairs Technical Committee, which retains its name and continues to be one of the most effective women's organizations, its value due to its cross-factional board of trustees, an intrinsic part of its original purpose.

37 Siniora, interview (December 16, 1997).

38 Lamia Lahoud, "United They Stand, Claim Disparate Palestinian Groups," *Jerusalem Post*, December 11, 1992.

39 Jon Immanuel, "Palestinian Returnees Accused of Connivance with US," *Jerusalem Post*, December 23, 1991.

40 Jon Immanuel, "UNL Leaflet no. 84 Attempts to Jump-Start Intifada, Condemns Rabin, Glorifies Stabbers," *Jerusalem Post*, July 6, 1992.

41 Jamal, *Palestinian National Movement*, 147.

42 Shlaim, *Iron Wall*, 511.

43 Khatib, interview (December 15, 1997).

44 Pappé, *History of Modern Palestine*, 242.

45 The Oslo process started informally with Israeli academician Yair Hirschfeld, who met in December 1992 in London with Afif Safieh, now representative of the PLO in Washington, and PLO treasurer Ahmad Qurei (Abu Ala). What became a back channel to Israel with Hirschfeld and Ron Pundik, another Israeli, was kept strictly confidential—Yossi Beilin was initially the sole Israeli official aware of the meetings. Prime Minister Yitzhak Rabin and Shimon Peres were informed after the first round. Hilde Henriksen Waage, "Norway's Role in the Middle East Peace Talks: Between a Strong State and a Weak Belligerent," *Journal of Palestine Studies* 136 (Summer 2005): 8. Yasir Arafat and Mahmoud Abbas monitored for the Palestinians. The talks became official when Uri Savir, director general of

the foreign ministry, became the chief negotiator for the Israelis, soon joined by Yoel Singer, an attorney with 20 years' experience in the IDF legal department. Ibid., 10. Abu Ala became the key Palestinian negotiator. President Jimmy Carter was the first American to be informed, or so said Arafat, when he flew to Yemen specifically to enlighten the former U.S. chief at the end of August 1993. Later the U.S. State Department and President Clinton were informed by Peres. Carter was in Sanaa to deliver a lecture on human rights and democracy. The author was the third person present.

46 Mahmoud Abbas (Abu Mazen), *Through Secret Channels* (Reading, England: Garnet Publishing, 1995), 113, 114-15.

47 A study by the foreign minister on civilian-based defense germane to this inquiry is Johan Jørgen Holst, *Civilian-Based Defense in a New Era*, Monograph Series no. 2 (Cambridge, Massachusetts: Albert Einstein Institution, 1990).

48 Waage, "Norway's Role," 14. "Holst was not only the messenger, passing on to the Palestinians what the Israelis told him to pass on, but also the formulator." Ibid.

49 Waage, "Norway's Role," 14-15.

50 Shehadeh, *From Occupation to Interim Accords*, 104-31, 157-169, esp. 127-31, 161-169.

51 Haider Abd al-Shafi, "Looking Back, Looking Forward: An Interview," *Journal of Palestine Studies* 125 (Autumn 2002): 28-35. The conceptual framework for the Israel-PLO accord was developed "without the knowledge of the official Israeli and Palestinian negotiators," then decamped in Washington. Avi Shlaim, "The Rise and Fall of the Oslo Peace Process," in *International Relations of the Middle East*, ed. Louise Fawcett (Oxford: Oxford University Press, 2005), 242. That team was intentionally ignored by the PLO leadership. Rashid Khalidi, *The Iron Cage: The Story of the Palestinian Struggle for Statehood* (Boston: Beacon Press, 2006), 161.

52 Jamal, *Palestinian National Movement*, 102.

53 Anthony Lewis, "Albright Can End the Leadership Vacuum in the Middle East," *International Herald Tribune*, August 16-17, 1997. See Serge Schmemann, "U.S. Mediators Get Support from Two Israeli Ex-Officials; Shimon Peres Backs the Creation of a Palestinian State by May 1999," *New York Times*, April 27, 1998, A8.

54 See Shimon Peres, *The New Middle East* (New York, Henry Holt and Company, 1993).

55 Shlaim, *Iron Wall*, 515.

56 Barton Gellman, "West Bank Pact Eases Way for Palestinian Statehood," *Washington Post*, September 27, 1995, A1.

57 Daniel Rubinstein, thirty-minute communication (Washington, D.C., October 17, 1993).

58 Pappé, *History of Modern Palestine*, 244.

59 Ibid.

60 Jadallah, interview (December 15, 1997).

61 Jon Immanuel, "Sari Nusseibeh: Palestinians Wrong to Rely on America," *Jerusalem Post*, March 19, 1993, 10.

62 Joel Greenberg, "Palestinian Offers Idea: Get Israelis On Our Side," *New York Times*, October 17, 2001; Clyde Haberman, " 'Pragmatic Palestinian' Draws Road Map to Peace," *New York Times*, December 23, 2001. Disenchantment often follows a popular upsurge. Guillermo A. O'Donnell and Philippe C. Schmitter, "Tentative Conclusions about Uncertain Democracies," *Transitions from Authoritarian Rule: Prospects for Democracy*, ed. Guillermo A. O'Donnell, Philippe C. Schmitter, and Lawrence Whitehead (Baltimore: Johns Hopkins University Press, 1986), pt. 4, 55-56.

63 Balfour, "11 August 1919 Memorandum," 132187/2117/44A, in Woodward and Butler, *Documents on British Foreign Policy*, 345.

64 Pressburg, interview (June 12, 1998). Numerous sources corroborate Pressburg's summation.

65 Simon, *Gramsci's Political Thought*, 24; Bobbio, "Gramsci and the Concept of Civil Society," 91-93.

66 Carnoy, *State and Political Theory*, 71.

67 Gramsci, *Selections from the Prison Notebooks*, 1971), esp. 3-23. Also see Simon, *Gramsci's Political Thought*, 18-19.

68 Simon, *Gramsci's Political Thought*, 93.

69 Ibid., 27, 73.

70 Ibid., 94.

71 Keith Tester, *Civil Society* (London: Routledge, 1992), 125.

72 Jean L. Cohen and Andrew Arato, *Civil Society and Political Theory: Studies in Contemporary German Social Thought* (Cambridge: Massachusetts Institute of Technology [MIT] Press, 1994), 566, 567.

73 The 1996 and 2006 Palestinian elections show development of such norms. The significance of elections ultimately lies in their meaning for the participating population. The Palestinian people,

including now Hamas, normatively accept balloting as the formal mechanism for bringing about institutionalized political change.

74 Wing, "Embryonic Self-Rule," 95-153, esp. pp. 98, 131, and 153.

75 Rema Hammami, "Palestinian NGOs since Oslo: From Politics to Social Movements?" in Beinin and Stein, eds., *Struggle for Sovereignty*, 86.

76 Robinson, *Palestinian Leadership in Transition?*

77 Charles Tilly, *From Mobilization to Revolution* (Reading, Massachusetts: Addison-Wesley, 1978), 54, 55.

78 Kaufman and Abed, "Relevance of Democracy to Israeli-Palestinian Peace," 47. Michael Walzer observes, "The civility that makes democratic politics possible can only be learned in the associational networks." Walzer, "Idea of Civil Society," 302.

79 O'Donnell and Schmitter, "Tentative Conclusions about Uncertain Democracies," in O'Donnell, Schmitter, and Whitehead, *Transitions from Authoritarian Rule*, pt. 4, 49-56.

80 Zvi Gilat, "The Leadership of the Uprising," *New Outlook*, March-April 1988, 13.

81 Joel Greenberg, "Notes from an Uprising," *Jerusalem Post*, February 12, 1988, 6. Global communications have lifted cloaks of secrecy in the Middle East. Augustus Richard Norton, "Toward Enduring Peace in the Middle East," in Fernea and Hocking, *Struggle for Peace*, 319. On the other hand, alternative institutions such as popular committees lacked the visual motion sought for television news. Stones thrown by children, however, made good daily footage, and they learned that if they threw stones, camera crews would rapidly appear.

82 Barton Gellman, "Palestinians Await Release of Prisoners," *Washington Post*, October 3, 1995, A12. Gellman cites Israeli official government sources for this figure, yet some may have been jailed more than once.

83 By 1992, Sarah Helm notes, virtually every family in the West Bank and Gaza had someone in an Israeli prison. Sarah Helm, "Palestinian Prisoners' Strike Fuels Violence," *Independent*, October 12, 1992, 12.

84 Illegal under Israeli statutes and the more than one thousand military orders promulgated after 1967 were most of the 198 nonviolent methods tabulated by Gene Sharp in 1973.

85 Hoffman, "Amid Setbacks, Slow Change in Israeli Attitudes," 1.

86 Awad, "Nonviolence" (excerpts in appendices, p. 349).

87 Kaufman, "Potential Impact of Palestinian Nonviolent Struggle on Israel."

88 Sayigh, "Armed Struggle and Palestinian Nationalism," 33. Also see Sayigh, *Armed Struggle and the Search for State*. While respectful of the scale of Sayigh's inquiry—in which the PLO is viewed as the non-territorial equivalent of a statist entity—the account here challenges his conclusion that armed struggle and the militarization of Palestinian society helped to "rebuild societal structure and reconstitute the body politic," enabling nation building. Ibid., 34. An altogether different historical instance of state formation is offered here. Sayigh correctly notes that during the 1980s and prior to the first intifada, the PLO viewed the populace of the territories as a target for co-optation. Yet, while cognizant of the growth of voluntary nongovernmental formations based on popular participation, he considers this an outgrowth of the work of leftists and critics of the PLO. A different reality prevailed, seen here. In addition to the communists and unaffiliated professionals who were trailblazers throughout the 1980s, Fateh-affiliated figures also played crucial roles in the several movements that preceded the intifada, e.g., Qaddourah Faris's successive yearly election to be leader of the prisoners' movement in chapter 6, and Sari Nusseibeh's roles in the student and faculty unions in chapter 8. Sayigh misses the breadth of such social mobilization, including women's organizing (which he admits), and does not recognize formative cognitive redefinition of concepts and symbols by Feisel Husseini. Nor does he note that open elections were slowly replacing clandestine military leadership training, although he fleetingly acknowledges that the stress on armed struggle, despite the persistency of its failures, led to "hostile disregard" for nonviolent resistance; Mubarak Awad's work appears in one footnote. Ibid., 612-13.

89 Muhammad Hallaj, "The Challenge of Life," *Journal of Refugee Studies* 2, no. 1 (1989): 18.

90 See Alfred Stepan, "State Power and the Strength of Civil Society in the Southern Cone of Latin America," *Bringing the State Back In*, ed. Peter B. Evans, Dietrich Rueschemeyer, and Theda Skocpol (Cambridge: Cambridge University Press, 1985), 317-43; Schmitter, "Introduction to Southern European Transitions," in O'Donnell, Schmitter, and Whitehead, *Transitions from Authoritarian Rule*, pt. 1, 6.

91 By rejecting the British White Paper of May 1939, an argument goes, Palestinians sacrificed their chances for an Arab state in Palestine. For examples, see Rubin, *Revolution until Victory?* 184-85; Quandt, "Political and Military Dimensions," 45.

92 Porath, "United Uprising," 7. Porath also notes, "Perhaps in 1937, they could have accepted [the Peel

Commission] proposals, which spoke of a Jewish state on 15 percent of Palestine's land and allocated 80 percent of the land to the Arabs. Maybe they could have and should have accepted this." Ibid.

93 Sharp, "*Intifada* and Nonviolent Struggle: An Assessment and Notes on Strategic Problems," 7. Nafez Assaily makes the same point in "The *Intifada* and Civil Resistance Strategies," paper presented at the conference "Nonviolent Possibilities for the Palestinian-Israeli Conflict," sponsored by Palestinians and Israelis for Nonviolence, Notre Dame, East Jerusalem, September 7-8, 1993, 2, 3.

94 As quoted in Ian Black, "Quiet but Not at Peace," *Guardian*, March 2, 1990, 10.

95 Z. A. Pelczynski, "Solidarity and 'The Rebirth of Civil Society' in Poland," in Keane, *Civil Society and the State: New European Perspectives*, 361ff.

96 John Feffer, "Uncivil Society," *In These Times*, November 15, 1993, 28.

97 In Poland in the 1970s, the Roman Catholic monthly *Wiez* published translations of Gandhi and King, and two underground publishing companies brought out translations of Gene Sharp. Zielonka, *Political Ideas in Contemporary Poland*, 95. See Adam Michnik, *Letters from Prison and Other Essays*, trans. Maya Latynski (Berkeley: University of California Press, 1985), 88-89.

98 See Roberts, *Civil Resistance in the East European and Soviet Revolutions*, 3-4.

99 Walzer, "Idea of Civil Society," 301.

100 Peter Ackerman and Christopher Kruegler, *Strategic Nonviolent Conflict: The Dynamics of People Power in the Twentieth Century* (Westport, Connecticut: Praeger, 1994), 345.

101 *An Eyewitness History, People Power: The Philippine Revolution of 1986*, ed. Monina Allarey Mercado (Manila: James B. Reuter, S.J., Foundation, 1986), 140-41, 143, 144-45.

102 Pelczynski, "Solidarity and 'The Rebirth of Civil Society,'" in Keane, *Civil Society and the State: New European Perspectives*, 372.

103 Mary Craig, *Lech Walesa: The Leader of Solidarity and Campaigner for Freedom and Human Rights in Poland* (Milwaukee, Wisconsin: Gareth Stevens, 1990), 40-41.

104 Rigoberta Menchú, *I, Rigoberta Menchú: An Indian Woman in Guatemala*, ed. Elisabeth Burgos-Debray, trans. Ann Wright (London: Verso Books, 1984), 129.

105 On physical obstruction, human and material, see Boserup and Mack, *War without Weapons*, 40-44.

106 Philip Kreager, "Aung San Suu Kyi and the Peaceful Struggle for Human Rights in Burma," *Freedom from Fear*, ed. Michael Aris (London: Penguin, 1991), 298.

107 Francis Meli, *A History of the ANC: South Africa Belongs to Us* (Bloomington: Indiana University Press: 1989), 146, 148.

108 Schock, *Unarmed Insurrections*, 59.

109 Janet Cherry, personal communication (e-mail from Port Elizabeth, February 19, 2007).

110 Walter Sisulu, two-hour interview (Johannesburg, June 3, 1994).

111 Stephen Zunes, "The Role of Nonviolence in the Downfall of Apartheid," in Zunes et al., *Nonviolent Social Movements*, 212.

112 Schock, *Unarmed Insurrections*, 160,161.

113 Kuttab, interview (November 4, 1994).

114 Nusseibeh, interview (November 5, 1994).

115 Sir Stephen King-Hall's review of the evidence available in 1958 suggests that while the efficacy of nonviolent struggle is always reduced by violence, a mingling of violent and nonviolent engagement is often found: "All of the cases of which we have records were combinations of violence and non-violence and (with the exception of certain racial episodes where no arms were available to the resisters) we have no evidence of a completely non-violent struggle." King-Hall, *Defence in the Nuclear Age*, 195-96.

116 Gene Sharp, *Power and Struggle*, vol. 1, in *Politics of Nonviolent Action*, 64-77. See esp. the chart, "Six Classes of Action in Conflicts," 66.

117 Jeffrey Z. Rubin, Dean G. Pruitt, and Sung Hee Kim, *Social Conflict: Escalation, Stalemate, and Settlement*, 2nd ed. (New York: McGraw-Hill, 1994), 63, 64.

118 Malki, interview (May 3, 1995). A PFLP spokesperson, Malki quit the faction due to his recognition that violent strategies do not work. Nusseibeh, communication (December 16, 1997). Malki "slowly realized that the hard-line approach ended negatively," Hanna Siniora suggests; "he was thrown out of the PFLP because he wanted to stand in the 1996 elections for the legislative council. When his party [PFLP] refused, because it was boycotting the Oslo accords, he dropped out." Siniora, interview (December 16, 1997).

119 Václav Havel, "The Power of the Powerless," originally published in 1978, *Living in Truth*, ed. Jan Vladislav (London: Faber and Faber, 1989), 93.

120 Gandhi canceled a nationwide campaign of civil resistance when a single village, Chauri Chaura, set fire to a police station, burning to death six policemen inside it. Jawaharlal Nehru, *Toward Freedom: The*

Autobiography of Jawaharlal Nehru (Boston: Beacon Press, 1958), 79. In later years, Gandhi realized that such cancellations were tantamount to granting veto power to insurgent groups and unfair to those striving to maintain nonviolent discipline. The American unrest had breakaway parties, sects, and counter-movements in the Black Muslims, Black Panthers, and other groups advocating armed self-defense.

Epilogue

1   Greenberg, "Where Is the *Intifada* Heading?" 42.
2   Zeev Schiff, "A Pessimist Optimist Ruminates on the *Intifada*," *Moment* (Washington, D.C.), January-February 1989, 57.
3   As cited in Youssef M. Ibrahim, "Syria's Tough Choice," *New York Times*, November 3, 1991.
4   Chris Hedges, "A Shadow over the Mideast: Arab Youths on a Short Fuse; If Talking Fails, Young Arabs Are Poised for a Deadly Revolt," *New York Times*, October 4, 1996, A1
5   Nusseibah, "In a Different Time Zone," 29.
6   ITN Evening News, London, November 13, 1995.
7   Khalidi, *Iron Cage*, 198.
8   Shlaim, *Iron Wall*, 530.
9   The Hamas hostile operations targeted civilians in Israel proper, with even more reprehensible implications than usual, not just for the larger conflict, but also in international law.
10 Shlaim, *Iron Wall*, 601-2; Pappé, *History of Modern Palestine*, 254.
11 Hammami, "Palestinian NGOs," 88.
12 Denis J. Sullivan, "NGOs in Palestine: Agents of Development and Foundation of Civil Society," *Journal of Palestine Studies* 99 (Spring 1996): 93-100, and Hammami, "Palestinian NGOs." Despite longstanding claims of the PLO that it favored democracy and was the most democratic entity in the Arab world, and even with a certain fidelity to parliamentary procedures and requirements for a quorum in functioning, the PA had no experience with civil society. Yet, Philippe Schmitter notes, "for political democracy to become and remain an alternative model of political domination, a country must possess a civil society in which certain types of self-constituted units are capable of acting autonomously in defense of their own interests and ideals. . . . [and are] organized for coherent collective action." Schmitter, "Introduction to Southern European Transitions," in O'Donnell, Schmitter, and Whitehead, *Transitions from Authoritarian Rule*, part 1, 6.
13 Sara Roy, "Civil Society in the Gaza Strip: Obstacles to Social Reconstruction," in Norton, *Civil Society*, vol. 2, 225.
14 A March 1996 videotape from a Nablus symposium shows PA planning minister Nabil Shaath vowing, "If the negotiations reach a dead end, we shall go back to the [armed] struggle and strife, as we did for forty years. . . . As long as Israel goes forward [with the process], there are no problems, which is why we observe the agreements of peace and non-violence. But if and when Israel will say, 'That's it, we won't talk about Jerusalem, we won't return refugees, we won't dismantle settlements, and we won't retreat from borders,' then all the acts of violence will return. Except that this time we'll have 30,000 armed Palestinian soldiers." "Shaath Threatens Armed Conflict If Peace Fails," *Jerusalem Post*, March 15, 1996, 4.
15 Husseini was still alive. On his 2001 death, see Deborah Sontag, "A Palestinian Champion of Living in Peace Is Dead," *New York Times*, June 1, 2001, A6; eadem, "A Funeral in Jerusalem Arouses Palestinian Nationalism," *New York Times*, June 2, 2001; Lee Hockstader, "PLO Official Faisal Husseini, 60, Dies," *Washington Post*, June 1, 2001, B7; Daniel Williams, "Death of a Man, Loss of a Philosophy."
16 Khalidi, *Iron Cage*, 163. The issue was not solely autocracy or attrition. Khalidi lists sixteen PLO leaders who were assassinated or disabled between 1968 and 1991. Ibid.
17 Gelvin, *Israel-Palestine Conflict*, 240.
18 Ben Kaspit, *Mariv*, September 6, 2002, as cited in Rema Hammami and Salim Tamari, "Anatomy of Another Rebellion: From Intifada to Interregnum," in Beinin and Stein, eds. *Struggle for Sovereignty*, 266.
19 Michel Warschawski, *Toward an Open Tomb: The Crisis of Israeli Society*, trans. Peter Drucker (New York: Monthly Review Press, 2004), 12.
20 Catherine Cook and Adam Hanieh, "The Separation Barrier: Walling Out Sovereignty," in Beinin and Stein, eds., *Struggle for Sovereignty*, 343.
21 Khalidi, *Iron Cage*, 198, 199.
22 Cook and Hanieh, "Separation Barrier," 343. The Israeli Central Bureau of Statistics reported 192,976 settlers residing in West Bank settlements in 2000, "Population in Israel and West Bank Settlements, 1995-2005," as cited in *Report on Israeli Settlement in the Occupied Territories*, September-October

2006, http://www.fmep.org/reports/overview.html. See Gershom Gorenberg, "Building Nowhereland," *Washington Post*, 1 October 2006, B7, on " the failed project of the settlements, which for nearly 40 years has drained Israel's energies, subverted its democracy and harmed its security."

23 Daoud Kuttab, "The Two Intifadas: Differing Shades of Resistance," February 8, 2001, Information Brief no. 66, Washington, D.C., Center for Policy Analysis on Palestine.

24 Arrested in April 2002, Marwan Barghouti was charged with killing twenty-six Israelis and membership in a terror organization. Beside acknowledged leadership of the *tanzim*, he was accused of commanding the al-Aqsa Martyrs' Brigade, which carried out suicide bombings, a charge that he denied. Rejecting the jurisdiction of the Israeli courts, he would not permit his lawyers to mount a defense, and in May 2004 was convicted for the murder of five persons and received a life sentence. Having once described the development of two political cultures, "one born of the Arab world and one born of Israeli occupation," Barghouti is among the few able to mediate between the PLO factions and Islamist revivalists on the one hand, and the PA on the other. Barghouti interview, *Middle East Report*, 22. Among Palestinians, he is admired for his democratic convictions. In prison in 2006, he negotiated a cross-factional agreement called the "Prisoners' Document" between Fateh, Hamas, and Islamic Jihad to stop attacks against Israeli citizens. The "Prisoner's Document" is seen by Amjad Atallah as "actually a platform for recreating a unified national movement. It accepts the concept of an Israel living in peace with not only Palestine but with all the Arab states, however, does not necessarily believe that this is an Israeli goal." Amjad Atallah, "The Politics of Chaos: The Palestinian-Israeli Conflict in Context of the United States' Middle East Wars," presentation to the Royal College of Defence Studies (London: Royal College of Defence Studies, September 4, 2006).

25 Rema Hammami and Salim Tamari, "Anatomy of Another Rebellion," in Beinin and Stein, eds., *Struggle for Sovereignty*, 267.

26 Robinson, *Palestinian Leadership in Transition?*

27 Michael Howard, "Terrorism Has Always Fed off Its Response: An Indiscriminate American Reaction Would Only Reinforce Her Enemies," *The Times* (London), September 14, 2001.

28 Hammami and Tamari, "Anatomy of Another Rebellion," 272.

29 Detailed maps and photographs are found in B'Tselem, "Land Grab, Israel's Settlement Policy in the West Bank", May 2002, also available at http://www.btselem.org.

30 See *Operation Defensive Shield: Soldiers' Testimonies, Palestinian Testimonies* (Jerusalem: B'Tselem, 2002).

31 Hammami and Tamari, "Anatomy of Another Rebellion," 274.

32 Pappé, *History of Modern Palestine*, 266.

33 Paul Scham, "Glimmers of Hope from the Israeli and Palestinian Civil Societies?" *Middle East Institute Perspective*, November 17, 2003. The statement of principles of the People's Voice initiative addresses the right of return through compensation for property claims and repatriation to a State of Palestine, not restitution of lost property. Fiercely debated among Palestinian refugees, it implies that any Palestinian who would move to the new Palestinian state would solely receive citizenship, but not compensation. To view the 2002 Nusseibeh-Ayalon proposal in historical context, see a concise breakdown of options in Fischbach, *Peace Process and Palestinian Refugee Claims*, 98.

34 *Under the Guise of Security: Routing the Separation Barrier to Enable the Expansion of Israeli Settlements in the West Bank* (Jerusalem: B'Tselem, December 2005), 5.

35 Cook and Hanieh, "Separation Barrier," 338. See Tim Morris, "Just a Wall?" *Forced Migration Review* 26 (August 2006).

36 *A Wall in Jerusalem: Obstacles to Human Rights in the Holy City* (Jerusalem: B'Tselem, 2006), 13.

37 "Court Orders Changes to West Bank Wall," *Guardian*, 30 June 2004.

38 Donald Macintyre, "Tear Down Israel's Illegal Barrier, Says World Court," *Independent* (London), July 10, 2004. In the same month, the General Assembly overwhelmingly reaffirmed the judgment of the International Court of Justice that the wall violates international law and called on Israel to demolish it or move it to the Green Line.

39 Tanya Reinhart, *The Road Map to Nowhere: Israel/Palestine since 2003* (London and New York: Verso Books, 2006), 31.

40 Nahi Alon, thirty minute personal communication (Bethlehem, December 30, 2005). In Jerusalem in December 2005, Gene Sharp and Jamila Raqib of the Albert Einstein Institution met extensively with Alon and Omer; Brigadier General Gershon Hacohen, who headed the military component of the Gaza withdrawal; and Raffi Lev, of the Israeli police, to discuss how study of nonviolent resistance had been useful in preparations for withdrawal. Albert Einstein Institution newsletter, spring 2006, 7-9. See Nahi Alon and Haim Omer, *The Psychology of Demo-*

nization: Promoting Acceptance and Reducing Conflict (Mahwah, New Jersey, and London: Lawrence Erlbaum Associates, 2006).

41 In Budrus and Deir Ballut, nonviolent resistance, combined with appeals to courts and third-party solidarity promotion, has altered the course of the wall, permitting communities to reclaim some pastures, vineyards, and water sources. By mid-2006, however, 200 had been injured in Bilin demonstrations. Gadi Algazi, "Settlers on Israel's Eastern Frontier," *Le Monde Diplomatique*, August 2006, 4. Concerning one of the Israeli participating peace protagonists, Nimrod Ronen, see Meron Rapaport, "Symbol of Struggle," *Haaretz*, 10 September 2005, available at http://www.haaretz.com/hasen/objects/pages/PrintArticleEn.jhtml?itemNo=622829.

42 Beshara Doumani, remarks at "The Palestinian Question Post-Oslo," a conference of the Palestine Center, Washington, D.C., October 27, 2006.

43 Nathan Brown, "The Changing Political Landscape: Reorganization of Power and Action," transcript of remarks, July 18, 2006, *For The Record*, no. 259, July 21, 2006, Washington, D.C., Palestine Center.

44 Wing, remarks at "The Future of Palestinian Society and Politics," a conference of the Middle East Institute and Elliott School of International Affairs, George Washington University, Washington, D.C., February 13, 1998.

45 Dajani, *Eyes without Country*, 114-53.

46 Ilan Pappé, "Post-Zionist Critique on Israel and the Palestinians, Part 1: The Academic Debate," *Journal of Palestine Studies* 26, no. 2 (Winter 1997): 33.

47 Ezrahi, *Rubber Bullets*, 275, 234.

48 Scott Wilson, "Textbooks in Israel to Designate West Bank: Cabinet Minister's Move Draws Anger," *Washington Post*, 6 December 2006, A15.

49 Jon Immanuel, "To Talk or Not to Talk," *Jerusalem Post*, November 9, 1990.

50 Avi Azrieli, "Talking to the Neighbors: It's Time Israel Embraced the Mideast," *International Herald Tribune*, August 30, 2006, 6.

Index

A

Abbas, Mahmoud (Abu Mazen), 272, 302, 442*n*45
Abd al-Hadi, Awni, 42, 88
Abd al-Hadi, Issam, 95
Abd al-Hadi, Mahdi, 120, 171, 216, 346, 413*n*70
Abd al-Hadi, Ouni, 91-92
Adbullah, King, 62, 70, 402*n*30
Abraham Fund, 425*n*2
Abu Ala (Ahmad Qurei), 273, 442*n*45
Abu Ammar. *See* Arafat, Yasir
Abu-Amr, Ziad, 49, 122, 289, 404*n*82, 408*n*166-67, 411*n*39, 441*n*10
Abu Ayyash, Radwan: about, 180-82, 414*n*94; on armed struggle, 288; and Fateh, 215, 281, 293; and Husseini, Feisel, 216, 220; imprisonment of, 324, 404*n*82; and Knesset, 276; on Palestinians' despair, 204-5; Sharon's terrorist charges against, 216, 415*n*103
Abu-Diab, Haj Abd, 147, 154-56, 216, 238, 259, 300
Abu Iyad (Salah Khalaf), 272, 283, 291, 376*n*26, 411*n*37, 436*n*169, 440*n*238
Abu Jihad (Khalil al-Wazir): on Arab states' abandonment, 388*n*78; assassination of, 219-20, 417*n*129-30, 418*n*134; and Awad, 144, 272; and Fateh, 63; and Husseini, Feisel, 175-76; and Jerusalem Paper, 198, 409*n*172; methods of, 417*n*127-28; on Palestinian-Jordanian Joint Committee, 176; political organizing in occupied territories, 78-79, 219; on white revolution, 413*n*70
Abu Rahme, Fayez, 194
Abul Abbas, Muhammed, 278, 284, 435*n*151
Abu-Sharif, Bassam, 79, 220, 376*n*38
Abu Shilbaya, Muhammad, 80, 381*n*169
Abu Zayyad, Ziad, 179-81, 267, 282, 290, 324, 409*n*169
Ackerman, Peter, 317
action methods. *See* nonviolent action methods
activist intellectuals: about, 1-4, 40, 386*n*26, 414*n*81; activism, 106-9, 190-93, 205, 376*n*37; and Birzeit University closure, 222; catalysts for frame transformation, 407*n*147; and the Command, 208; on declaring an independent state, 196; of East Jerusalem, 178-79, 183-84, 403*n*58, 403*n*68; and international community, 178-79, 198, 200-201; Islamic Jihad's threats to, 440*n*243; nonviolence of, 185, 201,

208-9, 213-15, 415*n*103; and Palestinian state, 85; on provisional government, 417*n*124, 440*n*4. *See also* Israeli-Palestinian cooperation; Palestinian civil society
administrative detention, 167-68, 170, 172, 194-95, 361*n*36, 401*n*14, 424*n*261
"aggressive nonviolence" of Husseini and Abu Jihad, 175
Ahad Haam (Asher Ginsburg), 68
Aharoni, Reuben, 434*n*106
Ahmad, Eqbal, 101, 140, 146, 281, 385*n*3
Aker, Mamdouh, 214, 218, 414*n*84
Al Azhar University of Cairo in Palestine, 108
Algerian model, 3, 64, 186-87, 279, 405*n*106
al-Haq (Law in the Service of Man), 85-86, 383*n*199, 389*n*93
Allenby, Edmund, 26, 364*n*6, 365*n*34
Alon, Nahi, 335, 447*n*40
Alpher, Yossi, 410*n*19
Amaari refugee camp, al-, 105
American Friends of Peace Now, 305
American Friends Service Committee, 271, 306
American University of Beirut, 376*n*37
Amirav, Moshe, 191-92, 406*n*130, 428*n*73
Anabta refugee camp, 115-16
Anderson, Benedict, 169
Andrews, Lewis, 373*n*215
Anish, Abu, 166
ANM (Arab Nationalist Movement), 64, 376*n*37-38
antiapartheid movement in South Africa, 19-20, 186-87, 279, 318-22, 338, 405*n*105
Antonius, Katy, 128-29
apartheid in Palestine, 186-87, 251, 405*n*105, 407*n*152
apartheid regime in South Africa, 19-20, 318, 320
"apology visits," 142
Aqsa Martyrs' Brigade, al-, 447*n*24
Arab Car-Owners' and Drivers' Committee, 50
Arab East Jerusalem. *See* East Jerusalem
Arab Executive Committee, 32-33, 39-43, 48
Arab Higher Committee, 50-54, 60. *See also* Husseini, Haj Amin al-
Arab League, 71, 339, 379*n*100
Arab National Committee, 50, 228
Arab Nationalist Movement (ANM), 64, 376*n*37-38
Arab states: Awad on, 154-55; and Fateh, 64-65, 377*n*41, 377*n*44; and fedayeen, 65; leaders

PDFLP, 72. *See also* Democratic Front for the Liberation of Palestine

peace agreements between Arabs and Jews, 60-61

Peace Now (Shalom Achshav), 115, 170, 252-54, 427*n*44, 437*n*179

peasant laborers (fellahin), 38-39, 47-48, 61-62, 89, 91, 371*n*181, 371*n*184, 374*n*5

Peel, Lord William Robert Wellesley, 31

Peel Commission, 54-58

Peel Commission Report (1937), 31, 54-55, 59-60, 366*n*42, 373*n*216, 444*n*92

Pellitreau, Robert, 274

People's Party, 73, 214. *See also* Palestine Communist Party

People's Voice Initiative, 447*n*33

Peres, Shimon, 181, 406*n*140, 442*n*45

Peretz, Don, 76, 111, 157, 408*n*166, 414*n*97

Permanent Mandates Commission at the League of Nations, 91

Petah Tiqvah, 25-26, 33-34, 49

Peteet, Julie M., 88

PFLP. *See* Popular Front for the Liberation of Palestine

PFLP-GC (Popular Front for the Liberation of Palestine-General Command), 204, 437*n*177

Phalangist massacre of refugees, 114-15

phone lines, cutting of, 424*n*277

Pickering, Thomas, 160

PLA (Palestine Liberation Army), 63, 376*n*38

PLF (Palestine Liberation Front), 283, 435*n*151

PLO. *See* Palestine Liberation Organization

PNC. *See* Palestine National Council

political detainees' (prisoners') movement, 116-19

political jujitsu, 249-50

political struggle versus civil society, 103

political systems, boycotts of social and, 35-36, 42-43, 54, 81, 91-93, 198, 237, 292, 384*n*21. *See also* tax resistance

Politics of Nonviolent Action, The (Sharp), 136-37, 154, 274

Popular Army, 431*n*45

Popular Front for the Liberation of Palestine-General Command (PFLP-GC), 204, 437*n*177

Popular Front for the Liberation of Palestine (PFLP): and communists, 78; end of nonviolent intifada encouraged by, 408*n*168; founding of, 72; Habash's leadership of, 72, 284, 376*n*37, 418*n*135, 437*n*187, 441*n*8; hijacking of El Al airliner, 379*n*110; and Jerusalem Paper, 197, 408*n*168; and labor unions, 75; leaflets published by, 439*n*217; and Malki, 163, 400*n*214; and Palestinian Women's Committees, 97; support for armed insurrection, 437*n*177

Porath, Yehoshua, 235, 314-15, 371*n*184, 372*n*212, 444*n*92

Posner, Michael, 255

PPS (Palestine Press Service), 180

Pressburg, Gail, 271, 306, 434*n*112

Prisoners' Document, 447*n*24

prisoners' movement, 116-19, 389*n*103. *See also* Palestinians imprisoned by Israel

Provisional Basic Law, 375*n*16

Pundik, Ron, 442*n*45

PWU (Palestinian Women's Union), 87, 383*n*4

Q

Qalandia refugee camp, 153, 209

Qassam, Izz al-Din al-, 45-49, 52, 65, 122

Qassamites, 45-49, 370*n*155, 372*n*197, 373*n*218, 433*n*78

Qastel, al-, 401*n*28

Qatanna olive trees episode, 148-51, 396*n*116

Quandt, William, 65, 75

Quds, al-. See Jerusalem Paper

Qurei, Ahmad (Abu Ala), 273, 442*n*45

R

Rabaia, Muhammad (Abu Tariq), 198, 211

Rabin, Yitzhak: "break their bones" mandate attributed to, 7-9; on cost of ruling another people, 428*n*77; on curfew policy, 418*n*142; on deportation of Awad, 399*n*196, 399*n*202; and Oslo process, 442*n*45; and PLO, 433*n*97

Rajoub, Jabril, 166, 167, 389*n*92, 401*n*14

Rakah (Israeli Communist Party), 69, 73, 95, 378*n*79, 379*n*103

Ramallah, 95-96, 104

Randle, Michael, 16

Raqib, Jamila, 447*n*40

Ratz (Citizens Rights), 221

Ravitzki, Avi, 429*n*86

Raviv, Dan, 220

Reagan, Ronald, 113-14

Reinhart, Tanya, 335

refugee camps. *See* Palestinian refugee camps

refugees. *See* Palestinian refugees

religious faiths in Palestine, 34-35, 120, 121, 128. *See also specific religions*

resistance. *See* nonviolent resistance

Richardson, David, 132-33, 138

Rida, Rashid, 45-46

Rigby, Andrew, 438*n*199

Robinson, Glenn, 331

Rogers, Carl, 136

Rolef, Susan Hattis, 123, 269, 296, 426*n*31

Roth, Kenneth, 255

Rothschild, Lord Lionel Walter, 26

Roy, Sara, 327

Rubenstein, Daniel, 172, 246, 305

Rustin, Bayard, 18

S

Sabra, A. I., 182-83

Sabra refugee camp massacre, 114-15

Sacred Struggle, 47-49, 55

sacred violence concept, 64

Sadat, Anwar al-, 75-77

Safed, 38, 368*n*94

CPSIA information can be obtained at www.ICGtesting.com
Printed in the USA
LVOW07s1229280716

497899LV00001B/23/P